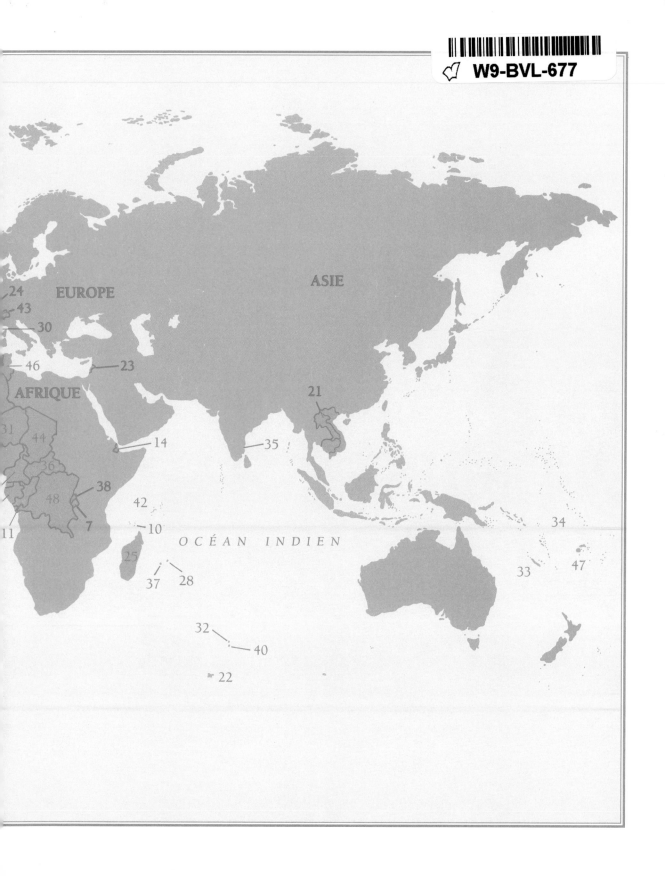

EUROPE

ASIE

24

43

30

46

23

AFRIQUE

31

44

36

48

38

11

7

14

35

21

42

10

OCÉAN INDIEN

34

25

33

47

37

28

32

40

22

Third Edition

Rapports

Language, Culture, Communication

Joel Walz

University of Georgia

Jean-Pierre Piriou

University of Georgia

D. C. Heath and Company
Lexington, Massachusetts   Toronto

Address editorial correspondence to:

D. C. Heath and Company
125 Spring Street
Lexington, MA 02173

Acquisitions Editor:	Denise St. Jean
Developmental Editor:	Denise St. Jean
Production Editor:	Rosemary R. Jaffe
Designer:	Judith Miller
Photo Researcher:	Nancy Hale
Production Coordinator:	Lisa Merrill
Permissions Editor:	Margaret Roll

Cover: *Café à Montmartre* by Yolande Ardissone. Photograph courtesy of Wally Findlay Galleries, New York. Cover design by Joanna Steinkeller.

About the cover: Yolande Ardissone, born in Normandy in 1927, completed her extensive studies in painting at the Ecole des Beaux-Arts. In 1949 she had her first exhibit at the Salon des Artistes Français and won honorable mention. She was also chosen a member of the Salon. Ardissone has gone on to win many distinguished honors for her work and is considered to be one of France's finest contemporary artists. Primarily a painter of landscapes and seascapes, she conveys a warm, optimistic view of life through her impressionistic style and vivid colors.

International Standard Book Number: 0–669–27711–8 (Instructor's Edition)
                                    0–669–27710–X (Student's Edition)

Library of Congress Catalog Number: 92–70171

10 9 8 7 6 5 4 3

PREFACE ....

Rapports, Third Edition, is a complete first-year French program for college and university students. It promotes the active command of spoken French without neglecting the development of your listening, reading, and writing skills. Because *Rapports* focuses on the practical use of French for communication in context, it also emphasizes the everyday life and cultures of the French and of French-speakers in other francophone countries.

The Text

Rapports consists of a brief preliminary chapter and eighteen chapters. After every three chapters is a review section with oral and written exercises for class work and interactive activities for pair and small group work.

The preliminary chapter permits you to begin talking in French with your fellow students on the very first day of class. In this chapter, you will learn greetings, leave-takings, and basic information about French pronunciation, and you will be introduced to the francophone world through a reading in English.

Each subsequent chapter contains the following features:

1. **Chapter Opener** The first page of each chapter introduces you to the theme and topics you will study.

   A. **Theme** Each chapter is centered around a theme. The chapter theme will be evident in the opening dialogue, vocabulary, language exercises and activities, functional / situational phrases, and the cultural reading. A unifying theme enhances your ability to understand and learn the language.

   B. **Objectives** The first page of each chapter sets forth the learning objectives for the chapter according to the textbook's three goals: *Language,* or the structures and vocabulary you will learn; *Culture,* information on the French-speaking world that provides an authentic context; and *Communication,* the notions, functions, and situational language that you will use to express yourself.

2. **Commençons** This section provides samples of language use, cultural information, active vocabulary related to the chapter's theme, and information on pronunciation, all of which will help you put the structures you will be learning to use in communicating in French.

   A. **Dialogue** Each chapter opens with a dialogue or other type of communication such as a phone conversation, a postcard, a formal letter, a poem, or a fable. The setting for each text is a situation that you might encounter or one that is typical of college-age people in francophone countries. A **Mots clés** section follows, listing all new active vocabulary. **Etudions le dialogue** then provides questions on the content of the opening text. A cassette icon at the beginning of the section indicates that the dialogue is recorded on the *Cassette Program*. A videocassette icon tells you that video clips are provided for each chapter of your textbook.

B. **Faisons connaissance**   This section presents cultural information in English that will help you understand the interaction in the dialogue. It is thematically related to the rest of the chapter and especially to the reading passage in the **Lecture culturelle** at the end of the chapter.

C. **Enrichissons notre vocabulaire**   Active vocabulary appears here in drawings and in conversational exchanges. The vocabulary will recur throughout the chapter in grammar exercises and activities and in the *Workbook / Laboratory Manual. Rapports* has tightly controlled vocabulary with active words appearing only in the dialogue, **Faisons connaissance, Enrichissons,** and grammar presentations when they pertain to the structure being taught. All other sections contain only passive vocabulary, which your teacher may ask you to learn.

D. **Prononciation**   This section offers detailed, yet simple explanations of the major features of French pronunciation along with exercises. You may go over the exercises in class or practice them in the language laboratory since they are recorded on the *Cassette Program* (as the cassette icon indicates).

3. **Grammaire**   The grammar sections present concepts that you can be expected to handle and use actively. The clear presentations in English allow you to prepare the lesson before coming to class and thus spend more class time using the language than talking about it.

A. **Usage statement**   Each presentation begins with a short explanation in English of *why* you would need to know the structure in order to communicate in French.

B. **Explanation**   The structure is explained in a clear fashion with numerous examples, which often come from the dialogue.

C. **Ce qu'ils disent**   Spoken French is not exactly like the more formal language taught in textbooks. While you should learn a fairly formal style, you can use these explanations to help you understand what you will hear in a French-speaking country.

D. **L'Orthographe**   This section describes the features of the French language that appear only in writing since written French sometimes differs from spoken French.

E. **Attention**   This section points out elements of the language that cause trouble for non-native speakers or that are easy to forget.

F. **Language / Langue**   The first group of exercises for each grammar point carries this name (the names as well as directions to all exercises, changes from English to French as of Chapter 7.) These exercises are all meaningful, that is, you must understand the French to produce the correct answer. Virtually all of these exercises also have a short context that unifies the items so that you practice each structure in an everyday situation.

G. **Culture**   For every point of grammar taught, *Rapports,* Third Edition, has at least one activity based on cultural similarities and differences between the United States and francophone cultures. You must understand not only the language but also the culture to produce a correct answer. The activities reflect a wide range of content involving everything from famous artists and historical figures to how French speakers conduct their daily lives. You will not know some of the information at first, but you can create sentences that seem logical, and your teacher will guide you to the correct answers.

H. **Communication**   Every grammar point also has a number of activities that allow you to express your own ideas and experiences. The formats always provide suggestions to get you started, but they also encourage originality. The personal questions revolve around a context, which helps you interact with your teacher and classmates in a way that more closely resembles natural conversation.

4. **Communiquons**   This section introduces a notion, a function, or a situation that is important to communication. A short paragraph in English introduces the topic. Then, you learn various common phrases so you can express your thoughts appropriately in French. The dialogue or **Interaction** that follows illustrates authentic usage of the phrases presented, and the communication activities allow you to practice using the new expressions in other contexts.

5. **Lecture culturelle**   Each chapter concludes with a reading passage on a topic related to the cultural theme introduced in the **Commençons** section. The pre-reading activities will help you develop skills so that you can read French more proficiently. The post-reading activities will check your comprehension of the reading passage and will enable you to discuss what you have learned in terms of your own life.

End-of-Text Reference Materials

1. Appendices include the International Phonetic Alphabet, the French names of and prepositions used with the fifty American states, supplemental grammar points, and verb conjugation charts.

2. The French-English vocabulary lists all active and passive vocabulary in *Rapports,* Third Edition. The English-French vocabulary lists all active

words and expressions. Each entry in the vocabularies is followed by a reference indicating the chapter in which it first appears.

3. An index provides ready access to all grammatical structures, vocabulary topics, and pronunciation points presented in the textbook.

The Workbook / Laboratory Manual and Cassette Program

The *Workbook / Laboratory Manual* is fully integrated with *Rapports,* Third Edition, to further develop your writing, speaking, and listening skills. Each chapter contains two sections—workbook exercises and laboratory activities. The *Workbook* section offers a variety of exercises that require you to write in French using the structures and vocabulary of the corresponding textbook chapter. Each *Workbook* section concludes with **Ecrivons,** a section devoted to directed compositions and open-ended, personalized writing assignments. The *Laboratory* section guides you through the *Cassette Program,* providing pronunciation explanations and exercises and cues for all of the listening-and-speaking and listening-and-writing activities that accompany each chapter. The *Workbook / Laboratory Manual* also provides workbook exercises and laboratory activities for the review sections, which appear after every three chapters.

The *Cassette Program* provides you with forty to fifty minutes of listening material for each textbook chapter and additional listening activities for each review section. The textbook dialogues and pronunciation exercises are recorded. They are followed by a series of listening-and-speaking and listening-and-writing activities for each grammar point. Each chapter concludes with a dictation and a global listening comprehension activity tied thematically to the content of the corresponding textbook chapter.

Acknowledgments

A major revision of this book would not have been possible without the help of many people. We would like to thank Denise St. Jean, Senior Acquisitions Editor at D. C. Heath and Company, who has been guiding us for many years and who served as developmental editor for this Third Edition. We would also like to thank Sharon Alexander, Managing Editor of Modern Languages; Patricia Angelo, Editorial Associate; Rosemary Jaffe, Senior Production Editor; Jacqueline Rebisz, Copyeditor; Judith Miller, Designer, Nancy Hale, Photo Researcher; Margaret Roll, Permissions Editor; Irene Cinelli, Supplements Typesetter; Lisa Merrill, Production Coordinator; and Michael O'Dea, Production Manager.

The one person who deserves special recognition is Christine Fau, *agrégée de l'université,* and Ph.D. candidate in the Department of Romance Languages at the University of Georgia, who read our manuscript with care, maintaining the French-English vocabulary list and making useful comments on language, culture, and pedagogy. Michael Lastinger, Assistant Professor of French at West Virginia University, once again revised the Testing Program.

Many of our colleagues and graduate students have offered advice, corrections, and realia to use in the Third Edition; we would like to mention Lisa Déchelette, Ben Drummond, Susan Guice, Teri Hernández, Valérie Huet, Lionel Lemarchand, Jean Ouédraogo, Kevin Telford, Francis Assaf, and Tim Raser. Many other graduate teaching assistants in our department as well as reviewers and adopters across the country have made helpful suggestions, and we are grateful.

Joel Walz
Jean-Pierre Piriou

Table des matières ....

Chapitre 3
AU RESTAURANT   51

REVISION A   Chapitres 1 à 3   73

Chapitre 4
LES VOYAGES   77

Chapitre préliminaire

BONJOUR!

«Bonjour, Isabelle! Ça va?»

1

COMMENÇONS ....

Philippe et Isabelle

PHILIPPE: Bonjour!

ISABELLE: Salut! Ça va?

PHILIPPE: Oui, ça va bien. Et toi?

ISABELLE: Ça va, merci.

PHILIPPE: Je m'appelle Philippe. Et toi?

ISABELLE: Isabelle.

Pierre et Madame Dumas

MME DUMAS: Bonjour, Pierre.

PIERRE: Bonjour, Madame. Comment allez-vous?

MME DUMAS: Je vais bien, merci. Et vous?

PIERRE: Très bien, merci.

Mots clés

Bonjour!	*Hello! / Good morning!*	**Je m'appelle...**	*My name is . . .*
Salut!	*Hi!*	**Madame**	*ma'am*
Ça va?	*How's it going?*	**Comment allez-vous?**	*How are you?*
oui	*yes*		
Ça va bien.	*Fine.*	**Je vais bien.**	*I'm fine.*
Et toi?	*And you?*	**Et vous?**	*And you?*
Merci.	*Thank you.*	**Très bien.**	*Very well.*

FAISONS CONNAISSANCE

The way people greet each other varies from culture to culture and depends on how well they know each other. When French people meet, they always make physical contact. Friends and business associates exchange a brief handclasp **(une poignée de main)** not only upon being introduced, but also upon seeing each other for the first time each day, and again upon parting. In France, women shake hands as often as men.

Salut, Ahmed, ça va?

When two French people who are relatives or good friends see each other, they may embrace lightly and kiss on both cheeks **(faire la bise).** It is not unusual for French men to greet each other this way, especially if they are celebrating an important occasion. In a French family, all children, no matter how old, will kiss both parents before leaving for the day or going to bed.

Relationships also influence the kind of language people use in greeting each other. For example, in the dialogue, two friends of the same age say **«Salut, ça va?»,** but a young person would say to an adult: **«Bonjour, comment allez-vous?».** In general, French people are more formal than Americans and they are less likely to act casually with new acquaintances.

Enrichissons notre vocabulaire

Faisons connaissance! *(Let's get to know each other!)*

Au revoir.	*Good-bye.*
Bonsoir.	*Good evening. / Good night.*
A bientôt.	*See you soon.*
A plus tard.	*See you later.*
—Comment ça va?	*How's it going?*
—Pas mal.	*Not bad.*
—Comme ci, comme ça.	*So, so.*
Quoi de neuf?	*What's up?*
Monsieur	*sir*
Mademoiselle	*miss*

Communication

Using the expressions you have just learned in the dialogue, greet the student next to you, introduce yourself, and ask how things are going.

Prononciation   Some Basic Information   `◦━◦`

A. Although French and English use the same alphabet, the combinations of letters and the sounds that they represent can be very different. Each language contains some sounds that do not exist in the other. French has no *th* sound as in *thank*, no *ch* sound as in *children*. English has no **u** sound, as in **une**, no **r** sound as in **merci**.

B. Both languages have words containing letters that are not pronounced.

> French: tar*d*, alle*z*, Madam*e*
> English: *i*sland, *k*nife, ni*gh*t

C. In French, as in English, one letter or one combination of letters can be pronounced more than one way.

> French: *c*omme, *c*i
> English: *c*all, *c*ircle

D. In French, as in English, one sound can be written more than one way.

> French: *ç*a, *s*alut, mer*c*i, profe*ss*eur
> English: con*qu*er, *k*itchen, *ch*aracter

LECTURE CULTURELLE ....

Le Monde francophone

The word **francophonie** refers to the use of the French language, and the expression **le monde francophone** (the French-speaking world) designates all the countries in the world where French is spoken. Only about half of the people who use French daily live in France. The others are scattered all over the
5 world, in Europe, North and South America, Asia, and Africa. Altogether, almost 106 million people speak French, and for more than 67 million of them, it is their mother tongue.

The French language derives from Latin, and its introduction into different areas of the world occurred at various times in history. In 1534, the Age of
10 Discovery brought Jacques Cartier to Canada, where French is now the official language of over 7 million **Québécois**; it also brought La Salle to Louisiana, where there are still a quarter of a million speakers of French. Later, when slave trading became a profitable enterprise, the French influence spread over West Africa and the Antilles. In the nineteenth century, France evolved as a

15 colonial power in Africa, the Near East, and Southeast Asia. The French colonial empire began to crumble in 1954 with the loss of Vietnam and continued to dissolve as one country after another declared its independence from France in the sixties. France has retained a certain number of territories known as **DOM (départements d'outre-mer)** and **TOM (territoires d'outre-mer).** The
20 **DOM** include **la Martinique, la Guadeloupe, la Guyane, la Réunion,** and **Saint-Pierre-et-Miquelon,** while the **TOM** consist of **la Nouvelle-Calédonie, Wallis-et-Futuna, la Polynésie française, les Terres australes et antarctiques françaises,** and **Mayotte.** The **DOM** and **TOM** elect representatives to the parliament in Paris and are represented by a minister in the French government.
25   You can find a map of the French-speaking world on the inside front cover of this book.

Chapitre 1

LA VIE UNIVERSITAIRE

En cours d'histoire

Commençons ....

A l'université, en cours d'anglais 🔲

LE PROFESSEUR: Commençons! Mademoiselle, comment vous appelez-vous?

L'ETUDIANTE: Je m'appelle Patricia Keller.

LE PROFESSEUR: Mais, alors, vous parlez bien anglais, n'est-ce pas?

PATRICIA: Non, juste un peu.

LE PROFESSEUR: Eh bien, ouvrez votre livre page neuf et lisez le dialogue. *(A la classe)* Ecoutez et répétez ensemble après Patricia.

Mots clés

à l'université *(f.)*	*at the university*	eh bien	*well then*
en cours *(m.)*	*in class*	Ouvrez votre livre.	*Open your book.*
anglais *(m.)*	*English*	page	*page*
professeur	*teacher*	neuf	*nine*
Commençons! (commencer)	*Let's begin!*	lisez (lire)	*read*
		dialogue	*dialogue*
Comment vous appelez-vous?	*What's your name?*	à	*to*
		classe	*class*
étudiant, -e *(m., f.)*	*student*	écoutez (écouter)	*listen (to)*
Mais, alors...	*But, then . . .*		
parlez (parler)	*speak*	répétez (répéter)	*repeat*
n'est-ce pas?	*don't you?*		
non	*no*	ensemble	*together*
juste un peu	*just a little bit*	après	*after*

Faisons connaissance

French universities are state-supported. Since 1968, new universities have been created in many French cities. However, in Paris and in other major cities, the universities are so big that they are divided and have numbers. For example, the former **Sorbonne** is now **Paris IV.** In addition to having numbers, many universities also have names. For instance, **Lyon III** is also called **l'université Jean-Moulin,** whereas **Montpellier III** is known as

La Sorbonne

l'université Paul-Valéry. Students use the term **la fac,** an abbreviation of **la faculté,** to refer to the university or any of its schools, such as **la faculté de Médecine,** *(School of Medicine)* or **la faculté des Lettres et des Sciences humaines** *(College of Arts and Sciences).*

Most French students go to the university nearest to their home and continue to live with their families. Students who cannot return home every night often have to rent a room from individuals because universities cannot provide housing for everyone who needs it. This also helps explain why there is little campus life. Students often go to cafés between classes and when classes are over to meet friends or simply study. Traditionally, one can stay in a café for an unlimited period of time without having to place another order. Near universities, however, a sign may indicate that orders will be taken again every two hours.

Etudions le dialogue

1. Repeat the dialogue after your teacher.
2. Read the dialogue with another classmate.
3. Ask one of your classmates to act out the dialogue with you in front of the class.

Enrichissons notre vocabulaire

Voilà la salle de classe. *(Here is the classroom.)*

Expressions utiles pour le cours de français *(Useful expressions for French class)*

Continuez la leçon.	***Continue*** *the lesson.*
Commencez ici et **répétez avec** Patricia.	***Start here*** *and repeat **with** Patricia.*
Commencez l'examen *(m.)* / vos **devoirs.** *(m.)*	*Start the **test** / **your homework**.*
Lisez **de** la page quatre à la page cinq et **répondez aux questions.**	*Read **from** page four to page five and **answer the questions**.*
Faites l'exercice A.	*Do exercise A.*
Parlez **beaucoup** en classe, mais **en français!**	*Speak **a lot** in class, but **in French!***
—**Qu'est-ce que c'est?**	*What is this?*
—**C'est le bureau de Madame Dumas.**	*It's Mrs. Dumas's desk.*
—**Ce sont** les livres.	*They're books.*

—**Comment dit-on** «good-bye»
  à Paris / au Québec?
—**Je ne sais pas.**
—A Paris, **on dit** «au revoir»,
  mais au Québec, on dit
  «bonjour».

—**Qu'est-ce que** «salut» **veut
  dire?**
—**Cela veut dire** «hi».

—**Voici** le livre de français.
—**Merci.**
—**Il n'y a pas de quoi. / De rien.**

*How do you say "good-bye" in
  Paris / in Quebec?*
I don't know.
*In Paris, you say "au revoir,"
  but in Quebec, you say
  "bonjour."*

What does "salut" mean?

It means "hi."

Here is the French book.
Thank you.
*Don't mention it. / You're
  welcome.*

Prononciation   The International Phonetic Alphabet

The International Phonetic Alphabet (IPA), which is used in the **Prononciation**
sections of this book, simplifies learning new words because each written symbol represents one specific sound. The International Phonetic Alphabet appears
in Appendix I.

The French alphabet

A. The French alphabet is the same as the English, but the names of the letters differ. The following chart gives the letters, the IPA symbols showing
  the pronunciation of each letter, and a short, imaginary word to help
  you remember the names.

a	/a/	ah	j	/ʒi/	ji	s	/ɛs/		esse
b	/be/	bé	k	/ka/	ka	t	/te/		té
c	/se/	sé	l	/ɛl/	elle	u	/y/		u
d	/de/	dé	m	/ɛm/	emme	v	/ve/		vé
e	/ø/	euh	n	/ɛn/	enne	w	/du blø ve/	double vé
f	/ɛf/	ef	o	/o/	oh	x	/iks/		iks
g	/ʒe/	jé	p	/pe/	pé	y	/i gʀɛk/	i grec
h	/aʃ/	ache	q	/ky/	ku	z	/zɛd/		zed
i	/i/	i	r	/ɛʀ/	erre				

B. The letters **k** and **w** are rare in French and occur only in words borrowed
  directly from other languages. Examples are **le week-end, le wagon, le
  kiosque.**

C. The letter **h** is always silent. Words that start with **h** sound as though
  they start with the vowel that follows. Two examples are **homme** /ɔm/
  and **hôtel** /o tɛl/.

Accent marks and punctuation

A. French has a system of written accent marks that are as important as the dot of an **i** or the cross of a **t**. Be sure to learn accents as part of the spelling of words.

accent	name		example
´	l'accent aigu	*acute accent*	poignée
`	l'accent grave	*grave accent*	très
^	l'accent circonflexe	*circumflex accent*	hôtel
¸	la cédille	*cedilla*	français
¨	le tréma	*dieresis*	Noël

B. Accents can indicate pronunciation.

commençons /kɔ mã sɔ̃/
classe, café /klas/, /ka fe/

C. Accents can differentiate words.

a *has* ou *or*
à *to* où *where*

You will not, however, see accents on capital letters. For example, you will see **à Paris,** but **A Paris.**

D. French uses almost the same punctuation marks as English; only quotation marks look different.

.	**le point**	*period*
,	**la virgule**	*comma*
-	**le trait d'union**	*hyphen*
'	**l'apostrophe**	*apostrophe*
«»	**les guillemets**	*quotation marks*

E. To spell words aloud in French, say the letter and any accent mark it may have immediately after it. If the word has a double consonant, say **deux** *(two)* before the letter that is doubled. A *capital* letter is **majuscule** and a *small* letter is **minuscule.**

ça c cédille a   accent a deux c e n t
café c a f e accent aigu   René r majuscule e n e accent aigu

Exercices

A. Repeat the French alphabet after your teacher.

B. In French, spell your full name, your mother's maiden name, and the name of the street where you live.

C. Team up with a classmate and ask each other to spell words from the dialogue. When giving the words, be sure your pronunciation is correct. When spelling the words, be sure to remember accents.

GRAMMAIRE . . . .

I. Nouns and Definite Articles

> You use nouns to name people, places and things.

A. In French, all nouns, whether they represent living or nonliving things, are either masculine or feminine. Nouns referring to male human beings are masculine. Nouns referring to female human beings are generally feminine.

B. An article almost always accompanies a noun in French. The article indicates the gender (masculine or feminine) and the number (singular or plural) of the noun. A masculine noun is introduced by a masculine article. A feminine noun is introduced by a feminine article. French has four forms that may correspond to the English definite article *the*.

L'étudiant parle bien.	*The student speaks well.*
Robert adore **le** français.	*Robert loves French.*

Definite Articles

	singular	plural
masculine	**le** dialogue	**les** dialogues
	l'étudiant	**les** étudiants
feminine	**la** porte	**les** portes
	l'étudiante	**les** étudiantes

C. **Le** /lø/ is used with masculine singular nouns that begin with a consonant.

le stylo	*pen*	**le** crayon	*pencil*
le café	*sidewalk café; coffee*	**le** français	*French (language)*

D. **La** /la/ is used with feminine singular nouns that begin with a consonant.

la radio	*radio*	**la** leçon	*lesson*
la télévision	*television*	**la** classe	*class*

E. **L'** is used with all singular nouns that begin with a vowel sound.

l'ami *(m.)*	/la mi/	*friend*	l'hôtel *(m.)*	/lo tɛl/	*hotel*
l'amie *(f.)*	/la mi/	*friend*	l'enfant *(m. or f.)*	/lã fã/	*child*

F. **Les** is used with plural nouns, masculine and feminine. It is pronounced /le/ before a consonant and /lez/ before a vowel sound.

les livres *(m.)*	/le livʀ/	*books*
les femmes *(f.)*	/le fam/	*women*
les hommes *(m.)*	/le zɔm/	*men*
les amies *(f.)*	/le za mi/	*friends*

CE QU'ILS DISENT

You are no doubt aware that people do not always use a language the way grammar books (or textbooks) describe it. For example, English has the verb *going to,* but most people say "gonna." To help you bridge the gap between written and spoken French, this section, **Ce qu'ils disent** *(What people say),* will appear throughout this book.

In conversations, French people often shorten words. Two that you have just seen are **la télévision,** which becomes **la télé** (often written **la TV**), and **le professeur,** which is shortened to **le prof.** While you must use the masculine **le professeur** for male and female teachers, both **le prof** and **la prof** exist.

▶ ## L'Orthographe

As with English, there are numerous differences in French between what you say and what you write. This section, **L'Orthographe** *(Spelling),* will appear throughout the book to explain forms that are present only when you write in French.

1. In French, the plural of most nouns is formed by adding an **s** to the singular noun. If the noun already ends in **s,** the singular and the plural are the same.

le disque	les disques	*records*
la leçon	les leçons	*lessons*
le cours	les cours	*classes*
l'autobus	les autobus	*buses*

2. The letter **x** is used for the plural of words ending in **-eau.**

le cadeau	les cadeaux	*gifts*
le bureau	les bureaux	*desks, offices*
le tableau	les tableaux	*chalkboards*

ATTENTION

Notice the similarity between **classe** and *class*. French and English words that are alike in sound, spelling, and meaning are *cognates*. There are, however, French words that are similar in spelling to English words but that differ in meaning. These are **faux amis,** or *false friends.* An example is **comment,** which means *how.*

Language

A. Make the following nouns plural.

1. l'enfant	3. le stylo	5. l'ami	7. l'étudiante
2. la carte	4. le disque	6. l'homme	8. l'affiche

B. Make the following nouns singular.

1. les cours	3. les femmes	5. les exercices	7. les livres
2. les radios	4. les étudiants	6. les hommes	8. les amies

C. Use the correct definite article with the following nouns. (Watch for the plural marker **s** or **x.**)

1. fenêtre	4. hommes	7. bureaux	10. amies
2. disques	5. crayon	8. alphabet	11. leçon
3. classe	6. ami	9. stylos	12. femmes

Culture

D. **L'hypermarché.** An **hypermarché** is a huge store that combines a supermarket and a discount store, such as K-Mart, under one roof. Two well-known French chains are **Carrefour** and **Mammouth.** Indicate whether or not you think the following items are available for sale in an **hypermarché** by adding a definite article and **Oui** or **Non.**

MODEL: livres *Les livres? Oui.*
          étudiants *Les étudiants? Non!*

1. cartes	3. disques	5. affiches	7. crayons
2. bises	4. enfants	6. cours	8. livres

Communication

E. Divide into pairs. Take turns pointing to classroom or personal objects asking, **Qu'est-ce que c'est?** Your partner will answer with **C'est,** a definite article, and a noun.

MODEL: Student 1: (Pointing to the window) *Qu'est-ce que c'est?*
          Student 2: *C'est la fenêtre.*

F. Team up with a classmate to study the nouns you have learned. When giving the French word, use the definite article.

MODEL: Student 1: *Comment dit-on «book»?*
          Student 2: *On dit «le livre.»*

Then choose a French word and ask your classmate English equivalent.

MODEL: Student 1: *Qu'est-ce que «le stylo» veut dire?*
Student 2: *Cela veut dire «pen.»*

II. Subject Pronouns and -er Verbs

A. Subject Pronouns

> You use pronouns to avoid repeating the names of people and things when the meaning is clear.

1. Subject pronouns replace noun subjects.

Paul chante. → *Il chante.*   **Paul** sings. → *He sings.*
Paul et Marie étudient. →   **Paul and Marie** study. →
   Ils étudient.   *They study.*

Subject Pronouns

je	*I*	nous	*we*
tu	*you*	vous	*you*
il	*he*	ils	*they (m.)*
elle	*she*	elles	*they (f.)*
on	*one, we, you, they*		

2. Note that there are two French forms for *you*: **tu** and **vous. Tu** is the singular, informal form. Use **tu** to address a person that you know well, such as a friend or a relative, or a child.

Tu parles français?   *Do **you** speak French?*

Vous can be singular or plural. Use **vous** to speak to one person you do not know well, or are unsure how to address, or wish to treat with respect. Also use **vous** to speak to more than one person, regardless of your relationship.

Vous parlez anglais, Madame?   *Do **you** speak English, ma'am?*
Philippe et Isabelle, **vous**   *Philippe and Isabelle, are **you***
   écoutez le professeur?   *listening to the teacher?*

CE QU'ILS DISENT

In the last few years, the French people have relaxed their constraints on the use of **tu**. Business associates who would have used **vous** in the past are now more likely to use **tu** with each other. As a foreigner, you should still use **vous** with native speakers until they use **tu** with you. It is generally acceptable, however, to use **tu** with another student.

In other parts of the French-speaking world, particularly Louisiana, rules for the **tu–vous** distinction are even more relaxed, with **tu** used for most occasions.

3. There is no specific word in French for *it*. Since all nouns have a gender, **il** refers to masculine nouns and **elle** refers to feminine nouns.

4. **Elles** refers to two or more females or feminine nouns.

Marie et Isabelle? **Elles** travaillent bien.	*Marie and Isabelle? **They** work hard.*
La porte et la fenêtre? **Elles** ferment mal.	*The door and the window? **They** close badly.*

5. **Ils** refers to two or more males or masculine nouns. **Ils** also refers to a combined group of males and females or masculine and feminine nouns.

Les étudiants? **Ils** écoutent en cours.	*The students? **They** listen in class.*
La carte et le livre? **Ils** sont ici.	*The map and the book? **They** are here.*

6. There is one impersonal subject pronoun in French: **on.** It is used in a general sense and has at least four English equivalents: *we, one, they, people.*

Ici **on** parle français.	*Here **we** speak French.*
	*Here **one** speaks French.*
	*Here **they** speak French.*
	*Here **people** speak French.*

CE QU'ILS DISENT

In conversational French, the pronoun **on** usually replaces **nous.**

On regarde la télévision?	*Shall **we** watch television?*
On commence!	*Let's begin!*

B. -er Verbs

> You use verbs to describe actions or states of being.

1. French verbs are classified by the ending of the infinitive. The infinitive consists of a stem (like **chant**) and an ending (like -er). The largest group of French verbs has an infinitive that ends in -er, like **chanter**.

infinitive	*chanter*	*to sing*
singular		
1st person	je **chante**	*I sing, I am singing, I do sing*
2nd person	tu **chantes**	*you sing, you are singing, you do sing*
3rd person	il **chante**	*he sings, he is singing, he does sing*
	elle **chante**	*she sings, she is singing, she does sing*
	on **chante**	*one sings, one is singing, one does sing*
plural		
1st person	nous **chantons**	*we sing, we are singing, we do sing*
2nd person	vous **chantez**	*you sing, you are singing, you do sing*
3rd person	ils **chantent**	*they sing, they are singing, they do sing*
	elles **chantent**	*they sing, they are singing, they do sing*

2. The present tense in French corresponds to three English forms as shown in the preceding verb chart.

En général, ils **chantent** bien, mais ce soir ils **chantent** mal.

*Generally, they **sing** well, but tonight they **are singing** badly.*

3. Conjugated -er verbs have only three pronunciations. The singular forms and the third-person plural forms (**ils / elles**) are pronounced alike. The listener must know from the context whether / il ʃãt / is singular or plural.

je	/ ʃãt /	nous	/ ʃã tõ /
tu	/ ʃãt /	vous	/ ʃã te /
il	/ ʃãt /	ils	/ ʃãt /
elle	/ ʃãt /	elles	/ ʃãt /

4. When a verb starts with a vowel sound, **je** becomes **j'**, the letter **n** of **on** is pronounced, and the final **s** of all plural subject pronouns is pronounced.

J'invite.	/ ʒɛ̃ vit /
On invite.	/ ɔ̃ nɛ̃ vit /
Nous invitons.	/ nu zɛ̃ vi tõ /
Vous invitez.	/ vu zɛ̃ vi te /
Ils invitent.	/ il zɛ̃ vit /
Elles invitent.	/ ɛl zɛ̃ vit /

▶ L'Orthographe

1. All regular -er verbs are conjugated the same way. Written present-tense endings for -er verbs are: **-e, -es, -e, -ons, -ez, -ent.**

2. In written French, verbs that end in **ger** add an **e** before the **-ons** ending (**nous mangeons**). Verbs that end in **cer** add a **cédille** to the c before the **-ons** ending (**nous commençons**). These small changes preserve the "soft" sounds of the g and c.

Mots clés Common and useful -er verbs

adorer	*to love; to adore*	fermer	*to close*
aimer	*to like*	fumer	*to smoke*
arriver	*to arrive*	habiter	*to live (in a place)*
commencer	*to begin*	inviter	*to invite*
continuer	*to continue*	jouer	*to play*
danser	*to dance*	manger	*to eat*
demander	*to ask (for)*	montrer	*to show*
donner	*to give*	parler	*to speak*
écouter	*to listen*	regarder	*to watch*
étudier	*to study*	terminer	*to end*
expliquer	*to explain*	travailler	*to work*

Language

A. **En cours.** Make complete sentences about the following classmates with each group of words provided.

MODEL: Pierre / aimer / université
Pierre aime l'université.

1. Je / écouter / professeur
2. Philippe / arriver / avec Marie
3. Nous / commencer / examen
4. étudiants / étudier / français
5. Hélène et Chantal / travailler / ensemble
6. Vous / terminer / devoirs

Culture

B. **Le Crazy Horse.** The **Crazy Horse Saloon** is a famous Parisian nightclub. Guess what people do there by using the verbs below with either **Oui** or **Non.**

MODEL: danser   *On danse? Oui.*
étudier le français   *On étudie le français? Non!*

1. fumer
2. manger
3. parler
4. travailler
5. regarder les hommes et les femmes
6. écouter la radio
7. regarder la télé
8. jouer

Communication

C. Make a list of five statements about yourself using the **-er** verbs and other vocabulary you have learned. Present your list to the class.

MODEL: *J'aime les enfants. Je chante bien. Je danse mal. Je regarde la télévision. J'étudie le français.*

D. **Questions personnelles.** A l'université

1. Le professeur de français explique bien la leçon?
2. Vous parlez français?
3. Vous étudiez beaucoup?
4. Les étudiants travaillent bien ici?
5. Vous écoutez bien le professeur?
6. Vous aimez les cours à l'université?

Carte Bleue Visa. Elle parle toutes les langues.

III. Yes-or-No Questions

> You use yes-or-no questions to find out information.

A. One of three basic ways to ask a yes-or-no question in French is to use intonation. This means that you make your voice rise, rather than fall, at the end of a sentence.

Statement:	Il travaille ici.	*He works here.*
Question:	Il travaille ici?	*He works here?*

B. You can add the phrase **Est-ce que** to the beginning of a sentence.

Statement:	Cécile parle bien.	*Cécile speaks well.*
Question:	Est-ce que Cécile parle bien?	
	Does Cécile speak well?	

When the subject of a sentence begins with a vowel, the **e** of **que** is not pronounced and is replaced with an apostrophe.

Est-ce **qu'il** regarde la télévision?   *Is he watching television?*
Est-ce **qu'on** parle français ici?   *Is French spoken here?*

C. You can add the phrase **n'est-ce pas?** to the end of a sentence.

Statement:	Je joue bien.	*I play well.*
Question:	Je joue bien, n'est-ce pas?	
	I play well, don't I?	
Statement:	Elle parle français.	*She speaks French.*
Question:	Elle parle français, n'est-ce pas?	
	She speaks French, doesn't she?	

CE QU'ILS DISENT

In conversation, rising intonation is the most frequently used type of question. The expression **n'est-ce pas?** is used often, but implies that the speaker expects an affirmative answer.

—Vous parlez anglais, n'est-ce pas?   *You speak English, don't you?*
—Oui, je parle anglais.   *Yes, I speak English.*

Language

A. Since you do not believe everything you hear, ask for a clarification of each of the following sentences, using yes-or-no questions.

MODEL: Patricia aime le français.
Patricia aime le français?
Est-ce que Patricia aime le français?
Patricia aime le français, n'est-ce pas?

1. Les enfants étudient la carte.
2. Le prof ferme la porte.
3. Les étudiants fument beaucoup.
4. Tu aimes danser.
5. Jean et Marie habitent ici.
6. On écoute beaucoup la radio.

B. You are circulating from group to group at a party and you overhear several conversations. Ask the question that elicited the following answers. Be sure to use the correct pronoun. You have a choice as to which question form to use.

MODEL: Oui, je travaille après le cours.
Tu travailles après le cours?
Est-ce que tu travailles après le cours?
Tu travailles après le cours, n'est-ce pas?

1. Oui, elles aiment la radio.
2. Oui, tu parles bien.
3. Oui, je chante bien.
4. Oui, vous mangez beaucoup.
5. Oui, on parle anglais ici.
6. Oui, elles jouent ensemble.

Culture

C. You are going to interview someone about the francophone world. Ask questions using **on** with the following expressions.

1. aimer les Américains
2. fumer beaucoup
3. regarder beaucoup la télé
4. aimer faire la bise
5. étudiants / travailler beaucoup
6. parler anglais à Paris
7. manger bien
8. parler français au Québec

Communication

D. Remember that in asking questions, you must indicate your relationship with the person to whom you are speaking by choosing between **tu** and **vous**. Use the following expressions to ask questions of your classmates and your teacher.

1. regarder beaucoup la télé?
2. aimer les étudiants?
3. adorer les enfants?
4. fumer?
5. aimer danser?
6. travailler beaucoup?

E. Prepare five questions using -er verbs from the list on page 18. Interview a classmate in a small group or in front of the class.

IV. Numbers from 0 to 20

0 zéro	6 six	11 onze	16 seize
1 un	7 sept	12 douze	17 dix-sept
2 deux	8 huit	13 treize	18 dix-huit
3 trois	9 neuf	14 quatorze	19 dix-neuf
4 quatre	10 dix	15 quinze	20 vingt
5 cinq			

A. Numbers can be used alone, as in telephone numbers, or they can be used with nouns, for example, **trois livres**. When used with nouns, many numbers require pronunciation changes. You will study this in Chapter 4.

B. To express math problems, use the following:

Combien font deux et trois?	*How much are two and three?*
ou	*or*
Combien font deux **plus** trois?	*How much are two and three?*
Deux plus trois font cinq.	*Two and three are five.*
Combien font vingt **moins** six?	*How much is twenty minus six?*
Vingt moins six font quatorze.	*Twenty minus six is fourteen.*
Combien font quatre **multiplié par** trois?	*How much is four multiplied by three?*
Quatre multiplié par trois font douze.	*Four multiplied by three is twelve.*
Combien font seize **divisé par** quatre?	*How much is sixteen divided by four?*
Seize divisé par quatre font quatre.	*Sixteen divided by four is four.*

Language

A. Count in French, continuing each series of numbers started below.

1. 1, 2, 3 . . . 20
2. 2, 4, 6 . . . 20
3. 1, 3, 5 . . . 19
4. 20, 19, 18 . . . 0
5. 20, 18, 16 . . . 0
6. 19, 17, 15 . . . 1

B. Do the following math problems in French.

1. $12 + 3 =$
2. $11 + 2 =$
3. $2 \times 2 =$
4. $15 \div 3 =$
5. $1 + 5 =$
6. $16 - 2 =$
7. $3 \times 5 =$
8. $20 \div 2 =$
9. $9 + 8 =$
10. $5 - 5 =$
11. $4 \times 4 =$
12. $18 \div 3 =$
13. $2 + 17 =$
14. $20 - 1 =$
15. $6 \times 3 =$
16. $10 \div 2 =$

Culture

C. In Quebec, people say telephone numbers one digit at a time. Read the numbers for the following places you might have to call while in Quebec.

    1. la Banque nationale du Canada   (416) 867-5000
    2. la Bibliothèque nationale du Québec   (514) 873-4553
    3. le Musée du Québec   (418) 643-4173
    4. *Le Devoir*   (514) 842-9645
    5. l'Hôpital général de Montréal   (514) 937-6011
    6. l'Université du Québec   (418) 657-3551

Communication

D. Divide into pairs and ask each other math problems, the answers to which range from 0 to 20.

    MODEL: Student 1: *Combien font sept et deux?*
                Student 2: *Sept et deux font neuf.*

                Student 1: *Combien font cinq multiplié par deux?*
                Student 2: *Cinq multiplié par deux font dix.*

E. Read aloud your Social Security number, and your classmates will write it. Then ask one of them to verify your number by reading it aloud.

COMMUNIQUONS ....

Commencer et terminer les conversations

The way people greet each other and manage conversations varies from culture to culture. An important consideration is the degree of familiarity between the speaker and the person being greeted. In France, people greet acquaintances (**les connaissances**) and business associates with a few words and a handshake. Good friends and relatives may embrace lightly and kiss on both cheeks (**faire les bises**). Formal situations require a word of greeting (e.g., **Bonjour**) and the title **Monsieur, Madame,** or **Mademoiselle,** but no last name.

      Small talk in French involves topics similar to those of American conversations: the speakers' health, their recent activities, and the weather. Like English speakers, French speakers use a variety of expressions to end a conversation. However, the expressions **Salut!** and **Bonsoir!** can be used for both arrival and departure. In Quebec, **Bonjour** is also used in this way.

On commence les conversations avec les amis / les connaissances.

Salut!	*Hi!*
Tiens!	*Hey!*
Dis donc!	*Say!*

On commence les conversations avec les personnes importantes.

Bonjour, Monsieur / Messieurs.	*Good morning / afternoon, sir / gentlemen.*
Bonjour, Madame / Mesdames.	*Good morning / afternoon, ma'am / ladies.*
Bonsoir, Mademoiselle / Mesdemoiselles.	*Good evening miss / ladies.*

On commence les conversations avec les inconnus (*strangers*).

Pardon, Monsieur.	*Pardon / Excuse me, sir.*
Excusez-moi, Madame.	*Excuse me, ma'am.*
Pardonnez-moi, Mademoiselle.	*Pardon me, miss.*

On continue les conversations.

Ça va? / Comment ça va? / Ça va bien?	*How's it going?*
Comment allez-vous?	*How are you?*
Qu'est-ce que tu deviens?	*What are you up to?*
Qu'est-ce que vous faites?	*What are you doing?*
Quoi de neuf?	*What's new?*
Il fait chaud!	*It's hot!*
Il fait froid!	*It's cold!*

On termine les conversations.

A bientôt.	*See you soon.*
A demain.	*See you tomorrow.*
A la prochaine.	*See you next time.*
A tout à l'heure.	*See you a little later.*
Bonne nuit.	*Good night. (when one is going to bed)*
Bonsoir.	*Good evening. / Good night.*
Salut.	*So long.*

Interaction   *Marie rencontre* (meets) *Monsieur Dupont.*

MARIE: Bonjour, Monsieur!

M. DUPONT: Bonjour, Marie. Comment ça va?

MARIE: Ça va, merci. Et vous?

M. DUPONT: Pas mal. Qu'est-ce que vous faites?

MARIE: J'étudie l'anglais à l'université.

M. DUPONT: Très bien. A la prochaine!

Activités

A. What would the person mentioned in the following situations be most likely to say?

   1. Jacques is kissing his mother good night.
   2. Patricia has just run into a friend on campus.
   3. Philippe and his English teacher arrive at the classroom at the same time.
   4. Isabelle is leaving class, but she will see her classmates the next day.
   5. Anne and Marie are going to different classes, but they have plans to study together later in the afternoon.
   6. The school year is over, and you may not see your friends for several months.
   7. You stop someone on the street to ask directions.
   8. Marc is leaving the room, but he will be back in an hour.

B. Greet the student next to you.

C. Go to the front of the class with a classmate. Greet each other and say good-bye.

D. Write a short dialogue with a classmate involving two friends who run into each other, and then present it in front of the class.

LECTURE CULTURELLE ....

Avant la lecture

French and American universities and university life (**la vie universitaire**) differ widely. Unlike their American counterparts, French students take a comprehensive examination at the end of secondary school. The two-thirds who pass are entitled to attend one of the numerous French universities, almost all of which are public. Tuition is practically free, and with the appropriate background students may select any field they wish.

Despite the increase in the number of suburban universities, French universities are principally located in large cities. Because they are often in the center of town, they do not have a campus as is common in the United States; there are no open, grassy areas or student unions to serve as gathering places.

Activité

Skim the reading passage to find the following information:

1. the name of the examination students take at the end of high school
2. what high school students and college students are called
3. where students live while attending the university

L'Université française

En France, le «college» *n'* existe *pas.* A la *fin* de l'*école* secondaire *(le lycée)*, *les Français passent* le baccalauréat (le «bac», le «bachot»), un examen très complet. *Maintenant*, le bac est le passeport *pour* entrer dans la vie professionnelle *ou* à l'université. En 20 *ans,* le nombre de *bacheliers* a triplé.

not / end / school / high school / French people take / Now / to

or / years / holders of the bac / Today / percent / young people / are / pupils / as / year / ends

5   *Aujourd'hui,* 25 *pour cent* des *jeunes* de 20 à 24 ans étudient dans les universités. Ils ne *sont* pas *élèves, comme* au lycée, mais étudiants. *L'année* universitaire commence en octobre et *finit* en mai. Les étudiants passent les examens en juin. *S'ils échouent,* ils repassent en septembre. Dans les universités, la présence aux cours n'est pas obligatoire.

If / fail

10   Dans le système français, les étudiants sont très indépendants. S'ils sont ambitieux, ils *vont toujours* aux cours et ils sont bien préparés. Les *autres* étudiants *sèchent* les cours et fréquentent les cafés et les cinémas, mais ils échouent *souvent* en juin.

go / always / other
cut
often

En France, l'université ressemble à la «graduate school» américaine.
15   Généralement, les étudiants n'habitent pas *sur* le campus. Ils habitent en famille ou ils *louent* une *chambre en ville.* Les activités extra-universitaires ne sont pas très *nombreuses.* Les «sororities» et «fraternities» et le «football américain» n'existent pas.

on
rent / room / downtown
numerous

La liste des cours à l'université Paris 1

Après la lecture

Questions sur le texte

1. Qu'est-ce que *(What is)* le bac?
2. Quand *(When)* est-ce que l'année universitaire commence en France? Et aux Etats-Unis?
3. Quand est-ce qu'elle finit?
4. Quand est-ce que les étudiants passent les examens en France?
5. Est-ce que la présence aux cours est obligatoire en France? Et aux Etats-Unis?
6. Généralement, est-ce que les étudiants habitent sur le campus en France?

Activité

Using the reading selection, make a list in French of differences (**différences**) and similarities (**similarités**) between university life in France and in the United States.

Chapitre 2

LA FAMILLE ET LES AMIS

Dans un parc à Paris

Commençons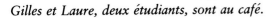

Au café °—○

Gilles et Laure, deux étudiants, sont au café.

GILLES: Tiens, voilà Monique!

LAURE: Oui, elle est avec Jacques.

GILLES: C'est le dernier petit ami?

LAURE: Oui, il est sympathique et studieux.

GILLES: Et Monique, elle n'est pas studieuse?

LAURE: Si, elle est toujours première. Ils étudient l'anglais ensemble.

GILLES: L'anglais? Tu es certaine?

LAURE: Oui, quand ils ne sont pas au café!

Devant une boîte

Des jeunes gens sont devant une boîte.

MONIQUE: Où est la sœur de Patrick?

LAURE: Chantal? Elle arrive avec un copain américain.

CHANTAL: Salut! *(Elle embrasse Monique et Laure.)* Voici Jim. Il est étudiant avec Patrick; ils sont ensemble en philo à la fac.

JIM: Enchanté. Je suis très heureux de passer la soirée avec vous. *(A Chantal)* Ton frère n'est pas là?

MONIQUE: Si. Il gare la voiture.

CHANTAL: Il est toujours en retard. Entrons sans lui.

Mots clés

sont (être)	*are*	devant	*in front of*
au	*at*	boîte	*(night)club*
Tiens!	*Hey!*	des jeunes	*some young*
est (être)	*is*	gens	*people*
dernier, -ère	*latest*	où	*where*
petit ami /	*boyfriend /*	sœur	*sister*
petite amie	*girlfriend*	copain (m.) /	*friend*
sympathique	*nice*	copine (f.)	
studieux, -euse	*studious*	américain, -e	*american*
Si.	*Yes, of*	embrasse	*kisses*
	course.	(embrasser)	
toujours	*always*	philo(sophie) (f.)	*philosophy*
premier, -ère	*first*	Enchanté, -e.	*Delighted.*
es (être)	*are*	suis (être)	*am*
certain, -e	*certain*	heureux, -se	*happy*
quand	*when*	passer	*to spend*
ne... pas	*not*	soirée	*evening*

ton frère *(m.)*	*your brother*	**Entrons.**	*Let's go in.*
là	*here*	(entrer)	
gare (garer)	*is parking*	**sans**	*without*
voiture	*car*	**lui**	*him*
en retard	*late*		

Faisons connaissance

In general, French families are much closer than American families. Many people remain in the areas where they were brought up as children, and families are not scattered all over the country as in the United States. Even after they are married, people continue to visit their parents regularly. The main meal on Sunday still provides an opportunity for family members to get together. The French calendar also has many holidays that constitute occasions for family reunions. In addition, it is not unusual for parents, married children, and sometimes grandparents to plan their summer vacations together.

Having friends is very important to French people. They tend, however, to have fewer friends than Americans do, because in their view, friendships take longer to get established and are not as casual as some relationships among Americans. The French still make a distinction between an acquaintance (**une connaissance**) and a friend (**un(e) ami(e))**. This is also true in the business world, where doing business with someone does not automatically turn the person into a friend. Most of the time, that person remains a business acquaintance (**une relation d'affaires).**

Un dîner en famille

Etudions les dialogues

A. Au café

1. Est-ce que Monique est la petite amie de Gilles?
2. Elle est studieuse, n'est-ce pas? Et Jacques?
3. Est-ce que Jacques est toujours premier?
4. Jacques et Monique étudient le français, n'est-ce pas?

B. Devant une boîte

1. Est-ce que Monique est la sœur de Patrick?
2. Jim est américain, n'est-ce pas?
3. Jim et Patrick sont en philo?
4. Patrick gare la voiture, n'est-ce pas?

Enrichissons notre vocabulaire

La famille de Marie *(Marie's family)*

le grand-père — Jean Leclair
la grand-mère — Renée Leclair
l'oncle — Jacques Leclair
la tante — Nicole Leclair
la mère — Anne Dupont
le père — Martin Dupont
le cousin — René Leclair
la cousine — Pauline Leclair
Marie Dupont
le frère — Louis Dupont
la sœur — Claire Dupont

la femme	*the wife*	la fille	*the daughter*
le mari	*the husband*	les enfants	*the children*
les parents	*the parents*	les petits-	*the grand-*
les grands-	*the grand-*	enfants	*children*
parents	*parents*	le neveu	*the nephew*
le fils	*the son*	la nièce	*the niece*

Les amis *(The friends)*

le / la **camarade de chambre**	*the roommate*
le / la **camarade de cours**	*the classmate*
la **fille**	*the girl*
le **garçon**	*the boy*

Quelques distractions favorites *(A few favorite pastimes)*

l'**art** *(m.)* **moderne**	*modern art*
le **rock**	*rock 'n' roll*
le **jazz**	*jazz*
la **musique classique**	*classical music*
les **sports** *(m.)*	*sports*
les **matchs** *(m.)* **de football**	*soccer games*
les **films** *(m.)* **à la télé**	*films on TV*

J'aime / Je déteste *(I like / I dislike)*

aimer / aimer **faire**	*to love / to like **to do***
aimer bien	*to like*
aimer mieux	*to prefer*
apprécier	*to appreciate*
désirer	*to want*
détester / détester faire	*to hate / to hate to do*
—**Qu'est-ce que** tu aimes / aimes faire?	***What do you like / like to do?***
—J'adore **fréquenter** les **boîtes de nuit.**	*I love **to go to nightclubs.***
—**Moi aussi,** je fréquente souvent les **clubs** *(m.).*	***Me too, I often** go to nightclubs.*
—Qu'est-ce que tu détestes?	*What do you hate?*
—Je déteste l'**hypocrisie** *(f.)* / l'**intolérance** *(f.).*	*I hate **hypocrisy / intolerance.***
—J'aime mieux la **sincérité.**	*I prefer **sincerity.***

Prononciation   Word Stress in French   [°━°]

A. Learners of English as a foreign language often have a great deal of difficulty putting stress on the proper syllables. Some words, such as *record* or *present,* can vary in pronunciation according to their meaning. Words can even vary according to region. For example, one says *laboratory* in England and *laboratory* in the United States. In French, however, all syllables receive the same stress except the last, which has a somewhat longer vowel.

Notice the difference in stress as you repeat the following pairs of English and French words after your teacher.

English	French
ex*am*ine	exa*mine*
*mer*chandise	marchan*dise*
a*part*ment	apparte*ment*

B. In French, each syllable has the same stress, and vowels maintain the same pronunciation throughout the word. This is not the case in English. For example, *Alabama* has the same written vowel throughout, but in its unaccented syllables (the second and the fourth), the vowel sound is reduced to /ə/, the "uh" sound. In French, vowel quality does not change.

Note the difference in the sound and quality of the italicized vowels as you repeat the following pairs of English and French words after your teacher.

English	French
un*i*versity	un*i*versité
tel*e*vision	tél*é*vision
labor*a*tory	labor*a*toire

Exercice

Read the following sentences aloud, taking care to put equal stress on all syllables.

1. Je regarde la télévision.
2. Paul examine l'itinéraire.
3. Nous visitons le laboratoire.
4. Elle enveloppe les marchandises.
5. La police occupe l'appartement.
6. Le professeur est intelligent.

GRAMMAIRE ....

I. Negation

> You use the negative to indicate that something is not true or does not occur.

A. To make a statement negative in French, place the words **ne... pas** around the conjugated verb.

Est-ce qu'ils sont au café?	*Are they at the café?*
Non, ils **ne** sont **pas** au café.	*No, they aren't at the café.*

B. If there are two consecutive verbs, you still place the **ne... pas** around the conjugated verb to make the statement negative.

Ils aiment travailler ensemble?	*Do they like to work together?*
Non, ils **n'**aiment **pas** travailler ensemble.	*No they **don't** like to work together.*

C. If the verb begins with a vowel sound, you do not pronounce the **e** of **ne**, and you write **n'**.

Elle **n'**est pas studieuse.	*She isn't studious.*
Tu **n'**es pas étudiant.	*You aren't a student.*

Even before a consonant, the **e** of **ne** is rarely pronounced.

Vous n*é* parlez pas bien.	*You don't speak well.*
Je n*é* ferme pas la fenêtre.	*I am not closing the window.*

The pronunciation of the **s** of **pas** before a vowel is optional.

Ils ne sont pas‿au café. ⎫	*They aren't at the café.*
Ils ne sont pas / au café. ⎭	

CE QU'ILS DISENT

In casual conversation, the French leave out the **ne** of the negation. This is particularly the case with young people. However, they would never write that way, and you must always use **ne** to maintain an appropriate style.

Speaking	**Writing**
On mange pas beaucoup.	On **ne** mange pas beaucoup.
Il écoute pas la radio.	Il **n'**écoute pas la radio.
C'est pas un stylo.	Ce **n'**est pas un stylo.

Language

A. **Mais non!** You think your friend Robert is always wrong. Contradict every sentence he says.

MODEL: Nadine joue avec les enfants.
Nadine ne joue pas avec les enfants.

1. Je danse avec les sœurs de Louise.
2. Le frère de Jean parle beaucoup.
3. Les parents de Michelle adorent la musique.
4. Tu apprécies l'art moderne?
5. Vous travaillez peu.
6. Marthe et Jean mangent souvent.

Culture

B. **En France?** Answer the following questions based on your knowledge of life in France.

    1. On parle anglais avec les copains?
    2. Les femmes travaillent?
    3. Les Français fument peu?
    4. Ils détestent la musique américaine?
    5. Les parents voyagent avec les enfants?
    6. Les Français fréquentent les cafés?

Communication

C. **En famille.** Complete the following statements as they apply to your family and you. If your answer is negative, give your own alternative or use one of the suggestions in parentheses.

    MODEL: J'aime l'art. (la musique)
               Non, je n'aime pas l'art. J'aime la musique.

    1. Je travaille mal. (bien / beaucoup / souvent)
    2. J'apprécie l'intolérance. (l'hypocrisie / la sincérité)
    3. Mes *(My)* parents aiment le rock. (jouer / danser)
    4. Mes frères / sœurs adorent étudier. (les sports / les cafés)
    5. Ma *(My)* famille et moi, nous regardons les matchs de football. (écouter la radio / fréquenter les clubs)
    6. Ma famille déteste mes copains. (adorer / apprécier)

D. Divide into groups of three or four and find someone who can answer truthfully each of the following questions in the negative.

    1. Tu chantes bien?   5. Tu manges bien?
    2. Tu écoutes souvent la radio?   6. Tu aimes regarder les films à
    3. Tu fumes?   la télé?
    4. Tu travailles beaucoup?

SOCIÉTÉ INSTALLATIONS TÉLÉPHONIQUES
MARNE-LA-VALLÉE recherche
1 RESPONSABLE SERVICE TRAVAUX
Il aura une bonne expérience du montage
et sera organisé, méthodique
Ses fonctions : gérer le planning travaux, suivi
de stock. Chantier, approvisionnement.
Tél. pour rendez-vous : 60.20.58.50

NANTERRE
Cuverture
nouvelle agence
travail temporaire
ABC I
GROUPE

PEINTRES CHEFS D'ÉQUIPE O.H.Q.
INTÉRIEUR ET BÂTIMENT
POSEURS REVÊTEMENTS MURAUX
ET REVÊTEMENTS DE SOL
POSEURS FAUX PLAFONDS - MENUISIERS
MAÇONS V.R.D. - MAÇONS BATIMENT
BOISEURS O.Q.3. ET O.H.Q. - ENDUISEURS
CONDUCTEURS D'ENGINS
ELECTRICIENS BATIMENT INDUSTRIEL

Chantal NEDELEC - Eric BOUCHER
184. avenue Georges-Clemenceau
Tél. 42.04.19.76
Accès R.E.R. La Défense
Bus 158, arrêt Félix-Faure

CHAMPAGNE
POMMERY
CRÉER POMMERY C'EST TOUT UN ART.

II. Etre / Etre and Occupation or Nationality

> You use **être** to indicate a state of being or to describe something.

A. Etre

1. **Etre** is an irregular verb, so you must memorize its forms.

être	*(to be)*				
je **suis**	/ʒø sɥi/	*I am*	nous **sommes**	/nu sɔm/	*we are*
tu es	/ty ɛ/	*you are*	vous **êtes**	/vu zɛt/	*you are*
il **est**	/i lɛ/	*he is*	ils **sont**	/il sɔ̃/	*they are*
elle **est**	/ɛ lɛ/	*she is*	elles **sont**	/ɛl sɔ̃/	*they are*
on **est**	/ɔ̃ nɛ/	*we are*			

2. The final written consonant of each form of **être** is usually not pronounced. When the verb occurs before a vowel, however, the **t** of the third-person forms is pronounced.

Elle est‿étudiante.   *She is a student.*
Ils sont‿en philo.   *They are philosophy majors.*

3. The other final consonants may be pronounced and linked before vowels, but it is not necessary.

Je suis‿étudiant. ⎫
Je suis / étudiant. ⎬   *I am a student.*

Tu es‿américaine. ⎫
Tu es / américaine. ⎬   *You are American.*

B. Etre with Occupation or Nationality

1. When **être** is used with occupation or nationality, no article is used—the noun or adjective follows the verb directly.

Marie **est médecin.**   *Marie is a doctor.*   (noun)
Christian **est allemand.**   *Christian is German.* (adjective)

▶ L'Orthographe

Note that adjectives of nationality are not capitalized in French. When used as nouns, however, they are capitalized.

Il invite trois **Français.**	*He is inviting three **French people.***
Les **Canadiens** travaillent beaucoup.	***Canadians** work a lot.*

2. Some occupations have one form for both the masculine and feminine.

Mme Dupont est **professeur.**	*Mrs. Dupont is **a teacher.***
L'**auteur** est aussi **actrice.**	*The author is also **an actress.***

Mots clés   Professions and Nationalities

Les professions (f.)

l'acteur (m.),
  l'actrice (f.)
l'agent de
  police (m.)
l'architecte
  (m.)
l'artiste (m.
  or f.)
l'auteur (m.)
l'avocat (m.),
  l'avocate (f.)
  lawyer
le diplomate

l'économiste (m.)
l'ingénieur (m.)
le / la journaliste
le médecin
  doctor
le musicien,
  la musicienne
le président,
  la présidente
le programmeur,
  la programmeuse
le / la secrétaire

Les nationalités (f.)

allemand,	espagnol,
allemande	espagnole
German	*Spanish*
américain,	français,
américaine	française
anglais,	italien,
anglaise	italienne
canadien,	
canadienne	

CE QU'ILS DISENT

1. In very informal conversation, the **u** of **tu** is often dropped with the verb **être.** This may occur in sentences in which the **ne** of the negative is also dropped.

T'es certain?	*Are you sure?*
T'es pas anglais!	*You aren't English!*

2. In Quebec, French speakers have invented the feminine form **écrivaine** because there are so many active women writers there. The **Québécois** in general are more relaxed about vocabulary than the French; one also sees **auteure** and **professeure.**

Language

A. **Les professions.** What do the following people do? Use the correct form of **être**.

MODEL: Je / étudiant(e)
        Je suis étudiant(e).

1. L'oncle de Jean / musicien
2. Les cousines de Patricia / profs
3. Vous / diplomate
4. Nous / étudiants
5. Elle / agent de police
6. La nièce de Robert / journaliste

Culture

B. **Des célébrités françaises.** Identify the professions of the following famous French-speaking people.

MODEL: Debussy
        Il est musicien.

1. Gérard Depardieu
2. l'Inspecteur Clouseau
3. Le Corbusier
4. Gauguin et Van Gogh
5. Isabelle Adjani
6. François Mitterrand
7. Gustave Eiffel
8. Dumas père et Dumas fils

C. **Familles célèbres.** Identify the following people by their famous French-speaking family members.

MODEL: la fille de Victor Hugo?
        C'est Adèle H.

1. le mari de Joséphine?
2. la femme de Louis XVI?
3. le père de Louis IX (Saint Louis)?
4. la copine de Sartre?
5. la femme de Louis Malle?
6. l'ex-femme de Roger Vadim?

Communication

D. Can you think of famous people of the following occupations and nationalities?

MODEL: Student 1: *Qui* (Who) *est acteur?*
        Student 2: *Alain Delon est acteur.*

actrice	français(e)	espagnol(e)	anglais(e)
médecin	américain(e)	diplomate	journaliste
artiste	avocat	étudiant(e)	auteur
canadien(ne)	italien(ne)	musicien(ne)	agent de police

E. **Mes connaissances.** Ask each other the following questions about people you know. Be sure to answer in complete sentences, and honestly!

1. Le professeur est français?
2. Est-ce que le président est intelligent? Et le vice-président?
3. Les parents de votre *(your)* copain / copine sont sympathiques?

4. Les camarades de cours sont américains?
5. Est-ce que vous êtes studieux (-euse)?
6. Tu es toujours premier (-ère)?

III. Descriptive Adjectives

> You use adjectives to describe people and things.

A. In French, adjectives are usually placed *after* the noun, and they may vary in pronunciation or spelling or both, to agree in gender and number with the nouns they describe.

B. Singular and Plural Forms

1. Most adjectives add a written -s to form the plural. The pronunciation does not change.

L'étudiant **intelligent** travaille beaucoup.	The **intelligent** student works a lot.
Les étudiants **intelligents** travaillent beaucoup.	**Intelligent** students work a lot.
Elle n'est pas **studieuse**?	She isn't **studious**?
Elles ne sont pas **studieuses**.	They aren't **studious**.

2. Masculine adjectives that end in a written -s or -x do not have a different plural form.

Le professeur **français** est **ambitieux**.	The **French** professor is **ambitious**.
Les professeurs **français** sont **ambitieux**.	The **French** professors are **ambitious**.

3. To describe a mixed group of masculine and feminine nouns, use the masculine plural form of the adjective.

Marie et Pierre ne sont pas **italiens**.	Marie and Pierre are not **Italian**.

C. Masculine and Feminine Forms

1. Masculine singular adjectives that end in a silent -e do not change in pronunciation or spelling in the feminine.

Le garçon est **sympathique**.	The boy is **nice**.
La fille est **sympathique**.	The girl is **nice**.

Some adjectives that have the same masculine and feminine forms are as follows:

agréable *pleasant*	**difficile**	**fantastique**
désagréable	**facile** *easy*	**formidable** *great*

hypocrite	pessimiste	sincère
impossible	possible	stupide
inutile *useless*	rapide	sympathique
magnifique	riche	timide
optimiste	simple	utile *useful*
pauvre *poor*		

2. Masculine singular adjectives that end in a pronounced vowel or a pronounced consonant are spelled differently in the feminine, although they are pronounced the same.

José est **espagnol.**	*José is **Spanish.***
Maria est **espagnole.**	*Maria is **Spanish.***

Some adjectives that change in spelling but not in pronunciation are as follows:

compliqué, **compliquée** *complicated*	**impoli, impolie** *impolite*
	poli, polie *polite*
espagnol, espagnole	**seul, seule** *alone*
fatigué, fatiguée *tired*	**vrai, vraie** *true*
fermé, fermée *closed*	

3. Many adjectives end in a silent consonant in the masculine. To form their feminine, add a written -e and pronounce the consonant.

Le livre **français** est magnifique.	*The **French** book is great.*
La musique **française** est magnifique.	***French** music is great.*

Some adjectives that end in a silent consonant in the masculine are as follows:

absent, absente	**intelligent, intelligente**
anglais, anglaise	**intéressant, intéressante**
charmant, charmante	**laid, laide** *ugly*
chaud, chaude *hot*	**mauvais, mauvaise** *bad (quality)*
compétent, compétente	
content, contente *happy*	**méchant, méchante** *bad (character)*
fascinant, fascinante	
français, française	**ouvert, ouverte** *open*
froid, froide *cold*	**présent, présente**
incompétent, incompétente	**prudent, prudente** *careful*
indépendant, indépendante	

ATTENTION

Pay particular attention to adjectives to which you add a sound to form the feminine. Final consonants are stronger in French than in English, so you must make a bigger effort to pronounce them. Otherwise, the people to whom you are speaking will not hear the difference between the masculine and feminine forms.

4. Some adjectives end in a nasal vowel in the masculine. To create their feminine forms, add a written **-e.** If the masculine ends in **-en,** however, double the **-n** before adding the **-e.** In both cases, the vowel loses its nasality and the **-n** is pronounced.

Il n'est pas **italien,** mais **américain.**　　*He's not **Italian,** but **American.***

Elle n'est pas **italienne,** mais **américaine.**　　*She's not **Italian,** but **American.***

Some adjectives of this type are as follows:

-ne	**-nne**
américain, américaine	**ancien, ancienne**　*old*
certain, certaine	**canadien, canadienne**
féminin, féminine	**italien, italienne**
masculin, masculine	**parisien, parisienne**
mexicain, mexicaine	

5. To form the feminine of adjectives that end in **-eux,** add the sound / z / and change the **-x** to **-se.**

Le garçon est **paresseux.**　　*The boy is **lazy.***
La fille est **paresseuse.**　　*The girl is **lazy.***

Some adjectives ending in **-eux, -euse** are as follows:

affectueux, **affectueuse**　*affectionate*	**généreux, généreuse**
affreux, affreuse　*terrible*	**heureux, heureuse**　*happy*
ambitieux, ambitieuse	**malheureux,** **malheureuse**　*unhappy*
courageux, courageuse	**paresseux, paresseuse**　*lazy*
dangereux, dangereuse	**sérieux, sérieuse**
ennuyeux, ennuyeuse　*boring*	**studieux, studieuse**

▶ ## L'Orthographe

Two quick rules of thumb that will work for spelling most French adjectives are as follows:

Plural:　　Add an **-s** to any letter except **s** or **x.**
Feminine:　Add an **-e** to any letter except unaccented **e, x,** or **en.**

Language

A. Describe the following people with the definite article and the adjective provided.

MODEL:　étudiant / français　*l'étudiant français*

1. actrice / formidable	4. enfant / paresseux
2. étudiante / intelligent	5. hommes / fatigué
3. auteur / ennuyeux	6. femmes / indépendant

B. Describe the following people and things with the verb **être** and the correct form of the adjective provided.

   MODEL: garçons / fatigué   *Les garçons sont fatigués.*

1. musique / affreux	5. professeurs / intéressant
2. filles / sympathique	6. Nous / fatigué *(two possibilities)*
3. livres / facile	7. Je / américain *(two possibilities)*
4. Ils / mexicain	8. Vous / poli *(four possibilities)*

Culture

C. **L'Amérique.** Describe what you believe are traditional French attitudes toward Americans and American culture, using the following nouns and adjectives.

   MODEL: les Américains: agréable / désagréable
   Les Américains sont agréables.

   1. Les Américains: sympathique / froid
   2. la musique: ennuyeux / fantastique
   3. la télévision: fascinant / affreux
   4. le café: mauvais / formidable
   5. les présidents: compétent / incompétent
   6. la politique *(politics):* prudent / dangereux

Communication

D. Use the adjectives listed below to describe the following people and things. You may also provide your own adjectives if you prefer.

   MODEL: *Les journalistes sont ambitieux et intelligents.*

sincère	ennuyeux	inutile	charmant
hypocrite	ambitieux	fantastique	intelligent
formidable	paresseux	fatigué	heureux
compliqué	utile	méchant	malheureux

1. secrétaires	4. télévision	7. médecins	10. hommes
2. professeurs	4. université	8. président	11. étudiants
3. rock	6. Français	9. femmes	12. Je

E. Tell your preferences by choosing one item from each of the columns on the next page and adding any necessary words.

   MODEL: *J'aime les hommes intelligents.*
   Je n'aime pas les enfants méchants.

A	B	C	
J'aime	femmes	désagréable	généreux
Je n'aime pas	hommes	compétent	stupide
	familles	incompétent	sérieux
	médecins	charmant	sympathique
	étudiants	impoli	sincère
	Français *(pl.)*	intelligent	méchant
			???

IV. Numbers from 21 to 69 / Ordinal Numbers

> You use cardinal numbers to count or quantify *(one, two, three . . .)* and ordinal numbers *(first, second, third . . .)* to rank people or things.

A. A few of the cardinal numbers from 20 to 69 are as follows:

20 vingt	30 trente	40 quarante
21 vingt et un	31 trente et un	41 quarante et un
22 vingt-deux	32 trente-deux	44 quarante-quatre
23 vingt-trois	36 trente-six	47 quarante-sept

50 cinquante	60 soixante
51 cinquante et un	61 soixante et un
55 cinquante-cinq	67 soixante-sept
58 cinquante-huit	69 soixante-neuf

1. **Et** is used with the numbers **21, 31, 41, 51,** and **61;** the **t** of **et** is never pronounced.

2. The succeeding numbers are hyphenated.

3. The **t** of **vingt** is pronounced from **21** to **29.**

4. In **soixante** (/swa sãt/), the **x** is pronounced /s/.

5. Except for **un / une,** numbers do not agree in either number or gender with the nouns they modify.

Quatre garçons habitent ensemble.	*Four boys live together.*
Voilà **neuf** filles.	*There are **nine** girls.*
but: **vingt et une** pages	***twenty-one** pages*

B. Ordinal Numbers

1. To form ordinal numbers, in most cases, simply add the suffix **-ième** to the cardinal number.

cardinal	**ordinal**	
deux	**deuxième**	*second*
trois	**troisième**	*third*

dix-sept	**dix-septième** *seventeenth*
vingt	**vingtième** *twentieth*
vingt et un	**vingt et unième** *twenty-first*

C'est le **troisième** médecin de la famille.	*He/She is the **third** doctor in the family.*
Nous terminons le **quatrième** exercice.	*We are finishing the **fourth** exercise.*

2. Three exceptions are as follows:

cardinal	**ordinal**
un, une	premier, première
cinq	cinquième
neuf	neuvième

In addition, for **deuxième** an alternate form, **second / seconde**, is used.

▶ L'Orthographe

1. If the cardinal number ends in **-e**, you must drop the written **-e** before adding the **-ième** suffix.

cardinal	**ordinal**
onze	**onzième**
trente	**trentième**
cinquante-quatre	**cinquante-quatrième**

2. Ordinal numbers may be abbreviated, as they often are in English.

premier → 1er première → 1ère
cinquième → 5ème or 5^{e}

Language

A. Count in French.

1. 30, 31, 32... 40	3. 25, 26, 27... 35	5. 21, 23, 25... 69
2. 21, 24, 27... 69	4. 20, 22, 24... 68	6. 60, 59, 58... 50

B. Do the following problems in French.

1. 10 + 11 =	4. 15 + 16 =	7. 30 + 15 =	10. 19 + 33 =
2. 14 + 16 =	5. 21 − 12 =	8. 20 + 29 =	11. 40 − 22 =
3. 47 − 19 =	6. 18 + 22 =	9. 24 + 27 =	12. 55 − 34 =

Culture

C. **Au lycée.** The French count years of schooling in reverse order of the American system. The *sixth grade* is **la sixième**, but *seventh grade* is **la**

cinquième. Give the French equivalent of the following grades. (The *senior year* is called **la terminale.**)

1. sixth grade
2. seventh grade
3. eighth grade
4. freshman
5. sophomore
6. junior

D. **Au téléphone.** You are in Paris and want to plan your visits to the following places in advance. Read the names and numbers to your hotel switchboard operator.

1. Air Canada   43.20.14.15
2. le Centre Georges
   Pompidou   45.08.25.00
3. Notre-Dame   40.33.22.63.
4. la tour Eiffel   47.05.44.13
5. La Tour d'Argent
   43.44.32.19
6. Le Moulin Rouge
   42.64.33.69

Communication

E. Rank the following things according to how important they are to you. Use the phrases **En premier:...**, **En deuxième:...**, and so on, to do so.

les amis
être riche
la famille

la profession
la nationalité
être heureux (-euse)

COMMUNIQUONS ....

Faire les présentations

The basic rules of politeness that exist in the United States are also observed in France. You must introduce people who do not know each other, and you must pay attention to the style of language you use. To introduce someone who is older than you, use one of the following formal expressions. For friends and relatives, one of the informal expressions is appropriate.

On présente les adultes.

Monsieur / Madame / Mademoiselle, je voudrais vous présenter Marie.	*Sir / Ma'am / Miss, I would like you to meet Marie.*
Permettez-moi de vous présenter Marie.	*Allow me to introduce Marie to you.*
Enchanté, Monsieur / Madame / Mademoiselle.	*Pleased to meet you, sir / ma'am / miss.*
Très heureux (-euse) (de faire votre connaissance).	*A pleasure (to meet you).*

On présente les amis.

Robert, je voudrais te présenter Marie.	*Robert, I'd like you to meet Marie.*
Robert, je te présente Marie.	*Robert, this is Marie.*
Robert, voilà Marie.	*Robert, this is Marie.*
Salut, Marie.	*Hi, Marie.*
Bonjour, Marie, ça va?	*Hello, Marie, how are you?*

Interaction *Solange et son père rencontrent un professeur sur le campus.*

SOLANGE:	Bonjour, M. Renaud!
M. RENAUD:	Bonjour, Solange. Comment allez-vous?
SOLANGE:	Très bien. Je voudrais vous présenter mon père.
M. RENAUD:	Enchanté, Monsieur.
LE PERE DE SOLANGE:	Très heureux.

«Irène, je vous présente Hélène.»

Activités

A. What would you say to introduce the following people?

1. your roommate and your teacher

3. your parents and your faculty advisor

2. your roommate and an old friend from high school

4. your sister and someone in your class

B. Divide into groups of three and practice introducing your classmates to each other.

LECTURE CULTURELLE ....

Avant la lecture

In a recent poll of the **INSEE (Institut national de la statistique et des études économiques)**, one finds that, at the end of the eighties, a typical French family had two children, and both parents worked. The number of divorces, which tripled between 1970 and 1985, is now stable, but a divorce still occurs in 30 out of each 100 marriages. France has one of the highest divorce rates in Europe.

French people today get married later than they used to. In general, men wait until they are 27, while the average age for women is 25. However, many couples live together before getting married.

Activité

Skim the reading passage for the following information:

1. Find five singular and five plural descriptive adjectives, and tell which ones are cognates and which are not.
2. Find all the numbers that are spelled out in the passage and write the figures they represent above them.
3. Find three things that have a great influence on the upbringing of French children outside their families.
4. Name the people French children prefer to confide in and rank them in descending order of importance.

La Famille française

L'*éducation* d'un enfant est le résultat d'une série d'influences extérieures *comme* l'*école*, les médias et les copains. Mais en France, la famille, et *surtout* les parents, constitue *encore* l'influence *la plus* importante. Les enfants observent *leurs* parents et ils développent leur conception de la *vie*. Les parents
5 français *d'aujourd'hui* sont *mieux* informés *que* leurs *propres* parents et très conscients des difficultés de la vie *actuelle*. Ils sont très préoccupés *par* l'éducation de leurs enfants.

upbringing
such as / school /
  particularly / still / the
  most / their / life
of today / better / than /
  own / present / by

On joue avec les enfants.

Cependant, la vie familiale est différente. Dans la majorité des familles, les grands-parents *n'*habitent *plus* avec leurs enfants et leurs petits-enfants, et les
10 jeunes ne profitent plus de leur expérience. *De plus,* le développement de *l'union libre* et le nombre important de divorces, la réduction du nombre des *naissances* jouent un rôle essentiel dans l'éducation des enfants français.

Aujourd'hui, un nombre *croissant* d'enfants est le résultat du deuxième mariage de la mère; les enfants *ont moins de* frères et de sœurs; un *sur* deux *a*
15 une mère *active. Parmi* les Françaises de 25 à 39 *ans,* trois femmes sur quatre travaillent. C'est aussi vrai *pour* les mères de deux enfants, mais avec trois enfants, une mère sur deux *reste* à la *maison.* A dix ans, un enfant sur dix a des parents séparés ou divorcés et un sur quatre habite encore avec sa famille à 24 ans.

20 Les *années quatre-vingts* signalent une *amélioration* des relations *entre* les générations. Les parents et les enfants sont très affectueux et ils communiquent *facilement.* On parle aux parents plus facilement qu'aux professeurs, mais on préfère discuter des problèmes de la vie avec les copains. Pour la majorité des enfants, la famille constitue *toujours* un refuge. A cinq ans, à vingt ans, ou à
25 vingt-cinq ans, les Français sont en général satisfaits de leur vie familiale.

However

no longer

Furthermore
living together
births

growing

have / fewer / out of /
has / working / Among /
years / for
stays / home

1980s / improvement /
between

easily

still

Après la lecture

Questions sur le texte

1. Est-ce que l'école, les médias et les copains sont les influences les plus importantes sur les enfants?
2. Est-ce que la vie est facile pour les parents d'aujourd'hui?
3. Les grands-parents habitent toujours avec leurs enfants et petits-enfants?
4. Beaucoup de Françaises de 25 à 39 ans travaillent?
5. Est-ce que les années soixante signalent une différence dans les relations familiales?
6. Généralement, les enfants français sont contents?

Activités

A. Using the reading selection, make a list in French of differences (**diff-érences**) and similarities (**similarités**) between family life in France and in the United States.

B. List the people you like and do not like to go to when you have problems.

   MODEL: *J'aime parler avec mes copains.*
            Je n'aime pas parler de mes problèmes avec mes grands-parents.

C. In your family, who are your favorite people? Why?

   MODEL: *J'aime ma sœur; elle est fantastique.*
            J'aime bien mon cousin; il est très intelligent.

AU RESTAURANT

On va manger un couscous.

Commençons ....

A La Goulette

Sylvie, programmeuse à IBM, et Maude, journaliste à Elle, *sont dans un restaurant tunisien à Paris. Elles regardent la carte.*

LE GARÇON: Bonsoir. Vous désirez?

SYLVIE: Je voudrais un apéritif. Vous avez du Martini?

LE GARÇON: Oui, mademoiselle. Rouge ou blanc?

SYLVIE: Rouge, s'il vous plaît.

LE GARÇON: Mademoiselle aussi?

MAUDE: Non, merci.

SYLVIE: J'ai faim ce soir. Je voudrais un couscous au mouton.

LE GARÇON: Vous aussi, mademoiselle?

MAUDE: Non, je ne mange pas de viande. Je voudrais un couscous aux légumes.

LE GARÇON: Et comme boisson?

SYLVIE: Apportez de l'eau minérale et un pichet de vin rouge.

LE GARÇON: Très bien. J'apporte l'apéritif tout de suite.

10, rue Christine, Paris 6ᵉ
☎ 326-13-45   Métro Odéon - Saint-Michel

vous propose

Restaurant Oriental, sympa! et pas cher...

le Grand Texel

sa cuisine * **Tunisienne** *
typique * et Française *

Mots clés

dans	*in*	**carte**	*menu*
restaurant	*restaurant*	**garçon**	*waiter*
tunisien	*Tunisian*	**je voudrais**	*I would like*
(-ienne)		**apéritif**	*before-dinner drink*

avez (avoir)	*have*	viande *(f.)*	*meat*
du	*any*	aux	*with*
rouge	*red*	légumes *(m.)*	*vegetables*
blanc	*white*	comme	*for*
s'il vous plaît	*please*	boisson *(f.)*	*drink*
J'ai faim.	*I am hungry.*	apportez	*bring*
(avoir faim)		(apporter)	
ce soir	*this evening*	eau minérale	*mineral water*
couscous	*couscous*	*(f.)*	
au	*with*	pichet	*carafe*
mouton *(m.)*	*mutton*	vin *(m.)*	*wine*
de	*any*	tout de suite	*immediately*

FAISONS CONNAISSANCE

France offers a variety of restaurants that range from very elegant and expensive establishments to little **bistrots** or **cafés** where people can go for a simple meal. Fast-food places have become popular, and McDonald's exist in all major French cities. Unlike their American counterparts, however, they do serve wine and beer.

Restaurants featuring foreign cooking are also very popular in France. Because of the French presence in North Africa, Tunisian, Algerian, and Moroccan specialties are particularly well-liked. Couscous is a typical Arab dish made with a wheat product called semolina **(la semoule),** which resembles rice somewhat. On top of the grain one puts a vegetable stew and a choice of meat. Mutton, lamb chops, or chicken are the usual choices.

Le fast-food en France

Traditionally, Arabs do not drink alcohol, but North-African restaurants in France do serve it. An **apéritif** usually contains alcohol and is drunk before meals to increase one's appetite. **Martini** is a brand of vermouth and is not to be confused with the American *martini*. **Un pichet** would be the house wine, which is less expensive than bottled wine. Many French people order mineral water in restaurants; they do not drink tap water even though there is nothing wrong with it.

Menus are posted in the windows of restaurants. Patrons often have a choice of ordering individual items from **la carte** or a three- or four-course meal from **le menu.** Many choose the latter because the fixed price (**prix fixe**) usually includes the tip (**service compris**) and often a beverage. The selection normally offers an appetizer (**le hors-d'œuvre**), a main course (**le plat principal**), a vegetable, and a choice of cheese, fruit, or dessert.

Etudions le dialogue

1. La Goulette est un restaurant anglais?
2. Maude aime l'apéritif?
3. Est-ce que Sylvie et Maude demandent du vin blanc?
4. Est-ce que Sylvie a faim ce soir?
5. Maude mange un couscous au mouton aussi?
6. Le garçon est poli ou impoli?

Enrichissons notre vocabulaire

Des boissons *(Drinks)*

du thé

de l'eau

du café

du coca

du vin

du lait

de la bière

du jus de fruit

De la nourriture *(Food)*

du poisson

du jambon

de la **viande**

de la **salade**

du poulet

de la **glace**

du **fromage**

des **légumes**

de la **soupe**

du beurre

des fruits

du **pain**

un hamburger

des **frites**

du **gâteau**

Quelques expressions utiles *(Some useful expressions)*

commander	*to order*
consommer	*to drink, to eat, to consume*
déjeuner	*to have lunch*
dîner	*to eat dinner or supper, to dine*
goûter	*to taste (a food), to have a snack*
préparer	*to prepare*
recommander	*to recommend*

—Comment **trouvez**-vous le couscous à La Goulette?

—Il est **délicieux;** c'est le **plat préféré** de Sylvie.

—**Quelle sorte de cuisine** est-ce qu'elle aime?

—La cuisine tunisienne.

*How do you **like** the couscous at La Goulette?*

*It is **delicious;** it is Sylvie's favorite dish.*

***What kind of cooking** does she like?*

Tunisian cooking.

Prononciation Silent Consonants ◦▬◦

A. As mentioned in the preliminary chapter, a large number of written consonants are not pronounced in French.

Il es~~t~~ paresseu~~x~~.	*He is lazy.*
Jacque~~s~~ e~~t~~ Gille~~s~~ étudie~~nt~~ l'anglai~~s~~.	*Jacques and Gilles are studying English.*

B. Final written consonants are rarely pronounced.

Nou~~s~~ ne travaillon~~s~~ pa~~s~~.	*We aren't working.*
Le~~s~~ livre~~s~~ sont ennuyeu~~x~~.	*The books are boring.*

There are, however, exceptions to this rule.

Mar*c* apporte un apériti*f*.	*Marc is bringing a drink.*
I*l* travaille seu*l*.	*He works alone.*

C. In general, a final silent **e** shows that the preceding consonant is pronounced.

El*le* regar*de* la car*te*.	*She is looking at the menu.*
Jea~~n~~ est présen~~t~~; Jea*nne* est absen*te*.	*Jean is present; Jeanne is absent.*

Remember that the final silent **e** marks the difference between masculine and feminine nouns and adjectives such as **étudiant / étudiante** and **froid / froide**.

Exercice

Read the following sentences aloud, paying particular attention to silent consonants.

1. Les trois Français étudient l'anglais.
2. Nous sommes très contents.
3. Jean est méchant et il n'est pas heureux.
4. Ils dansent très bien.
5. Tu es paresseux et tu n'étudies pas.
6. Mon amie canadienne est médecin.

G RAMMAIRE ·

I. Indefinite and Partitive Articles

> You use indefinite and partitive articles with names of people, things, and ideas to indicate something not specific or previously mentioned.

As mentioned in Chapter 1, an article almost always accompanies a noun in French. The most frequently used articles in French are *nondefinite*—they stand for a person, thing, or idea that is not specific and not defined.

There are two types of nondefinite articles because in French, as in English, there is a distinction between nouns that can be counted *(count nouns)*, and those that cannot *(mass nouns)*. *Indefinite articles* are used with count nouns. *Partitive articles* are used with mass nouns.

A. Indefinite Articles

Indefinite Articles

	singular		plural	
masculine	un	} a, an	des	} some
feminine	une		des	

1. Indefinite articles refer to one unspecified object or person or to an unspecified group of *countable* objects or persons.

Elles sont dans **un** restaurant tunisien.	*They are in a Tunisian restaurant.*
Je voudrais **un** apéritif.	*I would like a before-dinner drink.*

2. The indefinite articles **un** and **une** correspond to the English *a* or *an*. The masculine singular indefinite article is **un,** pronounced /ɛ̃/ before a consonant and /ɛ̃n/ before a vowel.

un bureau	/ɛ̃ by ʀo/	*a desk, **an** office*
un mur	/ɛ̃ myʀ/	*a wall*
un stylo	/ɛ̃ sti lo/	*a pen*
un élève	/ɛ̃ ne lɛv/	*a (male) student*

3. The feminine singular indefinite article is **une,** always pronounced /yn/.

une carte	/yn kaʀt/	*a map, a card, a menu*
une école	/y ne kɔl/	*a school*
une élève	/y ne lɛv/	*a (female) student*
une photo	/yn fo to/	*a photograph*

4. The plural indefinite article is **des,** pronounced /de/ before consonants and /dez/ before vowel sounds.

des chaises *(f.)*	*(some)* chairs
des examens *(m.)*	*(some)* exams

B. Partitive Articles

Partitive Articles

before masculine, singular nouns	**du**
before feminine, singular nouns	**de la** } *some, any*
before singular nouns beginning with a vowel	**de l'**

1. Partitive articles refer to an unspecified portion, or *part*, of an object that is measurable but not countable, such as water, wine, or meat. **Du, de la,** and **de l'** may be expressed in English as *some* or *any*, or may not be expressed at all.

Je désire **du** vin.	*I want wine.*
	or
	*I want **some** wine.*
Elle mange **de la** tarte.	*She is eating pie.*
	or
	*She is eating **some** pie.*
Apportez **de l'**eau minérale!	*Bring **some** mineral water!*

2. The masculine partitive article for mass nouns—those that are not counted—is **du,** pronounced /dy/.

du chocolat	*hot chocolate, chocolate candy*
du gâteau	*cake*
du sel	*salt*
du sucre	*sugar*

3. The feminine partitive article for mass nouns is **de la.**

de la confiture	*jam*
de la farine	*flour*
de la moutarde	*mustard*
de la crème	*cream*

4. The singular partitive article **de l'** is used with masculine or feminine mass nouns that start with a vowel sound.

de l'agneau *(m.)*	*lamb*
de l'alcool *(m.)*	*alcohol*
de l'argent *(m.)*	*money*
de l'huile *(f.)*	*oil*

5. When referring to a countable unit of a mass noun, such as *a bottle* of beer, *a loaf* of bread, or *two cups* of coffee, the indefinite article is used.

Mass		**Count**	
de la bière	*(some) beer*	**une** bière	*a bottle of beer*
du café	*(some) coffee*	**un** café	*a cup of coffee*
du couscous	*(some) couscous*	**un** couscous	*a meal of couscous*
du gâteau	*(some) cake*	**un** gâteau	*a cake*
du pain	*(some) bread*	**un** pain	*a (loaf of) bread*
de la pizza	*(some) pizza*	**une** pizza	*a pizza*

ATTENTION

In negative sentences, all indefinite and partitive articles change to **de** (**d'** before a vowel sound), except when the verb is **être**.

Elle mange **de la** viande.   Elle **ne** mange **pas de** viande.
Vous avez **des** disques?   Vous **n'**avez **pas de** disques?
J'ai **un** stylo.   Je **n'**ai **pas de** stylo.

but:

C'est **un** stylo.   Ce n'est **pas un** stylo.
Le Martini **est un** apéritif.   Le Perrier **n'**est **pas un** apéritif.

Language

A. Identify the following nouns as primarily count nouns or mass nouns and provide an indefinite or partitive article as appropriate.

1. stylo	4. homme	7. sucre	10. élève
2. crayon	5. photo	8. moutarde	11. fille
3. lait	6. crème	9. eau	12. sel

B. You are going to a supermarket and have begun a list of what you need. Finish your list by adding the correct partitive or indefinite article.

huile
confiture
lait
stylo
glace

beurre
eau minérale
bière
gâteau
apéritif

C. You are very disagreeable today! Contradict the following statements.

MODEL: J'invite des copains.
          Je n'invite pas de copains.

1. Marc commande du fromage.
2. Ils demandent du vin.
3. Le mouton est un légume.
4. Nous invitons des amis.
5. Je mange de la viande.
6. Catherine prépare de la salade.
7. Les enfants consomment des cocas.
8. Le couscous est un apéritif.

Culture

D. In a neighborhood grocery store in France, you may have to ask the grocer to get your supplies. What do you have on your shopping list for a party you are giving this weekend for French friends?

MODEL: *Je voudrais du pain, du beurre et du lait.*

E. What do the following companies headquartered in French-speaking countries sell? Can you think of others?

MODEL: Chanel? *Ils vendent du parfum.* (They sell perfume.)

1. Mouton Cadet?
2. Labatt?
3. Evian?
4. Larousse?
5. Nestlé?
6. Knorr?
7. Martini?
8. La Vache Qui Rit?
9. Godiva?
10. Bic?

Communication

F. Answer the following questions, using any of the suggested words below or your own ideas.

intéressant	ennuyeux	anglais	gâteau
simple	sérieux	formidable	vin
difficile	américain	de Paula Abdul	thé
fantastique	français	de rock	lait

MODEL: Quelle sorte de livres est-ce que tu aimes regarder?
          J'aime regarder des livres intéressants.

1. Qu'est-ce qu'on trouve dans votre *(your)* frigidaire?
2. Quelle sorte de boisson est-ce que vous consommez?
3. Qu'est-ce que vous aimez manger?
4. Quelle sorte de films est-ce que vous aimez mieux?
5. Quelle sorte de disques est-ce que vous écoutez?

G. Interview a classmate to find out what he or she likes to eat.

MODEL: Student 1:   *Est-ce que tu aimes manger de la tarte?*
          Student 2:   *Non, je ne mange pas de tarte.*

          Student 1:   *Est-ce que tu consommes du thé?*
          Student 2:   *Oui, je consomme du thé.*

II. The Irregular Verb avoir / Expressions with avoir

> You use **avoir** to state possession and to describe certain conditions.

A. Avoir

1. **Avoir** is an irregular verb, and you must memorize its forms.

	avoir	*(to have)*			
j' ai	/ ʒe /	*I have*	nous **avons**	/ nu za vɔ̃ /	*we have*
tu as	/ ty a /	*you have*	vous **avez**	/ vu za ve /	*you have*
il a	/ i la /	*he has*	ils **ont**	/ il zɔ̃ /	*they have*
elle a	/ ɛ la /	*she has*	elles **ont**	/ ɛl zɔ̃ /	*they have*
on a	/ ɔ̃ na /	*we have*			

2. The final **s** of **nous, vous, ils,** and **elles** is pronounced / z / and the **n** of **on** is pronounced / n / in the affirmative because the verb forms start with a vowel sound.

3. Before a vowel sound, **je** becomes **j'** and **ne** becomes **n'**.

J'ai du talent.	*I have talent.*
Je n'ai pas de patience.	*I don't have any patience.*

B. Expressions with avoir

Avoir is used in several idiomatic expressions.

Elle a chaud; ils ont froid.	*She is hot; they are cold.*
Je ne mange pas; je n'ai pas faim.	*I'm not eating; I'm not hungry.*
Elle désire de l'eau; elle a soif.	*She wants some water; she's thirsty.*
Vous n'avez pas raison, vous avez tort!	*You aren't right; you are wrong!*
—Quel âge avez-vous?	*How old are you?*
—J'ai dix-huit ans.	*I'm eighteen.*
Il y a une carte dans la classe.	*There's a map in the classroom.*
Il n'y a pas de vin.	*There isn't any wine.*

ATTENTION

Voilà is used to point out something; **il y a** merely indicates existence. Both take singular or plural objects.

Voilà le père de Luc!	*There's Luc's father! (over there)*
Il y a des légumes dans un couscous.	*There are vegetables in a couscous.*

Mots clés Expressions with avoir

avoir faim	*to be hungry*	avoir _____ ans	*to be _____ years old*
avoir soif	*to be thirsty*		
avoir chaud	*to be hot*	il y a	*there is, there are*
avoir froid	*to be cold*	il n'y a pas	*there isn't, there aren't*
avoir raison	*to be right*		
avoir tort	*to be wrong*		

CE QU'ILS DISENT

You saw in Chapter 2 that the **u** of **tu** often disappears in informal conversation when the verb is **être.** The same is true with **avoir.**

T'as froid?	*Are you cold?*
T'as pas faim?	*Aren't you hungry?*

Language

A. Chantal is talking to her friends about other people. Make complete sentences by adding any necessary words.

1. Ils / avoir / souvent / tort
2. Tu / ne / avoir / pas / faim?
3. Les enfants de Jacques / avoir / disques
4. On / ne / avoir / pas / froid
5. Tu / avoir / raison
6. Je / ne / avoir / pas / frère
7. Vous / ne / avoir / pas / 21 / ans?
8. Jeanne / avoir / amis

B. Name three things that you have with you, three things a classmate has with him or her, and one thing you do not have with you.

MODEL: *J'ai un stylo, deux crayons, et des livres.*
Anne et Jacqueline ont de l'argent, des photos, et un sac à dos.
Je n'ai pas de nourriture.

Culture

C. **En cours.** Look at the photograph of a French classroom on page 6, and state what there is and is not to be found.

MODEL: *Il y a des étudiants.*
Il n'y a pas de café.

Communication

D. Describe the kind of friends you have, using the suggestions provided below or your own ideas.

MODEL: *J'ai des amis sympathiques.*

intéressant	intelligent	ennuyeux	studieux
indépendant	paresseux	sympathique	???

E. Name famous people who have the following things. Can you think of someone who does not have them?

MODEL: du talent? *Paul Simon a du talent.*
   Barry Manilow n'a pas de talent.

1. de l'argent?
2. un restaurant?
3. beaucoup de femmes? maris?
4. des amis riches?
5. beaucoup d'enfants?
6. des étudiants intelligents?

F. Find out more about your classmates by asking them questions using the following expressions.

1. avoir froid ou chaud?
2. avoir soif ou faim?
3. avoir des frères ou des sœurs?
4. avoir quel âge?
5. avoir souvent raison ou tort?
6. avoir de la patience?

G. **Questions personnelles.** Parlez de vous!

1. Vous avez souvent faim? Qu'est-ce que vous mangez?
2. Quelle boisson est-ce que vous aimez mieux quand vous avez soif?
3. Quel âge avez-vous? Quel est l'âge idéal?
4. Est-ce que vous avez du talent? Quelle sorte?
5. Est-ce que vous avez de l'argent? Qu'est-ce que vous désirez avoir?
6. Vous désirez avoir des enfants? Combien de garçons et combien de filles?

III. Use of Articles

> You must always use articles with nouns, which name people, things, and ideas. The type of article you use determines the nature of the noun (specific or general, previously mentioned or not).

Now that you have learned the definite, indefinite, and partitive articles, it is essential to know when to use each kind.

A. Use of Definite Articles

1. Definite articles refer to one specific person or thing.

Elles regardent **la** carte.	*They are looking at **the** menu. (a specific menu)*
Tu as **le** livre?	*Do you have **the** book? (referring to a book just mentioned)*

2. They also refer to all of a given item in a generalized sense.

Les enfants aiment **le** chocolat.	*Children like chocolate. (in general)*
Je déteste **la** bière.	*I hate beer. (all beer)*

   Verbs that lend themselves to use in a generalized sense include **aimer, aimer mieux, adorer, apprécier, détester.**

B. Use of Indefinite and Partitive Articles

1. Indefinite articles refer to an entire, unspecified object or person.

Tu as **un** stylo?	*Do you have **a** pen? (any pen)*
Elles sont dans **un** restaurant tunisien.	*They are in **a** Tunisian restaurant. (an unspecified Tunisian restaurant)*

2. Partitive articles refer to an unspecified portion, or part, of an object that is measurable but not countable.

Apportez **de l'**eau minérale.	*Bring **some** mineral water. (not all of it)*
Jacques n'a pas **de** talent.	*Jacques doesn't have **any** talent. (none at all)*

   Many verbs almost always imply a portion of an item and therefore take a partitive article. These include **consommer, demander, désirer, manger,** and the expression **je voudrais.**

3. In the negative, all indefinite and partitive articles become **de** or **d',** but definite articles do not change.

   —Vous mangez **de la** viande?
   —Non, je **ne** mange **pas de** viande.

   —Tu aimes **le** café?
   —Non, je **n'**aime **pas le** café.

   ATTENTION

   Translating into English will not help you choose the proper article. In French, you must decide whether the item is considered in a general or specific sense or as a portion. For example, compare the following sentences:

*I like **wine**.* → J'aime **le** vin.
*I want **wine**.* → Je voudrais **du** vin.

Language

A. Contradict the following statements.

1. Il déteste la bière.
2. Ils mangent un couscous.
3. Tu aimes le pain français?
4. Nous avons du gâteau.
5. Christine et Michel demandent de la soupe.
6. Anne-Marie a de la salade.

B. **Les préférences.** Make complete sentences, adding any necessary words to indicate what the following people like.

1. Catherine / désirer / fromage
2. Je / demander / mouton
3. Elles / adorer / glace
4. enfants / détester / légumes
5. Vous / ne / apprécier / pas / vin français
6. Ils / ne / commander / pas / tarte

Culture

C. **Les végétariens.** Many French are extremely conscious about eating healthy foods, and some do not eat meat (**végétariens**) or do not eat anything of animal origin, such as fish, eggs, or milk (**végétaliens**). State their habits by making complete sentences from the words below.

MODEL: commander / fruits
           Ils commandent des fruits.

1. aimer / agneau
2. manger / légumes
3. détester / poulet
4. adorer / pain
5. désirer / salade
6. avoir / faim!

D. **Dînons dans un restaurant élégant.** Eating habits vary widely from one culture to another. Below is a list of eight items frequently associated with eating. Using the verb **avoir,** guess which ones you would have with dinner at a nice restaurant and which ones the restaurant would not have.

MODEL: eau   *Ils ont de l'eau.*
           «French dressing»   *Ils n'ont pas de «French dressing».*

1. thé froid
2. salade après la viande
3. café au lait
4. cocas
5. sucre avec du sel
6. fruits comme dessert
7. lait
8. tarte

Communication

E. State whether or not you have the following items.

sœur	enfants	camarade de chambre	carte de France
radio	disques	amis français	voiture
frère	stylo		

F. Express your opinions on the following subjects by completing the sentences in a logical manner.

1. Je n'aime pas...
2. J'apprécie...
3. Le professeur n'a pas...
4. Mon restaurant préféré prépare...
5. Je mange...
6. Les Français aiment...
7. Ma mère adore...
8. Mon frère / ma sœur a...

G. **Questions personnelles.** A table!

1. Qu'est-ce que vous mangez quand vous avez faim?
2. Qu'est-ce que vous consommez quand vous avez très soif?
3. Qu'est-ce que vous aimez comme boisson?
4. Qu'est-ce que vous détestez? appréciez?
5. Vous préparez le dîner? Qu'est-ce que vous aimez préparer?
6. Est-ce que vous êtes végétarien (-ienne)? Pourquoi *(why)* ou pourquoi pas?

IV. The Imperative

You use the imperative to give orders, advice, or suggestions.

A. Forms

1. To form the imperative, you simply drop the pronoun subject, except in the **tu** form in which the final **s** of the present indicative is also dropped.

Indicative: **Vous apportez** un pichet de vin rouge.
Imperative: **Apportez** un pichet de vin rouge.

Indicative: **Vous invitez** des étudiants.
Imperative: **Invitez** des étudiants.

Indicative: **Tu manges** du pain.
Imperative: **Mange** du pain.

2. There is also an imperative in the **nous** form. Equivalent to the English *Let's . . .* , it is used to suggest something.

Parlons!   *Let's talk!*
Travaillons ensemble.   *Let's work together.*

3. The negative imperative is formed with **ne... pas** like the other verb forms you have learned.

Ne regarde pas la télévision.	*Don't watch television.*
Ne parlez pas en classe.	*Don't talk in class.*
Ne mangez pas de sel.	*Don't eat salt.*

B. Irregular Verbs in the Imperative

The imperative forms of **être** and **avoir** are irregular.

Sois	⎱		**Aie**	⎱
Soyons	⎬ *Be*		**Ayons**	⎬ *Have*
Soyez	⎰		**Ayez**	⎰

Sois prudent!	*Be careful!*
Ne **soyez** pas méchante!	*Don't be mean!*
Ayez de la patience!	*Have patience!*

C. Politeness

In French, as in English, one normally adds *please* to the imperative for politeness. There are two such forms in French.

Ouvrez la porte, **s'il vous plaît.**	*Open the door, **please.** (formal)*
Ferme la fenêtre, **s'il te plaît.**	*Close the window, **please.** (familiar)*

Language

A. Give commands with the following expressions and address them to the people indicated.

MODEL: *(to your classmate)* parler avec le professeur
Parle avec le professeur.

1. *(to your brother)* danser avec Jacqueline
2. *(to your teacher)* fermer la porte
3. *(to a group of friends)* préparer un couscous
4. *(to your roommmate)* étudier beaucoup
5. *(to your family, including yourself)* écouter la radio
6. *(to your classmates)* travailler ensemble

Culture

B. **En vacances!** A large proportion of the French population goes on vacation around August 1, creating throughout the country enormous traffic jams and dangerous driving conditions, often due to driver fatigue. On the radio, you hear advice constantly about what to do to be a safe driver. Form sentences in the imperative to give this type of advice, and do not forget to use the negative when appropriate.

1. consommer / alcool
2. être / prudent
3. avoir / patience
4. manger beaucoup
5. consommer souvent / café
6. être «macho»
7. étudier / carte
8. demander / apéritifs au café

Communication

C. If you were to hear the following statements, what would your advice be? Use the imperative of the verbs listed below or those of your own choosing.

MODEL: J'ai chaud.
         Ouvrez la fenêtre.

étudier   manger   fermer   inviter   consommer   écouter

1. J'ai faim.
2. La leçon est difficile.
3. J'ai soif.
4. Nous avons froid.
5. Je suis seul.
6. J'adore le rock.

D. **Je suis stressé(e)!** Give advice to your classmates as to what they should do to relax and have a good time. You may refer to the following list for ideas, but feel free to add your own ideas.

MODEL: *Mangez de la glace. Ne travaillez pas.*

écouter les disques de...
regarder... à la télévision
manger...
(ne... pas) étudier...

inviter...
parler avec...
consommer...
(ne... pas) travailler

COMMUNIQUONS ....

Parler de la quantité

Being able to express quantity in French is very useful because these expressions apply to a variety of situations such as shopping for food and talking about people and objects. Quantity can be expressed with adverbs, adjectives, and nouns.

Trop de saumon

beaucoup de devoirs

pas assez de talent

On utilise les adverbes.

The preposition **de (d')** is used after adverbs of quantity even if the following noun is plural; no article is used. **Un peu de** is used with mass nouns, but **peu de** is used with either mass nouns or count nouns. Also note that, as in English, **un peu de** has a positive connotation, whereas **peu de** has a negative one.

Il n'a pas assez de talent.	*He doesn't have enough talent.*
Elle a beaucoup de devoirs.	*She has a lot of homework.*
Moins de sel, s'il vous plaît!	*Less salt, please.*
Je voudrais un peu de crème.	*I would like some / a little cream.*
Nous avons peu d'argent.	*We have little money.*
Un peu plus de café, Madame?	*A little more coffee, ma'am?*
Elle a trop de saumon.	*She has too much salmon.*

On utilise les adjectifs.

The adjectives **plusieurs** and **quelques** do not take the preposition **de**.

Il y a plusieurs cartes dans la salle de classe.	*There are several maps in the classroom.*
Marie invite quelques amis.	*Marie is inviting a few friends.*

On utilise les noms.

As with adverbs of quantity, the preposition **de (d')** is used after nouns of quantity; no article is used.

Ils commandent une bouteille de vin.	*They're ordering a bottle of wine.*
Un kilo de farine, s'il vous plaît!	*A kilo (2.2 pounds) of flour, please!*
Je voudrais un litre d'eau minérale.	*I would like a liter of mineral water.*
Elle désire une livre de beurre.	*She wants a pound of butter.*
Le garçon apporte une tasse de thé.	*The waiter is bringing a cup of tea.*
Sylvie commande un verre de vin rouge.	*Sylvie is ordering a glass of red wine.*

Interaction *Jacques et Monique sont au café.*

LE GARÇON: Vous désirez?

MONIQUE: Une tasse de thé et un verre de vin blanc.

LE GARÇON: Tout de suite.

Activités

A. Tell whether you would like more or less / fewer of the following items using **plus de** or **moins de**.

1. argent
2. devoirs
3. camarades de chambre
4. classes
5. exercices
6. amies
7. français en classe
8. étudiants sur le campus

B. Using expressions of quantity, tell to what degree you have the following qualities.

MODEL: *Je n'ai pas assez de patience.*

patience	talent	courage
ambition	énergie	tact
imagination	prestige	intelligence

LECTURE CULTURELLE ....

Avant la lecture

French cuisine is celebrated all over the world. In France, a meal is a ritual most people follow scrupulously. There are unwritten "rules" to observe, things that one does or does not do. For instance, salad comes with almost every meal, but usually *after* the meat and the vegetables, not with them. Many French people consider a meal without cheese incomplete. One always serves red wine with cheese, which comes after the meal but before dessert. A French proverb says that a meal without wine and cheese is like a day without sunshine.

Activités

A. What specialties of French cooking do you know? Do you know what goes into traditional French cooking that makes it French?

B. What courses are served during a formal dinner? In what order are they served in the United States?

C. Do you know any cooking terms that come from French? (**crêpes, béarnaise, vinaigrette,** etc.)

D. Try to guess what would follow these statements about French cooking. Then see if you can find the answers in the reading.

1. The French use butter and cream, but not . . .
2. Heavy cooking is being replaced by . . .
3. If you do not go to supermarkets, you . . .
4. The three meals each day are . . .
5. Between lunch and dinner, children have . . .
6. Popular foreign restaurants in France might include . . .

Quels beaux croissants!

Les Français et la cuisine

Les Français aiment la *cuisine raffinée*. En France, la *gastronomie* est une tradition ancienne et les spécialités régionales sont très appréciées. Dans la cuisine française, on utilise généralement du beurre et de la crème, mais peu d'huile. On mange toujours de la salade et du fromage, et on consomme du vin et de
5 l'eau minérale, ou de l'eau naturelle. En France, la cuisine est très importante, mais les *habitudes* changent. La *cuisine minceur* remplace le beurre et la crème et élimine des calories.

Il y a des supermarchés, mais certains Français aiment *acheter* du pain, de la viande et des légumes *tous les jours*. On a des *magasins* spécialisés, comme
10 la *boucherie* pour la viande et la *pâtisserie* pour les desserts, et il y a aussi des *marchés en plein air une ou deux fois par semaine* sur une place publique.

Chaque jour, on prépare trois *repas:* le *petit déjeuner,* le déjeuner et le dîner. Au petit déjeuner, on *prend* du café au lait, du thé ou du chocolat avec du *pain grillé,* du beurre et de la confiture ou des *biscottes.* Les petits déjeuners
15 copieux *à l'américaine* n'existent pas en France. On prend le déjeuner *entre midi* et *deux heures. Souvent,* quand les enfants *rentrent de* l'école, ils ont faim et ils goûtent: ils mangent du chocolat ou du pain et du beurre avec du café au lait. Le dîner commence à *sept heures et demie* ou à huit heures du soir, et traditionnellement tous les membres d'une famille mangent ensemble.
20 Les Français fréquentent aussi des restaurants où la cuisine n'est pas typiquement française. Les restaurants *étrangers*—chinois, italiens, vietnamiens et nord-africains—sont très populaires. Si on préfère manger rapidement, on a des McDonald's et des Burger King!

refined cooking / gourmet cooking

habits / low-calorie cooking
to buy
every day / stores
butcher shop / pastry shop
open-air markets / once or twice a week / Each / meals / breakfast / has toast / zwieback (dried toast) / American-style / between noon / two o'clock / Often / return from / seven thirty P.M.

foreign

Après la lecture

Questions sur le texte

1. Quelle sorte de cuisine est-ce que les Français aiment?
2. En général, est-ce qu'on utilise de l'huile en France? Qu'est-ce qu'on utilise?
3. Qu'est-ce qu'on consomme comme boisson en France?
4. Qu'est-ce que la cuisine minceur remplace?
5. Qu'est-ce que certains Français aiment acheter tous les jours?

6. Qu'est-ce qu'on prend au petit déjeuner?
7. Qu'est-ce que les enfants français mangent quand ils ont faim après l'école?
8. Quelles sortes de restaurants étrangers est-ce que les Français fréquentent?

Activité

Study the recipe below and try it out at home.

Crêpes (13 à la douzaine)

METTEZ DANS UN GRAND BOL
2 TASSES DE FARINE,
2 ŒUFS ENTIERS,
2 PAQUETS DE SUCRE VANILLÉ,
LE ZESTE RAPÉ D'UN CITRON
ET 1 *pincée* DE SEL.
AJOUTEZ *petit-à-petit*
2 3/4 TASSES D'EAU
EN MÉLANGEANT BIEN AVEC LE FOUET.

ALLUMEZ LE GAZ (*feu moyen*).
POSEZ LA POÊLE DESSUS.
METTEZ-Y 3 *cuillères à soupe* DE BEURRE.
AUSSITÔT LE BEURRE FONDU
VERSEZ-LE DANS UN PETIT BOL.
PRENEZ 1/2 LOUCHE DE PATE A CRÊPE.
VERSEZ-LA **HORS DU FEU** DANS LA POÊLE.
QUAND LA CRÊPE BOURSOUFLE
RETOURNEZ-LA ET
LAISSEZ CUIRE 15 SECONDES.
GLISSEZ LA CRÊPE SUR LE PLAT.
SUCREZ-LA AVEC
1 *cuillère à café* DE SUCRE EN POUDRE.

RECOMMENCEZ 13 FOIS.

œufs *eggs*

zest *rind*

mélangeant *mixing* /
  fouet *whisk*
Allumez *Light* / **feu**
  moyen *medium flame*
poêle *skillet* /
  dessus *on*
Aussitôt *As soon as* /
  fondu *melted*
Versez-le *Pour it*
louche *ladle* /
  pâte *batter*
hors *away from*
boursouffle *bubbles*
Retournez-la *Turn it over*
Laissez cuire *Let cook*
Glissez *Slide*
en poudre *powdered*

CLASS WORK

A. Rewrite the following sentences using the cues in parentheses. Make any necessary changes.

MODEL: Il est studieux.   (Elles...)
Elles sont studieuses.

Les gens *(People)*

1. Nous sommes généreux.   (Madeleine...)
2. Tu as froid.   (... fatigué.)
3. Vous invitez des Américains?   (Luc et Jeanne... Canadienne?)
4. Ils sont tunisiens?   (Marie... ?)
5. Je suis content.   (... chaud.)
6. Nous sommes sérieux.   (Claire, tu...)

Les boissons

7. Vous aimez le thé?   (... désirez...)
8. Elle aime les jus de fruit.   (... consommer...)
9. Il a soif.   (Marc et Marie...)
10. Jean-Pierre n'aime pas l'eau.   (... consommer...)

Les possessions

11. Un sac à dos est utile.   (... cartes...)
12. Nous adorons les enfants.   (... avoir...)
13. Tu as une affiche?   (Nous... affiches.)
14. Elles écoutent des disques.   (... avoir... radio.)

B. **La nourriture.** Answer the following questions using the cues provided.

MODEL: Vous avez des légumes?   (Non,...)
Non, je n'ai pas de légumes.

1. Qu'est-ce que vous mangez?   (Nous... frites.)
2. Vous avez des gâteaux?   (Non,...)
3. Qu'est-ce que tu détestes?   (... eau minérale.)
4. Vous aimez le couscous?   (Oui, nous...)
5. Jeanne et Sylvie ont faim?   (Non,... soif.)
6. Est-ce qu'elles aiment le coca?   (Oui,... demander...)
7. Qu'est-ce que Paulette prépare?   (... mouton.)
8. Est-ce que tu manges de la viande?   (Non,... détester...)

73

9. Est-ce qu'il y a du lait?   (Non,...)
10. Vous aimez la cuisine française?   (Non,... aimer mieux... américain...)
11. Vous mangez de la soupe?   (Non, nous... aimer mieux... salade.)
12. Est-ce que les enfants consomment de l'alcool?   (Non,...)
13. Tu désires de la crème?   (Non,... beurre,... vin et... huile.)
14. Quand est-ce que vous demandez un chocolat?   (... avoir froid...)

C. Create a complete sentence with each group of words below, making appropriate changes and adding any necessary words.

MODEL: étudiants / aimer / musique
Les étudiants aiment la musique.

A table! *(Let's eat!)*

1. enfants / adorer / glace
2. crème / et / sel / être / mauvais
3. On / avoir / eau / chaud?
4. Paul / ne... pas / manger / fromage
5. garçon / préparer / boissons

Les gens

6. La sœur de Philippe / avoir / talent
7. Vous / avoir / tort / Monsieur
8. Françoise et Marc / avoir / disques / américain
9. Est-ce que / elle / avoir / raison?
10. Monique / être / heureux

En cours

11. Nous / commencer / leçon / intéressant
12. Fermer / porte / s'il te plaît!
13. Ecouter / s'il vous plaît!
14. étudiant / avoir / examens / difficile

D. Complete the following sentences according to your opinion.

1. J'adore...
2. Je déteste...
3. Les Américains aiment...
4. Je voudrais...
5. Quand j'ai soif, je...
6. Je suis...
7. Je ne suis pas...
8. Le professeur est...

E. Translate the following sentences into French.

Bavardage *(Gossip)*

1. She likes a lawyer.
2. They watch football games.
3. Does he smoke a lot?
4. No, but he is lazy.
5. They are happy when they are together.

A la cuisine *(In the kitchen)*

6. Let's make *(préparer)* a cake!
7. You don't have any sugar?
8. We want butter and milk.
9. They hate milk and cream.
10. They are wrong. They are delicious!

F. Do the following math problems in French.

1. 5 + 7 =
2. 15 + 16 =
3. 51 − 27 =
4. 69 − 8 =
5. 6 + 45 =
6. 13 + 14 =
7. 49 − 10 =
8. 41 − 12 =
9. 3 × 4 =
10. 15 × 3 =
11. 48 ÷ 3 =
12. 66 ÷ 2 =
13. 11 × 3 =
14. 7 × 3 =
15. 42 ÷ 7 =
16. 39 ÷ 3 =

G. **Questions personnelles.** Qui êtes-vous?

1. Vous êtes optimiste? pessimiste? sincère? hypocrite?
2. Est-ce que vous avez des amis dans le cours de français?
3. Quelle sorte d'amis est-ce que vous avez?
4. Qu'est-ce que vous mangez quand vous avez faim?
5. Quelles boissons est-ce que vous aimez?
6. Est-ce que vous travaillez beaucoup? fréquentez des boîtes de nuit?
7. Est-ce que vous avez des frères et sœurs? Combien?
8. Vous désirez être avocat(e)? ingénieur? journaliste? ???

PAIR AND SMALL GROUP WORK

A. With a partner, practice spelling in French. Select ten words that you have learned thus far. Then, take turns spelling them to each other and guessing what each other's words are.

B. Say a word in English to your partner and ask for its French equivalent. Then, say a French noun, and your partner will give the noun with the correct definite, indefinite, or partitive article.

C. In groups of three or four, count from 1 to 20 in French, continuing around the group so that each person must give the next number. Then count, taking turns, from 20 to 40 by odd numbers and from 40 to 60 by even numbers.

D. With a partner, play the role of two people who disagree with each other. If one of you makes an affirmative statement, the other makes it negative and vice versa.

MODEL: Student 1: *J'ai du vin.*
Student 2: *Je n'ai pas de vin.*

Student 1: *Tu aimes faire la cuisine.*
Student 2: *Tu n'aimes pas faire la cuisine.*

E. In groups of four students, take turns describing yourself, using three adjectives. Then describe one of your classmates without naming him or her, and have the members of the group guess whom you are describing.

F. In groups of three or four students, take turns giving one or two students commands that they can carry out.

G. Interview your classmates to find out the following information. Be prepared to report your findings to the class.

    1. what they are like
    2. what their likes and dislikes are
    3. what they do every day and on weekends (**Le week-end...**)

I. Create a brief dialogue based on the following drawing.

LES VOYAGES

A la réception de l'hôtel

OBJECTIVES

OBJECTIVES

▸ *Language*
Vocabulary for travel and
vacations
Enchaînements and
liaisons
A and **de** with definite
articles
Place names
Aller and **futur proche**
Articles and prepositions
with place names
Numbers from 70 to
1,000,000,000

▸ *Culture*
Travel in France
Vacations

▸ *Communication*
Finding a hotel
Expressing future time
Counting
Asking directions

COMMENÇONS ·································

A Nice, au Syndicat d'Initiative

Robert et Eric, deux étudiants américains, rentrent de Corse et voyagent sur la Côte d'Azur. Ils arrivent à Nice et ils cherchent un hôtel près de la plage. Ils sont maintenant au Syndicat d'Initiative, où ils demandent des renseignements.

L'HOTESSE: Bonjour, Messieurs.

ERIC: Bonjour, Mademoiselle. Nous cherchons une chambre dans un hôtel près de la mer.

L'HOTESSE: A côté de la plage, cela va être difficile!

ROBERT: Pourquoi?

L'HOTESSE: Parce que les hôtels sont chers et parce qu'ils sont tous pleins aujourd'hui. Mais il y a de la place en ville. C'est près des restaurants et des cinémas; ce n'est pas loin du Casino et il faut dix minutes pour aller à la plage.

ROBERT: S'il n'y a pas de chambres au bord de la mer, nous n'allons pas rester à Nice. Nous allons visiter l'Italie. Est-ce que vous avez une liste des hôtels de San Remo?

L'HOTESSE: Ah, non, pas du tout! Nous n'avons pas de renseignements
sur l'Italie, mais vous avez une agence de voyages au coin
de la rue.

ERIC: Où ça?

L'HOTESSE: Là-bas, Monsieur. A côté de l'église.

ROBERT: Merci mille fois. Au revoir.

L'HOTESSE: Au revoir, Messieurs.

Mots clés

Syndicat d'Initiative *(m.)*	*Tourist Office*	**pleins**	*full*
		aujourd'hui	*today*
		mais	*but*
rentrent de (rentrer de)	*come back from*	**place**	*room*
		en ville	*downtown*
Corse *(f.)*	*Corsica*	**cinémas** *(m.)*	*movie theaters*
voyagent (voyager)	*are traveling*	**loin du Casino**	*far from the Casino*
sur	*on*	**il faut**	*it takes*
Côte d'Azur	*French Riviera*	**minutes** *(f.)*	*minutes*
cherchent (chercher)	*are looking for*	**pour aller à**	*to go to*
		s' (si)	*if*
près de	*near*	**au bord de la mer**	*at the seaside*
plage	*beach*		
maintenant	*now*	**rester**	*to stay*
renseignements *(m.)*	*information*	**visiter**	*to go to*
		Italie *(f.)*	*Italy*
hôtesse *(f.)*	*hostess*	**liste**	*a list*
Messieurs	*gentlemen*	**ah, non**	*of course not*
chambre	*room*	**pas du tout**	*not at all*
mer	*sea*	**agence de voyages**	*a travel agency*
à côté de	*next to*		
va être (aller être)	*is going to be*	**au coin de**	*at the corner of*
		rue	*street*
pourquoi	*why*	**Où ça?**	*Whereabout?*
parce que	*because*	**là-bas**	*over there*
chers (cher, -ère)	*expensive*	**église** *(f.)*	*church*
tous	*all*	**Merci mille fois.**	*Thanks a million.*

FAISONS CONNAISSANCE

Upon arrival in a French city or town, the useful thing to do is to go to the **Syndicat d'Initiative**, where you will get information about points of interest and a list of hotels arranged by categories. If you wish, someone at the **Syndicat** will call hotels for you to check for vacancies. There you can also find out about other areas in France you may wish to visit. Because the service is run by the French government, it does not include information about other countries.

Nice is the largest city on **la Côte d'Azur**, one of the principal vacation areas of France. You may also have heard of Cannes because of its international film festival in May. Saint-Tropez was made famous in the 1950s as the playground of Brigitte Bardot and other screen personalities. The tiny country of Monaco is also wedged into the Mediterranean coast to the east of Nice. San Remo, an Italian city, is farther along the coast.

While **la Côte d'Azur** is known throughout the world for its splendid beaches, Americans are often surprised to find many of them covered with smooth stones (**les galets**) rather than with sand.

Sur la Côte d'Azur

Etudions le dialogue

1. Où sont Robert et Eric?
2. Qu'est-ce qu'ils cherchent?
3. Ils désirent être loin de la plage, n'est-ce pas?
4. Est-ce qu'il y a de la place au bord de la mer?
5. Qu'est-ce qu'il y a en ville?
6. Où est-ce que Robert et Eric vont aller s'ils ne restent pas à Nice?

Enrichissons notre vocabulaire

En ville *(In the city)*

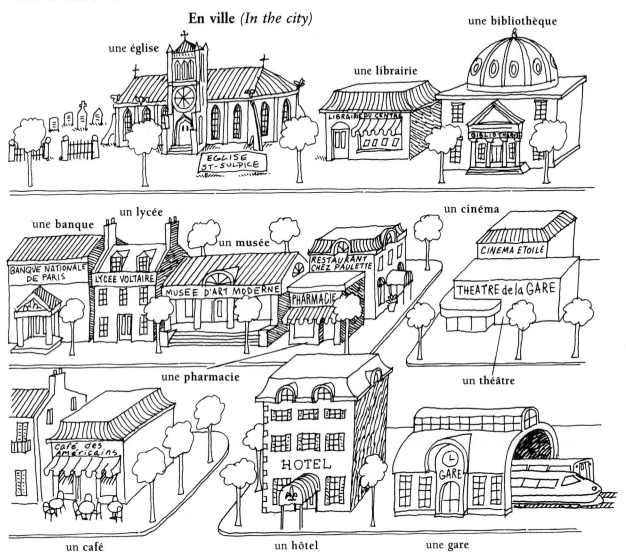

D'autres endroits *(m.)* *(Other places)*

un appartement	*apartment*	un parc	*park*
un arrêt d'autobus	*bus stop*	un parking	*parking lot*
		une piscine	*a swimming pool*
un bureau de poste	*post office*	une résidence universitaire	*dormitory*
un centre commercial	*shopping center*	un restau-U (restaurant universitaire)	*university restaurant*
un laboratoire	*a laboratory*		
un magasin	*store*	un stade	*a stadium*
une maison	*house*	une usine	*a factory*

Prononciation **Enchaînements et liaisons** 〔°━°〕

A. In spoken French, words flow together very smoothly. When a word begins with a vowel sound, French speakers pronounce the last consonant of the preceding word as if it were the first letter of the next word. This is **enchaînement.**

avec elle	/avɛ kɛl/	il a	/i la/
sept étudiants	/sɛ te ty djã/	elle est	/ɛ lɛ/

Practice **enchaînements** by repeating the following expressions after your teacher.

> neuf étudiantes / elle habite / il invite / cinq acteurs /
> l'artiste intelligent / le professeur intéressant

B. There is a separate category of **enchaînement** in which a written final consonant that is normally not pronounced must be sounded because a vowel sound follows it. Notice the difference in the pronunciation of: **nous travaillons** /nu tʀa va jɔ̃/ and **nous habitons** /nu za bi tɔ̃/.

The **s** of **nous** in **nous habitons** must be pronounced because the verb begins with the vowel sound /a/. This is **liaison.** It is limited to closely linked word groups (pronoun subject–verb, adjective–noun), and most often involves the /z/ sound.

Listen carefully and repeat the following paired words after your teacher, paying particular attention to the **liaisons.**

No liaison	*Liaison*	*No liaison*	*Liaison*
un livre	un ami	nous dansons	nous invitons
deux garçons	deux amies	ils sont	ils ont
trois cafés	trois hôtesses	des légumes	des hôtels
six portes	six étudiants	les filles	les enfants
dix cartes	dix hommes	en France	en Amérique

Exercice

Practice reading these sentences aloud, while concentrating on the **enchaînements** and **liaisons.**

1. Les Américains habitent en Amérique.
2. Nous étudions avec un professeur intéressant.
3. Vous avez une opinion d'elle?
4. Les enfants sont intelligents.
5. Ils invitent des amis sympathiques.
6. Elle donne une leçon d'anglais aux étudiants.

GRAMMAIRE ·······························

I. A and de with Definite Articles

> You use **à** to indicate location or direction and **de** to indicate origin or possession.

A. Two very common French prepositions are **à** *(to, in, at, or into)* and **de** *from or of).*

> Ils arrivent **à** Nice.   J'ai le stylo **de** Robert.
> Elle est **de** New York.

B. **A** and **de** are often used with the definite articles **l'** and **la.**

> Elle travaille **à l'**université.   Quel est le prix **de la** chambre?
> Ils sont **à la** maison.   C'est le livre **de l'**étudiant.

C. When **à** and **de** come before the definite articles **le** or **les,** the two words form a contraction.

> à + le = **au**   de + le = **du**
> à + les = **aux**   de + les = **des**

> Ils sont **au** Syndicat d'Initiative.   Il est **du** Canada.
> Je donne la glace **aux** enfants.   Elles ont les cahiers **des** étudiants.

Note that the **x** of **aux** and the **s** of **des** are pronounced / z / in front of a vowel sound, just like the **s** of **les.**

ATTENTION

The preposition **de** in combination with the definite articles has the same forms as the partitive articles and the plural indefinite article, which you learned in Chapter 3, but, unlike them, the preposition **de** never changes in the negative.

Indefinite article:

> J'ai **des** enfants.   *I have (**some**) children.*
> Je n'ai **pas d'** enfants.   *I **don't** have (**any**) children.*

Preposition de and the definite article les:

> Je parle **des** enfants.   *I'm talking **about the** children.*
> Je **ne** parle **pas des** enfants.   *I'm **not** talking **about the** children.*

D. The preposition **de** is part of some prepositional expressions, subject to the same rules regarding contractions.

> Ils cherchent un hôtel **près de** la mer.
> Ils trouvent un hôtel **en face de** l'agence de voyages.
> Ce n'est pas **loin du** Casino.
> C'est **près des** restaurants.

Mots clés

Prepositional phrases with **de**

à côté de	*next to*	loin de	*far (from)*
au coin de	*at the corner of*	près de	*near*
en face de	*across from*		

Other common prepositions that do not take **de**

chez	*at the home of*	entre	*between*
dans	*in*	sous	*under*
derrière	*behind*	sur	*on*
devant	*in front of*		

Language

A. **A la résidence.** Someone is calling your floor in the dorm, but everyone is out. Tell the caller where everyone is by forming complete sentences.

1. Marie / travailler / librairie
2. Marc / étudier / bibliothèque
3. Jacques et Jean / être / centre commercial
4. Monique / manger / restau-U
5. Jeanne et Chantal / être / près / cinéma
6. Je / être / dans / chambre de Paul

B. Describe the activities and locations of the people below, using an item from each of the four columns provided.

MODEL: Je / être / à / université
Je suis à l'université.

A	B	C	D
Les étudiants	travailler	à	bibliothèque
Je	habiter	de	cinéma
Vous	être	derrière	maison
Luc	étudier	à côté de	appartement
Mes amis	manger	devant	étudiants
Nous	parler	loin de	théâtre
agents de police		sous	université
		sur	magasin
Mes parents		près de	parc

Culture

C. **Visitons Paris.** Identify where various landmarks in Paris are located by adding être and a preposition to the places listed on page 85. For help, refer to the map of Paris on the inside back cover of this book.

MODEL: Le parc des Expositions / le palais des Sports
Le parc des Expositions est derrière le palais des Sports.

1. La tour Eiffel / le palais de Chaillot
2. Le Louvre / la Seine
3. Notre-Dame / le Palais de Justice
4. la gare Montparnasse / le Sacré-Cœur
5. L'Arc de Triomphe / la place Charles-de-Gaulle
6. La place de la Concorde / l'avenue des Champs-Elysées et les Tuileries

a. près de
b. à côté de
c. entre
d. sur
e. en face de
f. loin de

Communication

D. Using the map in **Enrichissons notre vocabulaire,** give the locations of the following places.

MODEL: Café des Américains / musée
Le Café des Américains est près du musée.

1. cinéma Etoile / théâtre de la Gare
2. église Saint-Sulpice / café des Américains
3. gare / hôtel
4. pharmacie / restaurant Chez Paulette
5. musée / pharmacie
6. librairie / église / bibliothèque
7. banque / lycée
8. restaurant Chez Paulette / cinéma Etoile

E. Tell where you do the following things:

MODEL: étudier? *J'étudie dans ma chambre.*

1. jouer
2. terminer les devoirs
3. dîner
4. travailler
5. regarder la télé
6. aimer danser

F. **Questions personnelles.** Votre ville *(Your town)*

1. Vous êtes de New York?
2. Où est-ce que vous habitez? C'est près de... ?
3. Qu'est-ce qu'il y a dans la ville où vous habitez?
4. Dans la ville où vous habitez, où est le musée? la gare? Où sont les cinémas? les cafés? les restaurants?
5. Vous aimez bien un restaurant? Où est-ce qu'il est?
6. Qu'est-ce que vous aimez à l'université où vous étudiez?

II. Aller / The futur proche

> You use **aller** to express the idea of going somewhere or to talk about health.

A. Forms of aller

1. **Aller** is an irregular verb, and you must memorize its forms.

aller *(to go)*	
je **vais**	nous **allons**
tu **vas**	vous **allez**
il / elle / on **va**	ils / elles **vont**

2. **Aller** is almost never used alone as it can be in English (*I'm going!*). It is often followed by expressions that indicate manner or direction.

Nous **allons en** France.
Je **vais au** café **avec** Marie.
Est-ce que vous **allez au** théâtre?

Pour étudier, elle **va à la** bibliothèque.

3. The formation of the imperative of **aller** is regular: **va, allons, allez.**

Allons au cinéma.

Ne va pas avec Jean.

4. You have already learned some idiomatic expressions with **aller.** Those and some other common expressions are listed below.

—**Comment ça va? Ça va?**
—**Ça va. Ça va bien.**

—**Comment allez-vous?**
—**Je vais bien.**

On y va? *Shall we go?*
Allez-y. Vas-y. *Go ahead.*
Allons-y! *Let's go!*

B. The futur proche

1. One very frequent use of **aller** is to express an action in the future by using a conjugated form of **aller** + an *infinitive*. This construction is similar to the English *to be going* + an *infinitive* and is called the **futur proche** (near future). The main action is expressed by the infinitive, which directly follows the conjugated verb **aller.**

Nous **allons visiter** l'Italie.

Je **vais travailler** demain.

2. To make negative sentences with the **futur proche,** you simply place **ne... pas** around the conjugated form of **aller.**

—Tu vas regarder la télévision?

—Non, je **ne vais pas regarder** la télévision.

3. The **futur proche** is frequently used with expressions of time.

aujourd'hui *today*

cet après-midi *this afternoon*

ce matin *this morning*

ce soir *tonight*

demain *tomorrow*

demain matin *tomorrow morning*

demain soir *tomorrow evening*

maintenant *now*

tous les jours *every day*

l'année prochaine *next year*

la semaine prochaine *next week*

le week-end prochain *next weekend*

Language

A. Say where the following people are going today, using the cues provided and the verb **aller**.

MODEL: Paul / cinéma *Paul va au cinéma.*

1. Tu / université
2. Nous / arrêt d'autobus
3. Mes amis / librairie
4. Je / bureau de poste
5. Vous / centre commercial
6. Françoise / maison

B. Tell what will happen to the following people in the future by changing the sentences from the present tense to the **futur proche**.

MODEL: Il arrive fatigué.
Il va arriver fatigué.

1. Je travaille en ville.
2. Elle est ingénieur.
3. Ils invitent des amis.
4. Jacques a chaud.
5. Est-ce que vous habitez ici?
6. Nous aimons le restaurant.
7. Tu vas au Canada.
8. Elles mangent un couscous.

Culture

C. **A l'Office de tourisme.** This office, located on the **Champs-Elysées** in Paris, gives tourist advice. Pretend you are working there by matching the interests of various tourists on the left with places to go on the right.

MODEL: la poésie   musée Victor-Hugo
Allez au musée Victor-Hugo.

1. l'impressionnisme
2. l'art classique
3. l'art moderne
4. le cubisme
5. la sculpture
6. le Moyen Age *(Middle Ages)*

a. musée Cluny
b. musée Rodin
c. musée d'Orsay
d. le Louvre
e. musée Picasso
f. Centre Pompidou

D. **En France ou aux Etats-Unis?** Form complete sentences, then state whether the action is more typical in France or in the U.S.

    1. Les touristes / aller / gare pour changer de l'argent.
    2. On / aller / café parce qu'on a soif.
    3. La famille de Jacqueline / aller / gare pour dîner.
    4. Les enfants / aller / pharmacie pour manger une glace.
    5. Les étudiants / aller / café pour étudier.
    6. Tu / aller / librairie / parce que tu désires avoir un tee-shirt.

Communication

E. Answer the following questions.

    1. Où est-ce que vous allez aujourd'hui pour étudier? pour manger? pour regarder un film?
    2. Où vont les étudiants de votre université pour dîner? pour danser? pour parler?
    3. L'année prochaine, est-ce que vous allez étudier le français?
    4. Vous allez regarder la télévision ce soir? écouter la radio? aller à l'église le week-end prochain?

F. Ask a classmate if he or she is going to do the following things.

    1. travailler à la maison cet après-midi?
    2. aller dans une boîte ce soir?
    3. rester à la résidence demain matin?
    4. déjeuner chez des amis le week-end prochain?

G. Ask your professor if he or she is going to do the following things.

    1. donner des devoirs pour demain?
    2. donner un examen facile la semaine prochaine?
    3. préparer un couscous en classe?
    4. être agréable ou désagréable?

III. Articles and Prepositions with Place Names

> You use articles, prepositions, and place names to indicate geographical location or destination.

A. Unlike English, French does not make a distinction between going *to* or being *in* a place. Instead, the correct preposition depends on the type of place name.

    1. Use **à,** meaning *to* or *in,* with cities.

    Nous n'allons pas rester **à Nice.**
    Robert est **à New York.**
    A Madrid on dîne à 22 heures.

2. Use **en**, meaning *to* or *in*, with feminine countries, all continents, and countries whose names begin with a vowel. (Most countries whose names end in a written **e** are feminine.)

Vous allez étudier **en France.**
Nous allons aller **en Italie.**
Ils désirent voyager **en Russie.**
En Asie, on parle français.
Le diplomate va voyager **en Israël, en Iraq,** et **en Iran.**

3. Use **au** (*pl.* **aux**), meaning *to* or *in*, with countries that are masculine. (Masculine countries have names that end in letters other than **e**, with the exceptions of **le Mexique, le Mozambique,** and **le Zaïre.**)

Ils désirent voyager **au Canada.**
Nous sommes **aux Etats-Unis.**
Au Portugal on trouve des universités très anciennes.

B. To express *from*, use **du** with masculine singular countries, **des** with plural countries, and **de** without an article for feminine countries and cities. Some verbs often followed by **de** are **arriver, être, rentrer,** and **aller** (to indicate origin).

Il est **du** Canada, mais elle est **des** Etat-Unis.
Mes parents rentrent **de** Paris la semaine prochaine.
Nous allons aller **de** Grande-Bretagne en Belgique.

Mots clés Cities, Continents, and Countries

Des Villes (f.)

Bruxelles	Mexico
Genève	Moscou
Lisbonne	La Nouvelle-Orléans
Londres	Varsovie *Warsaw*

Des Continents (m.)

l'Afrique	l'Asie
l'Amérique du Nord	l'Europe
l'Amérique du Sud	

Des Pays féminins

l'Algérie		la Grande-Bretagne	*Great Britain*
l'Allemagne	*Germany*	la Grèce	
l'Angleterre	*England*	la Hollande	
l'Australie		l'Irlande	
l'Autriche	*Austria*	l'Italie	
la Belgique		la Norvège	*Norway*
la Chine		la Pologne	
la Côte-d'Ivoire		la Russie	
l'Espagne		la Suède	*Sweden*
la Finlande		la Suisse	*Switzerland*
la France		la Tunisie	

Des Pays masculins

le Brésil	le Mozambique
le Canada	les Pays-Bas *the Netherlands*
le Danemark	le Portugal
les Etats-Unis[1] *U.S.A.*	le Sénégal
le Japon	le Tchad *Chad*
le Maroc *Morocco*	le Zaïre
le Mexique	

ATTENTION

If you are not expressing *to* or *in* a place, no preposition is necessary, but the definite article *must* be used with most countries. Do not use an article with cities unless the city name already contains an article, such as **La Nouvelle-Orléans.**

L'Italie est un pays fascinant.
Ils adorent **la Chine.**
Paris a des restaurants fantastiques.
Je vais visiter **La Nouvelle-Orléans** pour écouter du jazz.

Language

A. Form a sentence to describe where the people below are, based on the following model.

MODEL: Yves: Paris, France
Yves est à Paris, en France.

1. Carlo: Rome, Italie
2. Maria: Mexico, Mexique
3. Tom: Washington, Etats-Unis
4. Mamadou: Dakar, Sénégal
5. Rachel: Tel-Aviv, Israël
6. Robert et Line: Bruxelles, Belgique
7. Paul et Claire: Montréal, Canada
8. Fatima: Casablanca, Maroc

B. **Un peu de géo.** Identify the following countries by what continent they are on.

MODEL: *La France est en Europe.*

1. Mexique
2. Angleterre
3. Chine
4. Zaïre
5. Brésil
6. Tchad
7. Portugal
8. Japon

---

1. Articles and prepositions used with states of the United States are found in Appendix II.

Culture

C. **Voyages à l'étranger.** Cars crossing borders in Europe must have an oval sticker on the back that indicates the country where the car is registered. Name the country of the drivers of cars with the following stickers.

MODEL: F   *Il est de France.*

1. D	3. I	5. CH	7. E
2. B	4. DK	6. A	8. GB

Communication

D. Try to identify where you are, as another student chooses a number for a country or a letter for a city from the map of Europe on page 92.

MODEL: Student 1: *1*
Student 2: *Nous sommes en France.*

Student 1: *B*
Student 2: *Nous sommes à Madrid.*

E. With a classmate, plan a trip through Europe using the map on page 92. Then read your itinerary.

MODEL: *J'arrive à Paris. Je visite la France. Après, je vais en Suisse et en Italie. Je continue le voyage en Autriche et je termine à Berlin.*

F. Answer the following questions with complete French sentences.

1. Où est-ce que vous désirez aller en Europe? en Afrique?
2. Quelles *(Which)* villes et quels pays est-ce que vous désirez visiter?
3. Où est-ce que la vie *(life)* est agréable? désagréable? Pourquoi?
4. Quels pays est-ce que vous recommandez aux Américains? Pourquoi?

IV. Numbers from 70 to 1,000,000,000

70	soixante-dix	82	quatre-vingt-deux
71	soixante et onze	83	quatre-vingt-trois
72	soixante-douze	84	quatre-vingt-quatre
73	soixante-treize	85	quatre-vingt-cinq
74	soixante-quatorze	86	quatre-vingt-six
75	soixante-quinze	87	quatre-vingt-sept
76	soixante-seize	88	quatre-vingt-huit
77	soixante-dix-sept	89	quatre-vingt-neuf
78	soixante-dix-huit	90	quatre-vingt-dix
79	soixante-dix-neuf	91	quatre-vingt-onze
80	quatre-vingts	92	quatre-vingt-douze
81	quatre-vingt-un	93	quatre-vingt-treize

94	quatre-vingt-quatorze	200	deux cents
95	quatre-vingt-quinze	231	deux cent trente et un
96	quatre-vingt-seize	284	deux cent quatre-vingt-quatre
97	quatre-vingt-dix-sept	300	trois cents
98	quatre-vingt-dix-huit	400	quatre cents
99	quatre-vingt-dix-neuf	701	sept cent un
100	cent	1.000	mille
101	cent un	3.200	trois mille deux cents
108	cent huit	1.000.000	un million
172	cent soixante-douze	1.000.000.000	un milliard
199	cent quatre-vingt-dix-neuf		

A. Note that **et** is used with **21, 31, 41, 51, 61,** and **71** (**vingt et un, trente et un,...**), but not with **81, 91,** and **101** (**quatre-vingt-un, quatre-vingt-onze, cent un**).

B. **Cent** and **mille** are *never* preceded by **un**, but **un million** and **un milliard** *(one billion)* must be.

    100   cent
    1005   mille cinq
    1.500.000   un million cinq cent mille
    1.003.800.000   un milliard trois millions huit cent mille

C. When counting in millions or billions, you must use the preposition **de** (**d'**) before a noun. However, when **million** or **milliard** is followed by a number, the preposition is dropped.

un million d'habitants	*one million inhabitants*
quatre milliards de francs	*four billion francs*
deux millions cinq cent mille dollars	*two million five hundred thousand dollars*

▶ L'Orthographe

1. **Quatre-vingts** and multiples of **cent** take an **s** when they are not followed by another number. When they are followed by another number, there is no **s**.

quatre-vingts	quatre-vingt-cinq
deux cents	deux cent trente-quatre
quatre cents	quatre cent dix

2. **Mille** never takes an **s**.

   Mille, deux mille, trois mille...

3. Note that French uses a period to mark thousands, not a comma as in English. (Some French publications, however, mark thousands by leaving a space between digits: 1 000.) Decimals are the opposite: two and five-tenths (2.5 in English) is **2,5** in French (**deux virgule cinq**).

Language

A. Say the following numbers in French.

1. 71	5. 100	9. 391
2. 81	6. 102	10. 500
3. 89	7. 151	11. 544
4. 99	8. 274	12. 1.000

B. Say the following numbers in French.

1. 1.000	3. 2.000	5. 16.552	7. 1.000.000
2. 1.600	4. 10.000	6. 200.000	8. 100.000.000

Culture

C. Give the distances in kilometers to the following destinations in French-speaking Canada.

MODEL: New York—Montreal   613
New York est à six cent treize kilomètres de Montreal.

1. Montréal—Québec   270
2. Chicoutimi—Rivière-du-Loup   182
3. Gaspé—Rivière-du-Loup   499
4. Sherbrooke—Victoriaville   97
5. Trois-Rivières—Chicoutimi   367
6. Québec—Ville-Marie   918

D. **Trivia.** The annual publication *Quid* resembles *The World Almanac* and presents a great many statistics about France. Read the following in French.

1. Consommation annuelle de caviar: 50 tonnes
2. Ecrivains professionnels: 945
3. La dette nationale en France en 1984: 915.000.000.000 F
4. Escargots consommés: 40.000 tonnes
5. Sucre consommé: 1.865.000 tonnes
6. Nombre de bicyclettes: 1.958.000
7. Cigarettes consommées: 88.000.000.000 par an *(a year)*
8. Naturistes: 500.000

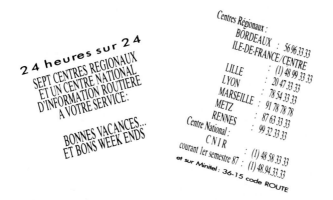

24 heures sur 24
SEPT CENTRES REGIONAUX
ET UN CENTRE NATIONAL
D'INFORMATION ROUTIERE
A VOTRE SERVICE:

BONNES VACANCES...
ET BONS WEEK ENDS

Centres Régionaux :
BORDEAUX   : 56 96 33 33
ILE-DE-FRANCE/CENTRE
LILLE   : (1) 48 99 33 33
LYON   : 20 47 33 33
MARSEILLE   : 78 54 33 33
METZ   : 91 78 78 78
RENNES   : 87 63 33 33
Centre National :   99 32 33 33
C.N.I.R
courant 1er semestre 87 : (1) 48 58 33 33
                           (1) 48 94 33 33
et sur Minitel : 36-15 code ROUTE

E. **La Loterie.** Answer the following questions about the results of a lottery drawing based on the newspaper report above.

1. Où est cette *(this)* loterie?
2. Quels numéros gagnent *(win)*?
3. Combien gagne-t-on avec les six numéros?
4. Combien de personnes ont quatre numéros?
5. Combien de personnes gagnent dix dollars?
6. Combien d'argent est-ce qu'on va gagner la prochaine fois *(time)*?

Communication

F. Give your phone number to the class. In France, you would read the first three digits as a whole number and break the other number into a pair of two-digit numbers.

MODEL: 549-8859

cinq cent quarante-neuf, quatre-vingt-huit, cinquante-neuf

G. Answer the following questions with complete French sentences.

1. Quel âge a le professeur?
2. Quel âge a le président des Etats-Unis?
3. Combien d'étudiants est-ce qu'il y a à la résidence? à l'université?
4. Combien de pages est-ce qu'il y a dans le livre de français?
5. Combien d'argent est-ce que vous avez à la banque?
6. Combien d'étudiants vont aux matchs de football?

Communiquons

Demander son chemin

When traveling in a new place, one must be able to ask for directions (**deman-der son chemin**) and understand them. In this situation, you need to know how to get someone's attention on the street and then ask for directions politely. Most French people are used to seeing tourists and are glad to help.

One custom of giving directions is very different in Europe. While Americans judge distances in cities by blocks, the French generally estimate the distance in meters. A meter is about three inches longer than a yard.

«Pardon, Messieurs, je cherche une banque.»

On demande son chemin.

S'il vous plaît, pourriez-vous me dire où se trouve la gare?	*Could you please tell me where the train station is located?*
Excusez-moi, pourriez-vous m'indiquer une banque?	*Excuse me, could you show me a bank?*
Pardon, où se trouve le bureau de poste?	*Pardon me, where is the post office?*

On indique le chemin.

Tournez à droite à 200 mètres d'ici.	*Turn right 200 meters from here.*
Vous tournez à gauche au coin de la rue.	*You turn left at the corner.*
Ensuite, continuez jusqu'à la rue Pascal.	*Then, continue until Pascal Street.*
Là, vous allez tout droit.	*There, you go straight ahead.*
Traversez la rue.	*Cross the street.*

On regarde une carte de la francophonie.

La Tunisie est à l'est de l'Algérie.	*Tunisia is east of Algeria.*
Le Sénégal est au sud de la Mauritanie.	*Senegal is south of Mauritania.*
Le Gabon est à l'ouest du Congo.	*Gabon is west of the Congo.*
Le Cameroun est au nord du Zaïre.	*The Cameroon is north of Zaire.*

Interaction   *Robert cherche la gare.*

ROBERT: Pardon, Monsieur...

UN *PASSANT*:   Oui?   *passer-by*

ROBERT: Pourriez-vous me dire où se trouve la gare?

UN PASSANT: Oui, mais c'est loin!

ROBERT: Mais, j'ai un train dans vingt minutes!

UN PASSANT: Alors, traversez cette rue, allez jusqu'au coin là-bas, et
               tournez à droite. Ensuite continuez jusqu'au coin de la rue
               Montaigne, à 400 mètres. Là, vous tournez à gauche et
               vous avez la gare en face de vous.

ROBERT: Merci beaucoup, Monsieur.

UN PASSANT: *Je vous en prie.*   *Don't mention it.*

Activités

A. Answer the following questions about your campus.

   1. Comment est-ce que vous allez de la bibliothèque au restau-U?
   2. Comment est-ce que vous allez de la salle de classe à la librairie?
   3. Pour aller de la salle de classe à la résidence, on va tout droit?
      Expliquez.

4. Le parking des étudiants est à quelle distance de la classe? Le parking des professeurs est loin ou près de la classe?

B. Act out the following situations with a classmate.

1. You are a French tourist who becomes lost in an American college town while looking for a local tourist attraction. Your partner is a French-speaking American who gives you directions to the landmark you are seeking.

2. You are an American tourist visiting the French town pictured in **Enrichissons notre vocabulaire**. Using the map, decide where you are in the town and choose a destination that you would like to visit. Your partner will play the role of the town resident whom you stop on the street to ask for directions to your chosen destination.

LECTURE CULTURELLE ....

Avant la lecture

In France, every person who has been employed for at least a year is entitled to five weeks of paid vacation. July and especially August are the months in which the vast majority of people take their annual leave. In August, the country comes almost to a standstill. Most plants, companies, and big corporations shut down completely, and the population migrates to summer resorts in France and abroad. Tourists who visit Paris in August are often irritated to see signs that say «**Fermeture annuelle**» on stores, theaters, and exhibits.

For years, the government has encouraged people to spread their vacations over a longer period of time. But most are reluctant to do so. Many still consider August the ideal vacation time because of better chances for good weather. It is also a question of status. In big companies, newly hired employees are forced to take their vacations in June or September because those with more seniority almost always pick July or August.

More and more people with school-age children take their vacations in two parts, four weeks in the summer and another in the winter, either during the Christmas holidays or in February, when children have a break.

Activités

A. Answer the following questions to prepare yourself for the reading.

1. What do you think vacations would be like in the U.S. if everyone had five weeks of paid vacation and took it at the same time?

2. Look at the map of France on page 94. Where would you go for a vacation at the beach? In the mountains?

3. Where could the French go to save money on a vacation? What could they do to cut down on expenses?
4. What measures can be taken to promote safe driving when many people are on the road?

D. The following words which you will see in the reading are closely related to English words. What do you think they mean?

nouns	adjectives	verbs
les salariés	payés	passent
en juillet	scolaires	constitue
la montagne		
les habitants		
une pause-café		

En août, les magasins ferment pour les vacances.

Les Conges

En France, les salariés ont cinq semaines de *congés payés*. Les vacances sco-   *paid vacation*
laires commencent en juillet et les *grandes entreprises* ferment en *août*. Juillet   *big companies / August*
et août sont les *mois* des *grandes vacances*. En août, à Paris, les magasins, les   *months / summer vacation*
théâtres et l'Opéra ferment.

5   Les Français aiment aller en vacances *à l'étranger*, particulièrement en Es-   *abroad*
pagne, en Italie et au Portugal. Ils vont aussi très loin et visitent les Antilles ou
les Seychelles. Les Français restent aussi en France et passent des vacances à la
mer, *à la montagne, à la campagne* et dans les villes. Les vacances à l'hôtel sont   *in the mountains / in the*
très chères et beaucoup de Français préfèrent camper ou voyager en *caravane*.   *country / motor home*
10 *L'été,* sur la Côte d'Azur, les terrains de camping sont toujours pleins, et beau-   *In summer*

Un terrain de camping
au bord de l'eau

coup de *vacanciers* campent dans les *champs* et sur la plage. C'est le «*camping sauvage*». Les habitants et les autorités de la région n'aiment pas *cette sorte* de camping parce que les *gens envahissent* les *propriétés* privées et *créent* des situations difficiles.

15   En vacances, les Français pratiquent beaucoup de sports; à la mer, ils aiment faire du *ski nautique* et de la *planche à voile*. *La plupart* aiment *nager* et *prendre des bains de soleil*.

    Les Français aiment aussi les vacances d'*hiver*. De décembre à mars, ils vont aux sports d'hiver. Ils restent en France ou ils vont en Suisse, en Autriche,

20 en Italie ou en Allemagne. Ils *font du ski*, du *patin à glace*, de la *luge* et ils jouent dans la *neige*. Le soir, ils dansent dans les boîtes.

    Les vacances sont très importantes pour les Français. Le premier août constitue un *véritable exode*. Les routes sont *encombrées* et la *circulation* est intense. A la radio, on recommande régulièrement des itinéraires supplémentaires

25 pour aller *plus vite*. On demande aux *chauffeurs* de ne pas consommer d'alcool, de faire souvent une pause-café et de respecter la *limite de vitesse*.

vacationers / fields / unauthorized camping / this kind / people / invade / properties / create

water skiing / wind surfing / Most people / to swim / to sunbathe

winter

go skiing / ice skating / sledding / snow

real exodus / jammed / traffic
faster / drivers
speed limit

Après la lecture

Questions sur le texte

1. En France, qui (*who*) a cinq semaines de congés payés?
2. Quand commencent les vacances scolaires en France?
3. En août à Paris, est-ce que les magasins, les théâtres, et l'Opéra sont ouverts?
4. Où vont les Français en vacances?
5. En général, est-ce que les Français vont à l'hôtel?

6. Pourquoi est-ce que les vacanciers campent dans les champs et sur les plages?
7. Où vont les Français aux sports d'hiver?
8. Qu'est-ce qu'on demande aux chauffeurs de faire?

Activités

A. Répondez aux questions suivantes.

1. Vous êtes prudent(e) quand vous êtes en vacances?
2. Vous aimez faire du camping? Où?

B. Regardez la carte d'Europe à la page 92. Montrez les endroits mentionnés dans le texte. Où est-ce que vous désirez aller?

C. Décrivez vos vacances idéales.

Chapitre 5

LE MONDE FRANCOPHONE

A Fort-de-France à la Martinique

103

COMMENÇONS ························

Lise et Gaëtan Morin font leurs bagages.

Lise et Gaëtan sont québécois. Ils habitent à Montréal et, tous les ans en hiver, ils font un voyage à la Martinique.

GAËTAN: Est-ce que tu as fait les valises?

LISE: Oui, mais je n'ai pas terminé les bagages à main; et toi, est-ce que tu as fait toutes tes courses?

GAËTAN: Bien sûr. Tu as pensé à mon short blanc et à mon tee-shirt de l'université de Montréal?

LISE: Si tu portes quelque chose comme cela, tu vas avoir l'air du parfait touriste!

GAËTAN: Tu as raison; ce n'est pas une bonne idée. Je vais faire des achats à Fort-de-France.

LISE: Moi aussi. Leurs maillots de bain sont super.

GAËTAN: Ça y est! Nous sommes prêts, mais où sont mes lunettes de soleil?

LISE: Dans la poche de ton veston. Fais attention; n'oublie rien!

Mots clés

font leurs bagages *(m.)* (faire ses bagages)	pack their luggage	portes (porter)	wear
		quelque chose	something
		avoir l'air	to look like
		parfait	perfect
québécois	from Quebec	touriste *(m., f.)*	tourist
tous les ans	every year	bonne (bon)	good
hiver *(m.)*	winter	idée *(f.)*	idea
font un voyage (faire un voyage)	to take a trip	faire des achats *(m.)*	to go shopping
		moi	I
as fait les valises *(f.)* (faire les valises)	packed the suitcases	maillots de bain *(m.)*	bathing suits
		super	terrific
		Ça y est!	That's it!
		prêts	ready
bagages à main	hand luggage	mes	my
toi	you	lunettes de soleil *(f.)*	sunglasses
as fait toutes tes courses *(f.)* (faire des courses)	did all your errands	poche	pocket
		ton	your
		veston	coat
Bien sûr.	Of course.	Fais attention. (faire attention)	Be careful.
as pensé à (penser à)	thought of		
mon *(m.)*	my	N'oublie rien. (oublier)	Don't forget anything.
short	shorts		
tee-shirt	T-shirt		

FAISONS CONNAISSANCE

French is the native language of more than seven million Canadians and the official language of Quebec. Montreal is the second largest French-speaking city in the world. It has a large, cosmopolitan population and exhibits cultural features of English- and French-speaking communities and many other ethnic groups. It is often the site of international meetings and events and in 1976 hosted the Summer Olympics.

The people of Quebec love to travel, and because of the long winters many take a vacation in a warmer climate. Some of their favorite places are Florida, and Guadeloupe and Martinique, two French **départements** in the Caribbean.

Discovered in 1495 by Christopher Columbus, the island of Martinique is part of the **Petites Antilles,** and it has always been a part of France except

La Martinique

for two short periods when it was occupied by English-speaking people. Fort-de-France is its administrative, commercial, and cultural capital. With its mild climate all year round and its beautiful sandy beaches, the island attracts many European and Quebec tourists. As in Guadeloupe, French is spoken in Martinique, but among themselves, the natives use **le créole**.

Etudions le dialogue

1. Est-ce que Lise et Gaëtan sont français? Où est-ce qu'ils habitent?
2. Pourquoi est-ce qu'ils font leurs bagages?
3. Pourquoi Lise n'aime pas le short blanc et le tee-shirt de Gaëtan?
4. Qu'est-ce que Gaëtan va faire à Fort-de-France?
5. Qu'est-ce que Lise aime aux Antilles? Pourquoi?
6. Qu'est-ce que Gaëtan cherche?

Enrichissons notre vocabulaire

Les vêtements *(m.) (Clothing)*

les bottes *(f.)*	*the boots*	le manteau	*the coat*
le chapeau	*the hat*	le parapluie	*the umbrella*
le costume	*the suit*	le pull	*the sweater*
l'écharpe *(f.)*	*the scarf*	la robe de	*the robe*
l'imperméable	*the raincoat*	chambre	
(m.)		les tennis *(m.)*	*the tennis shoes*

le chemisier
la cravate
la robe
la chemise
les jeans (m.)
les chaussettes (f.)
la jupe
le pantalon
les chaussures (f.)

Quelques expressions utiles *(Useful expressions)*

Quel polo est-ce que vous allez **acheter?**	*Which **polo shirt** are you going to **buy?***
Combien **coûte** le **pyjama** / la **chemise de nuit?**	*How much are the **pyjamas** / the **night gown?***
Quelles vestes / **ceintures** Christine va **emporter?**	*Which **jackets** / **belts** is Christine going to **take?***
Quels gants est-ce que Lise porte?	*Which **gloves** is Lise wearing?*

Les couleurs *(f.) (Colors)*

bleu / bleue	◼	gris / grise	◼
vert / verte	◼	jaune / jaune	◻
brun / brune	◼	noir / noire	◼
blanc / blanche	◻	rouge / rouge	◼

—**De quelle couleur** est la jupe?
—Elle est bleue.

What color is the skirt?
It is blue.

Prononciation   Vowel Tension   [🔲]

French vowels are pronounced with much more tension of the muscles in the tongue, lips, and jaw than English vowels. The gliding of one vowel sound into another is common in English, and the sound produced is called a *diphthong*. You must avoid tongue movement when pronouncing French vowel sounds, so that each is distinct.

Repeat the following English and French word pairs after your teacher, being careful to avoid any unwanted movement when pronouncing the French words.

English	French	English	French
see	si	day	des
D	dit	Fay	fait
boo	bout	foe	faut
do	doux	low	l'eau

Exercices

A. Repeat the following words after your teacher, paying attention to vowel tension.

/i/	/u/	/e/	/o/
1. si	où	et	l'eau
2. dit	bout	des	beau
3. Guy	cou	les	faut
4. J	fou	mes	mot
5. oui	vous	été	tôt

B. Read the following sentences, taking care to keep your muscles tense when you pronounce the vowels.

1. Vous travaillez au café?
2. Sylvie étudie le français.
3. Hervé va aller au musee.
4. Les Anglais vont visiter l'université.
5. Le bureau est à côté du tableau.
6. J'ai oublié mon idée.
7. Vous allez téléphoner cet après-midi?
8. Nous aimons le café de Colombie.

Grammaire ....

I. The Verb **faire**

> You use the verb **faire** to describe many activities and to ask other people what they are doing.

faire *(to do, make)*	
je **fais**	nous **faisons**
tu **fais**	vous **faites**
il / elle / on **fait**	ils / elles **font**

Imperative: **fais, faisons, faites**

All singular forms are pronounced alike: / fɛ /. The **nous** form is pronounced / fø zɔ̃ /.

Il ne **fait** pas de devoirs.   **Faisons** la cuisine ensemble!

Mots clés Common expressions with faire

A la maison

faire la cuisine	*to cook*	faire la lessive	*to do the washing*
des crêpes *(f.)*	*crepes*	faire le ménage	*to do housework*
une omelette	*omelet*		
un sandwich	*sandwich*	faire un régime	*to be on a diet*
des pâtes *(f.)*	*noodles*		
faire la grasse matinée	*to sleep late*	faire la vaisselle	*to do the dishes*

A l'université

faire attention à	*to pay attention to*	faire la queue	*to wait in line*
faire des devoirs	*to do homework*	faire du sport	*to play sports*

En ville

faire les bagages *(m.)* / la valise	*to pack one's bags / a suitcase*
faire des courses	*to go shopping, to do errands*
faire mal (à)	*to hurt*
faire une promenade / un tour	*to go for a walk*
faire un voyage	*to take a trip*

A l'extérieur *(Outside)*

The verb **faire** is also used with the impersonal pronoun **il** to talk about the weather.

Il fait beau.	*It is nice.*	**Il fait chaud.**	*It is warm.*
Il fait mauvais.	*The weather is bad.*	**Il fait froid.**	*It is cold.*

ATTENTION

As in English, the answer to a question using **faire** often has a different verb.

—Qu'est-ce que vous **faites** ce soir?
—Je **vais regarder** la télévision.

Language

A. **Des activités.** Indicate what people are doing or asking about by filling in the blanks with the appropriate form of **faire.**

1. Nous _____ des devoirs.
2. Il _____ la vaisselle.
3. Il va _____ un tour en ville.
4. Est-ce que vous _____ les bagages de Paul?
5. Tu _____ la grasse matinée?
6. On a faim; _____ des sandwichs!

B. **Interview.** You are being interviewed to find out about life in your home. Answer the following questions, using the cues provided.

1. Vous aimez faire des promenades?   (Oui, nous...)
2. Qu'est-ce que vous aimez faire le week-end?   (... des courses.)
3. Est-ce que les enfants font attention?   (Oui, mais Jacqueline ne...)
4. Vous faites la cuisine?   (Oui, mais ma mère... ce soir.)
5. Est-ce que vous faites la vaisselle?   (Non,... détester...)
6. Qui fait des voyages?   (Nous... ensemble.)

Culture

C. **Les fêtes.** Different areas of the French-speaking world have traditional dishes that people make for holidays. See if you can match the holiday with the dish from the list below, using the verb **faire.**

une bûche *(log cake)*	une fricassée de crabes de terre *(land crabs)*
une omelette à la créole	une galette *(King cake)*
des crêpes	une tourtière *(meat pie)*

1. Pour l'Epiphanie (le 6 janvier), les Français...
2. Pour la Chandeleur (le 2 février), on...
3. Pour Nöel en France, on...
4. Pour Nöel au Canada, les Québécois...
5. A Pâques *(Easter)* à La Nouvelle-Orléans, les gens...
6. A la Martinique, pour la Pentecôte (40 jours après Pâques), on...

Communication

D. Look at the list on page 111. What do these people do for a living? Can you think of other famous people and name their professions?

MODEL: *Louis Malle fait des films.*

1. Steffi Graf et Gabriela Sabatini	a. la cuisine
2. Justin Wilson et Paul Prudhomme	b. du théâtre
3. Evander Holyfield	c. du cinéma
4. Meryl Streep et Isabelle Huppert	d. de la politique
5. Hume Cronyn et Jessica Tandy	e. de la boxe
6. François Mitterrand	f. du tennis

E. What are your plans for next weekend? Indicate your activities for each time slot, using the suggestions provided or your own ideas.

des devoirs	la grasse matinée	aller danser
la cuisine	aller au cinéma	regarder la
des courses	travailler à la	télévision
une promenade	bibliothèque	

1. vendredi soir *(Friday night)*   3. samedi soir *(Saturday night)*
2. samedi *(Saturday)*   4. dimanche *(Sunday)*

F. Interview a classmate to find out the following information.

1. où il / elle fait des courses
2. où il / elle fait des promenades
3. s'il / si elle fait la cuisine / le ménage
4. s'il / si elle va faire un régime
5. quand il / elle aime faire le ménage
6. s'il / si elle fait attention au professeur / aux agents de police

II. The passé composé

> You use the **passé composé** to tell what happened in the past.

A. The **passé composé** refers to actions or events that the speaker views as completed in the past. To form the **passé composé,** use the present indicative forms of **avoir** and the past participle of the main verb.

travailler *(to work)*	
j'ai **travaillé**	nous **avons travaillé**
tu **as travaillé**	vous **avez travaillé**
il /elle / on **a travaillé**	ils / elles **ont travaillé**

J'ai tout **terminé** ce matin.   Tu **as acheté** un pantalon bleu?

B. To form the past participle of -er verbs, drop the -er of the infinitive and add é as in **travailler** → **travaillé.** (The pronunciation does not change.)

C. The **passé composé** has several English equivalents. For example, **elle a chanté** could be *she sang, she has sung,* or *she did sing.*

Elle a chanté la semaine dernière.	*She **sang** last week.*
Elle a chanté trois fois.	*She **has sung** three times.*
Elle a chanté?	***Did** she **sing**?*

D. In the negative, place the **ne... pas** around the auxiliary verb **avoir.**

Il **n'a pas** porté de costume.   Je **n'ai pas** trouvé les gants.

E. To ask a question in the **passé composé,** use the forms you learned in Chapter 1:

Elle a fait du sport?
Est-ce que tu as terminé les bagages à main?
Tu as fait tous les achats, **n'est-ce pas?**

F. Many verbs have irregular past participles. Here are the ones that you have studied so far.

avoir → eu	Il **a eu** une idée.	*He **had** an idea.*
être → été	Elle **a été** contente.	*She **was** happy.*
faire → fait	Tu **as fait** la vaisselle?	***Did** you **do** the dishes?*

G. Generally, expressions of time are placed either at the end or at the beginning of the sentence. Some frequent expressions indicating past time are the following:

hier	*yesterday*	**le mois dernier**	*last month*
récemment	*recently*		
le week-end dernier	*last weekend*	**l'été dernier**	*last summer*
		l'année dernière	*last year*
la semaine dernière	*last week*		

J'ai fait une promenade **hier.**
Hier il a fait le ménage pendant trente minutes.
Le week-end dernier nous avons fait la grasse matinée.

In contrast, many frequently used adverbs precede the past participle.

beaucoup	*a lot*	**peu**	*little*	**souvent**	*often*
bien	*well*	**mal**	*poorly, badly*	**toujours**	*always*
déjà	*already*	**pas encore**	*not yet*	**trop**	*too much, too many*

—Vous avez **déjà** acheté des vêtements de plage?
—Non, je n'ai **pas encore** pensé à cela.

—Ils ont **bien** dîné?
—Oui, mais ils ont **trop** mangé.

Language

A. **Un voyage.** Replace the infinitive with the **passé composé** in the following sentences.

1. Jean-Paul (faire) un voyage en Grande-Bretagne avec Christine.
2. Pierre (donner) un cadeau à Jean-Paul.
3. —Tu (être) content du cadeau?
4. —Nous (trouver) le livre sur l'Angleterre formidable.
5. Nous (visiter) Paris aussi.
6. —Tu (manger) un couscous?
7. —On ne... pas (aimer) cela.
8. Il (faire) froid en Angleterre.

B. **Pas du tout!** Change the following sentences to the negative to state that people did *not* do the following things.

1. Nous avons mal fait le ménage.
2. Il a beaucoup aimé le livre.
3. Michelle a trouvé l'hôtel.
4. Gaston a fait attention au prof.
5. Elles ont cherché une chambre.
6. On a souvent invité des amis.

C. Make complete sentences to show what people did at the times in column **A** by using these expressions with words from columns **B** and **C**.

A	B	C
hier	je	acheter une jupe
le week-end dernier	mes amis	faire froid
récemment	mes parents	avoir chaud
la semaine dernière	le professeur	visiter un parc
l'année dernière	vous	être fatigué(e)(s)
l'été dernier	???	???

Culture

D. What did the following French-speaking people do to become famous?

MODEL: *Valéry Giscard d'Estaing a été président de la République française.*

1. Marie Curie
2. Louis Pasteur
3. Edith Piaf
4. Pierre Trudeau
5. Gustave Eiffel
6. François Truffaut
7. Léopold Senghor
8. Simone Signoret

a. faire des films
b. être président du Sénégal et membre de l'Académie française
c. avoir le prix Nobel de physique et de chimie
d. développer des vaccins
e. être ingénieur
f. avoir un Oscar
g. être Premier ministre du Canada
h. chanter «La Vie en rose»

Communication

E. Tell your classmates one thing you did yesterday. Then, tell them something you did not do last week that you should have. Use the suggestions provided or your own responses.

MODEL: *Hier j'ai fait la lessive. La semaine dernière je n'ai pas préparé la leçon.*

préparer la leçon	faire la lessive
manger au restau-U	écouter les professeurs
parler à mes parents	terminer les exercices
faire le ménage	étudier à la bibliothèque

F. Divide into small groups and find out what your partners did or did not do last summer. Report your findings to the class. Some possible answers are listed below.

MODEL: *L'été dernier, Robert a étudié le français et il a visité la Floride.*

travailler à...	faire un voyage...
visiter l'état de...	inviter des amis à...
acheter...	parler au téléphone avec...
étudier...	???

G. **Questions personnelles.** Mes activités récentes

1. Où avez-vous été récemment?
2. Est-ce que vous avez acheté des vêtements? De quelle couleur?
3. Combien est-ce qu'ils ont coûté?
4. Est-ce que vous avez invité un(e) ami(e) à la maison?
5. Qu'est-ce que vous avez fait ensemble?
6. Quel pays est-ce que vous avez déjà visité?
7. Vous avez parlé avec une personne célèbre *(famous)*? Qui?
8. Quel film est-ce que vous avez regardé à la télévision récemment?

III. Possessive Adjectives

> You use possessive adjectives to show ownership.

A. In English, possessive adjectives show the ownership of an object (*my* coat) or of a quality (*your* honesty). They also show relationship: *his* girlfriend / *her* boyfriend.

In French, these adjectives show not only the possessor but also indicate the number (singular or plural) of the object or quality possessed. They can also show the gender (masculine or feminine) of the thing possessed.

mon pull	*my sweater* (**pull** is *m.* + *sing.*)
ma ceinture	*my belt* (**ceinture** is *f.* + *sing.*)
mes bottes	*my boots* (**bottes** is *pl.*)

B. Written Forms

		Singular		
Person	*English equivalent*	*Masculine*	*Feminine*	*Plural*
1st singular	*my*	mon	ma	mes
2nd singular	*your*	ton	ta	tes
3rd singular	*his, her its, one's*	son	sa	ses

		Plural		
1st plural	*our*		notre	nos
2nd plural	*your*		votre	vos
3rd plural	*their*		leur	leurs

French identifies the gender of the item possessed, not the gender of the person who owns the item(s).

—C'est l'imperméable de Marie?
—Oui, c'est **son** imperméable.

—C'est l'imperméable de Jacques?
—Oui, c'est **son** imperméable.

—C'est la robe de chambre de Lise?
—Oui, c'est **sa** robe de chambre.

—C'est la robe de chambre de Robert?
—Oui, c'est **sa** robe de chambre.

ATTENTION

1. The adjectives **ma, ta,** and **sa** are not used before a vowel. You must use **mon, ton,** and **son,** even if the word is feminine.

Vous êtes **son** étudiante?   Voilà **son** amie.

Therefore, **ton enfant** may refer to a male or female child.

2. To identify the possessor, use **c'est** (for the singular) or **ce sont** (for plurals) as the subject of the sentence.

—Mme Morin, **c'est** votre manteau?
—Oui, **c'est** mon manteau.

—**Ce sont** les chaussures de Jean?
—Oui, **ce sont** ses chaussures.

C. Oral Forms

The pronunciation of possessive adjectives changes according to whether the following noun starts with a consonant or a vowel sound.

1. The only final written consonant that is always pronounced is the **r** of **leur**. The pronunciation of all other possessive adjectives changes before a vowel sound.

   Où est **leur argent?**   / lœ ʀaʀ ʒɑ̃ /
   Voici **leur valise.**   / lœʀ va liz /

2. The **n** of **mon, ton, son** and the **s** of **mes, tes, ses, nos, vos, leurs** are pronounced before a vowel sound because of **liaison**.

Liaison		**No Liaison**	
leurs enfants	/ lœʀ zɑ̃ fɑ̃ /	leurs classes	/ lœʀ klas /
mon écharpe	/ mɔ̃ ne ʃaʀp/	mon frère	/ mɔ̃ fʀɛʀ /

3. The final **e** in **notre** and **votre** is not pronounced before a vowel; the adjective and noun should be pronounced as one word.

   notre appartement   / nɔ tʀa paʀ tø mɑ̃ /
   votre école   / vɔ tʀe kɔl /

4. Remember that **ma, ta,** and **sa** change the most: they become **mon, ton,** and **son** when the following noun begins with a vowel sound.

CE QU'ILS DISENT

In conversation, the **-re** of **notre** and **votre** is often dropped when it occurs before a consonant.

   Notre voiture est rouge.   / nɔt vwa tyʀ /
   Ils ont votre sac.   / vɔt sak /

   but: C'est votre imperméable?   / vɔ tʀɛ̃ pɛʀ me abl /

Language

A. **En cours.** Replace the italicized words with each of the suggested subjects and change the possessive adjective to reflect the new subject.

1. *Il* a demandé son cahier. (je)
2. *Pierre* a trouvé son stylo. (Ils)
3. *Elles* ont parlé à leurs amis. (Vous)
4. *J'*ai oublié mon sac à dos. (Tu)
5. *Vous* avez fait vos devoirs? (Anne)
6. *Elle* a expliqué ses idées. (Nous)

B. **Faisons la lessive!** Your friends did a load of laundry, but they washed everything together, so confusion reigns as they sort out the wash. Answer their questions using possessive adjectives and the cues provided.

MODEL: C'est le chemisier de Micheline? *Oui, c'est son chemisier.*

1. C'est la chemise de Jacques? (Oui,...)
2. Tu as trouvé les chaussettes de Monique? (... sont ici.)
3. Où est la jupe de Jeanne? (Voici...)
4. Tu cherches le pyjama de mon frère? (Oui,...)
5. Est-ce que c'est le jean de Pierre? (Oui,...)
6. Tu as la robe de Chantal? (Oui,...)

C. **A la douane.** A customs agent is going through your suitcase. Answer her questions according to the cues provided.

1. Est-ce que vous avez vos bagages à main? (Oui,...)
2. Vous êtes avec vos amis? (Non,... famille.)
3. Ce sont vos vêtements? (Oui,...)
4. Où est-ce que vous avez trouvé votre jean et vos chemises? (... à K Mart.)
5. Qu'est-ce qu'il y a dans vos chaussures? (... chaussettes.)
6. Vous avez fait votre lessive récemment? (Oui,... la semaine dernière.)

AIR CANADA
Téléphonez à Air Canada ou à votre agent de voyages pour des renseignements concernant nos tours-vacances.

AIR CANA

Culture

D. **Les préférences.** Try to guess the preferences of French people in the categories below.

MODEL: Vacances préférées des Français?
a. Italie b. Espagne c. Suisse
Leurs vacances préférées sont en Espagne.

1. Boisson préférée avec le dîner?
   a. eau   b. vin   c. bière
2. Activité préférée pour les jeunes?
   a. faire du sport   b. jouer   c. regarder la télé
3. Musique préférée des jeunes?
   a. le rock   b. le reggae   c. le jazz

4. Films préférés des Français?
   a. films comiques   b. films d'amour   c. films d'aventure
5. Sport préférés des jeunes?
   a. la gymnastique   b. le tennis   c. le football
6. Et avec qui est-ce que les jeunes parlent de leurs problèmes?
   a. frère ou sœur   b. amis   c. mère

Communication

E. If you were stranded on a desert island, which three of your possessions would you most like to have with you? Consult the following list
for ideas, but use your imagination!

MODEL: *Je voudrais avoir ma radio, mon short et mes tee-shirts.*

disques	petit(e) ami(e)	bière préférée
jean	parents	livre de français
cravates	professeurs	lunettes de soleil
radio	maillot de bain	???

F. Describe the members of your family, according to the ideas below.

MODEL: *Mon frère est sympathique.*
   Mes cousins habitent à New York.

Où est-ce qu'ils habitent?	Qu'est-ce qu'ils aiment?
Où est-ce qu'ils travaillent?	Qu'est-ce qu'ils détestent?
Quel âge est-ce qu'ils ont?	Où est-ce qu'ils aiment aller?

G. **Questions personnelles.** A l'université ou chez moi?
   1. Où est-ce que vos parents habitent?
   2. De quelle couleur est leur maison?
   3. Où est votre résidence universitaire ou votre appartement?
   4. Vous faites vos devoirs là ou à la bibliothèque?
   5. Vous aimez mieux faire votre lessive en ville ou chez vos
      parents?
   6. Qu'est-ce qu'il y a sur votre bureau?
   7. Quand vous n'étudiez pas, qu'est-ce que vous faites avec vos
      ami(e)s?
   8. Quel est votre restaurant préféré? Et le restaurant préféré de vos
      ami(e)s?

IV. Stressed Pronouns

> You use stressed pronouns to talk about people when it is clear
> whom you are talking about.

	Stressed Pronouns		
person	*singular*		*plural*
1st	**moi** I, me		**nous** *we, us*
2nd	**toi** you		**vous** *you*
3rd	**lui** *(m.)* *he, him, it*		**eux** *(m.)* *they, them*
	elle *(f.)* *she, her, it*		**elles** *(f.)* *they, them*

A. Stressed pronouns are used without a verb, in order to ask or answer a question with one word, or in a compound subject when separated from the verb.

> Et **toi**? Tu as fait tes courses?

> —Qui aime le vin?
> —**Moi**!

> **Elle** et **toi,** vous n'allez pas acheter cela!

B. Stressed pronouns are also used after a preposition.

> —Tu vas travailler avec **nous**?   —Est-ce qu'ils sont en retard?
> —Non, je travaille avec **elle**.   —Oui, le professeur a commencé
>   sans **eux**.

ATTENTION

Two of the few uses of the stressed pronoun after the preposition **à** are with the expressions **être à** *(to belong to)* and **penser à** *(to think about)*.

> —A qui est le polo rouge?
> —Il **est à moi**.

> —Est-ce qu'il pense souvent à sa petite amie?
> —Oui, il **pense** souvent **à elle**.

C. You also use stressed pronouns to put emphasis on a subject pronoun.

1. In French, you cannot simply emphasize a word by putting stress on it as you can in English (*I* don't care!). To emphasize a word in French, you use a stressed pronoun to repeat the subject.

> —J'adore les vêtements de Madonna.
> —**Moi**, je n'aime pas ses chemisiers.

> —Elles sont riches, **elles**.
> —Pas du tout! Elles sont professeurs.

2. This structure also allows you to contrast people:

   Lui, il est médecin; **elle,** avocate.

   Note that a stressed pronoun can come at the beginning or the end of a sentence, and that the intonation rises at the comma. If you want to emphasize a noun, however, the stressed pronoun must follow it.

   Les Canadiens, **eux,** ils sont sympathiques.

3. Another way to emphasize a subject pronoun is to use the stressed pronoun followed by **-même(s).** This is the equivalent of *-self* in English.

   —Est-ce que vous avez fait votre robe **vous-même?**
   —Oui, la semaine dernière.

   —Vous mangez au restaurant?
   —Non, nous faisons la cuisine **nous-mêmes.**

CE QU'ILS DISENT

1. Stressed pronouns appear very frequently in conversation and may serve almost as "fillers."

   Lui, Jacques, il est studieux.

2. The pronoun **moi** may appear unexpectedly to mean *in my opinion*.

   Moi, j'aime le sucre dans mon café.
   Moi, pas du tout.

3. Since **on** frequently replaces **nous** as a subject pronoun, you will hear the stressed pronoun **nous** used with it.

   On travaille beaucoup, **nous!**

Language

A. **Les possessions.** The following sentences all show possession with possessive adjectives. Change them by using the expression **être à.**

   MODEL: C'est mon livre.   *Il est à moi.*

   1. Ce sont leurs valises.
   2. C'est ton costume.
   3. Ce sont vos disques.
   4. C'est la robe de chambre de Sylvie.
   5. C'est mon argent.
   6. Ce sont nos tennis.
   7. C'est la maison des Morin.
   8. C'est le pyjama de l'enfant.

B. **Des opinions.** Daniel has very strong opinions about everything. How would he make the subjects of the following sentences more emphatic?

MODEL: Elle ne va pas au cinéma.
*Elle, elle ne va pas au cinéma. / Elle ne va pas au cinéma,
elle.*

1. Mes amis sont très intelligents.
2. Je déteste faire des courses.
3. Nous allons acheter des vêtements formidables.
4. Mes sœurs ont du talent.
5. Tu ne travailles pas beaucoup.
6. Vous n'habitez pas une maison magnifique.

Culture

C. **Les préférences.** American and French tastes are sometimes different,
sometimes similar. Form sentences from the elements below and add
stressed pronouns to indicate preferences.

MODEL: le lait avec le dîner
*Nous, nous aimons le lait; les Français, eux, ils aiment
mieux l'eau.*

1. aimer porter un jean
2. (ne... pas) aimer les westerns
3. avoir beaucoup d'amis
4. faire des promenades en voiture
5. consommer de l'eau naturelle au restaurant
6. aimer acheter beaucoup de vêtements
7. (ne... pas) faire souvent la bise
8. (ne... pas) manger souvent du fromage

Communication

D. Think about a person or a group of people who do the following things
and people who do not. Express the contrast using a stressed pronoun.

MODEL: parler français
*Moi, je parle français; mon camarade de chambre, lui, il
parle anglais.*

1. avoir du talent
2. parler espagnol
3. aimer le vin
4. chanter bien
5. faire bien la cuisine
6. porter des vêtements super

E. Question your classmates to find out the following information.

MODEL: Qui a acheté un tee-shirt récemment?
Robert, lui, il a acheté un tee-shirt.

1. Qui a des chaussures rouges?
2. Qui a deux frères?
3. Qui a visité l'Europe?
4. Qui habite une maison blanche?
5. Qui adore la cuisine
mexicaine?
6. Qui a fait la grasse matinée
aujourd'hui?

F. **Questions personnelles.** Et vous?

   1. Vous habitez chez vos parents?
   2. Vous parlez français avec votre professeur?
   3. Est-ce que le professeur parle français avec vous?
   4. Vous allez au cinéma seul(e) ou avec vos amis?
   5. Est-ce que vos camarades aiment étudier avec vous?
   6. Est-ce que vous pensez souvent à vos parents?

COMMUNIQUONS ....

Demander des renseignements

In Chapter 4 you learned how to ask for and give directions. There are many other types of information that you will have to ask for when traveling through or living in a French-speaking country. You will also have to clarify the meaning of what you hear and want to say, participate in basic conversations, and understand questions and provide information when it is asked of you.

«Vous aimez ce pantalon?»

En ville on demande...

—Comment vous appelez-vous? — *What's your name?*

—Je m'appelle Chantal Laforge. — *My name is Chantal Laforge.*

—Comment allez-vous? / — *How are you?*
Comment ça va? / Ça va?

—Je vais bien. / Ça va. — *I'm fine.*

—Quelle heure est-il? — *What time is it?*

—A quelle heure est-ce que — *At what time does the bus*
l'autobus arrive? — *arrive?*

—Il arrive à trois heures. — *It arrives at 3:00.*

—Quel temps fait-il / va-t-il — *What's the weather like / going*
faire? — *to be like?*

En cours on demande...

—Comment dit-on *coat* en — *How do you say* coat *in French?*
français?

—On dit «manteau». — *You say "manteau."*

—Qu'est-ce que cela veut dire? — *What does that mean?*

—Que veut dire «chaussures»? — *What does* chaussures *mean?*

—Ça veut dire «*shoes*». — *It means "shoes."*

—Que veut dire l'expression «à — *What does the expression* à tout
tout à l'heure»? — à l'heure *mean?*

—Ça veut dire «*see you soon*». — *It means "see you soon."*

Au magasin on demande...

—Est-ce que vous avez des — *Do you have gloves?*
gants?

—Oui, là-bas, au fond, — *Yes, over there, in the back, sir.*
Monsieur.

—C'est combien? — *How much is it?*

—C'est 125 francs. — *It's 125 francs.*

—Combien coûte l'écharpe — *How much is the blue scarf?*
bleue?

—Elle coûte 89 francs. — *It's 89 francs.*

—Combien coûtent les pulls — *How much are the sweaters*
là-bas? — *over there?*

—Le pull rouge coûte 430 — *The red sweater costs 430*
francs et les blancs 520. — *francs, and the white ones*
520.

Chez les amis on demande...

—Quoi de neuf?   *What's new?*
—Pas grand-chose!   *Not much.*

—Qu'est-ce qui se passe?   *What's going on?*
—Qu'est-ce qui s'est passé?   *What happened?*
—Rien d'important.   *Nothing much.*

—Qu'est-ce qu'il y a?   *What is the matter?*
—Qu'est-ce qui ne va pas?   *What's wrong?*
—Frédéric est malade.   *Fred is sick.*

Interaction   *Une touriste entre dans une boutique.*

L'EMPLOYEE: Vous désirez, Madame?

LA TOURISTE: Vous avez des robes de chambre?

L'EMPLOYEE: Oui, de quelle couleur?

LA TOURISTE: Noire, *de préférence.*   *preferably*

L'EMPLOYEE: Regardez; *ça vous plaît?*   *do you like it?*

LA TOURISTE: Oui, c'est combien?

L'EMPLOYEE: 670 francs *en solde.*   *on sale*

Activités

A. Interview a classmate to find out the following information:

   1. son nom   3. son adresse
   2. son âge   4. où il ou elle habite

B. You are traveling in Quebec. What question(s) would you ask in the
   following situations?

   1. You are in Pollack's department store in Quebec and are looking
      for an article of clothing that you do not see.
   2. You see an interesting person while going for a walk on the
      Terrasse Dufferin in Quebec and want to start up a conversation
      with him / her.
   3. You run into an old friend you haven't seen for several years.
   4. You are reading the menu in the dining room of the Reine
      Elisabeth Hotel in Montreal, and you come across the name of a
      dish with which you are not familiar.
   5. You want to go on a cruise on the Saint Lawrence
      (Saint-Laurent) but you are unsure of what weather to expect.
   6. You are in the lobby of your hotel, and you see a little boy
      crying.

LECTURE CULTURELLE ·······················

Avant la lecture

Although the adjective **francophone** appeared in *Le Grand Larousse de la langue française* as early as 1930, the noun **francophonie** was not found in French dictionaries until the sixties and seventies. This happened because it took a long time before a consensus on a definition could be reached. For many years, different people gave the term different connotations even though they agreed on a very broad meaning. However, after the first summit meeting of **francophone** heads of state held in Versailles in February 1986, the definition of the word became clearer. All parties recognized that **francophonie** had several meanings; in addition to the linguistic characteristic of people who all speak French, it took on a geographical meaning to designate the countries where French was spoken and a cultural meaning applying to communities in which people shared common values.

Activités

A. Where is English spoken in the world? Are the reasons that so many people speak English the same as the reasons people speak French? Does English sound the same everywhere?

B. French immigrants have had a strong influence in North America. What cities do you know that have French names? What family names do you know that have a French origin?

C. Guess the meanings of the following words that appear in the reading. The words in the left column are near cognates. Those in the right column are related to English words that come from the same word families.

occupé	célèbre *(celebrity)*
nombreuses	diable *(diabolic)*
langues	jour *(journal)*
esclaves	conservé *(conservation)*
emploient	monde *(mundane)*
nom	travail *(travail)*
	nouvelle *(novel)*
	vie *(vital)*

La Francophonie

La France, la Belgique, et la Suisse ne sont pas les seuls pays francophones. On parle français dans beaucoup de pays et sur *plusieurs* continents. En   *several*
Amérique du Nord, on utilise le français tous les jours au Québec, en Nouvelle-Angleterre et en Louisiane. Dans les Caraïbes, le français est parlé en
5 Haïti et dans deux départements français, la Guadeloupe et la Martinique. Un

autre département français, la Guyane, est situé en Amérique du Sud. Elle est célèbre pour sa prison de l'île du Diable et la base de missiles français à Kourou. Sur le continent africain, de nombreux pays, comme le Maroc, la Côte-d'Ivoire et le Sénégal, ont conservé l'usage de la langue française.

10   A l'origine, le français dérive du latin. Les Romains ont occupé la Gaule mais leur langue, le latin, a changé progressivement et *a cédé* sa place au fran-   *gave up*
çais. Dans leur histoire, les Français ont exporté leur langue aux quatre coins du monde. Ils ont colonisé de nombreuses régions et *la plupart de ces* pays sont   *most / those*
encore francophones.

15   Le français est *ainsi* la langue officielle de sept millions de Québécois. Ils   *thus*
emploient le français tous les jours à l'école ou à l'université, dans leur travail, et en famille. Le reste du Canada est officiellement bilingue et *même* l'*hymne*   *even / anthem*
national est en français et en anglais.

    Au cours de leur histoire, beaucoup de Québécois ont *quitté* leur pays pour   *left*
20 les Etats-Unis. En Nouvelle-Angleterre, il y a beaucoup de villes où on parle français. En Louisiane, on trouve trois langues à côté de l'anglais. Les aristocrates de La Nouvelle-Orléans parlent le «français grammatical», une variété du français standard. Quelques descendants d'esclaves emploient un créole similaire à la langue parlée en Haïti. Les descendants des Québécois, *chassés*   *forced out of*
25 *du* Canada au dix-huitième *siècle*, parlent le «cajun», une autre variété du   *century*
français. Le *mot* «cajun» dérive du mot «Acadien», nom donné à un habitant   *word*
de l'Acadie au Canada, la *terre* ancestrale des Cajuns.   *land*

    Dans les pays francophones d'Afrique, on utilise des langues africaines comme le ouolof et le bambara dans la vie de tous les jours. Les enfants étudi-
30 ent le français à l'école *car* on utilise la langue française dans l'administration.   *because*
Le français reste la langue littéraire des pays africains francophones. La majorité des écrivains publient leurs *romans* et leurs poèmes en français. *Pourtant*,   *novels / However*
on *assiste de plus en plus* au développement d'une littérature en langue   *witness / more and more*
indigène.   *indigenous*

35 Ainsi, dans le monde, plus de cent millions de *personnes* parlent le français *people*
comme langue maternelle ou comme langue officielle. En France, il y a un mi-
nistre chargé de la francophonie et des *organismes* spécialisés comme le *Haut* *organizations / High*
Conseil de la francophonie. Il y a aussi des sommets de chefs d'Etats franco- *Council*
phones. Le premier *a eu lieu* à Versailles en 1986, *suivi* par *ceux* de Québec et *took place / followed / the*
40 de Dakar. La francophonie a maintenant un rôle politique et économique *ones*
important.

Après la lecture

Questions sur le texte

1. Où est-ce qu'on parle français en Europe? En Amérique du Nord? En
   Afrique?
2. Le français dérive de quelle langue?
3. Est-ce que les Québécois parlent souvent français? Où?
4. Où est-ce qu'on parle français aux Etats-Unis?
5. Le ouolof et le bambara sont une variété du français?
6. Combien de personnes parlent français dans le monde?

Activité

The following famous people were associated with the French-speaking
world. Can you match the person with the modern name of the country?

1. le Dr. Albert Schweitzer
2. le Dr. David Livingstone and
   Sir Henry M. Stanley
3. Papillon
4. Jean-Jacques Rousseau
5. Georges Simenon
6. René Lévesque

a. le Zaïre (l'ancien [*former*]
   Congo belge)
b. la Guyane (l'île du Diable)
c. le Gabon
d. le Canada (Québec)
e. la Belgique
f. la Suisse

Chapitre 6

LES TRANSPORTS

Le TGV

Commençons ....

Dans le métro

Un soir au mois d'avril, Chantal a retrouvé ses amis Hélène et Richard à la station Châtelet. Ils ont décidé d'aller à un concert de rock à l'Olympia.

CHANTAL: Salut, les copains! Je suis là depuis longtemps, moi!

HELENE: Salut, Chantal! On a un gros problème. Richard a oublié nos billets dans la poche de son imperméable.

RICHARD: On a changé à Gare du Nord et quand je suis descendu, j'ai laissé mon imper sur la banquette.

HELENE: Nous sommes allés au bout de la ligne pour rien. Heureusement, le bureau des objets trouvés est ouvert le jeudi soir.

CHANTAL: C'est au métro Plaisance. Allons-y!

Au bureau des objets trouvés

Les trois jeunes gens sont arrivés au bureau et ils parlent avec l'employé.

L'EMPLOYE: C'est à qui?

HELENE: C'est à nous. Est-ce qu'on a rapporté un imperméable?

L'EMPLOYE: Comment est-il?

RICHARD: Il est beige avec une ceinture.

L'EMPLOYE: Est-ce qu'il est avec les manteaux là-bas?

RICHARD: Oui, justement.

L'employé donne l'imperméable à Richard. Richard cherche dans la poche et trouve les billets.

RICHARD: Quelle chance! Voilà les billets. Il est huit heures et on a encore le temps de prendre un pot avant le début du concert.

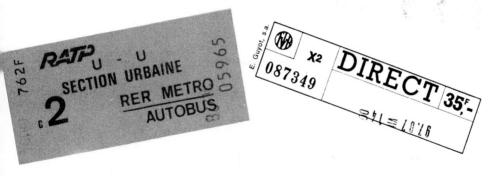

Mots clés

métro	subway	descendu	got off
avril	April	(descendre)	
retrouvé	met	laissé (laisser)	left
(retrouver)		imper	raincoat
station	metro stop	banquette	seat
ont décidé d'	decided	allés	went
(décider de)		bout	end
concert	concert	ligne	line
depuis	for a long time	pour rien	for nothing
longtemps		heureusement	fortunately
gros, -se	big	bureau des	lost and found
problème	problem	objets	
billets (m.)	tickets	trouvés	
changé	changed	jeudi	Thursday
(changer)		Allons-y!	Let's go!
employé (m.)	employee	Quelle chance!	What luck!
C'est à qui?	Whose turn is it?	huit heures	eight o'clock
rapporté	brought back	encore	still
(rapporter)		temps	time
Comment	What is it like?	prendre un pot	to have a drink
est-il?		avant	before
beige	beige	début	beginning
justement	as a matter of fact		

FAISONS CONNAISSANCE

The **métro** in Paris is a system of one hundred miles of rails plus the **RER (Réseau Express Régional),** a network of suburban lines. It is not only a very efficient system of transportation, it is also one of the easiest to use. Thanks to the numerous **correspondances** (stations where you can change lines), the **métro** is the fastest way to get from one point to another in Paris. Because you go any distance on one ticket, travel is very inexpensive. Rather than buy one ticket **(un ticket)** at a time, it is more economical to buy a booklet **(un carnet)** of ten tickets or a **carte orange,** which permits unlimited travel for specified periods of time. All of these are also valid on the bus system.

Work is constantly being done to enlarge and improve the **métro.** The old rails have been replaced, and most trains now run on rubber tires rather than on metal wheels. Several years ago, the ticket punchers in the **métro** were replaced with automatic turnstiles. Parisians complain that this system tempts certain people to jump over the turnstiles without paying for tickets and that it has caused an increase in the amount of crime in the **métro.** Some stations (**Louvre, Franklin Roosevelt,** and **Chaussée d'Antin**) are quite artistically decorated. Other stations (**Opéra**) are true commercial centers with many underground shops. Of course, the traditional accordion and guitar players playing for tips are still seen in the **métro.**

Etudions les dialogues

A. **Dans le métro**

1. Où est Chantal?
2. Qu'est-ce qu'elle va faire avec ses amis?
3. Quelle sorte de problème est-ce que Richard et Hélène ont?
4. Où est-ce que Richard a laissé son imperméable?

B. **Au bureau des objets trouvés**

1. Les trois amis, avec qui parlent-ils au bureau des objets trouvés?
2. Comment est l'imperméable de Richard?
3. Est-ce que l'employé a l'imperméable?
4. Est-ce que les billets sont toujours dans la poche de l'imperméable?

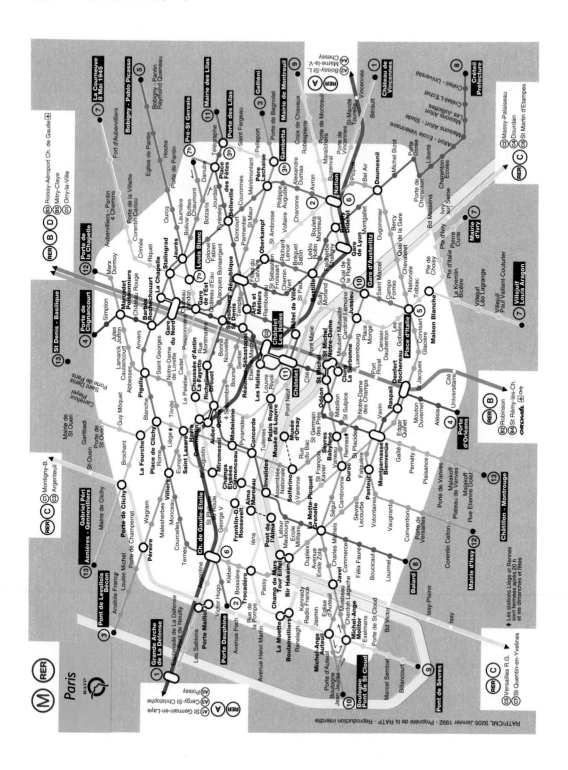

Enrichissons notre vocabulaire

Les transports *(m.) (Forms of transportation)*

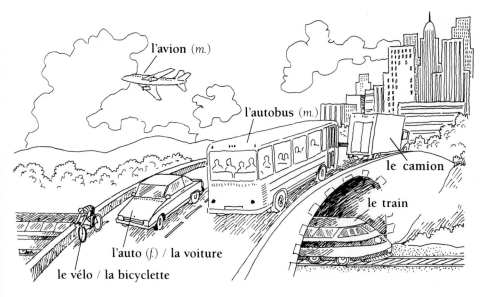

Comment est-ce qu'on voyage? *(How does one travel?)*

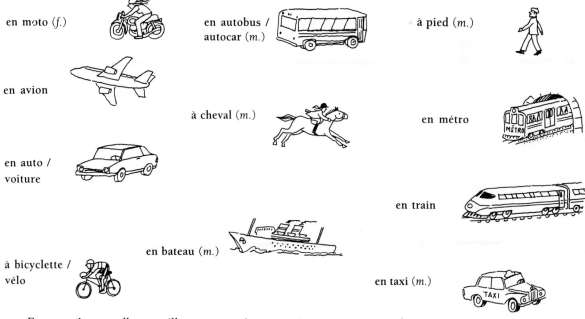

en moto *(f.)*

en avion

en auto / voiture

à bicyclette / vélo

en autobus / autocar *(m.)*

à cheval *(m.)*

en bateau *(m.)*

à pied *(m.)*

en métro

en train

en taxi *(m.)*

Est-ce qu'on va aller en ville en auto?
Non, **faisons du stop!**

Are we going to go to town by car?
*No, let's **hitchhike!***

Prononciation   The Sounds / y /, / u / and / ɥ /   ⊡

A. You have already encountered the sound / y / several times in words such as **tu** and **du**. It is always represented in writing by the letter **u** and must not be confused with the sound / u /, written **ou** (**nous, vous**). The / y / sound is produced with the tongue forward in the mouth and lips rounded. The easiest way to say it is to pronounce the / i / sound (as in **si**) and then round your lips without moving your tongue.

Repeat the following pairs of words, which differ only in lip rounding.

/ i / (unrounded)	/ y / (rounded)
si	su
dit	du
fit	fut
J	jus
qui	Q
rit	rue

Repeat these pairs, which differ only in tongue position, after your teacher.

/ u / (back)	/ y / (front)
où	U
bout	bu
nous	nu
sous	su
tout	tu
vous	vu

B. When the / y / sound is followed by another vowel sound, it is pronounced in a shorter fashion, but still with the lips rounded and the tongue forward. Many English speakers attempting to pronounce **lui** (/ lɥi /) say / lwi / instead, which is understood as **Louis**.

Practice the / ɥ / sound, called a *semi-vowel*, by repeating the following words after your teacher.

lui / cuisine / je suis / huit / huile / juillet / ennuyeux / affectueux / tout de suite / la Suisse

Exercice

Read the following sentences aloud, paying particular attention to the vowel sounds / y / and / ɥ /.

1. Je suis curieux.
2. Tu étudies avec lui?
3. Lucie trouve vos chaussures ridicules.
4. Ils sont étudiants à l'université de Tours.
5. Luc a eu huit amis chez lui.
6. Je suis allé avec lui au Portugal.

GRAMMAIRE ······························

I. Le Calendrier

> You use vocabulary related to the calendar to situate events in time.

A. Les Jours de la semaine *(The Days of the Week)*

lundi	*Monday*	**vendredi**	*Friday*
mardi	*Tuesday*	**samedi**	*Saturday*
mercredi	*Wednesday*	**dimanche**	*Sunday*
jeudi	*Thursday*		

1. On the French calendar, the week always begins with Monday (**lundi**), not Sunday (**dimanche**). Note that in French, another way of saying *one week* (**une semaine**) is **huit jours. Quinze jours** is *two weeks,* but after that you say **trois semaines** and **quatre semaines (un mois).**

2. Do not use a preposition to express the English *on* a day of the week.

   Je vais aller au bureau lundi.   *I'm going to the office on Monday.*

3. All of the days of the week are masculine nouns. They take the article **le** only to indicate a habitual action or repeated occurrence. In English, this is expressed by a plural.

   Le bureau est ouvert **le jeudi soir.**   *The office is open on **Thursday evenings.***
   Nous allons à l'église **le dimanche.**   *We go to church on **Sundays**.*

4. You can use **prochain** and **dernier** with the days of the week.

   Il y a un concert jeudi **prochain.**
   Ils n'ont pas travaillé mardi **dernier.**

B. Les Mois de l'année *(The Months of the Year)*

janvier	*January*	**mai**	*May*	**septembre**	*September*
février	*February*	**juin**	*June*	**octobre**	*October*
mars	*March*	**juillet**	*July*	**novembre**	*November*
avril	*April*	**août**	*August*	**décembre**	*December*

1. August (**août**) has two acceptable pronunciations, /u/ and /ut/.

2. To say *in a month,* you use **en** plus the month or **au mois de.**

   Les Français ne travaillent pas **en août.**
   Je vais aller en vacances **au mois de juin.**

▶ **L'Orthographe**

Days of the week and months of the year are not capitalized in French.

C. Les Quatre Saisons *(The Four Seasons)*

le printemps spring	**l'automne** *(m.)* *fall*
l'été *(m.)* *summer*	**l'hiver** *(m.)* *winter*

J'aime faire des promenades **au printemps**.
Je n'étudie pas **en été**.
Je vais aux matchs de football américain **en automne**.
Je reste chez moi **en hiver**.

D. La Date

1. To ask the date, you say:

   Quelle est la date aujourd'hui? *or* **Quel jour sommes-nous?**

2. To express a date in French, use a combination of the definite article **le,** the number, and then the month.

   La Saint-Valentin est **le 14 février.**
   En Belgique, la fête nationale c'est **le 21 juillet.**

3. Cardinal numbers, which you have already learned, are always used in dates, except for the first day of the month, **le premier.**

   Le premier mai est la fête du Travail en Europe.

4. If you wish to add the day of the week to a date, you may place it before or after the article.

   le jeudi 12 décembre   **dimanche, le 1ᵉʳ** novembre

E. Les Années *(Years)*

1. In French, there are two ways of expressing calendar years. Start with **mil** (a special spelling of **mille** used for years) and count in hundreds. You may also simply count in hundreds:

   1963   **mil neuf cent** soixante-trois or **dix-neuf cent** soixante-trois

2. When only the year is given, the preposition **en** is used.

   Il a visité la Chine **en 1981.**

   but: Il est arrivé en Chine **le 22 juin 1981.**

ATTENTION

1. The **e** of **le** is not dropped in front of numbers that begin with a vowel.

   le huit février   **le onze novembre**

2. No prepositions are used with days of the month or with **week-end**.

Ils vont arriver le 4 octobre.   Elles travaillent beaucoup le
                                   week-end.

▶ L'Orthographe

When dates are abbreviated, the day is always given before the month.

    10-3-94 → le 10 mars 1994   2-6-95 → le 2 juin 1995

Language

A. Read the following dates aloud in French.

   1. January 1, 1918   4. Thursday, August 1, 1881
   2. March 10, 1929   5. Friday, September 30, 1993
   3. April 23, 1776   6. Saturday, December 25, 1996

B. **Leurs projets.** What plans do Robert's friends have? Fill in the blanks
   with an appropriate word when necessary.

   1. Le copain de Robert va acheter une voiture _____ printemps.
   2. Paul va visiter l'Angleterre _____ été.
   3. Sylvie va inviter Luc _____ dimanche prochain.
   4. Les parents de Sylvie ne travaillent pas _____ samedi.
   5. Leurs vacances commencent _____ juillet.
   6. Robert dîne toujours au restaurant _____ vendredi.

Culture

C. **Examen d'histoire.** Match the following important events in French
   history with the dates on which they occurred.

   1. Jeanne d'Arc brûlée *(burned)*   a. 14-7-1789
   2. L'édit de Nantes   b. 30-5-1431
   3. Naissance *(birth)* de Louis XIV   c. 5-9-1638
   4. Libération de la Bastille   d. 16-10-1793
   5. Marie-Antoinette guillotinée   e. 13-4-1598
   6. Napoléon couronné *(crowned)*   f. 2-12-1804

D. **Les fêtes.** Americans have many of the same holidays as people in
   French-speaking countries, but often not at the same time. Make sentences contrasting American and other holidays in French-speaking
   countries by using the words below.

   1. les Américains / les Français: avoir la fête du Travail en
      septembre / en mai
   2. les Américains / les Canadiens: avoir *Thanksgiving* en novembre /
      en octobre
   3. les Américains / les Français: aller en vacances en été / en août

4. les Américains / les Suisses: avoir leur fête nationale en juillet / en août
5. En janvier, les Américains / les Français: la fête de Martin Luther King, Jr. / l'Epiphanie
6. Le 15 août, les Américains / les Français: travailler / ne... pas travailler (c'est l'Assomption.)

Communication

E. Using vocabulary related to the calendar, complete the following sentences as they pertain to you.

MODEL: Je n'étudie pas...
          Je n'étudie pas le dimanche.

1. J'aime aller danser...   4. Je regarde toujours la télévision...
2. Mes parents vont à l'église... 5. Je fais mes courses...
3. J'aime faire du sport...   6. Je vais en vacances...

F. **Questions personnelles.** Votre agenda

1. Qu'est-ce que vous allez faire l'été prochain?
2. Qu'est-ce que vous avez fait samedi dernier?
3. Quel mois est votre anniversaire *(birthday)*?
4. Quand est-ce que vous faites du sport? Quel sport?
5. Quelle est votre saison préférée? Pourquoi?
6. Quel est votre jour préféré? Pourquoi?

II. The passé composé with être

> You use the **passé composé** to tell what happened in the past.

A. In the last chapter, you learned the formation of the **passé composé** using the conjugated form of **avoir** and the past participle: **Chantal a retrouvé ses amis.**

B. There are about twenty verbs in French that use **être** and not **avoir** as the auxiliary verb in the formation of the **passé composé**. The verb **aller** is one of them; you will learn it and five other **être** verbs in this section.

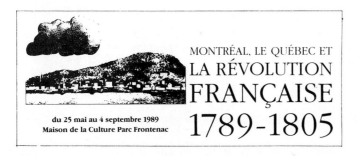

MONTRÉAL, LE QUÉBEC ET
LA RÉVOLUTION
FRANÇAISE
1789-1805

du 25 mai au 4 septembre 1989
Maison de la Culture Parc Frontenac

Passé composé of aller

je **suis allé(e)**	nous **sommes allé(e)s**
tu **es allé(e)**	vous **êtes allé(e)(s)**
il **est allé**	ils **sont allés**
elle **est allée**	elles **sont allées**
on **est allé(e)(s)**	

Nous **sommes allés** au bout de la ligne.

Mots clés   Some common verbs conjugated with être

Infinitives		Past Participles
aller	*to go*	allé
arriver	*to arrive*	arrivé
monter	*to get on; to go up*	monté
naître	*to be born*	né
rentrer	*to return*	rentré
rester	*to stay*	resté

Les trois jeunes gens **sont arrivés** au bureau.
Il **est rentré** chez lui et **est monté** dans sa chambre.
Ma mère **est née** le onze février.

▶ L'Orthographe

1. Note that, unlike verbs conjugated with **avoir**, verbs conjugated with **être** show agreement in number and gender between the subject and the past participle. This can lead to a number of forms with the same subject. You must use the correct agreement when writing to make your meaning clear.

Vous êtes **allé** au café?	*(if you are talking to a man)*
Vous êtes **allée** au café?	*(if you are talking to a woman)*
Vous êtes **allés** au café?	*(if you are talking to a group of men or of men and women)*
Vous êtes **allées** au café?	*(if you are talking to a group of women)*

2. The agreement of the past participle with the verbs listed above never causes a change in pronunciation: **Vous êtes arrivé** and **Vous êtes arrivées** are pronounced alike.

ATTENTION

With **aller** and **arriver** there is almost always a **liaison** with three forms of **être: suis, est,** and **sont.**

> Je suis allée à Québec.
> Il est arrivé en autobus.
> Elles sont arrivées de Paris.

Language

A. **Mon retour.** Chantal has just returned from vacation. Change her sentences to the **passé composé.**

1. Je rentre de vacances dimanche.
2. Nous arrivons à Paris en autocar.
3. Nous restons quinze jours.
4. Je montre mes photos à mes amis.
5. Vous allez en France en mai?
6. Chantal est contente de ses vacances!

B. Describe the activities of the following people by replacing the italicized words with each of the suggested phrases.

1. Jacqueline *est allée au musée.* (visiter une église / monter à la tour Eiffel / dîner au restaurant / rentrer à l'hôtel en taxi)
2. Georges *n'a pas trouvé son parapluie.* (chercher chez lui / aller au bureau des objets trouvés / rentrer chez lui)
3. Est-ce que tu *es arrivé en retard?* (faire tes devoirs / rester à la bibliothèque / avoir beaucoup à faire / déjà rentrer à bicyclette ou en moto)

Culture

C. **Personnages célèbres.** Match the famous French people with what they did.

1. Jacques Cartier
2. Jean-Jacques Rousseau
3. Napoléon
4. Marie Curie
5. Charlemagne
6. Clément Ader

a. aller jusqu'en Espagne
b. naître en Pologne
c. arriver au Canada en 1534
d. naître en Corse
e. monter en avion en 1890
f. rester en prison

D. **Les trains en France.** France is a world leader in public transportation. Form sentences with the words on page 141 and indicate what the French have already done (**... déjà...**) and have not yet done (**ne... pas encore...**) with trains.

MODEL: aller à 300 km/h
On est déjà allé à trois cents kilomètres à l'heure.

1. monter de Lyon à Paris en deux heures
2. aller en Angleterre
3. préparer des dîners élégants
4. aller à Nice et rentrer à Paris dans la journée *(day)*
5. arriver de Madrid à la gare du Nord
6. aller au sommet du mont Blanc

Communication

E. Say what you think your French teacher did the last time he or she was in Paris, based on the following cues.

Il / Elle... rester à l'hôtel? monter à la tour Eiffel?
acheter des souvenirs? aller en métro à l'Olympia?
oublier son passeport à la banque? visiter des musées?
consommer trop de vin? ne (n')... pas rentrer à l'hôtel?
fréquenter les bars?

F. Tell what you, your friends, and your family did at the times given below. Try to add original sentences also.

1. Hier, je (j')... aller à la bibliothèque? acheter... ? faire mon français? arriver en classe en retard? rester chez moi?
2. Dimanche dernier, mes amis... faire un tour en auto? aller au parc? monter à cheval? rentrer chez eux? faire du sport?
3. L'été dernier, mes parents et moi, nous... aller en vacances? rester en ville? monter en avion? voyager... ? faire beaucoup de promenades?

G. **Questions personnelles.** Vos activités récentes

1. Où est-ce que vous êtes allé(e) le week-end dernier? Comment?
2. Qu'est-ce que vous avez fait?
3. Combien de temps êtes-vous resté(e) là-bas?
4. Vous êtes rentré(e) chez vos parents récemment? Quand?
5. Est-ce que vous êtes resté(e) chez vous hier?
6. Est-ce que vous êtes arrivé(e) en retard ce matin? Pourquoi?

III. Inversion and Interrogative Adverbs

> You use interrogative adverbs to ask questions when you are seeking specific information. Inversion adds a more formal style to your questions.

A. Questions with Inversion

1. In Chapter 1 you learned three ways of asking a question in French: **rising intonation, Est-ce que,** and **n'est-ce pas.** Another way to form a question is through *inversion,* in which you invert the pronoun subject and the verb.

Vous travaillez samedi?	**Travaillez-vous** samedi?
Ils font un régime?	**Font-ils** un régime?

2. When the subject is a noun, you add a pronoun subject of the same number and gender, in the inverted position.

Les Français font du sport?	**Les Français font-ils** du sport?
Jacques et Marie vont au cinéma ce soir?	**Jacques et Marie vont-ils** au cinéma ce soir?

3. In the third-person singular, you must add a **t** between hyphens for all forms of verbs not ending in a written **t.**

Parle-t-on français ici?	**Ecoute-t-elle** la radio?
A-t-il chaud?	*but:* Etienne **est-il** arrivé à pied?

4. Inversion is usually avoided when **je** is the subject. Use **Est-ce que** instead.

   Est-ce que je suis en retard?

5. When there are two verbs in a sentence, as in the **futur proche** and the **passé composé,** you invert the conjugated verb and the pronoun.

Allons-nous faire du stop?	**A-t-elle visité** la Martinique?

6. In the negative interrogative, the **ne... pas** surrounds both the conjugated verb and the pronoun subject.

Ne va-t-il pas faire la vaisselle?	Les gens **ne sont-ils pas rentrés?**

7. You must pay attention to the style you use when asking questions. The most formal type would be one with inversion.

   Y a-t-il une pharmacie près d'ici?

   The next most formal is the use of **Est-ce que.**

   Est-ce qu'il y a une pharmacie près d'ici?

   The most informal is the use of rising intonation.

   Il y a une pharmacie près d'ici?

B. Inversion with Interrogative Adverbs

1. Inversion is frequently used with interrogative adverbs.

Combien de frères **as-tu?**
Comment vont-ils à Québec?
Où faites-vous du sport?

Pourquoi n'êtes-vous pas arrivés ensemble?
Quand vont-elles au restaurant?

Mots clés **Interrogative Adverbs**

Combien de?	*How much?, How many?*	**Pourquoi?**	*Why?*
Comment?	*How?*	**Quand?**	*When?*
Où?	*Where?*		

2. Inversion is common with **où,** and the repetition of the pronoun subject is not necessary with the present tense.

Où se trouve le bureau des objets trouvés?
Où habitent les Morin?

CE QU'ILS DISENT

1. Inversion is very common in English *(Is he studying? What is he studying?),* but in French, it shows a more formal style. In conversation, the use of intonation and **est-ce que** are more common.

2. In a very familiar style, the French do use interrogative adverbs without inversion or **est-ce que.** They also place all the interrogative adverbs except **pourquoi** at the end of the sentence. Be aware, however, that these two structures may be too informal for many situations you will encounter.

Où tu vas?
Comment il est, ton imper?

Tu arrives **quand?**
C'est **combien?**

Language

A. **On va au concert.** Change the following questions with **est-ce que** to the inverted form to make them more formal.

1. Est-ce que tu vas au concert ce soir?
2. Est-ce que Monique a invité ses amis?
3. Où est-ce que nous allons aller après?
4. Comment est-ce qu'on va aller en ville?
5. Quand est-ce que vous allez arriver ici?
6. Pourquoi est-ce que vos amis ne sont pas encore arrivés?

B. **Un procès.** You are a district attorney and are charged with eliciting the following information during a trial. What questions would you ask?

1. Je suis né le 15 novémbre 1952.
2. J'habite à New York.
3. Le 2 février je suis allé au cinéma.
4. Parce que j'aime le cinéma!
5. Un billet coûte huit dollars.
6. J'ai trouvé le film ennuyeux.

Culture

C. **Jean-Paul et sa famille.** You have just made friends with Jean-Paul, and he has invited you home to meet his family. Ask questions to find out the information listed below. Make two sets of questions, one in an informal style for Jean-Paul, and the other in a more formal style to ask Jean-Paul's parents about him.

MODEL: aimer / télévision
        (à Jean-Paul) Tu aimes la télé?
        (à ses parents) Jean-Paul aime-t-il la télévision?

1. Où / naître
2. Combien / frères / sœurs
3. Pourquoi / étudier l'anglais
4. Comment / aller en cours
5. Quand / arriver à la fac
6. Où / aller en vacances

Communication

D. Interview a classmate. Using inversion, ask questions to elicit the following information.

MODEL: son nom?
        Comment t'appelles-tu?

son âge?
où il / elle est né(e)?
où il / elle habite?
pourquoi il / elle est à l'université?

comment il / elle va en classe?
où il / elle est allé(e) en vacances?

E. **Questions personnelles.** Votre travail *(work)*
1. Avez-vous travaillé récemment?
2. Quelle sorte de travail avez-vous fait?
3. Comment êtes-vous rentré(e) chez vous après le travail?
4. Quels jours travaillez-vous?
5. Pourquoi aimez-vous / n'aimez-vous pas cela?
6. Avez-vous travaillé beaucoup avec le public? Comment sont vos clients?

IV. Telling Time

A. To ask about and tell time in French, use the following expressions.

Quelle heure est-il?	*What time is it?*
Il est une heure.	*It is one o'clock.*
Il est deux heures.	*It is two o'clock.*

B. To express minutes after the hour until the half hour, you add the minutes or the following expressions:

Il est **trois heures dix.**	*It is ten after three.*
Il est **six heures et quart.**	$\begin{cases} \textit{It is a quarter after six.} \\ \textit{It is six fifteen.} \end{cases}$
Il est **sept heures et demie.**	$\begin{cases} \textit{It is half past seven.} \\ \textit{It is seven thirty.} \end{cases}$

C. To express time falling within thirty minutes of the next hour, you subtract the time from the hour.

Il est **huit heures moins vingt.**	$\begin{cases} \textit{It is seven forty.} \\ \textit{It is twenty to eight.} \end{cases}$
Il est **onze heures moins cinq.**	$\begin{cases} \textit{It is ten fifty-five.} \\ \textit{It is five to eleven.} \end{cases}$
Il est **neuf heures moins le quart.**	$\begin{cases} \textit{It is eight forty-five.} \\ \textit{It is a quarter to nine.} \end{cases}$

D. There are special terms for *noon* and *midnight*.

Il est midi.	*It is noon.*
Il est minuit.	*It is midnight.*

▶ ## L'Orthographe

1. Because **heure** is feminine, **demie** following **heure** is also feminine: **une heure et demie.**

2. **Midi** and **minuit** are masculine, so **demi** does not take a final e with either term: **midi et demi, minuit et demi.**

3. **Demi(e)** is never plural: **trois heures et demie.**

4. When writing a time in numbers, the French separate the hours and minutes with an **h** or a period, not a colon.

   2 h 30   **deux heures et demie**   5.10   **cinq heures dix**

E. To express A.M. and P.M. in French, use **du matin** (from midnight to noon), **de l'après-midi** (from noon until about six), and **du soir** (from about six until midnight).

Il est trois heures **du matin**.	*It is 3 A.M.*
Il est quatre heures et demie de l'après-midi.	*It is 4:30 P.M.*
Il est onze heures **du soir**.	*It is 11 P.M.*

F. To express other time relationships, use the following expressions:

à *at, to*	**jusqu'à** *until*	**à l'heure** *on time*
de *from*	**en avance** *early*	**en retard** *late*
entre *between*		

—**A** quelle heure est-ce que vous dînez?	*At what time do you have dinner?*
—Je dîne **à** six heures et quart.	*I have dinner at 6:15.*
Je suis en cours **de** huit heures **à** trois heures.	*I'm in class from 8 to 3.*
J'étudie **jusqu'à** minuit.	*I study until midnight.*
Nous regardons la télé **entre** sept et dix heures.	*We watch TV between 7 and 10.*
—Arrivent-ils **en avance**?	*Do they arrive early?*
—Non, elle, elle est toujours **à l'heure**; lui, il est toujours **en retard**.	*No, she is always on time; he is always late.*

Language

A. Quelle heure est-il?

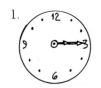

B. Robert and Marianne go out together, but Robert is always fifteen minutes late. If Marianne arrives at the following times, when does Robert arrive?

1. 11:00 A.M.	3. 8:15 P.M.	5. 3:30 P.M.
2. 12:00 P.M.	4. 11:45 P.M.	6. 10:20 P.M.

Culture

C. **Allons au cinéma.** You have only two days in Paris and must make the most of your time if you want to fit in a movie. To arrive exactly at the beginning of the film (**à deux heures et demie de l'après-midi**), count back to see when you must leave the hotel.

1. le film commence (2 h 30)
2. le début de la séance (15 minutes)
3. aller à pied jusqu'au cinéma, acheter le billet (6 minutes)
4. correspondance, deuxième métro (12 minutes)
5. monter dans le métro, aller à Châtelet (12 minutes)
6. aller de l'hôtel à la station de métro (15 minutes)

Communication

D. Tell at what time these things occur on your campus or in town.

1. Les premiers cours commencent à...
2. Moi, j'ai des cours entre... et...
3. Les films commencent à...
4. Les matchs de football américain sont à...
5. Les bars ferment à...
6. Les banques sont ouvertes jusqu'à...

E. **Questions personnelles.** Mon emploi du temps *(schedule)*

1. A quelle heure est-ce que vous arrivez en cours?
2. Arrivez-vous en avance ou en retard?
3. Jusqu'à quelle heure est-ce que vous êtes à l'université?
4. A quelle heure est-ce que vous dînez?
5. Jusqu'à quelle heure est-ce que vous étudiez le soir?
6. Vous parlez au téléphone / regardez la télé jusqu'à quelle heure?

COMMUNIQUONS ....

Utiliser l'heure officielle

The way that you just learned to tell time is called **l'heure conventionnelle,** and it is used primarily in informal conversations. In more formal situations such as those involving train or plane schedules, store hours, television schedules, and times of appointments, you will need to use **l'heure officielle** *(military time)*, which is based upon the twenty-four-hour clock.

In official time, times from midnight to noon are expressed as **zéro heure** to **douze heures.** To express a time from noon to midnight, continue counting the hours from twelve to twenty-four. Official time never uses the expressions **et quart, demi(e),** or **moins le quart.** You simply count the total number of minutes past the hour and use **quinze, trente,** and **quarante-cinq** respectively.

SUD-EST

Paris-Marseille-Nice   **Nice-Marseille-Paris**

★X	★X	★X	★X	★X	★X	★							★X	★X	★
7 00	7 30	7 40	10 23	10 41	11 42	12 55	Paris-Gare-de-Lyon ↑	6 21	6 25	7 42	8 13	{ 9 10	11 33	12 49
9 00	9 30			12 43			Lyon-Part-Dieu					7 06	9 28	
9 54		10 39			14 33	15 47	Valence		0 04			6 05	8 33	9 48
10 50		11 40	14 08		15 27	16 42	Avignon		23 02	0 04		5 05	7 38	8 55
11 46		12 37	15 03		16 22	17 39	Marseille		21 49	22 38			6 43	8 00
13 11	12 44	13 52	15 52	15 56	17 16	18 54	Toulon	21 51	20 46	21 44	23 04		6 00	{ 6 55
	13 35	14 43	16 59	16 46	18 05		St-Raphaël	20 54	19 25	20 43	22 11			
	13 59	15 08	17 23	17 09	18 29		Cannes	20 29	18 58	20 19	21 46			
	14 09	15 24	17 38	17 21	18 39		Antibes	20 16	18 40	20 02	21 31			
	14 25	15 44	17 58	17 37	18 56		Nice	19 58	18 20	19 46	21 14			

★X	★X	★X	★X	★X	★X	★X		X	X	★X	★X	★X	★	★
13 24	13 29	15 05	15 40	16 49	17 47	18 36	Paris-Gare-de-Lyon ↑	13 31	13 47	13 59	16 59	17 09	18 40	19 46
		17 05		18 57			Lyon-Part-Dieu					15 05		
	16 20		18 33	19 29	20 40	21 33	Valence	10 34	10 44		14 02		14 52	16 48
	17 15		19 25	20 49	21 39	22 29	Avignon	9 34	9 46		13 07			15 52
	18 10		20 25	21 44	22 35	23 25	Marseille	8 38	8 50		12 13		13 58	14 58
18 39		20 21	21 14	22 42	23 21	{ 0 28	Toulon	7 54	7 51	8 39	11 16	11 49	13 01	14 10
19 30		21 12	22 09	23 33			St-Raphaël		6 55	7 48	10 23	10 59	12 12	
19 55		21 35	22 32	23 57			Cannes		6 31	7 24	10 00	10 35	11 49	
20 05		21 45	22 44	0 08			Antibes		6 20	7 15	9 49	10 25	11 39	
20 22		22 01	23 00	0 24			Nice		6 03	7 00	9 34	10 10	11 24	

★X	★X	★X	★X	★X				X	★X	★X	X	X	★X
20 00	20 45	21 45	22 16	22 36			Paris-Gare-de-Lyon ↑	19 51	21 43	22 17	22 22	{ 23 20	
22 07							Lyon-Part-Dieu			20 11		21 07	
22 56							Valence		18 46		19 24	20 13	
				5 38			Avignon		17 46		18 28	19 19	
	5 05			7 20			Marseille		16 50		17 31	18 20	
	6 13		6 51	8 30			Toulon	14 34	15 54	16 59		{ 17 02	
	7 17	6 55	8 01	10 43			St-Raphaël	13 44	14 58	16 09			
	7 42	7 20	8 25	11 07			Cannes	13 20	14 35	15 45			
	7 58	7 38	8 41	11 18			Antibes	13 10	14 25	15 35			
	8 20	7 56	8 59	11 34			Nice	12 55	14 10	15 20			

26   a Heure d'arrivée.   b Horaires plus tardifs certains jours.

On donne l'heure de minuit à midi.

Le train arrive à six heures.	*The train arrives at 6 A.M.*
La classe commence à huit heures.	*The class begins at 8 A.M.*
Le camion arrive à onze heures quinze.	*The truck arrives at 11:15 A.M.*
On apporte le café à neuf heures trente.	*They bring the coffee at 9:30 A.M.*

On donne l'heure de midi à minuit

J'arrive à treize heures.	*I am arriving at 1 P.M.*
Le restau-U ferme à vingt et une heures.	*The university restaurant closes at 9 P.M.*
Le film commence à dix-neuf heures quarante-cinq.	*The film starts at 7:45 P.M.*
Le café ferme à vingt-quatre heures.	*The café closes at midnight.*

Interaction   *M. Robert va acheter un billet de train pour Marseille.*

M. ROBERT: Pardon, Monsieur, à quelle heure est le prochain train pour Marseille?

L'EMPLOYE: Il y a un *express* à quatorze heures cinq et un *rapide* à quinze heures trente.   *local / express*

M. ROBERT: A quelle heure arrivent-ils?

L'EMPLOYE: L'express à une heure dix, mais le rapide à zéro heure vingt-cinq.

M. ROBERT: L'express arrive après le rapide?

L'EMPLOYE: Oui, le rapide a moins d'arrêts.

Activités

A. Convert the following times in the conversational style to the more formal style (**l'heure officielle**).

1. deux heures du matin
2. trois heures et quart du matin
3. onze heures et demie du matin
4. midi vingt-cinq
5. une heure moins le quart de l'après-midi
6. quatre heures cinq de l'après-midi
7. neuf heures moins dix du soir
8. minuit moins le quart

B. Convert the following official times to the conversational style. Do not forget to indicate whether it is A.M. or P.M.

1. trois heures
2. cinq heures quinze
3. douze heures trente
4. quatorze heures quarante
5. vingt-deux heures dix
6. zéro heure quinze

C. Consult the schedule of trains from Paris to Nice on page 148 to answer the following questions. The arrows on each side of the names of the cities indicate in which direction the trains are traveling.

1. Où est-ce qu'on va à Paris pour avoir un train pour Nice?
2. Le train Paris-Toulon de 7.00 arrive à Marseille à quelle heure?
3. A quelle heure est-ce que le train du soir arrive à Nice?
4. Il faut combien de temps pour aller de Cannes à Nice?
5. Le train Marseille-Nice de 21.44 arrive à Antibes à quelle heure?
6. Est-il possible d'aller de Paris à Nice et de rentrer à Paris en une journée *(day)*? Expliquez.

L ECTURE CULTURELLE ....

Avant la lecture

French people are much more likely than Americans to take a train between cities. Trains in France are nationalized; they are fast, comfortable, and almost always on time. The company that operates the train system is **la SNCF (Société nationale des chemins de fer français)**.

In the sixties and seventies, when regional airports were built throughout France, the domestic airline, **Air Inter,** started competing very effectively for passengers with the SNCF. What made flying attractive to many people was the opportunity to travel faster. Today, however, thanks to the development of **TGV** lines, travel by rail is regaining its superiority. **TGV** stands for **train à grande vitesse,** or *high-speed train* in English.

Air travel in France, as in the rest of Europe, has always been very expensive. Very few flights operate during the night, whereas French trains run all night long and are often the best way to cover long distances without losing too much time and while enjoying the comfort of the **wagons-lits** *(sleeping cars)* or the much less expensive **couchettes.**

Another service provided by the SNCF is the **trains-autos-couchettes.** For instance, Parisians who are going to spend a vacation on the Riviera but who do not want to drive from Paris to Nice can take their car to a special station in Paris. The car is loaded on a flatbed railroad car while the passengers board a sleeping car. They spend the entire night traveling to Toulon, a town on the Mediterranean, and when they get off the train the next morning, their car is right there for them to pick up.

Activités

A. Imagine that in the year 2005 you decide to travel throughout Europe on **TGV** lines. You do not have much time, and you need to go from London to Seville, Spain. Using the map entitled **Le Réseau européen en 2005,** select an itinerary and pick the cities where you will stop.

B. In the following reading, many verbs are used in the **passé composé.** Scan the text to find the two instances of a **passé composé** with **être** and six examples of the **passé composé** with **avoir.**

Le TGV à l'heure européenne

En France, les trains ont toujours eu une excellente réputation *à cause de* leur ponctualité, et ils constituent depuis longtemps le *moyen* de transport public le plus populaire des Français. Pourtant, dans les années soixante-dix, *grâce à* la construction de *nouveaux* aéroports dans de *nombreuses* villes de province et
5 au développement de *liaisons aériennes* intérieures, Air Inter a commencé à *faire une concurrence* plus sérieuse à la SNCF (Société nationale des *chemins de fer* français).

Tout a *cependant* changé quand, le 27 septembre 1981, le TGV a inauguré une liaison entre Paris et Lyon et a transporté ses premiers passagers entre ces
10 deux villes. En quelques années, le TGV *est devenu* un succès incontesté. Il a causé à Air Inter une *baisse* de trafic de 60 pour cent entre Paris et Lyon. Il a transporté son cent millionième passager en 1989, et maintenant, une *moyenne* de 50.000 *voyageurs* l'utilisent tous les jours.

Le TGV a représenté pour la France un très grand succès technologique
15 *car,* contrairement à d'autres trains à grande vitesse conçus par des *concurrents étrangers,* il *roule* sur toutes les *voies* déjà existantes, *s'arrête* le long des

because of
means
thanks to
new / numerous
air routes
compete / railroads

however

has become
reduction
average
travelers

*because / foreign
competitors / runs /*

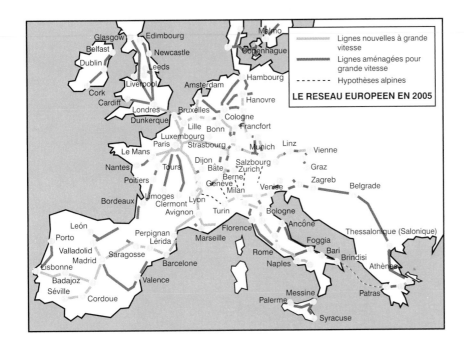

Glasgow
Edimbourg
Malmö
Belfast
Newcastle
Copenhague
Dublin
Leeds
Liverpool
Hambourg
Cork
Amsterdam
Hanovre
Cardiff
Londres
Bruxelles
Cologne
Dunkerque
Lille
Bonn
Francfort
Luxembourg
Paris
Strasbourg
Munich
Linz
Le Mans
Dijon
Salzbourg
Vienne
Nantes
Tours
Bâle
Zurich
Graz
Poitiers
Berne
Genève
Zagreb
Bordeaux
Limoges
Milan
Venise
Belgrade
Clermont
Lyon
Avignon
Turin
Bologne
León
Florence
Ancône
Thessalonique (Salonique)
Porto
Perpignan
Marseille
Foggia
Valladolid
Lérida
Rome
Bari
Madrid
Saragosse
Barcelone
Naples
Brindisi
Lisbonne
Valence
Athènes
Badajoz
Messine
Patras
Séville
Palerme
Cordoue
Syracuse

Lignes nouvelles à grande vitesse
Lignes aménagées pour grande vitesse
Hypothèses alpines

LE RESEAU EUROPEEN EN 2005

mêmes *quais* que *n'importe quel* train de *banlieue* et n'a pas demandé de modifications gigantesques du *réseau ferroviaire*. Sa vitesse moyenne, 270 km/h, donne aux *entreprises* la possibilité d'organiser des *réunions* plus
20 fréquentes *puisqu*'il est possible, par exemple, à des résidents lyonnais de monter à Paris pour la *demi-journée* et de *repasser* à leur bureau à Lyon avant de rentrer chez eux le soir.

Devant le succès de la ligne Paris-Lyon, la SNCF a *mis en service* d'autres TGV. Cette ligne a été *étendue* jusqu'à Marseille et Nice; en 1989, on a inau-
25 guré le TGV Atlantique entre Paris et Nantes et entre Paris et Rennes, et un an plus tard, en 1990, la liaison Paris-Bordeaux en deux heures cinquante-huit minutes *au lieu de* trois heures cinquante minutes *il y a* dix ans. Le nouveau TGV Atlantique apporte des *améliorations* techniques: il a *battu* le record du monde de vitesse avec des *pointes* à 482 km/h; mais il offre aussi de nouvelles
30 installations intérieures: par exemple, un coin *salon* pour les familles, une *salle de travail* avec équipement vidéo et deux *cabines* téléphoniques.

En 1993, c'est le tour d'un TGV Nord vers Lille, mais les projets de nouvelles lignes ne s'arrêtent plus aux *frontières* françaises. Beaucoup des *partenaires* de la France ont décidé de contribuer à l'établissement d'un grand ré-
35 seau TGV européen. On parle d'une ligne Londres-Cologne via le tunnel sous la *Manche*, d'une ligne Bruxelles-Amsterdam, et plus tard, d'un TGV Est pour *relier* Paris à Strasbourg et à l'Allemagne. A l'intérieur de pays comme la Grande-Bretagne, l'Italie et même l'Espagne, *qui doit* modifier complètement son réseau, des projets de TGV *font l'objet* de discussions.

40 Faut-il conclure que le TGV n'a que des admirateurs? Même en France, il est l'*enjeu* de rivalités politiques quand il faut décider de l'itinéraire d'une ligne. Mais c'est dans des pays comme la Grande-Bretagne et l'Allemagne où les groupes écologistes sont très puissants qu'il *rencontre* la plus grande opposition.

(Adapté de *L'Express* n° 1968)

tracks / stops / platforms / any / commuter rail network companies / meetings since / half a day go back
put into service
extended

instead of / ago
improvements / beat
top speeds
sitting room / workroom / booths

borders / partners

English Channel
link
which must
are the subject

stake

meets

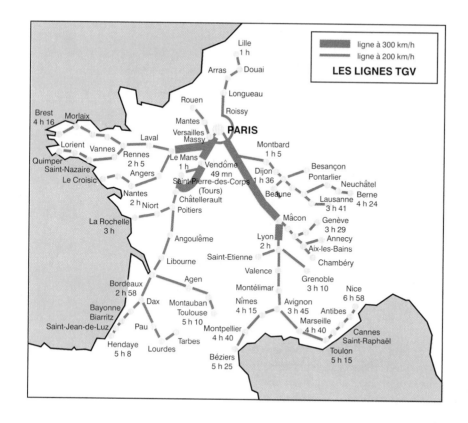

Après la lecture

Questions sur le texte

1. Pourquoi les trains sont-ils très populaires en France? Et le TGV en particulier?
2. Quels nouveaux TGV a-t-on inaugurés après la ligne Paris-Lyon?
3. Quelle est la vitesse du TGV Atlantique?
4. Quelles améliorations offre le TGV Atlantique?
5. Quelles lignes européennes vont être développées?
6. Est-ce que le TGV a seulement des admirateurs?

Activités

A. Utilisez la carte, «Les Lignes TGV», ci-dessus *(above)* et préparez un horaire *(schedule)* pour un voyage en TGV de Paris à Nice.

1. Si l'heure de départ est onze heures, à quelle heure est-ce que le train passe à Lyon, Avignon, Marseille et Toulon?
2. A quelle heure est-ce qu'il arrive à Nice?
3. Combien de temps va durer *(last)* le voyage?

B. In the reading passage, you came across two abbreviations, **SNCF** and **TGV**. French people use many abbreviations and acronyms, which are common in daily speech. Look at the following list of corresponding abbreviations and acronyms in French and in English. Try to match them.

French	**English**
1. ONU	a. AIDS
2. OTAN	b. SPCA
3. TVA	c. UFO
4. SIDA	d. UN
5. OVNI	e. VAT
6. SPA	f. NATO

C. Débats en classe.

1. Les avantages des voyages en train vs les avantages des voyages en avion.
2. Avantages et inconvénients des transports publics et des voitures personnelles.

RÉVISION B

Chapitres 4 à 6

CLASS WORK

A. Rewrite the following sentences using the cues in parentheses and making any necessary changes.

MODEL: Marie étudie le français.   (L'année prochaine...)
L'année prochaine Marie va étudier le français.

Des activités

1. Vas-tu au concert ce soir?   (... jeudi prochain?)
2. J'ai un examen aujourd'hui.   (Demain...)
3. Lise fait une promenade en auto le week-end?   (Les garçons... auto-stop... le week-end dernier?)
4. Christine a fait des courses en ville.   (Nous ne... pas... souvent...)
5. Nous allons à la bibliothèque cet après-midi.   (... hier.)
6. Les enfants écoutent-ils leurs parents?   (Isabelle... ?)
7. Etes-vous contents?   (... demain matin?)
8. Mes sœurs étudient beaucoup.   (La semaine dernière...)

En voyage

9. Claire passe un mois au Sénégal.   (... l'été prochain.)
10. Il fait froid ici.   (Le mois dernier... Europe.)
11. Les étudiants ne restent pas chez eux en été.   (Paul... l'été dernier.)
12. Il fait un voyage en Amérique.   (Vous... déjà...)

B. Answer the following questions using the cues provided.

MODEL: Où allez-vous?   (... université.)
Je vais à l'université.

Les possessions

1. C'est votre imper?   (Non,... cousine.)
2. Il donne des cadeaux à Mme Morin?   (Non,... frère.)
3. Ton jean est français?   (Non,... Etats-Unis.)
4. As-tu acheté une cravate bleue?   (Non,... verte.)
5. C'est ta jupe?   (Non,... ma mère.)
6. Où as-tu trouvé tes chemises?   (... Angleterre.)

D'autres activités

7. Où Pierre fait-il un voyage en été?   (... Mexique.)
8. Où étudiez-vous le soir?   (... bibliothèque.)
9. Est-ce que Sylvie visite la France?   (Non,... Tunisie.)
10. Où allez-vous le dimanche?   (... parc.)
11. Qu'est-ce que Jean va faire samedi?   (... grasse matinée.)
12. Tu as des amis en France?   (Non,... Maroc.)

C. Make complete sentences with each group of words below, adding any necessary words.

MODEL: Je / faire / promenade
         Je fais une promenade.

Dans ma ville

1. Quand / mon / parents / aller / cinéma?
2. tu / passer / vacances / ici?
3. Où / on / faire / lessive?
4. Marie / aller / toujours / église / dimanche
5. printemps / on / faire / promenades / parc
6. Mon / fille / naître / 1-12-93

Qu'est-ce qu'on a fait?

7. Pourquoi / Eric / rester chez lui / hier?
8. Jacques / monter / dans / voiture / et faire / tour
9. Nous / faire / ménage / hier matin
10. Elle / chercher / parapluie / sœur
11. Nous / ne / être / pas / restaurant / récemment
12. Lundi / Chantal / chercher / ceinture / pour / son / jupe / blanc

D. Fill in the blanks when necessary with the appropriate article or preposition.

MODEL: ... Rome est... Italie.
         Rome est en Italie.

1. ... Canada est un pays magnifique.
2. ... Madrid est une ville intéressante.
3. J'ai visité... Dakar,... Sénégal.
4. Avez-vous passé vos vacances... Japon?
5. ... Etats-Unis, les villes sont très grandes.
6. ... Florence, il y a beaucoup de musées.
7. ... Abidjan est... Côte-d'Ivoire.
8. ... été prochain, mes parents vont visiter... Mexique.
9. ... Italie est un pays fantastique.
10. Je suis allé au concert... lundi dernier.
11. Je vais visiter Washington... samedi.
12. Noël est... décembre.

E. Translate the following sentences into French.

1. Where is my book?
2. It is on your table.
3. Yesterday, your mother visited my school.
4. She likes our teacher a lot.
5. Their friends have my car.
6. And they left their bicycles at my house.
7. Her dorm is far from her parents' house.
8. She hates living at their house.

F. In French, read aloud or write the following numbers.

1. 71	5. 214	9. 891	13. 1.982	17. 1.000.000
2. 81	6. 321	10. 961	14. 2.600	18. 3.000.000
3. 95	7. 554	11. 1.000	15. 10.971	19. 10.500.000
4. 100	8. 742	12. 1.433	16. 259.500	20. 324.657.895

PAIR AND SMALL GROUP WORK

A. Form groups of three or four students, and find out the birthdays of everyone in your group.

B. Work with a partner to practice the **futur proche** and the **passé composé**. Take turns making statements in the **futur proche** and having your partner repeat your statements in the **passé composé**. Use the following verbs:

aller	inviter	acheter
oublier	rester	visiter
faire	manger	rentrer
monter	étudier	arriver

C. Write a number on a slip of paper starting with one digit and adding a digit each time (**7, 17, 175...**). Your partner will read your number aloud, and then you will reverse roles. Continue until one of you makes a mistake.

D. In groups of three or four, take turns identifying objects that belong to you, and point them out to your classmates using the expression **C'est...** or **Ce sont...** and possessive adjectives.

MODEL: *C'est mon stylo. Ce sont mes chaussures.*

E. Using the **Est-ce que** form or inversion and the verbs **avoir** and **être,** ask a question about your partner's feelings or present state of mind.

MODEL: Student 1: *Est-ce que tu as chaud?* or *As-tu chaud?*
Student 2: *Oui, j'ai chaud.*

F. With a classmate, make up a schedule of your daily activities. What things do you do at different times?

MODEL: *Notre premier cours commence à neuf heures, mais elle déjeune à midi et je déjeune à une heure.*

G. Interview a classmate about the following subjects. Be prepared to report your findings to the class.

1. Qu'est-ce que tu as fait le week-end dernier?
2. Comment va-t-on chez toi?
3. Où fais-tu tes courses? ta lessive?
4. Qu'est-ce que tu aimes?
5. Quel pays as-tu visité? Où désires-tu aller?
6. Aimes-tu faire la cuisine? Quelle est ta spécialité?
7. Où es-tu allé hier? Pourquoi?
8. Fais-tu toujours tes devoirs? Pourquoi ou pourquoi pas?

Chapitre 7

AU TELEPHONE

«Est-ce que je peux parler à Elisabeth?»

COMMENÇONS ....

C'est une erreur!

Le téléphone sonne chez Elisabeth Cambon.

UNE VOIX
FEMININE: Allô, 45.26.88.46, j'écoute.

BENJAMIN: Allô, est-ce que je peux parler à Elisabeth, s'il vous
plaît?

LA VOIX: Qui est à l'appareil?

BENJAMIN: Benjamin Ducaud.

LA VOIX: Ne quittez pas, je vais voir si elle est là.

Après une ou deux minutes...

LA VOIX: Allô, je suis désolée; elle est dans sa chambre et elle dort. Voulez-
vous laisser un message?

BENJAMIN: *(Il réfléchit.)* Je voudrais savoir si elle peut sortir avec moi ce soir.
Est-ce que je peux rappeler plus tard?

LA VOIX: Non, ce n'est pas la peine de téléphoner, Elisabeth n'est pas libre.
Au revoir.

BENJAMIN: Ne coupe pas! Elisabeth, c'est toi? Pourquoi est-ce que tu ne veux
pas sortir avec moi?

Mots clés

erreur	*wrong number*	voulez (vouloir)	*want*
téléphone	*telephone*	message	*message*
sonne (sonner)	*rings*	réfléchit	*thinks*
voix	*voice*	(réfléchir)	
Allô.	*Hello.*	savoir	*know*
J'écoute.	*Go ahead.*	peut (pouvoir)	*can*
peux (pouvoir)	*may*	sortir	*go out*
Qui est à	*Who's calling?*	rappeler	*call back*
l'appareil?		plus tard	*later*
Ne quittez	*Hold on.*	ce n'est pas la	*it's no use*
pas.		peine	
voir	*to see*	téléphoner (à)	*to phone*
désolée	*sorry*	libre	*free*
chambre	*bedroom*	Ne coupe pas.	*Don't hang up.*
dort (dormir)	*is sleeping*		

«Ne quittez pas!»

FAISONS CONNAISSANCE

In France the telephone system is run by **France Télécom,** an agency that administers one of the most sophisticated telephone systems in the world. One can call anywhere in France or the rest of the world in a matter of seconds, even from public phone booths. Since 91% of the population now has a phone, the French use the telephone much more than in the past. Their use of it, however, still tends to be more conservative than that of Americans. The French often do not have as many phones in a house as Americans do, and they refrain from calling at meal times and late in the evening.

To make a phone call, some people still go to a post office **(bureau de poste)** or a tobacco shop **(bureau de tabac),** where prior to the modernization of the phone system over the last twenty years, one traditionally went to use a phone. Today, however, with the installation of numerous phone booths **(cabines téléphoniques)** on the streets, in metro stations and other public places, the French can make a phone call from almost anywhere they are.

Les "TELECOMS" INTERNATIONALES, Les Aiguilleurs du Cœur.

COMMENT TELEPHONER DE FRANCE VERS LES USA.

PAR L'AUTOMATIQUE

DECROCHEZ TONALITE — 19 — TONALITE — 1 — INDICATIF DE ZONE — NUMERO DEMANDE

PRINCIPAUX INDICATIFS DE ZONE

ANCHORAGE (ALASKA) 907	DETROIT 313	NEW YORK 212
BOSTON 617	HONOLULU (HAWAI) 808	SAINT-LOUIS (MISSOURI) 314
CHICAGO 312	HOUSTON 713	SAN FRANCISCO 415
DALLAS 214	LOS ANGELES .. 213	WASHINGT. D.C. 202

IMPORTANT : après avoir composé le numéro d'appel de votre correspondant, vous ne percevez plus aucune tonalité. Ne raccrochez surtout pas. Ce n'est qu'après un délai de quelques secondes que vous percevrez un signal de sonnerie ou d'éventuelle occupation.

PAR L'INTERMEDIAIRE D'UN AGENT DES "TELECOMS"

DECROCHEZ TONALITE — 19 — TONALITE — 33 — 11 — Vous obtenez un agent des Télécommunications à qui vous formulez votre demande.

- pour obtenir des communications spéciales : cartes télécommunications, PCV...,
- pour connaître le numéro d'un abonné au téléphone à l'étranger,
- pour être renseigné sur un indicatif de zone.

OFFICE DU TOURISME DES ETATS-UNIS   AT&T Communications   DTRE

Etudions le dialogue

1. A qui est-ce que Benjamin veut parler?
2. Pourquoi est-ce qu'il ne peut pas parler à Elisabeth?
3. Quel message veut-il laisser?
4. Qu'est-ce qu'il veut faire plus tard?
5. Pourquoi est-ce que ce n'est pas la peine?
6. A qui est-ce que Benjamin parle au téléphone?

Enrichissons notre vocabulaire

Mes affaires *(f.)* *(My things)*

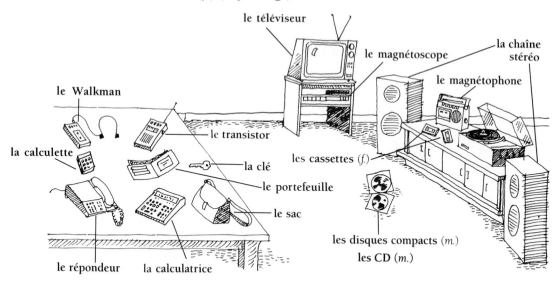

le téléviseur

le magnétoscope

la chaîne stéréo

le magnétophone

le Walkman

le transistor

la calculette

les cassettes *(f.)*

la clé

le portefeuille

le sac

les disques compacts *(m.)*
les CD *(m.)*

le répondeur

la calculatrice

Quelques expressions utiles

—Maman, je peux **allumer** la télé?
—**Range** ta chambre **d'abord!**
—Où est-ce que je **branche** le
   lecteur laser?
—Ce n'est pas **nécessaire;** il
   marche avec **des piles** *(f.)*

*Mom, can I **turn on** the TV?*
Pick up** your room **first!
*Where do I **plug in** the CD
   player?*
*It's not **necessary;** it **works**
   with **batteries.***

Prononciation Nasal Vowels

French has three vowel sounds that are nasalized. This means that air is allowed to pass into the nasal cavity and vibrate. If you pinch your nose and say the words **vin** and **va,** you will feel the vibrations as you say **vin,** but not **va.**

Repeat the following words, which are grouped according to the nasal vowel sound they contain, after your teacher.

/ã/ (Your lips are rounded, your tongue back.)
an / dans / gant / quand / sans / blanc / banque /
   chantez / changez / cent deux / je danse / il
   demande

/ɔ̃/ (Your lips are more rounded, your tongue
   farther back.)
on / blond / ton / non / son / ils vont / ils font /
   elles sont / faisons / travaillons / nous avons /
   mon

/ɛ̃/ (Your lips are spread, your tongue forward.)
pain / cinq / vin / un / brun / lundi / bien /
  impossible / important / loin / Alain /
  sympathique

Exercices

A. Repeat the following words after your teacher, paying particular attention to the nasal vowels.

allons / faisons / mes enfants / à demain /
  en France / invite / bonjour / sa maison /
  continuons / magasin / canadien / mexicain /
  examen / tu manges / décembre / pardon

B. Repeat each sentence after your teacher, paying particular attention to the nasal vowels.

1. Chantal danse bien.
2. Combien de garçons allons-nous inviter?
3. Les Américains sont-ils sympathiques?
4. Jean et Alain vont partir en vacances au printemps.
5. Mes enfants vont répondre aux questions.
6. Elles ont trouvé un restaurant mexicain fantastique.

GRAMMAIRE ·····························

I. Interrogative and Demonstrative Adjectives

> You use interrogative adjectives to ask someone to make a choice and demonstrative adjectives to point out or choose.

A. Interrogative Adjectives

1. In French, interrogative adjectives (*what?* or *which?* in English) ask for a choice. Like other French adjectives, they agree in gender and number with the nouns they modify. Either inversion or **est-ce que** is used with **quel.**

	singular	*plural*
masculine	**quel**	**quels**
feminine	**quelle**	**quelles**

Quel répondeur avez-vous acheté? •
A **quelle** heure est-elle arrivée?

Vous allez sortir avec **quels** amis?
Quelles sont vos cassettes préférées?

2. The plural **quels** and **quelles** call for a **liaison obligatoire.**

Quels‿artistes est-ce que tu apprécies?
Quelles‿universités vont-ils visiter?

B. Demonstrative Adjectives

1. French uses several forms of **ce** as demonstrative adjectives. They are equivalent to *this, that, these,* and *those* in English.

	singular	plural
masculine	ce, cet	ces
feminine	cette	ces

2. Cet is a special form of **ce** used with masculine singular adjectives or nouns beginning with a vowel sound.

Cet autocar va à Marseille.   A-t-elle invité **cet au**tre homme?

3. All the singular forms in the table above can mean *this* or *that,* and **ces** can mean *these* or *those.* The distinction between *this* and *that* and between *these* and *those* is rarely necessary in French.

—Quel Walkman recommandez-vous?
—**Ce** Walkman marche bien.

—Quand est-ce que vous allez arriver chez nous?
—**Cet** après-midi.

—Tu aimes **ces** CD?
—Quels CD?

When a distinction in meaning is necessary, you add **-ci** to the noun to express *this* or *these* and **-là** to express *that* or *those.*

—**Cette calculette-ci** est à toi?
—Non, elle est à mon frère.

—Vous désirez?
—Montrez-moi **ce téléviseur-là.**

Langue

A. Employez un adjectif interrogatif et un adjectif démonstratif avec les mots suivants *(following).*

MODELE: cassette *Quelle cassette? Cette cassette.*

1. idée
2. saison
3. magnétoscope
4. trains
5. chaînes stéréo
6. hôtel
7. examen
8. autobus
9. piles

B. **Suivons** (*Let's follow*) **M. et Mme Ducharme à un restaurant.** Formez des phrases complètes en employant (*using*) les mots donnés et en faisant (*making*) tous les changements nécessaires.

1. Tu / penser / quel / restaurant?
2. Tu / ne... pas / laisser / ce / imper / ici?
3. hôtesse / ne... pas / recommander / restaurant-là
4. quel / heure / nous / dîner?
5. Quel / viande / et / quel / légume / nous / commander / soir?
6. Aller / chercher / le / garçon; / ce / boissons / ne... pas / être / à nous

C. **Les Dupont font une promenade.** Répondez aux questions suivantes en employant les mots entre parenthèses et des adjectifs démonstratifs.

1. Est-ce qu'on va au parc ce matin? (Non,... après-midi)
2. Jacques a-t-il son parapluie? (Non,... porter... imper)
3. Est-ce que Louise va porter cette robe? (Oui, et... chaussures aussi)
4. Qu'est-ce que Pierre a oublié? (... transistor...)
5. Michel va rester à la maison pour faire la cuisine? (Non,... soir)
6. Est-ce que j'ai mes clés? (Non,... clé... être à moi!)

TABLE DE COMPARAISON DE TAILLES

Robes, chemisiers et tricots femmes.

F	36	38	40	42	44	46	48
GB	10	12	14	16	18	20	22
USA	8	10	12	14	16	18	20

Bas et collants femmes.

F	1	2	3	4	5
USA	8½	9	9½	10	10½

Chaussures femmes.

F	35½	36	36½	37	37½	38	39
GB	3	3½	4	4½	5	5½	6
USA	4	4½	5	5½	6	6½	7½

Chaussures hommes.

F	39	40	41	42	43	44	45
GB	5½	6½	7	8	8½	9½	10½
USA	6	7	7½	8½	9	10	11

Costumes hommes.

F	36	38	40	42	44	46	48
GB	35	36	37	38	39	40	42
USA	35	36	37	38	39	40	42

Chemises hommes.

F	36	37	38	39	40	41	42
USA	14	14½	15	15½	16	16½	17

Tricots hommes.

F	36	38	40	42	44	46
GB	46	48	51	54	56	59
USA	46	48	51	54	56	59

Culture

D. **Comparaison de tailles** *(size comparison)*. Regardez la table, et répondez aux questions suivantes sur les tailles des vêtements en employant des adjectifs démonstratifs.

MODELE: Les robes: Une Anglaise porte un dix.
En France, cette Anglaise porte un trente-six.

Les robes

1. Une Anglaise porte un quatorze. En France?
2. Une Américaine porte un seize. En France?
3. Deux Françaises portent un trente-six. Aux Etats-Unis?

Les chemisiers

4. Une Française porte un trente-huit. En Angleterre?
5. Trois Américaines portent un huit. En France?
6. Une Anglaise porte un douze. Aux Etats-Unis?

Les chemises d'homme

7. Un Français porte un trente-sept. Aux Etats-Unis?
8. Deux Américains portent un quinze et demi. En France?
9. Un Français porte un quarante-deux. Aux Etats-Unis?

Communication

E. **Questionnaire.** Formez des questions avec les mots suivants. Posez ces questions à vos camarades et n'oubliez pas d'attendre *(to wait for)* une réponse!

A	B		C
Quel	appartement	musée	habites-tu?
Quelle	disque compact	pays	aimes-tu mieux?
Quels	ville	villes	vas-tu visiter?
Quelles	film	café	fréquentes-tu?
	cours	cinéma	
	artistes	boîtes	

F. **Poursuite Triviale.** Répondez aux questions suivantes avec un adjectif démonstratif si vous savez *(know)* la réponse!

MODELE: Quelle femme a été pilote dans les années trente?
            Cette femme est Amelia Earhart.

1. Quelle actrice a joué le rôle de Scarlett O'Hara?
2. Quels journalistes ont été célèbres *(famous)* après Watergate?
3. Quelle a été la première université fondée aux Etats-Unis?
4. Quel explorateur français est arrivé au Canada en 1534?
5. Quel président a acheté la Louisiane?
6. Les Américains n'ont pas élu *(elected)* quel président?

G. **Questions personnelles.** Vos préférences

1. Dans quels restaurants est-ce que vous aimez manger?
2. Quelle cuisine aimez-vous?
3. Quel vin aimez-vous beaucoup?
4. Quelle boisson consommez-vous en été? en hiver?
5. Quelle sorte de musique aimez-vous écouter dans les boîtes?
6. A quelle heure est-ce que vous rentrez de ces boîtes?

II. -ir Verbs

> You use verbs to describe actions or activities.

In Chapter 1 you learned that French verbs are categorized according to the infinitive ending. In addition to -er verbs, there is a group ending in -ir. There are two distinct conjugations for this group.

A. -ir Verbs Conjugated like **finir**

Note the -iss- in the plural forms.

finir *(to finish)*	
je **finis**	nous **finissons**
tu **finis**	vous **finissez**
il / elle / on **finit**	ils / elles **finissent**

Mots clés Verbs conjugated like finir

choisir	*to choose*	**réussir (à)**	*to succeed; to pass*
désobéir à	*to disobey*		*(an exam)*
obéir à	*to obey*	**rougir**	*to blush*
punir	*to punish*		
réfléchir à	*to think (about),*		
	consider		

Je **finis** mes cours à dix-sept heures.
Elle va **choisir** une chaîne stéréo pour son frère.
M. Dupont ne **punit** pas ses enfants.
Elles **réussissent** toujours aux examens.

1. The imperative of this group of **-ir** verbs is regular: you simply delete the subject.

   Finis tes devoirs.   **Obéissez** à vos parents!

2. To form the past participle, drop the **r** of the infinitive.

   —Vous avez **choisi** votre dessert?
   —Non, nous n'avons pas **fini** notre fromage.

   —Pourquoi est-ce qu'ils ont **puni** leur fils?
   —Parce qu'il a **désobéi**.

3. Note that **obéir**, **désobéir**, and **réfléchir** must take the preposition **à** before a following noun. With **réussir**, however, **à** is optional.

   J'**obéis** toujours à mes parents.
   Ne **désobéissez** pas à l'agent de police.
   Je n'aime pas **réfléchir aux** problèmes difficiles.

Langue

A. **Des décisions.** Formez des phrases complètes avec les mots donnés. Faites les changements nécessaires.

1. Je / finir / ce / livre
2. Qu'est-ce que / tu / choisir / comme cours?
3. Tu / ne... / réfléchir / pas / quand / tu / étudier
4. parents / punir / enfants / quand / ils / désobéir
5. Il / ne... pas / réussir / examen
6. Tu / finir / ménage / demain

B. **Conversations à la résidence.** Refaites (*Redo*) les phrases suivantes en employant les mots donnés.

1. *Nous* finissons nos devoirs.   (Je...)
2. *Marc* ne va pas *finir* son examen ce matin.   (Vous... réussir...)
3. *Luc* a obéi à *l'agent.*   (Nous... agents)
4. Avez-*vous* fini à huit heures?   (Jacqueline...)
5. *Ce soir,* je vais choisir le restau.   (Hier soir,...)
6. *Jean* rougit souvent en classe.   (Jean et Marie...)

B. -ir Verbs Conjugated like **servir**

Note that you drop the last consonant of the infinitive stem in the singular forms of the present tense.

servir *(to serve)*	
je **sers**	nous **servons**
tu **sers**	vous **servez**
il / elle / on **sert**	ils / elles **servent**

Mots clés   Verbs conjugated like servir

dormir *to sleep* — je **dors**, nous **dormons**

mentir *to lie* — je **mens**, nous **mentons**

partir *to leave* — je **pars**, nous **partons**

sentir *to smell, to feel* — je **sens**, nous **sentons**

sortir *to go out* — je **sors**, nous **sortons**

Je **sors** avec des amis après.
Ce fruit **sent** mauvais.
Nous **allons dormir** tard ce week-end.
Elles **partent** aujourd'hui.
Tu **ne vas pas mentir** à ton frère.

1. The imperative of this group of **-ir** verbs is also regular.

   Servons du café à nos amis.   Ne **mentez** pas à vos parents.

2. To form the past participle, drop the **r** of the infinitive.

   Je n'ai pas **dormi** cette nuit.   Ils n'ont pas **servi** de vin.

3. The **passé composé** of **partir** and **sortir** take **être,** so the subject and past participle must agree.

   Elles sont **parties** hier.   Nous sommes **sortis** mardi soir.

Langue

C. **Les Français.** Formez des phrases complètes avec les mots donnés. Faites les changements nécessaires.

   1. Les Français / servir / souvent / vin
   2. Ils / partir / en vacances / août
   3. On / aime / sortir / le samedi
   4. enfants / dormir / huit heures
   5. Les Français / réfléchir / beaucoup
   6. Un jeune Français / ne... pas / mentir / parents

D. **M. et Mme Morin interrogent leur fils.** Mettez les phrases suivantes au présent.

   1. Tu vas sortir avec Marie ce soir?
   2. Tu vas dormir cet après-midi?
   3. Tu ne vas pas partir en retard?
   4. Elle va servir un dîner?
   5. Qu'est-ce que tu vas faire si le dîner ne sent pas bon?
   6. Tu ne vas pas mentir si tu n'aimes pas sa cuisine?

Culture

E. **La France ou les Etats-Unis?** Formez des phrases avec les mots donnés et dites *(say)* si l'activité est typique des Français ou des Américains.

   1. Les jeunes gens / sortir / en groupes, / pas à deux
   2. On / rougir / vite / devant la nudité
   3. Les élèves / réussir / moins au lycée
   4. On / choisir / les restaurants avec un livre
   5. Les parents / servir / vin aux enfants
   6. Les gens / partir en vacances / juin / juillet

Communication

F. **A mon avis.** Est-ce que les phrases suivantes sont vraies *(true)* ou fausses *(false)*? Si elles sont fausses, refaites des phrases vraies.

   1. Je dors cinq heures tous les jours.
   2. Mes amis choisissent des cours difficiles.

3. Je ne mens pas à mes parents.
4. Les étudiants réfléchissent quand ils font leurs devoirs.
5. Mes amis ne servent pas d'alcool.
6. Quand je fais la cuisine, cela sent toujours bon.

G. Complétez les phrases suivantes.

1. Je réussis à mes examens quand...
2. Nous sommes partis en vacances...
3. Comme restaurant, mes parents aiment choisir...
4. Je rougis toujours quand...
5. Le week-end, je dors jusqu'à...
6. Je voudrais sortir avec...

H. **Que choisissez-vous?** Répondez selon le modèle suivant et justifiez vos réponses.

MODELE: un restaurant chinois ou américain
         Moi, je choisis un restaurant chinois parce que j'adore cette cuisine.

1. un concert de musique classique ou un match de football
2. des vacances chez vos parents ou à la plage
3. du coca ou de la bière
4. un autocar ou votre voiture pour un voyage
5. le cinéma ou la télévision
6. une profession intéressante ou bien payée

I. **Questions personnelles.** Ma vie à l'université

1. A quelle heure partez-vous pour vos cours le matin?
2. Réussissez-vous toujours à vos examens? Et votre camarade de chambre?
3. Avez-vous rougi en cours? Quand?
4. Comment est-ce que votre professeur punit la classe quand les étudiants ne préparent pas la leçon?
5. Jusqu'à quelle heure dormez-vous le week-end?
6. Vous sortez beaucoup? Qu'est-ce que vous faites le samedi soir quand vous ne sortez pas?

AVEC LE BAC A, VOUS POUVEZ ENCORE VOUS INSCRIRE EN
LANGUES

AVEC LE BAC B, VOUS POUVEZ ENCORE VOUS INSCRIRE EN
ÉCONOMIE

AVEC LE BAC C, VOUS POUVEZ ENCORE VOUS INSCRIRE EN
MATHÉMATIQUES - PHYSIQUE - CHIMIE

AVEC LE BAC A, VOUS POUVEZ ENCORE VOUS INSCRIRE EN
LETTRES

III. Interrogative Pronouns

> You use interrogative pronouns to find out specific information about people and things.

In French, the form of an interrogative pronoun depends on whether the pronoun is the subject or the object of the verb. As in English, the form also varies according to whether you are asking about a person *(Who? Whom?)* or a thing *(What?).*

A. Persons

1. To ask about a person as the subject of a verb *(Who?)*, use **Qui est-ce qui** or **Qui.**

   —**Qui est-ce qui** a faim?   —**Qui** a téléphoné?
   —Moi!   —Benjamin.

2. If the person is an object of the verb *(Whom?)*, use **Qui est-ce que** or **Qui** with inversion.

   —**Qui est-ce que** vous admirez?   —**Qui est-ce que** tu as invité?
      Qui admirez-vous?   **Qui** as-tu invité?
   —J'admire mes parents.   —J'ai invité mes amis.

3. If the person is the object of a preposition *(Whom?)*, use the preposition plus **qui est-ce que** or **qui** with inversion.

   —**Avec qui est-ce qu'**ils ont joué?   —**A qui est-ce que** tu as parlé?
      Avec qui ont-ils joué?   **A qui** as-tu parlé?
   —Avec leurs enfants.   —J'ai parlé à la secrétaire.

B. Things

1. To ask about a thing as the object of a verb *(What?)*, use **Qu'est-ce que** or **Que** with inversion.

   —**Qu'est-ce que** vos frères cherchent?
   —Ils cherchent leurs clés.

   —**Qu'est-ce que** vous avez choisi?
      Qu'avez-vous choisi?
   —J'ai choisi un magnétoscope allemand.

2. A thing can be the subject of a sentence. In this case, the only interrogative pronoun that can be used is **Qu'est-ce qui** *(What?)*. This pronoun is often used with **arriver** *(to happen)* and **rester** *(to be left over; to remain).*

   —**Qu'est-ce qui** est arrivé?   —**Qu'est-ce qui** reste?
   —Mes parents sont partis.   —Un peu de coca.

3. If a thing is the object of a preposition *(What?)*, use **quoi,** which is followed by **est-ce que** or inversion.

—De **quoi** est-ce qu'ils parlent?
  De **quoi** parlent-ils?
—Ils parlent de leurs vacances.

C. Summary

	Persons (who? whom?)	*Things (what?)*
Subject of verb	**Qui** *or* **Qui est-ce qui**	**Qu'est-ce qui**
Object of verb	**qui** + inversion *or* **qui est-ce que**	**que** + inversion *or* **qu'est-ce que**
Object of prep.	Prep. + **qui** + inversion *or* Prep. + **qui est-ce que**	Prep. + **quoi** + inversion *or* Prep. + **quoi est-ce que**

Here are some examples of how you can use interrogative pronouns.

Person / Thing Contrasts

Qui est-ce qui reste?	*Who's left?*
Qu'est-ce qui reste?	*What's left?*
Qui est-ce que vous regardez?	*Whom are you looking at?*
Qu'est-ce que vous regardez?	*What are you looking at?*

Subject / Object Contrasts

Qui est-ce qui a invité Jacques?	*Who invited Jacques?*
Qui est-ce que Jacques a invité?	*Whom did Jacques invite?*
Qu'est-ce qui indique cela?	*What shows that?*
Qu'est-ce que cela indique?	*What does that show?*

Langue

A. **Interview avec des Français.** Vous allez interviewer des Français. Traduisez les questions suivantes en français.

1. What do you do?
2. What do you like to talk about?
3. What happened at your home last night?

4. What have you bought recently?
5. Whom do you phone often?
6. What does your family watch on TV?

B. Complétez les phrases suivantes avec un pronom interrogatif approprié *(appropriate)*.

1. __ a mangé ma glace?
2. A __ avez-vous donné l'argent?
3. __ est arrivé ce matin?
4. Avec __ a-t-on fait des crêpes?
5. __ il y a dans la chambre?
6. __ ont-ils regardé?

C. **Interview avec des étudiants.** Trouvez les questions qui ont provoqué les réponses en italique *(italics)*.

1. Nous sommes *étudiants.*
2. Nous étudions *l'anglais.*
3. *Marie et Jacqueline* sont absentes aujourd'hui.
4. *La résidence* est agréable.
5. Je vais téléphoner à *mon ami Luc* ce soir.
6. Luc va acheter *un téléviseur* samedi.

Culture

D. **Des célébrités francophones.** En utilisant les mots de la colonne de gauche *(left column)*, trouvez des questions qui décrivent *(describe)* les gens célèbres de la colonne de droite *(right)*.

1. chanter bien
2. danser bien
3. encourager les femmes
4. faire du cinéma
5. recommander un parfum
6. donner des leçons de cuisine

a. Catherine Deneuve
b. Paul Prudhomme et Justin Wilson
c. Simone de Beauvoir
d. Bertrand Blier
e. Joséphine Baker
f. Sylvie Vartan

E. Trouvez les questions qui correspondent aux renseignements en italique, et posez *(ask)* ces questions à un(e) camarade de classe.

MODELE: *Les Portugais* sont les immigrés les plus nombreux en France.
Qui sont les immigrés les plus nombreux en France?

1. 72% des parents français donnent *de l'argent de poche* à leurs enfants. (141 francs par mois en moyenne [*on average*])
2. 83% des Français ont de la sympathie *pour les Américains.*
3. Les Français regardent *la télévision* une heure et quarante-cinq minutes par jour.
4. *Les vêtements* représentent les achats les plus fréquents des jeunes Français (25%).
5. 50,7% des Français ne consomment pas *d'alcool.*
6. En France, il est possible de payer une contravention *(traffic ticket)* directement *à l'agent de police.*

Communication

F. Formez des groupes et posez des questions en utilisant des pronoms interrogatifs. Consultez les verbes donnés et inventez des questions originales. Informez vos camarades de cours des résultats.

MODELE: *Qui admires-tu?*
Qu'est-ce que tu as à la maison?

aimer bien	détester
porter en cours demain	faire le dimanche
téléphoner à	manger
oublier	regarder... à la télévision
faire bien	aller faire ce week-end

G. **Questions personnelles.** Votre passé

1. Qu'est-ce que vous avez fait l'été dernier?
2. Avec qui est-ce que vous avez fait un voyage?
3. Pour qui est-ce que vous avez voté en 1992?
4. De quoi avez-vous parlé avec vos amis le week-end dernier?
5. A qui avez-vous téléphoné?
6. Qui avez-vous invité chez vous cette semaine?
7. Qui a fait le ménage chez vous récemment? Cette année?
8. Qu'est-ce qui est arrivé d'intéressant ce mois-ci?

IV. Pouvoir and vouloir

> You use **pouvoir** to express ability or permission and **vouloir** to indicate a desire.

A. Pouvoir

1. **Pouvoir** *(to be able, can, may, to be allowed to)* is an irregular verb, so you must learn its forms.

je **peux**	nous **pouvons**
tu **peux**	vous **pouvez**
il / elle / on **peut**	ils / elles **peuvent**

2. **Pouvoir** is often followed by another verb in the infinitive.

—Est-ce que je **peux parler** à Elisabeth?
—**Pouvez**-vous **rappeler** plus tard?

—Est-ce que ton frère **peut partir** en vacances en hiver?
—Non, il ne **peut** pas **partir.**

3. The past participle of **pouvoir** is **pu.**

—Qu'est-ce que vous avez?
—Je n'ai pas **pu** dormir.

—Vous avez **pu** parler à Elisabeth?
—Non, elle est sortie.

B. Vouloir

1. **Vouloir** *(to want)* is also irregular and must be memorized.

je **veux**	nous **voulons**
tu **veux**	vous **voulez**
il / elle / on **veut**	ils / elles **veulent**

2. Like **pouvoir, vouloir** is frequently used with an infinitive.

—Tu **veux finir** mon dessert?
—Non, je ne **peux** pas.

3. The past participle of **vouloir** is **voulu.**

—Ils n'ont pas **voulu** partir le matin?
—Non, ils ont préféré faire la grasse matinée.

4. You have already seen the expression **je voudrais,** which is a form of **vouloir** used to say *I want* politely.

Je voudrais parler au médecin.
Je voudrais du café, s'il vous plaît.

5. The expression **vouloir bien** means *to be willing.*

—Tu veux sortir ce soir?
—Oui, je **veux bien.**

ATTENTION

Pouvoir and **vouloir** share a similar pronunciation.

1. The vowel sounds are the same.

je peux / je veux /ʒə pø/, /ʒə vø/
nous pouvons / nous voulons /nu pu võ/, /nu vu lõ/
ils peuvent / ils veulent /il pœv/, /il vœl/

2. Although the third-person vowels are written **eu,** the vowel sound changes from the singular to the plural. You must open your mouth wider to pronounce the sound for **eu** in the plural.

il peut, ils peuvent /il pø/, /il pœv/
il veut, ils veulent /il vø/, /il vœl/

Langue

A. **Jacques est difficile!** Dans les phrases suivantes, remplacez **vouloir** par **pouvoir** et vice versa.

1. Jacques ne veut pas aller en cours.
2. Vous ne pouvez pas téléphoner demain, Jacques?
3. Il n'a pas voulu parler.
4. Nous ne pouvons pas inviter des amis chez lui!
5. Ils veulent bien écouter la radio.
6. Je n'ai pas pu rester chez Jacques.

B. **Elodie et sa famille.** Formez des phrases complètes avec les mots donnés. Faites les changements nécessaires.

1. Elodie / ne... pas / pouvoir / sortir avec nous / parce que / parents / ne... pas / vouloir
2. week-end / dernier / ils / vouloir / aller / mer / ensemble
3. Samedi prochain / ils / pouvoir / aller en ville
4. Elodie / ne... pas / vouloir / ranger / sa chambre
5. Les parents d'Elodie / vouloir / inviter / son amie Juliette
6. Juliette / ne... pas / pouvoir / rester / chez eux

Culture

C. **Les élections en France.** Formez des phrases avec les mots donnés. Si une phrase est fausse, refaites une phrase vraie.

1. Les Français / pouvoir / voter / le mardi
2. Ils / pouvoir / voter / deux fois *(twice)* pour un candidat
3. En France, on / vouloir / communistes dans l'administration
4. Les Français / pouvoir / voter pour le président seulement *(only)* en novembre
5. On / pouvoir / voter à dix-huit ans
6. Les Français / vouloir / voter

Communication

D. Qu'est-ce que vous voulez faire et qu'est-ce que vous ne voulez pas faire? Utilisez les suggestions données ou vos propres idées.

MODELE: *Je voudrais manger de la glace.*
Je ne veux pas aller au parc.

téléphoner à   travailler le week-end
écouter mon Walkman   dormir jusqu'à midi demain
aller à la plage   acheter un lecteur laser
avoir une chaîne stéréo   sortir au restaurant avec mes amis

E. Regardez les listes des activités et des excuses page 178. Pourquoi ne faites-vous pas chaque activité? Choisissez ou inventez une excuse.

MODELE: *Je ne peux pas parler français aujourd'hui parce que j'ai mal dormi hier soir.*

Activités	**Excuses**
étudier ce soir	être fatigué(e), paresseux (-euse)
aller en cours	vouloir écouter mes disques
faire le ménage	dormir mal hier soir
parler français	préparer un examen important
???	???

F. Qu'est-ce que vous avez pu faire hier et qu'est-ce que vous avez voulu faire? Employez les suggestions données ou inventez des réponses originales.

MODELE: *Hier, j'ai pu terminer mes devoirs.*
J'ai voulu aller à la plage hier.

parler à un(e) ami(e)	oublier mes devoirs
aller en cours	acheter un vêtement
rester à la maison	téléphoner à mes parents
faire des courses	ranger mes affaires

G. **Questions personnelles.** Votre avenir

1. Qu'est-ce que vous voulez pour votre anniversaire?
2. Où pouvez-vous aller pour vos vacances d'été?
3. Pour qui voulez-vous voter en 1996?
4. Quelle profession voulez-vous avoir?
5. Où est-ce que vous voulez habiter?
6. Combien d'enfants voulez-vous avoir?

COMMUNIQUONS ······························

Donner un coup de téléphone

To make a telephone call in France, you can find a phone in post offices and some cafés, and, of course, there are telephone booths on the streets and in public buildings such as train stations. There had been a serious problem of vandalism of public phone booths, but it was solved with the introduction of the **télécarte**. This card has a set price encoded in a computer chip, and each time it is used, the phone electronically subtracts the cost of the call until the entire value is used up. You can buy a **télécarte** at all post offices and **bureaux de tabac**.

Telephone numbers in France consist of eight digits. For example, the number for the **bureau des objets trouvés** for the metro system is **45.31.82.10**, which is read **quarante-cinq, trente et un, quatre-vingt-deux, dix**. The number 08 would be read **zéro huit**.

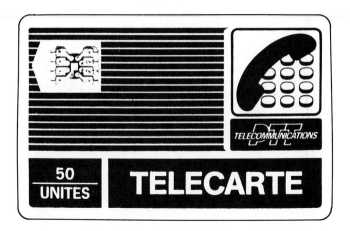

On donne un coup de téléphone.

Elisabeth donne / passe un coup de téléphone.	*Elisabeth is making a phone call.*
Elle cherche le numéro de téléphone dans l'annuaire / le bottin / le Minitel.	*She looks up the phone number in the phone book / the Minitel.*
Elle compose / fait le numéro des renseignements.	*She dials the number for information.*
Le téléphone sonne.	*The phone rings.*
On décroche le téléphone.	*Someone picks up the phone.*

On commence la conversation.

Allô!	*Hello!*
Qui est à l'appareil?	*Who's calling?*
C'est de la part de qui?	*May I say who's calling?*
Est-ce que je pourrais parler à Mlle Leclerc?	*May I speak to Ms. Leclerc?*
Poste 325.	*Extension 325.*
Ne quittez pas.	*Hold the line.*
Un instant, je vous prie.	*One moment, please.*

On finit la communication.

La ligne est occupée.	*The line is busy.*
Il / Elle n'est pas là.	*He / She isn't in.*
Il / Elle est sorti(e).	*He / She has gone / stepped out.*
Pouvez-vous rappeler dans une heure?	*Can you call back in an hour?*
Elisabeth raccroche.	*Elisabeth hangs up.*

Interaction   *Jacques téléphone à son ami François Morin.*

MME MORIN: Allô!

JACQUES: Bonjour, Madame. Est-ce que je pourrais parler à François?

MME MORIN: C'est de la part de qui?

JACQUES: C'est Jacques Calvet.

MME MORIN: Ne quittez pas, Monsieur.

Une minute plus tard

MME MORIN: Il n'est pas là. Pouvez-vous rappeler dans une heure?

JACQUES: Bien sûr. Merci, Madame.

MME MORIN: Merci et au revoir.

JACQUES: Au revoir.

Activités

A. Répondez aux questions suivantes.

1. Avez-vous le téléphone? Est-ce que le téléphone est essentiel?
2. Quel est votre numéro de téléphone? le numéro de la police? des renseignements?
3. En France, comment trouve-t-on un numéro de téléphone?
4. Vous êtes en France et vous voulez téléphoner à vos parents aux Etats-Unis. Que faites-vous?

B. Avec un(e) camarade, inventez des dialogues adaptés aux situations suivantes.

1. Call for an appointment with the doctor.
2. Call someone and ask him / her to go to the movies with you.
3. Call the train station to find out the schedule for trains from Paris to Bordeaux.
4. Call information for a phone number.
5. Call the lost and found office of your hotel to ask about your wallet, which you left in your room.
6. Call a restaurant to find out about their menu and hours.

LECTURE CULTURELLE ....

Avant la lecture

Today France has one of the best telephone systems in the world. The phone company has always been nationalized and is now operated by **France Télécom,** an agency created on January 1, 1991, and placed under the **ministre des Postes, des Télécommunications et de l'Espace,** or **ministre des PTE.**

A unique feature of the telephone system is the **Minitel,** a small computer terminal plugged into one's phone line and designed to replace the paper phone book (**l'annuaire** or **le bottin**). The people who invented the **Minitel** had the ingenious idea of supplying it for free and offering an introductory monthly rate for using it. Now the French type in codes to get phone numbers, train schedules, horoscopes, video games, or hundreds of other services.

Today, one French household out of four has a **Minitel.** There are more than five million sets throughout the country, and it is estimated that each one is used for an average of ninety minutes a month. The highly successful service is not without its critics, however. Some are shocked at the content of the personal message services, and one magazine reported that many people have had their phone disconnected when they could not pay their two-month bills, which were running as high as 20,000 francs ($3,300)!

Activités

A. You have a brand-new, sophisticated product to market. How would you get people to use it?

B. If you had a computer hooked up to phone lines, what services would you like to have? Number the following in order of importance to you, and add others you can imagine.

__ telephone numbers	__ sports results
__ weather forecast	__ horoscope
__ news	__ personal messages
__ ???	__ ???

C. It is easier to guess the meaning of new words if you know frequently used prefixes and suffixes. Study the definitions below and find the words in the reading passage that use the prefixes and suffixes given.

Prefixes

co = ensemble
mini = petit
télé = de loin
pseudo = faux

Suffixes

-ologue = une personne qui *(who)* étudie
-scope = regarder

Le Minitel: une révolution unique

Le compagnon indispensable de tous les «*branchés*», le Minitel est un paradis où *jeux* et messages personnels coexistent avec les annuaires *télématiques* et les services utilitaires.

cool people
games / computerized

Le mot **Minitel** est la contraction de «mini» et «télématique». Imaginez un
5 *petit écran* avec un *clavier à touches* branché sur votre téléphone. Imaginez toute la France à votre *portée*. Maintenant, il n'est pas nécessaire de sortir: on fait un numéro et on peut converser avec tout le monde.

small screen / keyboard
reach

L'idée est simple: France Télécom distribue *gratuitement* de petits terminaux dans les maisons françaises où il y a le téléphone. Ces terminaux ser-
10 vent d'annuaire téléphonique *informatisé* et remplacent les *vieux* bottins en papier. Pour chercher le numéro d'une personne, on *tape* son *nom* et le nom de sa
ville. Immédiatement, tous les gens de la même localité avec le même nom
passent sur l'écran, et vous pouvez choisir votre correspondant.

Mais le Minitel peut faire beaucoup mieux. Il ne sert pas seulement à com-
15 muniquer des listes d'*abonnés* au téléphone. Il *diffuse* un *produit* et le client
paie une taxe (0,74 francs ou 13 cents) toutes les 45 secondes à la compagnie
française des téléphones.

Avec un Minitel, on peut consulter son horoscope, son *compte en banque*,
la *météo*, un médecin, un vétérinaire, un psychiatre et même un sexologue. Le
20 Minitel donne aussi des *nouvelles* et remplace les journaux *écrits*. Si on veut
faire des courses sans quitter la maison, on tape le code «Télémarket» et on
peut acheter du beurre ou une *bouteille* d'huile par exemple.

Il ne faut pas oublier *non plus* les messages personnels échangés la nuit par
beaucoup d'abonnés. Les gens utilisent généralement un pseudonyme et par-
25 ticipent aux «*messageries roses*.»

without charge

computerized / old

types / name

subscribers / distributes /
product

bank account
weather forecast
news / written

bottle

either

adult messages

Après une heure de Minitel, votre *facture* de téléphone a *augmenté* de 60   bill / increased
francs ou 10 dollars. Généralement, les premiers mois après l'installation, la
facture téléphonique d'un abonné augmente considérablement. France-
Télécom donne aux compagnies *qui* offrent un service 38,40 francs pour   that
30 chaque heure de communication.

En somme, l'*affaire* Minitel est très sérieuse. La France, avant tous les   matter
autres pays expérimente avec la télématique de masse. Au bureau ou à la
maison, les Français *possèdent* les 5 millions de terminaux Minitel installés.   own
Entreprises, grandes banques, services publics et créateurs de programmes   Companies
35 spéciaux pour Minitel ne veulent pas *manquer* une *occasion*.   miss / opportunity

(Adapté de l'article «Le Minitel», Vol. 9, No. 5 du *Journal Français d'Amérique*.
Reprinted by permission)

Après la lecture

Questions sur le texte

1. Décrivez le Minitel.
2. Qui distribue le Minitel?
3. Qui peut avoir un Minitel?
4. Pour chercher un numéro, que faites-vous?
5. Combien coûte *(cost)* ce service?
6. Quels sont les autres services?
7. Qu'est-ce que «les messageries roses»?
8. Combien de terminaux Minitel y a-t-il en France?

Activités

A. Répondez aux questions suivantes.

1. Voulez-vous avoir un Minitel chez vous? Pourquoi ou pourquoi
   pas?
2. Quels services sont utiles pour vous?
3. Quel est le montant *(cost)* de votre facture téléphonique? Est-ce
   peu ou beaucoup?
4. Pourquoi est-ce que le Minitel existe en France et pas aux
   Etats-Unis?

B. Regardez l'extrait du *Minitel Magazine* page 184, et répondez aux
questions basées sur l'extrait.

1. A quoi sert le programme **Anglatel**?
2. Quand est-ce qu'on peut parler avec un professeur?
3. Quand on veut communiquer avec des professeurs du Centre,
   qu'est-ce qu'on peut employer?
4. Si on réussit bien, qu'est-ce qu'on peut gagner *(win)*?
5. Où trouve-t-on des renseignements sur les journaux et les
   cassettes en anglais?

6. Quels renseignements est-ce que «Au pair in America» donne?
7. Quand est-ce qu'on peut faire un stage *(training course)* d'anglais à Avignon ou à Aix-en-Provence?

36.15 + ANGLATEL

Au préalable, donner son pseudo et sa date de naissance, indispensable pour le suivi pédagogique.

INStructions

Faites les leçons et exercices, *Anglatel* vous indiquera si vous avez donné la bonne réponse. *Anglatel* comptabilisera et mémorisera vos points ; en cours d'exercice, la touche « guide » permet d'être assisté. Vous pouvez aussi pratiquer votre prononciation en lisant à haute voix la réponse correcte.

ABOnnements

Accès par le 36.14 à tarifs préférentiels.

ANGlatel lessons

Les différents niveaux (beging, pre-intermediate, intermediate, post-intermediate, pre-advanced, advanced) et les domaines (grammar, vocabulary, usage, pronunciation, reading comprehension, dialogues, idioms, etc).

DANgerous scoop

Le premier feuilleton d'aventure sur minitel.

SPEak with the professor

De 18 h 00 à 20 h 00 le lundi, mardi, mercredi et jeudi, salon « Anglatel » avec un professeur anglophone du Centre franco-américain de Provence.

BOOkshop

Consultation d'une liste de livres en anglais.

STAges d'anglais

Présentation des stages intensifs à Avignon et Aix-en-Provence, en juillet et août prochains.

SEE the top-scores

Les meilleurs scores réalisés par les usagers du service ; un aller/retour Paris-New York-Paris a été gagné par une personne en 1986.

MAIl-box

Boîtes aux lettres pour écrire aux profs du Centre.

TRIp to the USA

Conditions de participation au concours du meilleur score de l'année (1er prix : un voyage aux USA).

NEWs from the center

Présentation des activités du Centre franco-américain d'Aix-en-Provence.

FERnand Nathan

Informations de « Speakeasy Publications » (cassettes et journaux pour tous niveaux).

AUPair aux USA

Présentation de « Au pair in America », programme d'échanges culturels destiné aux jeunes européennes parlant anglais.

Chapitre 8

PARIS

Notre-Dame et un Bateau-Mouche

185

COMMENÇONS ....

Deux cartes postales

Roger Diallo est un étudiant sénégalais. Il est à Paris, et il va suivre des cours à la Sorbonne pendant l'année. Deux semaines après son arrivée, il passe le week-end à la campagne et il fait une carte postale à ses parents.

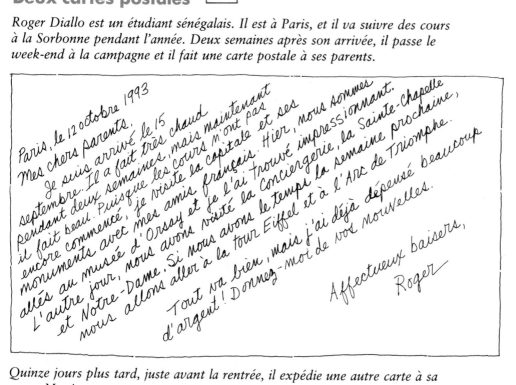

Paris, le 12 octobre 1993

Mes chers Parents,

Je suis arrivé le 15 septembre. Il a fait très chaud pendant deux semaines, mais maintenant il fait beau. Puisque les cours n'ont pas encore commencé, je visite la capitale et ses monuments avec mes amis français. Hier, nous sommes allés au musée d'Orsay et je l'ai trouvé impressionnant. L'autre jour, nous avons visité la Conciergerie, la Sainte-Chapelle et Notre-Dame. Si nous avons le temps la semaine prochaine, nous allons aller à la tour Eiffel et à l'Arc de Triomphe.

Tout va bien, mais j'ai déjà dépensé beaucoup d'argent! Donnez-moi de vos nouvelles.

Affectueux baisers,
Roger

Quinze jours plus tard, juste avant la rentrée, il expédie une autre carte à sa sœur, Monique.

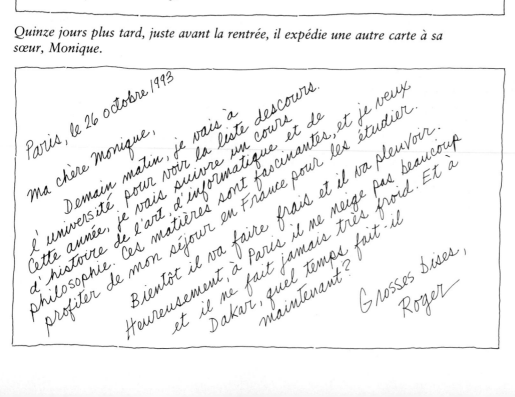

Paris, le 26 octobre 1993

Ma chère Monique,

Demain matin, je vais à l'université, pour voir la liste descours. Cette année, je vais suivre un cours d'histoire de l'art, d'informatique et de philosophie. Ces matières sont fascinantes, et je veux profiter de mon séjour en France pour les étudier.

Bientôt il va faire frais et il va pleuvoir. Heureusement, à Paris il ne neige pas beaucoup et il ne fait jamais très froid. Et à Dakar, quel temps fait-il maintenant?

Grosses bises,
Roger

Mots clés

cartes postales	*postcards*	affectueux baisers	*hugs and kisses*
sénégalais	*Senegalese*	juste	*just*
suivre des cours	*to take courses*	rentrée	*start of classes*
pendant	*during*	expédie (expédier)	*sends*
arrivée *(f.)*	*arrival*	histoire *(f.)* de l'art	*art history*
campagne	*country*	informatique *(f.)*	*computer science*
chers	*dear*		
puisque	*since*	matières *(f.)*	*subjects*
ne... pas encore	*not yet*	profiter de	*take advantage*
capitale	*capital*	séjour	*stay*
monuments *(m.)*	*monuments*	bientôt	*soon*
l'	*it*	Il va faire frais.	*It is going to be cool.*
impressionnant	*impressive*		
avons le temps (avoir le temps)	*have the time*	pleuvoir	*to rain*
		Il ne neige pas. (neiger)	*It doesn't snow.*
tout	*all*	ne... jamais	*never*
ai dépensé (dépenser)	*have spent*	Quel temps fait-il?	*What's the weather like?*
Donnez-moi de vos nouvelles.	*Let me hear from you.*	grosses bises	*love and kisses*

Faisons connaissance

Paris, the capital of France, is one of the most beautiful cities in the world and is renowned for its monuments, modern and historical, which millions of tourists come to visit each year. The **musée d'Orsay** is an art museum that opened in late 1986 in what used to be a train station, **la gare d'Orsay.** The museum houses a superb collection of over 4,000 pieces of nineteenth-century French art. It now attracts a large number of visitors (4 million in its first year)

Musée d'Orsay

Informations générales

Musée d'Orsay	répondeur
62, rue de Lille	informations
75007 Paris	générales : 45 49 11 11
tél. 45 49 48 14	

Entrée principale : 1, rue de Bellechasse.
Entrée des Grandes expositions du M'O :
place Henry-de-Montherlant (sur le quai).
Entrée du restaurant après la fermeture
du Musée : 62 bis, rue de Lille.

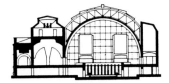

and has received great critical acclaim. The **Conciergerie,** the **Sainte-Chapelle,** and **Notre-Dame** cathedral, magnificent examples of Gothic art, are all located on the **île de la Cité** and surrounded by the river **Seine.** Nearby is the **Quartier latin,** so named because at the **Sorbonne,** the original university of Paris, classes were once conducted in Latin.

In addition to the tourists who flock to Paris, each year thousands of foreign students come to France. The main centers for study are Paris, Grenoble, and Aix-en-Provence, but all universities offer special courses for foreigners to learn French. These programs may last an academic year or varying lengths of time in the summer.

Etudions les cartes postales

1. Quand Roger est-il arrivé en France?
2. Quel temps fait-il en France?
3. Avec qui Roger visite-t-il Paris?
4. Quels monuments veut-il visiter?
5. A qui fait-il la deuxième carte postale?
6. Quels cours Roger va-t-il suivre cette année?

Enrichissons notre vocabulaire

Un ordinateur *(A computer)*

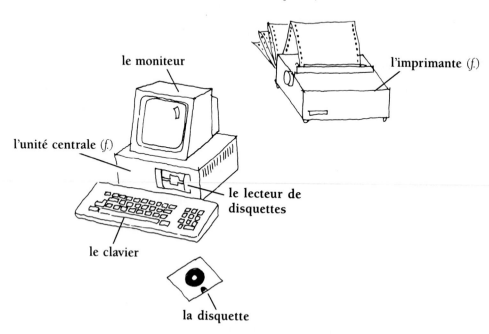

le moniteur

l'imprimante *(f.)*

l'unité centrale *(f.)*

le lecteur de disquettes

le clavier

la disquette

Faites-vous de l'informatique? *(Are you studying computer science?)*

—Qu'est-ce que tu penses du **matériel IBM**?	*What do you think of IBM* **hardware**?
—C'est formidable! J'ai acheté deux **logiciels**.	*It's fantastic! I bought two* **software programs**.
—Quelles sortes?	*What kind?*
—J'ai un **traitement de texte** pour mes **notes** et mes devoirs **écrits** et un **tableur**.	*I have a* **word processor** *for my* **notes** *and my* **written** *work, and a* **spreadsheet**.
—Tu as **rencontré** des problèmes?	*Have you* **met** *with any problems?*
—Non, et je vais **gagner** de l'argent si je **tape** les devoirs de mes amis.	*No, and I am going to* **earn** *money if I* **type** *my friends' papers.*
—Est-ce que je peux **emprunter** ton matériel et tes logiciels?	*May I* **borrow** *your equipment and your software?*
—Non, je ne les **prête jamais**; je les **utilise tout le temps**.	*No, I* **never lend** *them; I* **use** *them* **all the time**.

Au bureau de poste *(At the post office)*

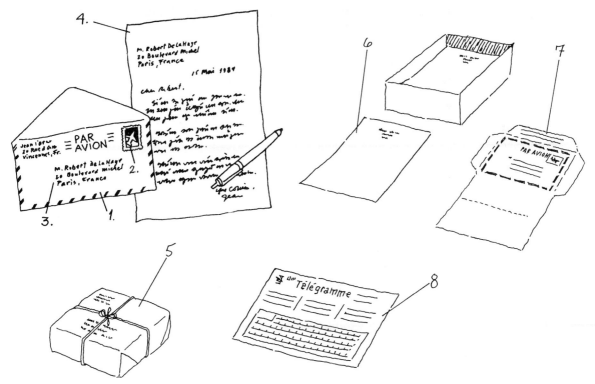

1. une **enveloppe**	5. un **paquet** / un **colis**
2. un **timbre**	6. du **papier à lettres**
3. l'**adresse** *(f.)*	7. un **aérogramme**
4. une **lettre**	8. un **télégramme**

Le **facteur:** Bonjour, Madame.

Mme Legrain: Vous avez du **courrier** pour moi?

Le facteur: Oui, une lettre **recommandée** et un **mandat**.

Mme Legrain: Tenez, merci beaucoup.

*The **mailman:** Good morning, ma'am.*

*Mme Legrain: Do you have any **mail** for me?*

*The mailman: Yes, a **registered** letter and a **money order**.*

Mme Legrain: There, thanks a lot.

Prononciation Oral Vowels and Nasal Consonants

A. In Chapter 7, you learned the pronunciation of the three nasal vowels in French: /ɛ̃/ (**pain**), /ã/ (**lent**), and /ɔ̃/ (**ton**). With nasal vowels, you never pronounce the letter **n** or **m** that follows.

Masculine	**Feminine**
américain	américaine
canadien	canadienne
italien	italienne

The masculine forms end in a nasal vowel, so the **n** is not pronounced. The **n** must be pronounced in the feminine, however, so the preceding vowel is oral instead of nasal.

B. The **n** or **m** must be pronounced if it is doubled (**sommes**) or followed by a vowel (**téléphone**).

Pronounce the following words and indicate whether the underlined vowels in boldface are oral or nasal.

je d**o**nne / t**o**n stylo / b**i**en / **e**n ville / s**o**nne / **a**nnée / v**i**n / mat**i**n / **i**nutile

Exercices

A. Pronounce the following pairs of words after your teacher, making a clear distinction between the oral and nasal vowels.

1. Jean / Jeanne
2. an / année
3. matin / matinée
4. plein / pleine
5. un / une
6. vietnamien / vietnamienne
7. gens / jeune
8. brun / brune

B. Read the following sentences aloud, taking care not to nasalize vowels before pronounced **n** and **m**.

1. Les usines anciennes consomment beaucoup d'énergie.
2. Elle aime un homme ambitieux.
3. Tiens! Etienne déjeune avec une Canadienne.
4. Anne et Micheline vont emprunter mon traitement de texte.
5. Jean et Jeanne ont acheté un ordinateur.
6. Yvonne expédie un télégramme à Lisbonne.

GRAMMAIRE ······························

I. The Weather (**La météo**)

A. In Chapter 5 you learned that the verb **faire** is often used to describe the weather.

Il fait beau.	**Il fait** chaud.
Il fait mauvais.	**Il fait** froid.

There are other descriptions of the weather that contain **faire:**

Il fait **du vent.**   Il fait **du brouillard.**

Il fait **du soleil.**   Il fait **de l'orage.**

Il fait **frais.**	*It is **cool.***
Il fait **bon.**	*It is **nice.***
Il fait **une chaleur insupportable!**	*The **heat** is **unbearable!***

B. In addition to **faire,** there are other verbs and terms used to describe weather:

être: **Le ciel est couvert.**	*The sky is overcast. / It's cloudy.*
neiger: **Il neige.**	*to snow: **It is snowing.***
pleuvoir: **Il pleut.**	*to rain: **It is raining.***
Il y a des **nuages** *(m.)*.	*There are **clouds.***

Il y a **des éclairs** *(m.)* **et du
  tonnerre.**
	*There is **lightning and
	  thunder.***

Il y a déjà beaucoup de **neige** *(f.)*.	*There is already a lot of **snow.***

Nous avons eu beaucoup de
  pluie *(f.)* cette année.
	*We've had a lot of **rain** this
	  year.*

C. The following examples show how weather expressions are used in other tenses.

Passé composé

Il **a fait** très chaud pendant deux semaines.
Le week-end dernier, il **a plu** mais il **n'a pas neigé**.

Futur proche

Il **va faire** frais et il **va pleuvoir**.
Il **va neiger** la semaine prochaine.

ATTENTION

1. **Il fait beau** is used for general weather conditions *(warm, sunny)*, while **il fait bon** refers to temperature and can refer to a room indoors.

    Il fait bon dans cette chambre.

2. **Chaud** and **froid** can be used with three different verbs, depending on what is being described.

weather (**faire**):	Il **fait chaud**. Il **fait froid**.
people (**avoir**):	J'ai **chaud**. Robert **a froid**.
things (**être**):	Cette eau **est chaude**. Ma bière n'**est** pas assez **froide**.

Langue

A. **Quel temps fait-il?** Faites deux phrases pour chaque dessin *(each drawing)*.

1

2

3

4

5

6

B. **La météo.** Refaites les phrases suivantes en employant les mots entre parenthèses.

1. Quel temps fait-il? (... hier?)
2. Il pleut. (... hier.)
3. Il neige beaucoup. (L'année dernière...)
4. Il ne fait pas froid. (... demain.)
5. Il fait de l'orage. (Le week-end dernier...)
6. Il va faire du brouillard. (... hier matin.)

C. **Le climat en Europe.** Caractérisez le climat des pays suivants en faisant des phrases complètes avec les mots donnés.

1. pleuvoir / beaucoup / Angleterre
2. neiger / beaucoup / Suisse
3. faire / soleil / Italie
4. Espagne / faire / chaud
5. faire / brouillard / Irlande
6. Norvège / faire / froid

Culture

D. **Les prévisions de la météo.** Regardez la carte météorologique ci-dessous (below) et répondez aux questions.

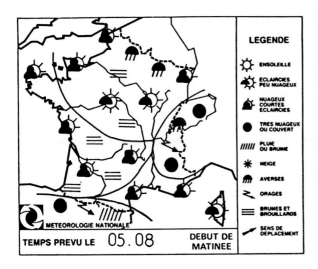

La carte

1. Est-ce qu'il va faire du soleil en France?
2. Quel temps va-t-il faire dans les Alpes?
3. Va-t-il faire beau sur une des plages en France?

La liste des villes

4. Dans combien de villes est-ce que le ciel va être couvert?
5. Est-ce qu'il va neiger?
6. Il va faire très froid à Tokyo?

Communication

E. Vos camarades partent en vacances. Suggérez des activités pour les différentes conditions météorologiques.

> MODELE: quand il fait bon
> *Quand il fait bon, faites une promenade!*

1. quand il pleut
2. quand il neige
3. quand il fait mauvais
4. quand il fait du soleil
5. quand il fait de l'orage
6. quand il fait très froid

F. Choisissez un(e) camarade et préparez ensemble un bulletin météorologique *(weather report)* pour une des situations suivantes.

1. votre ville cet après-midi
2. votre ville l'hiver dernier
3. votre région ce week-end
4. San Diego en hiver
5. le Sénégal
6. Montréal en hiver

G. **Questions personnelles.** Votre temps préféré

1. Etes-vous content(e) quand il fait froid? quand il fait chaud?
2. Aimez-vous faire une promenade quand il pleut?
3. Quelle saison aimez-vous mieux? Pourquoi?
4. Quel temps a-t-il fait le week-end dernier? Qu'est-ce que vous avez fait?
5. Quel temps voulez-vous avoir pour vos prochaines vacances?
6. Où est-ce qu'on trouve un climat idéal?

II. Suivre / Suivre des cours

> You use **suivre** to express the idea of *to follow (to follow a person; to follow an idea)* and to talk about taking an academic course.

A. Suivre

suivre *(to follow)*	
je **suis**	nous **suivons**
tu **suis**	vous **suivez**
il / elle / on **suit**	ils / elles **suivent**
Passé composé: il **a suivi**	

Nous allons **suivre** cette auto.
Suivez-moi, s'il vous plaît.
Vous **suivez** ce prof?

B. Suivre des cours

1. **Suivre** is often used with academic subjects (**suivre des cours, suivre un cours de...**) to express *to take a course or courses.*

   Il va **suivre des cours** à la Sorbonne.
   J'ai **suivi des cours** d'informatique.

   The following vocabulary can be used to talk about the school year:
   un trimestre *(a quarter)*, **un semestre** *(a semester)*, and **l'année scolaire** *(the school year)*.

2. There are three ways to state the subjects you study.

suivre un cours de (d'):	Mon ami **suit un cours** d'histoire.
faire du (de la, des, de l'):	Moi, je **fais de la** physique mais j'aime mieux la psychologie.
étudier le (la, les):	Ma sœur **étudie** le latin et le grec.

ATTENTION

You must be sure to use the correct article with each verb.

1. **Suivre un cours** takes only the preposition **de,** not an article.

2. **Faire** takes only the partitives **du, de la, de l', des.**

3. **Etudier** takes only the definite articles **le, la, l', les.**

Mots clés Academic Subjects

l'anthropologie *(f.)*	les langues étrangères	*foreign*
l'architecture *(f.)*		*languages*
l'art *(m.)*	l'allemand *(m.)*	le français
la biologie	l'anglais *(m.)*	le grec
la chimie *chemistry*	l'arabe *(m.)*	l'italien *(m.)*
le droit *law*	le chinois	le latin
l'éducation	l'espagnol *(m.)*	le russe
physique *(f.)*	la médecine	
la géographie	la musique	
la géologie	la philosophie	
la gestion *business*	la physique	
l'histoire *(f.)*	la psychologie	
l'informatique *(f.)*	les sciences économiques *(f.)*	
le journalisme	les sciences politiques *(f.)*	
la littérature	la sociologie	
les mathématiques *(f.)*		

Note that all languages are masculine and all sciences are feminine.

Ce qu'ils disent

1. When French students talk about the subjects that they study, they often use abbreviations. Most of them end in **o**.

philo philosophie   **psycho** psychologie
sciences éco sciences économiques   **socio** sociologie
sciences po sciences politiques   **les maths** mathématiques

2. To indicate their majors, students use the verb **être** with the preposition **en**.

Je **suis en socio** à la fac.   ***I'm a sociology major at the university.***

Langue

A. **Des présentations.** Faites des phrases en remplaçant les mots en italique par les mots entre parenthèses.

MODELE: Il fait du français. (étudier)
          Il étudie le français.

1. Luc *étudie* le russe. (suivre un cours)
2. Je *fais* du droit. (étudier)
3. Nous *allons suivre un cours* d'histoire. (faire)
4. Tu *vas étudier* la géologie. (suivre un cours)
5. Mon camarade de chambre *a fait* du chinois. (suivre un cours)
6. Julie et Kevin *ont étudié* la physique. (faire)

B. **Les études de Juliette.** Faites une phrase complète avec les mots donnés.

1. Juliette / suivre / cours / informatique / Etats-Unis
2. semestre dernier / elle / étudier / grec / et / latin
3. Sa sœur / faire / sciences économiques
4. année prochaine / elles / suivre / cours / psychologie?
5. Non, elles / ne... pas / étudier / sciences
6. trimestre prochain / Juliette / faire / informatique

Culture

C. **Au collège.** Un «collège» est l'équivalent d'un *high school* aux Etats-Unis. A la page 197, vous avez l'emploi du temps *(schedule)* de Caroline, une élève de cinquième qui habite à Lyon. Décrivez son emploi du temps en répondant aux questions suivantes.

1. Qu'est-ce que Caroline étudie le lundi matin?
2. Quand fait-elle du sport?
3. Dans quelle salle de classe a-t-elle son instruction civique?
4. Suit-elle un cours de philosophie?
5. Quelle langue étrangère Caroline étudie-t-elle? Combien d'heures par semaine?
6. Quand est-ce qu'elle n'a pas de cours?

		LUNDI	SALLE	MARDI	SALLE	MERCREDI	SALLE	JEUDI	SALLE	VENDREDI	SALLE	
8H.15												
MATIN	I	maths	15	Sciences Naturelles	50	maths	16	Histoire Géo	62	Français	10	I
	II	Anglais	26	1h 30 Sciences		Dessin	18	Enseignement religieux	23	Soutien de Français ou Hist-Géo	10 62	II
	III	musique	13	Physiques 1h 30	2	Français	36	Français	39	Hist-Géo	62	III
12H.15	IV					Français	36					IV
13H.30												
SOIR	I	Instruction Civique	62	Technologie	At			Soutien de maths		Maths	27	I
	II	Sport		Technologie	At			Anglais		Soutien. d'Anglais	26	II
15H.30	III	sport		Français	9			Sport		Anglais	26	III

Communication

D. Votre camarade de chambre a un livre d'un des auteurs suivants. Quelle langue étudie-t-il / elle?

MODELE: Dante *Il / Elle fait de l'italien.*
Il / Elle étudie l'italien.

1. Cervantes
2. Goethe
3. Jules César
4. Simone de Beauvoir
5. Homère
6. Confucius
7. Tolstoï
8. Emily Brontë

E. **Questions personnelles.** Vos études

1. Quels cours suivez-vous ce trimestre / ce semestre?
2. Qu'est-ce que vous allez étudier la prochaine année scolaire?
3. Faites-vous des sciences cette année?
4. Quels cours aimez-vous / détestez-vous?
5. Quel cours est trop difficile pour vous?
6. Qu'est-ce que vous faites quand vous n'allez pas aux cours?

III. **Direct Object Pronouns: Third Person**

You use direct object pronouns to refer to someone or something already mentioned in a conversation.

A. Direct Objects

1. In English, a direct object receives the action of the verb directly. In the following sentences, the words in boldface type are direct objects.

   He is buying **the apple.**   They are going to meet **Joe** at school.
   I like **your ideas.**   We saw **Jane** at the movies.

2. A direct object can be a person, an object, or an idea. It answers the question *whom?* or *what?* Direct object pronouns replace nouns that have already been mentioned.

   "Where is the jacket?"   "Are they going to get Joe?"
   "He is buying **it.**"   "Yes, they are going to get **him.**"

   "What do you think of his   "Has anyone seen Mary?"
     ideas?"   "I saw **her.**"
   "I like **them.**"

B. Third-Person Direct Object Pronouns

French also has direct objects. They may be replaced by direct object pronouns that are placed before the verb in an affirmative or negative present-tense statement.

   Roger visite **la capitale.** → Roger **la** visite.
   Il trouve **le musée** impressionnant. → Il **le** trouve impressionnant.
   Il aime **l'informatique.** → Il **l'**aime.
   Il suit **ses cours** à la Sorbonne. → Il **les** suit à la Sorbonne.

The following chart summarizes the third-person direct object pronouns.

	singular		plural	
masculine	le, l'	*him, it*	les	*them*
feminine	la, l'	*her, it*		

ATTENTION

Remember that every French noun has a gender, so *it* is expressed by either **le** or **la,** depending on the noun for which it stands. Both **le** and **la** become **l'** before a vowel, while the silent **s** of **les** becomes the sound /z/.

   —Vous faites du russe?
   —Je **l'**étudie, mais je ne **le** parle pas.

   —Pourquoi parle-t-il aux Dupont?
   —Il **les** invite chez lui.

C. Position of Direct Object Pronouns

1. As you have just seen, the direct object pronoun precedes the verb in an affirmative or negative present tense statement.

   —Vous avez **beaucoup d'argent?**
   —Non, je **le** dépense tout de suite.

   —Vous avez utilisé **ce logiciel?**
   —Oui, mais je ne **le** trouve pas intéressant.

2. The same is true of questions, including inversion.

   —Voilà **notre étudiant sénégalais!**
   —**L'**avez-vous en cours ce trimestre?

   —Où est **la lettre de Bernard?**
   —Est-ce que vous **la** voulez maintenant?

3. In any *helping verb plus infinitive* construction, the direct object pronoun precedes the infinitive, that is, the verb of which the pronoun is a direct object.

   —Il a **beaucoup de devoirs?**
   —Oui, mais il ne peut pas **les** faire.

   —Tu as **mes aérogrammes?**
   —Non, mais je peux **les** apporter demain.

4. In the **passé composé,** the pronoun precedes the auxiliary verb **avoir.**

   —Tu vas suivre **un cours** sur Corneille?
   —Non, je **l'**ai déjà étudié.

   —Avez-vous **votre Walkman?**
   —Non, je **l'**ai laissé chez moi.

▶ L'Orthographe

1. In the **passé composé,** the past participle must agree in gender and in number with a direct object pronoun that precedes it. This does not change the pronunciation of most past participles.

   —Tu as acheté **cette voiture?**   —Où as-tu trouvé **ces chaussures?**
   —Non, je **l'**ai empruntée à   —Je **les** ai trouvées à Montréal.
   un ami.

2. You have learned only one past participle whose masculine and feminine forms can be *audibly* distinguished **faire** (**fait / faite**).

   —Est-ce que je peux faire **la vaisselle?**
   —Non, nous **l'**avons déjà faite.

   —Ils vont faire **leurs courses** cet après-midi?
   —Non, ils **les** ont déjà faites.

Langue

A. Mettez les phrases suivantes au **passé composé** et au **futur proche.**

1. Nous les empruntons tous les jours.
2. Vous la suivez.
3. Il la laisse à la gare.
4. Les porte-t-on aujourd'hui?
5. Est-ce que vous l'invitez?
6. Je la regarde le soir.

B. **Qu'est-ce qu'on fait?** Remplacez les compléments d'objet direct *(direct objects)* par un pronom dans les phrases suivantes.

1. J'utilise mon ordinateur.
2. Julie emprunte-t-elle ton logiciel?
3. Jacques a fini son livre.
4. Tu vas inviter Sylvie et Monique?
5. Vous n'avez pas étudié l'allemand?
6. Henri n'aime pas prêter son imprimante.

Culture

C. **Les Français et la télévision.** Répondez aux questions suivantes en employant un pronom complément d'objet direct.

1. Est-ce que les Français regardent beaucoup la télévision?
2. Aiment-ils regarder la télé l'après-midi?
3. Ils aiment Jerry Lewis?
4. Ils aiment les westerns?
5. Est-ce qu'ils apprécient les jeux télévisés *(game shows)*?
6. Oublient-ils la télé pendant le dîner?

Communication

D. Vous entendez *(hear)* la dernière partie d'une conversation. Dans chaque situation, imaginez le sujet de cette conversation.

MODELE: Je ne peux pas la faire.
         Tu ne peux pas faire la vaisselle?

1. Pouvez-vous l'expédier?
2. Il ne va pas les inviter.
3. Tu ne l'as pas préparée?
4. Nous ne l'avons pas étudié.
5. Je ne les ai pas trouvés.
6. Je n'aime pas le faire.

E. Posez des questions à vos camarades avec les éléments donnés à la page 201. Ils / Elles vont répondre en employant des pronoms.

MODELE: Etudiant(e) 1: *Vas-tu préparer ton dîner ce soir?*
         Etudiant(e) 2: *Oui, je vais le préparer. / Non, je ne vais pas le préparer.*

	A	B
aller	consulter le médecin	oublier ton passé
désirer	acheter un ordinateur	préparer ton dîner ce soir
pouvoir	expédier une lettre à tes	finir tes cours cette année
vouloir	grands-parents	choisir ton / ta camarade
	étudier l'arabe ou le chinois	de chambre pour
	écouter tes parents	l'année prochaine
	expliquer tes absences	suivre le cours du même
	faire la cuisine chez toi	professeur le trimestre
	montrer tes photos	prochain

F. **Votre vie à l'université.** En petits groupes, préparez des réponses aux questions suivantes. Employez des pronoms et informez vos camarades de cours des résultats.

1. As-tu étudié la musique? l'informatique?
2. Aimes-tu tes cours ce trimestre?
3. Vas-tu étudier le français le trimestre prochain?
4. Où fais-tu tes devoirs?
5. Utilises-tu ton ordinateur pour faire tes devoirs?
6. Où expédies-tu ton courrier?

G. **Questions personnelles.** La vie moderne. Employez des pronoms compléments d'objet direct dans vos réponses.

1. Aimez-vous le jazz? le rock?
2. Quand écoutez-vous cette musique?
3. Votre camarade de chambre prête ses logiciels? ses vêtements?
4. Appréciez-vous l'art moderne?
5. Avez-vous étudié l'informatique?
6. Avez-vous utilisé les ordinateurs de votre université? Pourquoi?

IV. Voir

> You use the verb **voir** to indicate seeing as well as understanding.

	voir *(to see)*
je **vois**	nous **voyons**
tu **vois**	vous **voyez**
il / elle / on **voit**	ils / elles **voient**

Passé composé: il **a vu**
Imperative: **vois / voyons / voyez**

—**Avez**-vous **vu** mon sac?
—Oui, nous l'**avons vu** dans ta chambre.

—Tu **as vu** mes cartes postales?
—Non, je ne les **ai** pas **vues.**

A. The singular forms and the third-person plural (**voient**) have the same pronunciation, /vwa/.

—Son père a 82 ans! Comment va-t-il?
—Pas mal, mais il ne **voit** pas bien.

—Ils ne sont pas contents!
—Ils ne **voient** pas pourquoi tu es toujours en retard.

ATTENTION

1. The expression **aller voir** means *to visit* and is used with people. **Visiter** can only be used with places.

   Quand j'**ai visité** Paris l'année dernière, je **suis allé voir** des amis.

2. **Voir un film** is used for movie theaters. For films on television, use **regarder.**

   Ils ne veulent pas **regarder** ce film parce qu'ils l'**ont déjà vu** au cinéma.

B. Other verbs conjugated like **voir** are **prévoir** (*to foresee*) and **revoir** (*to see again* or *to review*).

   Il n'a pas **prévu** cela.   Elle va **revoir** ses leçons.

CE QU'ILS DISENT

The imperative form **Voyons!** changes meaning according to the speaker's tone of voice. With the simple declarative intonation, it means *Let's see* as when someone is looking for something or trying to think of something. With a slightly exasperated intonation, it means *Come on!*

   Voyons. Où est-ce que j'ai laissé mon parapluie?
   Voyons! Tu n'es pas sérieux!

Langue

A. **Voyage en Europe.** Faites des questions avec les mots donnés.

   1. Qu'est-ce que / tu / voir / en France / été dernier?
   2. Tu / revoir / amis parisiens?
   3. amis / prévoir / une visite d'une semaine?

4. Vous / voir / bon film / ensemble?
5. On / prévoir / ce / été / très chaud / n'est-ce pas?
6. Tu / vouloir / revoir / Paris?

B. **Après les vacances.** Répondez aux questions suivantes en employant des pronoms à la place des compléments d'objet direct.

1. A-t-on bien prévu *la météo* pour tes vacances?
2. Tu as revu *ta petite amie?*
3. Tes amis ont revu *leurs parents?*
4. Tu n'as pas vu *le dernier film d'Isabelle Adjani?*
5. Est-ce que je vais voir *tes photos de vacances?*
6. Est-ce que nous allons revoir *nos leçons de français* maintenant?

Culture

C. **Des sites pittoresques.** Qu'est-ce qu'on voit des sites suivants dans des pays francophones ou de quoi est-ce qu'on a une belle vue? Trouvez la réponse correcte dans la colonne de gauche.

MODELE: De la tour Eiffel
          De la tour Eiffel, on voit Paris.

1. Du Sporting Club	a. la mer des Caraïbes
2. Du mont du Lion	b. la mer Méditerranée
3. De la terrasse Dufferin	c. les Pyrénées
4. De Pau	d. la Seine et le Louvre
5. De la montagne Pelée	e. le Saint-Laurent
6. De la terrasse du musée d'Orsay	f. Waterloo

Communication

D. Qu'est-ce que vous voyez dans votre futur? Utilisez les suggestions suivantes et votre imagination!

MODELE: *Je vois cinq enfants, une profession fascinante et beaucoup d'argent.*

une maison blanche	une profession intéressante
une voiture de sport	des enfants intelligents
un appartement à Nice	des vacances à Tahiti
une femme / un mari riche	un yacht aux Antilles

E. Qui voulez-vous revoir ou ne pas revoir? Qu'est-ce que vous voulez revoir ou ne pas revoir?

MODELE: *Je ne veux pas revoir mon professeur d'éducation physique.*
          Je veux revoir le film Casablanca.

film	villes
ami(es)	chanteurs (-euses)
professeur(s)	émissions de télévision *(TV shows)*

F. **Questions personnelles.** Vos activités

1. Avez-vous vu vos parents récemment? Quand?
2. Allez-vous voir un film ce week-end? Quel film?
3. Est-ce qu'on voit souvent des films français dans votre ville?
4. Vous avez passé des vacances avec votre famille? Qu'est-ce que vous avez vu ensemble?
5. Qu'est-ce qu'on peut voir dans votre ville?
6. Qu'est-ce qu'on voit de la fenêtre de votre chambre?

C OMMUNIQUONS ······························

Aller au bureau de poste

The post office (le **bureau de poste, la poste** or **les P.T.T.**) is an institution in France that every visitor should know because it plays so many roles. You not only mail things there but also make phone calls. The French use the post office even for some banking needs, such as a checking account (**un compte-chèque postal** or CCP).

On expédie le courrier.

C'est combien pour envoyer une lettre aux Etats-Unis?	*How much is it to send a letter to the United States?*
Par avion, ça coûte quatre francs vingt les cinq grammes.	*Air mail is four francs and 20 centimes for each five grams.*
Je voudrais acheter un timbre à trois francs.	*I would like to buy a three-franc stamp.*

On donne un coup de téléphone.

Je voudrais téléphoner avec préavis à un ami à Lyon.	*I would like to make a person-to-person call to a friend in Lyon.*
L'étudiant va téléphoner à ses parents aux Etats-Unis en P.C.V.	*The student is going to call his parents in the U.S. collect.*
Allez dans la cabine numéro onze, Mademoiselle.	*Go into booth #11, miss.*
Je désire faire un appel interurbain / international.	*I want to make a long-distance / international call.*

On utilise la poste restante.

En France on peut recevoir son courrier à la poste restante.	*In France, you can receive mail at general delivery.*
Le préposé demande toujours une pièce d'identité.	*The employee always asks for an ID.*
Il faut payer la surtaxe.	*You must pay a charge.*

Interaction *Un étudiant américain va au bureau de poste.*

L'ETUDIANT: Est-ce que vous avez une lettre pour moi? Ma famille l'a envoyée à la poste restante.

LA PREPOSEE: Oui, s'ils ont bien indiqué ce bureau. Je vais chercher. Vous avez une pièce d'identité avec photo? Et il va y avoir une petite surtaxe à payer.

L'ETUDIANT: *D'accord.* Et est-ce que vous pouvez me donner un numéro de téléphone?   O.K.

LA PREPOSEE: Ah, non, Monsieur, mais vous avez le Minitel dans le hall à *gauche.*   left

Activités

A. Répondez aux questions suivantes.

1. Si vous allez en Europe, à qui allez-vous envoyer des cartes postales? des lettres?
2. Vous avez déjà envoyé des cartes postales? Avec une photo de quoi?
3. Avez-vous téléphoné d'un téléphone public? A qui? Comment avez-vous payé?
4. Où pouvez-vous recevoir du courrier en France? Et aux Etats-Unis? Est-ce que la poste restante est utile?

B. Jouez les scènes suivantes avec un(e) camarade de cours.

1. Vous voulez envoyer des cartes postales dans plusieurs pays.
2. Vous voulez téléphoner à vos parents, mais vous n'avez pas d'argent.
3. Vous pensez avoir une lettre à la poste restante, mais l'employé ne peut pas la trouver.
4. Vous voulez envoyer un télégramme.

LECTURE CULTURELLE ....

Avant la lecture

From one year to the next, Paris undergoes important transformations, and even tourists who visit the French capital regularly find that changes have occurred since their last trip. Recently, people have discovered the glass pyramid of the **Louvre,** the new opera house on the **place de la**
5 **Bastille,** the dome of the **Invalides** and the **Génie de la Bastille,** both glistening with the new gold leaves that were spread upon them for the celebration of the **bicentenaire de la Révolution.** But they also find that the number of fast-food establishments is steadily growing along the **Champs-Elysées,** which is one of the world's most famous avenues.
10   More recently, new architectural projects have developed in the eastern part of the city. The **quartier de la Villette** now has a new park which Parisians have already adopted. Anyone who enjoys strolling about the streets in **Belleville** or walking along the banks of the old **canal Saint-Martin** should hurry before promoters start tearing down all the old build-
15 ings to replace them with offices and luxury apartments.

Activités

A. Select a major American city that you visit frequently and identify the important changes that you have noticed from one trip to the next.

B. On the map of Paris on the inside back cover of your textbook, find as many as possible of the sites mentioned in the postcards at the beginning of the chapter, in the preceding **Avant la lecture** paragraphs, and in the following **Lecture culturelle**.

C. Scan the following reading passage and find ten nouns that refer to parts of a city or structures that one would find in a city (e.g., **rue, parc,** etc.).

Paris change

Petit à petit, les *vieux quartiers* parisiens changent d'aspect, et *ceux qui* les *connaissent* et les aiment depuis toujours *doivent se dépêcher* d'aller les revoir, parce qu'ils risquent de *perdre* bientôt cette originalité appréciée par des générations de Parisiens et de touristes. Regardez Montmartre par exemple: La
5 Butte a toujours beaucoup de visiteurs et elle *attire* de plus en plus d'artistes. Mais *puisque* la Ville de Paris est opposée à cette prolifération, elle *vient de* décider qu'ils doivent limiter leurs activités à la place du Tertre. Naturellement, les artistes ont refusé d'obéir, et *en attendant* une solution, ils continuent comme avant.

Little by little / old neighborhoods / those who / know / must / hurry / lose
attracts
since / has just

while waiting for

Place du Tertre et le Sacré-Cœur

10   Allez à Belleville, le quartier où Edith Piaf est née et *a grandi*. Quel change-   *grew up*
ment! Il y a maintenant un *étranger* sur cinq résidents et *lentement*, les *im-*   *foreigner / slowly*
meubles tombent et laissent la place à des buildings modernes. Des Arabes, des   *buildings / fall*
Africains, des Antillais et des Asiatiques habitent là depuis longtemps, et leurs
magasins et leurs restaurants *remplissent* les rues de parfums exotiques. Bientôt   *fill*
15   tout cela va *disparaître*.   *disappear*

A la Villette, le *nouveau* parc est presque terminé. Avec ses 55 *hectares* de   *new / hectares (2.47 acres)*
jardins, d'*aires de jeu,* de promenades, de *pelouses* et de fontaines, c'est le plus   *playgrounds / lawns*
grand espace vert *construit* depuis dix ans dans la capitale. Situé à côté du nou-   *built*
veau musée des sciences de la Villette, le parc fait partie d'un complexe *qui*   *which*
20   *mérite* plusieurs visites. Cependant, en même temps, d'autres espaces verts dis-   *is worth*
paraissent. La construction de parkings *souterrains* est souvent la cause de la   *underground*
disparition d'arbres parfois centenaires.   *removal / trees / sometimes /*
                                                                                                                        a hundred years old /

Et la Bastille? Est-ce qu'elle va résister? Elle a gardé son *côté* un peu anar-   *aspect*
chique; elle offre toujours beaucoup de cafés, de restaurants et de boîtes, mais
25   on peut observer de nombreuses transformations. On démolit les vieux immeubles et on les remplace par des immeubles *à grand standing*. On a placé   *deluxe*
beaucoup d'*espoir* sur le *nouvel* Opéra pour donner au quartier une certaine   *hope / new*
respectabilité, mais la voix des ténors et des sopranos *se mêle* encore au *bruit*   *mixes with / noise*
des bulldozers.

30   Beaucoup de Parisiens et de touristes étrangers voient toutes ces transformations avec regret, mais *même* si Paris est en train de changer de caractère,   *even*
elle reste la *Ville lumière,* l'endroit où tout le monde *rêve* d'aller un jour.   *City of Lights / dreams*

(Adapté de l'article «Paris», Vol. 13, No. 10 du *Journal Français d'Amérique*.
Reprinted by permission.)

Après la lecture

Questions sur le texte

1. Est-ce que Paris reste toujours Paris?
2. Est-ce que les artistes vont continuer à fréquenter toutes les rues de
Montmartre?
3. Qu'est-ce qui donne aux rues de Belleville un caractère original?
4. Pourquoi les Parisiens aiment-ils aller dans le quartier de la Villette?
5. Est-ce que le nouvel Opéra de la Bastille a changé le quartier?
6. Avec tous ces changements, est-ce qu'on ne va plus aimer Paris?

Activités

A. Make a list of famous Parisian sites and monuments that you know
and that have not been mentioned in this chapter.

B. With the help of the information about Paris provided in this chapter,
prepare your ideal itinerary of a one-day visit of the French capital.

LA CUISINE

Elle choisit des fruits.

COMMENÇONS ....

Au marché d'Antibes

*Anne Bryan passe ses vacances à Juan-les-Pins chez de bons amis de ses
parents, M. et Mme Leconte. Aujourd'hui, c'est jeudi et c'est le jour du
marché à Antibes. Nathalie, la fille des Leconte, a invité Anne à passer la
matinée au marché.*

NATHALIE: Commençons par les marchands de poissons et de fruits de mer!
Tu peux prendre des photos si tu veux.

ANNE: Regarde tous ces gros poissons. Et les crevettes! Comme elles sont
petites!

NATHALIE: Allons où ils vendent les fromages. Veux-tu apprendre leurs noms?

ANNE: C'est impossible, il y a trop de variétés. Est-ce qu'on peut vraiment
manger un fromage différent tous les jours de l'année?

NATHALIE: Bien sûr. Est-ce que tu aimes les olives? Moi, je les mange comme
des bonbons. Ici, c'est le coin de la viande. Tu vois, ça, ce sont des
lapins.

ANNE: Je n'aime pas voir cela. Et les poulets, on leur a laissé la tête et les
pattes!

NATHALIE: Ça là-bas, c'est un gigot. Maman va servir cela dimanche; j'espère
que tu es contente.

ANNE: Ma pauvre Nathalie, je ne mange jamais de viande; je suis
végétarienne!

Mots clés

marché	*market*	vraiment	*truly*
vacances *(f.)*	*vacation*	différent	*different*
bon(-ne)	*good*	olives *(f.)*	*olives*
matinée	*morning*	bonbons *(m.)*	*candy*
marchands *(m.)*	*merchants*	coin	*area*
fruits de mer *(m.)*	*seafood*	ça	*that*
prendre	*take*	lapins *(m.)*	*rabbits*
crevettes *(f.)*	*shrimp*	leur	*them*
comme	*how*	tête	*head*
petit(e)	*small*	pattes *(f.)*	*paws*
vendent (vendre)	*sell*	gigot	*leg of lamb*
apprendre	*learn*	espère que	*hope that*
noms *(m.)*	*names*	(espérer que)	
variétés *(f.)*	*varieties*	végétarien(-ne)	*vegetarian*

Faisons connaissance

Many French towns and villages are renowned for their open-air markets **(marchés en plein air).** They usually take place once a week and last from seven in the morning to one or two in the afternoon. **Le jour du marché** is always an important event for local people and tourists alike.

The **marché** is held on a square often named **la place du Marché,** and merchants are lined up in rows of temporary booths covered with a canopy in case of rain. The **marché** is principally a food market where people enjoy buying fresh vegetables and fruit that farmers bring and sell di-

Restaurant de fruits de mer

rectly to the consumers. Although it is not as common as it used to be, it is still possible to buy live chickens and rabbits in some markets.

Southern markets, like the one in Antibes, are very picturesque. The smell of olive oil and spices used in **Provençal** cooking fill the air. Other ingredients that characterize the cuisine of southern France, such as garlic, anchovies, and green and red peppers, are available in abundance at open-air booths.

Another enjoyable experience at open-air markets is the opportunity to taste various foods. For instance, before buying cheese, it is perfectly all right to sample several varieties. This is also true with other products such as **pâtés, saucissons,** and other foods available at the delicatessen.

Etudions le dialogue

1. Où Anne passe-t-elle ses vacances?
2. Qu'est-ce que Nathalie et Anne vont faire?
3. Pourquoi Anne ne veut-elle pas apprendre les noms des fromages?
4. Pourquoi Anne n'aime-t-elle pas voir les poulets?
5. Qu'est-ce que les parents de Nathalie vont servir dimanche?
6. Pourquoi Anne ne mange-t-elle pas de viande?

Enrichissons notre vocabulaire

Les repas *(Meals)*

le petit déjeuner	*breakfast*
le déjeuner	*lunch*
le dîner	*dinner*

Des hors-d'œuvre *(Appetizers)*

des carottes râpées	*grated carrots*	une salade de tomates	*a sliced tomato salad*
des crudités	*vegetable salad*	une salade de concombres	*a sliced cucumber salad*
un œuf, des œufs	*eggs*	du saucisson	*hard salami*
du pâté	*pâté*		

Des plats principaux *(Main dishes)*

du bœuf	*beef*	une côtelette de porc	*a pork chop*
un rosbif	*a roast*		
un bifteck	*a steak*	un rôti de porc	*a pork roast*
un filet de sole	*a filet of sole*	du veau	*veal*
une truite	*a trout*	une escalope de veau	*a veal steak*
du porc	*pork*		

Des légumes *(Vegetables)*

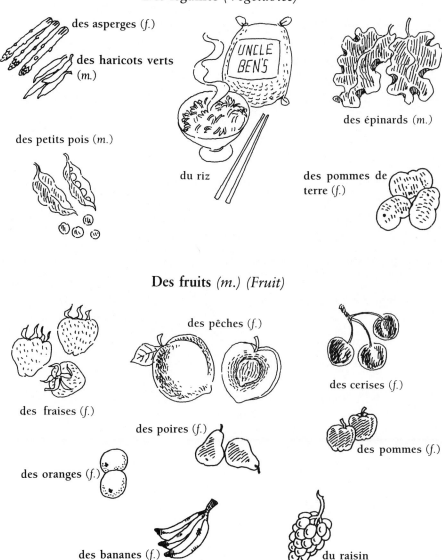

des asperges (f.)

des haricots verts (m.)

des petits pois (m.)

du riz

des épinards (m.)

des pommes de terre (f.)

Des fruits *(m.) (Fruit)*

des pêches (f.)

des cerises (f.)

des fraises (f.)

des poires (f.)

des pommes (f.)

des oranges (f.)

des bananes (f.)

du raisin

Prononciation   The French / R / Sound

To pronounce the French / R / sound, tuck in the tip of your tongue behind your lower teeth, and curve the back of your tongue toward the roof of your mouth. The words **gaz** (/ gaz /) and **rase** (/ Raz /) are almost identical, except that with the / g / sound, the back of your tongue touches the roof of your mouth, while with the / R / sound, there is a small gap that causes friction.

Exercices

A. Practice the /R/ sound preceded by a consonant in the following words by repeating them after your teacher.

> crème / cravate / grand / grammaire / groupe /
> crêpe / crevettes / crudités

B. Practice the /R/ sound in the middle of the following words by repeating them after your teacher.

> Marie / admirer / africain / agréable / heureux /
> parapluie / différent / marché

C. Practice the /R/ sound at the end of the following words by repeating them after your teacher.

> alors / lecture / lettre / mer / milliard / sur /
> porc / leur

D. Practice the /R/ sound at the beginning of the following words by repeating them after your teacher.

> radio / rapide / regarder / regretter / rentrer /
> repas / riz / rosbif

E. Repeat the following sentences after your teacher, paying particular attention to the /R/ sound.

1. Brigitte travaille au restaurant.
2. Il va faire du brouillard à Londres mardi.
3. Marie a perdu son portefeuille dans le parc.
4. Christine et son mari apprécient l'art moderne.
5. Beaucoup d'Américains vont avoir froid cet hiver.
6. La librairie ferme à trois heures le vendredi.

GRAMMAIRE ·

I. Prenominal Adjectives

> You use adjectives to describe people and things.

A. As you learned in Chapter 2, an adjective agrees in gender and number with the noun it modifies, and it usually follows the noun.

> Mes parents ont préparé un repas **délicieux** hier soir.
> On peut manger un fromage **différent** tous les jours.

There is, however, a group of frequently used adjectives that must precede the noun. The following chart gives the most common ones.

singular		plural		
masculine	**feminine**	**masculine**	**feminine**	**meaning**
ancien	ancienne	anciens	anciennes	*former, old*
autre	autre	autres	autres	*other*
beau	belle	beaux	belles	*beautiful, handsome*
bon	bonne	bons	bonnes	*good*
cher	chère	chers	chères	*dear*
dernier	dernière	derniers	dernières	*last*
grand	grande	grands	grandes	*big, great*
gros	grosse	gros	grosses	*big*
jeune	jeune	jeunes	jeunes	*young*
joli	jolie	jolis	jolies	*pretty*
mauvais	mauvaise	mauvais	mauvaises	*bad*
nouveau	nouvelle	nouveaux	nouvelles	*new*
pauvre	pauvre	pauvres	pauvres	*poor*
petit	petite	petits	petites	*small, little*
premier	première	premiers	premières	*first*
propre	propre	propres	propres	*own, clean*
vieux	vieille	vieux	vieilles	*old*

Regarde tous ces **gros** poissons.   Ce sont de **petites** crevettes.

B. Because these adjectives precede the noun, **liaison** is obligatory when the noun begins with a vowel sound.

> J'ai téléphoné à un **bon** ami.
> Les Wright ont fait le **premier** avion.
> Elle a invité ses **bons** amis.

C. Because of **liaison,** there are some irregular adjective forms. Before masculine singular nouns that begin with a vowel, you will find:

beau → **bel**	Le Concorde est un **bel** avion.
nouveau → **nouvel**	La classe a commencé un **nouvel** exercice.
vieux → **vieil**	Il a vu un **vieil** ami.

It will help you to remember that when a masculine singular noun begins with a vowel sound, the preceding adjective sounds like its feminine form. For example, in the following phrases, **bon** and **bonne** and **vieil** and **vieille** are pronounced the same.

> un **bon** étudiant, une **bonne**   un **vieil** ami, une **vieille** amie
> étudiante

D. A few adjectives may come either before or after the noun, but they change meaning according to their position.

un **ancien** professeur	*a former teacher*
une église **ancienne**	*an old church*
la **dernière** semaine	*the last week (of a series)*
la semaine **dernière**	*last week*
un **pauvre** homme	*a poor man (unfortunate)*
un homme **pauvre**	*a poor man (no money)*
ma **propre** voiture	*my own car*
une voiture **propre**	*a clean car*
un **cher** ami	*a dear friend*
un cadeau **cher**	*an expensive gift*

E. Adjectives can be used alone as nouns.

Les **pauvres** ne mangent pas bien.
Les **jeunes** vont aller voir les **vieux**.

ATTENTION

1. Whenever the indefinite article **des** is followed by an adjective, it becomes **de**.

Ils vendent **des** cerises.	Ils vendent **de belles** cerises.
Ce sont **des** amis	Ce sont **de vieux** amis.

but: Ce sont **des marchands désagréables.**

2. In **liaison**, the masculine form of **grand** is pronounced with a /t/ sound, and the masculine form of **gros** and other adjectives ending in s (**anciens, pauvres,** etc.) are pronounced with a /z/ sound.

un grand‿appartement, un grand‿homme
un gros‿oeuf, les gros‿avions
de bons‿amis, de belles‿olives

Langue

A. En ville. Donnez le contraire de l'adjectif en italique dans les phrases suivantes.

MODELE: J'ai une *petite* voiture.
            J'ai une grande voiture.

1. Il habite un *petit* appartement.
2. C'est un *bon* restaurant.
3. Ces *jeunes* employés travaillent beaucoup.
4. Je n'ai pas vu tes *dernières* photos de la ville.
5. Est-ce que c'est un *nouvel* hôtel?
6. Il a acheté une cravate *laide* dans ce magasin.

B. **Mon ami arrive.** Ajoutez la forme appropriée des adjectifs entre parenthèses aux noms en italique dans les phrases suivantes. Faites attention à la place de l'adjectif.

MODELE: Nous avons voyagé dans un *avion*   (gros)
   Nous avons voyagé dans un gros avion.

1. Un *ami* arrive de New York.   (bon)
2. Nous avons visité des *églises*.   (joli)
3. Nous avons parlé avec des *enfants*.   (jeune)
4. Avez-vous trouvé un *appartement* pour votre ami?   (beau)
5. Il a déjà invité des *amis*.   (sympathique)
6. Est-ce qu'il y a beaucoup d'*écoles* près d'ici?   (bon)

Culture

C. **En France ou aux Etats-Unis?** Formez des phrases avec les mots donnés et dites *(tell)* si la phrase décrit *(describes)* la France ou les Etats-Unis.

1. On / aimer / gros / voitures
2. jeune / gens / pouvoir / avoir / voiture / à seize ans
3. vieux / personnes / habiter / avec / leur / enfants
4. On / avoir / grand / universités / dans / petit / villes
5. On / prendre / bon / petit / déjeuner / tous les matins
6. «18» / être / très / bon / note
7. On / pouvoir / acheter / joli / petit / tartes / délicieux
8. nouveau / trains / être / rapide

Communication

D. **Votre vie à l'université.** Donnez votre opinion en repondant aux questions suivantes. Commencez vos réponses avec «**C'est...** » ou «**Ce sont...** ».

MODELE: Votre cours de français est facile ou difficile?
   C'est un cours facile.

1. Votre université est grande ou petite?
2. La cuisine du restaurant universitaire est délicieuse ou affreuse?
3. L'idée d'étudier l'informatique est bonne ou mauvaise?
4. Vos vêtements sont nouveaux ou vieux?
5. Votre professeur est jeune ou vieux?
6. Vos réponses en classe sont bonnes ou mauvaises? intelligentes ou stupides?

E. Qu'est-ce que vous avez acheté récemment? Qu'est-ce que vous avez depuis longtemps? Utilisez la liste page 218 ou vos propres idées.

MODELE: *J'ai un nouveau vélo.   J'ai une vieille voiture.*

appartement	cravate	imperméable	sac à dos
pantalon	auto	Walkman	robe
bicyclette	chaussures	chaîne stéréo	magnétophone
calculatrice	magnétoscope	cassette	répondeur

F. **Questions personnelles.** Vos préférences

1. Quels restaurants aimez-vous mieux? (simples ou chers?)
2. Quelles sortes d'amis avez-vous? (bons? sincères?)
3. Quelles sortes de villes voulez-vous visiter? (vieilles ou modernes?)
4. Quelle sorte de maison habitez-vous? (petite? grande? blanche?)
5. Quelles autos aimez-vous? (petites? grandes? économiques? chères?)
6. Quelle sorte de musique écoutez-vous? (classique? moderne?)

II. -re Verbs

You use verbs to describe actions or states of being.

A. Verbs with infinitives ending in **-re** drop the **-re** and add the following endings:

attendre *(to wait for)*	
j' **attends**	nous **attendons**
tu **attends**	vous **attendez**
il / elle / on **attend**	ils / elles **attendent**
Passé composé: il **a attendu**	

Mots clés

attendre	*to wait for*	rendre	*to give back, to*
descendre	*to go down,*		*return*
	come down;	rendre visite à	*to visit (a*
	to get off		*person)*
entendre	*to hear*	répondre à	*to answer*
perdre	*to lose*	vendre	*to sell*
perdre patience	*to lose patience*		

Où est-ce qu'on **vend** des fruits de mer?
Les étudiants **attendent** leur courrier.

B. The final **d** of the third-person singular of **-re** verbs has a /t/ sound with inversion, so using **-t-** with inversion is not necessary.

> **Répond-il** à ta lettre?

C. The imperative of **-re** verbs is regular; the **s** is not deleted from the **tu** form.

> **Descendons** maintenant!   **Attendez** le facteur.
> Ne **perds** pas ton portefeuille.

D. The past participle is formed by dropping **-re** and adding **u.**

> J'ai **perdu** mon parapluie.   Il a **vendu** sa maison.

E. **Descendre** is conjugated with **être** in the **passé composé.**

> Nous sommes **descendus** à Juan-les-Pins.

ATTENTION

The difference in pronunciation between the singular and plural third-person forms in the present tense is the /d/ sound. You must make an extra effort to pronounce this sound when using the plural form of the verb to distinguish it clearly from the singular form.

> il perd /il pɛʀ/   ils perdent /il pɛ ʀd/
> elle rend /ɛl ʀã/   elles rendent /ɛl ʀãd/

Langue

A. Mettez les phrases suivantes au passé composé.

1. Jacques perd beaucoup de temps.
2. A quelle heure va-t-il descendre ce soir?
3. Nous les attendons devant le café.
4. Le marchand va vendre beaucoup de fraises.
5. Entend-elle le téléphone?
6. Quand allez-vous rendre votre voiture?

B. **A l'aéroport.** Complétez le paragraphe suivant avec la forme appropriée d'un verbe en **-re.**

Je suis à l'aéroport Charles-de-Gaulle à Roissy, près de Paris. J(e) _____ l'avion pour New York. J(e) _____ mon imperméable et je demande à un employé où est le bureau des objets trouvés. Il _____ : « _____ . Vous allez le trouver en face du magasin où on _____ des timbres.» J(e) _____ et je vois un autre employé. «Pardon, Monsieur. J(e) _____ mon imperméable. L'a-t-on trouvé?» Il ne _____ pas et j(e) _____ patience.

Culture

C. **Au bureau de tabac.** Un bureau de tabac est un magasin où on vend beaucoup de choses, comme dans un *convenience store* aux Etats-Unis. Dites si on vend ou si on ne vend pas les choses page 220 dans un bureau de tabac. Suivez le modèle.

MODELE: Cigarettes?
Oui, on vend des cigarettes.

1. bonbons   3. télécartes   5. stylos   7. timbres
2. olives   4. cartes postales 6. ceintures   8. lapins

D. **Des confrontations célèbres.** Qui a perdu?

1. les Anglais / Guillaume le Conquérant en 1066
2. les Français / les Anglais dans la guerre de Sept Ans
3. Danton / Robespierre pendant la Révolution
4. Les Français / les Prussiens en 1871
5. les Allemands / les résistants en 1945
6. Jacques Chirac / Mitterrand en 1988

Communication

E. Qu'est-ce que vous avez perdu récemment? votre transistor? votre stylo? vos clés? votre portefeuille? votre argent? votre calculette? votre livre de français? Pendant combien de temps l'avez-vous cherché? L'avez-vous retrouvé? Où?

F. **Questions personnelles.** Vos habitudes

1. Vous rendez des cadeaux? Quelle sorte de cadeau rendez-vous toujours?
2. Quand vous empruntez quelque chose, est-ce que vous le rendez toujours?
3. Chez vous, qui répond au téléphone?
4. Quels musiciens avez-vous entendus cette année?
5. Faites-vous du sport? Dans quel sport perdez-vous souvent?
6. A qui allez-vous rendre visite ce mois-ci?

III. Indirect Object Pronouns: Third Person

> You use indirect object pronouns to refer to people and things already mentioned in a conversation that receive the action of the verb.

A. Introduction

In Chapter 8 you learned direct object pronouns, which receive the action of the verb (**La clé? Je l'ai perdue.**). An indirect object indicates *to whom* or *to what* this action is directed.

He sold the car *to John.* *or* He sold the car *to him.*
He sold *John* the car. *or* He sold *him* the car.

In these examples, *John* is the indirect object, since the action of selling the car is directed to him. The examples also show that the indirect object noun, *John,* may be replaced with an indirect object pronoun, *him.*

B. Third-Person Indirect Object Pronouns

	singular	plural
masculine		
feminine	lui	leur

1. A pronoun can also replace the indirect object noun in French.
   The masculine and feminine singular form, **lui,** means *(to) him /
   (to) her.*

   L'étudiant répond **au professeur?** → L'étudiant **lui** répond?
   Sylvie rend les CD **à son amie.** → Sylvie **lui** rend les CD.

   The masculine and feminine plural form, **leur,** means *(to) them.*

   On a demandé **aux enfants** leur nom. → On **leur** a demandé
   leur nom.
   Elle téléphone **à ses copines.** → Elle **leur** téléphone.

2. Indirect objects are somewhat easier to identify in French than in English because an indirect object noun is almost always preceded by the
   preposition **à.**

   Il a vendu des bonbons **à Jean-Paul.** → Il **lui** a vendu des bonbons.

C. Position of Indirect Object Pronouns

1. The correct position of indirect object pronouns is the same as that of
   direct object pronouns: they precede the verb from which the action is
   directed.

Present	**Passé composé**
Je **leur** apporte des fraises.	Nous ne **leur** avons pas téléphoné hier.
Luc ne **lui** prête pas son auto.	Elle **lui** a montré les lapins au marché.

2. Past participles do not agree with preceding indirect objects, as they
   do with preceding direct objects.

   A qui ont-elles donné la pomme?
   Elles l'ont donn**ée** au professeur.

   but: Elles lui ont donn**é** la pomme.

3. Indirect object pronouns follow helping verbs.

   Il va **leur** servir des crudités.　　　Vous ne pouvez pas **lui**
   répondre?

4. In negative commands, indirect object pronouns precede the verb.

Ne **lui** téléphonez pas
maintenant.

Ne **leur** montrez pas ma lettre.

5. The position of pronouns is irregular in affirmative commands. Both direct and indirect object pronouns are placed after the verb and joined with a hyphen.

Regarde-le!
Vendez-les tout de suite!

Apportez-lui une pêche.
Servons-leur du riz avec les crevettes.

Mots clés Verbs that take indirect objects

acheter	obéir
apporter / rapporter	parler
commander	passer
demander	poser une question *to ask a question*
désobéir	préparer
donner	présenter *to introduce*
emprunter / prêter	recommander
expédier	rendre
expliquer	répéter
faire mal	répondre
indiquer *to indicate*	ressembler *to resemble*
laisser	servir
mentir	téléphoner
montrer	vendre

ATTENTION

French verbs do not always take the same kind of object as their English equivalents. Translating will not always help determine whether a direct object pronoun or an indirect object pronoun should be used.

1. **Attendre, chercher, demander, écouter,** and **regarder** take a direct object in French, but are followed by a preposition in English.

Je cherche **le métro.** → Je le cherche.
Il a demandé **cette poire.** → Il l'a demandée.
Nous allons écouter **la radio.** → Nous allons l'écouter.
J'ai regardé **ses poissons.** → Je les ai regardés.

2. **Obéir à, désobéir à, téléphoner à, rendre visite à, répondre à,** and **ressembler à** take indirect objects in French but take direct objects in English.

Ils ont obéi **à l'agent de police.** → Ils **lui** ont obéi.
Téléphone **à Jacques.** → Téléphone-**lui.**
Elle ressemble **à sa mère.** → Elle **lui** ressemble.

Langue

A. **A la résidence.** Répondez aux questions suivantes en utilisant des pronoms compléments d'objet indirect.

1. Est-ce que Jacques a rendu ses devoirs à son prof?   (Oui,...)
2. Vous ne servez pas de bière à vos amis?   (Non,... cocas.)
3. Tu ne veux pas parler aux autres?   (Si,...)
4. On va servir des repas aux pauvres?   (Oui,...)
5. Paul a-t-il téléphoné à son copain.   (Non,...)
6. Peux-tu demander l'adresse à Jacqueline?   (Oui,...)

B. **Vous avez invité Monique hier soir?** Refaites les phrases suivantes selon les indications entre parenthèses.

1. Vous lui servez du bifteck et des haricots verts?   (... hier soir)
2. Je lui ai montré mon ordinateur.   (... nouveau...)
3. Ne lui demandez pas de sortir le week-end prochain!   *(make affirmative)*
4. Elle ressemble *à ses parents.*   *(use a pronoun)*
5. Je lui présente mes amis.   (Le week-end prochain...)
6. Nous lui donnons un beau cadeau.   *(give a command)*

Culture

C. **Les pourboires.** A qui est-ce qu'on donne un pourboire *(tip)* en France? Est-ce qu'on le donne toujours, pour un service spécial, ou jamais?

MODELE: garçon de café
On ne lui donne jamais de pourboire. (Le service est compris.)

1. le marchand
2. l'ouvreuse *(usher)*
3. le facteur
4. le médecin
5. les agents de police
6. les hôtesses du Syndicat d'Initiative
7. les chauffeurs de taxi
8. les garçons de restaurant

Communication

D. Vous avez vu un très bel homme / une très belle femme et vous voulez le / la revoir. Qu'est-ce que vous pouvez faire pour arranger un rendez-vous? Utilisez les suggestions données ou vos propres idées.

MODELE: *Je lui demande son nom.*

parler après la classe
téléphoner ce soir
demander s'il / si elle veut sortir
inviter chez moi
donner mon adresse

présenter mes amis
parler de son futur
servir...
montrer mes timbres
???

E. Voyez-vous souvent les personnes suivantes? Leur téléphonez-vous? Tous les combien *(How often)?* Utilisez les suggestions données ou vos propres idées.

MODELE: votre frère
Je ne le vois pas souvent, mais je lui téléphone toutes les semaines.

vos amis	tous les jours / mois / ans
vos parents	toutes les heures / semaines
votre frère / sœur	une / deux / trois fois
votre petit(e) ami(e)	par jour / semaine / mois
vos grands-parents	souvent / pas souvent
votre camarade de chambre	rarement
votre professeur	ne... jamais

F. Que pouvez-vous dire *(say)* à vos amis dans les trois situations suivantes?

1. Ils ont un invité *(guest)* important.

   MODELE: présenter vos amis   *Présentez-lui vos amis.*

   servir une boisson / montrer votre
       appartement / ne... pas demander leur âge /
       ne... pas laisser seul / parler du temps

2. Leur professeur les a invités à dîner.

   apporter un cadeau / demander comment il / elle va /
       admirer pour son travail / ne... pas
       demander d'argent / ne... pas expliquer vos
       absences / ne... pas parler de l'examen final

3. Ils vont visiter le campus avec des étudiants de première année.

   montrer la librairie / le laboratoire, etc. / ne... pas recommander
       le restaurant universitaire / parler des cours faciles / ne... pas
       inviter dans les bars / ne... pas vendre de billets pour la
       bibliothèque

G. **Questions personnelles: Vos habitudes.** Utilisez des pronoms compléments d'objet indirect dans vos réponses.

1. Avez-vous téléphoné à vos parents récemment? Pourquoi?
2. Qu'est-ce que vous allez demander au Père Noël *(Santa Claus)* cette année?
3. Prêtez-vous votre voiture à vos amis? vos CD? vos vêtements?
4. A qui désobéissez-vous souvent?
5. Qu'est-ce que vous servez à vos amis quand ils dînent chez vous?
6. Qu'est-ce que vous allez apporter à vos professeurs le dernier jour de cours?

IV. Prendre

> You use the verb **prendre** to express the idea *to take* and, when referring to food or drink, to express *to have* or *to eat*.

	prendre	*(to take; to have [food])*	
je **prends**	/pʀɑ̃/	nous **prenons**	/pʀø nɔ̃/
tu **prends**	/pʀɑ̃/	vous **prenez**	/pʀø ne/
il / elle / on **prend**	/pʀɑ̃/	ils / elles **prennent**	/pʀɛn/

Passé composé: il **a pris**

A. Although its infinitive ends in **-re**, **prendre** is not conjugated like the **-re** verbs you learned earlier in this chapter. In the present, the differences are in the plural forms. Because of these differences, **prendre** has three different vowel sounds in the present tense: /pʀɑ̃/, /pʀø nɔ̃/, and /pʀɛn/.

> On **prend** le métro pour aller au marché.
> Nous **prenons** quel autobus?
> Ils ne **prennent** pas le train aujourd'hui?

B. The verb **prendre** can also mean *to have* or *to eat* when used with foods and drinks, replacing **manger.** It *must* be used with the names of meals.

> Je ne **prends** pas de porc. Qu'est-ce que tu **prends?**
> Ils ne **prennent** pas de petit déjeuner.
> On **prend** le dîner à huit heures.

C. The past participle of **prendre** is **pris,** and its s is pronounced when preceded by a feminine direct object.

> Nous **avons pris** des poires.   Cette **photo?** Je ne **l'ai** pas **prise.**

D. Apprendre *(to learn)* and **comprendre** *(to understand)* are conjugated like **prendre.**

> —Est-ce que tu **comprends** le français?
> —Oui, je **l'ai appris** à l'école.

While **apprendre** means *to learn (how to),* **apprendre à** + *a person* means *to teach.* This expression can be followed by a noun or **à** plus an infinitive.

> Il apprend l'italien **aux** étudiants.
> Il apprend **aux** étudiants à parler italien.

ATTENTION

Since the letter **d** has a /t/ sound in **liaison,** there is no need to add **-t-** with inversion of the third-person singular form of **prendre** and verbs conjugated like it.

> **Prend-elle** l'avion ce matin?
> **Apprend-il** le russe?

Langue

A. **A l'université.** Substituez le verbe entre parenthèses dans les phrases suivantes.

1. On entend l'arabe à l'université? (apprendre)
2. On vend des livres de chinois à la librairie. (prendre)
3. Est-ce que vous avez emprunté mon livre de maths? (prendre)
4. Etudiez l'allemand! (apprendre)
5. Nous rendons les notes de Jean-Paul. (ne... pas comprendre)
6. Je parle très bien l'italien. (comprendre)

B. **Interview avec une étudiante américaine.** Répondez aux questions suivantes avec les mots donnés. Remplacez les compléments d'objet direct en italique par des pronoms.

MODELE: Avez-vous pris *votre voiture* ce matin?   (Oui,...)
Oui, je l'ai prise.

1. Les étudiants comprennent-ils *leurs leçons?*   (Non, ils...)
2. Peuvent-ils apprendre *le japonais?*   (Oui,... vouloir...)
3. Et vous, apprenez-vous *le chinois?*   (Non,...)
4. Comprenez-vous *l'informatique?*   (Non,...)
5. Avez-vous pris *votre petit déjeuner* ce matin?   (Non,... plus tard.)
6. Avez-vous pris *l'autobus* récemment?   (Oui, la semaine dernière...)

Culture

C. **Les habitudes gastronomiques des Français.** Les habitudes des Français sont différentes de celles *(those)* des Américains quand il est question de manger. Formez des phrases avec les mots donnés, et si la phrase ne représente pas la réalité en France, ajoutez *(add)* **ne... pas.**

1. Français / prendre / café au lait / au dîner
2. Français / prendre / toujours / asperges / froid
3. En France / on / aller / restaurant / pour / prendre / petit déjeuner
4. On / prendre / œufs / petit déjeuner
5. On / prendre / dîner / à six heures du soir
6. Beaucoup de Français / prendre / fruit / comme dessert
7. On / prendre / vin rouge / avec / rosbif
8. On / prendre / salade / après / dîner

Communication

D. Décrivez *(Describe)* vos repas typiques en utilisant les suggestions suivantes ou vos propres idées. Précisez *(Specify)* l'heure, les plats, et les boissons.

MODELE: *A midi je prends un sandwich et un coca.*

Les plats

riz	glace	pizza
bifteck	asperges	frites
veau	fromage	œufs
gâteau	salade	sandwich

Les boissons

eau	café	vin
eau minérale	thé	coca
bière	lait	jus de fruit

E. **Jeu de rôles.** Vous allez dîner au restaurant. Avec un(e) camarade, jouez une des scènes suivantes.

1. Vous êtes végétariens.
2. Votre camarade est au régime, mais vous avez très faim.
3. Vous êtes snobs.
4. Vous êtes pauvre, mais votre camarade veut dépenser beaucoup d'argent.

F. **Questions personnelles.** Vos études

1. Quelles langues comprenez-vous? Et dans votre famille?
2. Qu'est-ce que vous apprenez à l'université?
3. Qu'est-ce que vous avez pris ce matin avant vos cours?
4. Que prenez-vous avant un examen?
5. Après vos cours, qu'est-ce que vous aimez prendre avec vos amis?
6. Qu'est-ce que vous avez appris à votre frère / à votre sœur / à votre ami(e)?

COMMUNIQUONS ....

Prendre les repas

French people usually have three complete meals a day. Breakfast is very light, consisting of **café au lait** or tea and bread or **croissants.** Lunch is much more substantial, often consisting of meat, vegetables, cheese, and wine. The French have traditionally taken a two-hour lunch break to go home or to a restaurant while offices, banks, and stores closed. This tradition is rapidly changing. Lunch breaks are shorter, fast-food restaurants have gained in popularity, and more and more businesses stay open during the lunch hour.

On prend quelque chose au café.

The French usually eat dinner at home and often begin as late as 8 P.M. «A table!» signals to everyone that a meal is ready. The first course, **les hors-d'œuvre,** can be cold cuts (**de la charcuterie**) or **des crudités,** for instance. Then the **plat principal** is served. Normally meat or fish, it is accompanied by vegetables. The last part of the meal consists of salad, cheese and fruit or dessert.

There are many differences in eating habits between France and America. In France, you should keep both hands on the table rather than keeping one on your lap. At informal dinners in France, bread does not have a special plate, but is put directly on the table. You generally do not put butter on bread, but you do on radishes! Milk and hot beverages are not drunk with meals. Plates are changed several times during the meal, but some people wipe them with a piece of bread. Finally, French people, as do all Europeans, eat with the fork in their left hand.

On met le couvert. *(One sets the table.)*

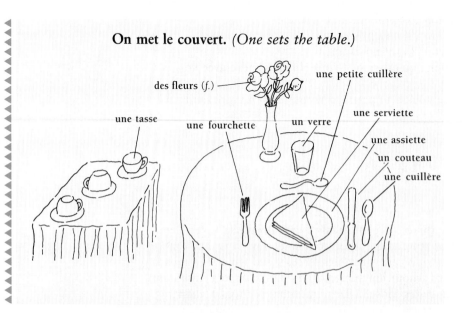

On parle pendant le repas.

Passe-moi du pain, s'il te plaît.	*Pass me the bread, please.*
Tu veux encore de l'eau?	*Do you want more water?*
Merci!	*No thanks.*
S'il te plaît!	*Yes, please.*

On est au restaurant.

Le maître d'hôtel leur montre leur table.	*The maître d' shows them to their table.*
Ils veulent voir la carte des vins.	*They want to see the wine list.*
Le garçon / La serveuse explique la carte et le menu.	*The waiter / The waitress explains the menu and the list of fixed-priced meals.*
Le plat du jour est délicieux.	*Today's special is delicious.*
On apporte l'addition.	*They bring the check.*
Ils donnent un pourboire au garçon.	*They give the waiter a tip.*
Boisson et service en sus.	*Drinks and tip are extra.*
Service compris.	*The tip is included.*
Payez à la caisse.	*Pay the cashier.*

Interaction *M. Marchand téléphone au restaurant Jamin pour réserver une table.*

LE MAITRE D'HOTEL: Allô, le restaurant Jamin.

M. MARCHAND: Bonjour, je voudrais réserver une table pour quatre ce soir.

LE MAITRE D'HOTEL: Attendez voir... Non, ce soir, nous sommes *complets*. Mais je veux bien prendre votre nom. Nous allons *peut-être* avoir une *annulation*.   *booked*   *perhaps / cancellation*

M. MARCHAND: Et demain soir?

LE MAITRE D'HOTEL: Oui, à quelle heure?

M. MARCHAND: Vingt heures trente?

LE MAITRE D'HOTEL: *C'est noté.* C'est à quel nom?   *I've got it.*

M. MARCHAND: Monsieur Marchand.

LE MAITRE D'HOTEL: *C'est convenu.* A demain soir.   *All right*

M. MARCHAND: A demain.

Activités

A. Expliquez comment vous préparez votre spécialité. Donnez votre recette *(recipe)* préférée à la classe.

   MODELE: *Je prends du sucre, de la farine...*

B. En petits groupes, demandez à vos camarades quels plats ils aiment et quels plats ils détestent. Ensuite, préparez un repas idéal et un repas affreux selon vos préférences et échangez vos idées avec vos camarades de cours.

C. Jouez les scènes suivantes avec un(e) camarade de cours.

   1. Vous êtes dans un restaurant et vous commandez un repas.
   2. Vous téléphonez à votre restaurant préféré pour réserver une table.
   3. Vous demandez au garçon / à la serveuse pourquoi votre repas est si *(so)* cher / froid / mauvais. (Choisissez!)

LECTURE CULTURELLE ....

Avant la lecture

Many French people love to travel during their free time, and they often use a detailed itinerary to help them with France's elaborate system of expressways, main highways, and secondary roads. Michelin, one of the world's major tire manufacturers, has a number of inexpensive publications to help travelers. Its maps and *Guides verts* help tourists find interesting places to visit in Europe. The company's best-seller, however, is the *Guide rouge* (the guides are named for the color of their covers). This guide is most known for its ratings of restaurants and hotels all across France. Just being mentioned in the guide is an honor for a restaurant, and receiving one, two, or three stars is a true distinction. In fact, there are only about twenty three-star restaurants in France.

Activités

A. Make a list of what kinds of information you would want to have before setting out on a long trip.

B. What would you want to know about a hotel or a restaurant before going in?

C. If you were writing a guidebook, what symbols would you use to indicate credit cards accepted, TV, a shower or bath in the room, a garage, and no pets?

Les Guides Michelin

En général, les Français ne partent pas en vacances sans prendre leurs guides et leurs cartes Michelin avec eux. La firme Michelin est célèbre *surtout* pour ses *pneus,* mais elle aide aussi les *voyageurs* en France et en Europe avec des *cartes routières* et des guides touristiques.

5   Les cartes Michelin sont excellentes. Elles indiquent *non seulement* les routes mais aussi les curiosités locales (de vieilles églises, de beaux panoramas, des sites pittoresques). Les cartes sont extrêmement *détaillées* et *permettent* aux touristes de choisir un itinéraire *selon* leurs préférences. Les touristes *pressés* prennent les autoroutes ou les routes nationales, mais les petites routes 10 servent aux touristes sérieux.

Si vous voulez visiter une région pendant plusieurs jours, vous pouvez acheter un *Guide vert.* Pour toute la France, Michelin offre une *vingtaine* de guides *(Châteaux de la Loire, Côte d'Azur, Alpes...).* Ils proposent des itinéraires variés selon la *longueur* de votre visite. Ils indiquent les monuments 15 historiques et expliquent l'architecture du pays. Ils sont très complets et *comportent* toujours une partie historique.

Michelin *publie* aussi le *Guide rouge.* Les Français l'appellent le *Guide Michelin* ou, simplement, *le Michelin.* En France, c'est la bible du voyageur. Une nouvelle édition sort tous les ans, et beaucoup de gens l'achètent 20 régulièrement. Toutes les villes et tous les villages sont présentés par ordre alphabétique. Il y a un plan de toutes les *agglomérations* importantes, mais on *insiste* surtout sur les hôtels et les restaurants. Le système de symboles adopté par Michelin *renseigne* les voyageurs sur la classe des *établissements* mentionnés.

25   Quand on cherche un hôtel dans une ville *inconnue, Le Michelin* donne les renseignements nécessaires sur la classe et le prix des établissements, mais il *contient* aussi un grand nombre de détails supplémentaires. Une série de symboles indique au voyageur si l'hôtel a un garage, un restaurant, l'*ascenseur.* On peut aussi savoir combien il y a de chambres; si elles sont avec *douche* ou avec 30 *salle de bains* et si elles ont le téléphone et la télévision. On apprend aussi si le petit déjeuner et les taxes sont compris. Il y a aussi une liste des cartes de crédit acceptées.

Le Michelin est célèbre principalement pour son évaluation des restaurants. Il accorde une, deux ou trois *étoiles* aux restaurants de qualité excep- 35 tionnelle. La France a seulement une vingtaine de restaurants trois étoiles. Dans ces restaurants on ne mange pas pour moins de cent dollars par personne, mais la cuisine et le service sont remarquables.

Après la lecture

Questions sur le texte

1. En général, qu'est-ce que les Français prennent quand ils partent en vacances?
2. Qu'est-ce que la firme Michelin fait?

---

particularly

tires / travelers

road maps

not only

detailed / allow

according to

in a hurry

around twenty

length

include

publishes

metropolitan areas

emphasize

informs / establishments

unknown

includes

elevator

shower

bathroom

stars

Annuellement vôtre

MICHELIN

	Grand luxe	XXXXX
	Grand confort	XXXX
	Très confortable	XXX
	De bon confort	XX
	Assez confortable	X
	Simple mais convenable	

	La table vaut le voyage
	La table mérite un détour
	Une très bonne table
R 70/110	Repas soigné à prix modérés
	Petit déjeuner
enf. 15	Menu enfant

	Menu à moins de 65 F

	Hôtels agréables
XXX...X	Restaurants agréables
	Vue exceptionnelle
	Vue intéressante ou étendue
	Situation très tranquille, isolée
	Situation tranquille

	Repas au jardin ou en terrasse
	Piscine en plein air ou couverte
	Jardin de repos - Tennis à l'hôtel

	Ascenseur
	Non fumeur
	Air conditionné
	Téléphone dans la chambre
	Téléphone direct
	Accessible aux handicapés physiques
	Parking - Garage
	Salles de conférence, séminaire
	Accès interdit aux chiens

Les plans

	Hôtels
	Restaurants

Curiosités

	Bâtiment intéressant et entrée principale
	Édifice religieux intéressant : Catholique - Protestant

Voirie

	Autoroute, double chaussée de type autoroutier échangeur : complet, partiel, numéro
	Grande voie de circulation
	Sens unique - Rue impraticable
	Rue piétonne - Tramway
Pasteur	Rue commerçante - Parc de stationnement
	Porte - Passage sous voûte - Tunnel
	Gare et voie ferrée
	Bac pour autos - Pont mobile

Signes divers

	Information touristique
	Mosquée - Synagogue
	Tour - Ruines - Moulin à vent - Château d'eau
	Jardin, parc, bois - Cimetière - Calvaire
	Stade - Golf - Patinoire - Hippodrome
	Piscine de plein air, couverte
	Table d'orientation - Vue - Panorama
	Funiculaire - Téléphérique, télécabine
	Monument, statue - Fontaine - Usine
	Port de plaisance - Phare
	Transport par bateau : passagers et voitures, passagers seulement

Bâtiment public repéré par une lettre :

A C	Chambre d'agriculture - Chambre de commerce
G H J	Gendarmerie - Hôtel de ville - Palais de justice
M P T	Musée - Préfecture, sous-préfecture - Théâtre
U	Université, grande école
POL	Police (commissariat central)

(3)	Repère commun aux plans et aux cartes Michelin détaillées
	Bureau principal de poste restante et téléphone
	Hôpital - Marché couvert - Caserne
	Tour ou pylône de télécommunications
	Aéroport - Station de métro - Gare routière
	Passage bas (inf. à 4 m 50) - Pont à charge limitée (inf. à 19 t.)
	Garage : Peugeot, Talbot, Citroën - Renault (Alpine)

Paris 137 – Bernay 14 – Évreux 35 – Lisieux 38 – Le Neubourg 16 – Pont-Audemer 33 – ✳Rouen 49.

XX **Soleil d'Or** avec ch, ℰ 32 45 00 08, 🐴 – ☎ 🅟 E 🆚🆇
fermé fév. et merc. du 1er sept. au 30 juin – **R** 83/195 – ☲ 32 – **12 ch** 160/280.

PEUGEOT-TALBOT Gar. Chaise, N 13 à Nassandres ℰ 32 45 00 33 🅽

ROANNE <🚗> 42300 Loire 🆒 🄸 ⑥ G. Vallée du Rhône – 49 638 h.

Env. Belvédère de Commelle-Vernay ❮ ✳ : 7 km au S par quai P. Sémard   BZ.

🏠 de Champlong ℰ 77 69 70 60 par ⑤.

🄸 Office de Tourisme avec A.C. cours République ℰ 77 71 51 77

Paris 390 ⑥ – Bourges 198 ⑤ – Chalon-sur-Saône 134 ① – ✳Clermont-Ferrand 105 ④ – ✳Dijon 202 ① – ✳Lyon 86 ⑥ – Montluçon 143 ⑤ – ✳St-Étienne 78 ③ – Valence 185 ③ – Vichy 74 ④.

🏨🏨🏨 **Côté 🄷 H. des Frères Troisgros** 🅼, pl. Gare ℰ 77 71 66 97, Télex 307507 – 🆎🆈 r
🔲 **rest** 🄴 🅐 🅓 E 🆚🆇 *fermé janv., merc. midi et mardi* – **R** (nombre de couverts limité - prévenir) 375/470
et carte – ☲ 60 – **17 ch** 475/600, 5 appart 1200
Spéc. Casse-tête aux truffes noires. Pièce de bœuf au Fleurie à la moelle. Strates au chocolat
guanaja Vins Pouilly-Fussé.

🏨🏨 **Gd Hôtel**, 18 cours République ℰ 77 71 48 82, Télex 300573 – 🛗 🅔 🅐 🅟 🅓 – 🔺 🆈🄵
100, 🄴 🅐 🅓 E 🆚🆇 *fermé 1er au 16 août et 23 déc. au 2 janv.* – **R** voir rest. L'Astrée ci-après – ☲ 30 –
38 ch 198/340.

🏨 **Terminus** sans rest, face gare ℰ 77 71 79 69, Fax 77 71 90 26 – 🛗 🐴 🅟 🅓 🅔 🆈🄵
🆚🆇 ☲ 25 – **55 ch** 175/280.

XX **L'Astrée** - Gd Hôtel, 17 bis cours République ℰ 77 72 74 22 – 🄴 🅐 🅓 E 🆚🆇   AY f
fermé 28 juil. au 21 août, 23 déc. au 11 janv., sam. et dim. – **R** 95/250.

XX **Côté Jardin**, 10 r. Benoit Malon ℰ 77 72 81 88 – 🄴 🆚🆇   BZ u
fermé sam. midi et dim. – **R** 89/220

au Coteau (rive droite de la Loire) – 8 380 h. – ☒ 42120 Le Coteau :

🏨🏨 **Artaud**, 133 av. Libération ℰ 77 68 46 44 – 🛗 🐴 🅟 🅓 – 🔺 150 E 🆚🆇   BZ e
fermé dim. – **R** (fermé 5 au 25 juil. et dim.) 85/260 🅙 – ☲ 25 – **25 ch** 205/350.

🏨 **Ibis** 🅼, 53 bd Ch. de Gaulle, ZI Le Coteau ℰ 77 68 36 22, Télex 300610, Fax
77 72 13 08 – 🐴 🅟 🅓 – 🔺 25 à 70 🄴 🅔 🆚🆇   BZ e
R (fermé dim. midi) carte 80 à 120 🅙 – ☲ 26 – **67 ch** 250/290.

XX **Aub. Costelloise** (Alex), 2 av. Libération ℰ 77 68 12 71 – 🄴 🆚🆇   BZ a
fermé 24 juil. au 24 août, 25 déc. au 4 janv., dim. et lundi – **R** carte 175 à 240
Spéc. Marinade de homard à infusion de marjolaine. Escalopes de foie gras chaud au gingembre.
Grande assiette des Côtes roannaises

X **Ma Chaumière**, 3 r. St-Marc ℰ 77 67 25 93 – 🆚🆇 🆐   BZ s
fermé 24 juil. au 20 août, dim. soir et lundi – **R** 80/220

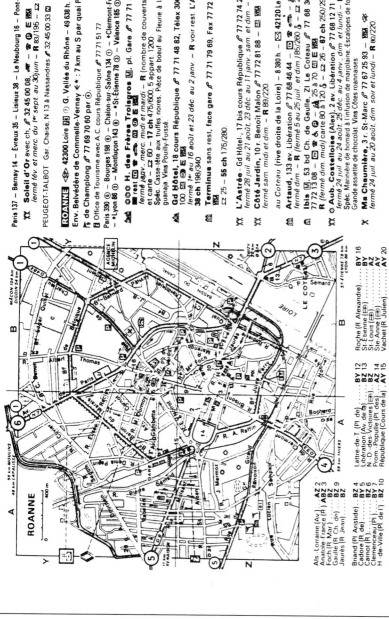

ROANNE

Als.-Lorraine (Av) .... **AZ** 2
Anatole-France (R.) ....) **ABZ** 3
Foch (R. Mar) .... **BZ** 9
Gaulle (R. Ch. de) .... **BZ**
Jaurès (R. Jean) .... **BZ**

Briand (Pl. Aristide) ...... **BZ** 4
Cadore (R. de) .... **BY** 5
Carnot (R.) .... **BZ** 6
Clemenceau (Pl.) .... **BY** 7
H.-de-Ville (Pl. de l') .... **BZ** 10

Lattre-de-T. (Pl. de) ...... **BY** 12
Libération (Av. de la) ..... **BY** 13
N.-D.-des-Victoires (🕂) ... **BZ**
Prom.-Populle (Pl. des) .... **AZ** 14
République (Cours de la) ... **BY** 15

Roche (R. Alexandre) .... **BY** 16
St-Étienne (🕂) .... **BY**
St-Louis (🕂) .... **AZ**
Ste-Anne .... **AY**
Vachet (R. Julien) .... **AY** 20

3. Qu'est-ce qu'elle publie?
4. Comment sont les cartes Michelin?
5. Pourquoi consulte-t-on un *Guide vert?*
6. Qu'est-ce qu'on trouve dans le *Guide rouge?*
7. Qu'est-ce que les symboles dans *le Michelin* indiquent?
8. Qu'est-ce que les étoiles du *Guide rouge* indiquent?

Activités

A. Obtain a guide of a motel chain or an AAA directory in North America and compare the symbols with those of the *Guide rouge* on page 232. What does the American guide not bother to indicate that is specified in the French guide?

B. Vous êtes à Roanne et vous consultez votre *Guide rouge* (page 233). Trouvez les renseignements suivants:

1. le numéro de téléphone de l'Office de Tourisme
2. la distance de Roanne à Paris
3. le nom d'un hôtel près de la gare
4. s'il est possible de manger à l'hôtel Terminus
5. le nom d'un très bon restaurant
6. le prix d'un repas dans ce restaurant
7. si le restaurant L'Astrée accepte les cartes de crédit
8. si ce restaurant est ouvert toute l'année

TOUS ENSEMBLE!

A. Refaites les phrases suivantes selon les indications entre parenthèses.

En cours

1. Il finit ses cours à onze heures. (Elles... midi.)
2. Elle a suivi un cours d'informatique. (... faire...)
3. Je ne comprends pas pourquoi ils dorment en classe.
   (Nous... il...)
4. Elle explique ce dialogue aux étudiants. (... apprendre...
   leçon...)
5. Ils font de l'italien. (... étudier...)

Au café

6. Ils finissent cette bière froide. (... servir... bon...)
7. Elle présente ses vieux amis à son fils. (... ami... fille.)
8. Nous allons voir nos copains ce soir. (... hier soir.)
9. Je prends du café quand il fait froid. (Ils... pleuvoir.)
10. Demain nous allons voir nos amis anglais ici. (Hier... bon...)

B. Répondez aux questions suivantes en employant les mots entre parenthèses.

En ville

1. Quel temps va-t-il faire demain? (... chaud et... pleuvoir.)
2. J'ai soif. Qu'est-ce que je peux prendre? (Prendre... eau!)
3. Qui choisit les films quand vous allez au cinéma?
   (Nos parents...)
4. Est-ce que vous êtes descendu en voiture? (Non,... prendre...
   taxi... parce que... brouillard.)
5. Qu'est-ce qu'ils font devant le café? (... attendre... amis.)

Chez vous

6. Est-ce que tes parents ont un répondeur? (Non... répondre
   eux-mêmes.)
7. Avez-vous donné de l'argent aux enfants? (Non... petit
   cadeau.)
8. Quels fruits prenez-vous? (... cerises.)
9. Va-t-il voir les filles? (Non... hier.)
10. Quelle sorte de vêtements a-t-il choisis? (... beau...)

C. Formez des phrases complètes en employant les mots donnés.

En famille

1. Ce / homme / ressembler / mère
2. Que / vous / voir / fenêtre?
3. Mes sœurs / sortir / souvent, / mais / elles / ne... pas / dormir assez
4. Qui / pouvoir / fermer / ce / porte?
5. Je / servir / thé / chaud / mon / père

Les études

6. Quel / cours / vous / choisir?
7. Nous / réussir / examen / maths?
8. Elle / vouloir / acheter / nouveau / ordinateur
9. Nous / faire / sciences économiques / automne
10. Ce / femmes / étudier / langues / étranger

D. Répondez aux questions suivantes selon les indications entre parenthèses et en remplaçant les mots en italique par des pronoms compléments.

1. Vous avez parlé *à vos amis?*   (Oui,...)
2. Avez-vous vu *son magnétophone?*   (Non,... pas encore...)
3. Elle apprend l'anglais *aux enfants?*   (Non,... le français.)
4. Est-ce que Christine veut acheter *cette robe?*   (Non,... détester.)
5. Nous allons inviter *les Ouellette* cette semaine?   (Non,... mois prochain.)
6. Il apprend *le chinois* à sa femme?   (Oui,...)
7. Est-ce qu'on fait *la vaisselle* maintenant?   (Non,... demain.)
8. Est-ce que j'ai perdu *mon livre de français?*   (Non,... oublier chez toi.)

E. Complétez les phrases suivantes logiquement *(logically)*.

1. Le dimanche à six heures, je...
2. Ce cours est...
3. En cours, nous ne pouvons pas...
4. Mes amis ne veulent pas...
5. Quand il pleut,...
6. Ce trimestre, je suis des cours...
7. De ma chambre, on peut voir...
8. Je ressemble à...

F. **Questions personnelles**

1. Quand vous mangez au restaurant, qu'est-ce que vous aimez prendre?
2. A quelle heure prenez-vous votre petit déjeuner?
3. Si vous allez en France l'été prochain, qu'est-ce que vous voulez manger?
4. Qu'est-ce que vous voulez apprendre?
5. Quel cours suivez-vous ce trimestre / semestre?

6. Quelles langues étrangères comprenez-vous?
7. A qui téléphonez-vous souvent?
8. Dans votre famille, qui désobéit souvent?
9. Où aimez-vous aller quand vous sortez?

ENTRE NOUS!

A. Avec un(e) camarade de cours, parlez de vos études le trimestre / semestre dernier, ce trimestre / semestre, et le trimestre / semestre prochain.

B. Interviewez un(e) camarade de cours sur ses rapports avec son / sa camarade de chambre. Utilisez les questions suivantes et des questions originales.

Vous l'aimez / le détestez? Vous l'écoutez toujours?
Vous lui téléphonez souvent? Vous lui avez présenté votre
Vous lui donnez des cadeaux? famille?
Vous lui prêtez des vêtements?

C. Quels bons films avez-vous vus? Choisissez un film et racontez-le à vos camarades de cours, mais ne leur donnez pas le titre *(title)*. Ils vont le deviner *(guess)*.

D. Avec un(e) autre étudiant(e), préparez un voyage pour le week-end prochain. Avec qui et comment allez-vous voyager? Qu'est-ce que vous voulez visiter? Qui est-ce que vous voulez voir?

E. En groupes de trois ou quatre personnes, faites des interviews pour connaître les réponses aux questions suivantes.

1. Qu'est-ce que tu voudrais apprendre à faire?
2. Où peux-tu aller pour l'apprendre?
3. Qu'est-ce que tu peux apprendre à une autre personne?
4. A qui veux-tu apprendre quelque chose?

F. **Jeu de rôles.** Jouez les scènes suivantes.

1. Vous sortez avec un(e) ami(e). Choisissez un restaurant et un film à voir.
2. Un(e) camarade de cours téléphone et il / elle veut sortir avec vous. Vous ne l'aimez pas. Trouvez des excuses.
3. Vous êtes journaliste et vous interviewez une célébrité.
4. Vous êtes au marché en plein air et vous achetez vos provisions.

Chapitre 10

EN VOITURE

A Louvain, en Belgique

COMMENÇONS ....

On loue une voiture.

Trois étudiants américains font un voyage en Europe pendant les grandes vacances. Ils viennent d'arriver à l'aéroport de Zaventem à Bruxelles et ils sont allés au bureau de la compagnie de location de voitures Avis.

L'EMPLOYEE: Bonjour, vous avez besoin d'une voiture?

JANE: Oui, nous l'avons réservée aux Etats-Unis et nous l'avons payée.

L'EMPLOYEE: Très bien. Mais vous savez, il faut régler la T.V.A. en Belgique quand vous rendez la voiture.

JANE: Nous ne savions pas cela quand nous l'avons louée. Est-ce qu'il y a d'autres frais?

L'EMPLOYEE: L'assurance tous risques est en plus. Elle n'est pas obligatoire, mais si vous ne connaissez pas bien les habitudes des conducteurs européens, elle est presque indispensable.

JANE: Oui, d'accord. Je vais payer avec ma carte de crédit. Est-ce que la voiture est automatique?

L'EMPLOYEE: Oui. C'est une Renault 25. Tenez, voilà les papiers à signer et les clés.

AVIS

LA CARTE CLE WIZARD,

LA LOCATION EN UN TEMPS RECORD

DEMANDE (ou MODIFICATION) DE CARTE-CLÉ WIZARD
Cette carte vous est délivrée gratuitement

> Veuillez compléter en lettres capitales.
> Si vous demandez une modification de votre carte Clé-Wizard, notez votre numéro Wizard ci-dessous ainsi que les éléments à corriger.
> ☐ Demande   ☐ Modification carte Clé-Wizard N° _____

> Veuillez indiquer le mode de paiement que vous préférez en cochant la case appropriée et en reportant, le cas échéant, le numéro de votre carte de crédit.
> ☐ AMERICAN EXPRESS   ☐ DINERS CLUB   ☐ CARTE BLEUE
> ☐ EUROCARD   ☐ AUTRE   ☐ PAIEMENT COMPTANT
> Numéro └┴┴┴┴┴┴┴┴┴┴┴┴┴┴┴┘

Mots clés

loue (louer)	*are renting*	frais *(m.)*	*costs*
grandes	*summer*	assurance tous	*full collision*
vacances *(f.)*	*vacation*	risques *(f.)*	*insurance*
viennent d'	*have just*	en plus	*extra*
(venir de)		obligatoire	*required*
aéroport *(m.)*	*airport*	connaissez	*know*
compagnie de	*rental*	(connaître)	
location	*company*	habitudes *(f.)*	*habits*
avez besoin de	*need*	conducteurs *(m.)*	*drivers*
(avoir besoin		européens	*European*
de)		presque	*almost*
réservée	*reserved*	indispensable	*indispensable*
payée	*paid for*	d'accord	*O.K.*
savez (savoir)	*know*	carte de crédit	*credit card*
régler	*pay*	automatique	*automatic*
T.V.A. (Taxe à	*value-added*		*(transmission)*
la valeur	*tax*	Tenez.	*Here.*
ajoutée)		papiers *(m.)*	*papers*
savions (savoir)	*did know*	signer	*sign*

La Grand-Place à Bruxelles

Faisons connaissance

Renting a car is an excellent, if expensive, way to see Europe. One reason that rentals are expensive is the **T.V.A.** This is a tax that many European countries add to purchases; it can be 33% of the total cost, or even more for luxury items. Another major expense in renting a car is additional insurance coverage. The deductible on standard coverage is quite high, making **assurance tous risques** a good idea for renters. In general, you must be at least 21 years old to rent a car in Europe; you must also produce a valid driver's license and a major credit card.

For many years, Belgium has been a popular point of arrival for American tourists who visit Europe. Sabena, the government-operated airline, was among the first European airlines to establish gateways in major American cities and to offer competitive transatlantic fares. Belgium also has a lot to offer to tourists. Cities like Brussels, **(Bruxelles),** Ghent **(Gand),** Bruges, and Liège contain historical treasures. Brussels is also very well known for its fine cuisine and for the luxury shops that line its **avenue Louise,** which is often compared to the **Champs-Elysées.**

Etudions le dialogue

1. Que font les trois étudiants américains à l'aéroport de Bruxelles?
2. Est-ce qu'ils ont déjà réservé une voiture? Où?
3. En Belgique, qu'est-ce qu'on paye en plus du prix de la location?
4. Quand paye-t-on la T.V.A.?
5. Quand est-il prudent de prendre une assurance tous risques?
6. Quelle sorte de voiture Jane et ses amis ont-ils louée?

Enrichissons notre vocabulaire

Une auto (A car)

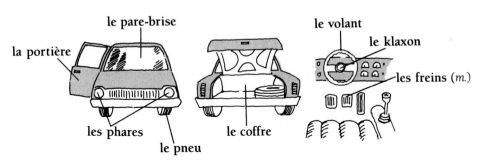

| les places (f.) | seats | | |
| le siège avant | front seat | le siège arrière | back seat |

La circulation (Traffic)

conduire	to drive	tomber en	to have a
démarrer	to start	panne	breakdown
un embouteillage	a traffic jam	une voiture	a brand-new
réparer	to repair	neuve	car
stationner	to park	une voiture	a second-hand
		d'occasion	car

Un accident *(An accident)*

la ceinture de sécurité	*seatbelt*
freiner	*to brake*
les gendarmes *(m.)*	*police officers*
le permis de conduire	*the driver's license*
la priorité à droite	*the right of way*
rouler à... kilomètres à l'heure	*to go... kilometers per hour*

Prononciation   The Mid Vowels / e / and / ɛ /

A. French has three pairs of mid vowels, so called because the mouth is neither fully open as with the / a / sound nor closed as with the / i / sound. With all three pairs, it is important to note whether a consonant sound follows the vowel sound.

B. The mid vowel sound / ɛ / is often followed by a consonant. It is pronounced with the mouth slightly open and the tongue forward.

Practice the / ɛ / sound by repeating the following words after your teacher.

treize / faire / laisse / cette / faites / laide

C. The mid vowel sound / e / is extremely tense, so you must be careful not to move your tongue or jaw when pronouncing it.

Repeat the following pairs of words after your teacher.

English	French
say	ses
day	des
bay	B

D. In French, a consonant sound never follows the / e / sound at the end of a word. Usual spellings for the / e / sound are -é, -ez, and -er. The letters z and r are silent.

Practice the /e/ sound by repeating the following words after your teacher.

allé / vous arrivez / réserver

Exercices

A. Repeat the following pairs of words after your teacher.

/e/	/ɛ/
1. les	laisse
2. B	bête
3. mes	mère

B. Now, practice the /e/ and /ɛ/ sounds in words of several syllables. Be sure to avoid diphthongizing the final /e/.

céder / chercher / acceptez / préféré / fermer / préparer

C. Read the following sentences aloud, keeping all vowels very tense.

1. Daniel fait des crêpes pour la fête de sa mère.
2. Cet employé a déjà fermé la fenêtre.
3. Visitez le musée près du café.
4. Merci pour ce verre de lait frais.
5. Elle est née en janvier l'année dernière.
6. Préférez-vous aller danser ou rester chez vous?

GRAMMAIRE ....

I. Savoir and connaître

> You use **connaître** and **savoir** to indicate that you know someone or something.

A. Forms

savoir	connaître
Present: je **sais**	je **connais**
tu **sais**	tu **connais**
il / elle / on **sait**	il / elle / on **connaît**
nous **savons**	nous **connaissons**
vous **savez**	vous **connaissez**
ils / elles **savent**	ils / elles **connaissent**
Passé composé: elle **a su**	il **a connu**

B. Uses

Savoir and **connaître** are rarely interchangeable.

1. **Savoir** means *to know a fact, to know very well,* or *to know how to do something.* Never use it to mean *to know people.*

   Je ne **sais** pas réparer cette voiture.
   Elle ne **sait** pas quelle sorte d'auto nous avons.
   Mais vous **savez,** il faut régler la T.V.A. en Belgique.

CE QU'ILS DISENT

In conversation, the French often drop the **ne** of **Je ne sais pas.** The **je** and **sais** combine to become / ʃe pa /

—Quelle heure est-il?
—J'sais pas.

2. **Connaître** means *to know, to be acquainted with,* or *to be familiar with.* Always use it to mean *to know people* or *places.*

   Je ne **connais** pas ce professeur.
   Connais-tu Bruxelles?

3. Another verb conjugated like **connaître** is **reconnaître,** *to recognize.*

   Il l'a vu mais il ne l'a pas **reconnu.**
   Reconnaissez-vous cette photo?

Mots clés   Words often used with savoir and connaître

Connaître

les étrangers *(f.)*	*foreigners*	quelqu'un	*somebody*
les gens *(m.)*	*people*	le roman	*novel*
la loi	*law*		

Savoir ou connaître

la chanson	*song*	la règle	*rule*
le numéro de téléphone	*phone number*	la réponse	*answer*
le poème	*poem*		

4. In some cases, both **savoir** and **connaître** can be used in similar sentences, but the meaning will then be different.

Connaissez-vous cette chanson?	*Do you **know** that song? (Are you familiar with . . .)*
Savez-vous cette chanson?	*Do you **know** that song? (Do you know the words . . .)*

ATTENTION

1. When implying knowledge rather than the presence or absence of an impediment, use **savoir**—not **pouvoir**. **Savoir** is the French equivalent of the verb *can* in English.

Elle **ne sait pas** chanter.	*She **can't** sing. (That is, she has a poor voice.)*
Elle **ne peut pas** chanter.	*She **can't** sing. (She has a sore throat.)*
Je **ne sais pas** conduire.	*I **can't** drive. (That is, I never learned.)*
Je **ne peux pas** conduire.	*I **can't** drive. (My car is in the shop.)*

2. The conjunction **que** introduces a fact; the verb **savoir** may precede it, but not **connaître**.

Ont-ils **su** que tu n'as pas 21 ans?
Je ne **connais** pas le professeur, mais je **sais** qu'il est sérieux.

Langue

A. **Notre prof.** Complétez les phrases suivantes avec la forme correcte du verbe **savoir** ou **connaître**, selon le cas.

1. _____ -vous son nom?
2. Oui, mais je ne _____ pas où il est né.
3. Nos camarades ne _____ pas qu'il est prof.
4. Où est-ce qu'il a _____ sa femme?
5. Il ne _____ pas parler italien.
6. Nous _____ ses enfants.
7. Est-ce que tu _____ ses livres?
8. Ses étudiants _____ chanter en français.

B. **Robert a changé.** Traduisez les phrases suivantes.

1. I saw Robert, but I didn't recognize him.
2. Does he know how to speak Spanish?
3. Can he play music?
4. We know he was born in Belgium.
5. Can he go out tonight?
6. He knows a good Italian restaurant near here.

Culture

C. **Des livres français.** Quel livre peut-on consulter pour connaître la France? Choisissez entre **savoir** et **connaître** dans vos réponses.

MODELE: *L'Argus*
On consulte L'Argus *pour savoir combien coûte une voiture d'occasion.*

1. le *Larousse*
2. le *Guide Michelin*
3. le *Quid*
4. *Le Bon Usage*
5. le *Bescherelle*
6. *Rapports*

a. de bons restaurants
b. comment conjuguer un verbe
c. des définitions
d. une règle de grammaire
e. des statistiques
f. parler français

Communication

D. Connaissez-vous... ?

MODELE: des villes   *Oui, je connais Londres.*

1. des villes loin d'ici
2. une autre culture
3. des gens célèbres *(famous)*
4. de bons films
5. un très mauvais restaurant
6. de bons poèmes
7. des étrangers sympathiques
8. des professeurs ennuyeux

E. **Interview.** Formez des questions avec un élément de chaque colonne et utilisez vos questions pour interviewer un(e) camarade de cours. Ensuite *(then)*, communiquez ses réponses aux autres.

A		**B**
Sais-tu...	danser	parler une langue étrangère
Connais-tu...	faire la cuisine	un numéro de téléphone
Peux-tu...	réciter un poème	important
	des gens en France	stationner une grosse voiture
	une chanson récente	dîner chez moi ce soir
	jouer du piano ici	reconnaître toutes les voitures américaines

F. **Questions personnelles.** Vos connaissances

1. Où avez-vous connu votre petit(e) ami(e)? votre camarade de chambre?
2. Connaissez-vous des poèmes français? Quels poèmes?
3. Savez-vous votre numéro de Sécurité sociale (sans vérifier)?
4. Qui n'avez-vous pas reconnu récemment? Avez-vous été embarrassé(e)?
5. Qui connaissez-vous le mieux *(the best)*?
6. Savez-vous réparer une voiture? Quels problèmes savez-vous régler *(solve)*?

II. Le passé composé (Review)

> You use the **passé composé** to relate events in the past.

A. The **passé composé** with **avoir**

1. In most cases, you form the **passé composé** with the present tense of **avoir** and the past participle of the verb. The past participle is based on the infinitive.

Infinitive	**Past participle**
chanter	chanté
choisir	choisi
répondre	répondu

2. You have also learned several irregular past participles.

apprendre	**appris**	pouvoir	**pu**
avoir	**eu**	prendre	**pris**
comprendre	**compris**	reconnaître	**reconnu**
connaître	**connu**	savoir	**su**
être	**été**	suivre	**suivi**
faire	**fait**	voir	**vu**
pleuvoir	**plu**	vouloir	**voulu**

3. Remember that in the **passé composé** with **avoir** construction, the past participle agrees with the direct object that *precedes* the verb.

—Quelle **robe** avez-vous choisie?
—J'ai choisi une **robe** rouge.

—Vous avez loué quelle voiture?
—La rouge. Nous l'avons réservée et nous
    l'avons payée.

" La femme la plus extraordinaire que j'ai rencontrée " ...

B. The **passé composé** with **être**

1. As you learned in Chapter 6, a small group of verbs forms the **passé composé** with the conjugated form of **être** and the past participle. Most of these are verbs of motion.

Mots clés   Verbs conjugated with être in the passé composé

Infinitive		Past participle
aller	to go	allé
arriver	to arrive	arrivé
descendre	to go down	descendu
*devenir	to become	devenu
entrer (dans)	to go in	entré
monter	to climb, go up	monté
mourir	to die	mort
naître	to be born	né
partir	to leave	parti
passer (par)	to pass (by)	passé
rentrer	to return; to run into	rentré
rester	to stay	resté
retourner	to return	retourné
*revenir	to come back	revenu
sortir	to leave	sorti
tomber	to fall	tombé
*venir	to come	venu

2. Remember that past participles of verbs conjugated with **être** agree in gender and number with their subjects.

Ils sont all**és** au bureau de la compagnie.
Quand **elle** est entr**ée**, **elle** est tomb**ée**.

ATTENTION

1. In spoken French, you hear past participle agreement with only one verb that takes **être**. That verb is **mourir**.

Il **est mort** (/i lɛ mɔʀ/) en 1967, et elle **est morte** (/ɛ lɛ mɔʀt/) en 1970.

---

* Verbs you will study later in this chapter.

2. **Passer** can mean *to spend (time)*, *to take (an exam)*, or *to pass (some-thing)*. When it takes a direct object, it forms the **passé composé** with **avoir**.

J'ai **passé** trois jours à Paris.   *I **spent** three days in Paris.*
Elle lui **a passé** le pain.   *She **passed** him / her the bread.*

When the verb indicates motion, it cannot have a direct object, so it forms the **passé composé** with **être**.

Des amis **sont passés** chez moi   *Some friends **came by** my*
   hier soir.   *house last night.*
Elle **est passée par** Marseille.   *She **went by** Marseille.*

3. **Retourner** indicates motion and is therefore conjugated with **être**.

Elle **est retournée** à la résidence.   *She **returned** to the dorm.*

The French equivalent of *to return (an object)*, **rendre**, is conjugated with **avoir**.

Elles **ont rendu** le parapluie.   *They **returned** the umbrella.*

Langue

A. **Les vacances de Marie-Claire et de sa famille.** Formez des phrases avec les mots donnés.

1. Tu / faire / voyage / agréable?
2. Oui, / nous / aller / Belgique
3. Combien de temps / vous / rester / là-bas?
4. Nous / passer / une semaine / Bruxelles
5. Quand / vous / rentrer?
6. Jeudi dernier. / Nous / passer / par / Montréal

B. **Conversation au téléphone.** Répondez aux questions suivantes en employant les mots entre parenthèses.

1. Est-ce que Pierre est à la maison?   (Non... sortir avec son frère)
2. Ont-ils fait un voyage?   (Non... aller à la plage)
3. Pourquoi n'ont-ils pas pris ta voiture?   (Elle... ne... pas... marcher; je... avoir... un accident)
4. Quand est-ce qu'on va voir tes parents?   (... arriver hier soir)
5. Ton père est-il vieux?   (Oui... naître en 1930)
6. Ils ont déjà vu l'appartement de Pierre?   (Oui,... passer le voir le mois dernier)

Culture

C. **Des personnages historiques célèbres.** Identifiez les personnages historiques dans la colonne de gauche *(left)* page 250 en formant une phrase avec les expressions verbales de la colonne de droite.

MODELE: Rimbaud
Rimbaud est parti pour l'Afrique.

1. de Gaulle
2. Napoléon
3. LaSalle
4. Camus
5. George Sand
6. Jean Genet

a. sortir de prison / devenir auteur
b. partir à Majorque avec Chopin
c. mourir dans un accident de voiture en 1960
d. descendre jusqu'en Louisiane en 1682
e. naître sur une île *(island)* / mourir sur une autre île
f. entrer dans le débat politique au Québec en 1967

Communication

D. Séparez-vous en petits groupes et interviewez vos camarades. Utilisez les expressions suivantes.

naître en quelle année? où?
arriver quand à l'université?
rentrer avant minuit samedi?
étudier le français pendant longtemps?

aller au cinéma récemment?
étudier ou sortir le week-end dernier?
connaître votre petit(e) ami(e) où?
???

E. Racontez votre journée *(Tell about your day)* d'hier. Utilisez les possibilités données ou vos propres idées.

prendre le petit déjeuner à... heures
partir pour...
prendre l'autobus / ma voiture
attendre mes amis à...
aller à mon cours de...
répondre à... questions
déjeuner avec...

voir...
rentrer chez moi à... heures
regarder la télévision l'après-midi
faire des courses à...
monter dans ma chambre à...
téléphoner à...
???

F. **Questions personnelles.** Vos activités extraordinaires

1. Où êtes-vous allé(e) plusieurs fois *(several times)*? Pourquoi?
2. Etes-vous déjà resté(e) seul(e) chez vous tout un week-end? Qu'est-ce que vous avez fait?
3. Etes-vous né(e) le même jour qu'une célébrité? Quelle célébrité?
4. Etes-vous descendu(e) en Amérique du Sud? Quels pays avez-vous visités?
5. Vous êtes allé(e) à New York? Par où êtes-vous passé(e)?
6. A quel monument très haut *(high)* êtes-vous monté(e)? La tour Eiffel? Le monument à George Washington?

III. The Imperfect

> You use the imperfect when you are describing conditions in the past.

A. Formation of the Imperfect

1. In addition to the **passé composé**, French has another past tense—**l'imparfait** (the imperfect). Its forms are based on the first-person plural (**nous** form) of the present tense: you drop the **-ons** and add the following endings.

parler (parlóns)	finir (finissóns)
je parlais	je finissais
tu parlais	tu finissais
il / elle / on parlait	il / elle / on finissait
nous parlions	nous finissions
vous parliez	vous finissiez
ils / elles parlaient	ils / elles finissaient

partir (partóns)	descendre (descendóns)
je partais	je descendais
tu partais	tu descendais
il / elle / on partait	il / elle / on descendait
nous partions	nous descendions
vous partiez	vous descendiez
ils / elles partaient	ils / elles descendaient

2. The imperfect of **il pleut** is **il pleuvait**.

ATTENTION

Because the imperfect tense is based on the first-person plural of the present tense, you must keep the pronunciation of the stem. Be careful especially with **je faisais** (/fø zɛ/) and **tu prenais** (/prø nɛ/). Note that the first vowel of each verb has the same sound as **je peux** (/ʒø pø/).

▶ L'Orthographe

1. Because four imperfect endings begin with the letter **a**, verbs ending in -**cer** and -**ger** undergo spelling changes in those forms. For infinitives ending in -**cer**, the **c** becomes **ç** before **a** or **o**. For verbs ending in -**ger**, the **g** becomes **ge** whenever the ending begins with an **a** or an **o**:

commen*cer* → commen**çons** → commen**çais**
man*ger*   → man**geons**   → man**geais**

2. Verbs with infinitives ending in -**ier** (**apprécier, étudier, expédier, oublier**) will have two **i**'s in the **nous** and **vous** forms.

Nous étud**ii**ons la gestion.   Vous appréc**ii**ez les gendarmes.

B. The Imperfect of **être**

Etre is the only verb that does not take its imperfect stem from the **nous** form of the present tense. Its imperfect stem (**ét-**) is irregular, but the endings are the regular imperfect tense endings.

	être	
j'étais		nous étions
tu étais		vous étiez
il / elle / on était		ils / elles étaient

C. Differences Between the Imperfect and the **Passé composé**

1. The difference between these two tenses depends on your perception of the action:

Imparfait: What was going on or what were the conditions?

Il **pleuvait** quand je suis sorti.	*It **was raining** when I went out.*
En 1962, nous **habitions** en Belgique.	*In 1962, we **lived** in Belgium.*
Quand j'**étais** petit, j'**allais** à l'école en autobus.	*When I **was** young, I **used to go** to school on the bus.*

Passé composé: What happened or what happened next?

Quand j'**ai vu** l'enfant, j'**ai freiné**.
Quand elle avait onze ans, elle **est allée** au Canada.
Il **a perdu** son permis de conduire parce qu'il **a eu** un accident.

2. Two actions going on at the same time cannot both be in the **passé composé**. The **imparfait** shows the conditions, and the **passé composé** indicates the events.

Condition	Event
Je **prenais** le petit déjeuner	quand le téléphone **a sonné.**
Il **était** minuit	quand Christine **est rentrée.**
Il y **avait** trop de gens chez Yves	et je **suis parti.**

D. Because the difference between the **imparfait** and the **passé composé** does not exist in English, English speakers must sometimes use different verbs to establish the distinction.

Il **connaissait** la femme.	He ***knew*** the woman.
Il **a connu** la femme.	He ***met*** the woman.
Elle **savait** la réponse.	She ***knew*** the answer.
Elle **a su** la réponse.	She ***found out*** the answer.
Je ne **voulais** pas le faire.	I ***didn't want*** to do it.
Je n'**ai** pas **voulu** le faire.	I ***refused*** to do it.

Langue

A. **Mon week-end.** Mettez le paragraphe suivant à l'imparfait. Commencez avec «**Le dimanche...** ».

Dimanche dernier, nous avons fait la grasse matinée. J'ai pris mon petit déjeuner à onze heures et je suis sorti. J'ai fait une promenade et je suis rentré à la maison. L'après-midi, j'ai regardé la télévision et j'ai écouté des disques. Ma femme a téléphoné à ses parents et elle les a invités chez nous.

B. **Monique rentre.** Dans les phrases suivantes, mettez les verbes au passé composé ou à l'imparfait, selon le cas. Faites les changements nécessaires.

1. Monique et nous, nous (visiter) la ville où nous (habiter) quand nous (avoir) dix ans.
2. Nous (avoir) froid quand nous (retourner) chez nous et nous (prendre) une boisson chaude.
3. Quand Monique (partir), nous (être) malheureux.
4. Je lui (téléphoner) quand elle (arriver) chez elle.
5. Quand elle (entendre) le téléphone, elle (savoir) que c'(être) nous.
6. Elle (vouloir) parler longtemps, mais moi, j'(avoir) des courses à faire.

C. **A la gare.** Mettez les verbes du paragraphe suivant au passé composé ou à l'imparfait, selon le cas.

Samedi dernier, il _____ (pleuvoir) et il _____ (faire) du brouillard. Nous _____ (arriver) à la gare à sept heures. Nous _____ (être) en avance car le train pour Paris _____ (aller) partir à huit heures. Mes parents _____ (avoir) froid et ils _____ (ne... pas vouloir) rester. Nous _____ (aller) au restaurant et nous _____ (prendre) un café bien chaud. A huit heures moins cinq, le train _____ (entrer) en gare

et il y _____ (avoir) beaucoup de gens. Nous _____ (monter) et
nous _____ (trouver) trois places ensemble. Le train _____ (partir).
Nous _____ (être) contents de rentrer.

Culture

D. **La France d'autrefois** *(of past time)*. Qu'est-ce qui a changé en France
et qu'est-ce qui n'a pas changé?

> MODELE: parler deux langues
> *On ne parlait pas deux langues, mais beaucoup de Français*
> *parlent deux langues maintenant.*

1. manger beaucoup à midi
2. regarder peu la télé
3. avoir des colonies en
   Afrique
4. divorcer peu
5. avoir un mauvais système
   téléphonique
6. utiliser peu le téléphone
7. avoir beaucoup d'enfants
8. consommer du coca

Communication

E. Quand vous étiez petit(e), que faisiez-vous pour embêter *(annoy)* les
gens? Utilisez les suggestions données ou vos propres idées.

manger du chewing gum
rentrer après dîner
désobéir
étudier peu

porter des vêtements bizarres
manger des insectes
écouter un transistor
???

F. Imaginez la vie *(life)* de l'homme préhistorique. Préparez des questions
et des réponses en utilisant les expressions données.

> MODELE: habiter dans une maison
> Etudiant(e) 1: *Est-ce que l'homme préhistorique habitait*
> *dans une maison?*
> Etudiant(e) 2: *Non, l'homme préhistorique n'habitait pas*
> *dans une maison.*

1. porter des chaussures
2. manger de la viande
3. regarder la télévision
4. parler français
5. avoir des cartes de crédit
6. fumer des cigarettes
7. avoir beaucoup de vacances
8. être artiste
9. voyager beaucoup
10. ???

G. **Questions personnelles.** Votre passé

1. Quand vous étiez petit(e), qu'est-ce que vous aimiez faire? Est-ce
   que vous étiez bon(ne) élève?
2. Qui admiriez-vous?
3. Quand vous alliez au lycée, où habitiez-vous?
4. Que faisiez-vous que *(that)* vous ne faites pas maintenant?
5. Quel âge aviez-vous quand vous êtes entré(e) à l'université?
6. Qui voyiez-vous souvent l'année dernière que *(whom)* vous ne
   voyez pas maintenant?

IV. Venir / Verbs Conjugated like Venir / Venir de + *Infinitive*

> You use the verb **venir** to express the idea of coming or to express a recent action.

A. Venir

venir *(to come)*	
Présent: je **viens**	nous **venons**
tu **viens**	vous **venez**
il / elle / on **vient**	ils / elles **viennent**
Passé composé: il **est venu**	

Tu **viens** chez nous ce soir? Je **suis venu** à huit heures.
Ils vont **venir** demain. Elle **venait** toujours avec une
amie.

B. Verbs Conjugated like **venir**

1. A number of verbs are conjugated like **venir** in the present tense.

appartenir à *to belong to*	Ce transistor ne lui **appartient** pas.
contenir *to contain*	Mon *Guide Michelin* **contient** les renseignements nécessaires.
devenir *to become*	Tu **deviens** impossible!
obtenir *to obtain*	Elle **obtient** son permis.
retenir *to hold back, to remember*	Je ne **retiens** pas les dates.
revenir *to come back*	Vous **revenez** le week-end prochain?
tenir *to hold, to keep*	Tu **tiens** l'enfant?
tenir à + *noun* *to be fond of*	Ils **tiennent à** leur vieille voiture.
tenir à + *verb* *to be anxious to, to insist on*	Nous **tenons à** partir tout de suite.
tenir de *to take after*	Elle **tient de** son père.

2. Like **venir**, **devenir** and **revenir** use **être** in the **passé composé**. All other verbs conjugated like **venir** use **avoir** in the **passé composé**.

Il **est devenu** méchant.
Elles **sont revenues** ensemble.

Elle **a tenu** à réparer sa voiture elle-même.
Il n'**a** pas **obtenu** son permis de conduire.

ATTENTION

1. **Devenir** is often used in the expression **Qu'est-ce que tu deviens?**, meaning *What are you up to?* In the **passé composé**, **Qu'est-ce qu'il est devenu?** means *Whatever became of him?* Like **être**, **devenir** does not take an article with professions that are not modified by adjectives.

   Elle est devenue **professeur**.   *She became a **teacher**.*

2. The verb **tenir** is used in the expressions **Tenez!** and **Tiens!**, which mean *Say! Here!*

   Tenez! Voilà vos papiers.
   Tiens! Je n'ai pas mon permis de conduire!

C. Venir de + *Infinitive*

The construction **venir de** + *infinitive* represents the **passé immédiat** and is used in two tenses: the present and the imperfect.

1. In the present tense, a conjugated form of **venir de** + *infinitive* indicates a recently completed action and is equivalent to the English *have just* + *past participle*.

   Je **viens** d'avoir un accident.   *I've just had an accident.*
   Ils **viennent** d'arriver à l'aéroport.   *They've just arrived at the airport.*

2. In the imperfect tense, a conjugated form of **venir de** + *infinitive* indicates an action that was completed just before another past action, which is expressed in the **passé composé**. In this case, the French **venir de** + *infinitive* is equivalent to the English *had just* + *past participle*.

   Il **venait** d'arriver quand je suis rentré.   *He **had just** arrived when I got home*
   Nous **venions** d'ouvrir la porte quand le téléphone a sonné.   *We **had just** opened the door when the telephone rang.*

Langue

A. **Promenade en auto.** Faites des phrases complètes avec les mots suivants.

   1. Ton / voiture / contenir / combien / personnes?
   2. Six / si / on / ne... pas / tenir / beaucoup de place
   3. Marc / venir / arriver / et nous / tenir / l'emprunter!
   4. Marc, / qu'est-ce que / tu / devenir?
   5. J(e) / obtenir / permis de conduire!
   6. Allez! / nous / venir / décider de partir

B. **Chez moi.** On téléphone pour parler avec les membres de votre famille. Mettez les phrases suivantes au passé immédiat en employant **venir de** au présent ou à l'imparfait, selon le cas.

1. Mon père part.
2. Ma sœur est tombée.
3. Robert finissait son dîner quand ma mère est arrivée.
4. Ma mère monte.
5. Elle finit son fromage.
6. Je faisais la vaisselle quand le téléphone a sonné.

Culture

C. **Les anciennes colonies.** A quel pays européen est-ce que les pays africains suivants appartenaient avant leur indépendance?

1. Le Zaïre	a. la Hollande
2. l'Algérie	b. le Portugal
3. le Mozambique	c. l'Italie
4. le Nigeria	d. la Belgique
5. l'Ethiopie	e. la Grande-Bretagne
6. l'Afrique du Sud	f. la France

Communication

D. **Un objet précieux.** A quoi tenez-vous? Quel objet aimez-vous beaucoup? Décrivez cet objet et expliquez pourquoi vous l'aimez beaucoup.

un vêtement (de vieilles chaussures?)	des livres anciens
une belle photo (de votre famille?)	un cadeau d'un(e) petit(e) ami(e)
	un poème
	???

E. Séparez-vous en petits groupes et répondez à la question «**Qu'est-ce que vous avez fait récemment?**» Employez **venir de** et utilisez les suggestions données ou vos propres idées.

prendre le petit déjeuner	parler avec un(e) camarade
obtenir une bonne note en...	arriver sur le campus
réussir à un examen de...	partir de la maison
rentrer de...	avoir un accident
finir un coca	???

F. **Questions personnelles.** Interviews

1. Vous allez partir ce week-end? Quand revenez-vous?
2. Avez-vous obtenu une bonne note? Quand? Dans quelle matière?
3. Venez-vous toujours en classe?
4. A quelles organisations appartenez-vous?
5. De qui tenez-vous?
6. Que voulez-vous devenir?

COMMUNIQUONS ....

Connaître le code de la route

In order to drive in France, you must be eighteen years old and take private lessons from an **auto-école.** The French driver's license is very difficult to obtain, but, once you have it, you never need to renew it. An American wishing to drive in France would do well to obtain an international driver's license before going and to become familiar with French traffic regulations (**le code de la route**).

The basic driving rules in France are the same as in North America for the most part, but there are some differences. For example, the right of way is usually given to the vehicle on the right unless otherwise indicated. In addition, to reduce noise in cities, it is forbidden to honk. Instead, drivers signal with high beams (**faire un appel de phares**) to warn others. To reduce casualties, the use of seat belts is mandatory and children under twelve are forbidden from riding in the front seat. Americans generally find French drivers very aggressive, so it is wise to be cautious when driving in France.

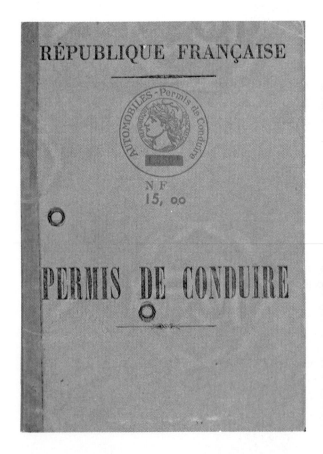

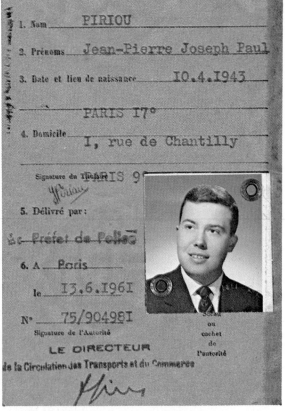

On conduit sa voiture.

Ce chauffeur fait du 100 kilomètres à l'heure.	*That driver is going 62 miles per hour.*
Ce chauffard a brûlé le feu.	*That reckless driver ran the red light.*
Ne doublez pas ici!	*Don't pass here!*
Cette auto a beaucoup de passagers (-ères) / occupants (-es).	*This car has a lot of passengers.*
J'ai pris le volant.	*I got behind the wheel.*

On entretient *(maintains)* sa voiture.

J'ai besoin de prendre de l'essence / de l'huile.	*I need to get some gas / oil.*
Faites le plein, s'il vous plaît.	*Fill it up, please.*
Le garagiste vérifie les pneus / l'eau.	*The mechanic is checking the tires / the water.*
Le mécanicien travaille à la station-service.	*The mechanic works at the gas station.*

Interaction   *M. Lafont fait le plein.*

M. LAFONT:	Le plein de *super*, s'il vous plaît.	*premium*
LA *POMPISTE*:	D'accord. Je vérifie l'huile?	*attendant*
M. LAFONT:	Oui, et le pneu *arrière droit*.	*right rear*
LA POMPISTE:	Vous allez loin?	
M. LAFONT:	Oui, nous allons à Aix. C'est à combien d'ici?	
LA POMPISTE:	Eh bien, par l'autoroute, il faut *compter* trois heures.	*plan on*

Elle roule à 3 à l'heure.

Activités

A. En France, on utilise **les panneaux routiers** *(road signs)* **internationaux.**
   Identifiez les panneaux correspondant aux définitions suivantes.

1. stop
2. stationnement interdit *(forbidden)*
3. chaussée glissante *(slippery)*
4. défense de *(forbidden)* tourner à droite
5. sens *(way)* unique
6. défense de doubler
7. vitesse *(speed)* limitée à cent kilomètres
8. sens interdit

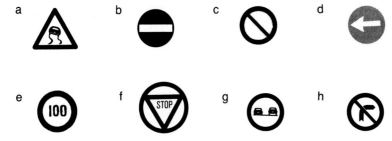

B. Répondez aux questions suivantes.

1. En général, roulez-vous vite? Du combien faites-vous sur
   l'autoroute *(interstate)*? En ville?
2. Brûlez-vous souvent les feux? Pourquoi?
3. Etes-vous un chauffard? A quelles lois désobéissez-vous souvent?
4. Aimez-vous mieux prendre le volant ou être passager (-ère)?
   Pourquoi?
5. Avez-vous déjà fait du stop? Pour aller où? Est-ce une bonne
   idée?
6. Où stationnez-vous à l'université? C'est près de votre salle de
   classe?
7. Etes-vous tombé(e) en panne? Dans quelles circonstances?
8. Quelle station-service fréquentez-vous? Pourquoi?
   Connaissez-vous un(e) bon(ne) mécanicien(ne)?
9. Que faites-vous à votre voiture avant de partir en vacances?
   Faites une liste.

consommation - consumption - consumo	
5 l/100 km	= 56,5 mi/gal
10 l/100 km	= 28,2 mi/gal
15 l/100 km	= 18,8 mi/gal
20 l/100 km	= 14,1 mi/gal
20 mi/gal	= 14,1 l/100 km
30 mi/gal	= 9,4 l/100 km
40 mi/gal	= 7,1 l/100 km
50 mi/gal	= 5,6 l/100 km

LECTURE CULTURELLE ·······················

Avant la lecture

French people have always been fascinated with cars. Today, three families out of four own an automobile, one out of three of these is an import, and the average yearly operating cost is $5,333. Lately, the French have been buying either small or big cars; the sales of medium-sized cars have dropped considerably. As in the United States, four-wheel drive vehicles are very popular; they are known as **les 4 × 4 (les quatre-quatre)**.

In spite of the high price of gasoline, insurance premiums, and the cost of the **vignette,** a sticker that must be purchased once a year from the government, French people continue to drive a lot, causing serious traffic problems on the roads and in the cities. It is estimated that each car owner drives an average of 8,100 miles per year, an impressive amount given the size of France.

Activités

A. Name five American cars that are extremely popular today because they are very economical, and indicate how many miles per gallon they go, both on the highway and in a city.

B. What cars do you know that have typified a style of life?

C. Look at the picture of the French car, called a **2 CV,** on page 262. What do you think the reading passage will tell you about the car?

La Dernière 2 CV

On a marqué la *fin* d'une *époque* quand la dernière «Deuche» est sortie de l'usine Citroën de Malgualde au Portugal. *(end / era)*

Depuis *plusieurs* années, on savait que la 2 CV était condamnée. L'agonie a commencé quand on a fermé l'usine de Levallois, près de Paris, où on la *fab-* *(several / manufactured)*
5 *riquait* depuis longtemps. Au Portugal, on avait déjà *diminué* sa production de *(lowered)* 70%, et on ne fabriquait plus que 85 voitures par jour. Commercialisée à 876 *exemplaires* en 1949, on a vendu la *célèbre* «*2 pattes*» à *plus de* 7 millions *(units / famous / legs / over)* d'exemplaires dans le *monde entier* pendant une carrière record de 41 ans. *(entire world)*

A l'automne 1935, les ingénieurs d'André Citroën ont reçu pour mission
10 de *concevoir* une voiture capable de transporter deux personnes et 50 kilo- *(devise)* grammes de pommes de terre *à soixante kilomètres à l'heure,* en consommant *(at 37 mph)* seulement *3 litres au cent*. Il *a fallu* attendre après la Seconde *Guerre mondiale* *(3 liters per 100 kms / was necessary / World War)* pour voir la voiture sortir.

A l'origine, on avait prévu un *toit* en *toile qui permettait* à une personne de *(roof / canvas that allowed)*
15 monter dans la voiture et de *garder* un *chapeau haut-de-forme* sur la tête. La *(keep / top hat)* voiture avait seulement un phare, *à gauche,* car c'était *tout ce que* le code de la *(on the left / all that)* route demandait. Quand on voulait tourner, *comme* il n'y avait pas de *cligno-* *(since / turn signal)* *tant,* il fallait *tendre le bras* par la *moitié* de la *vitre* qui *était relevable.* *(stretch one's arm / half / window / could be lifted)*

Finalement, le 7 octobre 1948, on a montré pour la première *fois* au pub- *(time)*
20 lic, en présence du président de la République, la voiture équipée d'un nouveau

Une 2 CV

moteur et d'un *véritable démarreur, au lieu* de la *manivelle* qu'on avait prévue.   *real starter / instead /*
Le succès a été immédiat, et *dès* 1950, *il fallait* attendre six ans entre le mo-   *crank / starting in / one*
ment de la *commande* et le moment de la *livraison*. Dans les années soixante,   *had to / order / delivery*
la production est passée de 5 à 1.000 voitures par jour, pour culminer en 1966
25 avec une production annuelle de 168.384 unités.

C'est l'époque de la gloire de cette voiture que les Allemands, les Hol-
landais et les Scandinaves baptisaient «le *vilain* petit *canard*». La «Deuche»   *ugly / duck*
passait *partout*, et on pouvait la réparer facilement. On raconte l'histoire d'un   *everywhere*
journaliste qui est tombé en panne avec sa 2 CV dans un désert en Bolivie et
30 qui a été *dépanné* quand un Chilien a mis des bananes dans le *carter!*   *rescued / gear box*

Pendant ses dernières années, la «Deuche» est devenue plus confortable.
Elle était plus rapide et on ne *gelait* plus quand on la conduisait en hiver.   *froze*
Même *embourgeoisée*, elle continuait à être un symbole, et avec sa *disparition*,   *gentrified / disappearance*
les 35–60 ans *ont enterré* une partie de leur *jeunesse*.   *have buried / youth*

(Adapted from the article "La dernière 2 CV," *Journal Français
d'Amérique*, Vol. 12, No. 17. Reprinted by permission.)

Après la lecture

Questions sur le texte

1. Qu'est-ce que la dernière «Deuche» a annoncé?
2. Quand est-ce qu'on a compris que la 2 CV était condamnée?
3. Combien de 2 CV a-t-on vendu pendant 41 ans?
4. En 1935, quelle sorte de voiture est-ce que les ingénieurs de Citroën
   devaient fabriquer?

5. Pourquoi avait-elle un toit en toile?

6. Combien de phares avait-elle?

7. Qu'est-ce qui montre que la voiture était un succès?

8. Comment est-ce que les Allemands appelaient la 2 CV?

Activités

A. Using popular French magazines, such as *Paris-Match, Le Point,* or *L'Express,* look up ads for popular French cars. Try to identify three models for the following makes: *Renault, Peugeot,* and *Citroën,* and make a list of the parts of the car mentioned in each ad.

B. Avez-vous déjà eu un accident de voiture? Qu'est-ce qui est arrivé?

1. Qui avait tort / raison?

2. Est-ce que les gendarmes sont venus?

3. Le conducteur était ivre *(drunk)*?

4. Une personne était blessée *(hurt)*?

5. Est-ce que la voiture marchait encore?

6. ???

C. **Débats en classe**

1. La voiture: un luxe ou une nécessité?

2. Les voitures électriques sont-elles possibles?

3. Les voitures personnelles ou les transports publics?

4. Solutions au problème des chauffards?

Chapitre 11

LA TELE

Interview pour la télévision

Commençons . . . .

Une Interview avec Simone Trudeau ▭

Simone Trudeau est journaliste à Antenne 2. Elle prépare un reportage sur les opinions des Français sur les grands problèmes de la vie contemporaine dans le monde. Elle discute avec Claude, 25 ans, cadre dans un grand magasin parisien, et avec Marc, 20 ans, étudiant en sciences politiques.

SIMONE: Qu'est-ce qui vous préoccupe le plus?

CLAUDE: Je suis contente que vous nous posiez cette question, mais j'ai peur qu'il ne soit pas facile de répondre. Il semble que la qualité de la vie soit le plus important.

MARC: Absolument! Selon moi, les gens ont peur qu'il y ait un désastre écologique et ils ne pensent pas qu'on réussisse à rendre la société plus juste.

SIMONE: Je suis surprise que vous ne me parliez pas de l'importance de l'argent et du succès!

CLAUDE: Tous les sondages d'opinion que je consulte montrent que la santé et le bonheur viennent avant le compte en banque et le travail pour un grand nombre de Français.

SIMONE: Je vous remercie pour votre franchise. N'oubliez pas de regarder le Journal de 20 heures demain soir.

Mots clés

interview	*interview*	important	*important*
reportage	*feature story*	absolument	*absolutely*
opinions *(f.)*	*opinions*	selon	*according to*
vie	*life*	il y ait (avoir)	*there might be*
contemporaine	*contemporary*	désastre	*disaster*
monde	*world*	écologique	*ecological*
discute	*is discussing*	rendre la société	*make society*
(discuter)		plus juste	*more just*
cadre *(m.)*	*middle-level*	surprise	*surprised*
	manager	importance	*importance*
grand magasin	*department*	succès	*success*
	store	sondages *(m.)*	*opinion polls*
vous *(direct*	*you*	d'opinion	
object		consulte	*consult*
pronoun)		(consulter)	
préoccupe	*preoccupies*	santé	*health*
(préoccuper)		bonheur	*happiness*
le plus	*the most*	compte en	*bank account*
nous *(direct*	*us*	banque	
object		travail	*work*
pronoun)		nombre	*number*
j'ai peur que	*I'm afraid that*	remercie	*thank*
(avoir peur)		(remercier)	
soit (être)	*is*	franchise	*candor*
Il semble	*It seems*	Journal	*news*
qualité	*quality*		

D'après un sondage I.P.S.O.S.-« J.D.D. », 5 % seulement des personnes interrogées accepteraient des « contributions à but politique »

ARGENT ET POLITIQUE

58 % DES FRANÇAIS REFUSENT DE FINANCER LES PARTIS

Les Français refusent à chaque fois qu'ils votent d'ajouter un chèque dans l'enveloppe !

Faisons connaissance

French people are avid readers of public opinion polls. These appear regularly in French newspapers and magazines and vary in content from the serious (national politics) to the frivolous (reactions to *Dallas* in *Paris-Match*). The French take polls so seriously that it is forbidden to publish the results of political polls immediately before an election.

On French television, many programs are devoted to round tables (**des tables rondes**) where journalists and personalities discuss the latest contemporary issues. During an election year, it is not unusual for all the channels to present such round tables several times a week. Amazingly, the viewers rarely seem to object.

The fears expressed by Marc reflect the opinions of a majority of his fellow citizens. In a recent poll, people ranked the following problems as sources of worry:

Problèmes	% des réponses affirmatives
la drogue *drugs*	54
le chômage *unemployment*	49
le Sida *AIDS*	46
la pollution *pollution*	39
la faim dans le monde *hunger*	33

Etudions le dialogue

1. Sur quoi est-ce que Simone Trudeau fait un reportage?
2. Qui sont Claude et Marc?
3. Qu'est-ce qui préoccupe Claude?
4. Selon Marc, de quoi les gens ont-ils peur?
5. Pourquoi est-ce que Simone est surprise?
6. Qu'est-ce qui est plus important que l'argent et le succès pour Claude?

Enrichissons notre vocabulaire

Le bonheur *(Happiness)*

—Qu'est-ce qu'**il te faut** pour être heureux?	*What do **you need** in order to be happy?*
—**Il me faut** de l'argent; je suis **matérialiste.**	*I **need** money; I'm **materialistic.***
—Nous avons besoin de **justice** *(f.)* et de **paix** *(f.).*	*We need **justice** and **peace.***
—Qu'est-ce que le bonheur pour vous?	*What is happiness for you?*
—L'**amour** *(m.)* de ma famille.	*Love of my family.*
—La sécurité d'un **emploi.**	*Job security.*
—L'**égalité** *(f.)* dans la société.	*Equality in society.*
—Des vacances à la **montagne.**	*A vacation in the **mountains.***

Les grands problèmes sociaux *(Major social problems)*

—Qu'est-ce qui vous préoccupe?	*What worries you?*
—La **criminalité** me **fait peur.**	*Crime scares me.*

—Le **trafic** des drogues.   *Drug **trafficking**.*
—La **politique**.   *Politics.*
—La **possibilité** d'une **guerre   *The **possibility** of **nuclear war**.*
   nucléaire**.
—L'**inflation** *(f.)*.   *Inflation.*
—Les **sans-logis** *(m.)* / **sans-abris**   *The **homeless**.*
   (m.)

Les petits inconvénients *(Annoyances)*

—Qu'est-ce qui t'**embête** le   *What **annoys** you the most?*
   plus?
—Beaucoup de **choses** *(f.)*!   *Many **things**!*
—Je ne peux pas **supporter** mes   *I can't **stand** my **neighbors**.*
   voisins *(m.)*.
   Ils **font du bruit**.   *They **make noise**.*
—L'**incertitude** *(f.)* de l'**avenir**   *The **uncertainty** of the **future**.*
   (m.).
—Mes parents n'**arrêtent** pas de   *My parents don't **stop giving me***
   me donner des **conseils** *(m.)*.   ***advice**.*

La télé *(TV)*

les actualités *(f.)*	*news*	un feuilleton	*series*
la chaîne	*channel*	un jeu télévisé	*game show*
un dessin animé	*cartoon*	le programme	*evening schedule*
les émissions *(f.)*	*shows*	la publicité	*commercials*
une émission de variétés	*variety show*		

Prononciation   **The Vowel Sounds / o / and / ɔ /**

A. The vowel sounds / o / and / ɔ / are pronounced with the tongue back and the lips very rounded. As with the sounds / e / and / ɛ /, the tongue is neither high nor low.

Repeat the following English and French word pairs after your teacher.

English	French	English	French
bow	beau	dough	dos
foe	faux	oh	eau

B. The / ɔ / sound is the same as the / o / sound, except that in the former, the mouth is held more open. You use the / o / sound when the word ends in a vowel sound. The / ɔ / sound is used when a pronounced consonant follows it.

Repeat the following pairs of words after your teacher.

l o l	*l ɔ l*	*l o l*	*l ɔ l*
beau	bonne	tôt	tort
faux	fort	trop	drogues
nos	notre	pot	poche

C. The spellings **au** and **ô** are almost always pronounced / o /, not / ɔ /. If the consonant that follows is a / z / sound, you also use / o /.

Repeat the following pairs of words after your teacher.

l ɔ l	*l o l*	*l ɔ l*	*l o l*
notre	autre	école	Côte d'Azur
botte	Claude	note	chose
pomme	pauvre	comme	cause

Exercice

Read the following sentences aloud, paying particular attention to the open / ɔ / sound and the closed / o / sound.

1. Robert veut un beau chapeau.
2. Donne-moi le téléphone!
3. A l'automne, nous faisons de bonnes promenades.
4. Paulette propose des choses idiotes.
5. Florence, donne-moi une pomme avec du coca.
6. Et comme fromage? —Du Roquefort!

GRAMMAIRE ....

I. Direct and Indirect Object Pronouns: First and Second Persons

> You use these pronouns to refer to yourself or to the person or people to whom or about whom you are speaking.

A. Direct and Indirect Object Pronouns: First and Second Persons

	singular	*plural*
1st person	me	nous
2nd person	te	vous

In contrast to the third person, in which the direct object pronoun forms (**le, la, les**) differ from the indirect object pronoun forms (**lui, leur**), first- and second-person pronouns have the same form. Note that **me** and **te** become **m'** and **t'** before a vowel.

Pronouns as direct objects

Tu **m'**as vu à la télévision?
Est-ce que ces problèmes **te** préoccupent beaucoup?
On ne **nous** consulte jamais quand on fait un sondage d'opinion.
Qu'est-ce qui **vous** embête le plus?

Pronouns as indirect objects

Vous **me** parlez de quelque chose d'important.
Le journaliste **t'**a posé des questions?
Tu **nous** fais peur.
Elle **vous** donne ses opinions?

B. Placement of Pronouns

First- and second-person object pronouns are placed in the same position as third-person object pronouns:

1. directly before the conjugated verb in the present, imperfect, and **passé composé** tenses:

   Vous **me** posez cette question?
   Marc **me** parlait quand Sylvie **nous** a vus.

2. in front of the infinitive when there is a helping verb:

   Elle ne veut pas **vous** embêter mais est-ce qu'elle
      peut **vous** parler maintenant?
   Cette réponse va **vous** rendre très heureux.

3. in front of the verb in the negative imperative:

Ne **me** parlez pas de l'importance de l'argent!
Ne **nous** fais pas peur!

4. after the verb in the affirmative imperative and linked to the verb with a hyphen:

Posez-**nous** des questions!

The pronoun **me** becomes **moi** in the affirmative imperative.

Ne **me** donnez pas votre opinion → Donnez-**moi**
 votre opinion!
Ne **me** laissez pas seul. → Laissez-**moi** seul.

ATTENTION

The distinction between direct and indirect object pronouns with **me, te, nous,** and **vous** is important only when determining past participle agreement in the **passé composé.** Only preceding *direct* object pronouns agree when the auxiliary verb is **avoir.**

Direct objects	**Indirect objects**
Elle **nous** a **regardés.**	On **vous** a **téléphoné?**
Je **vous** ai **vus** au cinéma.	Elle ne **nous** a pas **obéi.**

Langue

A. **La jalousie.** Pierre a vu sa petite amie Julie en ville et il est très jaloux *(jealous).* Jouez le rôle de Julie et répondez aux questions de Pierre en employant les mots entre parenthèses.

1. Je t'ai vue au café avec Robert?   (Oui, tu...)
2. Il t'a commandé une boisson?   (Oui,... coca.)
3. Est-ce que vous m'avez vu?   (Non, nous...)
4. Est-ce qu'il t'a parlé longtemps?   (Oui,...)
5. Est-ce qu'il va te téléphoner?   (Non,...)
6. Est-ce qu'il t'a donné son numéro de téléphone? (Non,...)
7. Est-ce que vous allez m'inviter demain?   (Non,...)
8. Est-ce que tu m'aimes?   (Non,... ne... pas pouvoir supporter.)

B. **Au téléphone.** Votre sœur parle au téléphone. Imaginez des questions pour les réponses suivantes.

MODELE: Oui, il m'aime.
  Est-ce que Paul t'aime?

1. Oui, elle m'a parlé hier soir.
2. Oui, elles vont nous inviter.
3. Non, ils ne peuvent pas te comprendre.
4. Oui, je t'ai présenté mon nouveau petit ami.
5. Non, nous ne vous avons pas oubliées.
6. Oui, apporte-moi tes photos.

Culture

C. **En famille.** Indiquez des différences culturelles entre votre famille américaine (vos parents et vous) et les familles françaises (les parents français et leurs enfants) en formant des phrases avec les mots donnés. Attention! Il y a aussi des similarités!

> MODELE: souhaiter *(wish)* une bonne fête *(saint's day)*
> *Mes parents ne m'ont jamais souhaité une bonne fête.*
> *Les parents français leur souhaitent une bonne fête tous les ans.*

1. donner de l'argent
2. punir souvent
3. téléphoner tous les jours
4. voir tous les dimanches
5. servir du vin quand on était jeune(s)
6. embrasser tous les soirs avant de dormir

Communication

D. Vous rencontrez un garçon / une fille charmant(e) dans une boîte. Imaginez la conversation. Utilisez les suggestions données ou vos propres idées.

> Est-ce que je vous ai déjà rencontré(e)?
> Comment vous appelez-vous?
> Vous venez souvent ici?
> Je peux vous offrir une boisson?
> Tu me donnes ton numéro de téléphone?
> Tu veux me laisser ton adresse?
> Je peux passer te voir?
> Je peux t'embrasser?

E. Vous êtes condamné(e) *(condemned)* et vous allez mourir demain matin. Qu'est-ce que vous demandez à la dernière minute?

> MODELE: donner du champagne.   *Donnez-moi du champagne.*
> laisser seul   *Ne me laissez pas seul.*

servir un bon dîner	parler
donner des cigarettes	faire un gâteau
prêter une Bible	montrer un film de...
apporter du vin	oublier
laisser partir	faire mal
écouter: «Je suis innocent!»	donner la clé

F. **Questions personnelles.** La famille et les amis

1. Comment est-ce que vos parents vous ont puni(e) quand vous étiez jeune?
2. Qu'est-ce que le Père Noël vous a apporté l'année dernière?
3. Vos parents vous posent quelles sortes de questions?

4. Qui vous téléphone souvent?
5. Qui est passé vous voir récemment?
6. Qui est-ce qui vous fait des lettres?
7. Qu'est-ce qui vous rend heureux (-euse)?
8. Qui est-ce qui ne peut pas vous supporter?

II. The Subjunctive of Regular Verbs and of avoir and être

> Until now, you have been using the indicative mood (**le présent**, **l'imparfait**, and **le passé composé**) to express facts and the imperative mood to express commands and requests. You use the subjunctive mood to express feelings, such as emotion, wishes, doubt, and judgment.

A. Introduction

Even though the subjunctive is used more frequently in French, it also exists in English:

I wish *that* he *were* home now.

As in English, the subjunctive in French is used mostly in subordinate clauses following a main clause. Both clauses are linked by **que** *(that)*.

Emotion:	Je suis contente **que** vous nous **posiez** cette question.
Wishing:	Je veux **que** vous me **parliez** de cela.
Doubt:	Les gens ne pensent pas **qu'on rende** la société plus juste.
Judgment:	Il semble **que** la qualité de la vie vous **préoccupe** le plus.

B. Forms of the Present Subjunctive

1. The subjunctive endings are the same for the four groups of regular verbs you know. They are added to the stem of the first-person plural (**nous** form) of the present indicative.

chanter (chant**ón**ś)	partir (part**ón**ś)
que je **chante**	que je **parte**
que tu **chantes**	que tu **partes**
qu'il / elle / on **chante**	qu'il / elle / on **parte**
que nous **chantions**	que nous **partions**
que vous **chantiez**	que vous **partiez**
qu'ils / elles **chantent**	qu'ils / elles **partent**

finir (finiss**óns**)	vendre (vend**óns**)
que je **finisse**	que je **vende**
que tu **finisses**	que tu **vendes**
qu'il / elle / on **finisse**	qu'il / elle / on **vende**
que nous **finissions**	que nous **vendions**
que vous **finissiez**	que vous **vendiez**
qu'ils / elles **finissent**	qu'ils / elles **vendent**

ATTENTION

Adding a written **-e** to the stem of **-ir** and **-re** verbs causes the final consonant to be pronounced:

dormir	→	**dorm-**	→	qu'il **dorme**
sortir	→	**sort-**	→	que tu **sortes**
attendre	→	**attend-**	→	qu'on **attende**
descendre	→	**descend-**	→	que tu **descendes**

2. Even though they are irregular in the present indicative, **connaître** and **suivre** are regular in the present subjunctive.

connaître	→	**connaiss-**	→	que je **connaisse**
suivre	→	**suiv-**	→	que tu **suives**

C. The Subjunctive of **avoir** and **être**

Two irregular verbs in the subjunctive are **avoir** and **être**. You will learn other irregular verbs in the subjunctive in Chapter 12.

avoir	être
que j'**aie**	que je **sois**
que tu **aies**	que tu **sois**
qu'il / elle / on **ait**	qu'il / elle / on **soit**
que nous **ayons**	que nous **soyons**
que vous **ayez**	que vous **soyez**
qu'ils / elles **aient**	qu'ils / elles **soient**

Les gens ont peur qu'il y **ait** un désastre écologique.
Il semble que la qualité de la vie **soit** très importante.

ATTENTION

The **nous** and **vous** forms of the subjunctive of **avoir** are pronounced with the /e/ sound: **nous ayons** /nu ze jɔ̃/, **vous ayez** /vu ze je/.

Langue

A. Remplacez les verbes en italique par les verbes donnés dans les phrases suivantes.

1. Je veux que vous *restiez*. (répondre, partir, réussir, parler, obéir, étudier)
2. Il faut que nous *chantions* ici. (travailler, dormir, finir, attendre, descendre, être)
3. Nous désirons que tu *finisses*. (écouter, ne pas fumer, partir, finir, avoir de la patience, être à l'heure)

B. **Le succès.** Formez des phrases complètes avec les mots donnés.

1. Vous / vouloir / que / nous / être / heureux?
2. Vos parents / désirer / que / vous / trouver / travail
3. Mon père / ne... pas vouloir / que / je / avoir / trop / argent
4. Il faut / que / tu / réussir / dans / vie
5. Nous / aimer mieux / que / vous / étudier / université
6. Mon prof / ne... pas vouloir / que / je / perdre / mon / temps

Culture

C. **Connaître un pays.** Vos amis veulent visiter un pays où on parle français. Qu'est-ce qu'ils peuvent faire pour connaître la culture de ce pays? Quels conseils pouvez-vous leur donner? Commencez avec **Il faut que vous...** et choisissez la meilleure *(best)* réponse.

1. rester...
   a. dans un petit hôtel b. dans un grand hôtel c. avec une famille
2. aimer...
   a. parler avec des gens b. observer les gens c. expliquer des traditions américaines
3. fréquenter...
   a. les musées b. les cafés c. les parcs
4. utiliser...
   a. le métro b. des taxis c. les autobus
5. passer... dans le pays.
   a. une semaine b. un mois c. une année
6. avoir...
   a. beaucoup de patience b. beaucoup d'argent c. beaucoup de temps
7. voyager entre les villes...
   a. en voiture b. en train c. en auto-stop
8. étudier
   a. leur langue b. leur art c. leur politique

Communication

D. Pour être un(e) bon(ne) étudiant(e), qu'est-ce qu'il faut faire?

> MODELE: étudier beaucoup
> *Il faut que nous étudiions beaucoup.*

écouter le professeur	finir tous les devoirs
passer beaucoup de temps à la bibliothèque	réussir aux examens
	ne... pas sortir le soir
être studieux (-euse)	répondre à toutes les questions
regarder des jeux télévisés tout le temps	réfléchir beaucoup
	???
dormir peu	

E. Vous allez faire une lettre au Président des Etats-Unis pour lui donner des conseils. Utilisez les suggestions données ou vos propres idées.

> MODELE: m'inviter à la Maison-Blanche
> *Je voudrais que vous m'invitiez à la Maison-Blanche.*

ne... pas oublier les pauvres	être plus patient avec les sénateurs
dépenser moins d'argent	encourager les gens sans travail
écouter les femmes	penser aux problèmes des sans-abris
voyager en autobus	
avoir moins de vacances	
répondre aux questions des journalistes	

F. **Questions personnelles.** Vos problèmes

1. Est-ce qu'il faut que vous passiez un examen cette semaine? Dans quelle matière?
2. Combien d'heures faut-il que vous étudiiez?
3. Est-ce qu'il est important qu'un professeur soit sévère? Pourquoi ou pourquoi pas?
4. Est-ce que votre petit(e) ami(e) veut que vous sortiez avec elle / lui trop souvent?
5. Est-ce qu'il est préférable que vous gagniez beaucoup d'argent ou que vous soyez heureux (-euse)?
6. De quoi avez-vous peur?

III. Uses of the Subjunctive

The verb in the main clause of a sentence determines whether you will use the indicative or the subjunctive in the subordinate clause. The indicative is the most frequent mood; it follows verbs indicating facts or certainty.

> Ils **savent** que vous **êtes** préoccupé.
> Les sondages **montrent** que le bonheur **vient** avant l'argent.

The subjunctive occurs in subordinate clauses after verbs of emotion, wishing, doubt, and uncertainty, and some impersonal expressions implying judgment.

A. Emotion

The subjunctive mood is used in subordinate clauses starting with **que** after verbs and expressions of emotion.

> Je **suis contente que vous nous posiez** cette question.
> J'**ai peur qu'il ne soit** pas facile de répondre.
> Je **suis surprise que vous ne me parliez** pas d'argent.

Mots clés   **Expressions of emotion**

avoir peur	*to be afraid*	**être heureux**	*to be happy*
être content(e)	*to be happy*	(**-euse**)	
être désolé(e)	*to be sorry*	**être surpris(e)**	*to be surprised*
être étonné(e)	*to be surprised*	**être triste**	*to be sad*
être furieux	*to be angry*	**regretter**	*to be sorry*
(**-euse**)			

ATTENTION

Note that, in order to use the subjunctive, the subject in the subordinate clause must be different from the subject of the main clause. If the subjects in both clauses are the same, the infinitive is used. In this case, all of the preceding expressions take **de** before an infinitive.

> J'ai peur qu'**elle** ait froid cet hiver.   *I'm afraid (that) **she**'ll be cold this winter.*
>
> J'ai peur d'**avoir** froid cet hiver.   *I'm afraid that **I**'ll be cold this winter.*

B. Wishing

The subjunctive is used in clauses starting with **que** after verbs and in expressions of wishing, desire, preference, and other impositions of will.

> Elle **veut que nous arrivions** à l'heure.
> Tu **aimes mieux que je choisisse** le restaurant?
> Nous **souhaitons que vous passiez** une bonne soirée.

Mots clés Verbs and expressions of will, wishing, and desire

aimer mieux	*to prefer*	désirer	*to want*
avoir envie (de)	*would like*	souhaiter	*to wish*
		vouloir	*to want*

C. Doubt and Uncertainty

The subjunctive is also used after verbs and expressions of doubt or uncertainty.

> Je **ne pense pas** que **nous ayons** envie de
>   beaucoup de choses.
> Elle **n'est pas sûre** qu'**il soit** là.

Mots clés Verbs and expressions of doubt and uncertainty

douter	*to doubt*
ne... pas penser	*not to think*
ne... pas être sûr (de)	*not to be sure, to be unsure*
ne... pas être certain (de)	*not to be certain, to be uncertain*

ATTENTION

1. Because they imply certainty, **penser** and **être sûr** in the affirmative are followed by a verb in the indicative.

   > Elle **pense** qu'il **est** beau.
   > *but:* Elle **ne pense pas** qu'il **soit** intelligent.

2. The verb **savoir** is always followed by a verb in the indicative.

   > Je **sais** que **vous êtes** italien.   Je **ne savais pas** que **vous étiez** cadre.

3. Several other verbs that you have learned, including **apprendre, décider, espérer, expliquer, indiquer, montrer, oublier,** and **répondre,** do not imply doubt. They are therefore followed by a verb in the indicative.

   > Le journaliste **a expliqué** que le Président ne **peut** pas
   >   venir.
   > N'**oublie** pas que nous **avons** du chômage.

D. Impersonal Expressions of Judgment

The subjunctive is used in the subordinate clause after expressions with no specific subject, that is, without a reference to any particular person or thing, if they express a judgment or opinion on the speaker's part.

Il **semble** que la qualité de la vie **soit** le plus important.

Il **faut** que nous **rendions** la société plus juste.

Mots clés   Impersonal expressions implying opinion or personal judgment

Il est bon[1] que	It is good that
Il est dommage[1] que	It's too bad that
Il est faux[1] que	It is untrue that
Il est important[1] que	It is important that
Il est juste[1] / injuste[1] que	It is fair / unfair that
Il est peu probable que[2]	It is unlikely that
Il est possible[1] / impossible[1] que	It is possible / impossible that
Il est préférable[1] que	It is preferable that
Il est rare[1] que	It is rare that
Il est temps[1] que	It is time that
Il faut[3] que / il est nécessaire[1] que	It is necessary that
Il semble[3] que	It seems that
Il se peut que[2]	It may be that / Perhaps / It's possible that
Il vaut mieux que[3]	It is better that

ATTENTION

The following verbs and expressions imply certainty in the speaker's mind and do *not* take the subjunctive.

Il est certain / sûr que	It is certain / sure that
Il est évident que	It is obvious that
Il est probable que	It is probable that
Il est vrai que	It is true that

Il est **certain** que vous n'**obéissez** pas.
Il est **probable** que Marc **est** très fatigué.

---

[1] Takes **de** with an infinitive.   [2] Cannot be used without a change of subject.
[3] Is followed directly by an infinitive.

Langue

A. **En vacances.** Formez des phrases complètes avec les mots donnés.

1. Je / souhaiter / vous / passer / bon / vacances
2. Elle / penser / nous / partir / demain
3. Ils / avoir peur / nous / avoir / mauvais / temps
4. Tu / aimer mieux / je / être / gare / sept heures?
5. Nous / être surpris / tu / avoir / quinze / jour / de vacances
6. Il / être / certain / elles / sortir / des Etats-Unis

B. **Il faut suivre ses propres conseils!** Changez les phrases suivantes pour indiquer que la première personne va penser à elle-même!

MODELE: Jacqueline veut qu'on parte maintenant.
           Jacqueline veut partir maintenant.

1. Robert aime que nous passions chez ses amis.
2. Marie a envie que tu sortes ce soir.
3. Claire est contente que nous ayons de bonnes notes.
4. Alain aime mieux que j'arrive en avance.
5. Yves n'est pas sûr qu'ils partent tout de suite.
6. Chantal veut que vous ayez de la patience.

C. **Les problèmes sociaux.** Dans les phrases suivantes, remplacez les mots en italique par les mots entre parenthèses.

1. Ils *pensent* que le Sida est un désastre.   (... avoir peur...)
2. Il est *vrai* que nous perdons patience avec les sans-logis.
   (... dommage...)
3. Il est *peu probable* que nous ayons une guerre nucléaire.
   (... possible...)
4. Ils *expliquent* que nous ne réfléchissons pas assez aux
   pauvres.   (... regretter...)
5. Je *doute* qu'ils aient faim.   (... apprendre...)
6. Il est *evident* qu'il y a trop de criminalité.   (... certain...)

Culture

D. **Connaître un pays.** Vos amis ont décidé de visiter un pays francophone, et ils veulent connaître cette culture. Donnez-leur des conseils.
Faites des phrases avec les mots donnés; ensuite *(then)*, mettez les
phrases dans l'ordre du plus important au moins important.

MODELE: Il est bon / préparer votre voyage en avance
           Il est bon que vous prépariez votre voyage en avance.

1. Il faut / goûter tous les vins
2. Il est important / choisir un bon guide
3. Il est évident / avoir besoin de parler leur langue
4. Il faut / parler avec beaucoup de gens
5. Il vaut mieux / manger avec une famille
6. Il est certain / aller chercher un bon café

Communication

E. Donnez votre opinion des situations suivantes en employant «**Je pense que...** » ou «**Je ne pense pas que...** ».

1. l'Amérique:
   a. Les Américains sont sympathiques.
   b. Ils parlent beaucoup de langues.
   c. Il y a trop de gens.
   d. L'argent est trop important pour eux.

2. les parents:
   a. Ils sont très sévères.
   b. Ils perdent souvent patience.
   c. Ils aiment mes amis.
   d. Ils ont toujours raison.

3. les grandes villes:
   a. Il y a trop de bruit.
   b. La pollution est un problème.
   c. Les habitants sont sympathiques.
   d. On dort bien en ville.

4. mes amis:
   a. Ils sont ennuyeux.
   b. Ils ont du talent.
   c. Ils réfléchissent aux problèmes importants.
   d. Ils sont préoccupés.

F. Dans les situations suivantes, complétez les phrases avec une bonne solution.

1. Vous avez un examen demain matin. Il vaut mieux que vous...
   a. étudier ce soir
   b. écouter des disques
   c. sortir avec des amis
   d. ???

2. Votre frère veut sortir avec une jolie fille. Il vaut mieux qu'il...
   a. lui téléphoner à trois heures du matin
   b. l'inviter chez lui
   c. lui parler en français
   d. ???

3. Vos amis veulent aller en France cet été. Il vaut mieux qu'ils...
   a. travailler le week-end
   b. dépenser beaucoup d'argent
   c. partir maintenant
   d. ???

4. Les restaurants sont fermés et vous avez faim. Il est probable que vous...
   a. demander un sandwich à vos voisins
   b. préparer quelque chose à la maison
   c. attendre le petit déjeuner
   d. ???

5. Votre grand-mère veut venir vous voir mais une amie vous a déjà invité(e). Il vaut mieux que vous...
   a. attendre votre grand-mère chez vous
   b. expliquer le problème à votre grand-mère
   c. partir tout de suite
   d. ???

G. Dans les situations suivantes, êtes-vous content(e) ou désolé(e)?

MODELE: Le professeur est sévère.
          Je suis désolé(e) que le professeur soit sévère.

1. Nous étudions le subjonctif.
2. Le professeur me choisit pour répondre à la question.
3. Nous donnons de l'argent aux pays pauvres.
4. Mon français (n')est (pas) très bon.
5. Il y a du chômage.
6. J'ai une voiture.

H. **Questions personnelles.** Votre personnalité

1. Avez-vous peur d'obtenir une mauvaise note? Dans quel cours?
2. Pensez-vous savoir parler français? Avec qui voulez-vous parler?
3. Est-ce qu'il est possible que vous changiez de personnalité?
4. De quoi avez-vous envie?
5. Quand êtes-vous furieux (-euse)?
6. Qu'est-ce que vous regrettez?
7. Etes-vous sûr(e) que vos études soient importantes?
8. Est-il vrai que vous pensiez aux autres?

COMMUNIQUONS ....

Exprimer l'incertitude

In English, when people are unsure of a person's name or simply wish to speak quickly without stopping to think of an exact name, they use a variety of expressions such as *What's-his-name* or *Mr. / Mrs. So-and-So.* These expressions of uncertainty also exist for talking about places and things. French has similar expressions, and you will find them useful for getting your ideas across in situations where you are not sure of precise terms to use for designating people, places, and things.

**pour tous
ou pour quelques-uns ?** ■

ENQUÊTE

On parle des gens.

1. Use **on** as the subject when you cannot name a specific person.

On nous a pris notre magnétoscope.	*They took our VCR.*
On a sonné à la porte.	*They rang the doorbell.*

2. Use **quelqu'un** to express the idea of *someone*. When used with an adjective, **quelqu'un** is followed by **de (d')** and a masculine adjective.

Quelqu'un m'a déjà posé cette question.	*Somebody already asked me that question.*
J'ai vu quelqu'un dans l'auto.	*I saw somebody in the car.*
Il a rencontré quelqu'un d'important.	*He met someone important.*

3. To express *Mr. So-and-So* and *Mrs. So-and-So*, use **Monsieur Untel** and **Madame Unetelle**. When you have forgotten a person's name, or when you do not want to be bothered saying it, use the names **Machin, Machin-Chouette** *(What's-his-name)* or **Chose**.

Madame Unetelle est déjà partie.	*Mrs. So-and-So has already left.*
Machin-Chouette m'a téléphoné.	*What's his-name phoned.*

On parle des endroits.

Use **quelque part** *(somewhere)*, **un coin** *(spot)*, or **un endroit** *(a place)* to talk about an unspecified place.

Les enfants sont allés quelque part.	*The kids went somewhere.*
Ils ont laissé mon parapluie dans un coin.	*They left my umbrella in some spot.*

On parle des choses.

1. Use **quelque chose** (*something*) to indicate a thing that cannot be specified. **Quelque chose** is always masculine and takes **de (d')** before an adjective.

Quelque chose a fait du bruit.	*Something made a noise.*
Je voudrais quelque chose pour ma mère.	*I'd like something for my mother.*
Vous me parlez de quelque chose d'important.	*You are talking to me about something important.*

2. There are several familiar French expressions that mean a *gadget*, a *thingamajig*, or a *doohickey*.

J'ai besoin d'un bidule pour ouvrir le coffre!	*I need a thingamajig to open the trunk.*
Je parle d'un engin pour prendre des messages au téléphone.	*I'm talking about a doohickey for taking messages on the phone.*
Qu'est-ce que c'est que ce machin?	*What's that gadget?*
Je cherche un truc pour réparer ma bicyclette.	*I'm looking for a gadget to repair my bicycle.*

3. Use **une chose** (*a thing*) for abstract nouns or ideas.

Le bonheur pour moi, c'est une chose simple.	*Happiness for me is a simple thing.*
Je voudrais vous expliquer une chose sérieuse.	*I would like to explain a serious thing to you.*

Interaction   *Simon va acheter un cadeau pour son frère.*

SIMON: Je cherche quelque chose de pas trop cher.

L'EMPLOYE: C'est pour quelqu'un de quel âge?

SIMON: Vingt-trois ans. Il aime les machins électroniques.

L'EMPLOYE: J'ai un truc pour prévoir l'avenir. Je viens de le *poser* quelque   *set down* part.

SIMON: Non, j'aime mieux les bidules amusants.

L'EMPLOYE: On va en avoir beaucoup à la fin de la semaine.

SIMON: D'accord. Je vais revenir samedi.

Activités

A. Refaites le paragraphe suivant en remplaçant les mots en italique par des expressions d'incertitude.

Un *homme* m'a téléphoné hier soir. C'était *Robert Ducroc*. Il voulait emprunter *ma voiture* parce qu'il avait des problèmes *en ville* et *les gens* ne voulaient pas l'aider à réparer sa voiture. *Une femme* lui a prêté de l'argent pour téléphoner *d'un café* près de l'hôtel. Je n'avais pas envie de sortir et je lui ai demandé d'aller voir *Mme Fantaisie* à l'hôtel.

B. Répondez aux questions suivantes.

1. Avez-vous déjà rencontré quelqu'un de célèbre? Qui?
2. Etes-vous allé(e) quelque part le week-end dernier?
3. Avez-vous visité un joli coin? Où?
4. Avez-vous fait quelque chose d'intéressant récemment?
5. Est-ce qu'on vous a invité(e) quelque part ce week-end?
6. Est-ce que quelqu'un va passer vous voir ce soir? Qui?

LECTURE CULTURELLE ....

Avant la lecture

Until 1992, six television channels broadcast programming in France. However, when the owners of **La Cinq** filed for bankruptcy, its future became uncertain. Of course, it is possible that new channels will be added; also, French people can access regional channels as well as channels from foreign countries, depending on the region where they live. Although they were once all nationalized, some French TV channels are now independent. They get their revenue from an annual tax on TV sets (**la redevance**) and from ever more frequent commercials, which are grouped together and interrupt shows less frequently than in the United States. One channel, **Canal +** (**Canal Plus**), requires a converter box and a monthly fee, much like movie channels on American TV. In many families, evening schedules follow television programming. One very popular show is **Le Bébête Show,** featured on **TF 1** before the evening news. Although it is not on every day, most French people look forward to it eagerly. It is a political satire: the characters are imitations of Muppets with each representing an easily recognizable French political figure. To enjoy the show, one must be very familiar with contemporary French political life.

The number of American TV shows broadcast on French TV and dubbed in French continues to increase. With so many channels competing for air time, producers have found it cheaper to buy American programs than to make their own. Some examples are *MacGyver, Santa Barbara, Shérif, fais-moi peur (Dukes of Hazard),* and *Kojak.* The French also copy American game shows, as with *La Roue de la fortune, Jeopardy!,* and *Une Famille en or (Family Feud.).*

Activités

The following readings are excerpts from a guide to French television, *Le Figaro TV Magazine*.

A. Based on your experience with American television, what kind of shows would you expect to be broadcast during the early evening hours? Now, scan the first reading, the listings for *Sélection de la semaine,* to find similarities and differences between your expectations and the French TV schedule. Next, answer the questions at the top of page 287.

La Télévision en France

SÉLECTION DE LA SEMAINE

TF1

VENDREDI 26 JUILLET

19.00 SANTA BARBARA
Feuilleton américain.
Avec **A. Martinez, Lane Davies.**
Eleanor persuade Cruz qu'Addison a essayé de l'empoisonner.

19.25 LA ROUE DE LA FORTUNE

19.50 LE BÉBÊTE SHOW

20.00 JOURNAL

20.30 MÉTÉO

20.35 TAPIS VERT

Questions sur le texte

1. Quelle sorte d'émission est *Santa Barbara?*
2. Comment joue-t-on à *La Roue de la fortune?*
3. A quelle heure présente-t-on *Le Journal?*
4. Qu'est-ce qui suit *Le Journal?*

B. The photograph accompanying the second reading, *La Planète miracle,* is a good indication that the program is about nature. Scan the passage and circle five words related to nature. Then, answer the questions at the top of page 288.

20.45

SÉRIE DOCUMENTAIRE EN DIX PARTIES — QUATRIÈME PARTIE

LA PLANÈTE MIRACLE

RÉALISATION : MASARU IKEO

La grande forêt

ERICH SPIEGELHALTER

Les séquoïas géants de Californie, les arbres les plus grands du monde, sont les témoins de l'intense relation qui existe entre le Soleil et la flore. Ils représentent à eux seuls des centaines d'années d'accumulation d'énergie solaire. Une énergie verte dont dépend toute vie animale. La flore n'est pourtant qu'une apparition relativement récente sur la planète, elle ne date que de 400 millions d'années environ. Pour quelles raisons la flore ne s'est-elle formée que si lentement ? Par quel processus la Terre a-t-elle fini par produire cette couverture végétale ? Comment les plantes, qui furent au début aquatiques, se sont-elles adaptées au milieu terrestre ? Autant de questions que soulève ce documentaire, qui sont d'autant plus importantes que la flore et l'énergie qui s'y est accumulée conditionnent toute vie animale et donc humaine.

Les fabuleux séquoïas de Californie.

---

essayé *tried*   empoisonner *to poison*   témoins *witnesses*   dont *upon which*   pourtant *however*   ne... que *only*   environ *about* couverture *cover*   furent *were*   Autant *As many*   soulève *raises* donc *therefore*

Questions sur le texte

1. Quelle sorte d'émission est *La Planète miracle?*
2. Qui a fait cette émission? Quelle est sa nationalité?
3. Pourquoi a-t-on choisi les séquoias pour cette émission?

Après la lecture

Activités

A. Répondez aux questions suivantes.

1. Est-ce que vous préférez les émissions sérieuses ou les émissions comiques?
2. Quelle est votre série américaine préférée? Résumez un épisode.
3. Quel(s) feuilleton(s) regardez-vous l'après-midi? Présentez le résumé du dernier épisode à la classe.

B. En petits groupes, jouez à *La Roue de la fortune*. Préparez une expression et demandez à vos camarades de trouver les consonnes et les voyelles.

LES ACHATS

Aux Galeries Lafayette, à Paris

COMMENÇONS ....

A la charcuterie

*Sophie et Annick louent un appartement au centre-ville. A midi, elles
mangent au restau-U, mais le soir, comme elles ne rentrent jamais de bonne
heure, elles aiment acheter des plats cuisinés dans une charcuterie et les
emporter chez elles pour dîner.*

LE CHARCUTIER: Bonjour, Mesdemoiselles, vous désirez?

ANNICK: Vous n'avez plus de pâté de foie?

LE CHARCUTIER: Si, nous avons reçu notre commande ce matin. Voulez-vous
que j'aille le chercher?

SOPHIE: Je ne sais pas; il vaut peut-être mieux que nous prenions
autre chose.

LE CHARCUTIER: J'ai de la très bonne choucroute garnie. Vous devriez
l'essayer.

ANNICK: Tiens! C'est une idée. Qu'est-ce que vous nous conseillez de
boire avec cela?

SOPHIE: Tu sais bien qu'avec la choucroute, il faut qu'on boive du
vin blanc sec ou de la bière.

ANNICK: Très bien. Donnez-nous 500 grammes de choucroute et une
bouteille de Riesling.

LE CHARCUTIER: Voilà, Mademoiselle!

SOPHIE: Combien je vous dois?

LE CHARCUTIER: Soixante-dix-neuf francs.

A la charcuterie alsacienne

Mots clés

charcuterie	*pork butcher shop*	autre chose	*something else*
centre-ville	*downtown*	choucroute garnie	*sauerkraut and assorted meat*
de bonne heure	*early*	devriez (devoir)	*ought*
plats cuisinés *(m.)*	*prepared dishes*	essayer	*to try*
charcutier	*pork butcher*	conseillez (conseiller)	*advise*
Mesdemoiselles	*ladies*	boire	*to drink*
n'... plus	*not . . . any more*	boive (boire)	*drink*
pâté de foie *(m.)*	*liver pâté*	sec	*dry*
reçu (recevoir)	*received*	grammes *(m.)*	*grams*
commande *(f.)*	*order*	bouteille	*bottle*
que j'aille (aller)	*me to go*	dois (devoir)	*owe*
peut-être	*perhaps*	francs *(m.)*	*francs*
prenions (prendre)	*take*		

FAISONS CONNAISSANCE

Although supermarkets **[supermarchés** *(m.)***]** are very popular in France, many people continue to buy food at specialty stores. They go to a neighborhood store at least once a day to pick up freshly baked bread, dairy products, or items they need for just one meal. **La charcuterie** specializes in pork products such as ham, sausages, and **pâté.** It also sells prepared dishes such as **hors-d'œuvre,** salads, and ready-to-eat foods that the shopper can warm up just before dinner. Bakeries are also specialized. You go to a **boulangerie** *(f.)* to buy bread and to a **pâtisserie** *(f.)* for pastries.

Galeries la carte.
Tout vous est dû !

600522 24 050 1234 5679
MLE DOMINIQUE LAFORÊT

French people also go to gigantic supermarkets called **hypermarchés** *(m.)*. Items that they commonly purchase include canned goods (**des conserves** *(f.)*), frozen foods (**des produits surgelés**), cleaning products, paper goods, and cases of beverages such as beer and mineral water. The French also like to shop in the department stores (**les grands magasins**). There, they usually purchase items such as clothes, furniture, and appliances. In Paris, the **Galeries Lafayette** and the **Printemps** are among the most popular. They have branches in large cities throughout France where they compete with other chains such as **Les Nouvelles Galeries.**

Etudions le dialogue

1. Est-ce que Sophie et Annick habitent à la campagne?
2. Qu'est-ce qu'elles aiment faire quand elles ne rentrent pas de bonne heure?
3. Est-ce que le charcutier a du pâté de foie?
4. Qu'est-ce qu'il recommande aussi?
5. Quelle sorte de vin consomme-t-on avec la choucroute?
6. Qu'est-ce qu'il est possible de boire aussi?

Enrichissons notre vocabulaire

Les boutiques *(Shops)*

une bijouterie   une boucherie   une crémerie   une épicerie

un magasin
d'articles de sports   un magasin de chaussures   une papeterie   une poissonnerie

la brasserie	*the café-restaurant*
le magasin de disques	*the record store*
la teinturerie	*the dry cleaners*

Les commerçants *(Shopkeepers)*

le boulanger / la boulangère	*the baker*
le boucher / la bouchère	*the butcher*
le pâtissier / la pâtissière	*the pastry maker*
l'épicier / l'épicière	*the grocer*
le poissonnier / la poissonnière	*the fishmonger*
le marchand de... / la marchande de...	*the person who sells . . .*
le / la buraliste	*the tobacco store operator*
le / la fleuriste	*the florist*

Dans un magasin *(In a store)*

le vendeur / la vendeuse	*the salesperson*
le rayon	*the department*
la caisse	*the cashier's*
les soldes	*sales*
en solde	*on sale*
une remise de 10%	*a 10% discount*

Prononciation   The Vowel Sounds /ø/ and /œ/

A. The third pair of mid vowels in French is /ø/ and /œ/. The /ø/ sound is pronounced with the mouth mostly closed, the tongue forward, and the lips rounded. It is represented by the letters **eu** and occurs in words such as **bleu** and **heureux**. The unaccented e in words such as **je, ne, ce,** and **que** approximates this sound.

B. You will notice that the /ø/ sound occurs when it is the last sound in a syllable. If the syllable ends in a consonant, you must pronounce the /œ/ sound by opening your mouth slightly. The /œ/ sound is also written **eu**, but it occurs only before a pronounced consonant in words such as **leur**, **veulent**, and **neuf**.

Repeat the following pairs of words after your teacher.

/ø/	*/œ/*		*/ø/*	*/œ/*
heureux	chauffeur		peu	peur
eux	heure		veut	veulent

C. There is only one frequent exception to the preceding rule. When the final consonant is the /z/ sound, usually written -se, you keep the vowel sound /ø/. In the following lists, the adjectives in the right column have the same final vowel sound as those in the left column.

Repeat the following pairs of words after your teacher.

/ø/	/øz/		/ø/	/øz/
affreux	affreuse		courageux	courageuse
ambitieux	ambitieuse		délicieux	délicieuse
dangereux	dangereuse		généreux	généreuse

Exercice

Read the following sentences aloud, distinguishing between the closed /ø/ sound and the open /œ/ sound.

1. Je veux aller chez eux.
2. Elle a peur que tu ne sois pas à l'heure.
3. Ils peuvent manger un seul œuf, pas deux œufs.
4. Cet acteur veut avoir deux répondeurs.
5. Le docteur peut venir à deux heures vingt-deux.
6. Je suis heureuse que ma sœur soit ambitieuse et studieuse.

GRAMMAIRE ....

I. Boire / Recevoir / Devoir

> You use these verbs to express the actions of drinking and receiving and the state of having to do something, respectively.

A. The irregular French verbs **boire**, **recevoir**, and **devoir** have similar conjugations.

	boire (to drink)	recevoir (to receive)	devoir (must, to have to, to be supposed to, to owe)
présent:	je **bois**	je **reçois**	je **dois**
	tu **bois**	tu **reçois**	tu **dois**
	il / elle / on **boit**	il / elle / on **reçoit**	il / elle / on **doit**
	nous **buvons**	nous **recevons**	nous **devons**
	vous **buvez**	vous **recevez**	vous **devez**
	ils / elles **boivent**	ils / elles **reçoivent**	ils / elles **doivent**
passé composé:	j'ai **bu**	tu as **reçu**	il a **dû**
imparfait:	nous **buvions**	vous **receviez**	elles **devaient**

Qu'est-ce que vous nous conseillez de **boire?**
Nous **avons reçu** notre commande hier.
Vous **devez** partir maintenant?

B. **Devoir** is a frequently used verb and has many English equivalents.

1. When followed by an infinitive, **devoir** has several possible meanings:

Je **dois aller** chez le charcutier.	*I **have to** / **am supposed to** go to the pork butcher's.*
Elle **a dû aller** à l'épicerie.	*She **had to** go / **must have gone** to the grocery store.*
Nous **devions acheter** quelque chose au supermarché.	*We **were supposed to** buy something at the supermarket.*

2. **Devoir** + a verb in the infinitive can replace the expression **il faut que** + a verb in the subjunctive.

Il faut que tu réussisses à cet examen.	**Tu dois** réussir à cet examen.

3. **Devoir** followed by a noun means *to owe.*

—C'est combien?
—Vous me **devez** 95 F.

4. **Devoir** is frequently used in the conditional mood to give advice, in which case it means *should* or *ought to.*

Je **devrais** téléphoner à ma mère.
Vous **devriez** aller à la boulangerie avant sept heures.

Langue

A. **Connaissez-vous Jacqueline?** Formez des phrases complètes avec les mots donnés.

1. Quand / elle / être / petit / elle / ne... pas / boire / lait
2. Qu'est-ce que / elle / devoir / faire / quand / pleuvoir?
3. Le week-end dernier / sa sœur / et / elle / devoir / rester / maison
4. Hier / Jacqueline / recevoir / lettre / de sa grand-mère
5. Est-ce que / son / parents / recevoir / souvent / son / amis?
6. Chez elle / on / ne... pas boire / souvent / alcool

B. **Conseils personnels.** Dans les phrases suivantes, remplacez **Il faut que** par la forme correcte du verbe **devoir**.

1. Il ne faut pas que je mente.
2. Il faut que vous finissiez votre travail.
3. Il faut que tu sois généreux.
4. Il faut que les gens connaissent leurs voisins.
5. Il faut que nous pensions aux sans-logis.
6. Il faut qu'on ait beaucoup de patience.

Culture

C. **Les boissons.** Qu'est-ce qu'on boit traditionnellement dans les régions francophones du monde? Faites des phrases en trouvant la bonne réponse dans la liste de possibilités.

du cidre	du vin blanc	du bourgogne
de la bière	du champagne	du rhum

1. Pour un anniversaire *(birthday)*, on...
2. A Dijon, les gens...
3. Avec les écrevisses *(crayfish)*, les Louisianais...
4. Avec une fondue, les Suisses...
5. En Bretagne, avec les crêpes, on...
6. Pour l'apéritif à la Martinique, les gens...

D. **Les obligations.** Si vous habitez en France, certaines choses sont obligatoires. Qu'est-ce qu'on doit faire dans les situations suivantes? Trouvez l'obligation dans la colonne de droite *(right)* et formez une phrase avec **devoir**.

MODELE: Pour acheter du pain / aller à une boulangerie.
Pour acheter du pain, vous devez aller à une boulangerie.

1. Si un Français vous invite à dîner chez lui,...
2. Si vous faites une promenade en auto,...
3. Quand on prend le TGV,...
4. Pour dîner dans un bon restaurant,...
5. Pour acheter un plat cuisiné,...
6. Pour obtenir un permis de conduire,...

a. attacher les ceintures de sécurité
b. attendre 7 h 30
c. apporter des fleurs *(flowers)* ou des bonbons
d. aller à une auto-école
e. faire une réservation
f. aller à une charcuterie

Communication

E. **Donnez des conseils.** Vous êtes assistant(e) dans une résidence universitaire et des étudiants vous parlent des problèmes suivants. Qu'est-ce que vous devriez leur recommander de faire dans ces situations?

MODELE: J'ai un examen de français demain.
Tu devrais étudier les verbes.

1. Il pleut beaucoup.
2. Mon / Ma camarade de chambre est très malheureux (-euse).
3. Je dois beaucoup d'argent à un(e) ami(e).
4. Je viens de faire des courses, mais j'ai oublié mon portefeuille.
5. Mon / Ma camarade de chambre et moi, nous ne recevons jamais de lettres.
6. Les étudiants font trop de bruit à la résidence.

F. **Questions personnelles.** Vos habitudes

1. Qu'est-ce que vous aimez boire le matin? à minuit?
2. Qu'est-ce que vous buvez quand vous avez très soif? Quand vous êtes fatigué(e)?
3. De qui recevez-vous souvent des colis?
4. Aimez-vous recevoir des amis chez vous ou aimez-vous mieux sortir?
5. A qui devez-vous de l'argent?
6. Qu'est-ce que vous devriez faire que vous n'allez pas faire ou que vous n'aimez pas faire?

II. Irregular Verbs in the Subjunctive

A. Verbs with One Subjunctive Stem

1. Some French verbs are irregular in the present subjunctive. In all forms, they use one stem.

faire (fass-)	
que je **fasse**	que nous **fassions**
que tu **fasses**	que vous **fassiez**
qu'il / elle / on **fasse**	qu'ils / elles **fassent**

2. The following verbs are also irregular in the subjunctive and use one stem in their forms.

pouvoir: que je **puisse** / que nous **puissions**
savoir: que je **sache** / que nous **sachions**

Je suis étonnée qu'ils **puissent** venir.
Il faut qu'on **sache** les réponses.

PREMIÈRE. LE MAGAZINE QUI PARLE DES FILMS AVANT QU'ILS NE FASSENT PARLER D'EUX.

Tous les mois, Première porte un certain regard sur le cinéma. Celui du cœur. Tous les mois, Première démontre que les films ont la vedette : on parle de l'Ours, du Grand Bleu, de Camille Claudel (films dont Première a parlé bien avant tout le monde...) au même titre qu'on parle de De Niro ou d'Adjani. Mais Première, c'est aussi un regard en profondeur sur le cinéma. Des critiques, des portraits d'acteurs et de réalisateurs, des repérages sur des petits films qui méritent souvent qu'on en parle en grand, et bien sûr des exclusivités. Première, le magazine qui parle des films comme personne n'en parle.

B. Verbs with Two Subjunctive Stems

1. Some verbs use both the **nous** and the **ils / elles** forms of the present indicative to create two different subjunctive stems—one for the **nous** and **vous** plural forms and one for the four other forms.

boire

Present indicative: ils **boivent**	*Subjunctive stems:* **boiv-**
nous **buvons**	**buv-**
que je **boive**	que nous **buvions**
que tu **boives**	que vous **buviez**
qu'il / elle / on **boive**	qu'ils / elles **boivent**

devoir	prendre	recevoir
stems: **doiv-,**	*stems:* **prenn-,**	*stems:* **reçoiv-,**
dev-	**pren-**	**recev-**
que je **doive**	que je **prenne**	que je **reçoive**
que tu **doives**	que tu **prennes**	que tu **reçoives**
qu'il / elle / on **doive**	qu'il / elle / on **prenne**	qu'il / elle / on **reçoive**
que nous **devions**	que nous **prenions**	que nous **recevions**
que vous **deviez**	que vous **preniez**	que vous **receviez**
qu'ils / elles **doivent**	qu'ils / elles **prennent**	qu'ils / elles **reçoivent**

venir	voir
stems: **vienn-, ven-**	*stems:* **voi-, voy-**
que je **vienne**	que je **voie**
que tu **viennes**	que tu **voies**
qu'il / elle / on **vienne**	qu'il / elle / on **voie**
que nous **venions**	que nous **voyions**
que vous **veniez**	que vous **voyiez**
qu'ils / elles **viennent**	qu'ils / elles **voient**

Il vaut mieux qu'on **boive** du vin blanc.
Il est temps que nous **recevions** du courrier.

2. The verbs that you have already learned that are conjugated like **prendre, venir,** and **voir** in the present indicative are conjugated like those respective verbs in the subjunctive.

apprendre:	que j'**apprenne** / que nous **apprenions**
comprendre:	que je **comprenne** / que nous **comprenions**
appartenir:	que j'**appartienne** / que nous **appartenions**
contenir:	qu'il **contienne**
devenir:	que je **devienne** / que nous **devenions**
obtenir:	que j'**obtienne** / que nous **obtenions**
retenir:	que je **retienne** / que nous **retenions**
revenir:	que je **revienne** / que nous **revenions**
tenir:	que je **tienne** / que nous **tenions**

3. The verbs **aller** and **vouloir** take one subjunctive stem from the **nous** form of the present indicative. It is used in the **nous** and **vous** forms of the subjunctive. The other subjunctive stem is irregular and is used in the other four forms.

aller	vouloir
stems: **aill-, all-**	*stems:* **veuill-, voul-**
que j'**aille**	que je **veuille**
que tu **ailles**	que tu **veuilles**
qu'il / elle / on **aille**	qu'il / elle / on **veuille**
que nous **allions**	que nous **voulions**
que vous **alliez**	que vous **vouliez**
qu'ils / elles **aillent**	qu'ils / elles **veuillent**

Voulez-vous que j'**aille** le chercher?
Il se peut qu'il **veuille** sortir ce soir.

C. Falloir and pleuvoir

1. The following verbal expressions are irregular in the subjunctive.

il faut → qu'il **faille**
il pleut → qu'il **pleuve**

Il est possible qu'il **faille** payer la TVA.
Je ne veux pas qu'il **pleuve** ce week-end.

2. In the indicative, **il faut** becomes **il a fallu** and **il fallait** in the past and **il va falloir** in the future.

Il **a fallu** que je prenne l'avion.
Il **fallait** que nous partions de bonne heure.
Il **va falloir** que tu fasses la vaisselle.

Langue

A. Remplacez les mots en italique avec les expressions données.

1. Il a fallu que nous *travaillions beaucoup.* (faire le ménage, aller à la charcuterie, boire de l'eau, voir ce film, retenir ces dates)
2. Elle a peur que vous *arriviez en retard.* (vouloir rester longtemps, ne... pas prendre le dernier métro, devenir furieux, ne... pas pouvoir répondre, la voir)
3. Il va falloir qu'on *rentre.* (aller à la charcuterie, faire des courses, recevoir ces gens, prendre un taxi, obtenir de bonnes notes)

B. **On va faire un pique-nique.** Formez des phrases complètes en employ-ant les mots donnés.

1. Notre / amis / vouloir / nous / aller / faire un pique-nique / demain
2. Je / avoir peur / Roland / ne... pas vouloir / venir / avec nous
3. Nous / être certain / vous / pouvoir / arriver à l'heure
4. Paul / douter / faire / froid / demain
5. Nous / penser / il / pleuvoir
6. Elles / être / désolé / leurs amies / ne... pas venir
7. Marie / aimer mieux / nous / faire des courses / l'hypermarché
8. Il faut / vous / voir / ces plats!

C. **Mes projets.** Formez des phrases en utilisant des expressions dans les deux colonnes.

MODELE: *Il est possible que je fasse la grasse matinée ce week-end.*

A	B
Etes-vous désolé	apprendre à jouer de la musique
Je suis certain	aller au cinéma ce soir
Il faut	vouloir aller au concert
Je pense	faire la cuisine
Il est probable	pleuvoir cet après-midi
Nous sommes sûrs	voir un film anglais
Il vaut mieux	devoir de l'argent à la banque
Nous ne savions pas	recevoir des amis

Culture

D. **Les habitudes des Français.** Qu'est-ce que les Français ont l'habitude de faire? Choisissez entre les deux possibilités dans la proposition *(clause)* principale pour former une phrase correcte.

MODELE: Il est probable / peu probable / / les Français / boire du vin blanc avec du fromage
Il est peu probable que les Français boivent du vin blanc avec du fromage.

1. Il est rare / certain / des vieux / suivre des cours à l'université
2. Il est vrai / faux / beaucoup de Français / savoir utiliser un ordinateur
3. Il est possible / impossible / on / aller de Paris à Londres en trois heures en train
4. Il est rare / n'est pas rare / un Français / devoir de l'argent
5. Il est sûr / peu probable / la majorité des Français / prendre leurs vacances en septembre
6. Je pense / ne pense pas / nous / voir beaucoup de Français aux Etats-Unis

Communication

E. **Quelles sont les possibilités?** Indiquez le degré de certitude des situations suivantes.

| certain | probable | possible | impossible |

MODELE: Il pleut ce soir.
Il est possible qu'il pleuve ce soir.

1. Je vais en Europe cet été.
2. Les étudiants sont contents de ce cours.
3. Je deviens professeur de lycée.
4. Je bois trop de café.
5. Nous voulons aller en classe samedi.
6. Mes amis peuvent me prêter de l'argent.

F. **Vos regrets.** Qu'est-ce que vous regrettez dans la vie? Choisissez vos réponses dans la liste suivante, ou exprimez vos propres regrets (*express your own regrets*).

MODELE: Mes professeurs sont trop sérieux.
Je regrette que mes professeurs soient trop sérieux.

Mon voisin reçoit trop d'amis.
On doit passer des examens.
Notre classe ne va pas au laboratoire tous les jours.
Mon / Ma camarade de chambre fait trop de bruit.
La banque ne veut pas me prêter d'argent.
???

G. **Vrai ou faux?** Que pensez-vous des affirmations suivantes? Doutez-vous / êtes-vous sûr(e) qu'elles soient vraies?

MODELE: Le pâté fait un bon hors-d'œuvre.
Je suis sûr(e) que le pâté fait un bon hors-d'œuvre.

1. On doit abolir la peine capitale (*capital punishment*).
2. On peut aller sur d'autres planètes.
3. Il y a une guerre nucléaire bientôt.

4. Nous allons connaître les causes du cancer au vingtième siècle *(century)*.
5. Certaines personnes prévoient l'avenir.
6. Nous ne tenons pas à notre passé.

H. **Questions personnelles.** Vos opinions

1. Est-il important qu'on apprenne des langues étrangères?
2. Pensez-vous qu'on voie de bons films à la télévision? de bonnes émissions?
3. Est-il nécessaire que vous alliez en classe tous les jours? Pourquoi?
4. Est-il possible que vous vouliez travailler pendant les vacances?
5. A quel âge pensez-vous qu'on doive pouvoir boire de l'alcool?
6. Est-ce qu'il vaut mieux pour l'économie que vous fassiez vos courses aux hypermarchés ou chez les petits commerçants?

III. Negatives

> You use negative expressions to state that people do not do certain things or that certain situations do not exist.

A. Forms

In addition to the general negative expression **ne... pas,** French has other negative expressions.

Affirmative	Negative
Ils prennent **quelque chose.**	Ils **ne** prennent **rien.**
*They are having **something**.*	*They are **not** having **anything**.*
Elle a **encore** de la patience.	Elle **n'a plus** de patience.
*She **still** has patience.*	*She does **not** have **any more** patience.*
Ils reçoivent des **gens** / **tout le monde.**	Ils **ne** reçoivent **personne.**
*They receive **people** / **everyone**.*	*They do **not** receive **anybody**.*

J'ai **beaucoup** d'argent.	Je **n'ai que** deux dollars.
*I have **a lot of** money.*	*I have **only** two dollars.*
Il va **souvent / toujours** en cours.	Il **ne** va **jamais** en cours.
*He **often / always** goes to class.*	*He **never** goes to class.*

Mots clés   Negative Expressions

ne... jamais	*never, not ever*
ne... personne	*no one, nobody, not anyone*
ne... plus	*no longer, no more, not any longer, not any more*
ne... rien	*nothing, not anything*
ne... que	*only*

B. Position of Negatives

1. The negative expressions **ne... jamais, ne... plus,** and **ne... rien** are used in exactly the same places in sentences as **ne... pas:** surrounding the conjugated verb and any object pronouns in declarative sentences and surrounding the verb and pronoun subject with inversion.

   Nous **n'**allons **plus** aller à cette bijouterie.
   Cette épicière **ne** m'a **jamais** servi!
   N'as-tu **rien** vu à la boutique?

2. The negative **ne... personne** surrounds the helping verb *and* the past participle in the **passé composé.** It surrounds the conjugated verb and the infinitive with double verbs.

   Nous **n'**avons reconnu **personne.**   Je **ne** veux oublier **personne.**

3. The **que** of **ne... que** immediately precedes the noun or preposition it modifies.

   Je **n'**ai pas de pâté; je **n'**ai **que** de la choucroute.
   Elles **n'**ont vu **qu'**un film français.
   Nous **n'**étudions **qu'**après les actualités.

4. **Rien** and **personne** can be the subject of a sentence. In this case, **ne** comes after them.

Rien n'est arrivé.	*Nothing happened.*
Personne n'est venu.	*No one came.*

5. **Jamais, personne,** and **rien** can be used alone as responses to statements or questions.

   Tu regardes les émissions de variété? —**Jamais!**
   Qui vous a invité? —**Personne!**
   Qu'est-ce qu'il a commandé? —**Rien.**

ATTENTION

1. Remember that the indefinite and partitive articles all become **de** in the negative. The only exception is **ne... que,** which does not require the article to change because it does not express complete negation.

   Ils ont toujours **des** idées; ils n'ont jamais **d'**argent.
   Je n'ai pas **de** dollars; je n'ai que **des** francs.

2. While it is possible to use two or more negative expressions in the same sentence, **pas** is never used with **jamais, plus, personne,** or **rien.**

   Elle ne mange **plus rien** le matin.   *She no longer eats anything*
   in the morning.

   Je ne vois **jamais plus personne.**   *I never see anyone anymore.*

3. To contradict a negative question or statement, use the word **si.**

   —Vous **n'**avez **plus** de hors-d'œuvre?
   —**Si,** j'ai encore du pâté.

CE QU'ILS DISENT

1. In conversations, French speakers often drop **ne** from the negation.

   J'ai plus de patience.   Ils ont vu personne.

2. **Que** can also be used entirely by itself to mean *only.*

   Que de l'eau, s'il vous plaît!

Langue

A. **Eric n'est pas comme son ami Luc.** Remplacez **Luc** par **Eric** et mettez les phrases suivantes à la forme négative.

   MODELE: Luc fait beaucoup de choses. *Eric ne fait rien.*

   1. Luc a encore du temps pour vous.
   2. Luc a perdu quelque chose.
   3. Luc a rencontré quelqu'un à la brasserie.
   4. Luc va acheter quelque chose pour sa mère.
   5. Luc aime toujours recevoir ses amis.
   6. Luc téléphone à quelqu'un samedi.

B. Répondez aux questions suivantes à la forme affirmative.

1. Tu ne manges jamais dans un parc?
2. Ton frère ne veut jamais m'inviter?
3. Tu n'es plus malheureux?
4. Personne ne te comprend?
5. Tes amis ne font rien?
6. Il n'y a personne chez toi?
7. Tu ne bois plus de vin?
8. Tu ne peux rien faire?

C. **J'ai été difficile hier.** Mettez les phrases suivantes au passé composé.

1. Je ne veux rien boire.
2. Je ne bois que de l'eau minérale.
3. Je ne fais jamais la vaisselle.
4. Je ne reçois personne chez moi.
5. Je ne suis jamais content.
6. Tu n'as plus peur de moi?

Culture

D. **Les magasins en France.** Qu'est-ce qu'on trouve dans les magasins suivants? Combinez les mots donnés pour former des phrases correctes en choisissant entre les mots entre parenthèses.

MODELE: trouver (souvent / jamais) / jambon / boucherie
On ne trouve jamais de jambon dans une boucherie.

1. (Tout le monde / Personne) / aller / bijouterie / pour acheter des disques
2. On / aller / (souvent / jamais) / papeterie / pour acheter un stylo
3. Les charcutiers / vendre / (toujours / jamais) / rôtis de veau
4. (Les gens / Personne) / aller à l'hypermarché pour acheter des vêtements
5. Les buralistes / vendre / (toujours / jamais) / viande
6. Si on / chercher / légumes, / on / trouver / (tout / rien) / dans une pâtisserie

Communication

E. **Mes habitudes.** Qu'est-ce que vous faites **souvent, assez souvent** ou **de temps en temps** *(from time to time)*, et qu'est-ce que vous ne faites jamais ou **presque jamais**? Utilisez les suggestions données ou vos propres idées.

MODELE: étudier le samedi soir   *Je n'étudie jamais le samedi soir.*
manger du poisson   *Je mange du poisson de temps en temps.*

avoir faim l'après-midi
boire de l'alcool
faire du sport
sortir avec un footballeur

écouter de la musique classique
fréquenter les pâtisseries
perdre mon temps
???

F. **Le snobisme.** Pour être snob, il ne faut faire ou utiliser que certaines choses. Qu'est-ce qu'on doit faire dans les situations page 306?

MODELE: servir / vin   *On ne sert que du vin français.*

1. porter / jean...
2. porter / chaussures...
3. aimer les... (autos)

4. sortir avec...
5. passer / vacances à...
6. faire des courses à...

MODELE: manger à   *Il ne faut jamais manger à McDonald's.*

7. fréquenter...
8. porter...
9. écouter des disques de...

10. inviter...
11. passer ses vacances...
12. utiliser...

G. **Questions personnelles.** Votre vie personnelle

1. Est-ce que vous allez inviter quelqu'un à dîner? Quand?
2. Est-ce que vous servez toujours du lait?
3. Quand est-ce que vous ne faites rien?
4. Quand est-ce que vous ne voulez voir personne?
5. Est-ce que vous devez de l'argent à quelqu'un?
6. Qu'est-ce que vous n'avez jamais fait?

COMMUNIQUONS ·····························

Parler d'argent

The monetary system in France is based on the franc. Francs are available as bills (**billets de banque**) in denominations of twenty, fifty, one hundred, two hundred, and five hundred francs and as coins (**pièces**) in denominations of one, two, five, ten, and twenty francs. In a **franc,** there are one hundred **centimes,** which are available only as coins in denominations of five, ten, twenty, and fifty **centimes.** Belgian and Swiss currency are also called **francs.**

De l'argent français

In contrast to American banknotes, French bills vary both in size and color according to the denomination and depict famous artists and writers as well as heads of state. In addition, French banknotes have a white spot, which contains a watermark to prevent counterfeiting.

It is possible to obtain French currency in exchange for dollars at large banks in many American cities. In France, francs are available in traveler's checks (**les chèques de voyage**), but some stores will not accept them. The most advantageous way of changing money in France is at a bank. After hours, you can find currency exchanges (**les bureaux de change**) at airports and large train stations. You may also change money at many hotels and restaurants, but at lower rates. The latest development in currency exchange is the installation of machines similar to American automated teller machines that change money automatically.

On fait des achats.

C'est combien?	*How much is it?*
Je vous dois combien?	*How much do I owe you?*
Combien coûte ce stylo / coûtent ces stylos?	*How much does this pen / do these pens cost?*
Quel est le prix de cette cassette?	*What's the price of this cassette?*
Quel est le taux de change du dollar?	*What's the exchange rate for the dollar?*
Gardez la monnaie.	*Keep the change.*
Le vendeur fait de la monnaie.	*The sales clerk is making change.*
Je vous rends la monnaie, Monsieur.	*I'm giving you the change, sir.*
Je vous remercie.	*Thank you.*
On ne marchande pas dans cette boutique.	*One doesn't bargain / haggle in this shop.*
Ça coûte soixante-quinze centimes.	*That costs seventy-five centimes.*
Ce stylo coûte un franc cinquante (1,50 F).	*That pen costs one franc and fifty centimes.*
Le prix? C'est trois francs dix (3,10 F).	*The price? It's three francs and ten centimes.*

On parle d'argent.

Mon père me donne de l'argent de poche chaque semaine.	*My father gives me an allowance every week.*
Il ne faut pas dépenser trop d'argent.	*One shouldn't spend too much money.*

J'économise / Je fais des économies. — *I'm saving my money.*

Je ne gaspille jamais mon argent. — *I never waste my money.*

Ce magnétoscope coûte cher. — *This VCR is expensive.*

Dix dollars pour cette chemise? C'est bon marché! — *Ten dollars for this shirt? That's cheap!*

Interaction *Un client fait des achats à la papeterie.*

LE PAPETIER: Voilà vos enveloppes et votre stylo.

LE CLIENT: Merci, je vous dois combien?

LE PAPETIER: Trente-sept francs cinquante, s'il vous plaît.

LE CLIENT: Je suis désolé, monsieur, mais je n'ai qu'un billet de cinq cents francs.

LE PAPETIER: *Cela ne fait rien.* Je vais vous rendre la monnaie... Trente-sept cinquante, trente-huit, quarante, cinquante, cent, trois cents, et cinq cents! Je vous remercie.

That doesn't matter.

Activités

A. Répondez aux questions suivantes.

1. Combien d'argent de poche recevez-vous chaque *(each)* mois?
2. Combien d'argent avez-vous sur vous en ce moment? Avez-vous la monnaie d'un dollar?
3. Avez-vous économisé de l'argent? Pourquoi? Qu'est-ce que vous avez fait pour avoir cet argent?
4. Qu'est-ce qui coûte trop cher? Qu'est-ce qui est bon marché?

B. Jouez les scènes suivantes avec un(e) camarade de cours.

1. Vous entrez dans une boulangerie pour acheter du pain et des croissants.
2. Vous voulez acheter un beau pantalon dans un marché aux puces *(flea market)* mais vous pensez qu'il coûte trop cher. Marchandez!
3. Dans un restaurant où vous venez de dîner, le garçon vous apporte l'addition *(check)*. Vous trouvez une erreur. Expliquez-la au garçon.
4. Vous avez une interview pour un travail. Demandez combien on va vous payer (**dollars de l'heure**). Est-ce que c'est assez?

LECTURE CULTURELLE ....

Avant la lecture

In the last twenty years, French attitudes toward spending money have changed radically. Because of inflation, changing habits, and the availability of new products, the French spend a much larger percentage of their income than before, and more of their money goes toward buying services, leaving less available for the purchase of durable goods (furniture, appliances, etc.). While Americans have experienced the same changes, the similarity stops there. The French save 13% of their income; Americans save only 4 to 6%.

Another interesting development in the way French people handle their money is their greater use of credit cards and checks. Cash transactions are now limited to small purchases in neighborhood stores. To pay for major purchases, a hotel or restaurant bill, and even gasoline, people routinely write checks or use a credit card. In addition, the French are ahead of North Americans in their use of electronic money. Using their **Minitel,** many French people perform a wide array of financial transactions from their homes without going to their bank.

Activités

A. What would be the major purchases for a family under the following categories?

Durable Goods	**Non-durable Goods**
1.	1.
2.	2.
3.	3.

B. Close or exact cognates, such as **l'impression,** are easy to identify. See if you can guess the meanings of the following words found in the **Lecture culturelle** even though they differ from English by several letters.

dépenses	en fait	diminuent
maintenir	éphémères	courant
typique	assurances	la somme

EUROCARD –
vous ouvre nombre de portes dans le monde entier.

Titulaire de la carte EUROCARD, vous serez cordialement bienvenu dans quelque 4,2 millions d'hôtels, restaurants, magasins et entreprises de services dans le monde entier. EUROCARD est en effet l'un des plus importants moyens de paiement internationaux vous permettant d'avoir toujours sur vous exactement ce qu'il vous faut et quelle que soit la monnaie.

Les Français et l'argent

Comment les Français dépensent-ils leur argent? Que font-ils de leurs *revenus* quand ils ont payé leurs *impôts?* Ils n'ont que deux solutions: dépenser ou *épargner*. Pendant longtemps, la majorité des gens a choisi de faire des économies, mais depuis les années 70, la crise économique a forcé les Français
5 à dépenser plus pour maintenir ou *améliorer* leur *niveau de vie*. En 1978, ils ne dépensaient que 82,5% de leurs revenus, mais maintenant, ce pourcentage est de 87%.

    Quand on examine le budget d'une famille française typique, on a l'impression qu'ils mangent de moins en moins et qu'ils n'achètent plus de
10 vêtements pour pouvoir *consacrer* plus d'argent à leur santé et à leurs *loisirs*. En fait, une analyse détaillée montre que les Français continuent à dépenser de plus en plus d'argent pour leur nourriture.

    Dans un budget, l'examen de la part des biens durables (*meubles, équipement ménager*, voiture, etc.) et de celle des dépenses plus éphémères (*ali-*
15 *mentation*, services) donne une idée de l'évolution du *mode de vie* des Français.

    Aujourd'hui, les biens durables représentent moins de 10% des dépenses des familles. La quantité de biens durables vendus a beaucoup augmenté jusqu'en 1972 avec la généralisation des télévisions, *machines à laver*, etc., et puis leurs *ventes ont baissé*. Il est probable que la nouvelle génération
20 d'équipement comme le magnétoscope, l'ordinateur personnel, le lecteur laser et le *four à micro-ondes*, provoque une nouvelle augmentation de la vente des biens durables.

    On remarque aussi que les Français dépensent de plus en plus pour les achats de services. Une distinction entre les achats de produits manufacturés et
25 ceux de services (assurances, *réparations, coiffeur*) montre que les premiers diminuent et les seconds augmentent.

income

taxes

save

improve / standard of living

devote / leisure

furniture

appliances / food

way of life

washing machines

sales / have dropped

microwave oven

repairs / hairdresser

Comment les Français réussissent-ils à continuer d'améliorer leur niveau de vie et à acheter plus? Ils le font *grâce* au crédit. Consommer avant de payer! Le principe est maintenant très *courant* en France et il donne à des millions de
30 Français la possibilité de posséder des biens qu'ils ne *pourraient* jamais avoir *autrement*. Personne ne veut attendre plusieurs années pour économiser la somme nécessaire pour acheter une voiture. Le crédit permet aussi à la majorité des gens de devenir propriétaires d'un *logement*. *Cependant*, le crédit n'a pas que des avantages, et beaucoup de gens sont allés trop loin sur la route de
35 l'*endettement* et ne peuvent plus *faire face à* leurs *engagements*.

    thanks

    common

    could

    otherwise

    apartment / However

    debts / face / commitments

Après un début assez lent dans les années 70, les Français sont maintenant plus de 10 millions à posséder au moins une carte de crédit, et la carte n'est plus considérée comme un privilège réservé aux *hommes d'affaires* et aux *cadres supérieurs*. *La plupart des* Français la considère aujourd'hui comme un
40 instrument utile et souvent indispensable. Aujourd'hui, ils l'utilisent pour acheter 25% des TV, 33% des magnétoscopes, 25% des *lave-vaisselle*, et 25% des machines à laver.

    businessmen

    upper-level managers /

      Most

    dishwashers

(Adapté de *Francoscopie 1991* / Larousse)

Après la lecture

Questions sur le texte

1. Pourquoi est-ce que les Français dépensent plus d'argent depuis 1970?
2. Quel pourcentage de leurs revenus est-ce qu'ils économisaient en 1978? Et maintenant?
3. Est-ce que les Français dépensent de moins en moins d'argent pour leur nourriture?
4. Quelle sorte d'équipement contribue à l'augmentation de la vente des biens durables?
5. Combien de Français possèdent au moins une carte de crédit?
6. Qu'est-ce que les gens achètent en utilisant le crédit?

Activités

A. Regardez la liste suivante des dépenses des Français. Ajoutez les pourcentages qui *(which)* correspondent à votre situation maintenant. Et si vous aviez une famille?

Les dépenses	Les Français	Moi	Avec une famille
Alimentation	21,3%	_____	_____
Vêtements	6,2%	_____	_____
Logement	17,9%	_____	_____
Santé	13,5%	_____	_____
Transports	13,6%	_____	_____
Loisirs	6,4%	_____	_____

B. Répondez aux questions suivantes.

1. Avez-vous acheté des biens durables récemment? Quoi? Les avez-vous achetés à crédit?
2. Avez-vous des cartes de crédit? Combien? Est-ce un avantage ou un désavantage?
3. Que pensez-vous de la nécessité des biens suivants? Indiquez s'ils sont indispensables, utiles ou si c'est un privilège de les avoir.

des meubles	un magnétoscope
une voiture	une machine à laver
un téléviseur	un lecteur laser
un ordinateur personnel	une chaîne stéréo

TOUS ENSEMBLE!

A. Répondez aux questions suivantes en employant les mots entre parenthèses.

Les amis

1. As-tu vu Françoise?   (Oui,... venir... hier)
2. Tu m'aimes?   (Oui,...)
3. Etes-vous étonnées que vos copains ne vous téléphonent jamais?   (Oui,...)
4. Qui a appris cela à ton ami?   (Personne...)
5. Est-ce que je peux te voir ce soir?   (Non, parler... demain)

Les activités

6. Est-ce que vous pouvez nous prêter votre auto?   (Oui,...)
7. Avez-vous peur qu'il fasse mauvais demain?   (Oui, je... pleuvoir)
8. Est-ce que vous venez me voir?   (Oui,...)
9. Est-il possible que vous partiez demain?   (Non, il faut que... partir aujourd'hui)
10. Est-ce que je vous ai vus à la boulangerie?   (Oui,...)

B. Refaites les phrases suivantes en utilisant les mots entre parenthèses.

Qu'est-ce qu'il y a?

1. Elle part à neuf heures et elle va à la charcuterie.   (Hier,...)
2. Quelque chose est arrivé au courrier.   (Rien...)
3. Je les vois quand ils sortent.   (... la semaine dernière.)
4. Il a attendu trois minutes.   (... ne... que...)
5. Elles connaissent des étrangers.   (L'année dernière,...)

Des opinions

6. Je suis sûr qu'il ne veut pas venir.   (... furieux...)
7. Il ne faut pas qu'on oublie les sans-abris.   (... devoir...)
8. Je doute qu'ils soient pauvres.   (... penser...)
9. Es-tu sûr que nous ayons un désastre écologique?   (Moi, je suis sûr...)
10. Je dois partir quand elle arrive.   (... hier.)

313

C. Faites des phrases complètes avec les mots donnés, en faisant les changements nécessaires.

Des activités

1. Jeanne / travailler / jamais / dans / boucherie
2. Hier / nous / descendre / en ville / avec / enfants
3. Paul / boire / jamais / eau
4. Hier soir / je / recevoir / personne
5. Tu / venir / répondre / téléphone?

La famille

6. Personne / devoir / rien / mes parents
7. Il / être / peu probable / tu / voir / ton / grands-parents
8. Quand / je / habiter / Québec / je / recevoir / souvent / cousins
9. Mon / sœurs / tenir / faire / promenade
10. Mes parents / ne... pas penser / guerre / être / possible

D. Complétez le paragraphe suivant avec la forme correcte des verbes donnés.

Le week-end dernier, Chantal et ses sœurs _____ (décider) d'aller au bord de la mer. Elle _____ (inviter) son petit ami Charles; il ne _____ (pouvoir) pas aller avec elles, mais il _____ (recommander) une belle plage près d'Arcachon.

Quand elles _____ (partir), il _____ (faire) du brouillard et il _____ (falloir) qu'elles _____ (faire) attention. Il _____ (être) cinq heures quand elles _____ (partir), mais dans la voiture personne ne _____ (dormir). Après deux heures, elles _____ (arriver) dans une petite ville. Il _____ (être) sept heures et tout le monde _____ (vouloir) continuer pour être à la mer avant les touristes. Mais Chantal _____ (être) fatiguée et elle _____ (vouloir) qu'on _____ (prendre) quelque chose. Elles _____ (chercher) un café ou un restaurant, mais comme il _____ (être) peu probable qu'elles _____ (pouvoir) trouver un café ouvert à cette heure, elles _____ (décider) de continuer.

Elles _____ (arriver) deux heures plus tard. Elles _____ (sortir) de la voiture et _____ (aller) sur la plage. Chantal _____ (comprendre) tout de suite pourquoi Charles aime cette plage: il n'y _____ (avoir) que des nudistes!

E. Complétez les phrases suivantes de manière logique.

1. Je ne pense pas que...
2. Il est probable que...
3. Mes parents veulent que...
4. A ma résidence, nous venons de...
5. Il ne faut pas que nous...
6. Je doute que mon professeur...
7. Hier, j'ai reçu...
8. Je suis sûr(e) que...
9. Les Américains pensent que...
10. Il se peut que...

ENTRE NOUS!

A. Interviewez un(e) camarade de cours et posez-lui les questions suivantes. Après, informez la classe des résultats.

1. Que veux-tu faire dans la vie?
2. Quelle sorte de travail as-tu déjà fait?
3. Où es-tu allé(e) le week-end dernier?
4. Qu'est-ce que tu as fait?
5. Qu'est-ce que tu ne fais jamais?
6. Qui te donne ton argent?

B. En petits groupes, interrogez vos camarades de cours sur leurs compétences. Qu'est-ce qu'ils savent faire? Quand est-ce qu'ils ne peuvent pas faire ces choses et pourquoi?

C. Racontez votre enfance *(childhood)* à un(e) camarade de cours. Employez les expressions suivantes ou vos propres idées.

jouer beaucoup   être méchant(e)
manger beaucoup de glace   dormir l'après-midi
regarder... à la télévision   ???

D. En petits groupes, expliquez vos réactions aux situations suivantes. Utilisez les suggestions suivantes ou d'autres expressions.

A	B
J'ai peur que	il y a un conflit international
Je pense que	le Président va à Moscou
Je ne pense pas que	le Canada veut coloniser les Etats-Unis
???	les jeunes peuvent influencer le gouvernement
	les athlètes russes ne sont pas compétitifs
	le Japon vend trop de voitures aux Etats-Unis
	l'inflation est un problème sérieux

E. Avec un(e) camarade de cours, faites une liste des activités que vous devez faire. Utilisez les suggestions suivantes ou vos propres idées.

étudier plus souvent?   faire une lettre à des amis?
téléphoner à mes parents?   aller à l'église?
dormir moins?   réparer ma voiture?

F. **Jeu de rôles.** Jouez les scènes suivantes avec un(e) camarade de cours.

1. Vous avez loué une voiture et vous la rendez à l'agence. Vous devez expliquer pourquoi vous êtes en retard.
2. Vous êtes journaliste. Interviewez trois personnes qui ont vu un accident de voiture.

3. Vous téléphonez au charcutier pour commander un dîner pour huit personnes. Quels plats voulez-vous servir?

4. Vous êtes dans un hypermarché et vous ne pouvez rien trouver. Demandez à un(e) employé(e) où vous pouvez trouver les choses que vous cherchez.

5. Vous cherchez du travail. Un(e) camarade de cours va prendre des renseignements sur votre identité (nom, âge, adresse...) et va vous poser des questions sur vos compétences.

6. Vous êtes journaliste et vous préparez un reportage sur les opinions des étudiants à votre université. Interrogez des camarades de cours pour voir s'ils sont optimistes ou pessimistes pour l'avenir. Qu'est-ce qui les préoccupe?

LA SANTÉ

On fait du sport derrière la tour Eiffel.

Commençons ....

Chez le médecin `▭`

Paul Prévot va consulter son médecin car il dort mal et il est très fatigué depuis deux semaines.

LE MEDECIN: Bonjour, Paul. Qu'est-ce qui ne va pas?

PAUL: Depuis quinze jours je suis très fatigué et le soir, je m'endors très tard.

LE MEDECIN: Est-ce que vous vous couchez de bonne heure? Est-ce que vous vous réveillez tôt le matin? Vous reposez-vous dans la journée?

PAUL: Je me couche généralement vers onze heures et je ne me lève jamais avant sept heures, mais je ne ferme pas l'œil de la nuit.

LE MEDECIN: Déshabillez-vous. Je vais vous examiner mais je ne pense pas que cela soit sérieux.

L'examen terminé, le médecin appelle Paul dans son bureau.

PAUL: Alors, docteur, j'espère que ce n'est pas trop grave!

LE MEDECIN: Je ne trouve rien. Il faut que vous vous détendiez davantage. Faites-vous de l'exercice régulièrement?

PAUL: Non, mais je me promène tous les soirs après dîner.

LE MEDECIN: Très bien. Ne vous inquiétez pas, mais suivez mon conseil: Evitez de boire du café avant de vous coucher, mais si cela ne va pas mieux, il va falloir qu'on vous fasse une prise de sang.

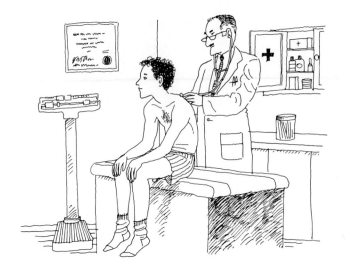

Mots clés

consulter	*visit*	Déshabillez-vous.	*Get*
Qu'est-ce qui ne va pas?	*What's wrong?*	(se déshabiller)	*undressed.*
		examiner	*examine*
m'endors (s'endormir)	*fall asleep*	appelle (appeler)	*calls*
		grave	*serious*
tard	*late*	vous détendiez	*relax*
vous vous couchez (se coucher)	*you go to bed*	(se détendre)	
		davantage	*more*
		Faites-vous de l'exercice?	*Do you exercise?*
vous vous réveillez (se réveiller)	*you wake up*	régulièrement	*regularly*
		me promène (se promener)	*go for a walk*
tôt	*early*		
reposez-vous (se reposer)	*you rest*	bien	*well*
		Ne vous inquiétez pas. (s'inquiéter)	*Don't worry.*
journée	*day*		
généralement	*generally*		
vers	*about, around*	évitez (éviter)	*avoid*
me lève (se lever)	*get up*	ne va pas mieux (aller mieux)	*do not feel better*
ne ferme pas l'œil	*can't sleep, don't close my eyes*	fasse une prise de sang	*do a blood test*
de la nuit	*all night long*		

FAISONS CONNAISSANCE

The medical profession remains a popular choice for young people in France, and medical students must go through a rigorous training that begins the year after high school. However, a surplus of physicians, particularly in the major urban centers, is beginning to create problems. Many physicians now have to compete for patients; their average income is decreasing; and the profession as a whole has lost some of its social prestige.

Many family doctors in France still follow the tradition of making house calls. A family would never go to a hospital first for an emergency—it would call the doctor. Many doctors work in their own apartments and do not have secretarial help. French citizens and foreigners working in France are reimbursed by the social security system for 80 percent of their medical expenses.

Dentistry does not have the same appeal as medicine. Unless they are specialists, dentists do not generally earn as much money as physicians. For the most part, French people wait until they have a problem before going to the dentist instead of going regularly for checkups.

A la pharmacie

   In France, many people consult pharmacists rather than doctors or dentists for minor problems. A pharmacist can offer advice and sell medicines over the counter that might not be available in this country without a prescription. Pharmacies are numerous in French cities and are easily identifiable by the green cross (**la croix verte**) that hangs above the store. When a pharmacy is closed, there is always a sign hanging on the door with the address of the nearest **pharmacie de garde** or **de nuit,** which is the pharmacy designated to stay open at night or on Sunday and holidays.

Etudions le dialogue

   1. Pourquoi Paul Prévot va-t-il chez le médecin?
   2. Combien d'heures est-ce qu'il dort?
   3. Est-ce que le docteur pense que c'est grave?
   4. Est-ce qu'il examine Paul?
   5. Qu'est-ce que le docteur recommande?
   6. Est-ce qu'il faut que Paul boive beaucoup de café?

Enrichissons notre vocabulaire

Les parties du corps *(Parts of the body)*

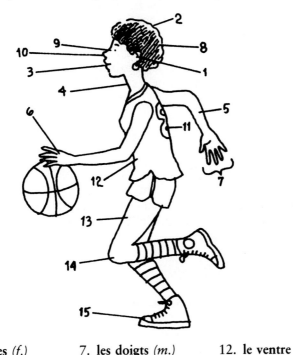

1. les oreilles *(f.)*	7. les doigts *(m.)*	12. le ventre
2. la tête	8. les cheveux *(m.)*	13. la jambe
3. la bouche	9. les yeux /	14. le genou
4. la gorge	l'œil *(m.)*	15. le pied
5. le bras	10. le nez	
6. la main	11. le dos	

La santé *(Health)*

être en bonne / mauvaise santé	*to be in good / bad health*
avoir bonne mine / mauvaise mine	*to look good / bad*
avoir mal à	*to hurt*
être malade	*to be ill*
avoir de la fièvre	*to have a fever*
se porter bien	*to be in good health*
être au régime	*to be on a diet*
aller chez le dentiste	*to go to the dentist*
—Qu'est-ce qui te fait mal? / Où as-tu mal?	*Where does it hurt?*
—J'ai mal aux dents *(f.)*, au cou, à l'épaule *(f.)*, à la cheville.	*My teeth, neck, shoulder, ankle hurt.*
—Tu es hypochondriaque!	*You're a hypochondriac!*

Prononciation   **Initial and Final Consonant Sounds**   `○━○`

A. If you place your hand in front of your mouth and pronounce an English word starting with the /p/, /t/, or /k/ sounds, you will feel a puff of air. This is *aspiration*, and you must avoid it in French when you pronounce such initial consonant sounds.

Listen carefully to your teacher and repeat the following pairs of words, trying to eliminate the aspiration in the French words.

English	French		English	French
Paul	Paul		two	tout
Paris	Paris		car	car

B. Final consonant sounds are stronger in French than in English. In French, it is very important to pronounce final consonant sounds clearly. As you know, some grammatical distinctions depend on the presence or absence of a final consonant sound in the oral form.

Gender: étudiant /e ty djã/, étudiante /e ty djãt/
Number: il descend /il dɛ sã/, ils descendent /il dɛ sãd/

Repeat the following pairs of words after your teacher, making the final consonant sound much stronger in French.

English	French		English	French
habit	habite		port	porte
bees	bise		long	langue
descend	descendent		mine	mine

Repeat the following words after your teacher, making sure to pronounce the final consonant sound clearly.

verte / sorte / verbe / servent / heureuse / tienne / sac /
    rendent / tête

Exercice

Read the following sentences aloud, avoiding the aspiration of initial consonant sounds and stressing final ones.

1. Le professeur pose une question intéressante.
2. Patrick passe l'été dans l'appartement de sa tante.
3. Au printemps, à Paris, les cafés sont pleins de monde.
4. Ces pays deviennent de plus en plus pauvres.
5. Un cours de psychologie demande beaucoup de travail.
6. Brigitte part faire des courses avec Monique.

GRAMMAIRE ....

I. Stem-Changing Verbs

> You use verbs to describe actions or states of being.

A. Two groups of common -er verbs have stem changes in the **je, tu, il,** and **ils** forms of the present indicative. These are verbs that have é or e at the end of their stem, such as **préférer** and **acheter**.

préférer	acheter
je préfère	j' achète
tu préfères	tu achètes
il / elle / on préfère	il / elle / on achète
nous préférons	nous achetons
vous préférez	vous achetez
ils / elles préfèrent	ils / elles achètent

Mots clés **Verbs conjugated like préférer and acheter**

Préférer		Acheter	
espérer	to hope	amener	to bring
inquiéter	to worry	emmener	to take
posséder	to own	enlever	to take off / away
répéter	to repeat	lever	to raise
sécher (un cours)	to cut class	promener	to walk

Je **préfère** la cuisine vietnamienne. Qu'est-ce que vous **préférez**?
Eux, ils n'**achètent** jamais rien, mais nous, nous **achetons** souvent des vêtements.

B. Note that in the **je, tu, il,** and **ils** forms, the vowel at the end of the stem is pronounced as a more open / ɛ / sound, thus causing a change from é or e to an **accent grave** (è) before a pronounced final consonant.

préférer → je préfère	/ ʒø pre fɛʀ /
répéter → tu répètes	/ ty ʀe pɛt /
acheter → elles achètent	/ ɛl za ʃɛt /
lever → il lève	/ il lɛv /

▶ L'Orthographe

1. **Appeler** *(to call)* uses a double **l** instead of an **accent grave** to make the vowel sound / ɛ / before a final consonant. Therefore, the **je, tu, il,** and **ils** forms of the present indicative exhibit this stem change.

   j'appelle, ils appellent   *but:* nous appelons

   Le médecin appelle Paul dans son bureau.

2. In the present indicative, only the **nous** and **vous** forms keep the same pronunciation and spelling as the infinitive because these forms end in a vowel sound and not in a consonant sound.

   espérer → nous espérons   / nu zɛ spe rɔ̃ /
   acheter → vous achetez   / vu za ʃte /

C. Since the present subjunctive has similar endings, the vowels change as in the indicative.

Il faut que je sèche	que j'enlève
que tu sèches	que tu enlèves
qu'on sèche	qu'il / elle / on enlève
que nous séchions	que nous enlevions
que vous séchiez	que vous enleviez
qu'ils sèchent	qu'ils / elles enlèvent

D. The past participle is pronounced like the infinitive; therefore, the vowels in the stem do not change.

   espérer → espéré   lever → levé
   posséder → possédé   appeler → appelé

E. Since the imperfect has a vowel ending in all forms of the verb, the vowel in the stem does not change.

   Je **possédais** une voiture, mais je l'ai vendue.
   Nous **appelions** Jacques quand il est arrivé.

Langue

A. **En classe.** Dans les phrases suivantes, mettez les verbes au singulier au pluriel et les verbes au pluriel au singulier.

   1. Répétez le dialogue!
   2. N'enlève pas tes chaussures en classe.
   3. Nous possédons une bonne calculatrice.
   4. J'espère qu'il va réussir.

5. Ils ont amené des amis.
6. Vous appelez son professeur?
7. Elle va sécher son cours d'espagnol.
8. Achète-lui un nouveau cahier.

B. Substituez les expressions données dans les phrases suivantes.

1. Tu sèches tes cours? (préférer l'eau minérale, espérer gagner le match, enlever ton manteau, promener tes amis, inquiéter ta famille)
2. Elle appelait sa sœur. (posséder une bicyclette, lever la main, espérer être heureuse, préférer aller au cinéma, répéter la question)
3. Je ne pense pas qu'elle achète une voiture. (emmener son ami, préférer les fraises, enlever son imperméable, appeler le docteur, amener les boissons)

Culture

C. **Les préférences des Français.** Choisissez la chose ou la personne que les Français préfèrent parmi *(among)* les trois possibilités.

MODELE: comme distraction: la télé / les livres / les sports
Les Français préfèrent la télé.

1. comme distraction: la radio / les cafés / le cinéma
2. à la télé: la fiction / les films / le journal
3. comme genre de film: les films d'amour / les films d'aventures / les films comiques
4. au cinéma: les westerns / la science-fiction / les films politiques
5. comme film: *E.T. l'Extra-terrestre* / *Les Dix Commandements* / *Dents de la mer*
6. comme acteur: Gérard Depardieu / Sylvester Stallone / Dustin Hoffman

D. **Le français québécois.** Comment est-ce que les Québécois appellent les choses suivantes?

MODELE: un week-end? *Ils l'appellent «une fin de semaine.»*

1. une voiture
2. un dîner
3. un match
4. du jambon
5. de l'auto-stop
6. un film

a. une vue
b. de la fesse
c. un char
d. un souper
e. une joute
f. du pouce

Communication

E. Etes-vous différent(e) de votre camarade de chambre? Choisissez entre les différentes possibilités. Suivez le modèle page 326.

MODELE: le jazz / la musique classique / le rock
Je préfère la musique classique.
Il / Elle préfère le jazz.

1. cinéma / théâtre / télévision
2. lait / thé / bière / vin
3. étudier / faire une promenade / aller danser / sécher les cours
4. la plage / les parcs / le centre-ville
5. avoir une profession bien payée / avoir une profession intéressante
6. parler de grands problèmes / parler de ses amis

F. Trouvez quelqu'un dans la classe qui possède les choses suivantes.

MODELE: un vélo   *Je possède un vélo.*
une calculette   *Marc possède une calculette.*

une auto jaune   un magnétoscope
un lecteur laser   un pantalon vert
des disques des Beatles   une photo de famille
un ordinateur personnel   un Walkman
une carte du monde   des chaussures rouges

G. **Questions personnelles.** L'avenir

1. Qu'est-ce qui vous inquiète? L'avenir? Votre santé?
2. Qu'est-ce que vous allez pouvoir acheter dans dix ans que vous ne pouvez pas acheter maintenant?
3. Combien d'enfants espérez-vous avoir? Préférez-vous des garçons ou des filles?
4. Préférez-vous un beau mari / une belle femme ou un mari / une femme intelligent(e)?
5. Qu'est-ce que vos amis espèrent avoir un jour? Et vous?
6. Quelle erreur n'allez-vous jamais répéter?

II. Reflexive Verbs: Present tense, futur proche, and the Infinitive

> Reflexive verbs in French describe an action that the subject performs upon itself.

A. Present Tense

1. Reflexive verbs are conjugated with a reflexive pronoun, which represents the same person as the subject. Reflexive pronouns have the same position as the other object pronouns you have learned.

se coucher *(to go to bed)*	s'amuser *(to have a good time)*
je **me** couche	je **m'**amuse
tu **te** couches	tu **t'**amuses
il / elle / on **se** couche	il / elle / on **s'**amuse
nous **nous** couchons	nous **nous** amusons
vous **vous** couchez	vous **vous** amusez
ils / elles **se** couchent	ils / elles **s'**amusent

2. In the negative, the reflexive pronoun precedes the conjugated verb.

Je **ne me lève jamais** avant sept heures.

3. With inversion in the interrogative, the reflexive pronoun precedes the conjugated verb.

Vous réveillez-vous tôt le matin?
Paul **se promène-t-il** tous les soirs?

Des lycéens à Orléans

Mots clés   Reflexive Verbs

se coucher

s'endormir

se réveiller

se lever

se laver

se brosser

s'habiller

se promener

s'amuser	to have a good time	se faire mal à	to hurt one's . . .
s'appeler	to be called / named	s'inquiéter	to worry
		s'occuper (de)	to take care of
se dépêcher	to hurry	se rappeler	to remember
se déshabiller	to get undressed	se reposer	to rest
se détendre	to relax	se sentir	to feel
		se trouver	to be located

ATTENTION

Note that definite articles, not possessive adjectives, are used with parts of the body: ownership is understood!

Elle se brosse **les** dents.   Ils se lavent **les** mains.

B. Le futur proche

1. To form the **futur proche,** you conjugate the verb **aller** and place the reflexive pronoun with the infinitive.

   Nous **allons nous reposer** ce soir.
   Tu **vas t'amuser** ce week-end?

2. In the negative, place the negative expression around the conjugated verb.

   Je **ne vais pas m'occuper** de la lessive.
   Nous **n'allons pas nous dépêcher** maintenant.

3. The interrogative with inversion is formed the same way as it is with other verbs in the **futur proche:**

   Vont-elles se promener après les cours?

C. The Infinitive

With an infinitive construction, the reflexive pronoun precedes the infinitive. Reflexive pronouns must represent the same person as the subject, even if the verbs are not conjugated.

Je ne peux pas **m'endormir.**
Tu as besoin de **te détendre!**
Evitez le café avant de **vous coucher.**
Pour **m'amuser,** j'aime passer la journée à la plage.

Langue

A. **Une journée typique de Monique.** Mettez les phrases suivantes à la forme interrogative en utilisant l'inversion.

1. Ton amie s'appelle
   Monique.
2. Elle se réveille tôt.
3. Elle se lave tout de suite.

4. Elle s'habille dans sa chambre.
5. Elle s'occupe de son fils.
6. Son bureau se trouve en ville.

B. **Un week-end à Arcachon.** Mettez les phrases suivantes au futur proche.

1. Nous nous dépêchons de partir.
2. Yvette se promène sur la plage.
3. Je ne me lève pas tôt.
4. Vous ne vous inquiétez pas si Yves amène des copains?
5. Jacques ne s'occupe pas de la vaisselle.
6. Nous nous amusons là-bas.

Culture

C. **La France ou les Etats-Unis?** Formez des phrases complètes avec les mots donnés et dites si l'activité est plus typique des Français ou des Américains.

1. On / faire / bises / avant / se coucher
2. grands-mères / s'appeler / «Mamy»
3. Certains / se dépêcher / payer les impôts *(income taxes)*
4. vieux / se promener / dans / centres commerciaux / pour leur santé
5. On / se déshabiller / sur / plage
6. On / se reposer / au déjeuner
7. Beaucoup de gens / s'inquiéter / leur poids *(weight)*
8. On / se promener / en auto / pour / se détendre

D. **Les provinces françaises.** Traditionnellement, la France est divisée en provinces. Dites *(Say)* dans quelle province on trouve les villes suivantes.

MODELE: Bordeaux   *Bordeaux se trouve en Aquitaine.*

1. Dijon	a. Provence
2. Reims	b. Normandie
3. Brest	c. Bretagne
4. Rouen	d. Bourgogne
5. Marseille	e. Alsace
6. Strasbourg	f. Champagne

Communication

E. **Une journée typique.** Racontez une journée typique dans votre vie. En-suite *(Next),* racontez une journée idéale. Si vous voulez, utilisez les mots de la liste suivante et un adverbe: **à... heure(s), tôt, tard, de bonne heure.**

se réveiller	se dépêcher	s'occuper de
se lever	partir pour les cours	se déshabiller
se laver	rentrer	se coucher
s'habiller	se reposer	???

F. Que faites-vous pour vous amuser? vous reposer? vous endormir? vous détendre? vous réveiller?

MODELE: *Pour me réveiller, je bois du café.*

G. **On s'inquiète.** Quand est-ce que les gens s'inquiètent? Répondez en utilisant un élément de chaque colonne.

A	B	C
Je	s'inquiéter	rentrer tard
Mes parents	quand	faire du stop
Mon petit ami		dépenser trop d'argent
Ma petite amie		sécher les cours
Mon professeur		ne pas répondre aux lettres
???		???

H. **Questions personnelles.** Réfléchissons!

1. Qu'est-ce que vous vous rappelez de votre enfance *(childhood)*?
2. Vous inquiétez-vous souvent? De quoi?
3. Préférez-vous vous coucher tôt ou tard et vous lever tôt ou tard?
4. Quand est-ce que vous vous sentez triste?
5. Où se trouve votre endroit préféré?
6. Qui doit s'occuper des pauvres?

III. Reflexive Verbs: **Passé composé** and Imperative

> You use reflexive verbs in the **passé composé** to describe personal actions that have been completed and in the imperative to give commands.

A. Passé composé

All reflexive verbs are conjugated with **être** in the **passé composé**.

Je **me suis levé** à sept heures.   Tu ne **t'es** pas **couché** hier soir?
Il **s'est inquiété.**   **Vous êtes-vous** déjà **lavé?**

▶ L'Orthographe

1. Unlike other verbs conjugated with **être** in the **passé composé**, the past participle agrees with the reflexive pronoun, which is usually a direct object and which is the same as the subject.

   Nous **nous** sommes habillés.   Elle ne s'est pas dépêchée.

2. There is no agreement with the past participle when a part of the body follows the verb.

   Elle s'est **lavé** les mains.   Nous nous sommes **brossé** les dents.

B. The Imperative

The reflexive pronoun follows the verb in the affirmative and precedes the verb in the negative.

Déshabillez-vous!   Ne te couche pas trop tard!
Dépêchons-nous!   Ne vous inquiétez pas trop!

ATTENTION
The pronoun **te** becomes **toi** when it *follows* the verb.

Ne **te** dépêche pas!   → Dépêche-**toi!**
Ne **t'**habille pas maintenant! → Habille-**toi** maintenant!

Langue

A. **Notre journée d'hier.** Mettez les phrases suivantes au passé composé.

1. Nous nous levons tôt.
2. Vous vous réveillez avant sept heures?
3. Nous ne nous promenons pas avant le déjeuner.
4. Robert et Julie s'amusent après notre promenade.
5. Lise se repose avant le dîner.
6. Jean se dépêche pour dîner avec nous.
7. Tu ne t'endors pas de bonne heure?
8. Je me couche tard.

B. **Des conseils.** Mettez les phrases suivantes à l'impératif pour donner des conseils à vos amis.

1. Tu ne te lèves pas trop tard.
2. Vous vous dépêchez pour aller en classe.
3. Tu te reposes cet après-midi.
4. Nous nous amusons ce soir.
5. Tu ne t'endors pas au concert.
6. Vous vous déshabillez avant de vous coucher.
7. Nous ne nous détendons pas avant l'examen.
8. Vous ne vous couchez pas à deux heures du matin.

Culture

C. **Des Américains ou des Français?** Avec un nom comme **Robert** ou **Michelle,** on peut être français ou américain. Formez des phrases complètes au passé composé pour décrire *(describe)* les activités des personnes suivantes. Ensuite dites si la personne est américaine ou française, selon l'activité.

1. Michelle / téléphoner / sa copine / avant se coucher
2. Robert / se laver / dans sa chambre
3. Michelle / s'amuser / bien / à la plage / pendant tout le mois d'août / avec ses parents
4. Robert / prendre des somnifères *(sleeping pills)* / et il / s'endormir
5. Michelle / s'habiller / très bien / pour aller en cours
6. Robert / laver / voiture / à côté de la rivière

Communication

D. **Expliquez-vous!** Trouvez des excuses ou des raisons pour les situations suivantes. Utilisez les suggestions données ou vos propres idées.

MODELE: Vous êtes très fatigué(e).
    Je n'ai pas pu m'endormir.

1. Vous arrivez en classe en retard.   (se lever tard / ne pas se dépêcher / se coucher à une heure / se faire mal au pied)
2. Un(e) camarade de classe n'a pas fait ses devoirs.   (s'amuser hier soir / s'endormir sur ses livres / se reposer après dîner / avoir mal aux yeux / emmener un ami chez le dentiste)
3. Votre ami(e) a l'air malheureux (-euse).   (s'inquiéter trop / ne pas se détendre assez / ne pas se reposer ce week-end)
4. Vos amis n'ont pas voulu vous recevoir.   (ne pas se laver / ne pas s'habiller / vouloir se promener en ville)

E. **Encore des conseils.** Quels conseils donnez-vous à quelqu'un pour les problèmes suivants? Si vous voulez, utilisez les verbes de la liste page 334 et des adverbes: **moins, plus souvent, plus tôt, plus tard.**

MODELE: Un ami ne veut pas aller en cours.
Promenons-nous!

se lever	se détendre	se réveiller
se coucher	s'amuser	s'endormir
se reposer	se promener	s'inquiéter

1. Vos amis n'ont pas d'énergie.
2. Un(e) ami(e) est trop sérieux (-euse).
3. Vos ami(e)s veulent sortir avec vous.
4. Vos ami(e)s ont peur de ne pas réussir aux examens.
5. Vos parents n'ont pas le temps de prendre le petit déjeuner.
6. Votre camarade de chambre a mal aux jambes.

F. Interrogez un(e) camarade de cours et ensuite racontez sa journée d'hier aux autres. Utilisez les mots de la liste et des adverbes: **heure(s), tôt, de bonne heure, tard.**

se lever	rentrer
se laver	se reposer
s'habiller	dîner avec
prendre le petit déjeuner	se coucher
partir pour l'université	s'endormir
étudier à la bibliothèque	???

G. **Questions personnelles.** Le week-end dernier

1. Est-ce que vous vous êtes réveillé(e) tôt le week-end dernier? A quelle heure?
2. A quelle heure vous êtes-vous levé(e) samedi? dimanche?
3. Vous êtes-vous détendu(e)? Comment?
4. Vos ami(e)s se sont-ils / se sont-elles bien amusé(e)s chez vous? Qu'est-ce que vous avez fait ensemble?
5. Comment est-ce que vous vous êtes habillé(e) dimanche?
6. De quoi est-ce que vous vous êtes occupé(e)?

COMMUNIQUONS ....

Parler de sa santé

The French are extremely health-conscious. For several years, eating healthful foods has been a major concern and each French person averages about six visits to the doctor a year. In addition to traditional medical care, the French believe in homeopathy, visits to health spas, and a close relationship with their pharmacist. Health spas (**stations thermales**) are so widely accepted that Social Security will reimburse a stay that was ordered by a doctor and approved by an examining board. Seeking such care is called **faire une cure** and the patients, **curistes.** Some of these spas are known in the U.S. because they also bottle their water for export (**Vichy, Evian**). Using sea water for therapy is also popular and is called **thalassothérapie.**

One tradition that remains in France is to blame a general malaise on one's liver. Because of the rich foods and alcoholic beverages that they consume, the French still complain of the stereotypical **crise de foie.**

Centre de Thalassothérapie

thalgo la baule

Dispense des cures de Thalassothérapie classiques (Médicale, Remise en Forme, Diététique) ou spécifiques (Anti-tabac, Vithalgo, Thalgo Beauté) pour prévenir ou traiter Troubles Ostéo-articulaires, Affections Cardio-vasculaires, Stress, Surmenage, Surcharges pondérales...

Hébergement privilégié à l'Hotel ROYAL**** du Groupe Lucien BARRIERE relié directement au Centre, ainsi que nombreuses possibilités hôtelières, para-hôtelières et locatives.

Possibilités forfaits séminaires sur demande.

On parle de la santé.

Comment allez-vous?	*How are you?*
Je vais bien.	*I'm fine.*
Je ne vais pas bien.	*I'm not well.*
Comme ci, comme ça.	*So-so.*
Mes grands-parents sont en bonne santé.	*My grandparents are in good health.*
Je suis malade.	*I'm sick.*
Vous sentez-vous bien?	*Do you feel well?*
Non, je me sens un peu fatigué.	*No, I feel a little tired.*

On indique où on a mal.

Les enfants ont mal au ventre.	*The children have a stomachache.*
Elle s'est cassé le bras quand elle est tombée.	*She broke her arm when she fell.*
Il s'est fait mal au genou dans un accident.	*He hurt his knee in an accident.*
Je me suis foulé le poignet.	*I sprained my wrist.*

Interaction   *Monique va chez le médecin.*

LE MEDECIN: Comment allez-vous, Monique?

MONIQUE: Pas très bien. Depuis deux jours j'ai mal *partout*.   *everywhere*

LE MEDECIN: Vous avez de la fièvre? Je vais prendre votre température.

MONIQUE: J'ai mal au dos et j'ai toujours froid. Et je commence à avoir mal à la gorge.

LE MEDECIN: C'est sans doute une petite *grippe*. Déshabillez-vous; je vais   *flu* vous *ausculter*.   *examine*

Activités

A. Où est-ce que les personnages historiques suivants ont eu mal?

  MODELE: Marie Antoinette?
  Elle a eu mal à la gorge.

  1. Van Gogh
  2. Le Cyclope
  3. Jesse James
  4. Socrate
  5. Isaac Newton
  6. Toulouse-Lautrec
  7. Le Capitaine Crochet *(Hook)*
  8. Quasimodo

B. Répondez aux questions suivantes.

  1. Comment allez-vous aujourd'hui?
  2. En général, êtes-vous en bonne ou en mauvaise santé?
  3. Avez-vous été malade récemment? Avez-vous consulté un médecin?
  4. Comment vous sentez-vous maintenant?
  5. Avez-vous souvent mal? Où?
  6. Est-ce que vous vous êtes déjà cassé quelque chose? Que faisiez-vous?

C. Avec un(e) camarade de cours, jouez les scènes suivantes.

  1. Vous êtes chez le médecin. Parlez-lui de vos problèmes de santé.
  2. Vous avez séché votre classe de français hier. Inventez une excuse médicale et présentez-la à votre professeur.
  3. Vous avez mal aux dents. Téléphonez chez le dentiste et prenez rendez-vous *(make an appointment)* avec lui.
  4. Vous travaillez dans une station thermale. Ecoutez les problèmes de vos curistes et donnez-leur de bons conseils.

LECTURE CULTURELLE ....

Avant la lecture

The largest private philanthropic organization dedicated to providing medical services is called **Médecins sans Frontières** *(Doctors Without Borders)* and is headquartered in France. It was founded in 1971 as a response to medical emergencies in various parts of the world.

Medical personnel are asked to volunteer for up to six months at a time. Those staying on site for at least three months receive a salary. The organization goes to areas that have been hit by a disaster, either natural (floods, earthquakes) or man-made (war). The name of the organization comes from the fact that aid is provided to everyone who needs it, regardless of politics, religion, or race.

Activités

A. It is often said that people who study foreign languages increase their vocabulary in their native language. What English words do you know that have the same origin as the following words that appear in the reading passage?

1. secours
2. belligérance
3. terre
4. urgence

5. exode
6. se poursuivent
7. dons
8. fournir

B. **Skimming.** Read the following reading passage without looking up any words. Then make two lists in English containing the following information.

1. types of disasters that cause medical problems
2. activities of **Médecins sans Frontières** in the field

Médecins sans Frontières

«Les Médecins sans Frontières apportent leur *secours* à toutes les victimes de catastrophes naturelles, d'accidents collectifs et de situations de belligérance, sans *aucune* discrimination de race, de politique, de religion ou de philosophie.»   *help*   *any*

(Extrait de la Charte de Médecins sans Frontières)

5   L'association Médecins sans Frontières (MSF) a été *créée* le 20 décembre 1971 par deux groupes de médecins: les uns revenus de mission au Biafra avec la Croix-Rouge Internationale, les autres rentrés du Bangladesh après les *inondations* causées en 1970 par un *raz-de-marée*. Dès le début, l'éthique de l'organisation est affirmée dans sa charte: «*soigner* de manière désintéressée et
10   sans discrimination... ».   *created*   *floods*   *tidal wave / From*   *to treat*

Médecins sans Frontières

Aujourd'hui les Médecins sans Frontières sont présents dans vingt-huit pays du monde. En se développant, l'association a *augmenté* son aide médicale *increased* et a diversifié son rôle: interventions dans des situations diverses comme les conflits armés, les camps de réfugiés, les catastrophes naturelles et les régions
15 sous-médicalisées.

Quand un conflit *éclate* dans un point du globe, les *équipes* de Médecins *breaks out / teams* sans Frontières, composées de *chirurgiens,* d'anesthésistes, d'*infirmières, inter-* *surgeons / nurses /* *viennent* très rapidement pour apporter les *premiers soins* aux *blessés,* dis- *intervene / first aid /* tinguer les cas critiques et assurer le traitement médico-chirurgical souvent *injured*
20 avec des *moyens* rudimentaires. Il faut, par exemple, installer une salle *means* d'opération dans une école, dans un parking ou sous une tente.

Pendant les années 70, on a commencé à voir *apparaître* de nombreux *appear* camps de réfugiés *partout* dans le monde: en Afrique, en Amérique centrale et *everywhere* en Asie du Sud-Est. Aujourd'hui, plus de dix millions de personnes ont *fui* leur *fled*
25 pays, victimes de l'oppression et de la violence.

Médecins sans Frontières a répondu à ce terrible problème humain. L'arrivée massive de milliers de personnes, souvent en mauvaise santé, dans des régimes *parfois* hostiles, pose des problèmes spécifiques: il faut développer *sometimes* rapidement des *soins* curatifs, prévoir l'hygiène et l'*assainissement* du camp, *treatments / disinfection*
30 prévoir et *enrayer* les épidémies favorisées par les mauvaises conditions sani- *stem* taires, éduquer la population et former des auxiliaires médicaux parmi les réfugiés.

L'intervention de Médecins sans Frontières est aussi cruciale dans le cas de catastrophes naturelles. *Tremblement de terre* à Mexico, raz-de-marée au *earthquake*
35 Bangladesh, inondations en Bolivie, éruption volcanique en Colombie,... sont des événements difficiles à prévoir. Ils demandent la mobilisation immédiate de chirurgiens et spécialistes en médecine d'*urgence*. *emergency*

Les missions de Médecins sans Frontières commencent souvent dans un contexte d'urgence (famine, exode) et *se poursuivent* à long terme. Selon les cas, *il s'agit de* reconstruire des hôpitaux ruraux, de les *équiper* de structures chirurgicales, d'installer de petits dispensaires dans la *brousse*, de développer un programme de vaccinations, d'organiser des centres de nutrition, et surtout aussi, de répondre aux besoins des médecins locaux.

continue
it is a question of / equip
bush

Qui sont les Médecins sans Frontières? Médecins, infirmières, *laborantins*, anesthésistes, *sage-femmes*, chirurgiens,... sont aux *avant-postes* des conflits et des cataclysmes. *Désintéressés*, ils sont *chaque* année sept cents à mettre leur professionnalisme au service d'autres hommes en détresse. Les compétences *requises* varient selon les postes, mais les diplômes, l'expérience professionnelle sur le terrain, la bonne connaissance de langues étrangères sont les principaux critères de recrutement.

lab technicians
midwives / outposts
Neutral / each

required

Le financement de Médecins sans Frontières est assuré à 75% par des *dons* individuels. Cette autonomie financière est la garantie de l'indépendance morale de l'organisation. Les autres 25% *proviennent* des financements des programmes médicaux spécifiques par des organisations internationales comme le Haut Commissariat aux Réfugiés des Nations unies, par exemple.

donations

come from

Comme l'indique la charte de l'association, les Médecins sans Frontières sont «anonymes et *bénévoles*. Ils n'attendent de l'exercice de leur activité aucune satisfaction personnelle ou collective. Ils mesurent les risques et les périls des missions qu'ils accomplissent et ne *réclameront*... aucune compensation autre que celle que l'association sera en mesure de leur *fournir*.»

volunteer

will demand
provide

(Adapté d'une annonce de presse de Médecins sans Frontières)

URGENCE AU SOUDAN.
AIDEZ-NOUS ! ➤➤

Tous les malheurs s'abattent à la fois sur un des pays les plus pauvres du monde.

Un million et demi de personnes sans abri dans ce pays déjà meurtri par la guerre et la famine.
Les journaux , la radio, la télévision vous en parlent.
Mais la réalité est pire, avec les cris, les pleurs et l'insoutenable silence, qui succède au désastre...

Les Médecins sans Frontières y sont.
La tâche est immense et les moyens sont infimes.
Mais ils savent que vous êtes avec eux.
Merci infiniment.

Rony Brauman

R. BRAUMAN
Président de Médecins sans Frontières

AGISSEZ DES AUJOURD'HUI

Après la lecture

Questions sur le texte

1. Pourquoi l'organisation s'appelle-t-elle «Médecins sans Frontières»?
2. Dans quelles situations est-ce que les MSF interviennent?
3. Comment sont composées les équipes de MSF?
4. Quels problèmes existent dans les camps de réfugiés?
5. Quelles catastrophes naturelles demandent l'aide des MSF?
6. Quel genre de personnes sont les MSF?
7. Qui paye pour les missions des MSF?
8. Est-ce que les MSF sont bien payés? Pourquoi font-ils cela?

Activités

A. Où est-ce qu'on a eu les désastres suivants?

1. un tremblement de terre	a. Ethiopie
2. un raz-de-marée	b. Johnstown en Pennsylvanie
3. une inondation	c. Irlande
4. une éruption volcanique	d. San Francisco
5. une famine	e. Pompéi
6. un exode	f. Krakatoa

B. Répondez aux questions suivantes.

1. A quelle organisation américaine ou internationale est-ce que MSF ressemblent? Quelles sont les différences entre les deux?
2. Avez-vous envie d'appartenir à une organisation comme MSF? A quelles activités des MSF pouvez-vous participer? Avez-vous déjà aidé une société bénévole? A quelle organisation donnez-vous de l'argent?
3. Quels désastres récents ont nécessité une intervention médicale importante?
4. Est-ce que le gouvernement des Etats-Unis aide les autres pays «sans aucune discrimination» politique? Etes-vous pour ou contre cette idée?

LES SPORTS

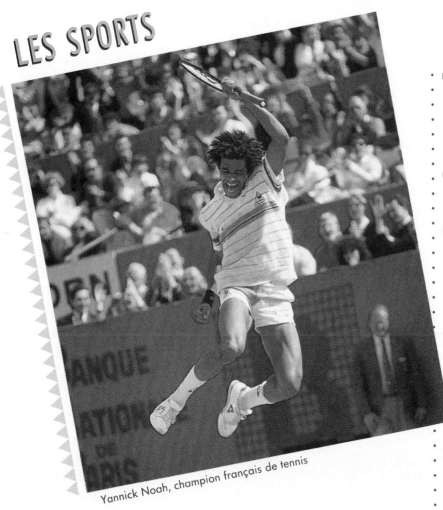

Yannick Noah, champion français de tennis

341

Commençons ....

Chez Ernest à l'heure du Tour de France

*Robert et Jean prennent l'apéritif dans leur café préféré et ils regardent les
informations à la télévision. Ils attendent le reportage sur le Tour de France.
Ernest, le patron, vient de servir un pastis et lève son verre à leur santé.*

ERNEST: A la vôtre, Messieurs!

ROBERT ET JEAN: A la tienne, Nénesse!

JEAN: Oh, regarde, ils vont montrer le film de l'étape d'aujourd'hui.

ROBERT: Celle d'hier était formidable! Le maillot jaune avait encore
deux secondes d'avance à cent mètres de l'arrivée, mais il a
perdu sa première place.

JEAN: J'ai lu dans *L'Equipe* que son contrôle anti-doping était
négatif, et tout le monde dit qu'il va gagner aujourd'hui.

ERNEST: Est-ce que je vous sers un autre pastis? Vos verres sont
vides.

ROBERT: Celui de Jean, oui, mais moi, je n'ai pas encore terminé le
mien.

JEAN: Non, merci. J'ai soixante kilomètres à faire ce soir et il faut
que je me dépêche parce que je n'aime pas conduire la nuit.

Mots clés

informations (f.)	the news	celle	that
patron	proprietor	maillot	jersey
pastis	anise-flavored alcoholic drink	d'avance	ahead
		mètre (m.)	meter (39.4 inches)
		place	place
verre	glass	lu (lire)	read
A la vôtre!	Here's to you! To your health!	contrôle anti-doping	drug test
		négatif	negative
		dit (dire)	says
A la tienne!	Here's to you! To your health!	gagner	to win
		vide	empty
		celui	that
Nénesse	(diminutive for Ernest)	le mien	mine
		kilomètre (m.)	kilometer (0.62 miles)
étape (f.)	stage		

FAISONS CONNAISSANCE

The **Tour de France,** one of the world's major bicycle races, preoccupies many French people each year during July. The race is a succession of day-long stages called **étapes.** Some are quite long and are run over flat countryside; others are much shorter and take place across steep mountainous terrain. The leader in the race, who wears a yellow jersey (**un maillot jaune**) for identification, is established by computing the lowest total time of all the competitors.

Une étape du tour de France

L'Equipe is a daily newspaper devoted entirely to sports. True devotees of the **Tour** rely on it for information during the race. In recent years, considerable emphasis has been placed on checking for drugs. As with all major sporting events, any drugs designed to enhance performance are illegal.

French television gives extensive coverage to the race. There are live broadcasts of each day's finish and filmed highlights on the evening news. Many French people go to cafés to watch the coverage with their friends. While there, they might order a **pastis,** a very popular drink, especially in southern France. It has a strong licorice flavor and is high in alcohol content.

Etudions le dialogue

1. Où sont Robert et Jean?
2. Que font-ils?
3. Qu'est-ce que Nénesse leur dit?
4. Qu'est-ce qu'on va montrer à la télévision?
5. Qu'est-ce que le maillot jaune a fait?
6. Que boivent Robert et Jean?
7. Est-ce que Robert veut encore un pastis? Pourquoi pas?
8. Pourquoi est-ce que Jean ne veut plus de pastis?

Enrichissons notre vocabulaire

Les sports *(Sports)*

l'alpinisme (m)

le base-ball

le basketball

le catch

le deltaplane

l'équitation (f.)

l'escrime (f.)

le football

le football américain

le golf

la gymnastique

le hockey

le jogging

le patinage

le patin à roulettes

la planche à roulettes

le ski

le ski nautique

le tennis

le volley-ball

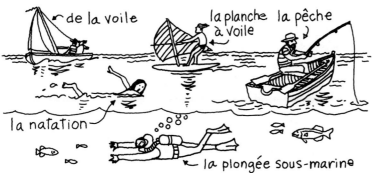

de la voile

la planche à voile

la pêche

la natation

la plongée sous-marine

Pratiquer un sport (To play a sport)

faire du, de la, de l'	to do / play (a sport)	le champion la championne	champion
jouer à	to play (a sport)	le championnat	championship
		l'équipe (f.)	team
nager	to swim	le joueur	player
patiner	to skate	sportif (-ive)	athletic / fond of sports

—Quels sports **pratiquez-vous?**
—Je joue à la **pétanque.**
—Je fais du **rugby.**

What sports do you play?
I play lawn bowling.
I play rugby.

—Nous allons à la **chasse**.	*We go **hunting**.*
—Nous adorons les **courses** *(f.)* de voiture / de bicyclette.	*We love **car races / bike races**.*
—Nous ne sommes pas sportifs; nous jouons seulement aux **cartes** *(f.)*!	*We aren't athletic; we only play **cards**!*

Prononciation   The Sounds /s/, /z/, /sj/ and /zj/   [°—°]

A. The distinction between the sounds /s/ and /z/ is very clear in French. A single letter **s** between two vowels is always pronounced /z/, while a double **s** represents /s/. This permits contrasts between words such as **le désert** and **le dessert**.

Repeat the following pairs of words, which have the same meanings in English and French, but vary between the sounds /s/ and /z/.

English	French	English	French
philosophy	la philosophie	disagreeable	désagréable
dessert	le dessert	disobey	désobéir
curiosity	la curiosité	resemble	ressembler

Now repeat the following words, which contain the sound /s/, the sound /z/, or both.

> ils choisissent / vous finissez / qu'il désobéisse /
> Nénesse / nous réussissons / la bise / tu laisses / la
> phrase / la boisson / la chasse / ennuyeuse /
> mes amis

B. In French, the sounds /s/ and /z/ may be followed by the /j/ sound, which is very similar to the initial sound in *yes*. In English, equivalent words usually have a /ʃ/ sound. In French, it is important to make two distinct sounds, /s/ or /z/, then the /j/ sound.

Repeat the following pairs of words, which contrast the sounds /s/ + /j/ and /z/ + /j/.

/sj/	/zj/	/sj/	/zj/
nous passions	nous faisions	traditionnel	vous lisiez
l'expression	la télévision	les sciences	les yeux
une émission	parisien	une description	une allusion

Now, pronounce the following pairs of words, which contrast the /ʃ/ sound in English with the /sj/ sound in French.

English	French	English	French
patience	la patience	essential	essentiel
pollution	la pollution	national	national
exceptional	exceptionnel	action	l'action

Exercice

Read aloud the following sentences, paying attention to the difference between the /s/ and /z/ sounds and pronouncing the sound /sj/ instead of /ʃ/.

1. Ma cousine a refusé son dessert.
2. Nous allons visiter une église suisse.
3. Les Parisiens préfèrent la conversation à la télévision.
4. Les Tunisiens ont réussi à supporter l'invasion romaine.
5. Il est essentiel que vous annonciez les résultats du championnat d'équitation.
6. Nous excusons son hypocrisie et sa curiosité excessives.

GRAMMAIRE ....

I. -ire Verbs

> You use verbs to describe actions.

A. Several verbs in French have infinitives that end in **-ire** and have similar conjugations.

écrire *(to write)*	conduire *(to drive)*
j'écris	je **conduis**
tu écris	tu **conduis**
il / elle / on écrit	il / elle / on **conduit**
nous écrivons	nous **conduisons**
vous écrivez	vous **conduisez**
ils / elles écrivent	ils / elles **conduisent**

B. To conjugate these verbs, you must learn which pronounced consonant appears in the plural forms. You then add the same endings used with **-ir** verbs like **servir** (Chapter 7).

Ils écrivent des poèmes. Nous ne conduisons pas la nuit.

ECRIVEZ LE FRANÇAIS COMME LES FRANÇAIS

GRAMR

Détecteur d'erreurs grammaticales, correcteur orthographique & conjugueur

Mots clés   -ire Verbs

conduire	*to drive*	nous conduisons
se conduire	*to behave*	nous nous conduisons
décrire	*to describe*	nous décrivons
dire	*to say / tell*	nous disons
écrire	*to write*	nous écrivons
lire	*to read*	nous lisons
produire	*to produce*	nous produisons
traduire	*to translate*	nous traduisons

Tout le monde **dit** qu'il va gagner.
Décrivez-moi l'étape d'aujourd'hui.
Ils **lisent** *L'Equipe* tous les jours.

ATTENTION

1. **Dire** has the irregular form **vous dites.**

2. **Dire** and **écrire** take indirect objects.

   Je vais dire cela **à mes amis.**
   Elle va écrire une lettre **au président.**

3. If a clause follows **dire, écrire,** or **lire,** you must use the conjunction **que (qu')** plus the indicative.

   Elle dit **qu'**elle va faire de la gymnastique.

C. In other tenses (the imperfect and subjunctive), **-ire** verbs follow the normal rules.

   Je **conduisais** déjà quand j'avais quinze ans.
   Elle veut que nous **lisions** ce livre.

D. The past participles of **-ire** verbs vary somewhat.

(se) conduire	**conduit**	lire	**lu**
décrire	**décrit**	produire	**produit**
dire	**dit**	traduire	**traduit**
écrire	**écrit**		

Mots clés   Words often used with -ire verbs

On écrit et on traduit...

un conte	*tale*	**de la poésie**	*poetry*
une phrase	*sentence*	**un texte**	*text*
une pièce	*play*		

On dit...		On lit...	
une bêtise / des bêtises	*dumb thing(s)*	un journal / des journaux	*newspaper(s)*
un mensonge	*lie*	un magazine	*magazine*
la vérité	*truth*	une revue	*magazine*

Langue

A. **Un voyage à la Martinique.** Mettez les verbes au temps indiqué entre parenthèses.

1. On produit du sucre ici. *(passé composé)*
2. Ils lisent un bon roman pendant le match de tennis. *(imparfait)*
3. Elles écrivent une carte postale. *(futur proche)*
4. Elles disent qu'elles adorent le ski nautique. *(passé composé)*
5. A l'hôtel nous avons écrit trois lettres. *(présent)*
6. J'ai lu le journal de Fort-de-France. *(imparfait)*
7. Vous me décrivez votre voyage. *(impératif)*
8. Vous avez dit que vous allez retourner à la Martinique? *(présent)*

B. **De la poésie.** Faites des phrases avec les mots donnés, en faisant tous les changements nécessaires.

1. Jacques et Marie / écrire / poèmes
2. Luc / les / lire / hier
3. Je / les / traduire / français
4. Louise / dire / ils / être / bon
5. Il / être / possible / ils / écrire / pièce / aussi
6. Vouloir / vous / écrire / poésie?

Culture

C. **Il n'y a pas que le vin!** Certaines régions francophones sont connues pour leurs produits. Regardez les listes, et identifiez les régions suivantes avec leur produit.

MODELE: En Suisse *En Suisse, on produit du chocolat.*

1. En Bourgogne
2. En Normandie
3. En Bretagne
4. En Provence
5. En Alsace
6. En Belgique

a. lait / crème
b. moutarde
c. huile d'olive
d. fruits de mer
e. bière
f. choucroute

E. **Le français cajun.** Le français parlé en Louisiane a beaucoup de mots qui n'existent pas en France. Comment est-ce que les Cajuns disent les choses suivantes?

MODELE: Il est mort.
            Pour «Il est mort», ils disent «Il est gone.»

1. maintenant
2. un bal *(a dance)*
3. un dollar
4. très
5. triste
6. un train

a. affreux
b. bleu
c. un grand char
d. asteur
e. un fais-dodo
f. une piasse

Communication

F. Demandez à un(e) étudiant(e) de vous décrire les choses suivantes.

MODELE: ta maison
            Etudiant(e) 1: *Décris ta maison.*
            Etudiant(e) 2: *Ma maison est grande et blanche.*

ta chambre
ton (ta) petit(e) ami(e)
ta voiture
ton professeur

tes dernières vacances
ton sport préféré
ton film préféré
ta pièce préférée

G. Que lisez-vous? Qu'est-ce que vous avez lu récemment? Qu'est-ce que les autres personnes lisent? Donnez des titres *(titles)*.

des journaux
des romans
des poèmes

des magazines de sport
un livre de français
des contes de...

1. Moi, je...
2. Mon (Ma) camarade de chambre...
3. En cours, nous...

4. Mes ami(e)s...
5. Mes parents...
6. Mes professeurs...

H. **Questions personnelles.** Vos habitudes

1. Comment vous conduisiez-vous quand vous étiez petit(e)? Qu'est-ce que vous faisiez de méchant? Quelles bêtises disiez-vous?
2. Avez-vous écrit une lettre à une personne importante? A qui? Pourquoi?
3. Qu'est-ce que vous lisiez quand vous étiez jeune? Qu'est-ce que vous lisez maintenant?
4. Qui a écrit votre roman préféré? Votre chanson préférée?
5. Quel journal lisez-vous? Pourquoi? Quel magazine?
6. Quand avez-vous dit un mensonge?

II. Demonstrative Pronouns

> You use demonstrative pronouns to refer to people or things already mentioned in the conversation, often to point them out or to make a distinction.

A. Demonstrative pronouns are similar to demonstrative adjectives (**ce, cet, cette, ces**) in that they point out something, but demonstrative pronouns *replace* nouns. They have the same number and gender as the nouns they replace.

	singular	*plural*
masculine	celui	ceux
feminine	celle	celles

B. Demonstrative pronouns have several equivalents in English, depending on how they are used *(this one, that one, these, those, the one[s])*. These pronouns are usually followed by one of two structures:

1. the suffixes **-ci** or **-là** to indicate degree of closeness.

   Ce livre-**ci** est bon, mais **celui-là** est ennuyeux.
   J'aime **cette** chanson-**ci**, mais je préfère **celle-là**.
   Donnez-moi **celle-ci** et **celle-là**.

2. the preposition **de**, which can show possession.

   —Vos verres sont vides?
   — **Celui de** Jean, oui.
   Ils vont montrer l'étape d'aujourd'hui. **Celle d'hier**
      était formidable.
   Préférez-vous l'équipe de Lyon ou **celle de** Marseille?

CE QU'ILS DISENT

When demonstrative pronouns refer to people, they can have a somewhat derogatory meaning.

Oh, **ceux-là**, je ne les aime pas.   *Those guys! I don't like them.*
Celui-là, il n'est jamais à l'heure.   *That character is never on time.*

Langue

A. **A la bibliothèque.** Dans les phrases suivantes, remplacez les mots en italique avec un pronom démonstratif.

> MODELE: Donnez-moi *ce livre*-là.
> *Donnez-moi celui-là.*

1. Aimez-vous *les pièces* de Molière?
2. Je préfère *les poèmes* de Ronsard.
3. Nous allons traduire *ces phrases*-ci.
4. Avez-vous lu *ce roman*-ci?
5. Voltaire n'a pas écrit *ces lettres*-là.
6. Voulez-vous voir *le journal* de Montréal?
7. Où produit-on *les films* de Bertolucci?
8. Elles n'écoutent jamais *ces cassettes*-ci.

B. **Où sont nos affaires?** Dans les phrases ci-dessous *(below)*, remplacez les mots en italique avec un pronom démonstratif pour indiquer la possession.

> MODELE: Tu as perdu *le stylo* du professeur?
> *Tu as perdu celui du professeur?*

1. *La bicyclette* de Luc est là.
2. J'ai oublié *le courrier* de Marie.
3. *La planche à roulettes* de Tim n'est pas dans la rue.
4. *Le maillot* de Robert n'est pas dans sa valise.
5. Tu as trouvé *les patins à roulettes* de ma sœur?
6. Passez-moi *le verre* de Jacqueline.
7. J'ai laissé *les devoirs* de mon copain chez moi.
8. *Le portefeuille* de Marie est dans son sac.

C. **Faisons du sport.** Refaites les phrases suivantes en remplaçant les noms par des pronoms démonstratifs.

1. Ce sport-là n'est pas très difficile.
2. Les voitures de sport des Italiens sont formidables!
3. Ce joueur-là me semble paresseux.
4. Les montagnes de Lyon ne sont pas assez grandes pour faire du ski.
5. Les vêtements des Galeries Lafayette sont excellents pour faire du sport.
6. Ce magazine de catch-ci est plein de bêtises.
7. Evite les cigarettes de mon père si tu veux jouer au football.
8. Le français des joueurs québécois est différent du français des joueurs marseillais.

Culture

E. **De grands mouvements artistiques.** Les tableaux *(paintings)* des artistes donnés à la page suivante représentent quel mouvement artistique?

MODELE: Matisse *Ceux de Matisse représentent le fauvisme.*

1. David
2. Delacroix
3. Monet
4. Seurat
5. Rousseau
6. Picasso
7. Dali
8. Rouault

a. le cubisme
b. le pointillisme
c. le primitivisme
d. le classicisme
e. le romantisme
f. l'impressionnisme
g. l'expressionnisme
h. le surréalisme

Communication

F. **Conversation interrompue.** Au moment où vous interrompez *(interrupt)* une conversation, vous entendez les phrases suivantes. Imaginez ce que *(what)* le pronom démonstratif peut représenter.

MODELE: J'ai trouvé ceux de Marc dans ma voiture.
Il a trouvé les livres / les CD de Marc.

1. Vous avez essayé ceux-ci? Ils sont délicieux!
2. Ceux du professeur sont sur son bureau.
3. Celle-là n'est pas très économique.
4. Moi, je préfère celui-ci.
5. Celle-là n'est pas assez jolie pour aller dîner.
6. Ils ont traduit celles-là en français.

G. **Qu'est-ce que vous achetez?** Vous pouvez commencer la réponse avec «Moi, j'achète... ».

1. Les chemises de Van Heusen ou les chemises d'Hawaï?
2. Les disques des U2 ou les disques de Dolly Parton?
3. Les jeans de Calvin Klein ou les jeans de Levi Strauss?
4. Les chaînes stéréo du Japon ou les chaînes stéréo d'Allemagne?
5. Le journal de New York ou le journal de chez vous?
6. Les robes de Coco Chanel ou les robes de Sears?
7. Les ordinateurs d'Apple ou les ordinateurs d'IBM?
8. Les frites de McDonald's ou les frites de Burger King?

H. **Questions personnelles.** Vos préférences

1. Préférez-vous les cours du matin ou les cours de l'après-midi?
2. Regardez-vous les reportages sportifs d'ABC, de CBS, de NBC, ou d'ESPN?
3. Aimez-vous mieux la musique des années quatre-vingt-dix ou la musique des années cinquante?
4. Vous voudriez avoir les cheveux de Don King ou les cheveux de Sinead O'Connor?
5. Avez-vous envie d'aller aux concerts de Pavarotti ou aux concerts des Grateful Dead?
6. Vous aimez recevoir les lettres de votre petit(e) ami(e) ou les lettres d'Ed McMahon?

III. Possessive Pronouns

> You use possessive pronouns to show ownership of something already mentioned in the conversation.

A. Possessive pronouns replace possessive adjectives and the items possessed.

> —**Vos verres** sont vides?
> —Non, je n'ai pas encore terminé **le mien.**

	m. sing.	*f. sing.*	*m. pl.*	*f. pl.*	*English*
1st sing.	le mien	la mienne	les miens	les miennes	*mine*
2nd sing.	le tien	la tienne	les tiens	les tiennes	*yours*
3rd sing.	le sien	la sienne	les siens	les siennes	*his / hers / its*
1st pl.	le nôtre	la nôtre	les nôtres		*ours*
2nd pl.	le vôtre	la vôtre	les vôtres		*yours*
3rd pl.	le leur	la leur	les leurs		*theirs*

> Mon sport préféré est l'escrime; **le sien** c'est l'équitation.
> Elle n'aime pas cette planche à voile. Elle préfère **la sienne.**
> Mes parents habitent à Paris. Et **les vôtres?**

B. Remember that possessive adjectives agree in gender and number with the thing possessed, not with the possessor as in English. The same is true of possessive pronouns.

> **son verre** = *his glass or her glass*   **le sien** = *his or hers*

ATTENTION

1. Note that with all possessive pronouns, *It's . . .* and *They are . . .* translate as **C'est...** and **Ce sont...** **Ils** and **Elles** are not used, except with the expression of ownership in the **être à** + *noun or pronoun* and **appartenir à** constructions.

> —**C'est** celui de Pierre?
> —Oui, **c'est** le sien.

> —Est-ce que **ce sont** vos livres ou les leurs?
> —Ce sont **les miens.**

> —A qui sont ces skis?
> —**Ils** sont à moi. / **Ils** m'appartiennent.

2. Don't forget that **le** and **les** combine with any preceding **à** or **de** in the ways you studied in Chapter 4.

> As-tu téléphoné **à** tes parents? Moi, je vais téléphoner
> **aux** miens.
> Vous voulez que je parle **de** mon avenir, mais vous ne
> parlez pas **du** vôtre.
> Leur vélo est à côté **des** nôtres.

Langue

A. **Nos possessions.** Dans les phrases suivantes, remplacez les mots en italique par des pronoms possessifs.

1. Je n'aime pas *tes vêtements.*
2. Veux-tu regarder *mes photos?*
3. *Ses chaussures* sont grandes.
4. *Mes disquettes* sont tombées dans l'eau.
5. Le facteur a oublié *celui de Jacques.*
6. Elle a retrouvé *son journal.*
7. *Vos gâteaux* sont excellents.
8. J'ai perdu *leur parapluie.*

B. **Pas de chance!** Complétez les phrases suivantes avec un pronom possessif.

1. J'ai fait mes devoirs; tu n'as pas fait _____!
2. Il n'a pas de voiture; il veut que je lui prête _____.
3. Ils viennent de recevoir leur courrier, mais nous n'avons pas encore reçu _____.
4. C'est son verre; donnez-moi _____.
5. Les Baillard ont vendu leur maison, mais M. Ducharme n'a pas pu vendre _____.
6. Garçon! Ce n'est pas ma boisson. C'est _____.

Culture

C. **Comparaison de cultures.** Comparez les phénomènes suivants comme ils existent en France et aux Etats-Unis. Utilisez les adjectifs donnés ou vos propres idées.

MODELE:　voitures: petit / grand
　　　　　Les leurs sont petites; les nôtres sont grandes.

1. églises: ancien / moderne
2. nourriture: bon marché *(cheap)* / cher
3. courses de bicyclettes: très apprécié / peu connu
4. conducteurs: prudent / agressif
5. vacances: moins long / plus long
6. billets d'avion: bon marché / très cher

Communication

D. Employez des pronoms possessifs pour décrire les choses suivantes.

> MODELES: tes week-ends   *Les miens ne sont pas assez longs.*
>
> votre équipe de football   *La nôtre perd ses matchs.*

1. ta famille
2. ton appartement
3. votre président
4. votre université
5. tes vacances
6. votre professeur
7. ta résidence
8. vos sports préférés
9. votre ville
10. tes cours

E. Séparez-vous en groupes de deux et comparez les villes où vous êtes né(e)s. Utilisez les suggestions données ou vos propres idées.

> MODELES: avoir beaucoup / peu de musées
> Etudiant(e) 1: *Ma ville a beaucoup de musées.*
> Etudiant(e) 2: *La mienne a peu de musées.*
> être calme / avoir du bruit
> Etudiant(e) 1: *Ma ville est très calme.*
> Etudiant(e) 2: *Il y a beaucoup de bruit dans la mienne.*

être petite / grande
être loin / près des montagnes
avoir peu / beaucoup de cinémas
avoir de bons / mauvais restaurants

avoir beaucoup / peu de pollution
avoir beaucoup / peu de parcs
être loin / près de la plage
???

F. **Questions personnelles.** Votre université

1. Comment s'appelait votre lycée? Et celui de votre petit(e) ami(e)?
2. Est-ce que votre université est trop grande ou trop petite?
3. Il y a souvent du bruit dans les résidences, et dans la vôtre?
4. Comment est votre chambre? Petite ou grande? Bien rangée?
5. Est-ce que vos week-ends sont agréables?
6. Est-ce que vos profs sont sympathiques? Qu'est-ce qu'ils n'aiment pas?

COMMUNIQUONS ··

Utiliser le système métrique

To function in most French-speaking countries, you must be familiar with the metric system, the official system of measurement in most of the world. It was first established by the French National Assembly in 1791, and the International Bureau of Weights and Measures is still located in France, just outside

Paris in Sèvres. The meter, the basic unit of length, is defined by the wavelength of krypton, while the kilogram, the basic unit of weight, is defined by a block of platinum that is housed at the bureau.

The following comparisons will help you do conversions from the U.S. system to the metric system and vice versa.

On exprime le poids *(weight)*.

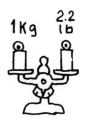

1. Here are some comparisons between metric weights and weights in the American system.

   28 grammes (g) = *1 ounce*   100 grammes = *4 ounces*
   454 grammes = *1 pound*   1 kilogramme (kg) = *2.2 pounds*
   500 grammes = une livre

2. To convert weights from the American system to the metric system and vice versa, use the following calculations as a guide.

   ? grammes = *3 ounces*
   Multipliez 28 par 3. Cela fait 84 grammes.

   50 kilogrammes = *? pounds*
   Multipliez 50 par 2,2. Cela fait 110 *pounds*.

3. The following expressions are used for weight.

   Je pèse quatre-vingts kilos.   *I weigh eighty kilos.*
   Ça coûte vingt francs le kilo.   *That costs twenty francs a kilo.*

On exprime la longueur *(length)*.

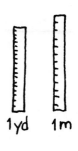

1. The following are some comparisons between metric lengths and those of the American system.

   2,54 centimètres (cm) = *1 inch*   1 centimètre = *about 0.4 inches*
   30 centimètres = *about 1 foot*   1 mètre = *about 39.4 inches*
   0,94 mètre (m) = *about 1 yard*   1 kilomètre = *about 0.62 miles*
   1,6 kilomètres (km) = *about*
       1 mile

2. To convert lengths from the metric system to the American system and vice versa, use the following calculations as a guide.

   ? mètres = *5 feet 8 inches*
   5 feet 8 inches = 68 inches. Multipliez 68 par 2,54.
       Cela fait 172,72 centimètres. Divisez par 10. Cela
       fait 1,73 mètres ou un mètre soixante-treize.

   525 kilomètres = *? miles*
   Multipliez 525 par 0,62. Cela fait 325,50 ou 325
       miles et demi.

3. These expressions are used for length or distance in French.

Paris est à 5.000 km d'ici.	*Paris is 5,000 kilometers from here.*
Ils habitent à 50 km de chez nous.	*They live 50 kilometers from our house.*
Jacques fait presque deux mètres.	*Jacques is almost two meters tall.*
Elle mesure un mètre soixante.	*She is one meter sixty centimeters tall.*

On exprime le volume.

1. Here are some comparisons between metric measurements of volume and those of the American system.

0,95 litre (l) = *1 quart*   1 litre = *1.06 quarts*
3,8 litres = *1 gallon*   25 centilitres (cl) = *about 1 cup*

2. To convert volume measurements from the metric system to the American system and vice versa, refer to these calculations.

? litres = *20 gallons*
Multipliez 20 par 3,8. Cela fait 76 litres.

0,75 litre = *? quarts*
Multipliez 0,75 par 1,06. Cela fait .795 *quarts.*

3. The following expression is used for volume.

Ma nouvelle voiture fait du 8   *My new car uses 8 liters (of gas)*
aux 100 km.   *per 100 kilometers.*

On exprime la température.

1. The following are some comparisons between the Celsius and Fahrenheit scales for measuring temperatures.

0° Celsius (C) = *32° Fahrenheit (F)*
100° C = *212° F*

2. To convert temperatures from the Celsius scale to the Fahrenheit scale, use the following formulas as guides.

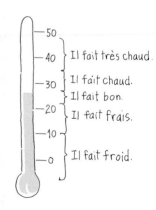

40°C = *? F*
degrés Fahrenheit = 9/5 C + 32
Multipliez 40 par 9 et divisez par 5. Cela fait 72.
    Ajoutez *(Add)* 32. Cela fait 104° F.

? C = *68° F*
degrés Celsius = 5/9 (F − 32)
68° moins 32 font 36. Multipliez 36 par 5 et divisez
    par 9. Cela fait 20° C.

3. The following expressions are used with temperatures.

Ma fille a trente-neuf.   *My daughter has a temperature of thirty-nine degrees Celsius.*

Il fait trente degrés aujourd'hui.   *It is thirty degrees Celsius out today.*

Interaction   *Monsieur Gosselin et son fils font des courses à l'hypermarché.*

M. GOSSELIN: Va acheter un rosbif pendant que je prends deux kilos de pommes de terre.

SON FILS: Pour nous cinq, quel poids est-ce qu'il faut?

M. GOSSELIN::   Oh, entre deux kilos et deux kilos cinq cents.

SON FILS: N'oublie pas non plus un litre de lait et une demi-livre de beurre.

M. GOSSELIN: Tu as raison. Et il nous faut aussi une bouteille de vin d'Alsace et 600 grammes de gruyère.

SON FILS: Chic! Maman va faire aussi une fondue.

Activités

A. Quelle unité de mesure détermine le prix des choses suivantes en France? Choisissez parmi *(among)* les possibilités données.

MODELE: du café à l'épicerie   *les 500 grammes*

3 ou 5 centilitres	le kilogramme
le litre	75 centilitres
le kilomètre	100 grammes
25 ou 33 centilitres	25 centilitres

1. des bananes
2. une bière au café
3. des bonbons
4. un vin de qualité
5. un vin de table
6. un pichet de vin au restaurant
7. du gigot
8. du fromage
9. des crevettes
10. de l'essence *(gasoline)*
11. l'apéritif au café
12. un billet de train

B. Répondez aux questions suivantes.

1. Combien pesez-vous en kilos? Combien mesurez-vous?
2. A combien de kilomètres habitez-vous de la maison de vos parents? de l'université?
3. En Amérique, on mesure l'économie d'une voiture en *miles per gallon*. En France, c'est en litres aux 100 kilomètres. Combien est-ce que votre voiture consomme?

4. Quelle est la température normale d'une personne en degrés Celsius? Quelle température avez-vous eue quand vous étiez malade?

5. Est-ce qu'il fait beau aujourd'hui? Combien fait-il en degrés Celsius?

Lecture culturelle ....

The **Tour de France** is not just the world's major bicycle race and a French passion. It requires considerable strategy and feats of incredible endurance. All participants are members of a team, which has a corporate sponsor, such as **La Vie Claire,** a chain of health-food stores. On a team, only one member has a chance of winning; the others provide support such as forming a windbreak or slowing down the pack (**le peloton**). But no one has help when it comes to **l'étape contre la montre**—a sprint in which the fastest time wins.

Activités

A. *Scanning* is the reading of a passage very quickly to find specific information. It will help you to learn to read faster and with more accuracy. Scan the reading passage for the names of French cities and locate each one on the map of France on page 94. Then, determine what **l'Hexagone** refers to in the reading passage.

B. Scan the reading passage in order to fill out this brief chronology of the **Tour** with the event associated with each date.

1903 _____

1926 _____

1930 _____

1951 _____

1954 _____

1969 _____

1986 _____

1992 _____

L'ÉQUIPE

AVEC NOS ENVOYÉS SPÉCIAUX

LE TOUR EN DIRECT!   VIVEZ L'ÉTAPE DU JOUR

Le Tour de France

Avec les Vingt-quatre Heures du Mans, le Grand Prix de Monaco, les Internationaux de tennis de Roland-Garros et la Coupe de France de football, le Tour de France est un des *événements* sportifs français les plus importants. *Chaque* année, pendant les trois premières semaines de juillet, cette course cycliste par étapes retient l'attention de l'opinion publique et des médias. Tous les après-midi, vers seize heures, la vie du pays semble *ralentir* et une grande partie de la population regarde ou écoute la retransmission de l'arrivée de l'étape *en direct* à la télévision ou à la radio. Le soir, les journaux télévisés des diverses chaînes *consacrent* une assez longue partie de leur émission à l'étape du jour.

Le Tour de France va bientôt être centenaire. Le 1er juillet 1903, il a pris le départ pour la première fois. En 1930, on a créé les équipes nationales et la *caravane publicitaire* a fait ses débuts. L'année 1955 est aussi une date importante, car pour la première fois, un même *coureur*, Louison Bobet, *remporte* une troisième victoire consécutive. Trois coureurs ont gagné le Tour cinq *fois:* Jacques Anquetil, Eddy Merckx, un Belge, et Bernard Hinault. Les équipes nationales ont été abandonnées en 1969, et on a formé des équipes de *marques* publicitaires. Enfin, en 1986, Greg LeMond a été le premier Américain à remporter le Tour. Depuis 1984, on organise chaque année un Tour de France féminin.

Depuis la fin de la Seconde Guerre mondiale, les organisateurs ne *s'efforcent* plus de passer par les six points de l'Hexagone. Aujourd'hui, le Tour de France n'a plus que l'apparence d'un tour, au sens où l'on va faire un tour, une promenade. Mais quelle promenade, quand on parle d'environ 3.000 kilomètres à bicyclette!

events / Each

slow down

live

devote

motorcade of sponsors

racer / won

times

brand names

attempt

Le maillot jaune sur les Champs-Elysées

25 Si le Tour n'est plus maintenant qu'une course à travers la France, à
l'origine, une *épreuve* ainsi appelée suivait un *parcours périphérique*. Imm-   *competition / itinerary /*
édiatement après le premier Tour où les seules villes *reliées* n'étaient que Paris,   *circular / linked*
Lyon, Marseille, Toulouse et Bordeaux, et où la *moyenne* des étapes était de   *average*
400 kilomètres, le Tour a suivi scrupuleusement les côtes et les frontières *afin*   *in order to*
30 *de* pouvoir justifier son nom. En 1926, les coureurs sont même partis d'Evian
et y sont revenus trois semaines plus tard pour compléter la *boucle* avant de   *circuit*
repartir enfin pour Paris. Cette année-là, l'itinéraire du Tour a établi le record
de la distance: 5.745 kilomètres!

Il a fallu attendre 1951 pour voir le Tour passer dans les montagnes du
35 Massif central par exemple, mais à partir de ce moment-là, les organisateurs
ont commencé la *recherche* d'itinéraires nouveaux et variés afin de pénétrer la   *search*
France profonde.   *heart of France*

Peu à peu, le Tour de France a commencé aussi à sortir des limites de
l'Hexagone. Le premier départ de l'étranger *a eu lieu* à Amsterdam en 1954.   *took place*
40 On a ensuite répété cette expérience avec des villes comme Bruxelles, Cologne,
Francfort, Bâle et Berlin.

L'*étalement* de la course sur trois semaines, la *foule* des participants et le   *spreading / crowd*
nombre de kilomètres *parcourus* à travers la France, quand ce n'est pas dans   *covered*
d'autres pays, font du Tour de France une grande épreuve sportive. C'est aussi
45 une gigantesque entreprise commerciale et une manifestation culturelle importante qui *exigent* une organisation phénoménale et des mois de préparation   *require*
intensive.

L'épreuve sportive est sans aucun doute la raison d'être du Tour de France.
L'endurance des coureurs est *mise à l'épreuve* tous les jours, et *à part* arriver   *tested / except for*
50 premier le soir à l'étape, rien n'est plus *convoité* que le maillot jaune, car celui   *coveted*
qui le porte encore à l'arrivée de la dernière étape sur les Champs-Elysées est
déclaré *vainqueur.*   *winner*

D'autre part, il ne faut pas minimiser l'aspect commercial de l'événement.
La caravane publicitaire qui accompagne le Tour *fournit* aux grandes marques   *provides*
55 françaises et internationales une occasion de *vanter* leurs produits *auprès du*   *brag about / to*
public. Et le soir, quand les coureurs se reposent, le Tour offre aux populations
locales des spectacles de variétés animés par des *vedettes* de la chanson et du   *stars*
music-hall.

Pendant près d'un siècle, le Tour de France *a subi* beaucoup de change-   *has undergone*
60 ments. *Cependant*, il reste un événement économique capital, il n'a jamais   *However*
perdu de sa popularité auprès des Français, et il continue même à les
passionner.

Après la lecture

Questions sur le texte

1. Quels sont les grands événements sportifs en France?
2. Comment sait-on que les Français trouvent le Tour de France
   fantastique?
3. Est-ce que tous les coureurs du Tour sont français?

4. Est-ce que le Tour reste en France?
5. Est-ce que le Tour de France n'est qu'une épreuve sportive?
6. Comment reconnaît-on le vainqueur du Tour?
7. Quels avantages économiques est-ce que le Tour offre?

Activités

A. Répondez aux questions suivantes.

1. Quels événements sportifs aux Etats-Unis retiennent l'attention des Américains comme le Tour en France? Fait-on trop attention aux sports aux USA?
2. Aimez-vous l'idée d'une course cycliste pour les femmes? Quels autres sports ont des compétitions féminines? Quels sports est-ce que les hommes et les femmes pratiquent ensemble?
3. Est-ce que les événements sportifs sont trop commercialisés? Quels sports en particulier? Quels sont les avantages et les désavantages de cet aspect des sports?
4. Quel rôle est-ce que les sports jouent dans votre vie? Expliquez.

B. Faites le plan d'un **Tour des Etats-Unis** imaginaire. Quelles sont les étapes de montagne? Expliquez votre itinéraire à la classe.

Chapitre 15

LES ARTS

Un peintre amateur

Commençons ....

Le Français en péril? `[ o━o ]`

La revue française L'Express *a consacré un reportage à la question suivante:*
«Sait-on encore parler le français?» Dans plusieurs articles, des journalistes
ont critiqué l'état du français parlé et écrit. Quelques semaines après, la revue
a publié la lettre d'un lecteur furieux. En voici un extrait.

9 / 12 / 93

Messieurs:

Qu'est-il arrivé à la langue de Voltaire et de Gide? [...] Moi, je pense que le
mal vient surtout d'un enseignement insuffisant et je dois dire que les fautes
de français entendues à la radio et à la télévision me font souffrir, comme des
atteintes à la beauté de notre langue. [...]

Je pense qu'il s'agit d'une volonté de certains milieux de contribuer à la
destruction d'une société par celle de sa langue. Parler et enseigner un
français correct est «bourgeois». Donc,... !

Moi, je dis que nous devons défendre notre langue car elle est vivace,
généreuse, et elle peut servir à toutes sortes d'usages.

Veuillez agréer, Messieurs, l'expression de mes salutations distinguées.

André Florion

(Adapté du *Débat des lecteurs,* L'Express, *numéros 1735 et 1736*)

Mots clés

en péril	*in danger*	fautes *(f.)*	*mistakes*
consacré	*devoted*	souffrir	*suffer*
(consacrer)		atteintes *(f.)*	*affronts*
suivante	*following*	beauté	*beauty*
plusieurs	*several*	il s'agit d'	*it's about /*
articles *(m.)*	*articles*		*it's a*
critiqué	*criticized*		*question of*
(critiquer)		volonté	*decision*
état *(m.)*	*state*	milieux *(m.)*	*circles*
publié	*published*	contribuer	*contribute*
(publier)		destruction	*destruction*
lecteur	*reader*	enseigner	*to teach*
en	*of it*	correct	*correct*
extrait *(m.)*	*excerpt*	bourgeois	*bourgeois*
arrivé (arriver)	*happened*	donc	*therefore*
mal	*evil*	défendre	*defend*
surtout	*above all*	vivace	*alive*
enseignement	*teaching*	usages	*uses*
insuffisant	*insufficient*		

Faisons connaissance

The French language is a constant preoccupation for the people who speak it daily. In France, many feel that their language has deteriorated: there is too much slang; people do not follow grammar rules; and too many words have been borrowed from English. Others think that languages are in a constant state of change and that it is useless to try to stop the process. The majority of the readers responding to that issue of *L'Express* agreed that the situation is deplorable. Yet a move to simplify French spelling, promoted by the government and endorsed by the **Académie française,** has been abandoned.

The French language is also an issue in other countries. Belgium is administratively divided into areas where one of two languages is official—French or Dutch, with the city of Brussels being the only officially bilingual area. A conflict exists between French and Dutch speakers, and it is so intense that it has led to riots in the past.

The province of Quebec in Canada has undergone profound changes. While the country is bilingual, the province has established French as its official language. For example, non-English-speaking immigrants must send their children to schools where classes are taught in French.

In Louisiana, several active groups have been working for years to reestablish the value of using French. The body of poetry, prose, music, and journalism in French is quite significant.

Etudions la lettre

1. De quoi est-ce qu'on parle dans cette lettre à *L'Express?*
2. D'où vient le problème selon le lecteur?
3. Comment est-ce que la radio et la télévision contribuent au problème?
4. Est-ce que le lecteur pense qu'on a tort ou qu'on a raison d'être «bourgeois»?
5. Finissez la phrase «Donc,... !»
6. Pourquoi faut-il défendre la langue française?

Enrichissons notre vocabulaire

Des instruments *(m.)* de musique *(Musical instruments)*

un orchestre / les instruments *(m.)*

un violon

une guitare

une flûte

un violoncelle

le chef d'orchestre

une trompette

un piano

—De quel instrument jouez-vous?

—Je joue du trombone.

What instrument do you play?

I play the trombone.

Des métiers *(m.)* artistiques *(Careers in the arts)*

Les **musiciens** *(m.)* écrivent des **opéras** *(m.)* et des **symphonies** *(f.)*.

Musicians write operas and symphonies.

Les **écrivains** *(m.)* produisent des **œuvres** *(f.)* littéraires.

Writers produce literary works.

Les **auteurs** *(m.)* dramatiques font des **pièces**: des **drames** *(m.)*, des **comédies** *(f.)* des **tragédies** *(f.)*, et des **comédies musicales.**

Playwrights write plays: dramas, comedies, tragedies, and musicals.

Les **danseurs** et les **danseuses** font de la **danse classique** (du **ballet**).	*Dancers perform ballet.*
Les **peintres** *(m.)* font des **tableaux** *(m.)*: des **peintures à l'huile** *(f.)* et des **aquarelles** *(f.)*.	*Painters make paintings: oil paintings and water colors.*
Les **sculpteurs** *(m.)* font des **sculptures** *(f.)* en **pierre** *(f.)* et en **bronze** *(m.)*	*Sculptors make stone and bronze sculptures.*

Prononciation   Intonation

A. Intonation is the change in the pitch of the voice. It enables a speaker to distinguish between sentences such as *She's going to the movies.* and *She's going to the movies?* French intonation is not radically different from that of English. The two basic kinds are rising intonation and falling intonation.

B. With rising intonation the pitch of the voice rises in yes-or-no questions and sentences when you pause for a breath at the end of a group of related words.

Repeat the following yes-or-no questions after your teacher.

Aimez-vous ce tableau? / Est-ce qu'il est parti?

Vous avez un violon?

Repeat the following sentences with pauses after your teacher.

Elle n'est pas venue parce qu'elle est malade.

J'ai acheté un parapluie, mais je l'ai perdu.

Nous sommes allés au cinéma et nous avons dîné après.

C. With falling intonation, the pitch of the voice drops in declarative and imperative sentences and in information questions (those that start with an interrogative or pronoun).

Repeat the following declarative sentences after your teacher.

Il va faire beau. / Marie n'est pas là.

Nous sommes très fatigués.

Repeat the following imperative sentences after your teacher.

Dépêche-toi. / Venez avec nous. / Allons au théâtre.

Repeat the following information questions after your teacher.

Qu'est-ce que vous allez faire? / Comment allez-vous?

Pourquoi fait-il cela?

Exercice

Read the following sentences aloud, paying particular attention to rising and falling intonation.

1. Voulez-vous danser?
2. Passez-moi le sucre.
3. Qui n'a pas pris de dessert?
4. Monique fait de la danse moderne.
5. J'ai lu un livre et j'ai téléphoné à un ami.
6. Couchez-vous plus tôt!

G RAMMAIRE ·

I. Verbs Followed by Infinitives

> Verbs describe action or states of being.

A. Verbs Followed Directly by an Infinitive

You have learned that it is possible to use two consecutive verbs in a sentence in French. Verbs and verbal expressions you already know that take an infinitive directly after the conjugated verb are as follows.

adorer	devoir	préférer
aimer	espérer	savoir
aimer mieux	il faut	sembler
aller	laisser	souhaiter
désirer	penser	il vaut mieux
détester	pouvoir	vouloir

Je **dois dire** que les fautes me font souffrir.
Sait-on encore **parler** le français?
Je **ne peux pas répondre**.

B. Verbs Followed by **à** and an Infinitive

Some verbs that take the preposition **à** before an infinitive are as follows.

s'amuser à	continuer à
apprendre à	hésiter à *to hesitate*
avoir du mal à *to have a hard time*	inviter à
chercher à *to try*	réussir à
commencer à	tenir à

Nous **avons du mal à nous lever** tôt.
Il **ne réussit pas à comprendre** la danse moderne.
Avez-vous **commencé à lire** cette comédie?

C. Verbs Followed by **de** and an Infinitive

Here are some examples of verbs that take the preposition **de** before an infinitive.

accepter de	essayer de
avoir besoin de	être + *adjective* + de
avoir envie de	éviter de
avoir peur de	finir de
avoir raison / tort de	oublier de
cesser de *to stop*	refuser de
choisir de	regretter de
décider de	rêver de *to dream*
se dépêcher de	venir de

As-tu **envie d'aller** au théâtre?
Alors, **dépêche-toi de t'habiller!**
J'ai décidé de faire une sculpture.

ATTENTION

1. If you use object pronouns with two verbs, remember that the pronoun precedes the verb of which it is an object. For example, in the first sentence below, **amis** is the object of **inviter,** and **orchestre** is the object of **écouter.**

   J'ai invité mes amis à écouter cet orchestre.
   Je **les** ai invités à l'écouter.

   Je vais essayer de téléphoner **aux lecteurs.**
   Je vais essayer de **leur** téléphoner.

2. Note that the prepositions **à** and **de** *do not* combine with the direct object pronouns **le** and **les.**

   Il regrette de vendre ce tableau.
   Il regrette **de le** vendre.

   Je n'ai pas encore commencé à faire **mes devoirs.**
   Je n'ai pas encore commencé **à les** faire.

Langue

A. Complétez les phrases suivantes avec une préposition, s'il y a lieu *(if necessary).*

   1. Détestez-vous _____ étudier?
   2. Elle regrette _____ arriver en retard.
   3. Nous continuons _____ regarder la télévision.
   4. Je viens _____ terminer le roman.
   5. Mes voisins s'amusent _____ jouer de la guitare.
   6. Mon père tient _____ écouter cet orchestre.
   7. Notre professeur ne nous laisse jamais _____ partir tôt.
   8. Ils vont _____ essayer _____ nous téléphoner ce soir.

B. **En famille.** Formez des phrases avec les mots donnés.

1. Mon mari / cesser / travailler / année / dernier
2. Notre fils / adorer / aller à la pêche avec lui
3. En semaine / nous / finir / dîner / huit heures
4. Notre fille / apprendre / jouer du violon
5. Nous / aimer mieux / se coucher / tôt
6. On / aller / visiter / Paris / printemps
7. Je / avoir du mal / décrire / nos vacances
8. Ma sœur / décider / aller voir / nos parents / Canada

Culture

C. **Au lycée.** Formez des phrases complètes avec les mots donnés et dites si la phrase est vraie ou fausse selon la vie des lycéens *(high school students)* français.

1. On / pouvoir / apprendre / conduire / au lycée
2. lycéens / adorer / écouter / musique américaine
3. On / devoir / étudier la religion
4. Ils / rêver / acheter / surtout / voiture
5. lycéens / ne... pas / chercher / travailler / après / classes
6. Parmi *(Among)* les langues étrangères, / ils / préférer / étudier / espagnol
7. Ils / avoir peur / passer le bac
8. La majorité des jeunes / obtenir le bac / et / choisir / aller / université

Communication

D. **Mes activités.** Qu'est-ce que vous préférez faire?

J'aime...	J'accepte...	Je déteste...	Je refuse...
me lever tôt		écrire des lettres	
préparer le petit déjeuner		lire des pièces / des romans	
sortir quand il pleut		conduire vite	
aller en classe en autobus		jouer à / de...	
suivre des cours le matin		???	

E. **L'avenir.** Posez des questions à un(e) camarade de cours sur ses projets pour l'avenir en employant un élément de la colonne A et de la colonne B. Ensuite, faites un résumé *(summary)* de ses réponses.

A	B
aller	suivre des cours pendant dix ans
tenir	gagner peu / beaucoup d'argent
décider	avoir peu / beaucoup de responsabilités
rêver	faire du cinéma / du théâtre
hésiter	devenir professeur / médecin
espérer	faire du deltaplane
avoir envie	écrire de la poésie
devoir	???

F. **Questions personnelles.** Vos préférences

1. Préférez-vous aller au cinéma ou au théâtre?
2. Avez-vous choisi d'habiter dans une résidence universitaire ou dans un appartement? Pourquoi?
3. Qu'est-ce que vous voulez apprendre à faire?
4. Qu'est-ce que vous avez du mal à faire?
5. Qu'est-ce que vous avez envie de faire ce week-end?
6. Où pensez-vous aller pour vos vacances?

II. Verbs Followed by Nouns

> Verbs describe actions or states of being.

A. Verbs are either transitive or intransitive. A transitive verb takes a direct object. An intransitive verb has no direct object, or it requires a preposition.

Les peintres font **des tableaux.**　　Elle est rentrée tôt.
On a critiqué **le président.**　　Nous allons **chez** le dentiste.

B. There are a number of verbs that are transitive in French but intransitive in English. The following are some transitive French verbs that you know.

attendre	écouter	payer
chercher	fréquenter	regarder
demander		

Elle fréquente un Italien.　　*She's going out with an Italian.*
Les enfants demandent du gâteau.　　*The children are asking for cake.*

C. There are also verbs that take **à** before a noun in French. Most of the following verbs are transitive in English.

désobéir à	répondre à
échouer à　*to fail*	ressembler à
entrer à / dans	réussir à
faire peur à	s'intéresser à　*to be*
jouer à + *sport*	*interested in*
obéir à	téléphoner à
penser à	tenir à
rendre visite à	

Ne désobéissez pas à vos parents!　　*Don't disobey your parents.*
Tenez-vous à ce vieux violon?　　*Are you fond of this old violin?*

D. Several verbs in French must take the preposition **à** before a noun and **de** before an infinitive.

conseiller **à** quelqu'un **de** faire quelque chose	*to advise someone to do something*
demander **à** quelqu'un **de** faire quelque chose	*to ask someone to do something*
dire **à** quelqu'un **de** faire quelque chose	*to tell someone to do something*
écrire **à** quelqu'un **de** faire quelque chose	*to write someone to do something*
rappeler **à** quelqu'un **de** faire quelque chose	*to remind someone to do something*
recommander **à** quelqu'un **de** faire quelque chose	*to recommend to someone to do something*

Conseillez **aux** étudiants **d'**apprendre à taper.
J'ai demandé **à** Mme Leblanc **de** jouer de la guitare.

E. Some verbs take the preposition **de** before a noun or a pronoun.

avoir besoin de	jouer de + *musical instrument*
avoir peur de	s'inquiéter de
changer de	s'occuper de
il s'agit de	

Il **s'occupe du** courrier des lecteurs.
Il **s'agit d'**une volonté de certains milieux.

ATTENTION

1. **Penser** takes the preposition **à** when it means *to have something in mind*. When **penser** means *to have an opinion*, it takes **de** and is almost always used in a question. You answer the question with **penser que...** .

   Je n'aime pas **penser aux** examens.
   —Que **pensez**-vous **de** l'art moderne?
   —Je **pense que** c'est fascinant.

2. When a verb that takes the preposition **de** is followed by a noun, the noun does not take an article if it is used in a general sense.

   Il **change** souvent **de vêtements**!
   Elle **s'occupe d'étudiants** étrangers.

3. **Il s'agit de** cannot take a noun subject. Use a prepositional phrase with **dans** instead.

   Dans ce magazine, **il s'agit de** la langue française.   *This magazine deals with the French language.*

Ce qu'ils disent

Se rappeler takes a direct object, but in daily speech, many French speakers add **de.**

Je ne me rappelle pas cela. → Je ne me rappelle pas **de** cela.

Langue

A. **Faisons attention au professeur.** Complétez les phrases suivantes avec une préposition ou un article, ou avec les deux s'il y a lieu.

1. Pour être professeur, on a besoin _____ patience.
2. Mon professeur a recommandé _____ étudiants _____ bien préparer la leçon.
3. Il a conseillé _____ ses étudiants _____ étudier le latin aussi.
4. Il leur a demandé pourquoi ils ont échoué _____ examen.
5. Moi, je vais réussir _____ examens de l'année prochaine.
6. J'écoute toujours _____ les conseils du professeur.

B. **Un agent de police donne des conseils aux touristes.** Formez des phrases complètes avec les mots donnés.

1. Dire / votre / amis / entrer / musée / avant six heures
2. Je / rappeler / gens / obéir / lois
3. Entrer / bureau de poste / pour / téléphoner / votre / famille
4. Je / dire / étudiants / adresse / du Louvre
5. Recommander / amis / regarder / ce / beau / église
6. Je / conseiller / Américains / visiter / musée d'Orsay

C. **Conversation avec votre camarade de chambre.** Répondez aux questions suivantes en utilisant les mots donnés.

1. Est-ce que c'est ton violoncelle?   (Non... appartenir... Marie)
2. Tu pars pour l'université?   (Non... revenir... supermarché)
3. Est-ce que tu as froid?   (Oui... demander... Robert... fermer... fenêtre)
4. Tu veux écouter de la musique?   (Non... préférer... regarder... film)
5. Alors, tu veux aller au cinéma?   (Oui... chercher... journal)
6. Qu'est-ce qu'on va faire après?   (... s'occuper... ménage)

Culture

D. **Au lycée.** Formez des phrases complètes avec les mots donnés et dites si la phrase est vraie ou fausse selon la vie des lycéens français.

1. Quand / deux lycéens / aller au cinéma, / garçon / payer / places
2. lycéens / regarder / souvent / télévision / l'après-midi
3. La majorité / lycéens / échouer / bac
4. On / demander / lycéens / étudier / deux langues étrangères

5. La majorité des lycéens / penser / football / et / penser / jouer / football
6. cours d'anglais / ressembler / cours de français aux Etats-Unis
7. beaucoup de lycéens / fréquenter / cafés / après les cours
8. Ils / téléphoner souvent / copains / après dîner

Communication

E. Racontez vos activités pendant une journée typique. Utilisez les verbes suivants ou vos propres idées.

téléphoner	chercher	revenir
écrire	penser	jouer
regarder	s'occuper	fréquenter
écouter	parler	changer

F. Séparez-vous en petits groupes et complétez les phrases suivantes. Ensuite expliquez à la classe les similarités et les différences entre vos réponses.

1. J'ai besoin _____ pour être heureux.
2. Je cherche _____ dans la vie.
3. Je pense souvent _____ .

4. Avec mes amis, je parle _____ .
5. Je tiens beaucoup _____ .
6. Pour l'avenir, je ne demande que _____ .

G. **Questions personnelles.** Décrivez-vous.

1. A quoi vous intéressez-vous?
2. A qui ressemblez-vous?
3. A qui téléphonez-vous souvent? A qui écrivez-vous?
4. A quoi pensez-vous en ce moment?
5. Quelle sorte de musique aimez-vous écouter?
6. Quels endroits fréquentez-vous?
7. Quels sports pratiquez-vous?
8. De quel instrument jouez-vous?

LE BON MOMENT
— *la Restauration du Voyage* —

*La SNCF vous propose de passer un Bon Moment
à bord des trains avec les restaurateurs du voyage,
qu'elle a choisis pour leur savoir-faire
et leurs qualités de service.
Pensez à réserver votre repas en même temps
que votre place en 1ère classe.*

III. The Pronouns y and en

Pronouns replace nouns. You use y when referring to places and things when the reference is clear, and you use **en** for things and occasionally people.

A. The Pronoun y

1. The pronoun y replaces prepositional phrases indicating a place. It means *there* and has the same position as the object pronouns you have already learned.

—Il habite **à Paris?**
—Oui, il y habite.

—Sylvie nous invite **chez elle.**
—Allons-y tout de suite!

—Ils vont travailler **au cinéma?**
—Oui, ils vont y travailler.

—Etes-vous allées **en France?**
—Oui, nous y sommes allées.

2. **Y** is also used with verbs taking the preposition **à** whenever the object is *not* a person.

—Avez-vous répondu **à sa lettre?**
—Oui, nous y avons répondu.

—Ils ne s'intéressent pas **à la sculpture?**
—Si, ils s'y intéressent.

Drôle de lieu de vacances: les sourires y sont naturels, pas saisonniers.

En Bretagne, les sourires ne naissent pas à Pâques pour s'éteindre en octobre, une fois BRETAGNE *achevée la saison touristique. En Bretagne, quand on vous gratifie d'un mot aimable, on ne s'y sent jamais forcé. Et quand on commerce avec vous, les raisons en sont rarement commerciales. Vous objecterez que les Bretons ne sourient pas toujours ? Réjouissez-vous-en : c'est parce que, chez eux, la spontanéité n'est pas affaire de saisonnalité. Renseignez-vous à la Maison de la Bretagne tél. : (I) 45.38.78.42*

BRETAGNE NOUVELLE VAGUE

ATTENTION

1. If the object of the preposition **à** is a person, you cannot use **y;** you must use an indirect object pronoun, **lui** or **leur.**

J'ai répondu **à la question.** → J'y ai répondu.
J'ai répondu **au professeur.** → Je **lui** ai répondu.

2. Two verbs you have learned require **à** plus the stressed pronoun when referring to people: **penser** and **s'intéresser.**

Elle pense souvent **à son frère.** → Elle pense souvent
à **lui.**
Je m'intéresse **aux musiciens de jazz.** → Je m'intéresse
à **eux.**

3. **Y** is used to indicate location. With some verbs, a place name receives the action of the verbs. In these cases, you must use a direct object pronoun.

Ils ont visité **la France.** → Ils **l'**ont visitée.
J'adore **le Québec.** → Je **l'**adore.

B. The Pronoun **en**

1. The pronoun **en** replaces any direct object modified by an indefinite or a partitive article. It is the equivalent of the English *some* or, in negative sentences, *any.*

Elle va écrire **des lettres?**	Non, elle **en** a déjà écrit.
Tu ne bois jamais **de vin?**	Non, je n'**en** bois jamais.

2. **En** can replace a noun modified by a number or an adverb of quantity. The number or adverb remains after the verb in the sentence.

Est-ce qu'elle connaît **beaucoup d'écrivains?**	Oui, elle **en** connaît **beaucoup.**
Ne donnez pas **trop de devoirs!**	Je n'**en** donne jamais **trop.**
Les Ducharme ont **deux voitures?**	Non, ils **en** ont **trois.**

3. **En** is also used when the object is preceded by the preposition **de.**

Tu as besoin **de vacances,** n'est-ce pas?	Oui, j'**en** ai besoin.
Je peux lui parler **de son travail?**	Non, elle n'aime pas **en** parler.

LE CHANT DU MONDE LDC 278 943
EDITION DAVID OISTRAKH

MENDELSSOHN
TRIOS POUR PIANO, VIOLON ET VIOLONCELLE

Ce qu'ils disent

If the object of the preposition **de** is a person, you do not use **en**; you must use **de** plus a stressed pronoun (**lui, elle, eux,** etc.). In casual conversation, however, **en** is often used for people.

> Des enfants? Oui, il s'occupe **d'eux.**
> Mon prof? Je n'**en** ai pas peur.

ATTENTION

1. There is no agreement between **y** or **en** and a past participle.

   > Ils ont habité **en Angleterre.** → Ils y ont habité.
   > Il a acheté **des romans.** → Il en a acheté.

2. **Liaison** is always obligatory between pronouns and **y** and **en.** The verbs that normally drop the **s** in the **tu** form of the imperative add it back in order to make a liaison possible.

   > Ils y sont allés l'année dernière.
   > Elles en ont trouvé au supermarché.
   > Vas-y. Achètes-en.

3. When **y** and **en** are used with a reflexive verb, they follow the reflexive pronoun.

   > Elle s'intéresse **à la musique classique.** → Elle s'y intéresse.
   > Il s'occupe **de la vaisselle.** → Il s'en occupe.

4. When **en** is used with **il y a,** it follows **y.**

   > Il y a des stylos dans le bureau. → Il y en a dans le bureau.
   > Y a-t-il des montagnes au Maroc? → Y en a-t-il au Maroc?

Langue

A. **Quelle bonne élève!** Remplacez les mots en italique par les pronoms **y** ou **en,** selon le cas.

1. Elle monte *dans l'autobus.*
2. Elle va *à l'école.*
3. Elle fait *des maths.*
4. Elle suit *sept cours.*
5. Elle s'intéresse *aux sciences.*
6. Elle n'échoue pas *aux examens.*
7. Elle rentre *chez elle* à l'heure.
8. Elle s'occupe *de ses devoirs.*

B. **Un voyage à Bruxelles.** Dans les phrases suivantes, remplacez les mots en italique par un pronom.

1. Nous sommes allés *en Belgique.*
2. Nous avons visité *la Grand-Place.*
3. Je m'intéresse *à cette architecture.*
4. On a bu trop *de bière.*
5. Laure a perdu *de l'argent.*

6. J'ai prêté cent francs *à Laure.*
7. On a joué *au tennis* dans un parc.

8. Tu veux parler *de tes vacances?*

C. **Un week-end à la résidence.** Votre camarade de chambre revient après un week-end chez ses parents et il / elle vous pose des questions. Répondez aux questions suivantes en utilisant les mots entre parenthèses et en remplaçant les noms par des pronoms.

1. As-tu répondu à la lettre de ta mère?   (Oui,...)
2. As-tu mangé une pizza?   (Non,...)
3. Tout le monde a obéi aux règles de la résidence?   (Non,... pas du tout...)
4. Tes amis et toi, vous avez écouté mes cassettes?   (Oui,...)
5. As-tu rencontré d'autres étudiants?   (Oui,... trois...)
6. On a pensé à moi?   (Non, personne... !)

Culture

D. **Les sports dans le monde francophone.** Certains endroits sont connus pour le sport qu'on y pratique. Identifiez les endroits suivants du monde francophone selon ce sport.

MODELE: Chamonix   *On y fait du ski.*

1. Roland-Garros
2. Le Mans
3. le stade Olympique
4. Dakar
5. les bayous de Louisiane
6. les Ardennes

a. aller à la pêche
b. jouer au tennis
c. faire des courses de voitures de Formule I
d. aller à la chasse
e. finir une course de voitures
f. jouer au base-ball

E. **Les arts dans le monde francophone.** Répondez aux questions suivantes en employant le pronom **en.**

MODELE: Qui a écrit des romans?   *Camus en a écrit.*

1. Qui a fait des sculptures?
2. Qui joue de la flûte?
3. Qui a fait des tableaux?
4. Qui a écrit des opéras?
5. Qui a écrit des chansons?
6. Qui joue de l'accordéon?

a. Clifton Chenier
b. Auguste Rodin
c. Jacques Brel
d. Jean-Pierre Rampal
e. Claude Monet
f. Georges Bizet

Communication

F. **Vos activités.** Que faites-vous très souvent? de temps en temps? rarement? jamais?

    MODELE: dîner au restaurant   *J'y dîne souvent. / Je n'y dîne jamais.*

1. boire du champagne
2. manger du caviar
3. aller à la chasse
4. jouer d'un instrument
5. écrire des poèmes
6. échouer aux examens
7. penser aux vacances
8. faire des tableaux

G. **Combien en avez-vous?** Interrogez vos camarades pour trouver qui a le plus grand nombre de...

    MODELE: frères et sœurs   *Marc en a six.*

1. camarades de chambre
2. instruments de musique
3. dollars dans son portefeuille
4. robes / pantalons
5. examens cette semaine
6. disques
7. tableaux
8. petit(e)s ami(e)s

H. **Questions personnelles.** Vos pensées

1. Vous intéressez-vous à la littérature?
2. Connaissez-vous des auteurs français? Que pensez-vous d'eux?
3. Allez-vous au restaurant universitaire? Qu'est-ce que vous en pensez?
4. Quand pensez-vous à vos parents?
5. Vous avez visité le musée d'art de votre ville? Pourquoi pas?
6. Est-ce que vous réfléchissez souvent à votre avenir? Etes-vous optimiste ou pessimiste?

santé magazine

le journal qui fait du bien !

Un problème de beauté, de diététique, d'enfant... il y a des solutions. Un symptôme, une maladie, un traitement...

SANTÉ MAGAZINE en a parlé.

Elle écrit une lettre.

C OMMUNIQUONS ·

Ecrire des lettres

The French observe a certain style when writing letters. The two basic types of letters, business and personal, are described below. Business letters are usually typed, but it is acceptable to write by hand if a typewriter is not available. A personal letter, however, should never be typed.

On écrit des lettres d'affaires.

1. To start a business letter, write or type your own name and address in the upper left corner. In the upper right corner, put your city and the date. Below them, you write the title and address of the person to whom you are writing. Note that the place of these elements is the reverse in English.

Jean-Michel Boirond
22, rue du Bac
75007 Paris

Paris, le 3 septembre 1993

Monsieur Henri Paulin
56, avenue Wagram
75017 Paris

Monsieur,

2. To begin the letter, use the person's title or simply **Monsieur, Mademoiselle,** or **Madame.** The standard English salutation *Dear* is generally not used in French business letters.

Monsieur le Directeur,	*(Dear) Director,*
Madame la Directrice,	*(Dear) Director,*
Monsieur le Maire,	*(Dear) Mr. Mayor,*
Madame la Présidente,	*(Dear) Madam President,*

3. The first sentence of a business letter is often a form of politeness.

J'ai l'honneur de vous...	*It's my privilege to . . .*
J'ai le plaisir de vous...	*I have the pleasure of . . .*
Je vous serais reconnaissant(e) de...	*I would be grateful if . . .*
Je vous prie de...	*I beg you to . . .*
Je vous remercie pour / de...	*I thank you for . . .*
Je vous suis reconnaissant(e) de...	*I thank you for . . .*

4. The closing sentence is usually a set expression in a very formal style. The person to whom you are writing must be addressed in the same way as in the opening.

Veuillez agréer, Monsieur le Directeur, l'expression de mes sentiments distingués.

Veuillez agréer, Madame la Présidente, l'expression de mes sentiments les meilleurs.

Veuillez agréer, Mademoiselle, l'expression de mes salutations distinguées.

On écrit des lettres personnelles.

1. To begin a personal letter, choose a heading that reflects how well you know the person to whom you are writing and his / her age. The following expressions progress from salutations used with people you do not know well to those used with friends and relatives.

Monsieur, / Madame, / Mademoiselle,	*Sir, / Madam, / Miss,*
Cher Monsieur,	*Dear Sir,*
Chère Madame, / Mademoiselle	*Dear Madam, / Miss,*
Cher Monsieur, Chère Madame,	*Dear Mr. and Mrs.———,*
Cher Jacques, / Cher ami,	*Dear Jacques,*
Chère Maman,	*Dear Mom,*
Chers tous, / tous deux,	*Dear folks,*

2. To conclude a personal letter, you can use a number of closing phrases. The following expressions progress from closures used with people you do not know well to those used with friends and relatives.

Amitiés,	*Fondly,*
Amicalement,	*Sincerely,*
Cordialement,	*Cordially,*
Je t'embrasse, / Je vous embrasse,	*Love,*
Affectueux baisers,	*Hugs and kisses,*
Grosses bises,	*XXX,*

Interaction   *Jacqueline écrit une lettre à sa mère.*

Toulouse, le 7 juillet, 1994

Chère Maman,
   J'espère que tout va bien à la maison.
La semaine prochaine, je vais venir
passer le <u>pont</u> du 14 juillet avec vous.   long weekend
Dis à Papa que je voudrais que nous
fassions un <u>pique-nique</u> et que nous   picnic
invitions les Fromentin.
   Tout va bien au travail. Mon nouvel
appartement est formidable. A bientôt!
              Affectueux baisers,
              Jacqueline

Activités

A. Comment allez-vous commencer et terminer une lettre dans les situations suivantes?

    1. à vos grands-parents: Vous voulez aller les voir.
    2. à votre voisin: Il joue de la trompette à minuit.
    3. à votre concierge: Vous n'avez pas d'eau.
    4. au doyen *(dean)*: Votre prof est formidable.
    5. à PBS: Vous aimez leurs émissions.
    6. à votre cousin: Vous l'invitez à venir.

B. Ecrivez une des lettres suivantes.

Destinataire	**Sujet**
1. secrétaire général de la faculté	*cours pour les étrangers*
2. une organisation charitable	*pourquoi vous admirez leur travail*
3. une revue	*pourquoi vous n'êtes pas d'accord avec eux*
4. votre journal préféré	*leur usage de l'anglais*
5. votre petit(e) ami(e)	*vos activités du week-end dernier*
6. vos parents	*pourquoi vous avez besoin d'argent*

LECTURE CULTURELLE ....

Avant la lecture

For the past twenty years, there has been a crisis in the French film industry. The high cost of tickets, uncomfortable theaters, and long lines at newly-released films have been gradually angering and alienating more and more movie-goers. In the mid-eighties, the French film industry reacted by trying to make tickets more affordable, modernizing the theaters, and creating new multi-theater complexes. These efforts resulted in a renewed interest in the movies. Unfortunately, this renaissance did not last, and around 1987 attendance began to decline again. Television and VCRs have been responsible in part for this second decline in movie attendance, but the French film industry must also share the blame. Lately, it has failed to produce many films that arouse the interest of French audiences, who turn more and more to foreign films.

    It would be wrong, however, to assume that no one goes to the movies in France. Adolescents and children continue to be avid movie-goers (although they are particularly attracted by the flashy, big-budget American films). Also, in the spring, the international film festival in Cannes overshadows all current events in France and steals the headlines of all French newspapers and magazines.

Activités

A. Try to name five films that won an Oscar for best movie at the Academy Awards in Hollywood.

B. Among the films mentioned in the following reading, you will find *Sexe, mensonges et vidéo.* In this case, you can probably guess that it stands for *Sex, Lies, and Videotape.* In many instances, however, the foreign title of a film does not resemble its original title. Look at the following list of French titles and try to match them with their English titles.

1. *Allô Maman, c'est encore moi*
2. *Le Cercle des poètes disparus*
3. *Danse avec les loups*
4. *Maman, j'ai raté l'avion!*
5. *Le Silence des agneaux*
6. *Chérie, j'ai rétréci les gosses*

a. *Honey, I Shrunk the Kids*
b. *Home Alone*
c. *Dead Poets Society*
d. *The Silence of the Lambs*
e. *Dances with Wolves*
f. *Look Who's Talking Too*

C. List the titles of five French films that you have seen in French or in their English version, or that you have heard of.

Le Festival de Cannes

Tous les ans au mois de mai, l'élite du cinéma *mondial se retrouve* à Cannes pour les deux semaines du Festival international du film. — *international / meets*

Créé en 1946, le festival de Cannes est pour les Français *ce que* le festival de Venise est pour les Italiens, et ce que les Oscars d'Hollywood sont pour les — *Created / what*
5 Américains. Mais, *alors qu'*on *décerne* des douzaines d'Oscars chaque année — *whereas / award*
en Californie, la Palme d'Or est la *récompense* suprême sur la Côte d'Azur. — *reward*
Elle est réservée aux *courts* et aux longs *métrages,* et elle peut être attribuée à — *short / features*
un film français ou à un film étranger. On se rappelle, par exemple, que dans
les dix dernières années, des films comme *Missing* du *réalisateur* Costa-Gavras, — *filmmaker*
10 *Sous le soleil de Satan,* inspiré du roman de Georges Bernanos, et *Sexe, mensonges et vidéo* ont reçu cette prestigieuse récompense.

On attribue aussi d'autres *prix* comme le Grand Prix spécial du jury, les — *prizes*
Prix d'interprétation masculine et féminine et le Prix de la *mise en scène.* — *directing*

Le *palmarès* du festival de Cannes est impressionnant et il ne faut pas ou- — *prize list*
15 blier que beaucoup de films comme, pour en citer quelques-uns, *Orfeu Negro*
de Marcel Camus, *La Dolce Vita* de Federico Fellini, *Blow up* de Michelangelo
Antonioni, ou *Les Parapluies de Cherbourg* de Jacques Demy, qui ont tous
reçu une Palme d'Or, sont maintenant considérés comme des classiques du
cinéma international.
20 Le choix des films *primés* au festival de Cannes n'est pas facile à faire. — *that receive a prize*
Cette *tâche* est *confiée* à un jury composé de célébrités, *pour la plupart,* du — *task / entrusted / for the*
monde du cinéma, mais aussi des milieux journalistiques, politiques et artis- — *most part*
tiques. Pendant deux semaines, les membres du jury *se réunissent* tous les jours — *meet*
et *assistent* à la *projection* d'un nombre considérable de films de toutes sortes. — *attend / viewing*

Gérard Depardieu au
festival de Cannes

25 Ils sont *épiés* et *assaillis* par une *meute* de journalistes qui *répandent* toutes
sortes de rumeurs et qui essayent de prédire quel film va recevoir la Palme
d'Or. Le suspense se termine à la *clôture* du festival, *lors* d'une grande soirée
de gala qui *se tient* dans le palais des Festivals et des Congrès sur la *célèbre*
Croisette, le boulevard *bordé* de *palmiers* qui *longe* le bord de mer et où se
30 trouvent les grands hôtels comme le Carlton, qui depuis des années *recueillent*
des milliardaires du monde *entier*.

    La soirée de gala et la *remise* des prix constituent, *bien entendu*, le *clou* du
festival. Comme à Hollywood, les gens *se pressent* autour du Palais des Festivals pour voir y arriver leurs acteurs et actrices favoris. Mais, les deux se-
35 maines où se fait la *délibération* du jury sont aussi passionnantes pour les
touristes qui *affluent* sur la Côte d'Azur à cette époque. Le festival attire les
vedettes déjà consacrées que les *chasseurs d'autographes* assez audacieux poursuivent, soit sur la plage, soit dans la rue, soit dans le hall d'un hôtel, *jusqu'à
ce qu*'ils aient obtenu satisfaction. Il permet également aux acteurs et actrices
40 encore inconnus de *se faire remarquer* par les journalistes présents en leur *ac-
cordant* des interviews sur la Croisette, ou même, *quelquefois*, sur la plage.

    Avec toutes ses joies, ses *déceptions*, ses rivalités, ses scandales, le Festival
international du film de Cannes continue à exercer la même fascination, et
l'intérêt que les gens lui *portent* montre bien qu'il est devenu une véritable in-
45 stitution française.

Glossary (right margin):

- spied upon / mobbed / swarm / spread
- closing / during
- is held / famous
- lined / palm trees / borders
- receive
- entire
- awarding / of course / peak
- huddle
- judging
- rush
- stars / autograph collectors
- until
- to be noticed
- granting / sometimes
- disappointments
- show

Après la lecture

Questions sur le texte

1. Depuis quand est-ce que le festival de Cannes existe?
2. Comment s'appelle le grand prix donné à un film?
3. Est-ce que seuls les films français peuvent gagner un prix?
4. Qui sont les membres du jury?
5. Quand et comment est-ce qu'on apprend la liste des gagnants *(winners)*?
6. Quels acteurs et actrices viennent au festival de Cannes?
7. Pourquoi beaucoup de touristes vont à Cannes pendant le festival?
8. Comment les artistes peu connus peuvent-ils devenir célèbres?

Activités

A. Répondez aux questions suivantes.

1. Quels sont vos acteurs et actrices préférés? Pourquoi?
2. Pourquoi allez-vous au cinéma? Quelles sortes de films préférez-vous?

B. Racontez l'histoire d'un de vos films favoris.

C. Formez deux groupes et organisez un débat sur la censure *(censorship)* au cinéma. Est-il nécessaire de séparer les films avec des lettres comme *G*, *PG*, *R*, and *NC 17* comme aux Etats-Unis?

RÉVISION E

TOUS ENSEMBLE!

A. **Les vacances de Christine et d'Eric.** Répondez aux questions suivantes en employant les mots entre parenthèses et des pronoms pour les mots en italique.

1. Comment vous appelez-vous?   (... Eric et Christine.)
2. Etes-vous déjà allés *en France?*   (... 1992.)
3. Est-ce que vous avez dû vous occuper de *vos billets d'avion?* (Oui,...)
4. Christine, t'es-tu promenée *dans Paris?*   (Oui,... déjà...)
5. Eric, tes parents étaient contents quand tu as voyagé?   (Non,... s'inquiéter beaucoup.)
6. Le soir, qu'est-ce que vous aviez envie de faire?   (... se détendre.)
7. Avez-vous fait *de la planche à voile?*   (Oui,... en Normandie.)
8. Quand il a plu, qu'est-ce que vous avez fait?   (... lire... livre et... écrire... lettres.)
9. Quand vous êtes en voyage, vous achetez beaucoup de choses? (Oui,... acheter des vêtements.)
10. Etes-vous allés *à l'Opéra?* (Oui,... aller trois fois.)

B. Faites des phrases avec les mots donnés.

La détente

1. Je / avoir / besoin / se détendre
2. Entrer / maison / et / se reposer!
3. Papa, / écouter / maman / Cesser / travailler / tard!
4. Elles / ne... pas / se dépêcher / parce que / elles / ne... pas / tenir / arriver / à l'heure
5. Nous / venir / se coucher

Au travail!

6. Nous / choisir / faire / métier / artistique
7. Nous / commencer / traduire / poème / hier
8. Elles / écrire / romans / et / contes

9. Je / venir / lire / ce / revue
10. Je / dire / enfants / continuer / étudier / piano

C. **Mes amis écrivains.** Remplacez les mots en italique par des pronoms.

1. Victor et Suzanne passent tout l'été *sur la Côte d'Azur.*
2. *Leur appartement* de Paris est petit, mais *leur maison* de Nice est grande.
3. Avez-vous lu *leurs livres?*
4. J'ai traduit *le poème de Victor* et *les poèmes* de sa femme.
5. Lui, il parle *de la mer;* elle, elle ne parle jamais *de cela.*
6. Voulez-vous que je vous montre *les poèmes* de Suzanne?
7. A Noël, j'ai acheté *le dernier livre* de Victor, et Suzanne m'a offert un *autre livre* pour mon anniversaire.
8. Je ne pense pas qu'ils aient beaucoup *d'argent.*
9. Ils s'intéressent *à la musique classique* aussi.
10. Ils invitent souvent *leurs amis* à écouter *des disques* avec eux.

D. **La matinée.** Complétez le paragraphe suivant avec la forme correcte des verbes donnés et des prépositions, s'il y a lieu.

Hier, Anne-Marie _____ (se réveiller) à sept heures et _____ (se lever) quelques minutes après. Elle _____ (se laver) et _____ (aller chercher) le journal. Elle le _____ (lire) rapidement et _____ (se dépêcher) _____ (s'habiller). Elle _____ (appeler) un taxi et l' _____ (attendre) pendant vingt minutes. Elle _____ (dire) à l'homme _____ (la conduire) au bureau. Dans le taxi elle _____ (écrire) des lettres à ses employés. Quand elle _____ (arriver) au bureau, elle _____ (appeler) son secrétaire; elle _____ (vouloir) qu'il _____ (commencer) taper ses lettres. Elle _____ (demander) son amie Andrée de déjeuner avec elle. Elles _____ (finir) travailler à 11 h 45 et _____ (partir) pour le restaurant.

E. **Réactions personnelles.** Complétez les phrases suivantes de manière logique.

1. J'aime lire...
2. J'espère être...
3. Pour le week-end, nous avons besoin...
4. Mon ami(e) a du mal...
5. Mon / Ma camarade de chambre se dépêche quand...
6. T'inquiètes-tu quand... ?
7. Pour me détendre...
8. Je refuse...

ENTRE NOUS!

A. Avec un(e) camarade de cours, décrivez une journée typique d'un(e) étudiant(e). Employez les suggestions données et vos propres idées.

se réveiller	lire le journal	rentrer
se lever	commencer	acheter
se laver	s'amuser	changer de vêtements
prendre le petit déjeuner	décider	écrire
s'habiller	jouer à / de	se coucher
partir	se détendre	s'endormir

B. Dans un petit groupe de trois ou quatre, parlez de vos projets pour demain, pour ce semestre et pour l'avenir. Parlez aussi des choses que vous n'allez pas faire. Ensuite, informez les autres des résultats de votre discussion.

MODELE: *Je tiens à apprendre le français.*
J'ai décidé de devenir médecin.
Je vais éviter de dépenser trop d'argent.

souhaiter	aller	éviter
rêver	commencer	refuser
chercher	avoir envie	choisir
tenir à	avoir peur	s'amuser
il faut que	devoir	vouloir

C. Un(e) camarade de cours et vous, vous vous trouvez sur une île *(island)* déserte. Qu'est-ce qu'il faut que vous ayez pour être heureux (-euse)? De quoi n'avez-vous pas besoin?

MODELE: *J'ai besoin d'une radio.*
Nous n'avons pas besoin d'argent.

D. Donnez le nom d'un(e) athlète ou d'un(e) musicien(ne) à votre camarade de cours. Ensuite, demandez-lui quel sport il / elle pratique ou de quel instrument il / elle joue.

MODELE: Jennifer Capriati   *Elle joue au tennis.*
Miles Davis   *Il jouait de la trompette.*
André le Géant   *Il fait du catch.*

E. **Questions personnelles.** Vos pensées

1. Que pensez-vous...

MODELE: des westerns? *Je pense qu'ils sont ennuyeux.*

a. des Beatles?	d. de la télévision?
b. du Président des Etats-Unis?	e. de votre cours de français?
c. des Français?	f. ???

2. Quand vous vous trouvez dans les situations suivantes, à quoi
ou à qui pensez-vous?

MODELE: Vous êtes en cours.
Quand je suis en cours, je pense à mes vacances.

a. Vous téléphonez à votre
   petit(e) ami(e).
b. Vous vous reposez.
c. Vous êtes en cours.
d. Vous êtes seul(e).

e. Vous passez un examen.
f. Vous recevez un
   télégramme.
g. Vous partez en vacances.
h. ???

F. **Jeu de rôles.** Jouez les scènes suivantes avec un(e) camarade de cours.

1. Vous êtes chez le médecin. Expliquez-lui vos problèmes. Le
   médecin vous donne des conseils.
2. Un journaliste français va vous interviewer. Il veut savoir
   comment est la journée typique d'un étudiant américain.
   Décrivez-lui la vôtre.
3. Vous jouez le rôle de votre athlète préféré. Un(e) autre
   étudiant(e) va vous interviewer après une compétition
   importante.
4. Vous êtes écrivain. Un(e) camarade de cours est journaliste et va
   vous interviewer. Parlez de vos créations littéraires.
5. Vous travaillez à la télévision. Faites de la publicité pour une
   marque *(brand name)* qui a une équipe dans le Tour de France.
6. Vous êtes guide dans un musée. Décrivez vos œuvres d'art
   (works of art) préférées. Un(e) camarade est touriste et va vous
   poser des questions.

Chapitre 16

LE FRANÇAIS EN AMERIQUE DU NORD

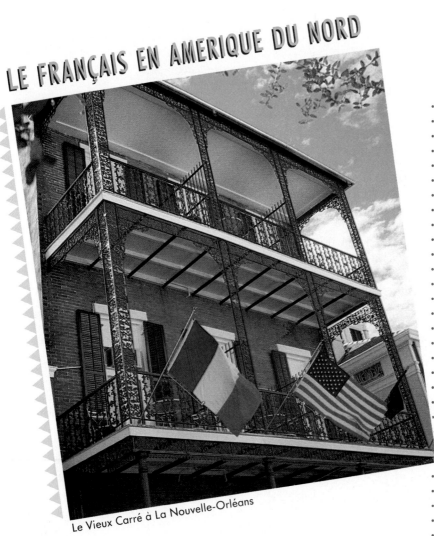

Le Vieux Carré à La Nouvelle-Orléans

Commençons ....

Réponse à une petite annonce

Un étudiant américain qui vient de Louisiane et qui s'appelle Daniel est à Lyon depuis une semaine. Il lit les petites annonces dans Le Progrès. *Il a trouvé des chambres à louer qui l'intéressent et il a téléphoné aux propriétaires pendant toute la matinée. Quelqu'un répond enfin.*

DANIEL: Allô, bonjour, Madame, J'ai lu la petite annonce que vous avez placée dans le journal et j'aimerais avoir des renseignements sur la chambre que vous voulez louer.

MME LUCAS: Bien sûr! C'est une grande chambre meublée qui donne sur le parc de la Tête d'Or et que je loue tous les ans à des étudiants étrangers. J'ai trouvé quelqu'un il y a un mois, mais il a dû rentrer chez lui.

DANIEL: Quel est le prix du loyer?

MME LUCAS: Quinze cents francs par mois charges comprises. Voudriez-vous aller voir la chambre maintenant?

DANIEL: Oui, mais je ne sais pas où elle se trouve. Pourriez-vous m'indiquer le chemin?

MME LUCAS: Connaissez-vous le musée Guimet? C'est juste en face, au numéro vingt et un. C'est au sixième étage, la troisième porte à gauche. Demandez la clé à la concierge.

DANIEL: Très bien, je vais y aller tout de suite et je vais vous rappeler dans la soirée.

Mots clés

qui	*who*	donne sur (donner sur)	*looks out on*
Louisiane	*Louisiana*	il y a	*ago*
petites annonces	*classified ads*	loyer	*rent*
qui intéressent (intéresser)	*that interest*	charges comprises	*utilities included*
propriétaires (m. / f.)	*owners*	Voudriez-vous... ? (vouloir)	*Would you like . . . ?*
enfin	*finally*	Pourriez-vous... ? (pouvoir)	*Could you . . . ?*
que	*that*	chemin	*way*
placée (placer)	*placed*	juste	*immediately*
aimerais (aimer)	*would like*	étage	*floor*
meublée	*furnished*	à gauche	*on the left*
		concierge	*concierge*

FAISONS CONNAISSANCE

Many French families rent rooms to students in their own homes or apartments or in property they own for purely financial reasons. This is particularly true of widows and older couples whose children have left home. They use the rent money to pay taxes and to supplement their incomes. This is a fortunate situation for students because few universities have enough student housing.

L'urbanisme moderne

A **concierge,** such as the one mentioned in the dialogue at the beginning of the chapter, is usually a woman responsible for distributing mail, helping visitors, and keeping the building clean. **Concierges** are rapidly disappearing, however, as building owners install automatic locks and individual mailboxes.

French people have a different way of counting floors. The first floor is **le rez-de-chaussée,** the second floor, **le premier étage,** and so on. In Quebec, however, people use the word **plancher,** which also means floor, for **étage,** and they count the floors the same way Americans do. Thus, to a person from Quebec or the United States, in the dialogue, the room **au sixième étage** would be on the seventh floor. On the top floor of many apartment buildings **(un immeuble)** there are maids' rooms **(des chambres de bonne),** which are often rented to students.

Etudions le dialogue

1. Qu'est-ce que Daniel lit? Pourquoi?
2. A qui téléphone-t-il?
3. Décrivez la chambre.
4. Quel est le prix du loyer?
5. Où se trouve la chambre?
6. Est-ce que Daniel la prend tout de suite?

Enrichissons notre vocabulaire

Les pièces de la maison *(The rooms of the house)*

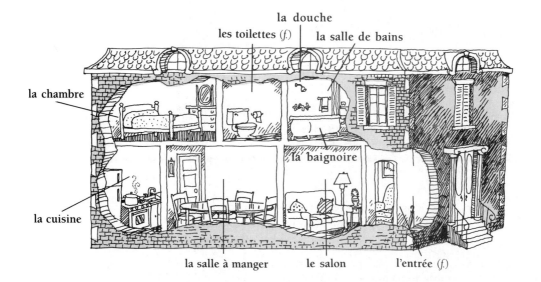

Les meubles et les appareils électro-ménagers
(Furniture and appliances)

un fauteuil
une lampe
une table

un divan / un canapé

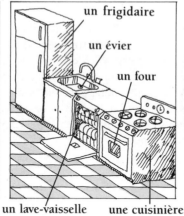

un frigidaire
un évier
un four

un lave-vaisselle / une cuisinière

une armoire
une étagère
une table de nuit
un lit
un tapis
un lavabo

une machine à laver

un sèche-linge

un four à micro-ondes

Prononciation Mute e

A. Mute **e** may or may not be pronounced, according to its position in the sentence. When pronounced, it is represented by the symbol /ə/ and is virtually identical to the /ø/ of **peu**.

B. Mute **e** is identified in written form by the letter **e** with no accent mark, and it is never followed by double consonants.

> **Devoirs** and **besoin** both contain mute **e**.
> **Derrière** has the /ɛ/ sound, as indicated by the double **r**.

C. In casual conversation, most French speakers drop as many mute **e**'s as possible, short of creating a string of unpronounceable consonants. One important rule is that mute **e** is never pronounced before a vowel sound.

> quatre heures / votre appartement / un autre étudiant /
> notre ami / une table immense / un pauvre homme

D. In general, a mute **e** is also dropped if it is preceded by only one pronounced consonant. For example, **trop de gens** is pronounced /tʀo dʒã/. The /ʒ/ is preceded by **d,** but **p** is not pronounced.

> beaucoup d̸e livres / sans c̸e livre / un kilo d̸e beurre /
> dans l̸e bureau / assez d̸e travail / Vous l̸e savez. /
> pas d̸e place / Tu n̸e bois pas.

E. If a mute **e** follows two pronounced consonants, however, it is better to keep the sound.

> Il ne̲ sait pas. / Regarde le̲ garçon. / avec le̲ couteau /
> Elles me̲ connaissent. / Jeanne te̲ voit / une pauvre̲
> femme / le gouverne̲ment / quatre̲ semaines de̲ vacances

Exercise

Read the following sentences aloud, dropping as many mute e's as possible.

1. Je ne sais pas si je veux cette table de nuit.
2. Beaucoup de gens se reposent le matin.
3. Elle me donne trop de travail.
4. A quatre heures nous décidons de préparer le dîner.
5. Qu'est-ce que vous allez me montrer?
6. Mon appartement se trouve au rez-de-chaussée près de la cuisine.

GRAMMAIRE ....

I. The Relative Pronouns qui, que, and où

> You use relative pronouns to connect two sentences or clauses
> into a single sentence.

A. In English, relative pronouns are used to combine two sentences or clauses into a single sentence. The relative pronoun introduces the second clause and refers to a word in the main clause. This word is called the *antecedent.*

> Here is the book. I read the book.
>
>   **antecedent   rel. pro**
>   ↓   ↓
> Here is the *book that* I read.
>
> Did you see the man? The man drove a red car.
>
>   **antecedent   rel. pro.**
>   ↓   ↓
> Did you see the *man who* drove a red car?

B. The Relative Pronoun **qui**

1. **Qui** *(who, which, that)* may refer to people or things and serves as the subject of the verb that follows it.

Nous avons demandé des renseignements à **Paul. Paul** connaît bien la ville.

Nous avons demandé des renseignements à Paul **qui** connaît bien la ville.

C'est **une grande chambre. La chambre** donne sur un parc.

C'est une grande chambre **qui** donne sur un parc.

2. The verb following **qui** agrees with the antecedent.

C'est **moi** qui **suis arrivé** à l'heure.   C'est **elle** qui **est montée.**

C. The Relative Pronoun **que**

1. **Que** *(whom, which, that)* also refers to people or things and serves as the direct object of the verb that follows it.

Je cherche **la chambre.** Vous louez **la chambre.**
Je cherche la chambre **que** vous louez.

Elle n'aime pas **l'émission.** Ils regardent **l'émission.**
Elle n'aime pas l'émission **qu'ils** regardent.

2. **Que** becomes **qu'** before a vowel sound.

Ma mère lit le roman **qu'elle** a trouvé sur le fauteuil.

▶ **L'Orthographe**

If the clause following **que** is in the **passé composé,** the past participle agrees with the antecedent of **que,** which is the preceding direct object.

Elle s'intéresse à **la robe** que tu lui as montrée.
Nous n'avons pas vu **les meubles** qu'ils ont achetés.
J'ai lu **les petites annonces** que vous avez placées dans le journal.

D. The relative pronoun **où**

1. **Où** *(where)* is used when the second clause indicates a place.

Il n'a pas dit **où** il allait.   Voilà la chambre **où** ils dorment.

2. If the antecedent is a place but is the *direct object* of the verb in the second clause, use **que** instead of **où.**

L'Espagne est un pays **que** nous n'avons jamais visité.
Le parc de la Tête d'Or est un parc **que** les Lyonnais
 fréquentent beaucoup.

E. In Chapter 15, you learned that demonstrative pronouns (**celui, celle, ceux, celles**) must be followed by **-ci, -là,** or the preposition **de.** They can also be followed by relative pronouns.

Elle n'aime pas ceux **que** j'ai achetés.
Prenez celui **qui** est sur la table.
Regardez cette maison. C'est celle **où** je suis née.

CE QU'ILS DISENT

1. French intonation and rhythm do not allow a speaker to emphasize a word in a sentence simply by saying it louder, as we do in English. To emphasize a word, you must put it just before a break in syntax. Relative pronouns are frequently used in this construction, which you hear very often in casual conversation. In the following examples, the word in boldface in the first sentence is emphasized in the second.

Jean cherche un appartement.   C'est Jean qui cherche un
                                                            appartement.
Je n'aime pas **tes meubles.**   Ce sont tes meubles que
                                                            je n'aime pas.
Madeleine travaille **là.**   C'est là où Madeleine travaille.

2. In this construction, stressed pronouns replace subject pronouns, and the verb in the second clause agrees with its subject in the first.

Tu achètes un lave-vaisselle?   **Il** ne va pas conduire!
C'est **toi** qui **achètes**   Ce n'est pas **lui** qui **va**
 un lave-vaisselle?   conduire!

Langue

A. **Dans notre appartement.** Complétez les phrases suivantes avec un pronom relatif.

  1. J'adore les appartements _____ il y a beaucoup de fenêtres.
  2. Apportez-moi le verre _____ j'ai laissé dans la cuisine.
  3. L'appartement _____ ma petite amie habite est derrière celui-ci.
  4. Je préfère les salons _____ n'ont pas trop de meubles.
  5. Nous n'apprécions pas les voisins _____ font du bruit.
  6. Le lit _____ ils veulent me prêter est trop petit.

B. **Une promenade en ville.** Complétez les phrases suivantes.

  1. Nous avons acheté des disques que...
  2. Je vous recommande un film qui...

3. J'ai visité une ville où...
4. Le restaurant sert des repas qui...
5. Allez-vous acheter les vêtements que... ?
6. Ils passent leur temps dans un magasin où...

C. **Préparatifs.** Dans les phrases suivantes, remplacez les noms avec un pronom démonstratif.

MODELE: Ce sont les amis que j'attends.
           Ce sont ceux que j'attends.

1. Ce n'est pas le plat que je vais servir.
2. Voilà les chaussures qui sont trop grandes.
3. As-tu perdu la cravate que Véronique vient de te donner?
4. J'aime la robe que tu as choisie.
5. Voilà la voiture de nos amis.
6. J'entends les amis qui viennent dîner.

Culture

D. **Où on travaille.** Comme aux Etats-Unis, on se réfère aux organisations gouvernementales françaises par le nom du bâtiment *(building)* où elles se trouvent. Trouvez le bâtiment pour chaque organisation.

MODELE: (aux Etats-Unis) la Maison-Blanche
           C'est là où le Président travaille.

1. Matignon
2. l'Elysée
3. le palais Bourbon
4. l'Hôtel de Ville
5. le palais du Luxembourg
6. le quai d'Orsay

a. le maire de Paris
b. le ministre des Affaires étrangères
c. le président
d. le Premier ministre
e. l'Assemblée nationale
f. le Sénat

Communication

E. **Mes préférences.** Formez des phrases logiques avec un élément de chaque colonne.

A	B	C
J'admire les gens	qui	être intéressant
Je ne peux pas supporter les gens	que	parler trop
J'aime visiter des pays	où	ne pouvoir rien faire
Je déteste les villes		être trop difficile
Je voudrais avoir un métier		donner mal à la tête
Je n'écoute jamais les gens		ne rien apprendre
Les étudiants s'intéressent aux cours		travailler beaucoup
On n'aime pas s'occuper de problèmes		être sincère
???		???

F. **Mes préférences (suite).** Complétez les phrases suivantes logiquement.

1. J'aime les filles / les garçons qui...
2. Je préfère les maisons qui...
3. J'adore les appartements où...
4. Je m'intéresse aux journaux que...
5. J'apprécie les étudiants qui...
6. Je tiens aux meubles que...

G. **Questions personnelles.** Votre logement

1. Dans quelle sorte de ville habitez-vous?
2. Habitez-vous dans une résidence, dans une maison, ou dans un appartement?
3. Décrivez votre chambre.
4. De quels meubles avez-vous besoin?
5. Vous avez cherché un(e) camarade de chambre? Qu'est-ce que vous avez demandé?
6. Vous aimez quelles sortes de voisins?

II. The Conditional Mood

> You use the conditional mood to express an occurrence that would exist under certain circumstances or to soften a request.

A. Formation of the Conditional: Regular Verbs

aimer	descendre
j' aimerais	je descendrais
tu aimerais	tu descendrais
il / elle / on aimerait	il / elle / on descendrait
nous aimerions	nous descendrions
vous aimeriez	vous descendriez
ils / elles aimeraient	ils / elles descendraient

choisir	écrire
je choisirais	j'écrirais
tu choisirais	tu écrirais
il / elle / on choisirait	il / elle / on écrirait
nous choisirions	nous écririons
vous choisiriez	vous écririez
ils / elles choisiraient	ils / elles écriraient

J'aimerais avoir des renseignements sur la chambre.

1. You form the conditional mood by adding the endings of the imperfect tense to the infinitive. If the infinitive ends in **-re**, you drop the **e** before adding the endings.

2. If the infinitive ends in **-r,** you pronounce the **r.**

   aimer → **j'aimerais**   louer → **tu louerais**

B. Formation of the Conditional: Irregular Verbs

1. Several verbs that you already know have irregular conditional stems:

aller	j'irais	pouvoir	elles **pourr**aient
avoir	tu **aur**ais	recevoir	vous **recevr**iez
devenir	on **deviendr**ait	savoir	elle **saur**ait
devoir	il **devr**ait	tenir	nous **tiendr**ions
être	nous **ser**ions	valoir	il **vaudr**ait (mieux)
faire	vous **fer**iez	venir	il **viendr**ait
falloir	il **faudr**ait	voir	tu **verr**ais
pleuvoir	il **pleuvr**ait	vouloir	je **voudr**ais

2. Stem-changing verbs use the **accent grave** or double consonant in the last syllable of the stem to keep the /ɛ/ sound. Verbs with an **accent aigu** in the last syllable of the stem keep the /e/ sound.

   acheter   →   elle ach**è**terait
   se lever   →   nous nous l**è**v**é**rions
   appeler   →   vous appe**ll**eriez

   but: préférer   →   je préf**é**rerais
           répéter   →   tu répéterais

C. Uses of the Conditional

1. The conditional mood expresses a possible occurrence that would exist under certain conditions.

   Nous **aimerions** habiter en Louisiane.
   A ce prix-là, ce **serait** trop cher.
   Il ne **viendrait** pas sans son ami.

2. Several expressions are frequently used with the conditional mood to show a condition that does not exist.

à ta / votre place:	A ta place, je **choisirais** un autre divan.
sans / avec cela:	Sans cela, nous ne **finirions** jamais.
si j'étais / si vous étiez:	Si vous étiez riche, vous ne **feriez** pas le ménage.

3. The conditional mood also softens a request or a statement.

   Voudriez-vous aller voir la chambre?
   Vous **devriez** consulter une carte.

Langue

A. **A la bibliothèque.** Mettez les phrases suivantes au conditionnel.

1. Pouvez-vous m'indiquer les renseignements?
2. Je veux savoir où se trouvent les revues.
3. Anne doit chercher un journal.
4. Où est-ce qu'on trouve les films?
5. Je suis heureux de pouvoir utiliser un ordinateur.
6. Il faut que j'aille au quatrième étage.

B. **Sans argent.** Formez des phrases avec les mots donnés. Mettez les verbes au conditionnel.

1. Sans argent / vous / ne... pas / pouvoir / acheter / fauteuil
2. Je / ne... pas / entrer / ce / magasin
3. Il / avoir peur / louer / voiture
4. Ce / enfants / ne... pas / pouvoir / aller / cinéma
5. Nous / ne... pas / appeler / médecin
6. Moi, / je / ne... pas / aller / ce / restaurant

C. **On invite nos voisins.** Répondez aux questions en employant les mots entre parenthèses et en mettant le verbe au conditionnel.

1. Vous voulez quelque chose?   (... vouloir du thé)
2. Que feriez-vous à ma place?   (... acheter un nouveau divan)
3. Est-ce que je peux ouvrir la fenêtre?   (Non,... avoir froid)
4. Est-ce que votre amie aimerait partir?   (Oui, mais... revenir tout de suite)
5. Est-elle en retard?   (Oui,... devoir se dépêcher)
6. Aimeriez-vous rester dîner?   (Non,... préférer rentrer)

Culture

D. **La politesse.** Si un Français vous invitait à dîner, que feriez-vous pour être poli(e)? Qu'est-ce que vous ne feriez pas?

MODELE: demander aux gens d'allumer la télé
        Je ne demanderais pas aux gens d'allumer la télé.

1. apporter des bonbons
2. arriver bien en avance
3. amener un ami
4. faire des bises à tout le monde
5. enlever mes chaussures
6. avoir les mains sous la table
7. demander encore de la viande
8. partir avant 11 heures

Communication

E. **Si les choses étaient différentes.** Avec les petits changements suivants dans votre vie, que feriez-vouz? Finissez les phrases.

1. Avec beaucoup d'argent,...
2. Si j'étais diplomate,...
3. Avec une voiture de sport,...
4. Avec de longues vacances,...
5. Sans ma famille,...
6. Sans cette classe,...

F. Si vous pouviez refaire votre vie, que feriez-vous de différent? Utilisez les suggestions données ou vos propres idées.

MODELE: *J'étudierais beaucoup plus. / J'habiterais en Europe.*

suivre plus / moins de cours de...   dépenser moins d'argent
aller à l'université de...   être plus / moins sympathique
apprendre à jouer du / de la...   louer un appartement
acheter un four à micro-ondes   ???

G. **Questions personnelles.** Votre avenir

1. Sans diplôme, que feriez-vous?
2. Quand est-ce que vous devriez commencer à travailler? Qu'est-ce que vous préféreriez faire?
3. Qu'est-ce que vous n'accepteriez jamais de faire?
4. Qu'est-ce que vous pourriez faire pour trouver une solution à un problème social?
5. Que faudrait-il que vous ayez pour être heureux (-euse)?
6. Avec un tapis volant *(flying carpet)*, où iriez-vous?

III. Expressing Time with **pendant, depuis,** and **il y a**

> You use time expressions to indicate when an action or a state began and whether or not it is still going on.

A. Pendant

Use **pendant** or no preposition at all to express the amount of time an action or a condition lasted in the past. The English equivalent is *for*.

J'ai téléphoné **pendant** toute la matinée.
or: J'ai téléphoné toute la matinée.

Les élèves ont attendu l'autobus **pendant** une heure.
or: Les élèves ont attendu l'autobus une heure.

B. Depuis

1. To describe the duration of an action that started in the past but is still going on, use the *present tense* of the verb and **depuis**. The English equivalent is *has / have been* or *has / have been doing*.

Daniel **est** à Lyon **depuis** une semaine.   *Daniel **has been** in Lyon **for** a week.*
Il **cherche** une chambre **depuis** longtemps.   *He **has been looking** for a room for a long time.*

2. **Depuis** may also be used with a specific time. In this case, its English equivalent is *since*.

| Mitterrand est président **depuis** 1981. | *Mitterrand has been president since 1981.* |
| Elle attend une lettre **depuis lundi.** | *She has been waiting for a letter since Monday.* |

C. Il y a... que and Voilà... que

Il y a... que and **Voilà... que** also express the duration of an action that started in the past but is still going on. They are used only with amounts of time. These two structures often show more impatience on the part of the speaker than **depuis** and must precede the subject and verb.

| **Il y a** trois jours **qu'**on n'a pas d'eau. | *We haven't had water for three days.* |
| **Voilà** une heure **que** nous téléphonons au propriétaire. | *We have been phoning the landlord for an hour.* |

D. Il y a

To describe the amount of time that has passed since an action took place, use **il y a** and a verb in a past tense. It may precede or follow the verb. The English equivalent is *ago.*

| **J'ai trouvé** un appartement **il y a** un mois. | *I found an apartment a month ago.* |
| **Il y a** trois jours, elle **était** encore en Europe. | *Three days ago, she was still in Europe.* |

ATTENTION

There are two differences between **il y a** meaning *for* and meaning *ago.* When **il y a** means *ago,* a past tense is used and there is no **que.**

| **Il y a** trois minutes, il **était** là. | *He was here three minutes ago.* |
| **Il y a** trois minutes **qu'**il **est** là. | *He's been here for three minutes.* |

E. Other Useful Time Expressions

1. **Dès** and **à partir de** *(from . . . on, as of . . . , beginning with . . .)* can be used at the beginning or at the end of the sentence.

   Dès maintenant, il faut que vous utilisiez un ordinateur.
   Les Français ont eu des vacances payées **à partir des** années 30.

2. **Pour** *(for)* is used with time only for projection into the future.

   Il est parti **pour** trois mois en Afrique.
   Elle va sortir **pour** une heure.

3. **Dans** *(in)* describes the amount of time before you do something; **en** *(in)* describes the amount of time it takes to do something.

   Je vais faire la vaisselle **dans** une heure.
   Il peut taper une page **en** trois minutes.

Langue

A. **Les petites annonces.** Complétez les phrases suivantes en traduisant le(s) mot(s) entre parenthèses.

1. Robert achète le journal ici _____ deux ans. *(for)*
2. Il lit les petites annonces _____ quelques minutes. *(in)*
3. _____ trois semaines _____ il cherche une voiture. *(for)*
4. _____ une semaine, il pensait en avoir trouvé une. *(ago)*
5. Il a téléphoné au propriétaire _____ plusieurs jours. *(for)*
6. Sa femme lui a dit qu'il venait de partir _____ une semaine en Angleterre. *(for)*
7. Il peut retéléphoner _____ mardi prochain. *(from Tuesday on)*
8. Il décide de chercher une autre voiture _____ demain. *(as of)*

B. **En première année à l'université.** Traduisez les phrases suivantes.

1. I have been here since September.
2. Classes started four weeks ago.
3. Every day, I stay in the lab for one hour.
4. From three o'clock on, I am in the library.
5. I have known my roommate for eight months.
6. I am going to have my last exam in three weeks.

C. **Fin du siècle.** C'est le vendredi 31 décembre 1999 à midi, et vous préparez les festivités pour le Nouvel An. Depuis quand ou depuis combien de temps faites-vous les choses suivantes? Ou bien, vous les avez faites il y a combien de temps?

1. attendre ce jour / des années
2. téléphoner / amis / mardi dernier
3. préparer / plats / huit heures du matin
4. choisir / musique / mois
5. acheter le champagne / semaine dernière
6. répéter «Ce n'est qu'un *au revoir*» / toute la matinée

Culture

D. **Prenons le train.** Vous êtes à Montréal et vous décidez de prendre le train pour aller à Ottawa. Consultez l'horaire *(schedule)* et répondez aux questions suivantes.

Connecting Train No. Correspondance ferroviaire		km				21 Ex. Sa. Su. Sauf sa. di.	23	23	
Québec, QC (Gare du Palais)		0	Dp			06 45	11 50	11 50	
Montréal, QC (Central Stn./Gare Centrale)		272	Ar			09 55	15 00	15 00	

		km							
Montréal, QC ET/HE (Central Stn./Gare Centrale)		0	Dp	07 20	09 30	13 05	16 30	17 50	19 40
Dorval		19		07 40	09 50	13 26	16 51	18 10	20 01
Coteau, QC		63				F 13 51			F 20 26
Alexandria, ON		100		F 08 32	F 10 35	F 14 16	F 17 36	F 18 55	F 20 58
Maxville		117		F 08 46	F 10 49				F 21 12
Casselman		140				F 14 41			
Ottawa, ON		187	Ar	09 29	11 32	15 22	18 40	19 49	21 58

1. On peut aller de Montréal à Ottawa en combien de temps?
2. Vous êtes dans le train de Montréal de 7 h 20 et vous venez de partir de Maxville. Vous voyagez depuis combien de temps?
3. Vous allez arriver à Ottawa dans combien de temps?
4. A Montréal vous montez dans le train de 13 h 05. Il y a combien de temps que les gens qui sont montés à Québec sont là?
5. Ils ont attendu à la Gare Centrale à Montréal pendant combien de temps?
6. Vous arrivez à la gare à huit heures du soir. Le dernier train est parti pour Ottawa il y a combien de temps?

Communication

E. **Mes études.** Complétez les phrases suivantes.

1. J'étudie le français depuis...
2. J'ai terminé mon dernier examen il y a...
3. Il y a... que je suis étudiant(e) à cette université.
4. Je vais rentrer dans...
5. Je vais commencer à chercher du travail dans...
6. J'ai préparé cette leçon pendant...

F. **Questions personnelles.** Votre logement

1. Pendant combien de temps est-ce que votre famille a habité sa maison?
2. Vous êtes parti(e) de chez eux il y a combien de temps?
3. Combien de temps avez-vous passé à chercher votre appartement / votre chambre?
4. Vous êtes là depuis combien de temps?
5. Vous faites le ménage en combien de temps?
6. Dans combien de temps pensez-vous acheter une maison?

C OMMUNIQUONS ....

Consulter la presse francophone

In France, most newspapers and news magazines can be associated with major political movements. For example, in Paris *Le Figaro* is rather conservative, but *Libération* is to the political left. One of the most respected dailies, *Le Monde,* has a liberal point of view, while *Le Canard Enchaîné,* a weekly newspaper, specializes in political satire. It uses many puns, innuendos, and allusions that only people who follow the daily political scene understand. Although these and other major Parisian newspapers are available throughout France, each region has its own paper. For example, Lyon has *Le Progrès,* Toulouse *La Dépêche du Midi,* and Rennes *Ouest-France.*

Other countries have their own daily papers in French, such as *Le Devoir*, which is published in Montréal. In many areas, residents have a choice of languages for their papers: French or Dutch in Belgium, French or German in Switzerland, French and English in Quebec.

There are also several types of weekly magazines (**les hebdomadaires**) and monthly publications (**les mensuels**). On a weekly basis, *L'Express*, *Le Point*, and *Le Nouvel Observateur* cover the news in sections (**les rubriques**) on the national and international scenes, while *Paris-Match* provides lighter, general information, emphasizing photographs and gossip about popular figures. Monthly magazines include those for fashion (**les journaux de mode**), such as *Marie-Claire* and *Marie-France*, or publications, such as *Femme*, that represent the feminist point of view. *Elle* is a magazine for women.

Numerous publications appeal to specific interests (**la presse spécialisée**). You have already learned that *L'Equipe* is a daily newspaper for sports fans and that *Télé 7 Jours* and *Télé-Poche* provide information on television programming. Other types of specialized publications include the Parisian magazines *Pariscope* and *L'Officiel des Spectacles*, which give a complete listing of the current movies, plays, and nightclub acts. In addition, most French hobbyists and sports lovers have publications for their individual interests. There is even a periodical for users of the **Minitel**!

On parle des rubriques d'un journal.

Les enfants lisent les bandes dessinées.	*Children read the comic strips.*
Je voudrais lire le courrier du cœur.	*I would like to read the advice column.*
Maman regarde l'économie.	*Mom reads the business section.*
Papa préfère l'éditorial.	*Dad is reading the editorial.*
Mon frère lit les faits divers.	*My brother reads human interest stories.*
Ma sœur lit seulement les gros titres.	*My sister reads only the headlines.*
Passe-moi l'horoscope.	*Pass me the horoscope.*
Il y a des mots croisés difficiles.	*There are difficult crossword puzzles.*
Les petites annonces ne m'intéressent pas.	*The classified ads don't interest me.*
J'ai vu le film décrit dans les spectacles.	*I saw the film described in the entertainment section.*
Tout le monde lit les sports.	*Everyone reads the sports section.*
Cette histoire est à la une.	*That story is on the front page.*

On emploie d'autres expressions journalistiques.

Un(e) abonné(e) à *L'Express* a
  écrit une lettre à la revue.
A subscriber to L'Express *wrote
  a letter to the magazine.*

J'ai un abonnement à
  Paris-Match.
*I have a subscription to
  Paris-Match.*

Tu t'abonnes à un magazine?
Do you subscribe to a magazine?

J'achète le journal au kiosque
  de journaux.
I buy the paper at the stand.

Le vendeur de journaux y
  travaille.
The news dealer works there.

Interaction   *Monsieur et Madame Legrand lisent le journal.*

M. LEGRAND: Tu as vu le journal?

MME LEGRAND: François l'a laissé sur le divan.

M. LEGRAND: Qu'est-ce qu'il y a d'intéressant à la une?

MME LEGRAND: *Pas grand-chose.* Le président a parlé de l'économie.   *Not much*

M. LEGRAND: Je veux regarder les sports.

MME LEGRAND: François a cette page dans la salle à manger. Il cherche
  une moto dans les petites annonces.

M. LEGRAND: Dans ce *cas*-là, j'espère qu'il trouve du travail aussi!   *case*

Activités

A. Quel journal ou quelle revue faut-il acheter dans les situations suivantes en France?

1. Vous voulez aller au cinéma.
2. Vous voulez savoir qui a gagné le match de football.
3. Vous voulez connaître la nouvelle mode.
4. Vous voulez des renseignements sur les événements *(events)*
  internationaux de la semaine.
5. Vous voulez regarder la télévision.

B. Quelle rubrique faut-il consulter dans les situations suivantes?

1. Vous cherchez un appartement.
2. Vous voulez connaître votre avenir.
3. Vous voulez savoir quelles sortes de problèmes personnels ont les
  Français.
4. Vous voulez vous détendre.
5. Vous voulez savoir qui a gagné l'étape du Tour de France.
6. Vous avez envie de sortir.

C. Répondez aux questions suivantes.

1. Quel journal lisez-vous? Quelles revues? Depuis quand?
2. Où se trouve votre vendeur de journaux préféré?
3. A quelles revues vous êtes-vous abonné(e)? Pour combien de temps?
4. Aimez-vous faire les mots croisés? Dans quel journal y a-t-il des mots croisés très difficiles? très faciles?
5. Lisez-vous votre horoscope? Souvent? Qu'est-ce que vous en pensez?
6. Avez-vous écrit une lettre au courrier du cœur? Pourquoi?
7. Consultez-vous les petites annonces? Que cherchez-vous?
8. Quelle bande dessinée préférez-vous? Pourquoi? Quel journal a de bonnes bandes dessinées?

LECTURE CULTURELLE ....

Avant la lecture

The fact that French is not really a "foreign" language in the United States, but a second language, is becoming widely known. For example, the cultural renaissance in Louisiana has produced, most noticeably, a popular style of cooking, as exemplified by Paul Prudhomme, and lively music, such as **zydeco.** American poets and novelists of French expression produce a diverse body of literature in their native French language. In the past, however, the French language was not viewed favorably. Earlier in the century, children were punished for speaking French in school. More recently, Hollywood has been guilty of much exaggerated stereotyping and inaccurate portrayals in such films as *Southern Comfort* and *Angel Heart*.

Most Americans of French origin owe their heritage not directly to France but to Canada. Many French speakers were forced to leave Canada after France lost the Seven Years' War (French and Indian War) in 1763. Again in the nineteenth century, economic conditions in Quebec forced many people to emigrate to the United States in search of work. There are still towns in New England where nearly eveyone speaks French. Close ties have always existed between Canada and the United States, as evidenced by the fact that we have the longest undefended border in the world.

Activités

A. Look at a map of Louisiana. Look for Lafayette, the francophone capital of Louisiana. What other names with a French origin can you see?

B. When the British drove the French away from Canada after 1763, why do you think the latter chose to go to Louisiana? What about nineteenth-century Quebec? Why did the people choose New England?

Bec Doux et ses amis,

*by Ken Meaux
and Earl Comeaux*

© *1980*

Le Français aux Etats-Unis

Des *vagues* successives d'immigration pendant plus de trois cents ans ont contribué à former la population américaine. *Parmi* celles-ci, l'*apport* français et canadien-français est prédominant par son ancienneté et son importance. Deux étapes principales en marquent l'histoire: l'installation en Louisiane et
5 l'émigration québécoise de 1840 à 1930.

waves
Among / contribution

La Louisiane

Ce grand territoire du sud des Etats-Unis a appartenu à la France de 1699 à 1763, *puis* de 1800 à 1802. Pendant cette période, trois mouvements d'immigration y ont constitué une population francophone importante. D'abord, il y a eu les Créoles, comme on appelait les *colons* français qui sont
10 arrivés aux dix-septième et dix-huitième *siècles*. Puis, les Cajuns (écrit aussi «Cadgin»), prononciation locale du mot «Acadien», expulsés d'Acadie en 1755 par les Britanniques, ont trouvé refuge sur les *bords* du golfe du Mexique. Enfin, les Créoles noirs, amenés comme *esclaves* d'Afrique et des Antilles, ont constitué *également* une partie importante de la population.

then

settlers
centuries

shores
slaves
also

15 De leur héritage français, les Créoles ont conservé leur religion catholique et ils ont converti une grande partie de la population anglophone, presque toujours à l'occasion d'intermariages. Ils ont développé une riche tradition musicale et théâtrale et, en 1808, ont fondé la première troupe d'opéra aux Etats-Unis. Les Créoles ont donné naissance à une cuisine qui est aujourd'hui une
20 adaptation de la cuisine française continentale traditionnelle où on a *ajouté* des *épices* et des ingrédients de la région. Cette culture a aussi produit une littérature francophone importante qui s'est *épanouie* surtout au dix-neuvième siècle.

added
spices
flourished

  Les Cajuns, eux, sont devenus une minorité francophone rurale. *Jusque*
25 vers le *milieu* des années 60, de plus en plus de jeunes Cajuns refusaient même de continuer à parler français car ils voulaient s'assimiler *au plus vite* à la majorité anglo-saxonne. Puis *soudain,* les choses ont changé. Comme beaucoup d'autres minorités, les Acadiens ont commencé à proclamer leur héritage, et ils sont maintenant très *fiers* de parler français et d'être cajuns.

Until
middle
as fast as possible
suddenly

proud

30   Après la *guerre de sécession,* les noirs francophones de La Nouvelle-Orléans ont formé une société stratifiée avec à sa tête une élite riche et cultivée. La vie sociale de cette élite ressemblait en tous points à celle de l'élite créole blanche. Ils voyageaient beaucoup et *envoyaient* fréquemment leurs enfants à l'école en France. Ils parlaient le même français que celui des blancs de La 35 Nouvelle-Orléans, comme le font encore leurs quelques descendants qui parlent encore français.

    Aujourd'hui, il n'est pas facile d'estimer l'importance de la population francophone de la Louisiane: en 1980, environ 947.000 personnes déclaraient être d'origine ethnique française, et on estime qu'à peu près 270.000 personnes 40 parlent encore le français. Ces statistiques sont incertaines, mais il est sûr que le français est devenu la principale langue seconde des Louisianais, même anglophones. *Ainsi, chaque* jour, des stations de télévision et de radio offrent plusieurs heures d'émissions en français.

Civil War

sent

Thus / each

Un million d'expatriés

De 1840 à 1930, près d'un million de Québécois se sont expatriés aux Etats-45 Unis pour y trouver un emploi. Dans une société surtout agricole, avec une *croissance* démographique explosive, les jeunes ne trouvaient plus de *terres* à cultiver et le chômage *hivernal* affectait cruellement les travailleurs agricoles. Deux *tiers* de ces immigrants se sont installés en Nouvelle-Angleterre, surtout dans le Massachusetts et dans le Connecticut, et un tiers dans le centre des 50 Etats-Unis, surtout au Michigan. Des chercheurs ont estimé l'*actuelle* population d'origine française du Québec sans cet exode historique. Ils pensent que dix millions de personnes habiteraient maintenant le Québec et qu'il y aurait quatre millions de Franco-Québécois de plus.

    Dans l'ensemble, on estime que treize millions d'Américains sont d'origine 55 française et qu'environ un million et demi d'entre eux parlent français à la maison. En plus de la Louisiane et de la Nouvelle-Angleterre, on trouve deux autres concentrations importantes de francophones aux Etats-Unis: l'une en Californie, l'autre en Floride, où plus de 100.000 habitants permanents

growth / land
winter
thirds

current

As a whole

seraient des immigrés francophones récents. Dans le cas de la Floride, pendant   *are thought to be*
60 la période hivernale, plus de 400.000 Québécois y *séjournent à la recherche du*   *stay / in search of*
soleil!

Après la lecture

Questions sur le texte

1. Quelles sont les deux étapes principales de l'immigration francophone aux Etats-Unis?
2. En quoi consiste la population francophone de Louisiane?
3. Quelles ont été les contributions des Créoles?
4. Où habitent principalement les Cajuns?
5. Quel français parlaient les Créoles noirs?
6. Pourquoi beaucoup de Québécois ont-ils émigré au dix-neuvième siècle? Où se sont-ils installés?
7. Combien d'Américains d'origine française parlent encore le français à la maison?
8. Quelles sont les autres régions où on trouve beaucoup de francophones aux Etats-Unis?

Activités

A. Quels aspects de la culture louisianaise francophone connaissez-vous personnellement? Avez-vous essayé un plat créole ou cajun? Avez-vous regardé une émission télévisée sur la cuisine ou sur la musique de cette région? Quels sont les chanteurs connus de la Louisiane francophone?

B. Quel contact avez-vous eu avec des francophones aux Etats-Unis? Si vous n'avez pas rencontré de gens qui parlent français, peut-être avez-vous été exposé(e) à une culture francophone?

C. Quel est votre héritage? D'où sont venus vos ancêtres? Avez-vous étudié votre arbre généalogique? Jusqu'où? Savez-vous pourquoi vos ancêtres sont venus aux Etats-Unis?

Chapitre 17

LE FRANÇAIS AU QUEBEC

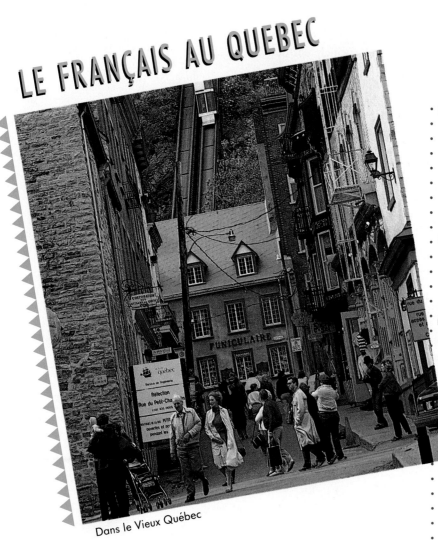

Dans le Vieux Québec

COMMENÇONS

Construire une maison

Un poète québécois rêve de la naissance d'un pays qu'il compare à la construction d'une maison.

Construire une maison
Qui soit un pays
Tous ensemble
Avec nos mains
Pour marquer la fin de l'exil

Dire le nom de ce pays
L'apprendre amoureusement
A tous les enfants
Avec leurs premiers mots
Répéter le nom du pays

Aimer ce pays
Comme on aime sa mère
Comme on aime une femme
Avoir en soi ce pays
Comme le sang dans les veines

Arrêter les plaintes
Bâtir
Nommer
Aimer
Ce pays qui est à l'horizon

(*Comme au retenue. Poèmes 1954–1963* de Jean-Guy Pilon)

Dans la campagne
québécoise

Mots clés

poète	*poet*	amoureusement	*lovingly*
naissance	*birth*	mots	*words*
compare	*compares*	soi	*oneself*
(comparer)		sang	*blood*
construction	*building*	veines (*f.*)	*veins*
construire	*to build*	plaintes (*f.*)	*complaints*
marquer	*to mark*	bâtir	*to build*
fin	*end*	nommer	*to name*
exil (*m.*)	*exile*	horizon (*m.*)	*horizon*

FAISONS CONNAISSANCE

Born in 1930 in Quebec, Jean-Guy Pilon graduated with a law degree from the University of Montreal. Later, he went to work for Radio-Canada, where he was first in charge of literary programs before assuming responsibility for all arts programming. As he started publishing poetry, he also traveled extensively throughout France and South America. He was elected to the **Société Royale du Canada** and received numerous prizes for his poetry. Guy Sylvestre, one of Pilon's contemporaries, wrote that Pilon's poetry sang the reconciliation of the poet with his country and his people after overcoming rejection and exile. Roger Duhamel, the French writer, said that Pilon was one of the most gifted poets of his generation.

The people of Quebec have always been very proud of their origins, their language, and their customs. Their profound attachment to their land is in evidence throughout their literature. For generations **québécois** poets have sung the beauty of the countryside and of the Quebec soul.

Today, Quebec and the rest of Canada are not just looking backward at their past; they are also oriented toward the future. Two examples of Canadian technological achievements are **Hydro-Québec,** one of the largest hydroelectric networks in the world, and the robotic arm **(le bras spatial)** used to manipulate objects outside the American space shuttle.

Québec, Montréal, même pays

A Québec, cité-refuge des valeurs francophones, et surtout à Montréal, on est en « presque Amérique ». Mais tout est dans ce « presque ».

Etudions le poème

1. Pour le poète Jean-Guy Pilon, à quoi est-ce qu'un pays ressemble?
2. Quelle est la première chose qu'on doit apprendre pour connaître un pays?
3. Pourquoi un pays est-il comme une mère? Pourquoi est-il comme une femme?
4. De quel pays est-ce que Pilon parle?

Enrichissons notre vocabulaire

La nature *(Nature)*

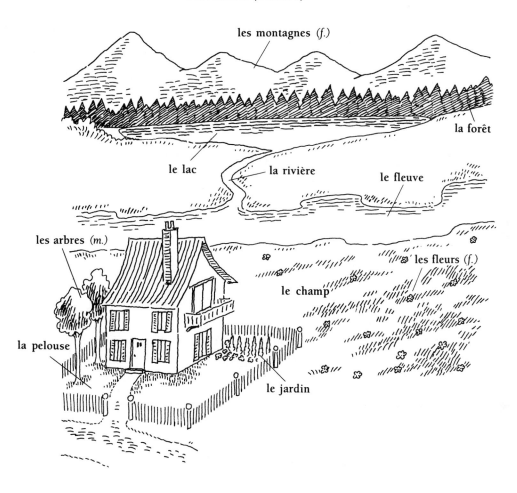

les montagnes *(f.)*

la forêt

le lac — la rivière

le fleuve

les arbres *(m.)*

les fleurs *(f.)*

le champ

la pelouse

le jardin

L'environnement *(m.)* *(The environment)*

l'écologie *(f.)* / les écologistes *(m., f.)*	*ecology / ecologists*
l'énergie *(f.)* solaire / nucléaire	*solar / nuclear energy*
les espaces *(m.)* habitables	*livable spaces*
la pluie acide	*acid rain*
La pollution **augmente** / **diminue**.	*Pollution **is increasing** / **decreasing**.*
le recyclage	*recycling*

Le futur *(The future)*

la biotechnologie	*biotechnology*
la lune, les étoiles *(f.)* les planètes *(f.)*	*the moon, the stars, the planets*
la navette spatiale	*the space shuttle*
la station spatiale	*the space station*

Prononciation   Liaisons   `[ ○━○ ]`

A. You learned in Chapter 4 that **liaisons** occur when a normally silent, final written consonant is pronounced because a word starting with a vowel follows. Often, a certain amount of flexibility is allowed when deciding whether or not to pronounce the consonant, but sometimes you must make a **liaison.**

B. **Liaisons** that you must make are called **liaisons obligatoires.** They fall into the following categories:

article + noun / article + adjective + noun

mes‿amis / un petit‿homme / des‿efforts /
   mon‿ordinateur / un grand‿appartement /
   d'autres‿exemples / un‿habitant /
   de vieilles‿églises / dix‿étudiants

pronoun + verb / verb + pronoun / pronoun + pronoun

ils‿habitent / Nous‿en voudrions. / Nous‿y allons. /
   Il va les‿inviter. / Donnez-en. / Vont-ils les‿acheter? /
   On‿en‿a. / Vous‿en‿avez vu. / Elles les‿ont.

Do not pronounce, however, the **liaison** between subject pronouns and verbs with inversion.

Sont-ils / arrivés?   Voulez-vous / en acheter? /
   Peuvent-elles / ouvrir?

after many one-syllable prepositions and adverbs

chez‿eux / trop‿aimable / dans‿un restaurant /
   très‿utile / sous‿un‿arbre / bien‿aimé /

C. Some **liaisons,** called **liaisons facultatives,** are optional. Generally, you should make more of them when speaking in a formal style. Some categories are as follows:

negation

pas‿avec moi	*or*	pas / avec moi
jamais‿au théâtre	*or*	jamais / au théâtre
plus‿à Paris	*or*	plus / à Paris

verbs + verbs / verbs + prepositions / verbs + articles

je dois‿aller	*or*	je dois / aller
il faut‿appeler	*or*	il faut / appeler

But with **est** and present-tense verbs ending in **-ont,** liaison is very frequent:

> Il est arrivé. / Ils font une erreur. /
> Elles ont un appartement.

two-syllable prepositions and adverbs

devant une église	*or*	devant / une église
beaucoup aimé	*or*	beaucoup / aimé
souvent excellent	*or*	souvent / excellent

Exercice

Read the following sentences aloud, making all **liaisons obligatoires.**

1. Ils en ont un.
2. Montrez-en aux enfants.
3. Elles y sont allées sans eux.
4. Je les ai emmenés avec leurs amis.
5. Etes-vous allés en Irlande cet été?
6. Les bons étudiants adorent étudier sous les arbres.

GRAMMAIRE ....

I. The Future Tense

> You use the future tense to talk about events and states that will occur in the future, but with a degree of uncertainty.

A. Forms

1. In French, the most frequent way of expressing a future action in conversation is by using the **futur proche,** but there is also a future tense that uses only one verb form. To conjugate a verb in the future tense, you add the following endings to the stems you learned for the conditional mood.

parler	finir	répondre
je parlerai	je finirai	je répondrai
tu parleras	tu finiras	tu répondras
il / elle / on parlera	il / elle / on finira	il / elle / on / répondra
nous parlerons	nous finirons	nous répondrons
vous parlerez	vous finirez	vous répondrez
ils / elles parleront	ils / elles finiront	ils / elles répondront

Nous **construirons** une maison ici.

*We **will build** a house here.*

Tu me **diras** le nom de ce vin?

*Will you **tell** me the name of this wine?*

Ils **apprendront** le recyclage aux enfants.

*They **will teach** recycling to the children.*

▶ L'Orthographe

Note that in the preceding examples you drop the **e** from infinitives ending in -re before you add the future endings: **répondre → ils répondront.**

2. All verbs that have irregular stems in the conditional mood also have the same irregular stems in the future tense. For these irregular stems, refer to the section on the formation of the conditional in Chapter 16.

B. Use

There is a slight difference in meaning between the **futur** and the **futur proche.** The **futur proche** expresses actions that are more certain than those in the **futur.**

Elle va avoir un enfant.

(She's pregnant.)

Elle aura un enfant.

(She hopes to have a child.)

Je vais écrire un poème.

(Now!)

J'écrirai un poème.

(When I have time.)

C. Expressions of Time

1. French has four expressions that are frequently used to introduce events in the future:

quand / lorsque

When

dès que / aussitôt que

as soon as

2. When you use these expressions in a sentence with future actions, you must use the **futur** in *both* clauses, even though you would use the present tense in English.

Je lui demanderai **quand il arrivera.**

*I will ask him **when he comes.***

Dès qu'elle partira, nous nous coucherons.

***As soon as she leaves,** we shall go to bed.*

3. An imperative used in the main clause of a sentence with an expression of time implies a future action; therefore, you must use the future tense.

Téléphonez **quand vous aurez le temps!**

*Call **when you have time.***

Langue

A. **Une promenade à la campagne.** Dans les phrases suivantes, mettez les verbes au futur.

1. Allez-vous faire un voyage?
2. Oui, nous allons partir samedi.
3. Je vais aller à la campagne.
4. Mais, il va pleuvoir!
5. Nos amis vont nous emmener en auto.
6. Nous allons voir de vieilles maisons.

B. **La visite d'une vieille amie.** Dans les phrases suivantes, changez les verbes du passé au futur.

1. Aussitôt que nous avons reçu sa lettre, nous avons su qu'elle revenait.
2. Quand elle a téléphoné de la gare, j'ai commencé à faire le ménage.
3. Dès qu'elle est arrivée, elle a sonné à la porte.
4. Dès que je l'ai vue, je l'ai embrassée.
5. Quand on a fini de parler, elle est allée se reposer.
6. J'ai été malheureux quand elle a dû partir.

C. **Notre avenir.** Formez des phrases complètes avec les mots donnés.

1. Nous / ne... pas / devenir / vieux
2. On / pouvoir / aller / dans la lune
3. Il / ne... plus / y / avoir / cancer
4. Président / recevoir / lettre / d'une autre planète
5. Il / falloir / vous / utiliser / énergie / solaire
6. Il / ne... plus / pleuvoir

Culture

D. **Que faire?** Que ferez-vous dans les situations suivantes en France? Trouvez la meilleure *(best)* solution.

MODELE: aller de Paris à Lyon / prendre le TGV
Quand j'irai de Paris à Lyon, je prendrai le TGV.

1. acheter des vêtements	a. aller dans une pharmacie
2. dîner chez des amis	b. aller dans un hypermarché
3. avoir mal à la gorge	c. dire «A vos souhaits»
4. quelqu'un éternue *(sneezes)*	d. dire «A la vôtre»
5. il pleut et vous allez à l'Opéra	e. falloir acheter des fleurs
6. prendre l'apéritif	f. valoir mieux prendre un taxi

Communication

E. Que ferez-vous...

1. aussitôt que le week-end arrivera?
2. quand vous serez en vacances?
3. lorsque vous pourrez avoir un appartement?

4. lorsque vous serez vieux / vieille?
5. dès que ce cours finira?
6. aussitôt que vous aurez beaucoup d'argent?

F. Imaginez la vie au vingt et unième siècle. Utilisez les suggestions données ou vos propres idées.

MODELE: *On passera le week-end sur la lune.*
Nous ne travaillerons plus.
Les gens resteront jeunes.

ne plus aller chez le dentiste
avoir des robots pour...
ne jamais être fatigué(e)
ne plus faire la vaisselle
falloir parler plusieurs langues
pouvoir travailler à la maison

ne plus avoir besoin de médecins
voir les gens au téléphone
vouloir retourner en 1990
(le bon vieux temps!)
???

G. **Questions personnelles.** Votre avenir

1. Où irez-vous cet été?
2. Quand commencerez-vous à travailler?
3. Quand aurez-vous trente ans?
4. Que ferez-vous ce jour-là?
5. Quand aurez-vous des enfants? Combien?
6. A quelle université iront-ils? A celle-ci?

II. Si Clauses

> You use **si** clauses to state the conditions under which things happen, even if only hypothetically.

Both French and English have sentences in which one action depends on a certain condition. In French, there is a sequence of verb tenses used in sentences that state a condition with **si**. At this point, you can construct three types.

A. Use the sequence **si** + *present tense* / *present tense* with general rules or typical conditions.

S'il **fait beau**, j'**emmène** mes enfants au parc.
Il **fait** ses devoirs s'il n'y a rien à la télé.

B. Use the sequence **si** + *present tense* / *futur* for a specific event.

Si on l'**invite**, elle **amènera** son copain.
Les élèves s'**endormiront** si le prof **est** ennuyeux.

C. Use the sequence **si** + *imperfect* / *conditional* for hypothetical situations.

S'il **faisait** attention, il **réussirait**.
La pollution **augmenterait** si nous ne l'**arrêtions** pas.

Langue

A. **Ce soir...** Dans les phrases suivantes, ajoutez l'expression **ce soir** et mettez le verbe en italique au futur.

MODELE: Si tu pars, je *viens* avec toi.
           Si tu pars ce soir, je viendrai avec toi.

1. S'il pleut, on *reste* à la maison.
2. Si nos amis veulent entrer, ils *peuvent* sonner.
3. Si on est fatigué, on *se couche* de bonne heure.
4. Si quelqu'un appelle, nous ne *répondons* pas.
5. Si tu ne travailles pas maintenant, *peux*-tu finir à l'heure?
6. Je ne *reviens* pas s'il n'y a pas d'autobus.

B. **Mais, ce n'est pas le cas!** Faites des phrases hypothétiques en mettant *(by putting)* les verbes à l'imparfait et au conditionnel, selon le cas.

MODELE: Si Marie est malade, nous irons sans elle.
           Si Marie était malade, nous irions sans elle.

1. S'il fait beau, ils iront à la montagne.
2. S'il y a des nuages, nous ne verrons pas les étoiles.
3. Nous ne prendrons pas la voiture s'il neige.
4. Tu auras mal à la tête si tu bois trop.
5. Si vous aimez la musique classique, nous irons au concert.
6. Nous n'irons pas dans la forêt si nous prenons ce chemin.

C. **Des projets pour ce soir!** Faites deux phrases différentes avec chaque groupe de mots.

1. Je / lui / écrire / si / je / recevoir / son / lettre
2. Si / elle / nous / poser / question, / nous / ne... pas / savoir / réponse
3. Les autres / ne... pas / vouloir / venir / si / je / inviter / Luc
4. Si / tout le monde / être en retard, / il / falloir / attendre
5. Si / elle / ne... pas / se dépêcher, / elle / ne... jamais / être / à l'heure.
6. Si / il / ne... pas / arriver à l'heure, / il / valoir mieux / partir / sans lui

Si le français vous intéresse...
...Le Québec vous passionnera!

Culture

D. **Allons au cinéma!** Vous êtes à Aulnay-sous-Bois, près de Paris, et vous voulez aller au cinéma avec des amis. Regardez l'extrait de *l'Officiel des Spectacles* et répondez aux questions suivantes.

AULNAY-SOUS-BOIS

CINE SOUS BOIS, ESPACE JACQUES PREVERT, 134, rue Anatole-France, 48 68 00 22. Pl. : 28 F, TR 25 F, 23 F, 20 F, 16 F.

Mer. 14h15, jeu. 18h30, dim., lun. 14h30, mar. 16h : ◆ **Fantasia.** — *Mer. 16h15, ven. 20h45, sam. 14h15, 18h30, 21h, dim., lun. 14h15, mar. 16h, 18h15 :* △ **Total recall.** — *Mer., sam. 18h30, jeu. 20h45, ven. 16h30, dim., lun. 16h15 :* **Bouge pas, meurs, ressuscite.** — *Mer. 20h45, jeu. 16h30, ven. 18h30, sam. 16h15, 20h45, dim., lun. 16h30, mar. 18h :* **La gloire de mon père.**

PARINOR, Centre Commercial, 48 65 44 11 et 36.15 UGC. C UGC 1 (112 F) et 2 (168 F). Pl. : 39 F TR : 30 F. Lun. C.V. 14h à 19h (sf sam. et dim.).

1) *Séances : 14h10, 16h10, 18h10, 20h10, 22h10. Sam., séance suppl. à 0h10 :*
◆ **Les tortues ninja**

2) *Séances : 13h40, 15h50, 18h, 20h10, 22h20. Sam. séance suppl. à 0h30 :*
Rocky n°5

3) *Séances : 13h30, 15h45, 18h, 20h15, 22h30. Sam. séance suppl. à 0h40 :*
Pretty woman

4) *Séances : 14h, 16h, 18h, 20h, 22h. Sam. séance suppl. à 24h :*
◆ **La petite sirène**

1. Si vous voulez voir un film américain, quel cinéma choisirez-vous?
2. Si vous sortez du restaurant à minuit et demi samedi, quel film pourrez-vous voir?
3. A quel film irez-vous si vous avez des enfants avec vous?
4. Si vous n'avez pas beaucoup d'argent, quel sera le cinéma le plus économique?
5. Si vos amis tenaient à voir Sylvester Stallone, à quelle heure devraient-ils arriver au cinéma l'après-midi?
6. Quelles possibilités auriez-vous si vous aviez envie de voir un film français?

Communication

E. **Mes habitudes.** Formez des phrases avec **si** pour décrire ce que *(what)* vous faites en géneral. Employez un élément de chaque colonne pour former des phrases logiques.

A		B	C
Si	avoir froid / chaud	avoir trop de travail	je
	avoir soif	pleuvoir	mes amis
	être fatigué(e)	échouer à un examen	ma famille
	le prof est absent	avoir de l'argent	mon copain
	faire beau	???	???

F. **Un peu d'imagination!** En quoi votre vie serait-elle différente...

1. si vous n'alliez pas à l'université?
2. si vous n'aviez pas de camarade de chambre?
3. si vous aviez une auto? / n'aviez pas d'auto?
4. si vous aviez des cours faciles?
5. si vous ne saviez pas lire?
6. si vous étiez très paresseux (-euse)?

G. **Questions personnelles.** Imaginez!

1. Si vous receviez vos amis, qu'est-ce que vous feriez pour vous amuser?
2. Où habiteriez-vous si vous pouviez choisir?
3. Si vous étiez président, quel serait votre première décision?
4. Si vous alliez prendre votre dernier repas, qu'est-ce que vous préféreriez manger?
5. Si vous pouviez voyager sans payer, où iriez-vous?
6. Si vous pouviez prévoir le futur, qu'est-ce qui vous intéresserait le plus?

III. Mettre / Verbs Conjugated like mettre

> You use these verbs to describe activities, such as placing something somewhere, putting on clothes, turning on the TV, giving permission, and making promises.

The irregular verb **mettre** means *to put, to put on (clothing), to set the table, to turn on (a TV),* or *to take (an amount of time to do something).*

	mettre	
présent:	je **mets**	nous **mettons**
	tu **mets**	vous **mettez**
il / elle / on **met**	ils / elles **mettent**
futur et conditionnel:	je **mettrai**	nous **mettrions**
passé composé:	il **a mis**	elles **ont mis**
subjonctif:	que je **mette**	que nous **mettions**
impératif:	**mets**	**mettons**	**mettez**

Où est-ce que je peux **mettre** mon parapluie?
Elle **a mis** sa robe neuve.
On ne **met** que trois heures et demie pour aller à Paris en Concorde.

Mots clés Verbs Conjugated like mettre

permettre	*to permit*
	to allow
promettre	*to promise*
remettre	*to postpone*
	to hand in
	to hand back
	to put back
se mettre à	*to begin*

Une navette nous **permettra** d'aller à une station spatiale.
Il **s'est mis** à pleuvoir.

ATTENTION

Permettre and **promettre** take **à** before a person and **de** before an infinitive.

Elle ne **permet** pas **aux** enfants **de** jouer dans la rue.
Je **lui** ai **promis d'**acheter des fleurs.

Langue

A. **Faisons la cuisine.** Formez des phrases complètes avec les mots donnés.

1. Je / ne... pas / mettre / lait / dans / gâteau
2. Tu / remettre / viande / dans le frigidaire / ce matin?
3. Ils / promettre / ne pas mettre / sel
4. Ne... pas / permettre / enfants / utiliser / cuisinière
5. Elle / se mettre / préparer / dîner
6. Nous / mettre / table / sept heures

B. **Habillons-nous.** Refaites les phrases suivantes en employant les mots entre parenthèses.

1. Cet automne nous mettrons des vêtements chauds.   (L'hiver dernier...)
2. Je n'aimerais pas que mon frère porte mes vêtements. (... permettre... mettre)
3. Tous les magasins vous recommandent d'essayer leurs vêtements.   (... permettre...)
4. Si tu mets ton imperméable, il ne pleuvra pas.   (... pleuvrait...)
5. Les enfants n'ont pas porté de chaussettes.   (... mettre...)
6. Regarde cette jupe; maman m'a promis de l'acheter.   (Mettre... permettre...)

Culture

C. **Le code de la route.** Vous préparez un voyage au Canada en voiture et vous avez besoin de connaître les différences entre les lois au Québec et celles des Etats-Unis. Qu'est-ce qu'on vous permet de faire et qu'est-ce qu'on ne vous permet pas?

MODELE: conduire à l'âge de seize ans?
On vous permet de conduire à l'âge de seize ans.

1. conduire et boire de l'alcool
2. conduire sans mettre sa ceinture de sécurité
3. transporter un jeune enfant sans siège de bébé
4. rouler à 105 à l'heure *(65 m.p.h.)*
5. tourner à droite à un feu *(light)* rouge
6. entrer dans le pays sans assurance

Communication

D. **Tenez-vous vos promesses?** Qu'est-ce que vous avez promis de faire que vous avez fait, et que vous n'avez pas fait? Utilisez un élément de chaque colonne et suivez le modèle.

MODELE: *J'ai promis à mon petit ami de lui téléphoner plus souvent.
(Je le fais.)
J'ai promis au professeur de venir en cours tous les jours.
(Je ne le fais pas.)*

à	de
parents	faire moins de bruit
petit(e) ami(e)	écrire toutes les semaines
camarade(s) de chambre	l' / les inviter au restaurant
voisin(e)(s)	être patient(e)
agents de police	rentrer le week-end
???	???

E. **Des enfants dans votre avenir?** Quand vous aurez des enfants, qu'est-ce que vous leur permettrez de faire et qu'est-ce que vous ne leur permettrez pas de faire?

MODELE: *Je leur permettrai de faire du vélo.
Je ne leur permettrai pas de jouer à table.*

manger du gâteau	mettre les pieds sur la table
jouer au football	regarder la télévision
sortir le soir	avoir un(e) petit(e) ami(e)
se promener sans vêtements	avoir une voiture
fumer	boire du / de la...
partir le week-end	???

F. **Questions personnelles.** Chez vous

    1. Quels disques mettez-vous le plus souvent?
    2. Permettez-vous aux gens de fumer chez vous?
    3. Quand est-ce que vous mettez la radio?
    4. Remettez-vous toujours une partie du ménage à plus tard?
    5. Quels vêtements mettez-vous quand vous êtes seul(e)?
    6. Qu'est-ce que vous avez promis de faire cette semaine?

COMMUNIQUONS ····························

Exprimer des émotions

In conversations, it is often necessary to express emotional reactions to statements or events. The following groups of words will help you express yourself in an authentic manner in French, particularly in informal situations.

On exprime l'étonnement *(surprise).*

Ça alors!	*I'll be darned!*
C'est pas vrai!	*No?!*
Comment?	*What?*
Quoi?	*What?*
Tiens!	*Hey!*
Nous avons du mal à croire qu'elle a dit cela.	*We have a hard time believing that she said that.*
Je suis étonnée qu'il refuse de le faire.	*I am surprised that he refuses to do it.*
Elle est surprise qu'ils n'en sachent rien.	*She is surprised that they don't know anything about it.*
Il s'étonne que la pluie acide soit si mauvaise.	*He is astonished that the acid rain is so bad.*
Tu ne sais pas que Jean a eu un accident?	*You don't know that John had an accident?*

On exprime la déception *(disappointment)*.

(Quel) dommage!	*That's too bad! / What a shame!*
Tant pis!	*Too bad!*
Zut alors!	*Darn!*
Nous sommes déçus qu'il n'y ait pas de jardin.	*We are disappointed that there isn't a yard.*
Il est désolé que nous n'allions pas à la rivière.	*He is sorry that we aren't going to the river.*
Je suis navrée que mon mari ne puisse pas venir.	*I'm sorry that my husband can't come.*
Je regrette que le lac soit si loin.	*I'm sorry that the lake is so far away.*

On exprime la satisfaction.

Bon!	*Good!*
Chouette alors!	*Great!*
Fantastique!	*Fantastic!*
Formidable!	*Great!*
Parfait!	*Perfect!*
Tant mieux!	*Good!*
Terrible!	*Super!*
Ils sont contents que nous nous promenions dans la forêt.	*They are happy we are walking in the forest.*
Vous êtes heureux que vos enfants arrêtent leurs plaintes?	*Are you happy that your children have stopped complaining?*
Je suis ravie que tu sois là!	*I am delighted that you are here!*
Elles sont satisfaites que tu réussisses.	*They are satisfied that you are passing.*

On exprime la colère *(anger)*.

Arrête!	*Stop!*
Ça suffit!	*Enough!*
Ça va pas, non?	*Are you crazy?*
Fiche-moi la paix! / Laisse-moi!	*Leave me alone!*
J'en ai assez!	*I've had it!*
J'en ai marre! / J'en ai ras le bol!	*I've had it up to here!*
Tu me casses les pieds!	*You really annoy me!*
Il est fâché que tu mentes.	*He is angry that you are lying.*
Elle est furieuse que les enfants jouent sur la pelouse.	*She is furious that the children are playing on the lawn.*

On exprime l'indifférence.

Ça m'est égal. / Je m'en fiche.	*I don't care.*
Ça ne fait rien.	*It doesn't matter.*
Ce n'est pas grand-chose.	*It's no big deal.*
Ce n'est pas grave.	*It's not serious.*
Comme ci, comme ça.	*So-so.*
Et après?	*So what?*
Ça m'est égal si tu fais cela.	*I don't care if you do that.*
Peu m'importe si tu ne viens pas.	*It doesn't matter if you don't come.*

Interaction   *Jean-Paul et Anne-Marie cherchent quelque chose à faire.*

JEAN-PAUL: Qu'est-ce que tu veux faire cet après-midi?

ANNE-MARIE: Ça m'est égal.

JEAN-PAUL: On peut aller au ciné.

ANNE-MARIE: Les films qu'on joue en ce moment ne sont pas terribles.

JEAN-PAUL: Tiens! Les étudiants vont avoir un débat sur l'énergie nucléaire.

ANNE-MARIE: J'en ai assez de la politique!

JEAN-PAUL: Alors, tant pis. Je vais y aller tout seul.

ANNE-MARIE: Chouette alors. Il y a Jean-François qui m'a invitée au café!

Activités

A. Quelqu'un va proposer quelque chose. Indiquez si la deuxième personne veut le faire ou non.

1. MARIE: On va aller au cinéma!
   ROBERT: Chouette!
2. PIERRE: J'ai acheté deux billets pour le concert de Patricia Kass.
   YVONNE: Elle est terrible!
3. MARIE-ANNE: Tu veux étudier à la bibliothèque?
   CHANTAL: Ça m'est égal!
4. JEAN-PAUL: On va écouter encore un disque.
   CLAUDE: Moi, j'en ai marre!
5. MME MORIN: Il reste encore un petit gâteau.
   SABINE: Tant mieux!
6. M. GILBERT: Nous avons loué un appartement à la plage et il y a un lit pour toi.
   ERIC: Formidable!

B. Que pourriez-vous dire dans les situations suivantes?

1. Votre camarade de chambre met la radio à minuit.
2. Vos ami(e)s veulent aller voir un western.
3. Vous trouvez cent dollars dans la rue.
4. Vous rencontrez un(e) ami(e) que vous n'avez pas vu(e) depuis trois ans.
5. Vous perdez votre Walkman.
6. Vos voisins parlent des problèmes de la pluie acide.
7. Quelqu'un veut que vous parliez de l'énergie solaire.
8. Un ami vous invite à passer le week-end à la campagne.

LECTURE CULTURELLE ....

Avant la lecture

Studies have shown that French speakers in Canada, and even in the province of Quebec, have often been treated as a minority. Their income is lower than that of English speakers, and they have not had the same opportunities for advancement in business. This situation was most fervently described by Pierre Vallières in his book, *Nègres blancs d'Amérique.*

In the 1960s and early 1970s, many French speakers began to develop a new pride in their heritage, as did many ethnic groups. Charles de Gaulle sent political shock waves through the world in 1967 with his «Vive le Québec libre» speech. The **Parti québécois** promoted separation from the confederation as the best way to improve the economic and social situation. While the **Québécois** voted against independence in 1980, the government of Quebec is still working to obtain a larger share of the economy and cultural autonomy for French speakers. The inability of the ten Canadian provinces to ratify the Meech Lake Accord by the June 23, 1990, deadline prevented the adoption of an amendment to the Canadian Constitution that would have officially declared Quebec "a distinct society." This failure triggered an immediate renewal of separatist feelings among the Quebec people.

Activités

A. By recognizing what family a word belongs to, you may be able to guess its meaning. In the chart below, the words on the left are found in the reading passage. Fill in the chart to become familiar with them.

Mot	Mot de la même famille	Sens	Autre mot de la même famille
pensable	*penser*	*thinkable*	pensée *(thought)*
banquier			bancaire
survie			survivre *(to survive)*
montée			
nationalisme			
natalité			natalistes
grossissaient			grossesse *(pregnancy)*
renouveler			
obligation			

B. The ending **-ment** often indicates an adverb (the *-ly* ending in English). Scan the reading passage to find the five adverbs that have this ending. Also find four words ending in **-ment** that are not adverbs. What is the first thing that tells you that each of these four words is not an adverb?

Le Débat linguistique au Québec

Pendant longtemps, les Québécois francophones ont connu une situation linguistique paradoxale. Ils considéraient naturellement que leur langue était le français, mais ils acceptaient le *fait* que cette langue ne se parlait qu'à la maison et en famille. Au travail, dans la vie économique, il n'était pas pensable
5 d'utiliser une langue autre que l'anglais, du moins si on espérait «faire de l'argent». Paul-André Comeau, ancien *rédacteur en chef* du *Devoir*, le prestigieux *quotidien* de langue française de Montréal, racontait un jour dans une *causerie* que son père qui était banquier dans une petite ville à 95 pour cent francophone ne pouvait pas imaginer qu'on puisse effectuer une transaction
10 bancaire dans une langue autre que l'anglais jusqu'au jour où, quand il était déjà à la *retraite,* son fils lui a fait connaître des banquiers français, et où il a découvert à sa grande surprise, que tous les termes de la banque et de la finance avaient des équivalents français.
　　Cette attitude a eu des conséquences sérieuses pour la *survie* des Québécois
15 francophones car la grande majorité des immigrants qui arrivaient au Québec voulaient *inscrire* leurs enfants dans des écoles anglophones et déclaraient appartenir à la minorité anglophone, même quand ils n'étaient pas capables de parler plus de quatre ou cinq mots d'anglais.
　　La *montée* du nationalisme québécois dans les années 70 et l'arrivée au
20 *pouvoir* du Parti québécois ont eu des conséquences immédiates sur le *statut* de la langue française. Le danger était très grand *car,* après avoir été un des pays

fact

editor-in-chief
daily
talk

retirement

survival

register

power / status
because

Le Château Frontenac

où la *natalité* était une des plus *fortes* du monde, le Québec était *tout d'un coup*, avec l'Allemagne, le pays du monde où le *taux de natalité* était le plus *faible*. De ce fait, en même temps que les nouveaux immigrants *grossissaient* les *rangs* des anglophones, la très forte *dénatalité réduisait* ceux des francophones.

birthrate / high / all of a sudden / birthrate low / swelled ranks / decline in birthrate / reduced

25

Sur le plan légal, c'est la promulgation de la *Charte de la langue française*, votée par le Parlement québécois en 1977, qui a eu l'impact le plus fort. *Sommairement*, cette loi faisait du français la seule langue officielle du Québec, et cette mesure s'appliquait à la vie culturelle, économique et sociale. En pratique, cela veut dire que les immigrants devront obligatoirement mettre leurs enfants dans des écoles francophones, *sauf* s'ils arrivent d'une des autres provinces canadiennes où leur *éducation* avait toujours été en anglais. S'ils viennent des Etats-Unis, de Grande-Bretagne, ou d'un autre pays anglophone au monde, ils doivent nécessairement étudier le français et *rallier* la majorité francophone. Cela ne signifie pas du tout que les *droits* de la minorité québécoise anglophone ne sont pas préservés puisque ceux-ci conservent leurs écoles et la possibilité d'*éduquer* leurs enfants en anglais. Dans la vie économique, cela veut dire que si on veut travailler au Québec, on doit être prêt à parler, à négocier et à *traiter* en français. Toutes les entreprises qui emploient cinquante employés ou plus doivent utiliser exclusivement le français. D'autre part, pour bien prouver que le gouvernement québécois prend ces mesures au sérieux, toute la publicité et tout l'*affichage* public se font à partir de ce moment-là en français, les seules exceptions étant faites pour les produits dits «culturels». Par exemple, dans le quartier chinois de Montréal, les magasins spécialisés dans la *vente* d'articles artisanaux chinois peuvent continuer à *promouvoir* leurs produits en chinois.

30

35

40

45

Briefly

except schooling

join
rights

raise

deal

posting

sale
promote

De toutes les mesures prises à la suite de la promulgation de la *Charte de la langue française*, celle concernant l'affichage public est celle qui cause encore le plus de controverse, car c'est celle qui est la plus symbolique et qui provoque
50 les réactions épidermiques les plus *sensibles*. La minorité anglophone a même *sensitive*
fait une sorte de *chantage* en affirmant que les touristes américains ne *blackmail*
viendraient plus au Québec si *subitement* le français remplaçait l'anglais dans *suddenly*
les rues. Cet argument fait *sourire* des Québécois comme Paul-André Comeau, *smile*
qui en parlait un jour à un groupe de professeurs de français américains et qui
55 leur demandait s'ils pensaient qu'un seul touriste américain pourrait un jour
décider de ne pas faire un voyage en Allemagne parce que toute la *signalisation* *road signs*
sur les autoroutes allemandes est en allemand!

Que peut-on prévoir pour l'avenir? Au mois de décembre 1988, la Cour suprême du Canada a déclaré que ces mesures étaient anticonstitutionnelles;
60 elle a affirmé que le Québec pouvait *exiger* que l'affichage soit en français, *require*
mais qu'il ne pouvait pas s'opposer à l'affichage en d'autres langues. Les
Québécois conservent *cependant* la possibilité d'utiliser des compromis: *however*
affichage en français à l'extérieur et affichage multilingue à l'intérieur ou *tra-* *translations*
ductions en langues autres que le français, mais en plus petits *caractères*. *printing*
65 *Quoi qu'il en soit*, les Québécois francophones se sentent *menacés*. Ils ne *Nevertheless / threatened*
font plus assez d'enfants pour renouveler leur population. L'obligation où se
trouvent les immigrants d'envoyer leurs enfants dans des écoles francophones
n'est pas une solution au problème, car on *s'aperçoit* de plus en plus que *finds out*
lorsque ces enfants se retrouvent dans la cour de récréation, ils parlent anglais
70 entre eux, et que c'est aussi la langue qu'ils parlent à la maison. Ceci est
d'autant plus ironique quand il s'agit de groupes d'origine francophone, *all the more*
comme les Haïtiens, par exemple. Si rien ne se passe, on peut *se demander*, s'il *wonder*
y aura encore des francophones au Québec en l'an 2060.

(Adapté d'une conférence faite par Paul-André Comeau devant un groupe de professeurs
de français américains.)

Après la lecture

Questions sur le texte

1. Quelle a été pendant longtemps la situation linguistique des Québécois?
2. Pourquoi la situation est-elle devenue dangereuse dans les années 70?
3. Quelle est la conséquence la plus importante de l'adoption de la *Charte de la langue française*?
4. Est-ce que la minorité anglophone a perdu ses droits?
5. Quelle est la mesure qui a causé le plus de controverse?
6. De quoi ont peur les anglophones si tout est écrit en français?
7. Pourquoi les Québécois francophones se sentent-ils menacés?
8. A votre avis, est-ce qu'on va continuer à parler français au Québec?

Activités

A. Répondez aux questions suivantes.

1. Au Québec, beaucoup de gens parlent une langue à la maison et une autre langue au travail. Même si vous ne parlez pas deux langues, pensez-vous parler de deux façons différentes à la maison et à l'université? Donnez des exemples.
2. Avez-vous connu une situation où vous aviez envie de savoir parler une autre langue? Racontez-la.
3. Voulez-vous que vos enfants apprennent une langue étrangère? A partir de quel âge? Quelle langue?

B. Parlez des avantages et des désavantages du nationalisme.

Chapitre 18

LES IMMIGRES

Un restaurant tunisien

Commençons ·

La Prière du Chacal

Voici un conte populaire du Maghreb.

Un matin, le Chacal voit le Coq qui chante sur une branche. Il s'approche et lui dit: «Que tu chantes bien! Quand je t'ai entendu, j'ai eu envie de devenir bon et de prier Dieu. Je suis venu tout de suite. Descends! Viens faire la prière avec moi.

—Oncle Chacal, répond le Coq, tu vois bien que j'appelle les gens à la prière!

—Oui, je vois, mais maintenant que tu as fini d'appeler, descends faire la prière avec moi!

—D'accord, dit le Coq. Mais j'attends l'imam.

—Qui est votre imam ici? demande le Chacal.

—Tu ne le connais pas? C'est le Chien de chasse.

—Au revoir! Au revoir! dit le Chacal. J'ai oublié de me laver avant la prière. J'y cours.»

(From Jean-Paul Tauvel, *Contes et histoires du Maghreb*. Paris: Hachette)

FAISONS CONNAISSANCE

Maghreb is an Arabic word meaning *sunset;* it is the name used to refer to the northern part of Africa, the area now occupied by Morocco, Algeria, and Tunisia. In France these countries are also known as l'Afrique du Nord, and because they were once French colonies, French is still used, together with Arabic, as an administrative and literary language.

According to statistics released by the French Ministry of the Interior, there are now 4.5 million foreigners residing in France. Approximately one third come from the **Maghreb,** including 710,000 **Algériens,** 575,000 **Marocains,** and 230,000 **Tunisiens.** Since 1954 the number of new European immigrants has decreased while the number of **Maghrébins** has constantly increased. They bring with them their ways of life and their Islamic religion.

La Prière du Chacal is set in a Muslim context where public prayer is conducted five times a day. The one who calls the faithful to assemble to pray is called the **muezzin,** but the **imam** is the one who leads the prayer.

This popular tale is reminiscent of the animal fables written by Jean de la Fontaine in the seventeenth century. Like those fables, its intent is to teach a lesson using animals as protagonists, a device used in literature since ancient times and featured in the fables of Aesop (ancient Greece), the *Roman de Renard,* popular in the Middle Ages, and more recently, in this country, the stories of Joel Chandler Harris.

Etudions la fable

1. A quelle sorte de personne est-ce qu'on pense quand on parle d'un chacal?
2. Comment le Chacal essaye-t-il de devenir ami avec le Coq?
3. Pourquoi est-ce que le Chacal veut que le Coq descende? Pour prier?
4. Qui est-ce que le Coq attend?
5. Pourquoi le Chacal décide-t-il de partir? Quelle raison donne-t-il?
6. Qui est plus intelligent, le Chacal ou le Coq? Pourquoi?

Enrichissons notre vocabulaire

Un animal / des animaux *(An animal / animals)*

un canard

une vache

une poule

un cheval

un oiseau *(m.)*

un mouton

un cochon

un chat

un lapin

Prononciation   Des mots difficiles

At this point you have learned all the main features of French pronunciation. There always remain a few individual words that are difficult to pronounce, however. One problem for people learning French is that they rely on spelling too much when they try to determine the correct pronunciation of a word. French spelling, as does English, represents the pronunciation of the language as it was spoken hundreds of years ago. The following words and phrases are among the most difficult to pronounce that you have learned in this book.

Repeat the following verbs after your teacher.

il peut, ils peuvent / je fais, nous faisons / tu achètes, vous achetez / je verrai, je ferai, je serai / que j'aille, que nous allions / qu'il veuille / soyons / choisissez, réussissez / ayez, aie / gagner / elle prend, elles prennent / j'aime

Repeat the following adjectives after your teacher.

un, une / ancien, ancienne / ennuyeux / bon, bonne / utile, inutile / ambitieux

Repeat the following nouns after your teacher.

les gens / un examen / ma sœur / la peur / le pays / mille, ville, fille / juin, juillet, août / un cours, un corps / monsieur, messieurs / une famille tranquille / la faim, la femme / l'Allemagne / la gare, la guerre / la psychologie / l'école / l'hiver, l'automne / un œil, des yeux / la campagne, la montagne / deux heures / Jean, Jeanne / un an, une année / les Etats-Unis / un franc / un œuf, des œufs

Exercice

Read the following sentences aloud, taking care to pronounce each word correctly.

1. Monsieur Martin utilise de l'huile et du beurre et sa cuisine est fantastique.
2. Je ne pense pas que Jean veuille gagner le match.
3. Nos familles prennent des vacances magnifiques en juin et en juillet.
4. Il est inutile de chercher un pays où les gens ne sont pas ambitieux.
5. Nous faisons une promenade ennuyeuse entre la gare et l'école.
6. En automne et en hiver ils peuvent suivre un cours de psychologie ou d'anthropologie.

GRAMMAIRE

I. Adverbs

You use adverbs to describe actions and to qualify descriptions.

A. Introduction

Adverbs are words that modify verbs, adjectives, or other adverbs. They usually indicate manner or degree and answer the questions *How?*, *How much?*, *When?*, and *Where?*

1. The following adverbs indicate manner, or degree.

assez *rather*	**ensemble**	**souvent**
beaucoup	**mal** *badly*	**surtout**
bien	**mieux** *better*	**très**
déjà	**peu**	**trop**
encore	**presque**	**vite** *quickly*

Le Coq chante **bien**.   Je l'aime **beaucoup**.

2. The following indications of time and place are also adverbs.

ailleurs *elsewhere*	**là**	**quelquefois** *sometimes*
aujourd'hui	**là-bas**	**tard** *late*
bientôt	**longtemps**	**tôt**
demain	**maintenant**	**toujours**
hier	**partout** *everywhere*	**tout de suite**
ici		

Demain il va appeler les gens à la prière.   Il chante **là-bas**.

B. Adverbs Created from Adjectives

Other adverbs may be created from adjectives by adding the ending
-ment (/ mã /).

1. Adjectives ending in a written vowel take **-ment** directly.

facile $\rightarrow$ **facilement**   rapide $\rightarrow$ **rapidement**
nécessaire $\rightarrow$ **nécessairement**   rare $\rightarrow$ **rarement**
probable $\rightarrow$ **probablement**   vrai $\rightarrow$ **vraiment**

2. Most adjectives that end in a written consonant add **-ment** to the
feminine form.

certain, certaine $\rightarrow$ **certainement**
complet, complète $\rightarrow$ **complètement**
général, générale $\rightarrow$ **généralement**
heureux, heureuse $\rightarrow$ **heureusement** *fortunately*
lent, lente $\rightarrow$ **lentement** *slowly*
malheureux, malheureuse $\rightarrow$ **malheureusement** *unfortunately*
parfait, parfaite $\rightarrow$ **parfaitement**
seul, seule $\rightarrow$ **seulement** *only*
sûr, sûre $\rightarrow$ **sûrement**
tel, telle $\rightarrow$ **tellement** *so*
traditionnel, traditionnelle $\rightarrow$ **traditionnellement**

3. Most adjectives ending in **-ent** or **-ant** (/ ã /) change those letters to
em or **am**, respectively, then add **-ment**. In both cases, / ã / becomes
/ amã /. The list on page 442 shows examples.

-ant	**-ent**
brillant → **brillamment**	évident → **évidemment**
indépendant → **indépendamment**	fréquent → **fréquemment**
insuffisant → **insuffisamment**	intelligent → **intelligemment**
méchant → **méchamment**	prudent → **prudemment**
suffisant → **suffisament**	récent → **récemment**
sufficiently	

C. Position of Adverbs

1. As a general rule, short, frequently used adverbs precede the words they modify, including past participles and infinitives, while longer adverbs follow the words they modify.

Il est **déjà** parti.   *but*   Elle a conduit **lentement**.
Je vais **vite** sortir.   Je suis venu **tout de suite**.

2. While there are exceptions to the above rule, two other rules always hold true.
   a. In French, a subject and conjugated verb are *never* separated by an adverb, as in English.

   Ils rentrent **souvent** tard.   *They **often** get home late.*
   (s.) (v.) (adv.)   **(s.) (adv.) (v.)**

   b. In French, adverbs of time and place always precede or follow the subject-verb group. Adverbs of time and place *never* occur between those elements.

   Nous allons commencer **demain**.   **Ici**, il n'y a pas de cafés.
   (s.-v. group)   (adv.)   **(adv.)   (s.-v. group)**

Langue

A. **On dîne chez Christine.** Changez les adjectifs entre parenthèses en adverbes, et ajoutez-les aux phrases données.

   1. Christine nous a préparé du poisson.   (récent)
   2. Il n'était pas bon.   (tel)
   3. Tu m'en parles!   (méchant)
   4. Vous avez mangé.   (beaucoup)
   5. Nous ne reviendrons pas.   (certain)
   6. J'ai d'autres amis.   (heureux)

B. **A la résidence.** Mettez les phrases suivantes au passé composé et faites attention à la place des adverbes.

   1. Mon camarade de chambre parle beaucoup.
   2. Nous finissons les cours aujourd'hui.
   3. Hélène s'habille rapidement.
   4. Jacques étudie peu.
   5. Mes copains viennent me voir souvent.
   6. Ils arrivent déjà.

Culture

C. **La société algérienne change.** La vie en Algérie a beaucoup changé depuis un certain temps. Caractérisez ces changements en parlant des choses qu'on fait **traditionnellement** et qu'on fait **aujourd'hui** dans ce pays.

> MODELE: boire de l'alcool
> *Traditionnellement on ne buvait pas d'alcool. Aujourd'hui certains en boivent.*

1. mettre les garçons et les filles ensemble à l'école
2. avoir l'enseignement primaire en français / en arabe
3. voir un voile *(veil)* sur toutes les femmes
4. rencontrer des femmes avec des responsabilités professionnelles
5. faire son service militaire obligatoirement
6. séparer la politique et la religion

Communication

D. Comment faites-vous les activités suivantes?

> MODELE: étudier (bien, longuement, rarement, vite)
> *J'étudie vite.*

1. faire le ménage (souvent, rapidement, mal, fréquemment, demain)
2. faire vos devoirs (sérieusement, tranquillement, attentivement, vite, bientôt)
3. dormir (peu, beaucoup, bien, longtemps)
4. s'habiller (simplement, curieusement, traditionnellement, bien)

Et l'année prochaine?

5. parler français (bien, mal, fréquemment, rarement)
6. voyager (souvent, partout, sûrement, longuement)
7. chercher un appartement (partout, peut-être, certainement, sérieusement, prudemment)
8. faire du sport (souvent, rarement, sûrement, régulièrement)

E. Comment avez-vous fait ces choses hier?

> MODELE: se réveiller
> *Je me suis réveillée lentement.*

1. se lever
2. manger
3. faire vos devoirs
4. conduire votre auto
5. s'habiller
6. lire le journal
7. travailler
8. s'endormir

F. **Questions personnelles.** Votre vie à l'université

1. Où allez-vous tout de suite après ce cours?
2. A qui avez-vous écrit récemment?
3. Qu'est-ce que vous faites particulièrement bien ou mal ce semestre / trimestre?
4. Allez-vous préparer l'examen final suffisamment?
5. Quelle note *(grade)* allez-vous probablement avoir dans ce cours?
6. Allez-vous étudier régulièrement le semestre / trimestre prochain?

II. The French Equivalents of *good* and *well, bad* and *badly*

> You use these adjectives and adverbs to make value judgments about people, things, ideas, and activities.

A. When expressing the equivalents of *good / well* and *bad / badly* in French, it is important to distinguish between adjectives and adverbs.

1. The adjectives **bon** and **mauvais** modify only nouns.

C'est un **bon** vin.   *It's a **good** wine.*
Cette bière est **mauvaise**.   *This beer is **bad**.*

2. The adverbs **bien** and **mal** modify verbs or adjectives.

Ce professeur parle **bien**.   *This teacher speaks **well**.*
Mais il s'habille **mal**.   *But he dresses **badly**.*

CE QU'ILS DISENT

In conversation, **bien** is used as an adjective to describe a person ("a fine person") or a thing ("a good thing").

Ton copain est **bien**.   Je connais un restaurant très **bien**.

B. To make a comparison, English uses *better* for both the adjective *good* and the adverb *well*. French, however, keeps the distinction between the adjective and the adverb. The comparative of the adjective **bon(ne)(s)** is **meilleur(e)(s)**. The comparative of the adverb **bien** is **mieux**.

C'est un **bon** vin. → C'est un **meilleur** vin.
Il parle **bien**. → Il parle **mieux**.

C. To complete a comparison, use **que** *(than)*.

M. Lebrun est un **très bon** professeur.
M. Ducharme est un **bon** professeur.
M. Lebrun est un **meilleur** professeur **que** M. Ducharme.

Les vins français sont **très bons.**
Les vins de Californie sont **bons.**
Les vins français sont **meilleurs que** les vins de Californie.

J'aime **bien** la viande.
J'aime **aussi** le poisson.
J'aime **mieux** la viande **que** le poisson.

Louise chante **très bien.**
Marc chante **bien.**
Louise chante **mieux que** Marc.

D. French also distinguishes between adjective and adverb forms to express the idea of *worse*. The adjective is **plus mauvais(e)(es),** the adverb **plus mal.** To complete the comparison, use **que.**

Robert a de **très mauvaises** idées.
Jacqueline a de **mauvaises** idées.
Robert a de **plus mauvaises** idées **que** Jacqueline.

Je dors **très mal.**
Mon camarade de chambre dort **mal.**
Je dors **plus mal que** lui.

E. To form the superlative *(best)*, use **le, la,** or **les** with **meilleur(e)(s)** and **le** with **mieux.** To express the idea of *in*, use **de.**

Baryschnikoff est **le meilleur** danseur **du** monde.
Non, c'est Noureïev qui danse **le mieux.**

Langue

A. **Au théâtre.** Ajoutez le mot entre parenthèses aux phrases suivantes. Faites attention à l'accord des adjectifs.

1. Michel est un acteur.   (bon)
2. Il a joué hier.   (bien)
3. Il est dans une pièce anglaise.   (mauvais)
4. J'ai entendu les acteurs.   (mal)
5. Moi, j'aime aller au cinéma.   (mieux)
6. J'adore voir des films étrangers.   (bon)

SORTIE LE 13 NOVEMBRE
OSCAR DU MEILLEUR FILM ÉTRANGER 1991
VOYAGE VERS L'ESPOIR
UN FILM DE XAVIER KOLLER

B. **Nos devoirs d'anglais.** Complétez les phrases suivantes avec la forme correcte de **bon, bien, mauvais, mal, meilleur** ou **mieux**, selon le cas.

1. Je viens de lire un _____ roman.
2. Mes camarades ont _____ fait leurs devoirs.
3. Ils parlent français _____ que moi.
4. Tu ne trouveras pas de _____ cours que celui-ci.
5. Elle écrit plus _____ que vous.
6. Est-ce que vous comprenez _____ ?

C. **Dînons ensemble.** Formez des phrases complètes avec les mots donnés.

1. Nous / s'amuser / bien / hier
2. Je / trouver / bon / restaurant / en ville
3. On / prendre / mon / voiture, / je / conduire / bien / toi
4. Ce / restaurant-là / être / bon / celui-ci
5. On / manger / bien / ici / là-bas
6. Nous / commander / bon / lapin

Culture

D. **Vos impressions.** Qui produit les meilleures choses, la France ou les Etats-Unis? Donnez vos opinions des catégories suivantes.

MODELE: le café *Le café français est meilleur que le café américain.*

la bière *La bière américaine est meilleure.*

1. la musique
2. le vin
3. les voitures
4. les vêtements
5. les films
6. les avions
7. la cuisine
8. les trains
9. les ordinateurs
10. les émissions de télévision

Communication

E. **Etes-vous sexiste?** Pensez-vous qu'il y ait des choses que les hommes font mieux que les femmes, ou vice versa?

MODELE: *Les femmes jouent au tennis mieux que les hommes.*
Les hommes font mieux les courses.

conduire
faire la cuisine
faire le ménage
jouer au football
réussir aux examens

nager
comprendre les mathématiques
apprendre les langues
retenir les dates
???

F. **Votre santé.** Est-ce que les choses page 447 sont bonnes ou mauvaises pour la santé?

MODELE: l'alcool *L'alcool est mauvais pour la santé.*

les cigarettes	les médecins
le vin	les œufs
le sport	le café
le sucre	le poisson
le sel	l'eau de votre ville

G. **Questions personnelles.** Vos souvenirs

1. Quel moment de votre vie vous rappelez-vous le mieux?
2. Que pensez-vous de votre lycée? Vous avez été mieux préparé(e) que d'autres étudiants?
3. Aimez-vous mieux votre vie au lycée ou votre vie ici?
4. Avez-vous connu un meilleur professeur que le vôtre?
5. Quand avez-vous mal dormi? Pourquoi?
6. Combien de très bons amis / bonnes amies avez-vous eu(e)s?

III. The Comparative and Superlative

> You use the comparative and superlative to rank people, places, things, and activities.

A. Comparative of Adjectives and Adverbs

1. With the exception of **bon** and **bien**, French adjectives and adverbs form the comparative with the expression **plus... que...** .

Ce chat est **plus** gros **que** le mien.	*This cat is **bigger than** mine.*
Ils sortent **plus** souvent **que** nous.	*They go out **more often than** we do.*

2. Two other comparative expressions are **aussi... que** *(as . . . as)* and **moins... que** *(less . . . than)*.

Il est **aussi** intelligent **que** sa sœur.
Elle tape **aussi** mal **que** nous.
Je comprends **moins** bien **que** toi.

B. Comparative of Nouns

To compare nouns, you use the following expressions; **plus de... que**, *(more . . . than)*, **autant de... que** *(as much / many . . . as)* and **moins de... que** *(less / fewer . . . than)*.

Elle a **plus de** patience **que** lui.	Nous avons **moins d'argent** qu'eux.
J'ai **autant de** talent **que** Marc.	

C. Superlative of Adjectives and Adverbs

1. To form the superlative, use the *definite article* before **plus** or **moins** followed by the adjective or adverb. Use **de** to express the idea of *in* or *of*.

Anne-Marie est **la plus artistique** de sa famille.	Anne-Marie is *the most artistic in her family.*
Pierre est **le moins insupportable** de tes amis.	Pierre is *the least annoying of your friends.*
Jean-Paul travaille **le plus régulièrement** de tous mes étudiants.	Jean-Paul works *the most consistently of all my students.*

2. If an adjective normally follows the noun it modifies, its superlative form uses the definite article twice, keeping the same number and gender.

J'habite **la** ville **la** plus intéressante de mon pays.
Ce sont **les** étudiants **les** plus sérieux de l'université.

ATTENTION

1. Note that in comparative constructions, you use **de**, not **que**, with numbers.

Nous avons moins **d'**une heure pour finir.
Il faut plus **de** deux cent mille dollars pour acheter cette maison.

2. The superlative of adverbs always takes **le** because adverbs have no number or gender.

Marie-France répond **le** moins souvent de toute la classe.
Nous habitons **le** plus loin de l'université de tous nos amis.

Langue

A. **Les impressions des touristes.** Formez des phrases complètes avec les mots donnés. Les symboles **+, −** et **=** représentent **plus, moins** et **aussi**, respectivement.

1. Les voitures / français / être / + petit / nôtre
2. théâtre / être / + cher / cinéma
3. hôtels / être / − bien / aux Etats-Unis
4. agents de police / être / = sympa / nôtre
5. Ce / église / être / + vieux / de la ville
6. pain / français / être / + bon / pain / américain
7. Le Louvre / être / musée / + connu / monde
8. La France / avoir / − plages / Etats-Unis

B. **Deux manières de dire la même chose.** Changez l'ordre des comparaisons sans changer la signification *(meaning)* de la phrase.

MODELE: Je suis plus riche que Paul. *Paul est moins riche que moi.*

1. Il parle plus vite qu'eux.
2. Tu as plus de problèmes que les autres.
3. Son français est moins bon que le tien.
4. Robert est aussi ennuyeux que Monique.
5. Jean traduit mieux que ses camarades.
6. Son fils est plus laid que le mien.

Culture

C. **La France: le pays et ses habitants.** Répondez aux questions suivantes sur la France en choisissant la bonne réponse.

1. Quelle est la plus grande montagne?
   a. le pic du Midi b. le Mont-Cenis c. le mont Blanc

2. Quel est le plus long fleuve?
   a. la Loire b. la Seine c. le Rhône

3. Quel est le pays d'origine du plus grand nombre d'immigrés?
   a. l'Algérie b. le Maroc c. le Portugal

4. Quel est l'auteur français le plus souvent étudié au lycée?
   a. Sartre b. Camus c. Proust

5. Quel est l'auteur que les élèves aiment le moins?
   a. Balzac b. Corneille c. Molière

6. Quelle est l'activité la plus fréquente des Français quand ils ne travaillent pas?
   a. lire b. faire une promenade c. regarder la télévision

7. Quel est le magazine qu'on achète le plus?
   a. *Télé 7 Jours* b. *Paris-Match* c. *L'Express*

8. Quel sport est-ce que les Français pratiquent le plus régulièrement?
   a. la natation b. la pêche c. le ski

Communication

D. **Des comparaisons.** Séparez-vous en groupes de deux. Comparez-vous en employant les expressions suivantes.

MODELE: Etudiant(e) 1: *Es-tu aussi grand(e) que moi?*
Etudiant(e) 2: *Je suis plus grand(e) que toi.*

avoir des sœurs / frères
habiter loin de l'université
se coucher tard
travailler bien
conduire vite

lire des romans
aller au cinéma souvent
être sérieux
dépenser de l'argent
???

E. **A votre avis.** Quel(le) est / Qui est, à votre avis,...

1. le plus grand écrivain?
2. la langue la plus difficile?
3. la voiture la plus rapide?
4. la ville la plus agréable de votre pays?
5. l'homme politique le moins honnête?
6. le cours le plus intéressant de votre université?
7. la profession la plus difficile?
8. la meilleure pizza de votre ville?

F. **Comparez-vous.** Dans votre cours, qui a autant d(e)...

cousins	cours aujourd'hui
dollars dans son portefeuille	examens finals
chiens	disques compacts
camarades de chambre	petit(e)s ami(e)s

G. **Questions personnelles.** Rêvez un peu.

1. Quel a été le jour le plus fantastique de votre vie?
2. Quelle personne admirez-vous le plus? Qui admirez-vous presque autant qu'elle?
3. Aimeriez-vous avoir autant d'argent que les Rockefeller? Qu'est-ce que vous en feriez?
4. Vous voudriez être aussi beau / belle / riche / connu(e) que quelle personnalité?
5. Préféreriez-vous avoir plus d'amis? Quelles caractéristiques font les meilleur(e)s ami(e)s?
6. Quelle est la chose la plus importante que vous avez entendue récemment?

COMMUNIQUONS . . . .

S'exprimer en français familier

Although the **Ce qu'ils disent** sections of this textbook have shown you many ways in which spoken French differs from the formal language, the French you have been studying is the standard variety used in more formal speech. If you go to a francophone country, you are more likely to hear colloquial, or popular, French (**le français familier**) in casual conversation. One characteristic of colloquial French is the frequent use of conversational fillers (**des remplisseurs de pause**) similar to words like *well, like,* or *ya know.* French speakers also omit or elide sounds (**élision**), just as English speakers replace *I am going to* with *I'm gonna.* Because so many sounds are dropped, this level of speech is often harder for foreigners to understand. In addition, colloquial French, like English, abounds in popular vocabulary. The following sections will review some features and describe others that characterize rapid, casual speech.

On fait des pauses.

—Euh	*Uh*
—Ben	*Um*
—M'enfin	*Well*
—M'alors	*So*
—Eh bien / Eh ben	*So*

On fait des élisions.

1. More mute e's than usual are dropped.

Jé te verrai demain.	*See ya tomorrow.*
Céla né sé fait pas.	*That isn't done.*

2. The **u** of **tu** is dropped.

T'es vraiment stupide.	*You're a dope.*
T'as fini?	*Finished?*

3. The **l** of **il** and **ils** is not pronounced.

Ils sont partis.	*They left.*
Il né sait pas.	*He doesn't know.*

4. The **ne** of negations is not used.

Jé peux pas venir.	*I can't come.*
Jé veux pas mé coucher.	*I don't wanna go to bed.*
C'est pas vrai!	*It isn't true!*

5. The consonant group **-re** at the end of words before a word beginning with a consonant is not pronounced.

Donne-moi l'autré stylo.	*Gimme the other pen.*
Il a quatré chiens.	*He's got four dogs.*
Le pauvré garçon!	*The poor guy!*

On emploie un vocabulaire familier.

1. Following are some popular words for common things.

C'est sa bagnole.	C'est son auto.
Il n'aime pas son boulot.	Il n'aime pas son travail / emploi.
De la flotte? J'en bois jamais!	De l'eau? Je n'en bois jamais!
J'ai pas de fric.	Je n'ai pas d'argent.
Où sont mes godasses *(f.)*?	Où sont mes chaussures?
C'est un bon pinard.	C'est un bon vin.

2. There are popular words used to talk about people.

Voilà des flics.	Voilà des agents de police.
T'as vu les gosses?	Tu as vu les enfants?
Elle parle avec un type / mec.	Elle parle avec un homme.
Il sort avec une nana.	Il sort avec une jeune femme.
C'est mon pote.	C'est mon ami.
Son père est toubib.	Son père est médecin.

3. The following expressions describe actions.

Ils bouffent au restau-U.	Ils mangent au restaurant universitaire.
Ta gueule!	Tais-toi! *(Shut up!)* *[vulgar]*

4. Several popular words are adjectives used to describe people or things.

T'es dingue?!	Tu es fou?! *(Are you nuts?!)*
C'est dégueulasse!	C'est dégoûtant! *(That's disgusting!)* *[vulgar]*
Il est moche.	Il est laid.

Interaction   *Julie et Etienne sont au restaurant universitaire.*

JULIE: Qu'est-ce qu'on a à bouffer aujourd'hui?

ETIENNE: Ben, les mêmes choses dégueulasses!

JULIE: Tu me cherches de la flotte?

ETIENNE: Pas moi! Je vais acheter du pinard.

JULIE: T'es dingue? C'est toi qui as la bagnole!

Activités

A. Mettez les phrases suivantes en français standard.

1. I' veut pas m' donner d' fric.
2. L' pauv' mec peut pas acheter d' bagnole.
3. T' as vu l'aut' nana?
4. Tu vas pas porter ces godasses au boulot?
5. T' es dingue? J'aime pas la flotte!
6. T' as pas encore fini d' bouffer?

B. Dans les phrases suivantes, remplacez autant de mots que possible avec du vocabulaire familier.

1. Les Américains sont fous. Ils mangent dans leur voiture!
2. Mon ami n'a jamais d'argent parce qu'il n'a pas de travail.
3. Qui a mis de l'eau dans mon vin? C'est dégoûtant!
4. Voilà un homme et une femme qui jouent avec leurs enfants.
5. Tais-toi! Tes chaussures sont beaucoup plus laides que les miennes.
6. Les agents de police ont trouvé la voiture de mon ami en ville.

Lecture culturelle ....

Avant la lecture

Racial tension has been a problem in France for a long time, just as it has been in most other countries. Many French people are concerned with the growing number of foreigners living and working in France. In the 1992 regional elections, a far-right candidate, Jean-Marie Le Pen, and his supporters won just over 14% of the vote on a primarily racist platform. The ruling Socialist party received only slightly more votes.

The efforts to combat racial tension are numerous, and one of the most effective groups doing this work is **S.O.S. Racisme,** which was organized by the descendants of both immigrants and native French people. One group that has traditionally borne the brunt of racism in France is the group of Arabs from the Maghreb. The young now call themselves **Beurs** (a reversal of the syllables in **Arabes**) and have developed a new pride in their heritage.

The following passage not only describes the origin of the group **S.O.S. Racisme,** but it also illustrates another tradition of youth: **l'engagement** or making a commitment to a cause.

Activités

A. In recent years, the French have borrowed a great deal of vocabulary directly from English. Scan the following reading to find the three examples of **franglais** that it uses.

B. This reading is about **xénophobie,** the fear or hatred of foreigners or anything that is foreign. What other phobias do you know? The words would be the same in French, because they come from ancient Greek. What would **francophobie** mean? What is the opposite?

C. You have learned that one should always use complete sentences (subjects, verbs, and perhaps an object) when writing. Occasionally, a writer will break this rule to achieve a specific effect. Scan the reading, and find four sentences that are not complete.

Touche pas à mon pote!

«Toucher» est un mot important dans la langue française. Surtout parce que c'est un des premiers mots que les petits Français entendent. *A travers* des expressions comme «Touche pas», «Il ne faut pas toucher», c'est tout un monde d'*interdictions* qui *se dresse* devant eux. On ne sera *donc* pas surpris qu'un slo-
5 gan comme «Touche pas à mon *pote*» ait obtenu une notoriété immédiate.

    Tout *remonte* au mois de novembre 1984: Diego, un jeune Sénégalais de la *banlieue* parisienne, se trouve dans le métro. *Tout à coup,* une jeune femme *affolée* se met à crier qu'on lui *a volé* son portefeuille. Aussitôt, sans qu'un mot soit prononcé, tous les *regards* accusateurs *se portent* sur Diego. C'est le seul
10 noir du *wagon*! La tension monte. Il n'y a pas de doute, Diego est *coupable.* Puis, miracle! Deux stations plus loin, la jeune femme retrouve le portefeuille «volé» *au fond* de son sac. Même silence, mais cette fois, c'est un silence *gêné.*

    Il s'agissait d'une scène de racisme ordinaire, mais ce jour-là, S.O.S. Racisme est né. Après l'incident, Diego est allé retrouver ses copains et copines
15 de fac, Fatima, Thaima, Jean-Pierre, Hervé et Harlem Désir. Immigrés, jeunes de la deuxième génération, Français ou *métis* comme Harlem Désir. De père *antillais* et de mère alsacienne, étudiant avant de devenir *animateur* de *centres de loisirs,* Harlem est devenu naturellement le président de l'association qui venait de naître à cause de Diego: S.O.S. Racisme.
20   Une association *de plus* contre le racisme? Justement pas. Copains de fac, fréquentant les mêmes *cités* tristes de la banlieue nord, Harlem, Fatima, Thaima, Jean-Pierre et Hervé ont déjà participé à la *lutte* contre la xénophobie à l'occasion de la *marche* des Beurs pour l'égalité. Pour eux, la société multi-culturelle, ce n'est pas une *découverte.* Quand on écoute Michael Jackson et
25 Sade, la symbiose des cultures, ce n'est pas un problème. Conclusion de Harlem, de Fatima et de leurs copains: les jeunes sont mieux équipés que les adultes pour résister à la *vague* raciste. S.O.S. Racisme donc. Mais il faut aussi trouver un slogan. Fatima dit que si Diego n'avait pas été seul dans le métro, les choses ne se seraient pas passées comme cela. C'est une idée! Le slogan naît:
30 «Touche pas à mon pote». Fini les slogans comme «Le racisme ne passera pas» ou les *discours* sur l'égalité des hommes, mais *plutôt* une réaction toute simple: touche pas à mes copains, qu'ils soient noirs, beurs ou portugais.

    «Touche pas à mon pote», c'est évidemment un *préalable.* Mais *ensuite,* s'il faut parler, on parle. Fatima, une Algérienne de la deuxième génération,
35 pourrait passer pour une Française du *Midi* de la France. Pourtant, elle porte le

---

Through

forbidden things / rises / thus / buddy
goes back / suburb / Suddenly frantic / stolen glances / converge car / guilty

at the bottom / embarrassed

mixed race / from the Antilles / organizer / community centers
another
high-rise projects
fight
protest march
discovery

wave

speeches / rather

preamble / then

South

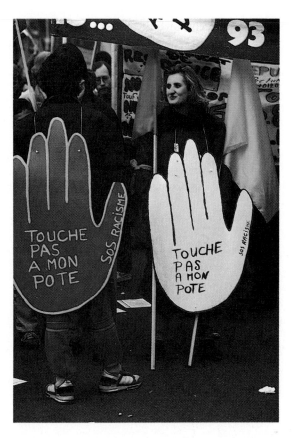

Manifestation contre le racisme

badge, une main ouverte avec le slogan inscrit dans la *paume*. «Je n'ai pas peur de parler aux racistes. Je connais les mots pour leur répondre», dit-elle. Et Fatima *ajoute* qu'elle *prend la parole*, en pensant à ses parents algériens qui, «eux, n'ont pas les mots pour se défendre». «Touche pas à mes parents.»

40 Avait-elle une chance, Fatima? Y avait-il une possibilité pour que cette campagne «Touche pas à mon pote» soit un peu plus qu'un gadget antiraciste *sans lendemain*? *Autrement dit,* la montée de Le Pen n'était-elle pas irrésistible dans les lycées comme ailleurs? Pas sûr... Dans de nombreux lycées, des élèves *ont fait grève* pour indiquer leur opposition à «un racisme rampant».

45 Paradoxe: y aurait-il un bon usage de Le Pen? Dans un océan d'indifférence, Le Pen par ses *formules grossières* et brutales a été le seul homme politique à faire *réagir, contre* lui, les jeunes. Annick Percheron, auteur de nombreuses études sociologiques sur la politique et les jeunes, observe: «Pour s'affirmer, ils n'ont pas trente-six solutions. La plus immédiate: *s'emparer* des 50 thèmes *délaissés* par les partis politiques. La faim dans le monde, c'est leur *truc*. L'altruisme et la générosité sont une manière *douce* d'entrer en politique sans *singer* les adultes.» Le succès d'organisations comme Médecins sans Frontières *auprès* des jeunes est significatif. Quand on a quinze ans, on ne dit plus: «Je voudrais être guérillero ou *pilote d'essai*», mais plus souvent, «J'ai envie 55 d'être médecin-sans-frontières».

palm

adds / speaks

without a future / In other words
went on strike

crude slogans
react / against

to pick up
abandoned
thing / gentle
aping
with
test pilot

L'aventure, certainement, mais l'aventure utile. Et la politique *là-dedans?* *therein*
Le militantisme d'hier impliquait une *remise en question* de soi et de sa culture. *reexamination*
Aujourd'hui, ce n'est plus l'idéologie qui passe en premier. *Ce qui* a fait le pres- *What*
tige d'Amnesty International, c'est sa grande impartialité qui lui a fait éviter
60 les passions idéologiques. C'est aussi le fait qu'elle *exige* de *chacun* de ses *requires / each one*
membres la *prise en charge* individuelle d'un prisonnier politique. «Touche pas *responsibility*
à mon prisonnier.» Responsabilité, *efficacité.* *effectiveness*

Ce à quoi on *assiste,* c'est un *élan du cœur.* Les organisations charitables *What / witnesses /*
sont *débordées* par les *dons* et les offres de service des jeunes. «Touche pas à *emotional commitment /*
65 mon pote», c'est avant tout un grand mouvement de solidarité de la jeunesse *overwhelmed / gifts*
qui a compris qu'elle seule possède la clé aux problèmes que pose une société
de plus en plus multiculturelle.

(Adapté d'un article de *L'Express,* no. 1058)

Après la lecture

Questions sur le texte

1. Pourquoi le slogan «Touche pas à mon pote» a-t-il eu un succès immédiat?
2. Quel incident a eu lieu dans le métro? A la fin, pourquoi les gens sont-ils gênés?
3. Qui sont les jeunes qui ont fondé S.O.S. Racisme? D'où viennent-ils?
4. Pourquoi ces jeunes gens sont-ils particulièrement bien préparés pour s'occuper d'une association comme S.O.S. Racisme?
5. Quel est, avec le slogan, l'autre symbole de l'association?
6. Selon Annick Percheron, que font les jeunes pour s'affirmer?

Activités

A. Répondez aux questions suivantes.

1. Est-ce qu'on vous a volé quelque chose? Avez-vous accusé quelqu'un? Est-ce que cette personne était coupable? Racontez l'aventure.
2. Avez-vous observé un événement raciste? Décrivez-le. Vous a-t-on accusé de quelque chose à cause de *(because of)* votre race, de votre âge ou de votre sexe? Expliquez.

B. Débats en cours.

1. On a dit que les tensions raciales augmentent sur les campus des Etats-Unis. Qu'en pensez-vous? Quelles solutions à ce problème pourriez-vous proposer?
2. Y a-t-il d'autres problèmes sociaux dans le monde que les jeunes pourraient aider à résoudre *(resolve)*?

TOUS ENSEMBLE!

A. Répondez aux questions suivantes en employant les mots entre parenthèses.

Conversation avec mes parents quand je rentre tard

1. A ta place, est-ce que nous rentrerions après minuit? (Non,... ne... pas faire cela.)
2. Qu'est-ce que vous avez fait ensemble? (Nous... danser... pendant... heures)
3. Qu'est-ce que tu as promis? (... revenir avant minuit.)
4. Vous êtes rentrés lentement? (Non,... vite...)
5. Quand nous téléphoneras-tu? (... aussitôt que... je... savoir quand je... arriver)

Un vieil ami

6. L'avez-vous connu? (Oui,... bien...)
7. Depuis quand êtes-vous amis? (... 1987.)
8. Est-ce qu'il sait parler français? (Oui,... + bien... que moi.)
9. Vous allez voyager ensemble pendant les vacances? (Oui,... partir... quinze jours.)
10. Est-ce qu'il est très riche? (Oui,... promettre... payer le voyage.)

B. **Parlez-moi de votre chambre.** Refaites les phrases suivantes en employant les mots entre parenthèses.

1. Il faut que tu viennes la voir. (Demain... vous...)
2. Je la loue depuis trois mois. (Il y a... que...)
3. Je n'ai pas souvent envie de sortir. (rarement)
4. Mon frère a fait le ménage il y a peu de temps. (récemment)
5. On met dix minutes pour aller en ville. (L'année prochaine,...)

C. **Connaissez-vous l'amie mystérieuse de Jacques?** Combinez les phrases suivantes.

1. Vous ne connaissez pas la jeune femme? La jeune femme sort avec Jacques.
2. Il refuse de me présenter cette femme fascinante. Il vient de décrire la femme.
3. Elle habite un village formidable. Il y a trois ans, j'ai passé mes vacances dans ce village.

457

4. Elle sait bien faire de la planche à voile. Jacques ne sait pas aussi bien en faire.
5. Elle joue très bien au tennis. Jacques joue moins bien.

D. Formez des phrases complètes avec les mots donnés. Les symboles = et + représentent **aussi** et **plus,** respectivement.

Allons voir Robert

1. Si / nous / avoir / temps / nous / aller voir / Robert
2. Il / permettre / gens / passer le voir / sans téléphoner
3. Il / ne... pas / être / = / sympa / Jean
4. Son / chien / être / = / méchant / tien

Chez Robert

5. Vouloir / vous / je / mettre / musique?
6. Regarder / divan / je / venir / acheter
7. Si / vous / avoir / faim / je / pouvoir / vous / servir / mouton
8. Dire / moi / quand / vous / avoir envie / partir

E. Complétez les phrases suivantes de manière logique.

1. Je n'aime pas les gens qui...
2. Ma mère ne ferait jamais...
3. J'aime les animaux qu(e)...
4. Je ne sais pas où...
5. Si j'étais en retard...
6. Je partirai vendredi, dès que...
7. Je ferai mieux si...
8. J'ai plus de talent...

ENTRE NOUS!

A. Avec un(e) camarade de cours, comparez des gens que vous connaissez. Employez un élément de chaque colonne, mais n'hésitez pas à utiliser vos propres idées.

A	B	C	D	E
je	être	plus	bien	moi
mes amis	avoir	moins	mauvais	vous
mon professeur	conduire	aussi	mal	mes amis
	comprendre	autant	beau	la ville
mes voisins	manger		brillant	l'université
mes parents	jouer		talent	le cours
mon frère / ma sœur	danser		???	???
???				

B. Interviewez un(e) camarade de cours. Parlez des sujets suivants.

1. la ville où tu habites
2. les cours que tu suis
3. les gens que tu aimes
4. les choses les plus importantes de ta vie
5. le genre de film que tu préfères
6. les endroits où tu vas
7. les animaux que tu as eus
8. les gens qui t'ont influencé(e)

C. Dans en groupe de trois ou quatre étudiants, imaginez votre vie quand vous aurez cent ans.

MODEL: se lever à cinq heures du matin
         Nous nous lèverons à cinq heures du matin.

ne pas se rappeler les gens   ne pas bien entendre / voir
manger peu   ne plus rien remettre à plus tard
ne pas sortir   se coucher de bonne heure
ne boire que du lait   prendre beaucoup d'aspirine

D. Interrogez vos camarades de cours. Demandez-leur depuis quand ils font les choses suivantes ou pendant combien de temps ils les ont faites.

avoir un chien / un chat   être étudiant(e) dans cette université
boire du lait   connaître ton / ta meilleur(e) ami(e)
se coucher à huit heures   savoir nager
jouer au docteur   habiter la ville où tu es né(e)
posséder une voiture   ???

E. Avec un(e) camarade de cours, imaginez ce que *(what)* vous feriez si vous étiez de l'autre sexe.

mettre une robe / cravate   avoir les cheveux plus / moins longs
(ne plus) jouer au football   dire aux personnes du sexe opposé qu(e)...
(ne plus) faire la cuisine   trouver... formidable / affreux (-euse)
payer au restaurant   ???

F. Dans un petit groupe, décrivez comment vous avez fait des choses le semestre / trimestre dernier.

vite   méchamment   brillamment
souvent   horriblement   le mieux
bien   fréquemment   le plus mal
mal   rarement   ???

G. **Jeu de rôles.** Jouez les scènes suivantes avec un(e) camarade de cours.

1. Vous êtes journaliste pour une revue spécialisée. Choisissez le sujet (sports, mode *[fashion]*, pêche, etc.) et interviewez un(e) camarade qui le connaît mieux que vous.
2. Vous voulez louer un appartement. Téléphonez au / à la propriétaire et posez-lui des questions.

3. Vous venez de gagner 100.000 francs dans un jeu télévisé. Discutez avec votre femme / mari ce que *(what)* vous allez faire avec cet argent.

4. Vous avez besoin d'emprunter de l'argent à un(e) ami(e). Faites beaucoup de compliments.

5. Vous voulez que votre camarade s'engage *(makes a commitment)* pour une cause. Expliquez-lui celle que vous préférez.

6. Vous êtes guide dans un musée de l'avenir. Décrivez la vie qu'on y représente.

7. Essayez d'être plus snob que votre ami(e). Mentionnez toutes les choses que vous achetez qui sont de la meilleure qualité.

8. Vous êtes professeur de français, et vous parlez avec un étudiant qui n'est pas sérieux. Expliquez-lui comment il peut réussir dans votre cours.

APPENDICES ....

I. International Phonetic Alphabet

Consonants

/p/	Pierre		/v/	vous
/t/	tu		/z/	bise
/k/	comme		/ʒ/	bonjour
/b/	bonjour		/l/	la
/d/	de		/ʀ/	garçon
/g/	garçon		/m/	main
/f/	fille		/n/	Anne
/s/	merci, professeur		/ɲ/	poignée
/ʃ/	chez			

Vowels

/i/	bise		/y/	une
/e/	café		/ø/	de, peu
/ɛ/	appelle		/œ/	heure
/a/	va		/ɛ̃/	bien, un, main
/ɔ/	comme		/ã/	connaissance
/o/	au		/ɔ̃/	faisons
/u/	vous			

Semivowels

/j/	Pierre
/w/	oui
/ɥ/	nuit

Mute e

/ə/	je, ferai

II. Les Etats-Unis

ETAT	in or to	ETAT	in or to
l'Alabama *(m.)*	dans l'Alabama / en Alabama	le Michigan	dans le Michigan
l'Alaska *(m.)*	dans l'Alaska / en Alaska	le Minnesota	dans le Minnesota
l'Arizona *(m.)*	dans l'Arizona / en Arizona	le Mississippi	dans le Mississippi
l'Arkansas *(m.)*	dans l'Arkansas / en Arkansas	le Missouri	dans le Missouri
la Californie	en Californie	le Montana	dans le Montana
la Caroline du Nord	en Caroline du Nord	le Nebraska	dans le Nebraska
la Caroline du Sud	en Caroline du Sud	le Nevada	dans le Nevada
le Colorado	dans le Colorado / au Colorado	le New Hampshire	dans le New Hampshire
le Connecticut	dans le Connecticut	le New Jersey	dans le New Jersey
le Dakota du Nord	dans le Dakota du Nord	l'état de New York	dans l'état de New York
le Dakota du Sud	dans le Dakota du Sud	le Nouveau-Mexique	au Nouveau-Mexique
le Delaware	dans le Delaware	l'Ohio *(m.)*	dans l'Ohio
la Floride	en Floride	l'Oklahoma *(m.)*	dans l'Oklahoma
la Géorgie	en Géorgie	l'Oregon *(m.)*	dans l'Oregon
Hawaii *(m.)*	à Hawaii / aux îles Hawaii	la Pennsylvanie	en Pennsylvanie
l'Idaho *(m.)*	dans l'Idaho	le Rhode Island	dans le Rhode Island
l'Illinois *(m.)*	dans l'Illinois / en Illinois	le Tennessee	dans le Tennessee
l'Indiana *(m.)*	dans l'Indiana	le Texas	au Texas
l'Iowa *(m.)*	dans l'Iowa	l'Utah *(m.)*	dans l'Utah
le Kansas	dans le Kansas	le Vermont	dans le Vermont
le Kentucky	dans le Kentucky	la Virginie	en Virginie
la Louisiane	en Louisiane	la Virginie-Occidentale	en Virginie-Occidentale
le Maine	dans le Maine	l'état de Washington	dans l'état de Washington
le Maryland	dans le Maryland	le Wisconsin	dans le Wisconsin
le Massachusetts	dans le Massachusetts	le Wyoming	dans le Wyoming

Adapted from Nachtmann, Francis W., "French Prepositions with American Place Names." *French Review*, Vol. 55, No. 1 (October, 1981), 88–92.

III. Double Pronoun Objects

A. If you use two pronoun objects in a sentence or a negative command, you must keep the following order:

me				
te	le	lui		
se	la	leur	y	en
nous	les			
vous				

Il prête ses livres à ses amis. → Il **les leur** prête.
J'ai donné de l'argent aux enfants. → Je **leur en** ai donné.
Nous allons vendre l'auto à notre voisin. → Nous allons **la lui** vendre.

B. Object pronouns in the first and third columns above cannot be used together. Use a tonic pronoun instead.

Il m'a présenté à Robert.   Il m'a présenté **à lui.**

C. In affirmative commands, use the following order:

		moi / m'		
	le	toi / t'		
	la	lui	y	en
verb	les	nous		
		vous		
		leur		

D. Me and te become **moi** and **toi** when they are the final elements of the command. If y or en is included, **me** and **te** become **m'** and **t'**.

Donnez-moi trois stylos. → Donnez-**m'en** trois.
Montrez-moi vos photos. → Montrez-**les-moi.**
Apportez-nous le journal. → Apportez-**le-nous.**

IV. Le passé simple

A. This tense may replace the **passé composé** in formal writing. There are three sets of endings:

-er verbs		-ir verbs		-re verbs	
je	chantai	je	partis	je	vendis
tu	chantas	tu	partis	tu	vendis
il	chanta	il	partit	il	vendit
nous	chantâmes	nous	partîmes	nous	vendîmes
vous	chantâtes	vous	partîtes	vous	vendîtes
ils	chantèrent	ils	partirent	ils	vendirent

B. Irregular verbs add the following endings to their stems:

-s   -^mes
-s   -^tes
-t   -rent

C. The irregular stems of the verbs you know are:

avoir → eu-   être → fu-   prendre → pri-
boire → bu-   faire → fi-   savoir → su-
conduire → conduisi-   lire → lu-   suivre → suivi-
connaître → connu-   mettre → mi-   venir → vin-
devoir → du-   mourir → mouru-   voir → vi-
dire → di-   naître → naqui-   vouloir → voulu-
écrire → écrivi-   pouvoir → pu-

Annibal **voulut** traverser les Alpes.	*Hannibal **wanted** to cross the Alps.*
Il **fit** ses devoirs.	*He **did** his homework.*
Nous **vîmes** un accident.	*We **saw** an accident.*
Napoléon **naquit** en Corse; il **mourut** à Sainte-Hélene.	*Napoleon **was born** in Corsica; he **died** on St. Helena.*
Elles ne **dirent** jamais la vérité.	*They never **told** the truth.*

V. Conjugaison des verbes

Regular Verbs

Infinitif	Indicatif				Impératif	Subjonctif	Conditionnel
	Présent	Passé Composé	Imparfait	Futur			
-ER chanter							
je / j'	chante	ai chanté	chantais	chanterai		chante	chanterais
tu	chantes	as chanté	chantais	chanteras	chante	chantes	chanterais
il / elle / on	chante	a chanté	chantait	chantera		chante	chanterait
nous	chantons	avons chanté	chantions	chanterons	chantons	chantions	chanterions
vous	chantez	avez chanté	chantiez	chanterez	chantez	chantiez	chanteriez
ils / elles	chantent	ont chanté	chantaient	chanteront		chantent	chanteraient
-IR servir							
je / j'	sers	ai servi	servais	servirai		serve	servirais
tu	sers	as servi	servais	serviras	sers	serves	servirais
il / elle / on	sert	a servi	servait	servira		serve	servirait
nous	servons	avons servi	servions	servirons	servons	servions	servirions
vous	servez	avez servi	serviez	servirez	servez	serviez	serviriez
ils / elles	servent	ont servi	servaient	serviront		servent	serviraient
-IR finir							
je / j'	finis	ai fini	finissais	finirai		finisse	finirais
tu	finis	as fini	finissais	finiras	finis	finisses	finirais
il / elle / on	finit	a fini	finissait	finira		finisse	finirait
nous	finissons	avons fini	finissions	finirons	finissons	finissions	finirions
vous	finissez	avez fini	finissiez	finirez	finissez	finissiez	finiriez
ils / elles	finissent	ont fini	finissaient	finiront		finissent	finiraient

Regular Verbs

Infinitif		Indicatif				Impératif	Subjonctif	Conditionnel
	Présent	Passé Composé	Imparfait	Futur				
-RE vendre								
je / j'	vends	ai vendu	vendais	vendrai			vende	vendrais
tu	vends	as vendu	vendais	vendras		vends	vendes	vendrais
il / elle / on	vend	a vendu	vendait	vendra			vende	vendrait
nous	vendons	avons vendu	vendions	vendrons		vendons	vendions	vendrions
vous	vendez	avez vendu	vendiez	vendrez		vendez	vendiez	vendriez
ils / elles	vendent	ont vendu	vendaient	vendront			vendent	vendraient
-IRE conduire								
je / j'	conduis	ai conduit	conduisais	conduirai			conduise	conduirais
tu	conduis	as conduit	conduisais	conduiras		conduis	conduises	conduirais
il / elle / on	conduit	a conduit	conduisait	conduira			conduise	conduirait
nous	conduisons	avons conduit	conduisions	conduirons		conduisons	conduisions	conduirions
vous	conduisez	avez conduit	conduisiez	conduirez		conduisez	conduisiez	conduiriez
ils / elles	conduisent	ont conduit	conduisaient	conduiront			conduisent	conduiraient
-IRE écrire								
j'	écris	ai écrit	écrivais	écrirai			écrive	écrirais
tu	écris	as écrit	écrivais	écriras		écris	écrives	écrirais
il / elle / on	écrit	a écrit	écrivait	écrira			écrive	écrirait
nous	écrivons	avons écrit	écrivions	écrirons		écrivons	écrivions	écririons
vous	écrivez	avez écrit	écriviez	écrirez		écrivez	écriviez	écririez
ils / elles	écrivent	ont écrit	écrivaient	écriront			écrivent	écriraient

Auxiliary Verbs

Infinitif	Indicatif				Impératif	Subjonctif	Conditionnel
	Présent	Passé Composé	Imparfait	Futur			
avoir							
j'	ai	ai eu	avais	aurai		aie	aurais
tu	as	as eu	avais	auras	aie	aies	aurais
il / elle / on	a	a eu	avait	aura		ait	aurait
nous	avons	avons eu	avions	aurons	ayons	ayons	aurions
vous	avez	avez eu	aviez	aurez	ayez	ayez	auriez
ils / elles	ont	ont eu	avaient	auront		aient	auraient
être							
je / j'	suis	ai été	étais	serai		sois	serais
tu	es	as été	étais	seras	sois	sois	serais
il / elle / on	est	a été	était	sera		soit	serait
nous	sommes	avons été	étions	serons	soyons	soyons	serions
vous	êtes	avez été	étiez	serez	soyez	soyez	seriez
ils / elles	sont	ont été	étaient	seront		soient	seraient

Reflexive Verb

Infinitif	Indicatif				Impératif	Subjonctif	Conditionnel
	Présent	Passé Composé	Imparfait	Futur			
se laver							
je	me lave	me suis lavé(e)	me lavais	me laverai		me lave	me laverais
tu	te laves	t'es lavé(e)	te lavais	te laveras	lave-toi	te laves	te laverais
il / elle / on	se lave	s'est lavé(e)	se lavait	se lavera		se lave	se laverait
nous	nous lavons	nous sommes lavé(e)s	nous lavions	nous laverons	lavons-nous	nous lavions	nous laverions
vous	vous lavez	vous êtes lavé(e)(s)	vous laviez	vous laverez	lavez-vous	vous laviez	vous laveriez
ils / elles	se lavent	se sont lavé(e)s	se lavaient	se laveront		se lavent	se laveraient

Verbs with Stem Changes

Infinitif	Présent	Passé Composé	Imparfait	Futur	Impératif	Subjonctif	Conditionnel
acheter							
j'	achète	ai acheté	achetais	achèterai		achète	achèterais
tu	achètes	as acheté	achetais	achèteras	achète	achètes	achèterais
il / elle / on	achète	a acheté	achetait	achètera		achète	achèterait
nous	achetons	avons acheté	achetions	achèterons	achetons	achetions	achèterions
vous	achetez	avez acheté	achetiez	achèterez	achetez	achetiez	achèteriez
ils / elles	achètent	ont acheté	achetaient	achèteront		achètent	achèteraient
appeler							
j'	appelle	ai appelé	appelais	appellerai		appelle	appellerais
tu	appelles	as appelé	appelais	appelleras	appelle	appelles	appellerais
il / elle / on	appelle	a appelé	appelait	appellera		appelle	appellerait
nous	appelons	avons appelé	appelions	appellerons	appelons	appelions	appellerions
vous	appelez	avez appelé	appeliez	appellerez	appelez	appeliez	appelleriez
ils / elles	appellent	ont appelé	appelaient	appelleront		appellent	appelleraient
posséder							
je / j'	possède	ai possédé	possédais	posséderai		possède	posséderais
tu	possèdes	as possédé	possédais	posséderas	possède	possèdes	posséderais
il / elle / on	possède	a possédé	possédait	possédera		possède	posséderait
nous	possédons	avons possédé	possédions	posséderons	possédons	possédions	posséderions
vous	possédez	avez possédé	possédiez	posséderez	possédez	possédiez	posséderiez
ils / elles	possèdent	ont possédé	possédaient	posséderont		possèdent	posséderaient

Irregular Verbs

Infinitif	Indicatif				Impératif	Subjonctif	Conditionnel
	Présent	Passé Composé	Imparfait	Futur			
aller							
je / j'	vais	suis allé(e)	allais	irai		aille	irais
tu	vas	es allé(e)	allais	iras	va	ailles	irais
il / elle / on	va	est allé(e)	allait	ira		aille	irait
nous	allons	sommes allé(e)s	allions	irons	allons	allions	irions
vous	allez	êtes allé(e)(s)	alliez	irez	allez	alliez	iriez
ils / elles	vont	sont allé(e)s	allaient	iront		aillent	iraient
boire							
je / j'	bois	ai bu	buvais	boirai		boive	boirais
tu	bois	as bu	buvais	boiras	bois	boives	boirais
il / elle / on	boit	a bu	buvait	boira		boive	boirait
nous	buvons	avons bu	buvions	boirons	buvons	buvions	boirions
vous	buvez	avez bu	buviez	boirez	buvez	buviez	boiriez
ils / elles	boivent	ont bu	buvaient	boiront		boivent	boiraient
connaître							
je / j'	connais	ai connu	connaissais	connaîtrai		connaisse	connaîtrais
tu	connais	as connu	connaissais	connaîtras	connais	connaisses	connaîtrais
il / elle / on	connaît	a connu	connaissait	connaîtra		connaisse	connaîtrait
nous	connaissons	avons connu	connaissions	connaîtrons	connaissons	connaissions	connaîtrions
vous	connaissez	avez connu	connaissiez	connaîtrez	connaissez	connaissiez	connaîtriez
ils / elles	connaissent	ont connu	connaissaient	connaîtront		connaissent	connaîtraient

Infinitif	Indicatif				Impératif	Subjonctif	Conditionnel
	Présent	Passé Composé	Imparfait	Futur			
devoir							
je / j'	dois	ai dû	devais	devrai		doive	devrais
tu	dois	as dû	devais	devras	dois	doives	devrais
il / elle / on	doit	a dû	devait	devra		doive	devrait
nous	devons	avons dû	devions	devrons	devons	devions	devrions
vous	devez	avez dû	deviez	devrez	devez	deviez	devriez
ils / elles	doivent	ont dû	devaient	devront		doivent	devraient
dire							
je / j'	dis	ai dit	disais	dirai		dise	dirais
tu	dis	as dit	disais	diras	dis	dises	dirais
il / elle / on	dit	a dit	disait	dira		dise	dirait
nous	disons	avons dit	disions	dirons	disons	disions	dirions
vous	dites	avez dit	disiez	direz	dites	disiez	diriez
ils / elles	disent	ont dit	disaient	diront		disent	diraient
faire							
je / j'	fais	ai fait	faisais	ferai		fasse	ferais
tu	fais	as fait	faisais	feras	fais	fasses	ferais
il / elle / on	fait	a fait	faisait	fera		fasse	ferait
nous	faisons	avons fait	faisions	ferons	faisons	fassions	ferions
vous	faites	avez fait	faisiez	ferez	faites	fassiez	feriez
ils / elles	font	ont fait	faisaient	feront		fassent	feraient

Infinitif		Indicatif				Impératif	Subjonctif	Conditionnel
		Présent	Passé Composé	Imparfait	Futur			
falloir	il	faut	a fallu	fallait	faudra		faille	faudrait
mettre	je / j'	mets	ai mis	mettais	mettrai		mette	mettrais
	tu	mets	as mis	mettais	mettras	mets	mettes	mettrais
	il / elle / on	met	a mis	mettait	mettra		mette	mettrait
	nous	mettons	avons mis	mettions	mettrons	mettons	mettions	mettrions
	vous	mettez	avez mis	mettiez	mettrez	mettez	mettiez	mettriez
	ils / elles	mettent	ont mis	mettaient	mettront		mettent	mettraient
pleuvoir	il	pleut	a plu	pleuvait	pleuvra		pleuve	pleuvrait

Infinitif	Indicatif				Impératif	Subjonctif	Conditionnel
	Présent	Passé Composé	Imparfait	Futur			
pouvoir							
je / j'	peux	ai pu	pouvais	pourrai		puisse	pourrais
tu	peux	as pu	pouvais	pourras		puisses	pourrais
il / elle / on	peut	a pu	pouvait	pourra		puisse	pourrait
nous	pouvons	avons pu	pouvions	pourrons		puissions	pourrions
vous	pouvez	avez pu	pouviez	pourrez		puissiez	pourriez
ils / elles	peuvent	ont pu	pouvaient	pourront		puissent	pourraient
prendre							
je / j'	prends	ai pris	prenais	prendrai		prenne	prendrais
tu	prends	as pris	prenais	prendras	prends	prennes	prendrais
il / elle / on	prend	a pris	prenait	prendra		prenne	prendrait
nous	prenons	avons pris	prenions	prendrons	prenons	prenions	prendrions
vous	prenez	avez pris	preniez	prendrez	prenez	preniez	prendriez
ils / elles	prennent	ont pris	prenaient	prendront		prennent	prendraient
recevoir							
je / j'	reçois	ai reçu	recevais	recevrai		reçoive	recevrais
tu	reçois	as reçu	recevais	recevras	reçois	reçoives	recevrais
il / elle / on	reçoit	a reçu	recevait	recevra		reçoive	recevrait
nous	recevons	avons reçu	recevions	recevrons	recevons	recevions	recevrions
vous	recevez	avez reçu	receviez	recevrez	recevez	receviez	recevriez
ils / elles	reçoivent	ont reçu	recevaient	recevront		reçoivent	recevraient

Infinitif	Indicatif				Impératif	Subjonctif	Conditionnel
	Présent	Passé Composé	Imparfait	Futur			
savoir							
je / j'	sais	ai su	savais	saurai		sache	saurais
tu	sais	as su	savais	sauras	sache	saches	saurais
il / elle / on	sait	a su	savait	saura		sache	saurait
nous	savons	avons su	savions	saurons	sachons	sachions	saurions
vous	savez	avez su	saviez	saurez	sachez	sachiez	sauriez
ils / elles	savent	ont su	savaient	sauront		sachent	sauraient
suivre							
je / j'	suis	ai suivi	suivais	suivrai		suive	suivrais
tu	suis	as suivi	suivais	suivras	suis	suives	suivrais
il / elle / on	suit	a suivi	suivait	suivra		suive	suivrait
nous	suivons	avons suivi	suivions	suivrons	suivons	suivions	suivrions
vous	suivez	avez suivi	suiviez	suivrez	suivez	suiviez	suivriez
ils / elles	suivent	ont suivi	suivaient	suivront		suivent	suivraient
tenir							
je / j'	tiens	ai tenu	tenais	tiendrai		tienne	tiendrais
tu	tiens	as tenu	tenais	tiendras	tiens	tiennes	tiendrais
il / elle / on	tient	a tenu	tenait	tiendra		tienne	tiendrait
nous	tenons	avons tenu	tenions	tiendrons	tenons	tenions	tiendrions
vous	tenez	avez tenu	teniez	tiendrez	tenez	teniez	tiendriez
ils / elles	tiennent	ont tenu	tenaient	tiendront		tiennent	tiendraient

Infinitif		Indicatif				Impératif	Subjonctif	Conditionnel
		Présent	Passé Composé	Imparfait	Futur			
venir								
	je	viens	suis venu(e)	venais	viendrai		vienne	viendrais
	tu	viens	es venu(e)	venais	viendras	viens	viennes	viendrais
	il / elle / on	vient	est venu(e)	venait	viendra		vienne	viendrait
	nous	venons	sommes venu(e)s	venions	viendrons	venons	venions	viendrions
	vous	venez	êtes venu(e)(s)	veniez	viendrez	venez	veniez	viendriez
	ils / elles	viennent	sont venu(e)s	venaient	viendront		viennent	viendraient
voir								
	je / j'	vois	ai vu	voyais	verrai		voie	verrais
	tu	vois	as vu	voyais	verras	vois	voies	verrais
	il / elle / on	voit	a vu	voyait	verra		voie	verrait
	nous	voyons	avons vu	voyions	verrons	voyons	voyions	verrions
	vous	voyez	avez vu	voyiez	verrez	voyez	voyiez	verriez
	ils / elles	voient	ont vu	voyaient	verront		voient	verraient
vouloir								
	je / j'	veux	ai voulu	voulais	voudrai		veuille	voudrais
	tu	veux	as voulu	voulais	voudras	veuille	veuilles	voudrais
	il / elle / on	veut	a voulu	voulait	voudra		veuille	voudrait
	nous	voulons	avons voulu	voulions	voudrons	veuillons	voulions	voudrions
	vous	voulez	avez voulu	vouliez	voudrez	veuillez	vouliez	voudriez
	ils / elles	veulent	ont voulu	voulaient	voudront		veuillent	voudraient

VOCABULAIRES ....

Français-anglais

The French-English vocabulary contains all the French words in this text except obvious cognates that are not active vocabulary items.

A number following a definition of a word indicates the chapter in which it first appears as an active vocabulary item. (P) indicates **Chapitre Préliminaire.**

A number-letter combination indicates the appearance of a new word in a chapter's **Lecture culturelle** (L) or **Communiquons** (C) section. Your instructor may or may not require you to include these entries in your active French vocabulary. Passive vocabulary has no chapter reference.

All nouns have gender markers (*m.* or *f.*). All adjectives appear in the masculine form followed by the feminine ending or feminine form. Plural forms of nouns or adjectives are indicated by the abbreviation *pl.*

Irregular verbs are followed by chapter references indicating when each verb first appears. If the infinitive or a verb form appears in the textbook prior to the presentation of the complete conjugation of the verb, the chapter in which the conjugation of the verb form appears is indicated by the reference forms + chapter number. An asterisk indicates aspirate **h.**

(Compiled by Christine Fau, Ph.D. candidate, University of Georgia.)

A

à   at, in, to (1)
—— bientôt   see you soon (P)
—— cause de   because of (6–L)
—— cheval   on horseback (6)
—— côté de   next to (4)
—— demain   see you tomorrow (1–C)
—— droite   right, to the right (4–C)
—— gauche   left (16)
—— ...kilomètres de   . . . kilometers away (14–C)
—— l'américaine   American-style (3–L)
—— la prochaine   see you next time (1–C)
—— la tienne / à la vôtre   cheers; to your health (14)
—— l'étranger   abroad (4–L)
—— l'extérieur   outside (5)
—— l'heure   on time (6)
—— partir de   starting with; from (16)
—— pied   on foot (6)
—— plus tard   until later (P)
—— qui   to whom (7)
—— tout à l'heure   see you a little later (1–C)
—— travers   through (18–L)
abonné(e) m., f.   subscriber (7–L)
abonnement m.   subscription (16–C)
s'abonner   to subscribe (16–C)
aborder   to approach (11–L)
absent(e)   absent (2)
absolument   absolutely (11)
accent m.   accent
—— aigu   acute accent
—— circonflexe   circumflex accent
—— grave   grave accent
accepter   to accept (15)
accident m.   accident (10)
accord m.   agreement
d'——   O.K. (10)
être d'——   to agree (15–C)
accorder   to grant (15–L)
accueillir   to receive (11–L)

achat m.   purchase (5)
faire des ——s   to go shopping (5)
acheter   to buy (3–L; 5)
acteur m.   actor (2)
actif (-ive)   working (2–L)
actrice f.   actress (2)
actualités f. pl.   news (11)
actuel(le)   present (2–L)
addition f.   check (in a restaurant) (9–C)
adorer   to adore (1)
adresse f.   address (8)
aérogramme m.   air letter (8)
aéroport m.   airport (10)
affaire f.   business (7–L)
——s f. pl.   possessions, things (7)
affectueux (-euse)   affectionate (2)
affichage m.   posting (17–L)
affiche f.   poster (1)
affluer   to rush (15–L)
affolé(e)   frantic (18–L)
affreux (-euse)   awful (2)
afin de   in order to (14–L)
Afrique f.   Africa (4)
—— du Nord   North Africa (18)
âge m.   age (3)
agence de voyages f.   travel agency (4)
agenda m.   calendar
agent de police m.   police officer (2)
agglomération f.   metropolitan area (9–L)
agneau m.   lamb (3)
agréable   pleasant (2)
agréer   to accept (15–C)
ah non   oh no (4)
ailleurs   elsewhere (18)
aimer   to like, to love (1)
—— bien   to be fond of, to like (2)
—— faire   to like to do (2)
—— mieux   to prefer (2)
ainsi   thus (5–L)
air
avoir l'——   to look, to appear to be (5)
aire de jeu f.   playground (8–L)

ajouter   to add (14–C)
alcool m.   alcohol (3)
Algérie f.   Algeria (4)
algérien(ne)   Algerian (18)
alimentation f.   food (12–L)
Allemagne f.   Germany (4)
allemand(e)   German (2)
aller   to go (4)
—— mieux   to feel better (13)
—— voir   to visit (8)
allez-y!   go ahead! (4)
allons-y!   let's go! (4)
on y va?   shall we go? (4)
vas-y!   go ahead! (4)
allô   hello (7)
allumer   to turn on (light; TV) (7)
alors   then (1)
—— !   well (13)
—— que   while (15–L)
alphabet m.   alphabet (1)
alpinisme m.   mountain climbing (14)
ambitieux (-euse)   ambitious (2)
amélioration f.   improvement (2–L)
améliorer   to improve (12–L)
amener   to bring (6–L; 13)
américain(e)   American (2)
Amérique f.   America (4)
—— du Nord   North America (4)
—— du Sud   South America (4)
ami(e) m., f.   friend (1)
amicalement   sincerely (15–C)
amitiés f. pl.   fondly (15–C)
amour m.   love (11)
amoureusement   lovingly (17)
s'amuser   to have a good time (13)
an m.   year (1–L; 3)
tous les ——s   every year (5)
ancien(ne)   older, former (2)
anglais(e)   English (1)
Anglais(e)   English person (2)
Angleterre f.   England (4)
anglophone   English-speaking (16–L)
animal m. (pl. -aux)   animal (18)
animateur m.   organizer (18–L)
année f.   year (1–L; 4)
—— scolaire   school year (8)

anniversaire *m.* birthday (9–C)

—— **de mariage** wedding anniversary (9–C)

annonce *f.*: petite —— classified ad (16)

annuaire *m.* phone book (7–C)

annulation *f.* cancellation (9–C)

anthropologie *f.* anthropology (8)

Antillais(e) from the Antilles (18–L)

août *m.* August (4–L; 6)

s'apercevoir to find out (17–L)

apéritif *m.* before-dinner drink (3)

apparaître to appear (13–L)

appareil *m.*

à l'—— on the phone (7)

—— **électro-ménager** appliance (16)

appartement *m.* apartment (4)

appartenir (à) to belong to (10)

appeler to call (13)

s'—— to be called, named (13)

apport *m.* contribution (16–L)

apporter to bring (3)

apprécier to appreciate (2)

apprendre to learn (9)

—— **(à)** to teach (15)

s'approcher (de) to get closer (18)

après after (1)

après-midi *m.* afternoon (4)

aquarelle *f.* watercolor (15)

arabe Arabic (8)

arbre *m.* tree (17)

architecte *m., f.* architect (2)

architecture *f.* architecture (8)

argent *m.* money (3)

—— **de poche** allowance (12–C)

armoire *f.* armoire (16)

arrêt *m.*

—— **d'autobus** bus stop (4)

arrêter to stop (11)

s'—— to stop (6–L)

arrivée *f.* arrival (8)

arriver to arrive (1); to happen (7)

arrondissement *m.* district (8–L)

art *m.* art (8)

article *m.* newspaper article (15)

—— **de sport** *m.* sports article (12)

artiste *m., f.* artist (2)

artistique artistic (15)

ascenseur *m.* elevator (9–L)

Asie *f.* Asia (4)

asperge *f.* asparagus (9)

assaillir to attack

assainissement *m.* decontamination (13–L)

assez rather (18)

—— **de** enough (3–C)

j'en ai ——! I've had it! (17–C)

assiette *f.* plate (9–C)

assister (à) to witness (5–L); to attend (15–L)

assurance *f.*

—— **tous risques** full collision insurance (10)

attacher to fasten

atteinte *f.* affront (15)

attendre to wait for (9)

attention *f.*: faire —— to pay attention (5)

attirer to attract (8–L)

—— **l'attention** to draw attention (4–C)

au (*contraction* **à** + **le**) to the, in the, at the (2)

—— **bord de** alongside (4)

—— **coin de** at the corner of (4)

—— **fond** at the bottom (18–L)

—— **lieu de** instead of (6–L)

—— **revoir** good-bye (P)

aucun(e) not any (13–L)

augmenter to increase (7–L; 17)

aujourd'hui today (1–L; 4)

auprès with (18–L)

—— **de** to (14–L)

aussi also, too (2)

——... **que** as . . . as (18)

aussitôt que as soon as (17)

autant as much, as many (11–L; 18)

auteur *m.* author (2)

—— **dramatique** playwright (15)

auto *f.* car (6)

autobus *m.* bus (1)

autocar *m.* inter-city bus (6)

auto-école *f.* driving school (10–C)

automatique automatic (10)

automne *m.* fall (6)

autoroute *f.* interstate highway (17–L)

autre other (1–L; 4)

—— **chose** something else (12)

autrefois in the past (8–L)

autrement otherwise (12–L)

—— **dit** in other words (18–L)

Autriche *f.* Austria (4)

avance *f.* advance (6)

d'—— ahead (14)

en —— early (6)

avant before (6)

avant-poste *m.* outpost (13–L)

avec with (1)

avènement *m.* advent (6–L)

avenir *m.* future (11)

avion *m.* airplane (6)

avocat(e) *m., f.* lawyer (2)

avoir to have (2–L; 3)

——... **an(s)** to be . . . years old (3)

——... (*degrees*) to have a temperature of (14–C)

avril *m.* April (6)

B

bac (bachot, baccalauréat) *m.* exam at the end of high school (1–L)

bachelier (-ère) *m., f.* holder of the bac (1–L)

bagages *m. pl.* baggage (5)

—— **à main** hand luggage (5)

faire les —— to pack (5)

bagnole (*fam.*) *f.* car (18–C)

baignoire *f.* bathtub (16)

bain

prendre des ——s de soleil to sunbathe (4–L)

baiser *m.* kiss (8)

baisse *f.* decrease (6–L)

baisser to drop (12–L)

bal *m.* dance

balle (*fam.*) *f.* franc (12–C)

ballet *m.* ballet (15)

banane *f.* banana (9)

bande dessinée *f.*   comic strip (16–C)

banlieue *f.*   suburb (18–L)

banque *f.*   bank (4)

banquette *f.*   seat (6)

bas(se)   low

base-ball *m.*   baseball (14)

basket-ball *m.*   basketball (14)

basque *m.*   Basque language

bateau *m. (pl.* **-eaux)**   boat (6)

bâtiment *m.*   building

bâtir   to build (17)

battre   to break (a record) (6–L)

beau (bel, belle[s], beaux)   handsome, beautiful (9)

   faire ——   to be nice (weather) (5)

beaucoup   much, many, a lot of (1)

beauté *f.*   beauty (15)

beige   beige (6)

Belgique *f.*   Belgium (4)

belle *f.*   beautiful (7)

ben *(fam.)*   um (18–C)

bénévole   voluntary (13–L)

besoin *m.*   need (10)

   avoir —— de   to need (10)

bêtise *f.*   dumb thing (14)

Beur *(fam.) m., f.*   Arab immigrant (18–L)

beurre *m.*   butter (3)

bibliothèque *f.*   library (4)

bicyclette *f.*   bicycle (6)

bidule *(fam.) m.*   thingamajig (11–C)

bien   well (P)

   —— entendu   of course (15–L)

   —— sûr   of course (5)

bientôt   soon (8)

bière *f.*   beer (3)

bifteck *m.*   steak (9)

bijouterie *f.*   jewelry store (12)

billet *m.*   ticket (6)

   —— de banque   bank note (12–C)

biologie *f.*   biology (8)

biotechnologie *f.*   biotechnology (17)

biscotte *f.*   zwieback (3–L)

bise *f.*   kiss (8)

   faire la ——   to kiss (P)

bistrot *m.*   café (3)

blanc (-che)   white (3)

blessé(e) *m., f.*   injured person (13–L)

bleu(e)   blue (5)

bœuf *m.*   beef (9)

boire   to drink (12)

boisson *f.*   drink (3)

boîte *f.*   club (2)

   —— de nuit   nightclub (2)

bon(ne)   good (9)

   faire ——   to be nice (temperature) (8)

   —— marché   cheap (12–C)

bonne nuit   good night (1–C)

bonbon *m.*   candy (9)

bonheur *m.*   happiness (11)

bonjour   hello (P); bye (in Quebec) (1–C)

bonsoir   good evening, good night (P)

bord *m.*   shore (16–L)

   —— de la mer   seashore (4)

bordé(e)   lined (15–L)

botte *f.*   boot (5)

bottin *m.*   phone book (7–L)

bouche *f.*   mouth (13)

boucher (-ère) *m., f.*   butcher (12)

boucherie *f.*   butcher shop (3–L; 12)

boucle *f.*   buckle, loop, circular itinerary (14–L)

bouffer *(fam.)*   to eat (18–C)

boulanger (-ère) *m., f.*   baker (12)

boulangerie *f.*   bakery (12)

bouleverser   (6–L) to change completely

boulot *(fam.) m.*   job (18–C)

bourgeois(e)   middle-class (15)

Bourgogne *f.*   Burgundy

bout *m.*   end (6)

bouteille *f.*   bottle (7–L; 12)

boutique *f.*   shop (12)

branche *f.*   branch (18)

branché(e) *(fam.) m., f.*   someone in the know (7–L)

brancher   to plug in, to connect (7)

bras *m.*   arm (13)

brasserie *f.*   bar-restaurant (12)

Brésil *m.*   Brazil (4)

breton *m.*   Breton language

brillamment   brilliantly (18)

brillant(e)   brilliant, shiny (18)

bronze *m.*   bronze (15)

se brosser   to brush (13)

brouillard *m.*   fog

   faire du ——   to be foggy (8)

brousse *f.*   bush (13–L)

bruit *m.*   noise (8–L; 11)

   faire du ——   to make noise (11)

brûlé(e)   burned

brûler un feu   to run a red light (10–C)

brun(e)   brown (5)

Bruxelles   Brussels (4)

bulletin météorologique *m.*   weather report

buraliste *m., f.*   tobacco shop owner (12)

bureau *m. (pl.* **-eaux)**   desk (1); office (2)

   —— de change   currency exchange (12–C)

   —— de poste   post office (4)

   —— des objets trouvés   lost and found (6)

   —— de tabac   tobacco shop (7)

C

ça   that, it (9)

   —— alors!   I'll be darned (17–C)

   —— m'est égal   I don't care (17–C)

   —— ne fait rien   it doesn't matter (17–C)

   —— suffit!   enough! (17–C)

   —— va?   how is it going? (P)

   —— va bien   I'm fine (P)

   —— va pas, non?   are you crazy? (17–C)

   —— y est   that's it (5)

cabine *f.*   booth (6–L)

   —— téléphonique   phone booth (7)

cadeau *m. (pl.* **-eaux)**   gift (1)

cadre *m.* middle-level manager (11)

—— **supérieur** upper-level manager (12–L)

café *m.* café (1); coffee (3)

cahier *m.* notebook (1)

caisse *f.* cash register (12)

calculatrice *f.* calculator (7)

calculer to calculate (12–C)

calculette *f.* pocket calculator (7)

calendrier *m.* calendar (6)

camarade *m., f.* friend (2)

—— **de chambre** roommate (2)

—— **de cours** classmate (2)

camion *m.* truck (6)

campagne *f.* country (8)

à la —— in the country (4–L)

camping sauvage *m.* unauthorized camping (4–L)

Canada *m.* Canada (4)

canadien(ne) Canadian (2)

canapé *m.* sofa (16)

canard *m.* duck (18)

capitale *f.* capital (8)

car because (5–L)

caractères *m. pl.* printing (17–L)

caravane *f.* motor home (4–L)

—— **publicitaire** accompanying sponsors' cars and trucks on the Tour de France (14–L)

carnet *m.* book (of tickets) (6)

carotte *f.* carrot (9)

—— **s râpées** grated carrots (9)

carte *f.* map (1); menu (3); card (14)

—— **de crédit** credit card (10)

—— **des vins** wine list (9–C)

—— **postale** postcard (8)

—— **routière** road map (9–L)

carter *m.* gear box (10–L)

casino *m.* casino (4)

casser to break

se —— **le (la, les)...** to break one's . . . (13–C)

tu me casses les pieds! you really annoy me! (17–C)

cassette *f.* cassette (7)

catalan *m.* Catalan language

catch *m.* wrestling (14)

causerie *f.* talk (17–L)

CD *m.* CD (7)

ce this, that, it (7)

—— **n'est pas grand-chose** it's no big deal (17–C)

—— **n'est pas grave** it's not serious (17–C)

—— **n'est pas la peine** it's not necessary (7)

—— **que** what (15–L)

—— **qui** what (18–L)

—— **soir** tonight (1)

c'est à qui? whose turn is it? (6)

c'est, ce sont it is, they are (1)

c'est convenu all right (9–C)

c'est de la part de qui? may I say who's calling? (7–C)

c'est noté I've got it (9–C)

c'est pas vrai! no! (17–C)

ce (cet, cette) this, that (7)

céder to give up (5–L)

ceinture *f.* belt (5)

—— **de sécurité** seat belt (10)

cela that, it (1)

—— **ne fait rien** it doesn't matter (12–C)

célèbre famous (10–L)

célébrité *f.* famous person

celle(s) *f.* this one, that one; these, those (14)

celui *m.* that, that one, this one (14)

censure *f.* censorship (15–L)

cent one hundred (4)

centenaire hundred-year-old (14–L)

centime *m.* 1/100th of a franc (12–C)

centre commercial *m.* shopping center (4)

centre de loisirs *m.* community center (18–L)

centre-ville *m.* downtown (12)

cependant however (2–L)

cerise *f.* cherry (9)

certain(e) certain (2)

certainement certainly (18)

ces these, those (7)

cesser (de) to cease to (15)

cet (cette) this, that (7)

ceux (celles) these, those (5–L; 14)

chacal *m.* jackal (18)

chacun(e) every, each (18–L)

chaîne *f.* channel (11)

—— **stéréo** stereo system (7)

chaise *f.* chair (1)

chaleur *f.* heat (8)

chambre *f.* bedroom (1–L; 4)

—— **de bonne** maid's bedroom (16)

champ *m.* field (4–L; 17)

champion(ne) *m., f.* champion (14)

championnat *m.* championship (14)

chance *f.* luck (6)

changement d'avis *m.* change of mind

changer (de) to change (6)

chanson *f.* song (10)

chantage *m.* blackmail (17–L)

chanter to sing (1)

chapeau *m.* (*pl.* -eaux) hat (5)

—— **haut de forme** top hat (10–L)

chapitre *m.* chapter (14)

chaque each (3–L)

charcuterie *f.* pork butcher shop, cold cuts (9–C; 12)

charcutier (-ère) *m., f.* pork butcher (12)

charges *f. pl.* utilities (16)

charmant(e) charming (2)

chasse *f.* hunting (14)

chassé(e) de forced out of (5–L)

chasseur *m.* hunter (15–L)

chat *m.* cat (18)

château *m.* (*pl.* -eaux) castle (9–L)

chaud(e) hot (1–C; 2)

avoir —— to be hot (3)

faire —— to be warm (weather) (5)

chauffard *m.* reckless driver (10–C)

chauffeur *m.* driver (4–L)

chaussette *f.* sock (5)

chaussure *f.* shoe (5)

chef d'orchestre *m.* conductor (15)

chemin *m.* way (16)

—— **de fer** railway (6–L)

chemise *f.* shirt (5)

—— **de nuit** nightgown (5)

chemisier *m.* blouse (5)

chèque de voyage *m.* traveler's check (12–C)

cher (-ère) expensive (4); dear (8)

chercher to look for (4)

———— **à** to try to (15)

chercheur *m.* researcher (16–L)

cheval *m.* (*pl.* -aux) horse (18)

cheveux *m. pl.* hair (13)

cheville *f.* ankle (13)

chez at the home of (4)

chien *m.* dog (18)

chimie *f.* chemistry (8)

Chine *f.* China (4)

chinois(e) Chinese (8)

chirurgien(ne) surgeon (13–L)

chocolat *m.* chocolate (3)

choisir to choose (7)

———— **de** to choose to (15)

chômage *m.* unemployment (11)

chose *f.* thing (11)

choucroute *f.* sauerkraut (12)

———— **garnie** sauerkraut with meat (12)

chouette alors! great! (17–C)

ci-dessous below

ciel *m.* sky (8)

le ———— **est couvert** it's cloudy (8)

cinéma *m.* cinema, movie theater (1–L; 4)

cinq five (1)

cinquante fifty (2)

cinquième fifth (2)

circulation *f.* traffic (4–L; 10)

cité *f.* high-rise project (18–L)

classe *f.* classroom (1)

classique classical (2)

clavier *m.* keyboard (8)

———— **à touches** keyboard (7–L)

clé *f.* key (7)

client(e) *m., f.* customer (12–C)

clignotant *m.* car signal (10–L)

clôture *f.* end (15–L)

clou *m.* climax (15–L)

club *m.* club (2)

coca *m.* Coca-Cola (3)

cochon *m.* pig (18)

code de la route *m.* traffic regulations (10–C)

coffre *m.* trunk (10)

coiffeur (-euse) *m., f.* hairdresser (12–L)

coin *m.* corner, area (5–L; 9)

colère *f.* anger (17–C)

colis *m.* package (8)

colon *m.* settler (16–L)

combien how many, how much (1)

———— **de** how many, how much (6)

———— **de temps?** how long (6)

———— **font?** how much are (1)

comédie *f.* comedy (15)

———— **musicale** musical (15)

commande *f.* order (10–L; 12)

commander to order (3)

comme as, like (3); how (9)

———— **ci,** ———— **ça** so-so (P)

commencer to begin (1)

———— **à** to begin to (15)

comment how (6)

———— **allez-vous?** how are you? (P)

———— **ça va?** how is it going? (P)

———— **dit-on?** how does one say? (1)

———— **est-il?** what is it like? (6)

———— **vous appelez-vous?** what's your name? (1)

commerçant(e) *m., f.* merchant (12)

communication *f.*

———— **internationale** international call (8–C)

———— **interurbaine** long-distance call (8–C)

———— **locale** local call (8–C)

compagnie de location *f.* rental agency (10)

comparer to compare (17)

compétent(e) competent (2)

complet (-ète) complete, full (1–L; 18)

complètement completely (18)

compliqué(e) complicated (2)

comporter to include (9–L)

composer un numéro de téléphone to dial a number (7–C)

comprendre to understand (9)

compris(e) included (9–L; 16)

compte en banque *m.* bank account (7–L; 11)

concert *m.* concert (6)

concierge *m., f.* concierge (16)

concombre *m.* cucumber (9)

concurrence: faire ———— to compete with (6–L)

concurrencer to compete with (6–L)

concurrent *m.* rival (6–L)

conducteur *m.* driver (10)

conduire to drive (10; forms 14)

se ———— to behave (14)

confier to entrust (15–L)

confiture *f.* jam (3)

congés *m. pl.* vacation (4–L)

connaissance *f.* acquaintance (1–C; 2)

faire la ———— **de** to meet (2–C)

connaître to know (8–L; 10)

consacré(e) devoted (15)

consacrer to devote (12–L)

conscient(e) aware (2–L)

conseil *m.* piece of advice (11)

conseiller to advise (12)

conserver to keep, to preserve (16–L)

conserves *f. pl.* canned foods (12)

consommer to drink (3)

construction *f.* construction (17)

construire to build (17)

construit(e) built (8–L)

consulter to consult (11)

conte *m.* tale (14)

contemporain(e) contemporary (11)

contenir to include, to contain (9–L; 10)

content(e) happy (2)

continent *m.* continent (4)

continuer to continue (1)

———— **à** to continue to (15)

contravention *f.* traffic ticket

contre against (18–L)

contribuer to contribute (15)

contrôle anti-doping *m.* drug test (14)

convenir to be suited (11–L)

convoité(e) coveted (14–L)

copain *m.* pal, buddy (male) (2)

copine *f.* pal, friend (female) (2)

coq *m.* rooster (18)

cordialement cordially (15–C)

corps *m.* body (13)

correct(e) correct (15)

correspondance *f.* subway station with connecting lines (6)

corriger to correct

Corse *f.* Corsica (4)

corse *m.* Corsican language

costume *m.* suit (5)

côte *f.* coast (14–L)

Côte d'Azur *f.* Riviera (4)

Côte-d'Ivoire *f.* Côte d'Ivoire (4)

côtelette *f.* chop (9)

cou *m.* neck (13)

se **coucher** to go to bed (13)

couchette *f.* train seat for sleeping (6–L)

couleur *f.* color (5)

coupable guilty (18–L)

couper to hang up (7)

courageux (-euse) courageous (2)

courant(e) widespread

coureur *m.* racer (14–L)

courir to run (18)

couronné(e) crowned

courrier *m.* mail (8)

—— **du cœur** advice column (16–C)

cours *m.* class (1); course (8)

en —— in class (1)

course *f.* errand (5); race (14)

—— **de bicyclettes** bicycle race (14)

—— **de voitures** car race (14)

faire des ——s to run errands (5)

couscous *m.* couscous (3)

cousin(e) *m., f.* cousin (2)

couteau *m.* (*pl.* -eaux) knife (9–C)

coûter to cost (5)

——... **le kilo** to cost ... a kilo (14–C)

couvert *m.* table setting (9–C)

couverture *f.* cover (11–L)

craie *f.* chalk (1)

cravate *f.* tie (5)

crayon *m.* pencil (1)

créer to create (4–L)

crème *f.* cream (3)

crémerie *f.* dairy shop (12)

créole Creole (5)

crêpe *f.* crepe (5)

crevette *f.* shrimp (9)

criminalité *f.* crime (11)

crise de foie *f.* liver attack (13–C)

critiqué(e) criticized (15)

croire to believe (17–C)

croissance *f.* growth (16–L)

croissant(e) increasing (2–L)

croix verte *f.* green cross (for a drug store) (13)

crudités *f. pl.* vegetable salad (9)

cuillère *f.* spoon (9–C)

petite —— teaspoon (9–C)

cuisine *f.* cooking (3); kitchen (16)

—— **minceur** *f.* low-calorie cooking (3–L)

faire la —— to cook (5)

cuisinière *f.* stove (16)

cure *f.*

faire une —— to go to a health spa (13–C)

curiste *m., f.* person going to a health spa (13–C)

D

d'abord at first (7)

d'accord O.K. (10)

être —— to agree (15–C)

dame *f.* lady (8)

Danemark *m.* Denmark (4)

dangereux (-euse) dangerous (2)

dans in (3); in (time) (16)

—— **l'ensemble** as a whole (16–L)

danse classique *f.* ballet (15)

danser to dance (1)

danseur (-euse) *m., f.* dancer (15)

date *f.* date (6)

d'autant plus all the more (17–L)

d'avance ahead (14)

davantage more (13)

de, de l', de la some, any (3)

de of, from, about (1)

—— **bonne heure** early (12)

—— **plus** furthermore (2–L)

—— **plus en plus** more and more (5–L)

—— **rien** you're welcome (1)

débordé(e) overwhelmed (18–L)

début *m.* beginning (6)

décembre *m.* December (6)

déception *f.* disappointment (15–L)

décerner to award (15–L)

décider (de) to decide to (6)

découverte *f.* discovery (14–L)

découvrir to discover

décrire to describe (14)

décrocher to pick up (the phone) (7–C)

déçu(e) disappointed (17–C)

défaut *m.* fault

défendre to forbid (15)

défense *f.* prohibition (10–C)

dégueulasse *(fam.)* disgusting (18–C)

dehors outside (2–L)

en —— outside (2–L)

déjà already (5)

déjeuner to have lunch (3)

déjeuner *m.* lunch (9)

délaissé(e) abandoned (18–L)

délibération *f.* deliberation (15–L)

délicieux (-euse) delicious (3)

deltaplane *m.* hang glider (14)

demain tomorrow (4)

—— **matin** tomorrow morning (4)

—— **soir** tomorrow night (4)

demander to ask (1); to ask for (15)

—— **son chemin** to ask directions (4–C)

se —— to wonder (17–L)

démarrer to start (car) (10)

démarreur *m.* starter (10–L)

demi(e) half (6)

demi-journée *f.* half day (6–L)

dénatalité *f.* decline in birth rate (17–L)

dent *f.* tooth (13)

dentiste *m., f.* dentist (13)

dépanner to make an emergency repair (10–L)

départ *m.* start (14–L)

département *m.* administrative division in France (5)

se dépêcher to hurry (8–L; 13)

dépenser to spend (8)

depuis since, for (6)
——— **longtemps** for a long time (6)
dernier (-ère) last (2)
derrière behind (4)
des some (3)
dès from . . . on, as of (10–L; 16)
——— **que** as soon as (17)
désagréable unpleasant (2)
désastre *m.* disaster (11)
descendre to get off (6); to go down (9)
se déshabiller to undress (13)
désintéressé(e) unselfish (13–L)
désirer to want (2)
désobéir to disobey (7)
désolé(e) sorry (7)
dessin animé *m.* cartoon (11)
destinataire *m., f.* addressee (15–C)
destruction *f.* destruction (15)
se détendre to relax (13)
détente *f.* relaxation
détester to detest, to hate (2)
——— **faire** to hate to do (2)
deux two (1)
——— **heures** two o'clock (3–L)
deuxième second (2)
devant in front of (2)
devenir to become (10)
devenu(e) become (6–L)
deviner to guess
devoir to have to, to owe (12)
devoirs *m. pl.* homework (1)
——— **écrits** written work (8)
dialogue *m.* dialogue (1)
Dieu *m.* God (18)
différent(e) different (9)
difficile difficult (2)
diffuser to broadcast (7–L)
dimanche *m.* Sunday (6)
diminuer to decrease (10–L; 17)
dîner to have dinner (3)
dîner *m.* dinner (9)
dingue *(fam.)* nuts (18–C)
diplomate *m., f.* diplomat (2)
dire to tell, to say (6–L; 14)
  comment dit-on? how do you say? (1)

ce qu'ils disent what they say (1)
vouloir ——— to mean (1)
direct: en ——— live (14–L)
directement directly
discours *m.* speech (18–L)
discuter to discuss (11)
dis donc! say! (1–C)
disparaître to disappear (8–L)
disparition *f.* disappearance (8–L)
dispensaire *m.* community clinic (13–L)
disque *m.* record (1)
——— **compact** compact disk (7)
disquette *f.* disk (8)
distingué(e) distinguished (15–C)
distraction *f.* entertainment, amusement (2)
divan *m.* sofa (16)
divertir to entertain (11–L)
divisé(e) divided (1)
diviser to divide (14–C)
dix ten (1)
dix-huit eighteen (1)
dix-neuf nineteen (1)
dix-sept seventeen (1)
d'occasion used (10)
doigt *m.* finger (13)
DOM (départements d'outre-mer) *m. pl.* overseas departments (P–L)
dommage *m.*
  il est ——— it's too bad (11)
don *m.* donation (13)
donc so, therefore (6–L; 15)
donner to give (1)
——— **un coup de fil** to make a phone call (8–C)
——— **sur** to look out on (16)
dont upon which (11–L)
dormir to sleep (7)
dos *m.* back (13)
douane *f.* customs
doubler to pass (in traffic) (10–C)
douche *f.* shower (16)
douter to doubt (11)
doux (-ce) gentle (18–L)
douze twelve (1)
doyen *m.* dean
drame *m.* drama (15)

se dresser to rise (18–L)
drogue *f.* drug (11)
droit *m.* law (8); right (17–L)
du some, any (3); of the (4)

E

eau *f.* water (3)
——— **minérale** mineral water (3)
écharpe *f.* scarf (5)
échouer à to fail (1–L; 15)
éclair *m.* lightning (8)
éclater to break, to explode (13–L)
école *f.* school (1–L; 3)
——— **secondaire** secondary school (3)
écologie *f.* ecology (17)
écologique ecological (11)
écologiste *m., f.* ecologist (17)
économies *f. pl.:* **faire des** ——— to save money (8)
économiser to save (12–C)
économiste *m., f.* economist (2)
écouter to listen (1)
  j'écoute go ahead (on the phone) (7)
écran *m.* screen (7–L)
écrevisse *f.* crayfish
écrire to write (14)
——— **à** to write someone (15)
écrit(e) written (7–L)
écrit *m.* writing (8)
écrivain *m.* writer (15)
écrivaine *f.* woman writer (Quebec) (2)
éducation *f.* upbringing (2–L); schooling (17–L)
——— **physique** physical education (8)
éduquer to raise (17–L)
effectuer to carry out, to make (17–L)
efficacité *f.* effectiveness (18–L)
s'efforcer de to try (14–L)
également also (16–L)
égalité *f.* equality (11)
église *f.* church (4)
eh bien well then (1)
élan du cœur *m.* emotional commitment (18–L)

élève *m., f.*   pupil (1–L; 3)

élevé(e)   high

elle   she, it (1)

elles   they (1); them (5)

élu(e)   elected

embêter   to annoy (11)

embourgeoisé(e)   gentrified (10–L)

embouteillage *m.*   traffic jam (10)

embrasser   to kiss (2)

émission *f.*   program, show (5–L; 11)

emmener   to take (someone) (13)

s'emparer   to pick up (18–L)

emploi *m.*   job (11)

———— **du temps**   schedule

employé(e) *m., f.*   employee (6)

empoisonner   to poison (11–L)

emporter   to carry (5)

emprunter   to borrow (8)

en   to, in (4); some, any (15); in (time) (16)

———— **face de**   in front of (4)

enchanté(e)   pleased (2)

encombré(e)   jammed (4–L)

encore   still, again (2–L; 6); more (9–C)

endettement *m.*   debt (12–L)

s'endormir   to fall asleep (13)

endroit *m.*   place (4)

énergie *f.*   energy (3–C; 17)

enfance *f.*   childhood

enfant *m., f.*   child (1)

enfin   at last (16)

engagement *m.*   commitment (12–L)

engin *(fam.) m.*   thingamajig (11–C)

enjeu *m.*   stake (6–L)

enlever   to remove (13)

ennuyeux (-euse)   boring (2)

enrayer   to stop, to check (13–L)

enseignement *m.*   teaching, education (15)

enseigner   to teach (15)

ensemble   together (1)

ensuite   then (4–C)

entendre   to hear (9)

entier (-ère)   whole (15–L)

entre   between (2–L; 4)

entrée *f.*   entrance, hall (16)

entreprise *f.*   company (4–C)

entrer (à, dans)   to enter, to go in (1–L; 2)

entretien *m.*   maintenance (10–C)

envahir   to invade (4–L)

enveloppe *f.*   envelope (8)

envie *f.*: avoir ———— **de**   to feel like (11)

environ   about (11–L)

environnement *m.*   environment (17)

envoyer   to send (8–C)

s'épanouir   to flourish (16–L)

épargner   to save (12–L)

épaule *f.*   shoulder (13)

épice *f.*   spice (16–L)

épicerie *f.*   grocery store (3–C; 12)

épicier (-ère) *m., f.*   grocer (12)

épidermique   immediate (17–L)

épier   to watch, to spy on (15–L)

épinards *m. pl.*   spinach (9)

époque *f.*   era (10–L)

épreuve *f.*   test (14–L)

   mettre à l'————   to test (14–L)

équipe *f.*   team (13–L; 14)

équipement électro-ménager *m.*   household appliances (12–L)

équitation *f.*   horseback riding (14)

erreur *f.*   wrong number (7)

escalope (de veau) *f.*   veal steak (9)

esclave *m., f.*   slave (5–L)

escrime *f.*   fencing (14)

espace *m.*   space (17)

Espagne *f.*   Spain (4)

espagnol(e)   Spanish (2)

espérer   to hope (9)

espoir *m.*   hope (8–L)

essayer   to try (12)

essence *f.*   gas (10–C)

est *m.*   east (4–C)

est-ce que   is, are, does, do, . . . (1)

estimer   to believe, to think (16–L)

et   and (P)

———— **après?**   so what? (17–C)

———— **toi**   and you (P)

———— **vous**   and you (P)

établissement *m.*   establishment (9–L)

étage *m.*   floor (16)

étagère *f.*   shelf (16)

étalement *m.*   spreading (14–L)

étape *f.*   stage (14)

———— **contre la montre**   part of a race where the fastest time wins (14–L)

état *m.*   condition (15)

Etats-Unis *m. pl.*   United States (4)

été *m.*   summer (5)

étendu(e)   extended (6–L)

éternuer   to sneeze

étoile *f.*   star (9–L; 17)

étonné(e)   surprised (11)

étonnement *m.*   surprise (17–C)

s'étonner   to be astonished, to wonder (17–C)

étranger (-ère)   foreign (3–L; 8)

étranger (-ère) *m., f.*   foreigner (8–L; 10)

être   to be (2)

———— + *adj.* + **de...**   to be . . . to (15)

———— **à**   to belong to (5)

étudiant(e) *m., f.*   student (1)

étudier   to study (1)

euh   uh (18–C)

Europe *f.*   Europe (4)

européen(ne)   European (10)

eux   they, them (5)

événement *m.*   event (14–L)

évidemment   obviously (18)

évident(e)   obvious (11)

évier *m.*   sink (16)

éviter   to avoid (13)

exactement   exactly (8)

examen *m.*   exam (1)

examiner   to examine (13)

excusez-moi   pardon me (1–C)

exemplaire *m.*   copy (10–L)

exercice *m.*   exercise (1)

   faire de l'————   to exercise (13)

exiger   to demand, to require (14–L)

exil *m.*   exile (17)

s'expatrier   to move to a foreign country (16–L)

expédier   to send (8)

expliquer   to explain (1)

explorateur *m.*   explorer

expression *f.*   expression (7)

exprimer   to express

expulsé(e)   expelled (16–L)

extrait *m.*   selection (15)

F

fabriquer to make (10–L)
fac (*fam.*) *f.* college (1)
fâché(e) angry (17–C)
facile easy (2)
facilement easily (2–L; 18)
facteur *m.* postman (8)
facture *f.* bill (7–L)
faculté *f.* college (1)
faible low (17–L)
faim *f.* hunger
  avoir ——— to be hungry (3)
faire to make, to do (5)
  ——— (measure) to be . . . tall (14–C)
  ——— (number) to be . . . degrees (weather) (14–C)
  ——— du (kilomètres/heure) to go (km/hour) (10–C)
  ——— du... aux 100 to get 100 kilometers per . . . liters (10–C)
  ——— du, de la, de l', des to study (8); to play (sport) (14)
  ——— face à to face up to (12–L)
fait *m.* fact (17–L)
  ———s divers human interest stories (16–C)
falloir to be necessary (12)
familier (-ère) colloquial (18–C)
famille *f.* family (2)
  en ——— as a family (1–L)
fantastique fantastic (2)
farine *f.* flour (3)
fascinant(e) fascinating (2)
fatigué(e) tired (2)
fauché(e) (*fam.*) broke (12–C)
faute *f.* mistake (11)
fauteuil *m.* armchair (16)
faux (fausse) false, untrue (11)
  ——— ami *m.* false cognate (1)
favori(te) favorite (2)
féminin(e) feminine (2)
femme *f.* woman (1); wife (2)
fenêtre *f.* window (1)
fermé(e) closed (2)
fermer to shut, to close (1)
  ne pas ——— l'œil not to be able to sleep (13)
fête *f.* holiday (6)

  ——— des Mères Mother's Day (9–C)
  ——— du Travail Labor Day (6)
  ——— nationale national holiday (6)
feu rouge *m.* red light
feuilleton *m.* TV series (11)
février *m.* February (6)
ficher
  fiche-moi la paix! leave me alone! (17–C)
  je m'en fiche! I don't care (17–C)
fier (-ère) proud (16–L)
fièvre *f.* fever (13)
  avoir de la ——— to have a fever (13)
filet *m.* filet (9)
fille *f.* girl, daughter (2)
film *m.* film (2)
fils *m.* son (2)
fin *f.* end (1–L; 17)
finir to end (1–L; 7)
Finlande *f.* Finland (4)
fleur *f.* flower (9–C; 17)
fleuriste *m., f.* florist (12)
fleuve *m.* river (17)
flic (*fam.*) *m.* policeman (18–C)
flotte (*fam.*) *f.* water (18–C)
flûte *f.* flute (15)
fois *f.* time (14–L)
fonder to found (16–L)
football *m.* soccer (2)
  ——— américain football (14)
forêt *f.* forest (17)
formidable wonderful (2)
formule *f.* slogan (18–L)
fort(e) strong, high (17–L)
foule *f.* crowd (14–L)
se fouler le, la... to sprain one's . . . (13–C)
four *m.* oven (16)
  ——— à micro-ondes microwave oven (12–L; 16)
fourchette *f.* fork (9–C)
fournir to provide (13–L)
frais *m. pl.* costs (10)
  faire ——— to be cool (8)
fraise *f.* strawberry (9)
franc *m.* franc (12)
français(e) French (1)
  en ——— in French (1)

France *f.* France (4)
franchise *f.* candor (11)
francophone French-speaking (P–L)
francophonie *f.* French-speaking countries (P)
frein *m.* brake (10)
freiner to brake (10)
fréquemment frequently (18)
fréquent(e) frequent (18)
fréquenter to visit (1–L; 2)
frère *m.* brother (2)
fric (*fam.*) *m.* money (12–C)
frigidaire *m.* refrigerator (16)
frites *f. pl.* French fries (3)
froid(e) cold (1–C; 2)
  avoir ——— to be cold (3)
  faire ——— to be cold (*temperature*) (5)
fromage *m.* cheese (3)
fruit *m.* fruit (3)
  ——— de mer seafood (9)
fuir to flee (13–L)
fumer to smoke (1)
furieux (-euse) furious (11)
futur *m.* future (17)

G

gagnant *m.* winner
gagner to earn (8); to win (14)
galet *m.* pebble (4)
gant *m.* glove (5)
garagiste *m.* mechanic (10–C)
garçon *m.* boy (2); waiter (3)
gare *f.* station (4)
garer to park (2)
gaspiller to waste (12–C)
gastronomie *f.* gourmet cooking (3–L)
gâteau *m.* (*pl.* -eaux) cake (3)
gauche *f.* left (4–C; 16)
  à ——— on the left (4–C; 16)
geler to freeze (10–L)
gendarme *m.* policeman (10)
gêné(e) embarrassed (18–L)
général(e) (*pl.* -aux, -ales) general (18)
  en ——— in general (1)
généralement generally (1–L; 13)
généreux (-euse) generous (2)
Genève Geneva (4)

genou *m.* (*pl.* **-oux**) knee (13)
gens *m. pl.* people (4–L; 10)
—— **d'affaires** business people (6–L)
géographie *f.* geography (8)
géologie *f.* geology (8)
gestion *f.* business (8)
gigantesque gigantic (14–L)
gigot *m.* leg of lamb (9)
glace *f.* ice cream (3)
glissant(e) slippery (10–C)
godasse (*fam.*) *f.* shoe (18–C)
golf *m.* golf (14)
gorge *f.* throat (13)
gosse (*fam.*) *m.* child (18–C)
goûter to taste; to have a snack in the afternoon (3)
grâce à thanks to (6–L)
gramme *m.* gram (12)
grand(e) large, big, tall (9)
—— **es vacances** summer vacation (4–L; 10)
—— **magasin** department store (11)
—— **standing** deluxe (8–L)
grand-chose: ce n'est pas —— it's no big deal (17–C)
Grande-Bretagne *f.* Great Britain (4)
grandir to grow up (8–L)
grand-mère *f.* grandmother (2)
grand-père *m.* grandfather (2)
grands-parents *m. pl.* grandparents (2)
gratuitement for free (7–L)
grave serious (13)
grec (grecque) Greek (8)
Grèce *f.* Greece (4)
grève *f.* strike
faire —— to strike (18–L)
gris(e) gray (5)
gros(se) large, big (6)
—— **titre** *m.* headline (16–C)
grossesse *f.* pregnancy (17–L)
grossier (-ère) crude (18–L)
grossir to augment (17–L)
guerre *f.* war (11)
—— **de Sécession** Civil war (16–L)
—— **mondiale** world war (10–L)

—— **nucléaire** nuclear war (11)
guillemet *m.* quotation mark
guitare *f.* guitar (15)
gymnastique *f.* gymnastics (14)

H

s'habiller to get dressed (13)
habitable livable (17)
habiter to live (1)
habitude *f.* habit, custom (3–L; 10)
hamburger *m.* hamburger (3)
***haricot vert** *m.* green bean (9)
***haut(e)** high
***Haut Conseil** *m.* High Council (5–L)
hebdomadaire *m.* weekly publication (16–C)
hectare *m.* hectare (2.47 acres) (8–L)
hésiter (à) hesitate to (15)
heure *f.* hour, time (6)
de bonne —— early (12)
—— **conventionnelle** conventional time (6–C)
—— **officielle** military time (6–C)
heureusement fortunately (6)
heureux (-euse) happy (2)
Hexagone *m.* France (14–L)
hier yesterday (5)
histoire *f.* history (8)
—— **de l'art** art history (8)
hiver *m.* winter (4–L; 5)
hivernal(e) (*pl.* **-aux, -ales**) winter (16–L)
***hockey** *m.* hockey (14)
***Hollande** *f.* Holland (4)
homme *m.* man (1)
—— **d'affaires** businessman (12–L)
honneur *m.* honor (15–C)
horaire *m.* schedule (6–L)
horizon *m.* horizon (17)
horodateur *m.* parking meter (12–C)
***hors-d'œuvre** *m.* appetizer (3)
hôtel *m.* hotel (1)
hôtesse *f.* hostess (4)
huile *f.* oil (3)

huit eight (1)
hymne *m.* anthem (5–L)
hypermarché *m.* giant supermarket (12)
hypochondriaque hypochondriac (13)
hypocrisie *f.* hypocrisy (2)
hypocrite hypocrite (2)

I

ici here (1)
idée *f.* idea (5)
bonne —— good idea (5)
il he, it (1)
—— **faut** it's necessary (4)
—— **faut que** it's necessary that (11)
—— **n'y a pas de quoi** don't mention it (1)
—— **s'agit de** it's a matter of (15)
—— **se peut que** it's possible that (11)
—— **semble que** it appears that (11)
—— **vaut mieux que** it's better that (11)
—— **y a** there is, there are (3); since, ago (6–L; 16)
île *f.* island
ils they (1)
imam *m.* imam (prayer leader) (18)
immédiatement immediately (14–L)
immeuble *m.* building (8–L; 16)
immigré(e) *m., f.* immigrant (18)
imparfait *m.* imperfect tense (10)
imper (*fam.*) *m.* raincoat (6)
imperméable *m.* raincoat (5)
impoli(e) impolite (2)
importance *f.* importance (11)
important(e) important (11)
impossible impossible (2)
impôt *m.* tax (12–L)
impressionnant(e) impressive (8)
imprimante *f.* printer (8)
incertitude *f.* uncertainty (11)
incompétent(e) incompetent (2)
inconnu *m.* unknown person (1–C)

inconnu(e)   unknown (9–L)
inconvénient *m.*   annoyance (11)
indépendamment   independently (18)
indépendant(e)   independent (1–L; 2)
indiquer   to indicate (9)
indispensable   indispensable (10)
infirmière *f.*   nurse (13–L)
inflation *f.*   inflation (11)
informations *f. pl.*   news (14)
informatique *f.*   computer science (8)
informatisé(e)   computerized (7–L)
ingénieur *m.*   engineer (2)
injuste   unfair (11)
inondation *f.*   flood (13–L)
inoubliable   unforgettable
inquiéter   to worry (13)
   s'———   to worry (13)
inscrire   to register (17–L)
installation *f.*   settlement (16–L)
s'installer   to settle (16–L)
instrument de musique *m.*   musical instrument (15)
insuffisamment   insufficiently (18)
insuffisant(e)   insufficient (15)
insupportable   unbearable (8)
intelligemment   intelligently (18)
intelligent(e)   intelligent (2)
interdiction *f.*   forbidden thing (18–L)
interdit(e)   forbidden (10–C)
intéressant(e)   interesting (2)
intéresser   to interest (16)
   s'——— à   to be interested in (15)
intermariage *m.*   mixed marriage (16–L)
interroger   to ask questions
interrompre   to interrupt
interrompu(e)   interrupted
interview *f.*   interview (11)
intolérance *f.*   intolerance (2)
inutile   useless (2)
invité(e) *m., f.*   guest
inviter   to invite (1)
Irlande *f.*   Ireland (4)
Italie *f.*   Italy (4)
italien(ne)   Italian (2)
ivre   drunk

J

jalousie *f.*   jealousy
jambe *f.*   leg (13)
jambon *m.*   ham (3)
janvier *m.*   January (6)
Japon *m.*   Japan (4)
jardin *m.*   garden (17)
jaune   yellow (5)
jazz *m.*   jazz (2)
je, j'   I (1)
   ——— écoute   go ahead (7)
   ——— m'appelle   my name is (P)
   ——— ne sais pas   I don't know (1)
   ——— vais bien   I'm fine (P)
   ——— voudrais   I would like (3)
   ——— vous en prie   don't mention it (4–C)
jean *m.*   jeans (5)
jeu *m.* (*pl.* jeux)   game (7–L)
   ——— télévisé   game show (11)
jeudi *m.*   Thursday (6)
jeune   young (9)
   ———s gens *m. pl.*   young people (2)
jeunes *m. pl.*   young people (1–L)
jeunesse *f.*   youth (10–L)
jogging *m.*   jogging (14)
joli(e)   pretty (9)
jouer   to play (1)
   ——— à   to play (*game, sport*) (14)
   ——— de   to play (*instrument*) (15)
joueur (-euse) *m., f.*   player (14)
jour *m.*   day (6)
   tous les ———s   every day (3–L; 4)
journal *m.* (*pl.* -aux)   newspaper (14); news on TV (6–C; 11)
journalisme *m.*   journalism (8)
journaliste *m., f.*   journalist (2)
journée *f.*   day (6–C; 13)
juillet *m.*   July (6)
juin *m.*   June (1–L; 6)
jupe *f.*   skirt (5)
jus de fruit *m.*   fruit juice (3)
jusqu'à   until (4–C; 6)
   ——— ce que   until (15–L)
juste   just, fair (11)

   ——— avant   just before (8)
   ——— un peu   just a little (1)
justement   as a matter of fact (6)
justice *f.*   justice (11)

K

kilomètre *m.*   kilometer (10)
kiosque (à journaux) *m.*   newspaper stand (16–C)
klaxon *m.*   horn *(car)* (10)
klaxonner   to honk

L

la (l')   the (1); her, it (8)
là   there (2)
là-bas   over there (4)
laborantin(e) *m., f.*   laboratory assistant (13–L)
laboratoire *m.*   laboratory (4)
lac *m.*   lake (17)
là-dedans   therein (18–L)
laid(e)   ugly (2)
laisser   to leave, to allow (6)
lait *m.*   milk (3)
lampe *f.*   lamp (16)
langage familier *m.*   slang (12–C)
langue *f.*   language (8)
lapin *m.*   rabbit (9)
latin *m.*   Latin (8)
lavabo *m.*   sink (16)
se laver   to wash, to bathe (13)
lave-vaisselle *m.* (*pl.* lave-vaisselle)   dishwasher (12–L; 16)
le (l')   the (1); him, it (8)
   ——— plus   the more (11)
leçon *f.*   lesson (1)
lecteur (-trice) *m., f.*   reader (15)
   ——— de disquettes *m.*   disk drive (8)
   ——— laser *m.*   CD player (7)
lecture *f.*   reading
légume *m.*   vegetable (3)
lendemain *m.*   next day (18–L)
lent(e)   slow (18)
lentement   slowly (8–L; 18)
les   the (1); them (8)
lessive *f.*   washing
   faire la ———   to wash clothes (5)
lettre *f.*   letter (8)
leur   to them (9)

leur(s) their (5)
  le, la, les ———(s) theirs (14)
lever to raise (13)
  se ——— to get up (13)
liaison aérienne *f.* air route (6–L)
librairie *f.* bookstore (4)
libre free (7)
lieu *m.:* **avoir ———** to take place (5–L)
ligne *f.* line (6)
limite de vitesse *f.* speed limit (4–L)
lire to read (14)
Lisbonne Lisbon (4)
lisez read (1)
liste *f.* list (4)
lit *m.* bed (16)
littéraire literary (15)
littérature *f.* literature (8)
livraison *f.* delivery (10–L)
livre *m.* book (1)
livre *f.* pound (3–C)
location *f.* rental (10)
logement *m.* housing (12–L)
logiciel *m.* software (8)
loi *f.* law (10)
loin de far from (4)
loisirs *m. pl.* free time (12–L)
Londres London (4)
longer to follow (15–L)
longtemps a long time (6)
longueur *f.* length (9–L)
lors de during (15–L)
lorsque when (17)
louer to rent (1–L; 10)
Louisiane *f.* Louisiana (16)
loyer *m.* rent (16)
luge *f.* sled (4–L)
lui to her, to him, to it (2, 9)
lundi *m.* Monday (6)
lune *f.* moon (17)
lunettes de soleil *f. pl.* sunglasses (5)
lutte *f.* fight (18–L)
luxe *m.* luxury
lycée *m.* high school (1–L; 4)
lycéen(ne) *m., f.* high school student

M

ma my (5)
machin *(fam.) m.* thingamajig (11–C)

Machin-chouette What's-his-name (11–C)
machine à laver *f.* washing machine (12–L; 16)
Madame *f.* Mrs. (P)
  ——— Unetelle Mrs. So-and-So (11–C)
Mademoiselle *f.* Miss (P)
magasin *m.* store (3–L; 4)
  grand ——— department store (11)
magazine *m.* magazine (14)
Maghreb *m.* North Africa (18)
Maghrébin(e) North African (18)
magnétophone *m.* tape recorder (7)
magnétoscope *m.* video cassette recorder (7)
magnifique magnificent (2)
mai *m.* May (1–L; 6)
maillot *m.* jersey (14)
  ——— de bain bathing suit (5)
main *f.* hand (13)
maintenant now (1–L; 4)
maire *m.* mayor (15–C)
mais but (1)
maison *f.* house (2–L; 4)
maître d'hôtel *m.* maitre d' (9–C)
mal *m.* evil (15)
  avoir ——— to hurt (5)
  avoir ——— à to have an ache (13)
  avoir du ——— à to have trouble (doing) (15)
  faire ——— to hurt (5)
  se faire ——— à to hurt oneself (13)
mal badly (18)
malade sick (13)
malgré despite (6–L)
malheureusement unfortunately (18)
malheureux (-euse) unhappy (2)
Manche *f.* English Channel (6–L)
mandat *m.* money order (8)
manger to eat (1)
manivelle *f.* crank (10–L)
manquer to miss (7–L)
manteau *m.* (*pl.* -eaux) coat (5)
marchand(e) *m., f.* shopkeeper (9)
marchander to bargain (12–C)

marche *f.* protest march (18–L)
marché *m.* market (9)
  ——— aux puces flea market (12–C)
  ——— en plein air open-air market (3–L; 9)
marcher to work, to function (7)
mardi *m.* Tuesday (6)
mari *m.* husband (2)
Maroc *m.* Morocco (4)
Marocain(e) Moroccan (18)
marque *f.* brand (14–L)
marquer to mark (16–L; 17)
marre: j'en ai———! I've had it up to here! (17–C)
mars *m.* March (6)
masculin(e) masculine (2)
match de football *m.* football game (2)
matérialiste materialistic (11)
matériel *m.* hardware (8)
mathématiques *f. pl.* mathematics (8)
matière *f.* subject (8)
matin *m.* morning (4)
matinée *f.* morning (9)
  faire la grasse ——— to sleep late (5)
mauvais(e) bad (2)
  faire ——— to be bad weather (5)
mec *(fam.) m.* guy (18–C)
mécanicien *m.* mechanic (10–C)
méchamment out of meanness (18)
méchant(e) mean, bad (2)
médecin *m.* doctor (2)
médecine *f.* medicine (8)
médias *m. pl.* mass media (14–L)
meilleur(e) better (18)
se mêler to mingle (8–L)
même self (5); even (5–L)
menacé(e) threatened (17–L)
ménage *m.:* **faire le ———** to do housework (5)
mensonge *m.* lie (14)
mensuel *m.* monthly publication (16–C)
mentir to lie (7)
menu *m.* menu, fixed-price meal (3)
mer *f.* sea (4)

merci thank you (P)

———— **mille fois** thanks a million (4)

mercredi *m.* Wednesday (6)

mère *f.* mother (2)

merguez *f.* North African spicy red sausage (3)

mes my (5)

Mesdames *f. pl.* Ladies (1–C)

Mesdemoiselles *f. pl.* Ladies (1–C; 12)

message *m.* message (7)

messagerie rose *f.* adult message service (7–L)

Messieurs *m. pl.* Gentlemen (4)

Messieurs-Dames Ladies and Gentlemen (1–C)

mesure *f.* measurement

mesurer to be . . . tall (14–C)

météo *f.* weather forecast (7–L; 8)

métier *m.* career (15)

———— **artistique** career in the arts (15)

métis *m.* person of mixed race (18–L)

métrage *m.*: **long** ———— full-length feature (11–L)

mètre *m.* meter (14)

métro *m.* subway (6)

mettre to put (17)

se ———— (**à**) to start to (17)

meuble *m.* piece of furniture (12–L; 16)

meublé(e) furnished (16)

meute *f.* herd (15–L)

mexicain(e) Mexican (2)

Mexico Mexico City (4)

Mexique *m.* Mexico (4)

midi *m.* noon (3–L; 6)

Midi *m.* south of France (18–L)

mien(ne) mine (14)

mieux better (2–L; 18)

milieu *m.* (*pl.* -eux) circle (15); middle (16–L)

mille thousand (4)

milliard *m.* billion (4)

million *m.* million (4)

mine *f.*

avoir bonne ———— to look healthy (13)

avoir mauvaise ———— to look sick (13)

Minitel *m.* telephone-linked computer terminal (7–L)

minuit *m.* midnight (6)

minute *f.* minute (4)

moche (*fam.*) ugly (18–C)

mode de vie *m.* life-style (12–L)

moderne modern (2)

moi me (2); myself (9)

moins less (1)

mois *m.* month (4–L; 5)

moitié *f.* half (5–L)

mon my (5)

monde *m.* world (5–L; 11)

mondial(e) (*pl.* -aux, -ales) worldwide (15–L)

moniteur *m.* monitor (8)

monnaie *f.* change (12–C)

Monsieur *m.* Mr., Sir (P)

———— **Untel** Mr. So-and-So (11–C)

montagne *f.* mountain (11)

montant *m.* cost

montée *f.* rise (17–L)

monter to go up (6)

montrer to show (1)

monument *m.* monument (8)

Moscou Moscow (4)

mot *m.* word (5–L; 17)

————**s croisés** *m. pl.* crossword puzzle (16–C)

moto *f.* motorcycle (6)

mourir to die (10)

moutarde *f.* mustard (3)

mouton *m.* mutton (3); sheep (18)

moyen *m.* means (6–L)

Moyen Age *m.* Middle Ages

moyenne *f.* average (14–L)

Mozambique *m.* Mozambique (4)

muezzin *m.* muezzin (18)

multiplié(e) multiplied (1)

multiplier to multiply (14–C)

mur *m.* wall (3)

musée *m.* museum (4)

musicien(ne) *m., f.* musician (2)

musique *f.* music (2)

———— **classique** classical music (2)

N

nager to swim (4–L; 14)

naissance *f.* birth (2–L; 17)

naître to be born (2–L; 6)

nana (*fam.*) *f.* girl (18–C)

natalité *f.* birth rate (17–L)

natation *f.* swimming (14)

nationalité *f.* nationality (2)

nature *f.* nature (17)

naturellement naturally (17–L)

navette *f.* shuttle (17)

navré(e) sorry (17–C)

ne (*negation*) (2)

————**... jamais** never (8)

————**... pas** not (2)

————**... pas encore** not yet (8)

————**... personne** nobody, no one, not anyone (12)

————**... plus** no more, not anymore (12)

————**... que** only (12)

————**... rien** nothing (12)

né(e) born (6)

nécessaire necessary (7)

nécessairement necessarily (18)

négatif (-ive) negative (14)

neige *f.* snow (4–L; 8)

neiger to snow (8)

n'est-ce pas isn't it, aren't they, etc. (1)

neuf nine (1)

neuf (-ve) new (10)

neuvième ninth (2)

neveu *m.* (*pl.* -eux) nephew (2)

nez *m.* nose (13)

nièce *f.* niece (2)

n'importe quel any (6–L)

niveau de vie *m.* standard of living (12–L)

Noël Christmas

noir(e) black (5)

nom *m.* name (5–L; 9)

nombre *m.* number (1–L; 11)

nombreux (-euse) numerous (1–L)

nommer to name (17)

non no (1)

———— **plus** neither (7–L)

———— **seulement** not only (9–L)

nonante ninety (*Swiss and Belgian French*) (12–C)

nord *m.* north (4–C)
Norvège *f.* Norway (4)
nos our (5)
note *f.* note (8)
notoriété *f.* publicity (18–L)
notre our (5)
nôtre ours (14)
nourriture *f.* food (3)
nous we (1); us (11)
**nouveau (nouvel, nouvelle[s], nou-
veaux)** new (6–L; 9)
nouvel new (8–L; 9)
nouvelle *f.* a piece of news
(7–L; 8)
Nouvelle-Angleterre *f.* New England (5–L)
Nouvelle-Orléans (La) *f.* New Orleans (4)
novembre *m.* November (6)
nuage *m.* cloud (8)
nucléaire nuclear (11)
nuit *f.* night (1–C)
de la ——— all night long (13)
numéro de téléphone *m.* phone
number (7–C; 10)

O

obéir (à) to obey (7)
objet *m.*
———**s trouvés** *m. pl.* lost and
found (6)
faire l'——— **de** to be the object of (6–L)
obligatoire required (1–L; 10)
obtenir to obtain (10)
occasion *f.* opportunity (7–L)
d'——— second-hand (10)
occupant(e) *m., f.* passenger
(10–C)
s'occuper (de) to take care of (13)
octante eighty (*Swiss and Belgian
French*) (12–C)
octobre *m.* October (1–L; 6)
œil *m. (pl.* **yeux)** eye (13)
ne pas fermer l'——— not to be
able to sleep (13)
œuf *m.* egg (9)
œuvre *f.* work (15)
oiseau *m. (pl.* **-eaux)** bird (18)
oisiveté *f.* idleness (11–L)

olive *f.* olive (9)
omelette *f.* omelet (5)
on one, people, they, we (1)
——— **dit** you say (1)
——— **y va** let's go (4)
oncle *m.* uncle (2)
onze eleven (1)
onzième eleventh (2)
opéra *m.* opera (15)
opinion *f.* opinion (11)
optimiste optimistic (2)
orage *m.* storm
faire de l'——— to storm (8)
orange *f.* orange (9)
orchestre *m.* orchestra (15)
ordinateur *m.* computer (8)
oreille *f.* ear (13)
organisateur *m.* organizer (14–L)
organisme *m.* organization (5–L)
orthographe *f.* spelling
ou or (1)
où where (2) (16)
——— **ça?** whereabouts? (4)
——— **se trouve... ?** where is
. . . located? (4–C)
oublier to forget (5)
ouest *m.* west (4–C)
oui yes (P)
ouvert(e) open (2)
ouvreuse *f.* usher
ouvrir to open (1)

P

page *f.* page (1)
pain *m.* bread (3)
——— **grillé** toast (3–L)
paix *f.* peace (11)
palmarès *m.* hit parade (15–L)
Palme d'or *f.* Golden Palm (15–L)
palmier *m.* palm tree (15–L)
panneau routier *m. (pl.* **-eaux)**
road sign (10–C)
pantalon *m.* pants (5)
papeterie *f.* stationery store (12)
papetier *m.* stationery store owner
(12–C)
papier *m.* paper (10)
——— **à lettres** stationery (8)
paquet *m.* package (8)
par by (1)

parapluie *m.* umbrella (5)
parc *m.* park (4)
parce que because (4)
parcours *m.* run (14–L)
parcouru(e) covered (14–L)
pardon excuse me (1–C)
pardonnez-moi excuse me (1–C)
pare-brise *m.* windshield (10)
parents *m. pl.* parents (2)
paresseux (-euse) lazy (2)
parfait(e) perfect (5)
parfaitement perfectly (18)
parfois sometimes (8–L)
parisien(ne) Parisian (2)
parking *m.* parking lot (4)
parler to speak (1)
parmi among (2–L)
parole *f.*: **prendre la** ——— to
speak (18–L)
partie *f.* part (13)
partir to leave (7)
partout everywhere (10–L; 18)
pas not (2)
——— **du tout** not at all (4)
——— **encore** not yet (5)
——— **mal** not bad (P)
passager (-ère) passenger (10–C)
passant(e) passerby (4–C)
passé *m.* past
——— **composé** compound past
tense (5)
passer to spend (2); to pass (10)
——— **un coup de fil** to make a
phone call (7–C)
——— **un coup de téléphone** to
make a phone call (8–C)
——— **un examen** to take an
exam (1–L; 10)
se ——— to happen (7)
passionner to fascinate (14–L)
pastis *m.* licorice-flavored
drink (14)
pâté *m.* pâté (9)
——— **de foie** liver pâté (12)
pâtes *f. pl.* pasta (5)
patience *f.* patience (3)
avoir de la ——— to be patient (3)
perdre ——— to lose patience (9)

patin à glace *m.*   ice skating (4–L)

patin à roulettes *m.*   roller skate (14)

patinage *m.*   skating (14)

patiner   to skate (14)

pâtisserie *f.*   pastry shop (3–L; 12)

pâtissier (-ère) *m., f.*   pastry shop owner (12)

patron(ne) *m., f.*   boss (14)

patte *f.*   paw (9)

paume *f.*   palm (18–L)

pauvre   poor (2)

payé(e)   paid (4–L)

payer   to pay (10)

pays *m.*   country (4)

Pays-Bas *m. pl.*   the Netherlands (4)

pêche *f.*   peach (9); fishing (14)

peine *f.*   trouble (7)

———— **capitale**   capital punishment

ce n'est pas la ————   it's not worth it (7)

peintre *m.*   painter (15)

peinture *f.*   painting (15)

———— **à l'huile**   oil painting (15)

peloton *m.*   pack (of racers) (14–L)

pelouse *f.*   lawn (8–L; 17)

pendant   during (8)

pensable   thinkable (17–L)

pensée *f.*   thought (17–L)

penser   to think (5)

———— **à**   to think about (5)

———— **de**   to think of (15)

perdre   to lose (8–L; 9)

père *m.*   father (2)

Père Noël *m.*   Santa Claus

péril *m.*   danger (15)

périphérique   peripheral (14–L)

permettre   to allow (2–C; 17)

permis de conduire *m.*   driver's license (10)

peser   to weigh (14–C)

pessimiste   pessimistic (2)

pétanque *f.*   lawn bowling (14)

petit(e)   small, little (9)

————**à petit**   gradually (8–L)

————**(e) ami(e)** *m., f.*   boyfriend, girlfriend (2)

———— **annonce** *f.*   classified ad (16)

———— **déjeuner** *m.*   breakfast (3–L; 9)

———— **pois** *m.*   pea (9)

Petites Antilles *f. pl.*   Lesser Antilles (5)

petits-enfants *m. pl.*   grandchildren (2)

peu   little (3–C; 5)

———— **m'importe**   it doesn't matter (17–C)

un ———— **de**   a little, a few (3–C)

peur *f.*   fear (11)

avoir ————   to be afraid (11)

faire ————   to scare (11)

peut-être   maybe (9–C; 12)

phare *m.*   headlight (10)

faire un appel de ————**s**   to signal with high beams (10–C)

pharmacie *f.*   drugstore (4)

———— **de garde**   emergency drugstore (13)

———— **de nuit**   all-night drugstore (13)

philo *(fam.)* *f.*   philosophy (2)

philosophie *f.*   philosophy (2)

photo *f.*   photo (3)

phrase *f.*   sentence (14)

physique *f.*   physics (8)

piano *m.*   piano (15)

pichet *m.*   pitcher (3)

pièce *f.*   play (14); coin (12–C); room (16)

———— **d'identité**   ID (8–C)

pied *m.*   foot (13)

pierre *f.*   stone (15)

pile *f.*   battery (7)

pilote d'essai *m.*   test pilot (18–L)

pinard *(fam.)* *m.*   wine (18–C)

pique-nique *m.*   picnic

piscine *f.*   swimming pool (4)

pizza *f.*   pizza (3)

place *f.*   room (4); seat (14); place (16)

à ta/votre ————   in your place (16)

———— **du marché**   market square (9)

placer   to place (16)

plage *f.*   beach (4)

plainte *f.*   complaint (17)

plaisir *m.*   pleasure (15–C)

planche à roulettes *f.*   skateboard (14)

planche à voile *f.*   wind surfing (4–L; 14)

plancher *m.*   floor (Quebec) (16)

planète *f.*   planet (17)

plat *m.*   dish (3)

———— **cuisiné**   prepared dish (12)

———— **du jour**   special of the day (9–C)

———— **principal**   main course (3)

plein(e)   full (4)

faire le ————   to fill up (10–C)

———— **air**   outdoor (9)

pleuvoir   to rain (8)

plongée sous-marine *f.*   scuba diving (14)

pluie *f.*   rain (8)

———— **acide**   acid rain (17)

plupart (la)   most (4–L)

plus   more (1)

en ————   in addition (10)

———— **de**   another (18–L)

———— **tard**   later (7)

plusieurs   several (3–C; 15)

plutôt   rather (18–L)

pneu *m.*   tire (9–L; 10)

poche *f.*   pocket (5)

poème *m.*   poem (10)

poésie *f.*   poetry (14)

poète *m.*   poet (17)

poids *m.*   weight (14–C)

poignée de main *f.*   handshake (P)

pointe *f.*   maximum speed (6–L)

poire *f.*   pear (9)

poisson *m.*   fish (3)

poissonnerie *f.*   fish market (12)

poissonnier (-ère) *m., f.*   fish vendor (12)

poli(e)   polite (2)

politesse *f.*   politeness

politique *f.*   politics (11)

pollution *f.*   pollution (11)

polo *m.*   polo shirt (5)

Pologne *f.*   Poland (4)

pomme *f.*   apple (9)

———— **de terre**   potato (9)

populaire   popular (18)

porc *m.*   pork (9)

porte *f.*   door (1)

portée *f.*   reach (7–L)

portefeuille *m.*   wallet (7)

porter   to wear (5); to bear (15–L)

se ——— to converge (18–L)

se ——— **bien**   to be in good health (13)

portière *f.*   car door (10)

Portugal *m.*   Portugal (4)

poser   to put (9)

——— **une question**   to ask a question (9)

posséder   to own (7–L; 13)

possibilité *f.*   possibility (11)

possible   possible (2)

poste *m.*   extension (7–C)

poste restante *f.*   General Delivery (8–C)

pot *m.*: **prendre un** ——— *(fam.)* to have a drink (6)

pote *(fam.) m.*   friend, buddy (18–C)

poule *f.*   hen (18)

poulet *m.*   chicken (3)

pour   for (1–L; 16); to, in order to (4)

——— **cent**   per cent (1–L)

——— **rien**   for nothing (6)

pourboire *m.*   tip (9–C)

pourquoi   why (4)

pourriez-vous m'indiquer... ?   could you indicate to me . . . ? (4–C)

pourriez-vous me dire... ?   could you tell me . . . ? (4–C)

pourtant   however (5–L)

pouvoir *m.*   power (17–L)

pouvoir   to be able to (7)

pratiquer   to practice (14)

préalable *m.*   preamble (18–L)

préférable   preferable (11)

préféré(e)   favorite (3)

préférer   to prefer (13)

premier (-ère)   first (2)

prendre   to take (3–L; 9)

préoccuper   to preoccupy (11)

préparé(e)   prepared (1–L)

préparer   to prepare (3)

près de   near (4)

présent(e)   present (2)

présentation *f.*   introduction (people) (2–C)

présenter   to introduce (2–C; 9)

président(e) *m., f.*   president (2)

presque   almost (10)

pressé(e)   in a hurry (9–L)

presse spécialisée *f.*   specialized publications (16–C)

se presser   to flock (15–L)

prêt(e)   ready (5)

prêter   to lend (8)

prévisions de la météo *f. pl.*   weather forecast (6–C)

prévoir   to predict, to foresee (8)

prier   to beg (15–C); to pray (18)

prière *f.*   prayer (18)

primé(e)   awarded a prize (15–L)

printemps *m.*   spring (6)

priorité à droite *f.*   right of way on the right (10)

prise de sang *f.*   blood test (13)

prise en charge *f.*   responsibility (18–L)

prix *m.*   price (3); prize (15–L)

——— **fixe**   menu (3)

probable   probable (11)

peu ———   unlikely (11)

probablement   probably (18)

problème *m.*   problem (6)

procès *m.*   trial

prochain(e)   next (4)

proclamer   to proclaim (16–L)

produire   to produce (14)

produit *m.*   product (7–L; 12)

——— **surgelé**   frozen food (12)

professeur *m.*   professor, teacher (1)

profession *f.*   profession (2)

profiter (de)   to take advantage of (8)

profond(e)   deep (14–L)

programme *m.*   TV schedule (11)

programmeur (-euse) *m., f.*   programmer (2)

projection *f.*   showing (15–L)

projet *m.*   plan

promenade *f.*   walk (5)

faire une ———   to go for a walk (5)

promener   to walk (13)

se ——— to take a walk (13)

promettre   to promise (17)

promouvoir   to promote (17–L)

propre   clean, own (9)

propriétaire *m., f.*   owner (16)

propriété *f.*   property (4–L)

Provençal(e) *(pl. -aux, -ales)*   Provençal (9)

provenir de   to come from (13–L)

prudemment   carefully (18)

prudent(e)   careful (2)

psychiatre *m.*   psychiatrist

psychologie *f.*   psychology (8)

publicité *f.*   commercials (11)

publié(e)   published (15)

publier   to publish (9–L)

puis   then (16–L)

puisque   since (6–L; 8)

pull *m.*   sweater (5)

punir   to punish (7)

pyjama *m.*   pajamas (5)

Q

quai *m.*   platform (6–L)

qualité *f.*   quality (11)

quand   when (2)

quarante   forty (2)

quart d'heure *m.*   quarter of an hour (6)

quartier *m.*   neighborhood (8–L)

quatorze   fourteen (1)

quatre   four (1)

quatre-quatre *m.*   four-wheel-drive vehicle (10–L)

quatre-vingts   eighty (2–L)

quatrième   fourth (2)

que   what (7); that, which, whom (16); how, than (18)

québécois(e)   from Quebec (P–L; 5)

quel(le)   what, which (5)

quelle chance!   what luck! (6)

quel dommage!   what a shame! (17–C)

quelle heure est-il?   what time is it? (6)

quelle sorte de   what kind of (3)

quel temps fait-il?   what's the weather like? (8)

quelque(s)   some, any, a few (2)

——— **chose**   something (5)

——— **part**   somewhere (11–C)

quelquefois   sometimes (18)

quelqu'un someone (10)
qu'est-ce que what (7)
——— **ça veut dire?** what does it mean? (1)
——— **c'est?** what is it? (1)
——— **tu deviens?** what are you up to? (1–C)
qu'est-ce qu'il y a? what is the matter? (5–C)
qu'est-ce qui what (7)
——— **ne va pas?** what's wrong? (5–C)
——— **se passe?** what's going on? (5–C)
——— **s'est passé?** what happened? (5–C)
question *f.* question (1)
queue *f.*
faire la ——— to stand in line (5)
qui who, which (7); whom (16)
——— **est-ce que** whom (7)
——— **est-ce qui** who (7)
quinze fifteen (1)
quitter to leave (5–L)
ne quittez pas! hold on! (7)
quoi what (7)
——— **de neuf?** what's new? (P)
——— **qu'il en soit** nevertheless (17–L)

R

raconter to tell (17–L)
radio *f.* radio (1)
raffiné(e) refined (3–L)
raisin *m.* grape (9)
raison *f.*
avoir ——— to be right (3)
ralentir to slow down (14–L)
rallier to join (17–L)
rang *m.* rank (17–L)
ranger to pick up (7)
rapide fast (2)
rapidement rapidly (18)
rappeler to call back (7)
——— **à** to remind (15)
se ——— to remember (13)
rapport *m.* relationship
rapporter to bring back (6)

rare rare (11)
il est ——— it's unusual (11)
rarement rarely (18)
ras le bol: j'en ai ———! I've had it up to here! (17–C)
ravi(e) delighted (17–C)
rayer to cross out
rayon *m.* department (12)
raz-de-marée *m.* tidal wave (13–L)
réagir to react (18–L)
réalisateur *m.* director (film) (15–L)
récemment recently (5)
récent(e) recent (18)
recette *f.* recipe
recevoir to receive (8–C; 12)
recherche *f.* search (16–L)
réclamer to demand (13–L)
recommandé(e) registered (8)
recommander to recommend (3)
récompense *f.* award (15–L)
reconnaissant(e) grateful (15–C)
reconnaître to recognize (10)
recueillir to collect (15–L)
recyclage *m.* recycling (17)
rédacteur en chef *m.* editor-in-chief (17–L)
redevance *f.* fees, tax (11–L)
réduire to reduce (17–L)
réfléchir to think about (7)
refuser (de) to refuse to (15)
regard *m.* glance (18–L)
regarder to look at (1)
régime *m.* diet (13)
être au ——— to be on a diet (13)
faire un ——— to follow a diet (5)
règle *f.* rule (10)
régler to pay (10)
regretter (de) to regret (11)
régulièrement regularly (13)
relation d'affaires *f.* business acquaintance (2)
relevable folding (10–L)
relié(e) linked (14–L)
relier to link (6–L)
remarquer: se faire ——— to be noticed (15–L)
remercier to thank (11)

remettre to put back, to hand in, to hand back, to postpone (17)
remise *f.* discount (12); awarding (15–L)
——— **en question** reexamination (18–L)
remonter to go back to (18–L)
remplir to fill (8–L)
remplisseur de pause *m.* conversational filler (18–C)
remporter to win (14–L)
rencontrer to meet (6–L; 8)
rendre to return, to give back (9); to make (11)
rendu(e) made (8–L)
renouveler to renew (17–L)
renseignement *m.* a piece of information (4)
renseigner to inform (9–L)
rentrée *f.* beginning of the school year (8)
rentrer to go in, to come back (3–L; 4)
répandre to spread (15–L)
réparation *f.* repair (12–L)
réparer to repair (10)
repas *m.* meal (3–L; 9)
repasser to retake (a test) (1–L)
répéter to repeat (13)
répétez! repeat! (1)
répondeur *m.* answering machine (7)
répondez! answer! (1)
répondre to answer (9)
réponse *f.* answer (10)
reportage *m.* report (11)
se reposer to rest (13)
requis(e) required (13–L)
réseau ferroviaire *m.* (*pl.* -eaux) railway system (6–L)
réservation *f.* reservation (7–C)
réserver to reserve (9–C; 10)
résidence universitaire *f.* university dorm (4)
résoudre to resolve
ressembler à to resemble, to look like (1–L; 9)
restaurant *m.* restaurant (3)
restau-U *m.* university cafeteria (4)
rester to stay (2–L; 4); to remain (7)
résultat *m.* result (2–L)

**retard: en ——— ** late (2)

retenir to hold back, to remember (10)

retour *m.* return

retourner to return (10)

retraite *f.* retirement (17–L)

retransmission *f.* broadcast (14–L)

retrouver to find again, to meet (6)

se ——— to meet (15–L)

se **réunir** to meet (15–L)

réussir (à) to succeed (7)

se **réveiller** to wake up (13)

revenir to come back (10)

revenu *m.* income (12–L)

rêver to dream (15)

revoir to see again (8)

revue *f.* magazine (14)

——— **de mode** fashion magazine (16–C)

rez-de-chaussée *m.* ground floor (16)

riche rich (2)

rien nothing (5)

rire *m.* laughter (11–L)

rivière *f.* river (17)

riz *m.* rice (9)

robe *f.* dress (5)

——— **de chambre** robe (5)

rock *m.* rock'n'roll (2)

roman *m.* novel (5–L; 10)

rosbif *m.* roast beef (9)

rôti *m.* roast (9)

rouge red (3)

rougir to blush (7)

rouler à to go (m.p.h.) (10)

route *f.* road

rubrique *f.* section of a newspaper (16–C)

rue *f.* street (4)

rugby *m.* rugby (14)

russe Russian (8)

Russie *f.* Russia (4)

S

sa his, her, its (5)

sac *m.* bag (7)

——— **à dos** backpack (1)

sage-femme *f.* midwife (13–L)

Saint-Valentin *f.* Valentine's Day (6)

saison *f.* season (6)

salade *f.* salad (3)

salle *f.* room

——— **à manger** dining room (16)

——— **de bains** bathroom (16)

——— **de classe** classroom (1)

——— **de travail** work room (6–L)

salon *m.* living room (6–L; 16)

——— **de l'auto** new car show (10–L)

salut hi (P); so long (1–C)

salutation *f.* greeting (15–C)

samedi *m.* Saturday (6)

sandwich *m.* sandwich (5)

sang *m.* blood (17)

sans without (2)

——— **lendemain** without a future (18–L)

sans-abri *m.* homeless person (11)

sans-logis *m.* homeless person (11)

santé *f.* health (11)

**être en bonne ——— ** to be in good health (13)

**être en mauvaise ——— ** to be in bad health (13)

satisfait(e) satisfied (17–C)

saucisson *m.* hard salami (9)

sauf except (17–L)

savoir to know (7)

sciences économiques *f. pl.* economics (8)

sciences politiques *f. pl.* political science (8)

scrupuleusement scrupulously (14–L)

sculpteur *m.* sculptor (15)

sculpture *f.* sculpture (15)

sec (sèche) dry (12)

**être à ——— ** to be broke (12–C)

sèche-linge *m.* dryer (16)

sécher to cut (class) (1–L; 13)

second(e) second (2)

secrétaire *m., f.* secretary (2)

sécurité *f.* security (11)

seize sixteen (1)

séjour *m.* stay (6–L; 8)

séjourner to stay (16–L)

sel *m.* salt (3)

selon according (9–L; 11)

semaine *f.* week (4)

sembler to seem (11)

semestre *m.* semester (8)

semoule *f.* semolina (3)

Sénégal *m.* Senegal (4)

sénégalais(e) Senegalese (8)

sens *m.*

——— **interdit** do not enter (10–C)

——— **unique** one way (10–C)

sensible sensitive (17–L)

sentiment *m.* feeling (15–C)

sentir to feel (7)

se ——— to feel (13)

séparer to separate

sept seven (1)

septante seventy (Swiss and Belgian French) (12–C)

septembre *m.* September (1–L; 6)

série *f.* series (TV) (6–C)

sérieux (-euse) serious (2)

serveuse *f.* waitress (9–C)

service *m.* service

——— **compris** tip included (3)

boisson et ——— en sus drink and tip extra (9–C)

serviette *f.* napkin (9–C)

servir to serve (7)

ses his, her, its (5)

seul(e) alone (2)

seulement only (18)

short *m.* shorts (5)

si of course (2); if (1–L; 4)

Sida *m.* AIDS (11)

siècle *m.* century (5–L)

siège *m.* seat (10)

——— **arrière** back seat (10)

——— **avant** front seat (10)

sien(ne) his, hers, its (14)

signalisation *f.* road signs (17–L)

signer to sign (10)

signification *f.* meaning

s'il te plaît please (3)

s'il vous plaît please (3)

simple simple (2)

sincère sincere (2)

sincérité *f.* sincerity (2)

singer to ape (18–L)

sinon if not

se **situer** to be situated (12–L)

six six (1)

ski *m.* ski, skiing (14)

   faire du ——— to ski (4–L)

   ——— **nautique** water skiing (4–L; 14)

social(e) *(pl.* **-aux, -ales)** social (11)

société *f.* society (11)

sociologie *f.* sociology (8)

sœur *f.* sister (2)

soi oneself (17)

soif *f.* thirst (3)

   avoir ——— to be thirsty (3)

soigner to treat (13–L)

soin *m.* care (13–L)

soir *m.* evening (3)

soirée *f.* evening (2)

soixante sixty (2)

solaire solar (17)

soldat *m.* soldier

solde *m.* sales (12)

   en ——— on sale (12)

sole *m.* sole (9)

soleil *m.* sun

   faire du ——— to be sunny (8)

sommairement briefly (17–L)

son his, her, its (5)

sondage *m.* poll (11)

   ——— **d'opinion** opinion poll (11)

sonner to ring (7)

sortir to go out (7)

sou *m.* money, cent (Canadian French) (12–C)

   avoir de gros sous to be rich (12–C)

   être près de ses sous to be stingy (12–C)

   ne pas avoir le sou to be broke (12–C)

soudain suddenly (16–L)

souffrir to suffer (15)

souhaiter to wish (11)

soulever to raise (11–L)

soupe *f.* soup (3)

sourire to smile (17–L)

sous under (4)

souterrain(e) underground (8–L)

souvent often (2)

spatial(e) *(pl.* **-aux, -ales)** space (17)

spectacle *m.* performance, show (14–L)

   ———**s** entertainment section (of a newspaper) (16–C)

sport *m.* sport (2)

   faire du ——— to play sports (5)

sportif (-ive) athletic (14)

stade *m.* stadium (4)

station *f.* station (6)

   ——— **service** service station (10–C)

   ——— **thermale** health spa (13–C)

stationnement interdit no parking (10–C)

stationner to park (10)

stop: faire du ——— to hitch-hike (5)

studieux (-euse) studious (2)

stupide stupid (2)

stylo *m.* pen (1)

subir to undergo (14–L)

subitement suddenly (17–L)

succès *m.* success (11)

sucre *m.* sugar (3)

sud *m.* south (4–C)

Suède *f.* Sweden (4)

suffisamment sufficiently (18)

suffisant(e) sufficient (18)

Suisse *f.* Switzerland (4)

suivant(e) following (15)

suivi(e) followed (5–L)

suivre to follow, to take (a class) (8)

super super (5)

supermarché *m.* supermarket (12)

supporter to stand (11)

sur on (1–L; 4); out of (2–L)

sûr(e) sure (11)

sûrement surely (18)

surgelé(e) frozen (12)

surpris(e) (11)

surtaxe *f.* fee (8–C)

surtout particularly (2–L; 15)

survie *f.* survival (17–L)

survivre to survive (17–L)

sympathique nice (2)

symphonie *f.* symphony (15)

Syndicat d'Initiative *m.* tourist information bureau (4)

T

ta your (5)

table *f.* table (16)

   mettre la ——— to set the table (9–C)

   ——— **de nuit** nightstand (16)

   ——— **ronde** round table (discussion) (11)

tableau *m. (pl.* **-eaux)** chalkboard (1); painting (15)

tableur *m.* spreadsheet (8)

tâche *f.* task (15–L)

taille *f.* size

talent *m.* talent (3)

   avoir du ——— to be talented (3)

tant mieux! good! (17–C)

tant pis! too bad! (17–C)

tante *f.* aunt (2)

taper to type (7–L; 8)

tapis *m.* carpet (16)

   ——— **volant** flying carpet

tard late (13)

tarte *f.* pie (3)

tasse *f.* cup (3–C)

taux *m.* rate (12–L)

   ——— **de change** exchange rate (12–C)

   ——— **de natalité** birth rate (17–L)

taxi *m.* taxi (6)

Tchad *m.* Chad (4)

tee-shirt *m.* T-shirt (5)

teinturerie *f.* dry cleaner (12)

tel(le) such, like (18)

télé *f.* TV (2)

télécarte *f.* pay phone card (7–C)

télégramme *m.* telegram (8)

télématique tele-computing (7–L)

téléphone *m.* telephone (7)

téléphoner to telephone, to call (7)

   ——— **avec préavis** to make a person-to-person call (8–C)

   ——— **en P.C.V.** to call collect (8–C)

téléviseur *m.* TV set (7)

télévision *f.* television (1)

tellement really (18)

témoin *m.* witness (11–L)

temps *m.* time (6); weather (8)

de ——— en ——— from time to time

tendre le bras to extend one's arm (10–L)

tenir to hold (10)

——— **à** to be fond of, to be anxious to (10)

——— **de** to take after (10)

tennis *m.* tennis (14); (*pl.*) tennis shoes (5)

terminale *f.* senior year of high school

terminer to end (1)

terre *f.* land (5–L)

terrible! super! (17–C)

tes your (5)

tête *f.* head (9)

texte *m.* text (14)

T.G.V. *m.* high-speed train (6–L)

thalassothérapie *f.* sea water therapy (13–C)

thé *m.* tea (3)

théâtre *m.* theater (4)

ticket *m.* ticket (6)

tien(ne) yours (14)

tiens! here! (1–C; 2)

tiers *m.* third (16–L)

timbre *m.* stamp (8)

timide shy (2)

titre *m.* title (8)

toi you (P)

toile *f.* canvas (10–L)

toilettes *f. pl.* restroom (16)

toit *m.* roof (10–L)

TOM (territoires d'outre-mer) *m. pl.* French overseas territories (P–L)

tomate *f.* tomato (9)

tomber to fall (8–L; 10)

——— **en panne** to break down (car) (10)

ton your (2)

tonnerre *m.* thunder (8)

tort: avoir ——— to be wrong (3)

tôt early (13)

toubib (*fam.*) *m.* doctor (18–C)

toujours always (1–L; 2); still (2–L)

tour: faire un ——— to go for a walk (5)

Tour de France *m.* annual bicycle race (14)

touriste *m., f.* tourist (5)

tous all (4)

tout (toute, tous, toutes) all (8)

——— **à coup** suddenly (18–L)

——— **d'un coup** all of a sudden (17–L)

——— **de suite** immediately (3)

——— **droit** straight ahead (4–C)

——— **en** while (13–L)

——— **le monde** everybody (12)

——— **le temps** all the time (8)

traditionnel(le) traditional (18)

traditionnellement traditionally (18)

traduction *f.* translation (17–L)

traduire to translate (14)

trafic *m.* trafficking (11)

tragédie *f.* tragedy (15)

train *m.* train (6)

——— **de banlieue** commuter train (6–L)

trait d'union *m.* hyphen

traitement de texte *m.* word processor (8)

traiter to deal (17–L)

transistor *m.* transistor radio (7)

transport *m.* transportation (6)

travail *m.* work (5–L; 11)

travailler to work (1)

traverser to cross (4–C)

treize thirteen (1)

tréma *m.* dieresis

tremblement de terre *m.* earthquake (13–L)

trente thirty (2)

trentième thirtieth (2)

très very (P)

——— **bien** very well (P)

trimestre *m.* quarter (8)

triste sad (11)

trois three (1)

troisième third (2)

trombone *m.* trombone (15)

trompette *f.* trumpet (15)

trop too, too much (3–C; 5)

trouver to find (3)

comment trouvez-vous? how do you like (3)

se ——— to be located (13)

truc (*fam.*) *m.* thingamajig (11–C)

truite *f.* trout (9)

tu you (1)

Tunisie *f.* Tunisia (4)

tunisien(ne) Tunisian (3)

T.V.A. *f.* value-added tax (10)

type (*fam.*) *m.* guy (18–C)

U

un(e) one, a (1)

à la une on the front page (16–C)

union libre *f.* living together (2–L)

unité centrale *f.* central processing unit (8)

universitaire university (1–L)

université *f.* university (1)

urgence *f.* emergency (13–L)

usage *m.* use, usage (15)

usine *f.* factory (4)

utile useful (2)

utiliser to use (8)

V

vacances *f. pl.* vacation (9)

grandes ——— summer vacation (10)

vache *f.* cow (18)

vague *f.* wave (16–L)

vainqueur *m.* winner (14–L)

vaisselle *f.* dishes

faire la ——— to do the dishes (5)

valeur *f.* value (12–C)

valise *f.* suitcase (5)

faire les ———s to pack (5)

valoir to be worth (16)

il vaut mieux it is better (11)

vantard *m.* braggart

vanter to brag about (14–L)

variété *f.* variety (9)

———s variety show (11)

Varsovie Warsaw (4)

vas-y! go ahead! (4)

veau *m.* veal (9)

vedette *f.* star (11–L)

végétarien(ne) vegetarian (9)

veine *f.* vein (17)

vélo *m.*   bicycle (6)

vendeur (-euse) *m., f.*   salesperson (12)

——— **de journaux**   news dealer
(16–C)

vendre   to sell (9)

vendredi *m.*   Friday (6)

venir   to come (10)

——— **de**   to have just (10)

vent *m.*: **faire du** ———   to be
windy (5)

vente *f.*   sale (12–L)

ventre *m.*   stomach (13)

vérifier   to check (10–C)

véritable   true (4–L)

vérité *f.*   truth (14)

verre *m.*   glass (3–C; 14)

vers   about, around (13)

vert(e)   green (5)

veste *f.*   jacket (5)

veston *m.*   coat (5)

vêtements *m. pl.*   clothes (5)

viande *f.*   meat (3)

vide   empty (14)

vie *f.*   life (1–L; 11)

**vieux (vieil, vieille, vieux,
vieilles)**   old (7–L; 9)

vignette *f.*   (10–L)

vilain(e)   ugly (10–L)

villageois(e)   villager (8–L)

ville *f.*   city (1–L; 4)

en ———   in town (4)

vin *m.*   wine (3)

vingt   twenty (1)

vingtaine *f.*   about twenty (9–L)

vingtième   twentieth (2)

violon *m.*   violin (15)

violoncelle *m.*   cello (15)

virgule *f.*   comma

visite *f.*: **rendre** ———**à**   to visit
(9)

visiter   to visit (4)

vite   quickly (18)

vitesse *f.*   speed (10–C)

——— **moyenne**   average speed
(6–L)

vitre *f.*   window (10–L)

vivace   lively (15)

voici   here is, here are (1)

voie *f.*   track (6–L)

voilà   there is, there are (1)

——— **... que**   for (time) (16)

voile *f.*   sail (14); *m.* veil

voir   to see (7)

voisin(e) *m., f.*   neighbor (11)

voiture *f.*   car (2)

voix *f.*   voice (7)

volant *m.*   steering wheel (10)

prendre le ———   to get behind
the wheel (10–C)

voler   to steal (18–L)

volley-ball *m.*   volleyball (14)

volonté *f.*   will (15)

vos   your (5)

votre   your (5)

vôtre(s)   yours (14)

vouloir   to want to (7)

——— **bien**   to agree to (7)

vous   you (P)

voyage *m.*   trip (4)

——— **organisé**   tour (5)

faire un ———   to take a
trip (5)

voyager   to travel (4)

voyageur *m.*   traveler (6–L)

voyons!   let's see! come on! (8)

vrai(e)   true (2)

vraiment   really (9)

W

wagon *m.*   train car (18–L)

wagon-lit   sleeping car (6–L)

Walkman *m.*   Walkman (7)

week-end *m.*   weekend (4)

Y

y   there (15)

yeux *m. pl.*   eyes (13)

Z

Zaïre *m.*   Zaire (4)

zéro *m.*   zero (1)

zut alors!   darn! (17–C)

Anglais-français

The English-French Vocabulary contains only active vocabulary.

A

a un(e) (1)

able: to be —— to pouvoir (7)

about de (1); vers (13)

absent absent(e) (2)

absolutely absolument (11)

[to] accept accepter de (15)

accident accident *m.* (10)

according to selon (11)

ache: to have an —— avoir mal à (15)

acquaintance connaissance *f.* (2)

actor acteur *m.* (2)

actress actrice *m.* (2)

address adresse *f.* (8)

[to] adore adorer (1)

advance avance *f.* (6)

advantage: to take —— of profiter de (8)

advice (piece of) conseil *m.* (11)

[to] advise conseiller (12)

affectionate affectueux (-euse) (2)

affront atteinte *f.* (15)

afraid: to be —— avoir peur (11)

Africa Afrique *f.* (4)

after après (1)

afternoon après-midi *m.* (4)

again encore (6)

age âge *m.* (3)

ago il y a, voilà... que (16)

[to] agree to vouloir bien (7)

ahead d'avance (14)

AIDS Sida *m.* (11)

air letter aérogramme *m.* (8)

airplane avion *m.* (6)

airport aéroport *m.* (10)

alcohol alcool *m.* (3)

Algeria Algérie *f.* (4)

Algerian algérien(ne) (18)

all tous (4); tout (8)

—— the time tout le temps (8)

[to] allow permettre (17)

almost presque (10)

alone seul(e) (2)

alongside au bord de (4)

alphabet alphabet *m.* (1)

already déjà (5)

also aussi (2)

always toujours (2)

ambitious ambitieux (-euse) (2)

America Amérique *f.* (4)

American américain(e) (2)

and et (P)

animal animal *m.* (*pl.* -aux) (18)

ankle cheville *f.* (13)

[to] annoy embêter (11)

annoyance inconvénient *m.* (11)

answer réponse *f.* (10)

[to] answer répondre (9)

answering machine répondeur *m.* (7)

anthropology anthropologie *f.* (8)

any quelque(s) (2); du, de la, de l', des (3); en (15)

apartment appartement *m.* (4)

[to] appear: it ——s that il semble que (11)

appetizer *hors-d'œuvre *m.* (3)

apple pomme *f.* (9)

appliance appareil électro-ménager *m.* (16)

[to] appreciate apprécier (2)

April avril *m.* (6)

Arabic arabe (8)

architect architecte *m., f.* (2)

architecture architecture *f.* (8)

area coin *m.* (9)

arm bras *m.* (13)

armchair fauteuil *m.* (16)

armoire armoire *f.* (16)

around vers (13)

arrival arrivée *f.* (8)

[to] arrive arriver (1)

art art *m.* (8)

—— history histoire de l'art *f.* (8)

article article *m.* (15)

artist artiste *m., f.* (2)

artistic artistique (15)

as comme (3)

—— much (many) autant (18)

—— soon as aussitôt que, dès que (17)

Asia Asie *f.* (4)

[to] ask demander (1)

—— a question poser une question (9)

—— for demander (15)

asleep: to fall —— s'endormir (13)

asparagus asperge *f.* (9)

at à (1)

—— first d'abord (7)

—— last enfin (16)

—— the au, à la, à l', aux (2)

—— the corner of au coin de (4)

—— the home of chez (4)

athletic sportif (-ive) (14)

August août *m.* (6)

aunt tante *f.* (2)

Austria Autriche *f.* (4)

automatic automatique (10)

[to] avoid éviter (de) (13)

awful affreux (-euse) (2)

B

back dos *m.* (13)

—— seat siège arrière *m.* (10)

backpack sac à dos *m.* (1)

bad mauvais(e), méchant(e) (2)

to be —— weather faire mauvais (5)

badly mal (18)

bag sac *m.* (7)

baggage bagages *m. pl.* (5)

baker boulanger (-ère) *m., f.* (12)

bakery boulangerie *f.* (12)

ballet ballet *m.* (15)

banana banane *f.* (9)

bank banque *f.* (4)

—— account compte en banque *m.* (11)

bar-restaurant brasserie *f.* (12)

baseball base-ball *m.* (14)

basketball basket-ball *m.* (14)

bathing suit maillot de bain *m.* (5)

bathroom salle de bains *f.* (16)
bathtub baignoire *f.* (16)
battery pile *f.* (7)
[to] be être (2)
———**... to** être + *adj.* + de (15)
———**... years old** avoir... an(s) (3)
beach plage *f.* (4)
beautiful beau, bel, belle(s), beaux (7)
beauty beauté *f.* (15)
because parce que (4)
[to] become devenir (10)
bed lit *m.* (16)
to go to ——— se coucher (13)
bedroom chambre *f.* (4)
beef bœuf *m.* (9)
beer bière *f.* (3)
before avant (6)
just ——— juste avant (8)
before-dinner drink apéritif *m.* (3)
[to] begin commencer à (1)
beginning début *m.* (6)
——— **of the school year** rentrée *f.* (8)
[to] behave se conduire (14)
behind derrière (4)
beige beige (6)
Belgium Belgique *f.* (4)
[to] belong to être à (5); appartenir à (10)
belt ceinture *f.* (5)
better meilleur(e), mieux (18)
it's ——— **that** il vaut mieux (11)
between entre (4)
bicycle bicyclette *f.*, vélo *m.* (6)
——— **race** course de bicyclettes *f.* (14)
big gros(se) (6)
billion milliard *m.* (4)
biology biologie *f.* (8)
biotechnology biotechnologie *f.* (17)
bird oiseau *m.* (*pl.* -eaux) (18)
birth naissance *f.* (17)
black noir(e) (5)
blood sang *m.* (17)
——— **test** prise de sang *f.* (13)
blouse chemisier *m.* (5)

blue bleu(e) (5)
[to] blush rougir (7)
boat bateau *m.* (6)
body corps *m.* (13)
book livre *m.* (1); *(of tickets)* carnet *m.* (6)
bookstore librairie *f.* (4)
boot botte *f.* (5)
boring ennuyeux (-euse) (2)
born: to be ——— naître (6)
[to] borrow emprunter (8)
boss patron(ne) *m., f.* (14)
bottle bouteille *f.* (12)
boy garçon *m.* (2)
boyfriend petit ami *m.* (2)
brake frein *m.* (10)
[to] brake freiner (10)
branch branche *f.* (18)
Brazil Brésil *m.* (4)
bread pain *m.* (3)
[to] break down tomber en panne (10)
breakfast petit déjeuner *m.* (9)
brilliant brillant(e) (18)
brilliantly brillamment (18)
[to] bring apporter (3); amener (13)
——— **back** rapporter (6)
bronze bronze *m.* (15)
brother frère *m.* (2)
brown brun(e) (5)
[to] brush se brosser (13)
Brussels Bruxelles (4)
[to] build bâtir, construire (17)
building immeuble *m.* (16)
bus autobus *m.* (1)
——— **stop** arrêt d'autobus (4)
business gestion *f.* (8)
——— **acquaintance** relation d'affaires *f.* (2)
but mais (1)
butcher boucher (-ère) *m., f.* (12)
——— **shop** boucherie *f.* (12)
butter beurre *m.* (3)
[to] buy acheter (5)
by par (1)

C

café café *m.* (1); bistrot *m.* (3)
cake gâteau *m.* (*pl.* -eaux) (3)
calculator calculatrice *f.* (7)

calendar calendrier *m.* (6)
[to] call appeler (13)
——— **back** rappeler (7)
Canada Canada *m.* (4)
Canadian canadien(ne) (2)
candor franchise *f.* (11)
candy bonbon *m.* (9)
canned foods conserves *f. pl.* (12)
capital capitale *f.* (8)
car voiture *f.*, auto *f.* (2)
——— **door** portière *f.* (10)
——— **race** course de voitures *f.* (14)
card carte *f.* (14)
career métier *m.* (15)
careful prudent(e) (2)
carefully prudemment (18)
carpet tapis *m.* (16)
carrot carotte *f.* (9)
grated ———**s** carottes râpées *f. pl.* (9)
[to] carry emporter (5)
cartoon dessin animé *m.* (11)
cash register caisse *f.* (12)
casino casino *m.* (4)
cassette cassette *f.* (7)
cat chat *m.* (18)
CD CD *m.* (7)
——— **player** lecteur laser *m.* (7)
[to] cease cesser de (15)
cello violoncelle *m.* (15)
central processing unit unité centrale *f.* (8)
certain certain(e) (2); sûr(e) (11)
certainly certainement (18)
Chad Tchad *m.* (4)
chair chaise *f.* (1)
chalk craie *f.* (1)
chalkboard tableau *m.* (*pl.* -eaux) (1)
champion champion(ne) *m., f.* (14)
championship championnat *m.* (14)
[to] change changer de (6)
channel chaîne *f.* (11)
chapter chapitre *m.* (14)
charming charmant(e) (2)
cheese fromage *m.* (3)
chemistry chimie *f.* (8)
cherry cerise *f.* (9)

chicken poulet *m.* (3)
child enfant *m.*, *f.* (1)
China Chine *f.* (4)
Chinese chinois(e) (8)
chocolate chocolat *m.* (3)
[to] choose choisir (7)
chop côtelette *f.* (9)
church église *f.* (4)
cinema cinéma *m.* (4)
circle milieu *m.* (*pl.* -ieux) (15)
city ville *f.* (4)
class cours *m.* (1)
classical classique (2)
classified ad petite annonce *f.* (16)
classmate camarade de cours *m.*, *f.* (2)
classroom classe *f.*, salle de classe *f.* (1)
clean propre (9)
[to] close fermer (1)
closed fermé(e) (2)
clothes vêtements *m. pl.* (5)
cloud nuage *m.* (8)
cloudy (sky) couvert (8)
  it's ——— le ciel est couvert (8)
club boîte *f.*, club *m.* (2)
coat manteau *m.* (*pl.* -eaux) (5); veston *m.* (5)
Coca-Cola coca *m.* (3)
coffee café *m.* (3)
cold froid(e) (2)
  to be ——— avoir froid (3); faire froid (5)
  ——— cuts charcuterie *f.* (12)
college fac *f.* (*fam.*); faculté *f.* (1)
color couleur *f.* (5)
[to] come venir (10)
  ——— back revenir (10)
  ——— near s'approcher de (18)
  ——— on! voyons! (8)
comedy comédie *f.* (15)
commercial publicité *f.* (11)
compact disk disque compact *m.*, CD *m.* (7)
[to] compare comparer (17)
competent compétent(e) (2)
complaint plainte *f.* (17)
complete complet (-ète) (18)
completely complètement (18)
complicated compliqué(e) (2)

computer ordinateur *m.* (8)
  ——— science informatique *f.* (8)
concert concert *m.* (6)
concierge concierge *m.*, *f.* (16)
condition état *m.* (15)
conductor chef d'orchestre *m.* (15)
construction construction *f.* (17)
[to] consult consulter (11)
[to] consume consommer (3)
[to] contain contenir (10)
contemporary contemporain(e) (11)
continent continent *m.* (4)
[to] continue continuer à (1)
[to] contribute contribuer (15)
[to] cook faire la cuisine (5)
cooking cuisine *f.* (3)
cool: to be ——— faire frais (8)
correct correct(e) (15)
Corsica Corse *f.* (4)
[to] cost coûter (5)
costs frais *m. pl.* (10)
Côte d'Ivoire Côte-d'Ivoire *f.* (4)
country pays *m.* (4); campagne *f.* (8)
courageous courageux (-euse) (2)
couscous couscous *m.* (3)
cousin cousin(e) (2)
cow vache *f.* (18)
cream crème *f.* (3)
credit card carte de crédit *f.* (10)
creole créole (5)
crepe crêpe *f.* (5)
crime criminalité *f.* (11)
criticized critiqué(e) (15)
cucumber concombre *m.* (9)
[to] cut (a class) sécher (13)

D

dairy shop crémerie *f.* (12)
damage dommage *m.* (11)
[to] dance danser (1)
dancer danseur (-euse) *m.*, *f.* (15)
danger péril *m.* (15)
dangerous dangereux (-euse) (2)
date date *f.* (6)
daughter fille *f.* (2)
day jour *m.* (6); journée *f.* (13)
dear cher (chère) (8)
December décembre *m.* (6)

[to] decide décider de (6)
[to] decrease diminuer (17)
delicious délicieux (-euse) (3)
Denmark Danemark *m.* (4)
dentist dentiste *m.*, *f.* (13)
department rayon *m.* (12)
  ——— store grand magasin *m.* (11)
[to] describe décrire (14)
desk bureau *m.* (*pl.* -eaux) (1)
destruction destruction *f.* (15)
[to] detest détester (2)
devoted consacré(e) (15)
dialogue dialogue *m.* (1)
[to] die mourir (10)
diet: to be on a ——— faire un régime (5); être au régime (13)
different différent(e) (9)
difficult difficile (2)
dining room salle à manger *f.* (16)
dinner dîner *m.* (9)
  to have ——— dîner (3)
diplomat diplomate *m.* (2)
disaster désastre *m.* (11)
discount remise *f.* (12)
[to] discuss discuter (11)
dish plat *m.* (3)
  prepared ——— plat cuisiné (12)
dishes: to do the ——— faire la vaisselle (5)
dishwasher lave-vaisselle *m.* (*pl.* lave-vaisselle) (16)
disk disquette *f.* (8)
  ——— drive lecteur de disquettes *m.* (8)
[to] disobey désobéir à (7)
divided divisé(e) (1)
[to] do faire (5)
doctor médecin *m.* (2)
dog chien *m.* (18)
don't mention it il n'y a pas de quoi (1)
door porte *f.* (1)
[to] doubt douter (11)
downtown centre-ville *m.* (12)
drama drame *m.* (15)
[to] dream rêver (15)
dress robe *f.* (5)
drink boisson *f.* (3); pot *m.* (6)

[to] **drink**   consommer (3); boire (12)

[to] **drive**   conduire (14)

driver   conducteur *m.* (10)

———'s **license**   permis de conduire *m.* (10)

drug   drogue *f.* (11)

——— **test**   contrôle anti-doping *m.* (14)

drugstore   pharmacie *f.* (4)

all-night ———   pharmacie de nuit (13)

emergency ———   pharmacie de garde (13)

dry   sec (sèche) (12)

dry cleaner   teinturerie *f.* (12)

dryer   sèche-linge *m.* (16)

duck   canard *m.* (18)

dumb thing   bêtise *f.* (14)

during   pendant (8)

E

ear   oreille *f.* (13)

early   en avance (6); de bonne heure (12); tôt (13)

[to] **earn**   gagner (8)

easily   facilement (18)

easy   facile (2)

[to] **eat**   manger (1)

ecological   écologique (11)

ecologist   écologiste *m., f.* (17)

ecology   écologie *f.* (17)

economics   sciences économiques *f. pl.* (8)

economist   économiste *m., f.* (2)

egg   œuf *m.* (9)

eight   huit (1)

eighteen   dix-huit (1)

eleven   onze (1)

eleventh   onzième (2)

elsewhere   ailleurs (18)

employee   employé(e) *m., f.* (6)

empty   vide (14)

end   bout *m.* (6); fin *f.* (17)

[to] **end**   terminer (1); finir (7); finir de (15)

energy   énergie *f.* (17)

engineer   ingénieur *m.* (2)

England   Angleterre *f.* (4)

English   anglais(e) (1)

[to] **enter**   entrer (2)

entertainment   distraction *f.* (2)

entrance   entrée *f.* (16)

envelope   enveloppe *f.* (8)

environment   environnement *m.* (17)

equality   égalité *f.* (11)

errand   course *f.* (5)

Europe   Europe *f.* (4)

European   européen(ne) (10)

evening   soirée *f.* (2); soir *m.* (3)

every   chaque

——— **day**   tous les jours (4)

——— **year**   tous les ans (5)

everybody   tout le monde (12)

everywhere   partout (18)

evil   mal *m.* (15)

exactly   exactement (8)

exam   examen *m.* (1)

to take an ———   passer un examen (10)

[to] **examine**   examiner (13)

exercise   exercice *m.* (1)

[to] **exercise**   faire de l'exercice (13)

exile   exil *m.* (17)

expensive   cher (chère) (4)

[to] **explain**   expliquer (1)

expression   expression *f.* (7)

eye   œil *m.* (*pl.* yeux) (13)

F

factory   usine *f.* (4)

[to] **fail**   échouer à (15)

fall   automne *m.* (6)

[to] **fall**   tomber (10)

——— **asleep**   s'endormir (13)

false   faux (fausse) (11)

family   famille *f.* (2)

fantastic   fantastique (2)

far from   loin de (4)

fascinating   fascinant(e) (2)

fast   rapide (2)

father   père *m.* (2)

favorite   favori(te) (2); préféré(e) (3)

fear   peur *f.* (11)

February   février *m.* (6)

[to] **feel**   sentir (7); se sentir (13)

——— **better**   aller mieux (13)

——— **like**   avoir envie de (11)

feminine   féminin(e) (2)

fencing   escrime *f.* (14)

fever   fièvre *f.* (13)

to have a ———   avoir de la fièvre (13)

few: a ———   quelques (2)

field   champ *m.* (17)

fifteen   quinze (1)

fifth   cinquième (2)

fifty   cinquante (2)

filet   filet *m.* (9)

film   film *m.* (2)

[to] **find**   trouver (3); retrouver (6)

fine: I'm ———   je vais bien (P)

finger   doigt *m.* (13)

Finland   Finlande *f.* (4)

first   premier (-ère) (2)

fish   poisson *m.* (3)

——— **market**   poissonnerie *f.* (12)

——— **vendor**   poissonnier (-ère) *m., f.* (12)

fishing   pêche *f.* (14)

five   cinq (1)

floor   étage *m.*, plancher *m.* (16)

florist   fleuriste *m., f.* (12)

flour   farine *f.* (3)

flower   fleur *f.* (17)

flute   flûte *f.* (15)

foggy: to be ———   faire du brouillard (8)

[to] **follow**   suivre (8)

——— **a diet**   faire un régime (5)

following   suivant(e) (15)

fond: to be ———   aimer bien (2); tenir à (10)

food   nourriture *f.* (3)

foot   pied *m.* (13)

football   football américain *m.* (14)

——— **game**   match de football *m.* (2)

for   depuis (6); pendant (8); pour (16)

——— **nothing**   pour rien (6)

[to] **forbid**   défendre (15)

foreign   étranger (-ère) (8)

foreigner   étranger (-ère) *m., f.* (10)

forest   forêt *f.* (17)

[to] **forget**   oublier (5); oublier de (15)

former   ancien(ne) (2)

fortunately   heureusement (6)

forty   quarante (2)

four quatre (1)
fourteen quatorze (1)
fourth quatrième (2)
franc franc *m.* (12)
France France *f.* (4)
free libre (7)
French français(e) (1)
———— **fries** frites *f. pl.* (3)
frequent fréquent(e) (18)
frequently fréquemment (18)
Friday vendredi *m.* (6)
friend ami(e) *m., f.* (1); camarade
  m., f., copain *m.,* copine *f.* (2)
from de (1); à partir de, dès (16)
front seat siège avant *m.* (10)
frozen surgelé(e) (12)
fruit fruit *m.* (3)
———— **juice** jus de fruit *m.* (3)
full plein(e) (4)
———— **collision insurance**
  assurance tous risques *f.* (10)
[to] function marcher (7)
furious furieux (-euse) (11)
furnished meublé(e) (16)
furniture (piece of) meuble *m.* (16)
future avenir *m.* (11); futur *m.* (17)

G

game match *m.* (2)
———— **show** jeu télévisé *m. (pl.*
  jeux) (11)
garden jardin *m.* (17)
general général(e) (*pl.* -aux,
  -ales) (18)
generally généralement (13)
generous généreux (-euse) (2)
Geneva Genève (4)
gentlemen messieurs *m. pl.* (4)
geography géographie *f.* (8)
geology géologie *f.* (8)
German allemand(e) (2)
Germany Allemagne *f.* (4)
[to] get
———— **dressed** s'habiller (13)
———— **off** descendre (6)
———— **up** se lever (13)
gift cadeau *m.* (*pl.* -eaux) (1)
girl fille *f.* (2)
girlfriend petit amie *f.* (2)
[to] give donner (1)
glass verre *m.* (14)

glove gant *m.* (5)
[to] go aller (4)
———— **... m.p.h.** rouler à... (10)
———— **down** descendre (9)
———— **in** rentrer (4); entrer (2)
———— **out** sortir (7)
———— **up** monter (6)
———— **ahead!** allez-y! (4);
  j'écoute (7)
God Dieu *m.* (18)
golf golf *m.* (14)
good bon(ne) (9)
———— **evening** bonsoir (P)
———— **night** bonsoir, bonne
  nuit (P)
good-bye au revoir (P)
gram gramme *m.* (12)
grandchildren petits-enfants
  m. pl. (2)
grandfather grand-père *m.* (2)
grandmother grand-mère *f.* (2)
grandparents grands-parents
  m. pl. (2)
grape raisin *m.* (9)
gray gris(e) (5)
Great Britain Grande-Bretagne
  f. (4)
Greece Grèce *f.* (4)
Greek grec (grecque) (8)
green vert(e) (5)
———— **bean** *haricot vert
  m. (9)
grocer épicier (-ère) *m., f.* (12)
grocery store épicerie *f.* (12)
ground floor rez-de-chaussée *m.*
  (16)
guitar guitare *f.* (15)
gymnastics gymnastique *f.* (14)

H

habit habitude *f.* (10)
hair cheveux *m. pl.* (13)
half demi(e) (6)
ham jambon *m.* (3)
hamburger hamburger *m.* (3)
hand main *f.* (13)
———— **luggage** bagages à main
  m. pl. (5)
[to] hand back remettre (17)
[to] hand in remettre (17)
handshake poignée de main *f.* (P)

handsome beau, bel, belle(s),
  beaux (9)
hang glider deltaplane *m.* (14)
[to] hang up couper (7)
[to] happen arriver, se passer (7)
happiness bonheur *m.* (11)
happy content(e), heureux (-euse)
  (2)
hard salami saucisson *m.* (9)
hardware matériel *m.* (8)
hat chapeau *m.* (*pl.* -eaux) (5)
[to] hate to do détester faire (2)
[to] have avoir (3)
———— **just** venir de (10)
———— **to** devoir (12)
he il (1); lui (9)
head tête *f.* (9)
headlight phare *m.* (10)
health santé *f.* (11)
  to be in bad ———— être en
  mauvaise santé (13)
  to be in good ———— être en
  bonne santé (13)
healthy: to be ———— se porter
  bien (13)
[to] hear entendre (9)
heat chaleur *f.* (8)
hello bonjour (P); allô, j'écoute (7)
hen poule *f.* (18)
her son, sa, ses (5); la (l') (8)
  to her lui (2)
here ici (1)
———— **is (are)** voici, voilà (1)
here! tiens! (2)
hers le sien, la sienne, les
  sien(ne)s (14)
[to] hesitate hésiter à (15)
hi salut (P)
high school lycée *m.* (4)
him le (l') (8)
  to him lui (9)
his son, sa, ses (5); le sien, la
  sienne, les sien(ne)s (14)
history histoire *f.* (8)
[to] hitch-hike faire du stop (6)
hockey *hockey *m.* (14)
[to] hold tenir (10)
———— **back** retenir (10)
———— **on!** Ne quittez pas! (7)
holiday fête *f.* (6)
Holland *Hollande *f.* (4)

homeless person sans-abris *m., f.*; sans-logis *m., f.* (11)
homework devoirs *m. pl.* (1)
　do ——— faire des devoirs (5)
[to] hope espérer (9)
horizon horizon *m.* (17)
horn (car) klaxon *m.* (10)
horse cheval *m.* (*pl.* -aux) (18)
horseback riding équitation *f.* (14)
hostess hôtesse *f.* (4)
hot chaud(e) (2)
　to be ——— avoir chaud (3)
hotel hôtel *m.* (1)
hour heure *f.* (6)
house maison *f.* (4)
housework: to do ——— faire le ménage (5)
how comment (6); comme (9); que (18)
　——— **are you?** comment allez-vous? (P)
　——— **do you say . . . ?** comment dit-on... ? (1)
　——— **is it going?** ça va?, comment ça va? (P)
　——— **many (much)** combien (1); combien de (6)
　——— **much are?** combien font? (1)
hundred cent (4)
hungry: to be ——— avoir faim (3)
hunting chasse *f.* (14)
[to] hurry se dépêcher (13); se dépêcher de (15)
[to] hurt avoir mal (5); faire mal (5)
　——— **oneself** se faire mal à (13)
husband mari *m.* (2)
hypochondriac hypochondriaque (13)
hypocrisy hypocrisie *f.* (2)
hypocrite hypocrite (2)

I

I je (1)
　I'm fine ça va bien (P)
ice cream glace *f.* (3)
idea idée *f.* (5)

good ——— bonne idée *f.* (5)
if si (4)
imam imam *m.* (18)
immediately tout de suite (3)
immigrant immigré(e) *m., f.* (18)
impolite impoli(e) (2)
importance importance *f.* (11)
important important(e) (11)
impossible impossible (2)
impressive impressionnant(e) (8)
in à, en (1); dans (4); (+ *time*) en, dans (16)
　——— **addition** en plus (10)
　——— **class** en cours (1)
　——— **danger** en péril (15)
　——— **French** en français (1)
　——— **front of** devant (2); en face de (4)
　——— **general** en général (1)
　——— **the** au, à la, à l', aux (2)
　——— **town** en ville (4)
included compris(e) (16)
incompetent incompétent(e) (2)
[to] increase augmenter (17)
independent indépendant(e) (9)
independently indépendamment (18)
[to] indicate indiquer (9)
indispensable indispensable (10)
inflation inflation *f.* (11)
information renseignement *m.* (4)
instrument instrument *m.* (15)
insufficient insuffisant(e) (15)
insufficiently insuffisamment (18)
intelligent intelligent(e) (2)
intelligently intelligemment (18)
intercity bus autocar *m.* (6)
[to] interest intéresser (16)
interested: to be ——— s'intéresser à (15)
interesting intéressant(e) (2)
interview interview *f.* (11)
intolerance intolérance *f.* (2)
[to] introduce présenter (9)
[to] invite inviter (1); inviter à (15)
Ireland Irlande *f.* (4)
isn't it n'est-ce pas (1)
it il, elle (1); ce (7); le, la, l' (8); ça (9)
　——— **is** c'est (1)

　——— **'s not necessary** ce n'est pas la peine (7)
Italian italien(ne) (2)
Italy Italie *f.* (4)
its son, sa, ses (5)

J

jackal chacal *m.* (18)
jacket veste *f.* (5)
jam confiture *f.* (3)
January janvier *m.* (6)
Japan Japon *m.* (4)
jazz jazz *m.* (2)
jeans jean *m.* (5)
jersey maillot *m.* (14)
jewelry store bijouterie *f.* (12)
job emploi *m.* (11)
jogging jogging *m.* (14)
journalism journalisme *m.* (8)
journalist journaliste *m., f.* (2)
July juillet *m.* (6)
June juin *m.* (6)
just juste (11)
justice justice *f.* (11)

K

key clé *f.* (7)
keyboard clavier *m.* (8)
kilometer kilomètre *m.* (10)
kind: what ——— of quelle sorte de (3)
kiss baiser *m.*, bise *f.* (8)
to kiss faire la bise (P); embrasser (2)
kitchen cuisine *f.* (16)
knee genou *m.* (*pl.* -oux) (13)
[to] know savoir (7); connaître (10)
　I don't ——— je ne sais pas (1)

L

laboratory laboratoire *m.* (4)
Labor Day fête du Travail *f.* (6)
ladies mesdemoiselles *f. pl.* (12)
lady dame *f.* (8)
lake lac *m.* (17)
lamb agneau *m.* (*pl.* -eaux) (3)
lamp lampe *f.* (16)
language langue *f.* (8)
large gros(se) (6)
last dernier (-ère) (2)

late en retard (2); tard (13)
later plus tard (7)
Latin latin *m.* (8)
law droit *m.* (8); loi *f.* (10)
lawn pelouse *f.* (17)
—— **bowling** pétanque *f.* (14)
lawyer avocat(e) *m.*, *f.* (2)
lazy paresseux (-euse) (2)
[to] learn apprendre (9)
—— **how to** apprendre à (15)
[to] leave laisser (6); partir (7)
left gauche (16)
on the —— à gauche (16)
leg jambe *f.* (13)
—— **of lamb** gigot *m.* (9)
[to] lend prêter (8)
less moins (1)
Lesser Antilles Petites Antilles *f. pl.* (5)
lesson leçon *f.* (1)
let's go on y va, allons-y (4)
letter lettre *f.* (8)
library bibliotèque *f.* (4)
licorice-flavored drink pastis *m.* (9)
lie mensonge *m.* (14)
[to] lie mentir (7)
life vie *f.* (11)
lightning éclair *m.* (8)
like comme (3)
[to] like aimer (1)
I would —— je voudrais (3)
how do you ——? comment trouvez-vous? (3)
—— **to do** aimer faire (2)
line ligne *f.* (6)
Lisbon Lisbonne (4)
list liste *f.* (4)
[to] listen écouter (1)
literary littéraire (15)
literature littérature *f.* (8)
little peu (5); petit(e) (9)
livable habitable (17)
[to] live habiter (1)
lively vivace (15)
liver pâté pâté de foie *m.* (12)
living room salon *m.* (16)
located: to be —— se trouver (13)
London Londres (4)
[to] look regarder (1); avoir

l'air (5)
—— **at** regarder (1)
—— **for** chercher (4)
—— **good** avoir bonne mine (13)
—— **out on** donner sur (16)
[to] lose perdre (9)
—— **patience** perdre patience (9)
lost and found bureau des objets trouvés *m.* (6)
lot: a —— **of** beaucoup de (1)
Louisiana Louisiane *f.* (16)
love amour *m.* (11)
[to] love aimer (1); adorer (1)
lovingly amoureusement (17)
luck chance *f.* (6)
lunch déjeuner *m.* (9)
to have —— déjeuner (3)

M

magazine magazine *m.* (14)
magnificent magnifique (2)
maid's bedroom chambre de bonne *f.* (16)
mail courrier *m.* (8)
main course plat principal *m.* (3)
[to] make faire (5); rendre (11)
man homme *m.* (1)
many beaucoup de (1)
map carte *f.* (1)
March mars *m.* (6)
[to] mark marquer (17)
market marché *m.* (9)
masculine masculin(e) (2)
materialistic matérialiste (11)
math maths *f. pl.* (8)
mathematics mathématiques *f. pl.* (8)
matter
it's a —— **of** il s'agit de (15)
as a —— **of fact** justement (6)
May mai *m.* (6)
maybe peut-être (12)
me moi (2); me (13)
meal repas *m.* (9)
mean méchant(e) (2)
[to] mean vouloir dire (1)
meanness: out of ——
méchamment (18)
meat viande *f.* (3)

medicine médecine *f.* (8)
[to] meet rencontrer (8)
menu carte *f.*, menu *m.*, prix fixe *m.* (3)
merchant commerçant(e) *m.*, *f.* (12)
message message *m.* (7)
meter mètre *m.* (14)
Mexican mexicain(e) (2)
Mexico Mexique *m.* (4)
Mexico City Mexico (4)
microwave oven four à micro-ondes *m.* (16)
middle-class bourgeois(e) (15)
middle-level manager cadre *m.* (11)
midnight minuit *m.* (6)
milk lait *m.* (3)
million million *m.* (4)
mine le mien, la mienne, les mien(ne)s (14)
mineral water eau minérale *f.* (3)
minute minute *f.* (4)
Miss Mademoiselle *f.* (P)
mistake faute *f.* (11)
modern moderne (2)
Monday lundi *m.* (6)
money argent *m.* (3)
—— **order** mandat *m.* (8)
monitor moniteur *m.* (8)
month mois *m.* (5)
monument monument *m.* (8)
moon lune *f.* (17)
more plus (1); davantage (13)
morning matin *m.* (4); matinée *f.* (9)
Moroccan marocain(e) (18)
Morocco Maroc *m.* (4)
Moscow Moscou (4)
mother mère *f.* (2)
motorcycle moto *f.* (6)
mountain montagne *f.* (11)
—— **climbing** alpinisme *m.* (14)
mouth bouche *f.* (13)
Mozambique Mozambique *m.* (4)
Mr. Monsieur *m.* (P)
Mrs. Madame *f.* (P)
much beaucoup (1)
muezzin muezzin *m.* (18)
multiplied multiplié(e) (1)

museum musée *m.* (4)
music musique *f.* (2)
   classical ——— musique classique (2)
musical comédie musicale *f.* (15)
   ——— **instrument** instrument de musique *m.* (15)
musician musicien(ne) *m., f.* (2)
mustard moutarde *f.* (3)
mutton mouton *m.* (3)
my mon, ma, mes (5)
myself moi-même (9)

N

name nom *m.* (9)
   my ——— **is** je m'appelle (P)
[to] name nommer (17)
   [to] be ———**d** s'appeler (13)
nationality nationalité *f.* (2)
national holiday fête nationale *f.* (6)
nature nature *f.* (17)
near près de (4)
necessarily nécessairement (18)
necessary nécessaire (7)
   it's ——— il faut (4); il est nécessaire (11)
   [to] be ——— falloir (12)
neck cou *m.* (13)
need besoin *m.* (10)
[to] need avoir besoin de (10)
negative négatif (-ive) (14)
neighbor voisin(e) *m., f.* (11)
nephew neveu *m.* (*pl.* -eux) (2)
Netherlands Pays-Bas *m. pl.* (4)
never ne... jamais (8)
new nouveau, nouvel, nouvelle(s), nouveaux (9); neuf (-ve) (10)
New Orleans La Nouvelle-Orléans *f.* (4)
news actualités *f. pl.* (11); informations *f. pl.* (14)
   a piece of ——— nouvelle *f.* (8)
   ——— **on TV** journal *m.* (11)
newspaper journal *m.* (*pl.* -aux) (14)
   ——— **article** article *m.* (15)
next prochain(e) (4)
   ——— **to** à côté de (4)
nice sympathique (2)
   to be ——— (*temperature*) faire

bon (8); (*weather*) faire beau (5)
niece nièce *f.* (2)
nightclub boîte de nuit *f.*, club *m.* (2)
nightgown chemise de nuit *f.* (5)
nightstand table de nuit *f.* (16)
nine neuf (1)
nineteen dix-neuf (1)
ninth neuvième (2)
no non (1)
   ——— **more** ne... plus (12)
   ——— **one** ne... personne (12)
nobody ne... personne (12)
noise bruit *m.* (11)
   to make ——— faire du bruit (11)
noon midi *m.* (6)
North Africa Afrique du Nord *f.*, Maghreb *m.* (18)
North African Maghrébin(e) (18)
North America Amérique du Nord *f.* (4)
Norway Norvège *f.* (4)
nose nez *m.* (13)
not ne... pas (2)
   ——— **anyone** ne... personne (12)
   ——— **at all** pas du tout (4)
   ——— **bad** pas mal (P)
   ——— **yet** pas encore (5)
note note *f.* (8)
notebook cahier *m.* (1)
nothing rien (5); ne... rien (12)
novel roman *m.* (10)
November novembre *m.* (6)
now maintenant (4)
nuclear nucléaire (11)
   ——— **war** guerre nucléaire *f.* (11)
number numéro *m.* (10); nombre *m.* (11)
   wrong ——— erreur *f.* (7)

O

[to] obey obéir à (7)
[to] obtain obtenir (10)
obvious évident(e) (11)
obviously évidemment (18)
October octobre *m.* (6)
of de (1)

——— **course** bien sûr (5)
office bureau *m.* (*pl.* -eaux) (1)
often souvent (2)
oh no ah non (4)
oil huile *f.* (3)
   ——— **painting** peinture à l'huile *f.* (15)
O.K. d'accord (10)
old vieux (vieille) (9)
olive olive *f.* (9)
omelet omelette *f.* (5)
on sur (4)
   ——— **foot** à pied (6)
   ——— **horseback** à cheval (6)
   ——— **sale** en solde (12)
   ——— **the phone** à l'appareil (6)
   ——— **time** à l'heure (6)
one un(e) (1); (*subject pronoun*) on (1)
oneself soi (17)
only ne... que (12); seulement (18)
open ouvert(e) (2)
[to] open ouvrir (1)
opera opéra *m.* (15)
opinion opinion *f.* (11)
   ——— **poll** sondage d'opinion *m.* (11)
optimistic optimiste (2)
or ou (1)
orange orange *f.* (9)
orchestra orchestre *m.* (15)
order commande *f.* (12)
[to] order commander (3)
other autre (4)
our notre, nos (5)
ours le/la nôtre (14)
outdoor en plein air (9)
outside à l'extérieur (5)
oven four *m.* (16)
over there là-bas (4)
[to] owe devoir (12)
own propre (9)
[to] own posséder (13)
owner propriétaire *m., f.* (16)

P

[to] pack faire les bagages, faire les valises (5)
package colis *m.*, paquet *m.* (8)
page page *f.* (1)

painter peintre *m.* (15)

painting peinture *f.*, tableau *m.* (*pl.* -eaux) (15)

pajamas pyjamas *m.* (5)

pal copain *m.*, copine *f.* (2)

pants pantalon *m.* (5)

paper papier *m.* (10)

parents parents *m. pl.* (2)

Parisian parisien(ne) (2)

park parc *m.* (4)

[to] park garer (2); stationner (10)

parking lot parking *m.* (4)

part partie *f.* (13)

particularly surtout (15)

[to] pass réussir à [a test] (7); passer (10)

pasta pâtes *f. pl.* (5)

pastry shop pâtisserie *f.* (12)

———— **owner** pâtissier (-ère) *m.*, *f.* (12)

pâté pâté *m.* (9)

patience patience *f.* (3)

patient: to be ———— avoir de la patience (3)

paw patte *f.* (9)

[to] pay payer, régler (10)

———— **a visit** rendre visite à (9)

———— **attention** faire attention à (5)

peace paix *f.* (11)

peach pêche *f.* (9)

pear poire *f.* (9)

peas petits pois *m. pl.* (9)

pebble galet *m.* (4)

pen stylo *m.* (1)

pencil crayon *m.* (1)

people gens *m. pl.* (10); (*subject pronoun*) on (1)

perfect parfait(e) (5)

perfectly parfaitement (18)

pessimistic pessimiste (2)

philosophy philosophie *f.* (2)

phone booth cabine téléphonique *f.* (7)

phone number numéro de téléphone *m.* (10)

photo photo *f.* (3)

physical education éducation physique *f.* (8)

physics physique *f.* (8)

piano piano *m.* (15)

[to] pick up ranger (7)

pie tarte *f.* (3)

pig cochon *m.* (18)

pitcher pichet *m.* (3)

pizza pizza *f.* (3)

place endroit *m.* (4)

in your ———— à ta/votre place (16)

[to] place placer (16)

planet planète *f.* (17)

play pièce *f.* (14)

[to] play jouer (13)

———— (game, sport) jouer à (14)

———— (instrument) jouer de (15)

———— **sports** faire du sport (5)

player joueur *m.*, *f.* (14)

playwright auteur dramatique *m.* (15)

pleasant agréable (2)

please s'il te plaît, s'il vous plaît (3)

pleased enchanté(e) (2)

[to] plug in brancher (7)

pocket poche *f.* (5)

———— **calculator** calculette *f.* (7)

poem poème *m.* (10)

poet poète *m.* (17)

poetry poésie *f.* (14)

Poland Pologne *f.* (4)

police officer agent de police *m.* (2); gendarme *m.* (10)

polite poli(e) (2)

political science sciences politiques *f. pl.* (8)

politics politique *f.* (11)

poll sondage *m.* (11)

pollution pollution *f.* (11)

polo shirt polo *m.* (5)

poor pauvre (2)

popular populaire (18)

pork porc *m.* (9)

pork butcher charcutier (-ère) *m.*, *f.* (12)

———— **shop** charcuterie *f.* (12)

Portugal Portugal *m.* (4)

possessions affaires *f. pl.* (7)

possibility possibilité *f.* (11)

possible possible (2)

it's ———— **that** il se peut que (11)

postcard carte postale *f.* (8)

poster affiche *f.* (1)

postman facteur *m.* (8)

post office bureau de poste *m.* (*pl.* -eaux) (4)

[to] postpone remettre (17)

potato pomme de terre *f.* (9)

[to] practice pratiquer (14)

[to] pray prier (18)

prayer prière *f.* (18)

[to] predict prévoir (8)

[to] prefer aimer mieux (2); préférer (13)

preferable préférable (11)

[to] preoccupy préoccuper (11)

[to] prepare préparer (3)

present présent(e) (2)

president président *m.* (2)

pretty joli(e) (9)

price prix *m.* (3)

printer imprimante *f.* (8)

probable probable (11)

probably probablement (18)

problem problème *m.* (6)

[to] produce produire (14)

product produit *m.* (12)

profession profession *f.* (2)

professor professeur *m.* (1)

programmer programmeur (-euse) *m.*, *f.* (2)

[to] promise promettre (17)

Provençal Provençal(e) (*pl.* -aux, -ales) (9)

psychology psychologie *f.* (8)

published publié(e) (15)

[to] punish punir (7)

pupil élève *m.*, *f.* (3)

[to] put poser (9); mettre (17)

———— **back** remettre (17)

Q

quality qualité *f.* (11)

quarter trimestre *m.* (8)

———— **of an hour** quart d'heure *m.* (6)

Quebec (from) québécois(e) (5)

question question *f.* (1)

quickly vite (18)

R

rabbit lapin *m.* (9)
race course *f.* (14)
radio radio *f.* (1)
rain pluie *f.* (8)
  acid —— pluie acide *f.* (17)
[to] rain pleuvoir (8)
raincoat imperméable *m.* (5); imper *m. (fam.)* (5)
[to] raise lever (13)
rapidly rapidement (18)
rare rare (11)
rarely rarement (18)
rather assez (18)
[to] read lire (14)
reader lecteur *m.* (15)
ready prêt(e) (5)
really vraiment (9); tellement (18)
[to] receive recevoir (12)
recent récent(e) (18)
recently récemment (5)
[to] recognize reconnaître (10)
[to] recommend recommander (3)
record disque *m.* (1)
recycling recyclage *m.* (17)
red rouge (3)
refrigerator frigidaire *m.* (16)
[to] refuse refuser de (15)
registered recommandé(e) (8)
[to] regret regretter de (11)
regularly régulièrement (13)
[to] relax se détendre (13)
[to] remain rester (7)
[to] remember retenir (10); se rappeler (13)
[to] remind rappeler à (15)
[to] remove enlever (13)
rent loyer *m.* (16)
[to] rent louer (10)
rental location *f.* (10)
  —— agency compagnie de location *f.* (10)
[to] repair réparer (10)
[to] repeat répéter (13)
report reportage *m.* (11)
required obligatoire (10)
[to] resemble ressembler à (9); tenir de (10)
[to] reserve réserver (10)
residence résidence *f.* (4)
[to] rest se reposer (13)

restaurant restaurant *m.* (3)
restroom toilettes *f. pl.* (16)
[to] return rendre (9); retourner (10)
rice riz *m.* (9)
rich riche (2)
right juste (11)
  to be —— avoir raison (3)
right of way on the right priorité à droite *f.* (10)
[to] ring sonner (7)
river fleuve *m.*, rivière *f.* (17)
Riviera Côte d'Azur *f.* (4)
roast rôti *m.* (9)
  —— beef rosbif *m.* (9)
robe robe de chambre *f.* (5)
rock 'n' roll rock *m.* (2)
roller skate patin à roulettes *m.* (14)
room place *f.* (4); pièce *f.* (16)
roommate camarade de chambre *m.*, *f.* (2)
rooster coq *m.* (18)
round table (discussion) table ronde *f.* (11)
rugby rugby *m.* (14)
rule règle *f.* (10)
[to] run courir (18)
  —— errands faire des courses (5)
Russia Russie *f.* (4)
Russian russe (8)

S

sad triste (11)
sail voile *f.* (14)
salad salade *f.* (3)
sale solde *m.* (12)
salesperson vendeur (-euse) *m.*, *f.* (12)
salt sel *m.* (3)
sandwich sandwich *m.* (5)
Saturday samedi *m.* (6)
sauerkraut choucroute *f.* (12)
  —— with meat choucroute garnie *f.* (12)
sausage saucisse *f.*
  North African spicy red —— merguez *f.* (3)
[to] save money faire des économies (8)

[to] say dire (14)
  how do you ——? comment dit-on? (1)
  what they —— ce qu'ils disent (1)
[to] scare faire peur (11)
scarf écharpe *f.* (5)
school école *f.* (3)
  secondary —— école secondaire *f.* (3)
  —— year année scolaire *f.* (8)
scuba diving plongée sous-marine *f.* (14)
sculptor sculpteur *m.* (15)
sculpture sculpture *f.* (15)
sea mer *f.* (4)
seafood fruit de mer *m.* (9)
seashore bord de la mer *m.* (4)
season saison *f.* (6)
seat banquette *f.* (6); siège *m.* (10); place *f.* (14)
  —— belt ceinture de sécurité *f.* (10)
second deuxième, second(e) (2)
second-hand d'occasion (10)
secretary secrétaire *m.*, *f.* (2)
security sécurité *f.* (11)
[to] see voir (7)
  let's —— voyons (8)
  —— again revoir (8)
  —— you soon à bientôt (P)
[to] seem sembler (11)
selection extrait *m.* (15)
self même (5)
[to] sell vendre (9)
semester semestre *m.* (8)
semolina semoule *f.* (3)
[to] send expédier (8)
Senegal Sénégal *m.* (4)
Senegalese sénégalais(e) (8)
sentence phrase *f.* (14)
September septembre *m.* (6)
series (TV) feuilleton *m.* (11)
serious sérieux (-euse) (2); grave (13)
[to] serve servir (7)
seven sept (1)
seventeen dix-sept (1)
several plusieurs (15)
she elle (1)
shelf étagère *f.* (16)

shiny brillant(e) (18)

shirt chemise *f.* (5)

shoe chaussure *f.* (5)

shop boutique *f.* (12)

[to] shop faire des achats (5)

shopkeeper marchand(e) *m., f.* (9)

shopping center centre commercial *m.* (4)

shorts short *m.* (5)

shoulder épaule *f.* (13)

show émission *f.* (11)

[to] show montrer (1)

shower douche *f.* (16)

shrimp crevette *f.* (9)

shuttle navette *f.* (17)

shy timide (2)

sick malade (13)

    to look —— avoir mauvaise mine (13)

[to] sign signer (10)

simple simple (2)

since depuis (6); puisque (8); il y a (16)

sincere sincère (2)

sincerity sincérité *f.* (2)

[to] sing chanter (1)

sink évier *m.* (kitchen), lavabo *m.* (bathroom) (16)

sister sœur *f.* (2)

six six (1)

sixteen seize (1)

sixty soixante (2)

[to] skate patiner (14)

skateboard planche à roulettes *f.* (14)

skating patinage *m.* (14)

ski ski *m.* (14)

skirt jupe *f.* (5)

sky ciel *m.* (8)

[to] sleep dormir (7)

    not to be able to —— ne pas fermer l'œil (13)

    —— **late** faire la grasse matinée (5)

slow lent(e) (18)

slowly lentement (18)

small petit(e) (9)

[to] smoke fumer (1)

snack: to have a —— **in the afternoon** goûter (3)

snow neige *f.* (8)

[to] snow neiger (8)

so donc (15)

soccer football *m.* (2)

social social(e) (*pl.* -aux, -ales) (11)

society société *f.* (11)

sociology sociologie *f.* (8)

sock chaussette *f.* (5)

sofa canapé *m.,* divan *m.* (16)

software logiciel *m.* (8)

solar solaire (17)

sole sole *m.* (17)

some quelque(s) (2); du, de la, de l', des (3); en (15)

someone quelqu'un (10)

something quelque chose (5)

    —— **else** autre chose (12)

sometimes quelquefois (18)

son fils *m.* (2)

song chanson *f.* (10)

soon bientôt (8)

sorry désolé(e) (7)

so-so comme ci, comme ça (P)

soup soupe *f.* (3)

South America Amérique du Sud *f.* (4)

space espace *m.* (17)

space spatial(e) (*pl.* -aux, -ales) (17)

Spain Espagne *f.* (4)

Spanish espagnol(e) (2)

[to] speak parler (1)

[to] spend passer (temps) (2); dépenser (8)

spinach épinards *m. pl.* (9)

sport sport *m.* (2)

    ——**s article** article de sport *m.* (12)

spreadsheet tableur *m.* (8)

spring printemps *m.* (6)

stadium stade *m.* (4)

stage étape *f.* (14)

stamp timbre *m.* (8)

[to] stand supporter (11)

    —— **in line** faire la queue (5)

star étoile *f.* (17)

[to] start démarrer (10); se mettre à (17)

station gare *f.* (4); station *f.* (6)

stationery papier à lettres *m.* (8)

    —— **store** papeterie *f.* (12)

stay séjour *m.* (8)

[to] stay rester (4)

steak bifteck *m.* (9)

steering wheel volant *m.* (10)

stereo system chaîne stéréo *f.* (7)

still encore (6)

stomach ventre *m.* (13)

stone pierre *f.* (15)

[to] stop arrêter (11)

store magasin *m.* (4)

[to] storm faire de l'orage (8)

stove cuisinière *f.* (16)

strawberry fraise *f.* (9)

street rue *f.* (4)

student étudiant(e) *m., f.* (1)

studious studieux (-euse) (2)

[to] study étudier (1)

stupid stupide (2)

subject matière *f.* (8)

subway métro *m.* (6)

    —— **station with connecting lines** correspondance *f.* (6)

[to] succeed réussir à (7)

success succès *m.* (11)

such tel(le) (18)

[to] suffer souffrir (15)

sufficient suffisant(e) (18)

sufficiently suffisamment (18)

sugar sucre *m.* (3)

suit costume *m.* (5)

suitcase valise *f.* (5)

summer été *m.* (5)

    —— **vacation** grandes vacances *f. pl.* (10)

Sunday dimanche *m.* (6)

sunglasses lunettes de soleil *f. pl.* (5)

sunny: to be —— faire du soleil (8)

super super (5)

supermarket supermarché *m.* (12)

    giant —— hypermarché *m.* (12)

sure sûr(e) (11)

surely sûrement (18)

surprised étonné(e), surpris(e) (11)

sweater pull *m.* (5)

Sweden Suède *f.* (4)

[to] swim nager (14)

swimming natation *f.* (14)

    —— **pool** piscine *f.* (4)

Switzerland Suisse *f.* (4)
symphony symphonie *f.* (15)

T

table table *f.* (16)
—— **setting** couvert *m.* (8)
[**to**] **take** prendre (9)
—— (**someone**) emmener (13)
—— **after** tenir de (10)
—— **care of** s'occuper de (13)
tale conte *m.* (14)
talent talent *m.* (3)
talented: to be —— avoir du talent (3)
tall grand(e) (9)
tape recorder magnétophone *m.* (7)
[**to**] **taste** goûter (3)
taxi taxi *m.* (6)
tea thé *m.* (3)
[**to**] **teach** enseigner (15); apprendre à (15)
teaching enseignement *m.* (15)
team équipe *f.* (14)
telegram télégramme *m.* (8)
telephone téléphone *m.* (7)
[**to**] **telephone** téléphoner à (7)
television télévision *f.* (1)
[**to**] **tell** dire (14)
—— **someone** dire à (15)
ten dix (1)
tennis tennis *m.* (14)
—— **shoes** tennis *m. pl.* (5)
test contrôle *m.* (14)
text texte *m.* (14)
than que (18)
[**to**] **thank** remercier (11)
thank you merci (P)
thanks a million merci mille fois (4)
that cela (1); ce (7); ça (9); celui (14); que (16)
—— **'s it** ça y est (5)
the le, la, l', les (1)
theater théâtre *m.* (4)
their leur(s) (5)
theirs le/la leur, les leurs (14)
them elles, eux (5)
to —— leur (9)
then alors (1)

there là (2); y (15)
—— **is (are)** voilà (1); il y a (3)
therefore donc (15)
these ces (7); ceux (14)
they elles, ils, on, elles, eux (5)
thing chose *f.* (11)
[**to**] **think** penser (5)
—— **about** penser à (5); réfléchir à (7)
—— **of** penser de (15)
third troisième (2)
thirst soif *f.* (3)
thirsty: to be —— avoir soif (3)
thirteen treize (1)
thirtieth trentième (2)
thirty trente (2)
this ce, cet, cette (7)
—— **one** celui, celle (14)
those ces (7); ceux (14)
thousand mille (4)
three trois (1)
throat gorge *f.* (13)
thunder tonnerre *m.* (8)
Thursday jeudi *m.* (6)
ticket billet *m.*, ticket *m.* (6)
tie cravate *f.* (5)
time heure *f.*, temps *m.* (6)
a long —— longtemps (6)
tip included service compris *m.* (3)
tire pneu *m.* (10)
tired fatigué(e) (2)
to à (1); en (4)
—— **the** au, à l', à la, aux (2)
—— **whom** à qui (7)
—— **your health** à la tienne, à la vôtre (14)
to (in order to) pour (4)
tobacco shop bureau de tabac *m.* (*pl.* -eaux) (7)
—— **owner** buraliste *m.* (12)
today aujourd'hui (4)
together ensemble (1)
tomato tomate *f.* (9)
tomorrow demain (4)
—— **morning** demain matin (4)
—— **night** demain soir (4)
tonight ce soir (1)
too aussi (2); trop (5)

it's —— **bad** il est dommage (11)
—— **much** trop (5)
tooth dent *f.* (13)
tour voyage organisé *m.* (5)
tourist touriste *m., f.* (5)
—— **information bureau** Syndicat d'Initiative *m.* (4)
toward vers (13)
traditional traditionnel(le) (18)
traditionally traditionnellement (18)
traffic circulation *f.* (10)
—— **jam** embouteillage *m.* (10)
trafficking trafic *m.* (11)
tragedy tragédie *f.* (15)
train train *m.* (6)
transistor radio transistor *m.* (7)
[**to**] **translate** traduire (14)
transportation transport *m.* (6)
[**to**] **travel** voyager (4)
travel agency agence de voyages *f.* (4)
tree arbre *m.* (17)
trip voyage *m.* (4)
to take a —— faire un voyage (5)
trombone trombone *m.* (15)
trouble peine *f.* (7)
have —— avoir du mal à (15)
trout truite *f.* (9)
truck camion *m.* (6)
true vrai(e) (2)
trumpet trompette *f.* (15)
trunk coffre *m.* (10)
truth vérité *f.* (14)
[**to**] **try** essayer de (12); chercher à (15)
T-shirt tee-shirt *m.* (5)
Tuesday mardi *m.* (6)
Tunisia Tunisie *f.* (4)
Tunisian tunisien(ne) (3)
[**to**] **turn on** allumer (7)
TV télé *f.* (2)
—— **schedule** programme *m.* (11)
—— **set** téléviseur *m.* (7)
twelve douze (1)
twentieth vingtième (2)

twenty   vingt (1)
two   deux (1)
[to] type   taper (8)

U

ugly   laid(e) (2)
umbrella   parapluie *m.* (5)
unbearable   insupportable (8)
uncertainty   incertitude *f.* (11)
uncle   oncle *m.* (2)
under   sous (4)
[to] understand   comprendre (9)
[to] undress   se déshabiller (13)
unemployment   chômage *m.* (11)
unfair   injuste (11)
unfortunate   malheureux (-euse) (2)
unfortunately   malheureusement (18)
United States   Etats-Unis *m. pl.* (4)
university   université *f.* (1)
—— cafeteria   restau-U *m.* (4)
—— dorm   résidence universitaire *m.* (4)
unlikely   peu probable (11)
unpleasant   désagréable (2)
until   jusqu'à (6)
—— later   à plus tard (P)
untrue   faux (fausse) (11)
unusual   rare (11)
[to] use   utiliser (8)
use   usage *m.* (15)
   it's no —— ce n'est pas la
      peine (7)
used   d'occasion (10)
useful   utile (2)
useless   inutile (2)
utilities   charges *f. pl.* (16)

V

vacation   vacances *f. pl.* (9)
Valentine's Day   Saint-Valentin
   f. (6)
value-added tax   TVA *f.* (10)
variety   variété *f.* (9)
—— show   variétés *f. pl.* (11)
veal   veau *m.* (9)
—— steak   escalope *f.* (9)
vegetable   légume *m.* (3)
—— salad   crudités *f. pl.* (9)
vegetarian   végétarien(ne) (9)
vein   veine *f.* (17)

very   très (P)
—— well   très bien (P)
video cassette recorder
   magnétoscope *m.* (7)
violin   violon *m.* (15)
[to] visit   fréquenter (2); visiter,
   aller voir (4)
voice   voix *f.* (7)
volleyball   volley-ball *m.* (14)

W

[to] wait for   attendre (9)
waiter   garçon *m.* (3)
[to] wake up   se réveiller (13)
walk: to go for a ——   faire un
   tour (5); faire une promenade (5)
   to take a ——   faire une
      promenade (5); se promener
      (13)
[to] walk   promener, se promener
   (13)
Walkman   Walkman *m.* (7)
wall   mur *m.* (3)
wallet   portefeuille *m.* (7)
[to] want   désirer (2); vouloir (7)
war   guerre *f.* (11)
warm: to be ——   *(weather)*
   faire chaud (5)
Warsaw   Varsovie (4)
[to] wash   se laver (13)
—— clothes   faire la lessive
   (5)
washing machine   machine à laver
   f. (16)
water   eau *f.* (3)
—— skiing   ski nautique
   m. (14)
watercolor   aquarelle *f.* (15)
way   chemin *m.* (16)
we   nous, on (1)
[to] wear   porter (5)
weather   temps *m.* (8)
—— forecast   météo *f.* (8)
Wednesday   mercredi *m.* (6)
week   semaine *f.* (4)
weekend   week-end *m.* (4)
well   bien (P); alors (13)
—— then   eh bien (1)
what   qu'est-ce que, qu'est-ce qui,
   que, quoi (7); quel(le) (5)

—— does it mean?   qu'est-ce
   que cela veut dire? (1)
—— is it?   qu'est-que c'est?
   (1)
—— luck!   quelle chance!
—— 's new?   quoi de neuf? (P)
—— 's your name?   comment
   vous appelez-vous? (1)
when   quand (2); lorsque (17)
where   où (2); où ça (4)
which   quel(le) (5); que (16)
white   blanc(he) (3)
who   qui, qui est-ce qui (7)
whom   qui est-ce que (7); que (16);
   qui (16)
whose is it?   c'est à qui? (6)
why   pourquoi (4)
wife   femme *f.* (2)
will   volonté *f.* (15)
[to] win   gagner (14)
window   fenêtre *f.* (1)
windshield   pare-brise *m.* (10)
windsurfing   planche à voile *f.* (14)
windy: to be ——   faire du
   vent (8)
wine   vin *m.* (3)
winter   hiver *m.* (5)
[to] wish   souhaiter (11)
with   avec (1)
without   sans (2)
woman   femme *f.* (1)
wonderful   formidable (2)
word   mot *m.* (17)
—— processor   traitement de
   texte *m.* (8)
work   travail *m.* (11); œuvre *f.*
   (15)
[to] work   travailler (1)
world   monde *m.* (11)
[to] worry   inquiéter, s'inquiéter
   (13)
—— about   s'inquiéter de (15)
wrestling   catch *m.* (14)
[to] write   écrire (14); écrire à (15)
writer   auteur *m.* (2); écrivain
   m. (15)
—— woman ——   *(Quebec French)*
   écrivaine *f.* (2)
writing   écrit *m.* (8)
wrong: to be ——   avoir tort
   (3)

Y

year   an *m.* (3); année *f.* (4)
yellow   jaune (5)
yes   oui (P)
yesterday   hier (5)
you   vous (P); tu (1); te (2); toi (P)
———— **say**   on dit (1)

————'**re welcome**   de rien (1)
young   jeune (9)
———— **people**   jeunes gens *m. pl.* (2)
your   ton (2); ta, tes, vos, votre (5)

yours   le tien, la tienne, les tien(ne)s, le (la, les) vôtre(s) (14)

Z

Zaire   Zaïre *m.* (4)
zero   zéro *m.* (1)

CREDITS ·······························

Text and Illustrations

p. 72, Recipe and illustrations from «Crêpes» from *la pâtisserie* text and drawings by Michel Oliver. Used by permission of Librairie Plon.

p. 132, Map of the Parisian subway system, «Le Métropolitain.» Used with permission from La Régie Autonome des Transports Parisiens.

pp. 151, 152, Two maps adapted from p. 48, «Les Lignes TGV en 1993» and from p. 53, «Le Réseau européen en 2005» from *L'Express* International, number 1968, 31 March 1989. Copyright 1989, *L'Express* International. Distributed by The New York Times Special Features.

pp. 151, 152, maps drawn for *Rapports,* Third Edition by Publication Services.

pp. 310–311, Adapted from articles «Bonheur» and «Dépenses» in *Francoscopie,* 1987. Used with permission from Francoscopie, Larousse.

p. 415, Poem «Construire une maison» by Jean-Guy Pilon from *Comme au retenue. Poèmes 1954–1963,* p. 138. Copyright Editions de l'Hexagone. Reprinted with permission.

p. 451, «Les triplés» by Nicole Lambert published in *Figaro Madame* magazine, issue number 1476, p. 14, March 9, 1991. Copyright © 1991 Nicole Lambert. Used with permission.

All other illustrations by George M. Ulrich

Photographs

p. 1, The Image Works; *p. 3,* © 1987 Pierre Valette; *p. 5,* Gamma Liaison; *p. 6,* Photo Researchers, Inc.; *p. 8,* The Image Works; *p. 27,* © J. Douglas Guy; *p. 28,* © Judy Poe; *p. 31,* The Image Works; *p. 47,* © Ulrike Welsch 1988; *p. 49,* Photo Researchers, Inc.; *p. 51,* The Picture Cube © B. & J. McGrath; *p. 53,* Andrew Brilliant; *p. 71,* The Picture Cube © Frank Siteman 1989; *p. 77,* Photo Researchers, Inc.; *p. 80,* Liaison Int'l © Kip Brundage; *p. 97,* The Picture Cube © Ellis Herwig; *p. 100,* The Image Works © Philippe Gontier; *p. 101,* Cameramann Int'l, Ltd.; *p. 103,* Gamma Liaison © Ag. Speranza; *p. 122,* © MCMXCII Ulrike Welsch; *p. 128,* The Image Works; *p. 158,* The Image Works; *p. 160,* The Image Works © Philippe Gontier; *p. 185,* Rapho Div./Photo Researchers, Inc.; *p. 204,* The Image Works; *p. 206,* The Image Works © Philippe Gontier; *p. 209,* Photo Researchers, Inc. © Christian Petit, Vandystadt; *p. 211,* © Lee Snider/Photo Images; *p. 228,* Photo Researchers, Inc. © George Haling; *p. 238,* Photo Researchers, Inc. © Robert E. Murowchick; *p. 240,* © Lee Snider/Photo Images; *p. 259,* The Image Works © MCMLXXXIII Mark Antman; *p. 262,* © Kathy Squires; *p. 264,* © Judy Poe; *p. 289,* The Image Works © Raymond Stott; *p. 290,* The Image Works © Snider; *p. 306,* The Picture Cube © Mikki Ansin; *p. 312,* Stock Boston © Mike Mazzaschi; *p 317,* Photo Researchers, Inc. © Richard Martin/Agence Vandystadt; *p. 320,* The Image Works © Mat Jacob; *p. 327,* Photo Researchers, Inc. © Ulrike Welsch; *p. 338,*

INDEX ....

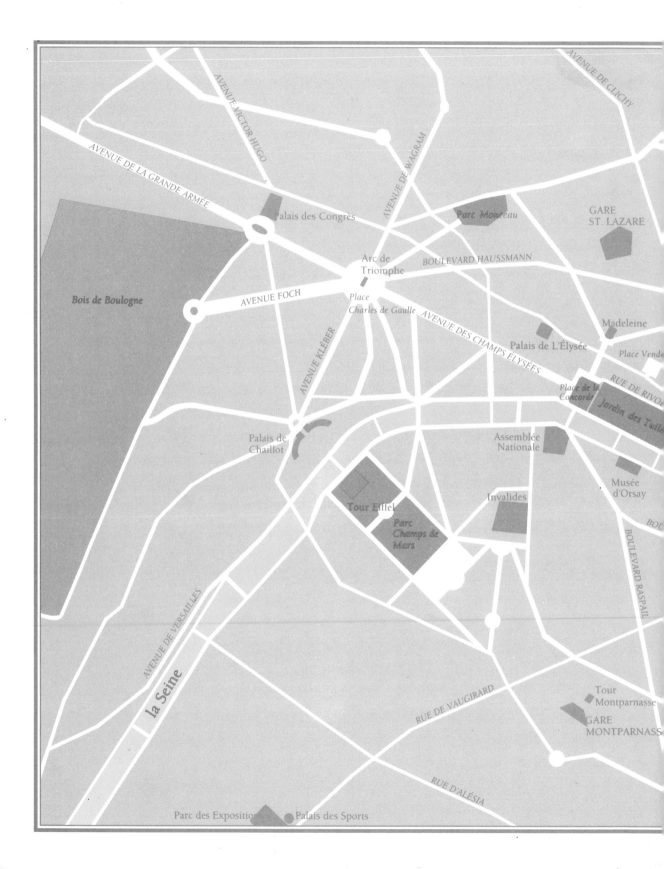